THE YELLOWSTONE STORY

THE YELLOW

A HISTORY OF OUR

BY AUBREY L. HAINES

YELLOWSTONE LIBRARY AND
IN COOPERATION
COLORADO ASSOCIATED

STONE STORY
FIRST NATIONAL PARK

VOLUME TWO

MUSEUM ASSOCIATION
WITH
UNIVERSITY PRESS 1977

Cover illustrations: Volume I, Castle Geyser; Volume II, Yellowstone Lake. Watercolor sketches by Thomas Moran, reproduced from Ferdinand V. Hayden, *Yellowstone National Park and the Mountain Regions of Portions of Idaho, Nevada, Colorado and Utah* (Boston: L. Prang & Co., 1876).

To Jack Ellis Haynes,
known to his friends as "Mr. Yellowstone"
from his long and helpful association
with our first National Park.

ILLUSTRATIONS

Photographs are courtesy Yellowstone National Park Museum unless otherwise credited.

MAPS AND CHARTS

CONTENTS

PREFACE

The Yellowstone Story is an outgrowth of a work begun with Jack Ellis Haynes shortly before his death in 1962. Those who knew "Mr. Yellowstone," as Jack was often called from his long association with the Park, also know of his deep and abiding interest in its history, but even they are not always aware that he lived in the area part of each year except two of his seventy-seven. It was there that he summered in his boyhood, worked in his father's business enterprises as a young man, and became an outstanding concessioner in his own right. During those years he met many characters of the Yellowstone past, saw much of its history made and had a hand in some of the making—sometimes by helping shape events and sometimes by recording them.

Jack's interest in an accurate re-creation of the Yellowstone of yesterday progressed from furnishing historical comments, which were always a feature of his Yellowstone Park guide book, to writing those scholarly accounts that provide a charming coverage of such outstanding events as President Arthur's visit in 1883, the Haynes Winter Expedition of 1887, and the five stagecoach holdups. It was his desire to do even more, by turning his former guidebook feature, "Tid-bits of History," into a "Yellowstone Story" (his title), and it was there our collaboration began.

With Jack's passing, just as the work was fairly launched, I was at once deprived of an old friend and a co-author who has been sorely missed. There are places where the story could have been better told by him, for Jack was a delightful storyteller; but, if his style is missing, much of what he knew survives in secondhand form. Thus, though he was not spared to have a hand in the writing, Jack's influence is here and he is truly an authority for this book.

Of course, a book is always the end product of much encouragement and assistance. In this case, Superintendent Lemuel A. Garrison—who was aware of the need for a centennial history a decade ago—gave the project a push by arranging for my transfer from an engineering assignment into a newly created position of Park historian. That moved the Yellowstone Story from a private hobby to an official basis, probably saving it from oblivion after Jack's death.

Others of the Park staff who have had more than a little influence on this work are the four chief Park naturalists, Robert N. McIntyre, John M. Good, William W. Dunmire, and R. Alan Mebane; Dr. Mary Meagher, whose services as curator and pro tem librarian were constantly requisitioned to dig something out of museum storage or sleuth the library for a hard-to-find reference; Bill Keller, whose camera and darkroom were always as available as his technical knowhow, and the succession of typists who copied reams of notes and labored over rough drafts and final manuscript pages (among them, Ann Martin, Jean Swearingen, Cathy McPherson, and my wife, Wilma, stand out prominently).

Outside the Park, helping hands were extended by historians Ray H. Mattison and Roy E. Appleman, of the regional and Washington offices of the National Park Service. Others whose assistance deserves special notice are Dr. Merrill G. Burlingame, Montana State University (Bozeman); Dr. Duane V. Hampton, University of Montana (Missoula); Dr. Richard A. Bartlett, Florida State University (Tallahassee); Miss Mary K. Dempsey and Miss Leslie B. Heathcote, former librarians, respectively, of the Montana State Historical Society, Helena, and the Montana State University Library here at Bozeman. Lastly, those persons too numerous for particular mention—the sons and grandsons of early ·explorers, the stagecoach drivers, old soldiers, former employees and early visitors—who stopped at Park headquarters to share their knowledge of other days, and thus put flesh upon the bare bones of history.

If this work has succeeded in what was proposed—re-creation of enough of Yellowstone's past to typify the whole of it—it is because the author has had the assistance of so many people, as well as the help of others, now gone, who wrote about our first and largest national park. In this regard, the reader should not expect an exhaustive treatment of any phase of Yellowstone's complex and extensive history; rather the intent has been to do only as much as is necessary to an understanding of the flow of events. There *are* occasional drier-than-dust factual treatments—for they could not always be avoided—but these are leavened with interludes intended to show the drama and comedy, also, as typical of life in Wonderland as elsewhere.

Should it seem to some that this work has been a long time in the writing, I take refuge in not being the first to struggle with the problem of how to present adequately a subject so large in a compass as small as the covers of two volumes. Another Yellowstone historian, Hiram M. Chittenden, was troubled by this problem, in a day when the Park's history was not nearly so long or so involved. In a letter to Acting Superintendent Anderson on March 28, 1895, he remarked: "I am afraid that you think I have been a good while at this work, but I came to the conclusion that I might better not do it at all than to do it poorly." As the truth of his statement bore upon me through familiarity with the Park's vast literature, I came to understand that strange supplication of an unknown newspaper correspondent of nearly a century ago, who wrote in his "Cactus Canticle,"

> Come, gentle Muse, my furnace fill with coal,
> Oil-up the heavy journals of my soul,
> File sharp my tongue, and belt-up my jaw bone,
> I sing an idyl of the Yellowstone.

Bozeman Avant Courier
February 18, 1876

May you enjoy the Yellowstone Story, finding something of the spirit of a great Park in it—despite the fact that you have every right to exclaim with the Queen of Sheba, "the half was not told me!"

Bozeman, Montana   Aubrey L. Haines
February 15, 1977

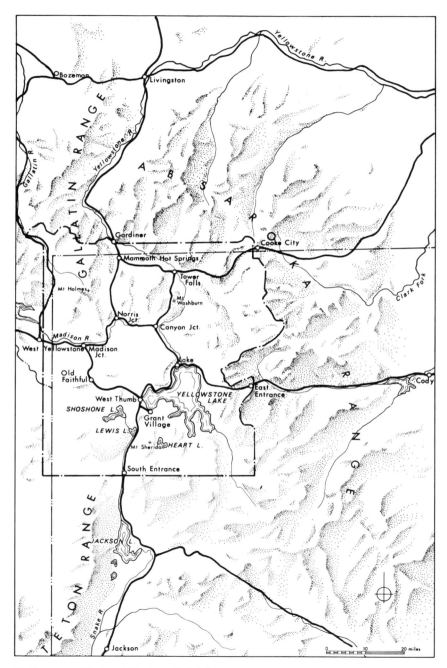

Yellowstone National Park and vicinity.

NOTE TO VOLUME II

An Introduction to the history of Yellowstone National Park may be found in Volume I of this two-volume work. The following is a chapter summary of Volume I: WHAT'S IN A NAME?—how the name Yellowstone has evolved to the present day. OUT OF THE MISTS OF TIME—prehistoric and Indian occupation of the Yellowstone Plateau and vicinity. IN PURSUIT OF PELTRY—John Colter, the first trapper, is followed by others who contribute knowledge of an unexplored wilderness. PICK AND SHOVEL PILGRIMS—during the 1860s the wilderness is penetrated by prospectors. BEYOND THE RANGES—definitive explorations by Folsom, Washburn, and the Hayden Survey confirm the existence of "wonders." THE NEW CREATION—legislation for a national park becomes law in 1872. MARKING TIME—the Park remains an unmanaged wilderness threatened by abuse. WARFARE IN WONDERLAND—Indian wars delay improvements. PIONEERING IN A PARK—P.W. Norris as superintendent makes improvements and resists monopolists. PETERFUNK'S GHOST—monopolies gain a foothold with P.H. Conger as superintendent. OF RABBIT CATCHERS—through misguided law enforcement and official chicanery the park experiment, and the wilderness park concept along with it, is on the verge of extinction.

III
RESCUED BY THE ARMY

In pleasing contrast to the noisy, ever-changing management, or mismanagement, of blundering, plundering, money-making, vote-sellers who received their places from boss politicians as purchased goods, the soldiers do their duty so quietly that the traveller is scarcely aware of their presence.

—*John Muir*
Our National Parks *(1902)*

CHAPTER 12

ORDER OUT OF CHAOS

Order is Heav'ns first law.
—Alexander Pope

In prompt compliance with Special Orders No. 79, Headquarters, Department of Dakota, issued at Fort Snelling, Minnesota, August 13, 1886, Captain Moses Harris marched the fifty men of Company M, First United States Cavalry, from Fort Custer, Montana Territory, to Mammoth Hot Springs, where they arrived on the evening of August 17.[1] A tent camp was established at the foot of the hot spring terraces,[2] and the captain assumed the duties of the superintendency on August 20, 1886. Accompanied by former Superintendent Wear, he made a hasty tour of the Park, stationing small detachments of his men at the places formerly occupied by members of the force of assistant superintendents: the Norris Geyser Basin, Lower and Upper Geyser Basins, Riverside on the Madison, the Grand Canyon, and Soda Butte on the road to Cooke City. Some of these stations had already been abandoned by assistants who had hurried home as soon as word was received that Congress had failed to appropriate money for their salaries; but at others, the assistants had remained until relieved (for which they were later rewarded through a deficiency bill). It was a hasty turnover of authority, which put untrained troops into a strange and difficult situation, and yet, there were urgent reasons why it should be done so.

The repeal, on March 10, 1886, of the Wyoming law of 1884 as it applied to Yellowstone National Park, left the area in a worse plight than it had ever been. The frontiersmen who lived in its vicinity, as well as the employees and visitors within, were emboldened by the obvious fact that they could once more defy the rules and regulations with impunity. To that, some of the worst added a desire for revenge, which surfaced in the form of grass and forest fires deliberately set to embarrass Superintendent Wear and his assistants. Of this state of affairs, Captain Harris says:

> I regret to have to report that destructive forest fires have been raging in the park during the greater portion of the present season. The most destructive one, which was burning when I arrived in the park, originated on the 14th of August last, near the east fork of Gardner River, in full view from the Mammoth Hot Springs hotel and about 7 miles distant. This fire is still burning, and has extended over a tract of country some ten or twelve miles in length by three to five in width.[3]

Faced with such cogent evidence of the serious situation that had developed within the Park, Captain Harris reacted vigorously.

Details were sent out to fight the fires; C.J. Baronett was retained as a scout to cover the back country (Captain Harris asked for three such positions, but only one was allowed him); and the soldiers were given clear instructions as to the manner of enforcing the park regulations. According to Orders No. 5, issued at Camp Sheridan on August 21, 1886, they were to make sure that the following were observed:

> (1) The cutting of green timber, or the removal or displacement of any mineral deposits or any natural curiosities, is forbidden.
>
> (2) Hunting or trapping and the discharge of firearms within the limits of the park is prohibited. Fishing is forbidden except with hook and line, and the sale of fish so taken is also disallowed.
>
> (3) Wagon tires on all wagons used for freighting purposes on the roads by the government are required to be at least 4 inches in width.
>
> (4) Camping parties will only build fires when actually necessary, and must carefully extinguish them when no longer required.
>
> (5) The sale of intoxicating liquors, except by hotel proprietors to their guests, for their own use, is strictly prohibited.
>
> (6) Trespassers within the park for illicit purposes, or persons wantonly violating the foregoing rules, will be summarily removed from the park.
>
> (7) No stock will be allowed to run loose in the vicinity of the various points of interest within the park frequented by visitors.
>
> (8) No rocks, sticks, or other obstructions, must be thrown into any of the springs or geysers within the park.

It is enjoined upon all soldiers, when on duty at points frequented by tourists, to be vigilant and attentive in the foregoing regulations, and also to see that the stage drivers and other employees of the hotels do not use abusive language to, or otherwise maltreat, the visitors to the park. They will also at all times exert themselves to preserve peace and order at the points where they are stationed.

They will in the enforcement of their orders conduct themselves in a courteous and polite, but firm and decided manner. They will not hesitate to make arrests when necessary, reporting at once by telephone to the commanding officer.[4]

Recognizing that the rules and regulations then in force (those of May 4, 1881, amended January 15, 1883) were largely outmoded, the captain recommended adoption of new rules and regulations that would cover the current problems.

Aware also that, in the absence of any other appropriate legislation, law enforcement would have to rest upon the provision of the organic act that allowed the expulsion of trespassers, Captain Harris prepared the way for the use of extra-legal methods by assuring the secretary of the interior that, though they might "at times appear harsh and arbitrary," such procedures were "indispensable to the proper protection of life and property."[5] An earnest of his methods was soon given in the eviction of M. E. Metcalf, a former justice of the peace under Wyoming law, and a Mrs. Crary, both of whom had settled at Mammoth Hot Springs with evident intentions of remaining; and also, in the expulsion from the Park of a number of disreputable characters with no visible means of support.

Despite this vigorous beginning, the management of the Park by the military was almost immediately criticized. Former Superintendent D. W. Wear stated to a correspondent of the *Pioneer Press* that the troops were not taking proper care of the Park and were "allowing the indiscriminate killing of game and the desecration of the formations above the mineral springs." Captain Harris answered that unfair allegation (which seems to have arisen from Wear's pique at being displaced, rather than from provable facts) with a careful investigation which established to his satisfaction that the troopers were performing their duties well. An equally baseless charge, for he was not there to observe actual conditions, came from Special Agent W. Hallett Phillips, who claimed that the geyser cones "were more hacked and injured while the soldiers were stationed there, than at any time since 1882-3."[6] Similar attacks, representing the disappointment of otherwise well-meaning people, continued for a year or more, and, though hard to endure, they did no real damage.

A lack of instructions as to how long Company M was to remain in Yellowstone Park led Captain Harris to inquire whether his men would overwinter there. Early in September he was informed that the quartermaster general, Department of Dakota, had been ordered to "provide such temporary shelter for the command as may be necessary for the comfort of the troops and the protection of public property."[7] Under that authorization, Camp Sheridan was soon turned into a cantonment which, though roughly built, was adequate.

Five buildings were completed before the end of December: a T-shaped barracks, 130 feet along the front and 24 feet wide, with a back extension; a storehouse, a guardhouse, a cavalry stable, and a quartermaster stable. These buildings were all of frame construction, 10 feet high and finished on the outside with vertical boards and bats. The following year a headquarters building, duplex officers' quarters, and an L-shaped post hospital were added. The buildings constructed the first fall are numbered 1 through 5 on the accompanying plan of Camp Sheridan.[8]

The detachments were brought in from all the outposts except Soda Butte by November 1, and it was well that there was "good and sufficient protection for men, animals, and supplies," for the winter of 1886-87 was one of the worst ever known in the northern Rocky Mountains.

It was a savage winter that burst upon the northern plains in January in a succession of bitter blizzards accompanied by temperatures as severe as 50 degrees below zero—a lethal cold which took the life of Alexander "Mormon" Brown on the trail near Gardiner. In the mountains the snow accumulated to unheard of depths. The snow-buried mining town of Cooke City was isolated, except for a weekly mail carried on skis, and there was constant fear of destructive avalanches from the slopes above; indeed, one slide of snow one-half mile wide and one mile long passed directly over the Republic mine, sweeping Anthony Wise and Clarence Martin to oblivion.

The garrison at Camp Sheridan did not suffer but they were entirely isolated. Beyond a few roads in the immediate vicinity of the post which they were able to keep open with horse-drawn drags—creating elevated roadways from which a tumble into snowy depths was always possible—there was no traveling except by the long skis called "snow shoes" in that day.

Down the Yellowstone Valley conditions were truly terrible. As the haystacks and wood piles dwindled, the stock died (sometimes frozen upright in fence corners), and homesteaders resorted to such expedients as burning their fences and furniture. The train that left

CAMP SHERIDAN: 1886-1891

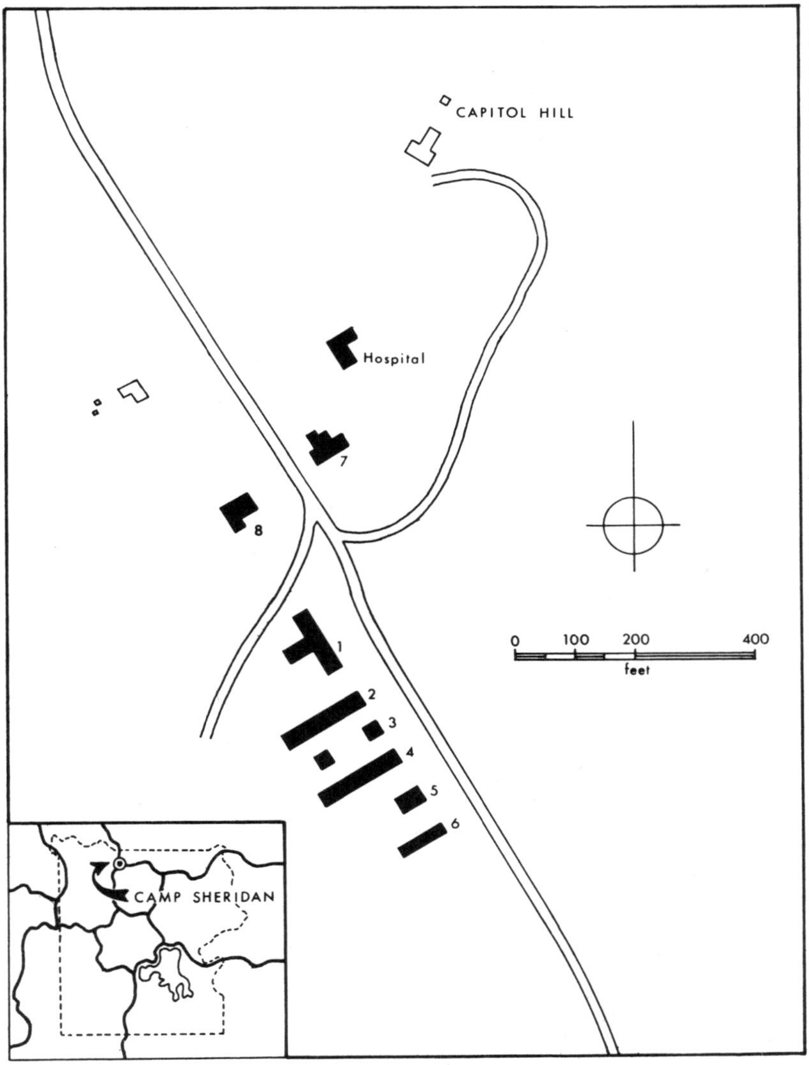

CAPITOL HILL

Hospital

7

8

1

2

3

4

5

6

CAMP SHERIDAN

0   100   200   400
feet

BUILDING KEY TO ORIGINAL USE

1 Barracks
2 Warehouse
3 Guardhouse
4 Cavalry Stable
5 Quartermaster Stable
6 (unknown)
7 Headquarters
8 Officer's Quarters

Livingston for the Cinnabar terminus of the park branch line on the last Saturday in January was not heard from until the following Wednesday, when the conductor reached Livingston after walking the last twelve miles. A locomotive plow brought in the stalled train which had been derailed many times by wind-packed drifts—and that was the last train to run on the park branch for six weeks. But before the true character of that awful winter could be clearly seen, a plan for a winter journey through the Park was put in motion.

The Yellowstone winter expedition of 1887 was organized by Lieutenant Frederick Schwatka, a 38-year-old cavalry officer who had gained considerable fame in Arctic ventures about which he had written several interesting books. His winter visit to Wonderland was made under the auspices of the *New York World*, for which he was to write a story. A sketch artist by the name of Bosse and photographer Frank J. Haynes were to accompany him.

The party of eight men, with far too much equipment, left Mammoth Hot Springs on the morning of January 2, 1887, in deceptively mild weather.[9] Lieutenant Tutherly assisted the party through the Golden Gate and as far as Swan Lake with mules, but there the drifts became too deep for his animals and he left the expeditioners to man-haul their loaded toboggans. This proved unexpectedly difficult, for the snow was too soft to bear up under their skis, and that day they got only to Indian Creek, where they camped as the temperature fell to 37 degrees below zero. The second day they did little better, making four miles to a camp near Obsidian Cliff. Another mile of grueling travel on the third day convinced them they would have to abandon the toboggans and their heavy outfit; taking what food they could carry in their pockets, and the photographic and sketching equipment, they pushed on toward the Norris Geyser Basin, knowing they could shelter with the winter keeper of the hotel built there the previous summer by the Yellowstone Park Association.

A day was spent at Norris, photographing Monarch Geyser and other steamy features, and the party again set forth over the snow for the Lower Geyser Basin. But Lieutenant Schwatka's lungs had been affected by the cold during the first three fatiguing days of travel, and about four miles south of the hotel, near where the Gibbon River enters its canyon, his lungs began to hemorrhage profusely. A brief consultation was held, and the sick man was persuaded to return to the Norris hotel. He released two members of his expedition, Charles A. Stoddard and David Stratton, to continue on into the Park with photographer Haynes (who called Ed Wilson on the telephone to join him at the Upper Geyser Basin). Then Lieutenant Schwatka and the

The Schwatka winter expedition, 1887, photographed by F. J. Haynes at Obsidian Cliff. *Photograph used with permission of the Haynes Foundation.*

remainder of his party made their way back to Mammoth Hot Springs and the railroad, where they arrived just in time to depart on the last train to operate on the park branch line that winter.[10]

With Lieutenant Schwatka's departure, his "Yellowstone winter expedition" became the "Haynes winter expedition," which certainly had an inauspicious beginning. Five days and nights of continuous storm kept Frank Haynes indoors at the Upper Geyser Basin, but the weather cleared on the sixteenth and seventeenth, allowing him to do the photography that was the object of his trip. He photographed several large geysers in eruption, and magnificent views of the frost-laden trees sparkling in the winter sun near Castle Geyser. Then, facing into the wind-driven snow of the renewed storm, the little party retraced the route to Norris Geyser Basin, where they rested for a day before continuing on to the Grand Canyon. There, the snow was so deep that they found the hotel only because the winter keepers— Major Lyman and William Thone—had been attempting to remove the snow from the roof of their temporary building.[11] They were hospitably entertained by those lonely men, as they had been at the other occupied points, while awaiting a favorable opportunity to photograph the ice encrusted Falls of the Yellowstone. With that accomplished, they decided to return to Mammoth Hot Springs by crossing the Washburn Range to Yancey's way station on the Cooke City Road.

They set out on January 23 without compass, ax, or blankets, and with only enough food for one meal, not realizing that the sparkling sunlight of that Sunday morning would soon give way to a leaden sky and bitter, snow-laden north winds which would prevent them from holding a course between the Grand Canyon and the summit of Mount Washburn. By ten o'clock in the morning they were shut within a blustery, grayish little world entirely devoid of landmarks. Objects became invisible beyond thirty feet, and "the snow from the air and the snow from the earth waltzed together in a bewildering whirl." As night settled upon them, they knew only that they were in the national park and somewhere on Mount Washburn.

Several wanted to keep moving, but they fortunately sought shelter in one of those natural arbors found beneath clumps of alpine firs. Within that "living tepee," the four men cleared away the snow and gathered pieces of the dry outer bark and bits of dead limbs for a feeble fire; and there they crouched through the bitter night, telling stories to keep each other awake. At daylight they set out into a storm which, if anything, was more violent than the previous day, and the second evening found them on a bare, bleak hillside, lacking even the drafty sort of shelter they had had the previous night. They were forced to keep themselves in motion all night or freeze to death, and that effort rapidly consumed their remaining strength, leaving in its place "a kind of giddiness." In the morning they ate the last bit of bread reserved from their small lunch, fearing they would soon have no further need of food. At that ebb point in their hopes, the wind abated and the sun came out, showing them hills and valleys newly clothed in snow. They were on the slope above Tower Creek, and from there it took them but an hour to reach Yancey's cabin at Pleasant Valley.

"Uncle John" Yancey put the four exhausted and famished men to bed, and "fed them a weak broth despite their threats to kill him if he did not give them food—lots of it!" He knew how to take care of them and they were soon able to travel on to Mammoth Hot Springs with those first winter pictures taken in the Yellowstone. Such was the conclusion of the tour that Superintendent Harris thought "is not to be recommended as a winter diversion."[12]

The soldiers, also, were forced to go adventuring in the Park that winter. In mid-April, information reached Captain Harris that a man named William James was probably poaching in the vicinity of Norris Geyser Basin. James was a teamster who had been employed in the late fall of 1886, with several others, hauling materials from Norris Geyser Basin to the Grand Canyon for construction of a hotel at that point. In the course of this work, James had frequently seen mountain lions and lynx along the route he traveled, and when George W. Wakefield, the contractor, stopped the hauling late in December, James did not move out of the Park but merely went to Gardiner and obtained some traps, a gun, and additional supplies. Returning to Norris Geyser Basin, he set up a winter camp in a tent near the hotel and proceeded to do a little poaching.

Upon hearing of that, Captain Harris sent Sergeant John Swan and a detail of men to Norris Geyser Basin on skis the night of the twentieth, with orders to make a thorough investigation and to arrest Mr. James if they found any evidence of wrongdoing. Evidence was soon found; there were three beaver traps set in the Gibbon River near the hotel, and a search of the premises revealed five beaver skins and one lynx skin in an outbuilding used by James as a storehouse. This was cause enough for arresting him, and he was brought into Mammoth Hot Springs on April 22.

When examined by Captain Harris, James readily admitted his guilt and also implicated two employees of the Yellowstone Park Association. One of these, a man named Brown, had helped James kill an elk near the Yellowstone Falls and haul in the meat, while the winter keeper at the Norris hotel was cognizant of his illegal activities.

All three men were summarily expelled from the Park, and the property of James, listed as "one Marlin rifle, three beaver traps (number four), five beaver skins, one lynx skin, four horses, two sleds, four sets of harness, three chains, two pairs of blankets, one A-tent, one whip, one coffee pot, one frying pan, and also a small quantity of bacon, flour, coffee, and sugar—about four days' supply for one man,"[13] was held pending the decision of the secretary of the interior concerning their disposition. In this regard, Captain Harris recommended outright confiscation of all items belonging to James (the two sleds and two of the horses were said to belong to the Yellowstone Park Association).

William James continued to hang around the town of Gardiner without visible means of support, for he was no longer considered reliable. Occasionally he wrote Captain Harris in an attempt to have his "little effects" restored to him. However, he prejudiced his case by entering the Park several times in spite of the order excluding him and by consorting with such suspected poachers as Page and Garfield. In his letter of August 27, James asked the captain not to believe "anything Thomas Garfield may say or write."[14] He had reason to be fearful for Garfield had knowledge of a serious crime that James had committed in the Park. But Garfield did not betray him; the denouement was his own doing.

On the evening of July 4, 1887, the six-horse stagecoach Bighorn, driven by Thea Hamm, was held up by two masked men about one mile inside the northern boundary of the Park while enroute to Mammoth Hot Springs. It was an amateurish bit of business, in which the robbers got only $16 for their trouble, and at the time there was nothing to indicate who they might be. The stage carried a number of passengers, three of whom are known: J. B. Kirkbride of Minneapolis occupied the box with a Mr. Watson of San Francisco, and Judge John F. Lacey of Oskaloosa, Iowa, was inside with the remaining passengers. Kirkbride says they were stopped by a man who stepped into the road and covered them with two pistols while he cried, "Halt and dismount!" The passengers inside the coach were covered by a confederate at the side of the road. After dwelling at length on a multitude of small details which added up to exactly nothing, Mr. Kirkbride admitted "the whole performance was such a surprise and so quickly done that time was not given us to take in the situation and get a correct impression of the parties committing the assault."[15] Judge Lacey was more helpful because he was carrying a distinctive pocket piece: "one napoleon coinage of 1811. Head of

Napoleon on one side. One Lira coinage of Pius IX."[16] That pocket piece was all it took to trip up the robbers.

About the sixth of September, William James decided to go to the Madison Basin with Frank Moore and H. C. Hinkley, and at their camp the first night out of Gardiner the talk around the fire turned to money. While pursuing that subject, James said, "If I don't get it one way I'll get it another. If you don't believe me, I'll show you!"[17] Upon saying that, James took a piece of money from a paper inside his stocking and handed it to Frank Moore with the comment: "I am the little son-of-a-bitch that held up that stage." Frank passed the piece of money to Hinkley who looked at it and returned it to James. Though Hinkley told him he would not have shown that to any man in the world, James put it back in his sock to keep "as long as he lived."

James then proceeded to tell his companions all about the robbery. He and Charley Higgenbotham had planned the holdup when they heard that the quartermaster was coming to pay off the troops at Camp Sheridan. He told Charley as they started out to be sure and get hold of the quartermaster's little satchel, as that was all they wanted; that the rest could go to hell. But things went awry. Soon after they had taken their stand at the "split rock" (across the Gardner River from the Eagle Nest Rock and somewhat above it, where the road used to bridge the stream), a buggy passed by driven by E. J. Lamartine, a foreman for the army engineers in the Park. The man riding with Lamartine was the paymaster, but the two highwaymen didn't know that; instead, they waited for the evening stage.

When the coach came up, James stepped out from behind the split rock and stopped it by presenting his pistols; he then ordered the ladies to get out on the left and the gents on the right. But Charley stepped up and changed that order to "all get out on the right," and ordered the ladies to walk around on the left.[18] Charley frisked the passengers, sticking one of his pistols in the top of a long boot to free a hand for that purpose. Neither of them took anything from the ladies, although one tried to give a watch to James. In hustling the passengers back into the stagecoach, Charley accidentally discharged a pistol, which served to get the coach off to a good start; but it also unnerved James, who tripped over a sagebrush and went sprawling, losing one of his pistols.

The following morning, James took a fishing rod and went up the Gardner River, pretending to fish as he looked for the pistol lost the evening before. He was searching when George Wakefield rode up with the driver of the stagecoach they had robbed. Recognizing James, Wakefield asked him if he had heard about the robbery, and

James said he had, but thought it was all a joke. Upon which, Wakefield said, "he did not know, but that he might have heard something." Meanwhile, the two horses were fretting and one nearly stepped on the pistol James was looking for, but he did not dare to pick it up then and had to return that evening to "put it where they would never find it."

Hinkley and Moore decided they had better tell the authorities what they had heard, and that led to the arrest of William James and Charley Higgenbotham in mid-October. They were tried in the United States District Court for the Third Judicial District, were found guilty, and each was fined $1,000 and sentenced to serve one year in the Montana Territorial Penitentiary at Deer Lodge.[19] This thoroughly bungled robbery would not have been nearly so important in the history of the Park if it had gone off as planned. The man whose foreign coin eventually tripped up the robbers, Judge John F. Lacey of Oskaloosa, Iowa, was later elected as a representative to Congress from the state of Iowa; when the way was at last cleared for passage of legislation that would give Yellowstone National Park effective legal machinery, it was Representative Lacey who initiated it by introducing H.R. 6442—"an act to protect the birds and animals in Yellowstone National Park, and to punish crimes in said park, and for other purposes." It is poetic justice that the Lacey Act, which brought law and order to the Yellowstone, was authored by a man who had experienced lawlessness in the Park.

The holdup incident spawned a legend. Jefferson Jones told it this way:

> The circumstances of the holdup, as I recall them, were somewhat as follows. Major McDougle, paymaster of the army in the park, traveling in an ambulance with a bodyguard of six soldiers rounded a turn in the road at Eagles Nest on the Gardner River to find himself confronted by nine mounted road agents, dressed in military uniform, carrying army carbines and their horses bore regulation army saddles and saddle-bags. Until the command "Hands up" was issued, Major McDougle thought he was looking at a cavalry patrol out on a morning maneuver. With the McDougle party covered by rifles, one road agent dismounted and searched the group for rifles and revolvers, which he took from the men and heaved in the nearby Gardner River. He then went to work in breaking open the army chest containing $40,000 in gold, all sacked. As the road agent lifted out a sack he would place it in the saddle-bag of one of his confederates. When the robbery was completed the men saluted the Major and rode down the road toward Gardiner. The robbery created much talk at this time but the men were never apprehended nor the money recovered.[20]

It is a beautiful little story, but there is no truth in it.

The quarters provided for the enlisted men at Camp Sheridan were adequate, but the officers' quarters were not. Second Lieutenant William Cannon Rivers and Dr. Galen L. Cline, the post surgeon, preferred lodgings in the National Hotel. This was particularly advantageous for Dr. Cline, who was a "contract surgeon" and, according to the custom of the day, was allowed the privilege of carrying on a private medical practice because, as Captain Harris later pointed out, "His services were at times indispensable to the resident population here as well as to the tourist visitors."[21] But the doctor's frequent presence at the hotel ultimately involved him in a difficult situation.

The beginning of this affair is described by Captain Moses Harris:

> There was at this time in the employ of the Hotel, as a clerk, a man by the name of Moore, who was a comrade and associate of [D.G.] Stivers. On the evening of the 9th of September 1888, Moore while partially under the influence of liquor, grossly insulted Dr. Cline, whereupon the Doctor struck him; a citizen interfered and the affair was terminated. The matter was reported to me and I fully investigated the circumstances. I found that Moore had been drinking for several days and had quarrelled with others; and although I did not approve of the course pursued by Dr. Cline, I believed that he had some justification in the insulting abuse heaped upon him by this drunken man. The next morning when Dr. Cline stepped from the door of his room, which opened into the main corridor of the hotel, he was confronted by Moore and Stivers, who informed him they were going to whip him. He was immediately assaulted by Moore, and a fist fight ensued in the Hotel corridor in the presence of many of the Hotel guests. Stivers stood by and encouraged Moore, and prevented the bystanders from interfering. Neither party was much injured in this contest and they soon separated. As soon as I heard of this affair, I decided to at once order the expulsion of Moore from the park, as he had previously offended by drunken and disorderly conduct, and had only been permitted to remain in the park upon expression of future good behavior. In the case of Stivers, desiring to avoid the necessity of ordering his expulsion, I called upon the General Manager of the Park Association to discharge him from employment in conformity with the provisions of Article 5 of Charles Gibson's lease, under which the Park Association carries on its business. This the General Manager, Mr. E. C. Waters promised to do: but evaded the spirit of the provision by retaining both men in the employment of the Park Association at Cinnabar, the Railroad terminus, eight miles from this place. Both of these men continued to make threats against Dr. Cline and Lieutenant Rivers, and came at least once, to this place after night, and having armed themselves laid in wait for Dr. Cline.[22]

Such was the state of affairs on the fifteenth of September when Dr. Cline drove down to Gardiner to visit a patient, unaware that Moore and Stivers were in town for the particular purpose of waylaying him.

Dr. Cline finished his professional call about one o'clock and was on his way to his buggy when Moore and Stivers approached him with drawn pistols. The doctor backed toward his vehicle, but before he could reach it, Stivers knocked him down and then jumped on him and began pummeling him with his fists. Meanwhile, Moore stood over the struggling pair with his pistol cocked, attempting to get a shot at Dr. Cline; but before he could do so, he was seized by some bystanders and disarmed. Though at a disadvantage, the doctor finally got his pistol out of his pocket and fired three or four shots, one of which struck Stivers in the groin, ending the fight.

It was at first thought that Stivers was seriously wounded, but an examination by Dr. Alton at Livingston, where he was rushed by train, proved that his wound was not dangerous. Charges were placed against both assailants, with Moore receiving a small fine and Stivers none—a leniency that was dependent upon their leaving the country as soon as possible.[23] This should have put an end to the Cline affair, but it didn't.

The following spring Stivers inquired of Captain Harris if there was an order of expulsion in force that would prohibit him from entering the Park. Stivers stated that he had found no such order on file in the Department of the Interior in Washington, adding, "I have no intention of reentering the employ of the Yellowstone Park Ass'n, and do not expect to be longer in the park than a day or so at a time."[24] Captain Harris saw in that letter an inclination on Stivers' part to pursue his vendetta against Dr. Cline, and perhaps Lieutenant Rivers also, both of whom were yet members of the garrison of Fort Yellowstone. So he hastened to put such an order of exclusion on the books, with the full approval of the secretary of the interior.[25] Stivers, who was an "army brat" (the son of Captain E. J. Stivers of the Twenty-fifth U.S. Infantry) considered that the order of expulsion increased "the degradation of being outlawed (practically) from the premises," and he was ingenious enough to find a way to circumvent it. He obtained a position as private secretary to the Honorable W.W. Dixon, congressman for Montana, then used his position as an argument for having the order of expulsion rescinded. However, all Stivers was able to accomplish was to get permission "to visit the Yellowstone National Park at any time in company with Hon. W. W. Dixon and in the capacity of stenographer to him."[26] In a letter of explanation to Congressman Dixon, it was pointed out that Stivers' offense "was of such character as forbids the policy of revoking the order of expulsion against him or of modifying it further than is done in this permit." Expulsion, as a method of law enforcement in the Park, had passed its most severe test.

An immediate consequence was the expulsion of Dr. Cline, Lieutenant Rivers, and Foreman Lamartine from their lodgings at the National Hotel by Manager E. C. Waters. He claimed that development of a very bitter feeling toward them among employees of the hotel made it necessary for him to ask them to move "for the purpose of avoiding any further trouble."[27] Subsequent events will show that the "very bitter feeling" mentioned by Mr. Waters was largely his own.

The bitterness expressed by Mr. Waters was really the second stage of a rocketing animosity that was touched off in the Upper Geyser Basin earlier that summer. The power of soap to excite certain thermal features to the point of eruption was discovered in 1885 when a Chinese employed as a laundryman at Upper Geyser Basin accidentally got some soap in the hot spring from which he was drawing his supply of water. Bob Burdet, a widely read correspondent of the day, gives a description:

> It is written in the Archives of Yellowstone Park that a child of the Flowery Kingdom, wearing the usual smile on his child-like face, and his shirt outside of his trousers, came to the Upper Geyser Basin to establish a laundry, because there was enough hot water there to run a Presidential Campaign. He pitched his tent over a thermal Spring, wrote his name in wierd characters upon a sign board, and when the raiments of the native and pilgrim came in, he chucked the whole invoice into the bubbling spring. Then he threw in a bar of soap, and smiled to see the great forces that upheave mountains and shake continents, and toss the mighty Globe into convulsions most awful, doing plain washing in a Chinese laundry. But this spring was a slumbering geyser. The soap awakened the imprisoned giant; with a roar that made the earth tremble, and a shriek of a steam whistle, a cloud of steam and a column of boiling water shot up into the air a hundred feet, carrying soap, raiment, tent and Chinaman along with the rush, and dropping them at various intervals along the way. "Hookee-la," said John, when he came down—way down! "Joss he no like washee for China-boy. Too muchee bubblee make." And since that day men have known the way to arouse a slumbering geyser is to give the monster soap.[28]

This discovery created a local demand for soap all out of proportion to the standard of cleanliness in vogue in the Park at that time. Every impatient tourist (and there were a great many of them even then) wanted soap to feed his favorite geyser, but with the establishment of the military detachment in Upper Geyser Basin the business of "soaping" geysers was frowned upon (this attitude was explained by supposing the government objected to the stimulating effect of soap).

> You see, if a geyser becomes addicted to the use of soap, it won't go off without it; it will sulk for months, just waiting for some man to come along with a plug of soap in his clothes, then it will go off with a grand hurrah and keep up the racket as long as the soap lasts; and one of these days some geyser that has been treated too often will have the delirium tremens, and that will be an end to the National Park.[29]

That was the situation in Upper Geyser Basin in the summer of 1888, when Burdet was loitering about the area "with a lot of other plebians": soaping geysers was forbidden, and there was a detail of soldiers there to see the rules were obeyed. At this time, Vice President Oakes and Division Superintendent Law of the Northern Pacific Railroad arrived there in the course of a park tour under the guidance of E. C. Waters. As their time was too valuable to waste waiting for the eruption of a common geyser, Mr. Waters soaped the Beehive. The geyser "went off—grandly. So did the great men— ignobly." They were arrested by a private soldier of Company M, taken before Captain Moses Harris and ordered out of the Park. Bob Burdet thought it was a "mighty sick transit" for such great men, but he also admits to being glad they soaped the geyser, "because it kept itself on exhibition twice a day after the soaping as long as we stayed." He was thankful to have been provided with a committee of great men to get into trouble for him, and adds "don't tell me that a railroad president isn't good for something." It was the slow burn left by this humiliation before his superiors that caused Waters to act as he did in the Cline affair. Indeed, he was set upon a course of vengeful uncooperation wherever the military was concerned, and this stubbornness eventually led to the ruin of all his enterprises.

It would appear that the board of directors of the Yellowstone Park Association did not hold Waters to account for his collisions with the authorities in the Park, for the minutes of the board meeting of January 26, 1889, record that "on motion of Mr. Oakes, the salary of the General Manager was fixed at $4,000 per annum."[30]

The confidence of the board in their employee was shown in another way. Interest in a steamboat service on Yellowstone Lake was reviving, and the association was willing to let Mr. Waters put a boat on the lake and operate it under the company's franchise.[31] The project got underway in the summer of 1889, when E. C. Waters hauled into the Park the steel hull for a steamboat of 40 tons. This vessel—the *Zillah*—was originally launched on the Great Lakes in 1884, and was transported to the Park in segments and reassembled at Lake Yellowstone. The equipment of the assembling crew, who were to work throughout the winter fitting up the little vessel, seems to have included guns, traps, and poison—an arrangement that came to the attention of the military authorities. Captain Frazier Augustus Boutelle, who had replaced Captain Moses Harris as acting superintendent of the Park, found that "all of the principal employees of the Yellowstone Park Association were implicated" in this attempt to make poaching a profitable sideline.[32] The captain attempted to exclude Waters from the Park for his part in this scheme, but may have been outmaneuvered; anyhow, the captain's assignment to other duty at this particular time was considered as evidence that politics had been introduced into the management of the Park. A House committee later looked into this charge, coming to the conclusion in its 300-page report that such was the case, although a minority of Republicans denied it.[33] According to H. D. Hampton's digest of that report, Waters went to Russell B. Harrison, son of the president, and requested that political pressure be applied so that "Captain Boutelle would be suspended and would not superintend the park another year."[34]

Historian Hiram Chittenden appears to subscribe to the foregoing explanation of Captain Boutelle's downfall, stating, "For causes not publicly understood, he [Boutelle] was unexpectedly relieved from duty January 21, 1891, and Captain George S. Anderson, 6th U. S. Cavalry, the present superintendent, was assigned in his place."[35] Even if the attempt to expell E. C. Waters was not the cause of Captain Boutelle's replacement, the secretary of the interior certainly had other good reasons for wanting to be rid of him.

Captain Boutelle took over the administration of the Park at the beginning of a busy summer and his attempts to get some necessary answers from the Department of the Interior were so frustrating that he lost his cool and said some very blunt things. He had written the secretary concerning the disposition of some confiscated property and had requested the installation of a telephone in his office and the purchase of fire buckets and axes for his troopers on patrol in the Park, all without result. Becoming impatient with bureaucratic lethargy, Boutelle wrote the secretary as follows:

> If you do not think it proper to give me such things as I asked for, I certainly am entitled to recognition. I take the liberty of enclosing this letter under personal cover, in order that I may feel sure that it reaches you in person and wish . . . that in the future I shall not be ignored. In the department in which I have served for 28 years I have been accustomed to have some respectful actions taken on my papers.[36]

The secretary's angry rejoinder to the effect that the captain was inclined to be troublesome and quick to find fault might have ended the matter, except that Captain Boutelle raised the issue again in his annual report. His reference to the failure to provide equipment for fighting forest fires was particularly galling. He said:

> Up to a late date last season there was no fire equipment in the Park. The few axes and shovels supplied the troops for garrison purposes were the only tools available. Application was made for funds for the purchase of axes, shovels, and folding rubber buckets, but through some misunderstanding the authority was not promptly received, and the work was doubly hard from want of proper tools.
>
> While at the hotel communicating with a fire party by telephone, an incident occurred which I think should be mentioned in this report. I was greatly troubled that I had not what was needed, and mentioned to a party of gentlemen that I did not know what I should do. I had exhausted all men and implements under my control and was afraid that the Park would burn in spite of every possible effort. I remarked that I had applied for rubber buckets and had failed to get them; that I supposed the Secretary had no funds, etc.; whereupon Mr. J. Lewis, of Mauch Chunk, Pa., exclaimed that "if this great United States Government or the Secretary of the Interior has not money to buy you a few rubber buckets for the protection of this wonderful and beautiful country I have." He handed me $40 from his purse. In three days I was supplied with two dozen buckets, which were of incalculable service during the remainder of the season. Would that Congress would take such an interest in the protection of the Park before it is too late.[37]

The secretary returned that acidulous report to Captain Boutelle hoping he would revise it, not only with regard to the foregoing statement, but also in his references to a proposed elevator at the Grand Canyon.[38]

In 1889, D. B. May of Billings, Montana, had applied to the secretary of the interior for permission to build an elevator to the bottom of the Grand Canyon immediately below the Lower Falls. The site—the first gulch south of Lookout Point—was examined that fall by Captain Boutelle and Arnold Hague of the United States Geological Survey, and they came to the conclusion that the elevator would not be objectionable if it followed the alignment of the gulch. However, the lease granted Mr. May allowed the building of a structure that would proceed in a straight line from top to bottom, rearing into view "a very unsightly structure." Thus, the captain saw fit to revise his earlier opinion, stating, "I recommend that the lease be either cancelled or that the incline be made to conform to the changes of direction of the gulch, and that no building of any kind be required or permitted at the bottom of the Canyon." The direct result was revocation of the objectionable lease on October 15, 1890.[39] It was probably a combination of all three of the foregoing incidents that caused Captain Boutelle's superintendency to be so brief—only a little over a year and eight months; but he seems not to have greatly minded the change, which he anticipated in these words:

> I was selected for it without being consulted and came here against my wish. My selection may have been unfortunate but being here I take great interest in my work, and, as has been the rule of my life, do as well as I can. It is not the first time I have paid the penalty of efficiency . . . While my interest in the park is great and I have here an importance which I should not enjoy at an ordinary frontier post where I should play a very subordinate role, I shall for many reasons be glad when my relief comes. I should be glad to remain and see some of the work which I have inaugurated carried to a successful termination, but at a military post I am able to please my commanding officer while here I have the world to consider and appear to be about as successful as the old man with the ass in the fable.[40]

It was not only in such special cases that the Park was protected by the military. There were minor cases also, such as the woman who was expelled from the Park for persisting to throw stones into the crater of Old Faithful Geyser; the man expelled for his "insufferable insolence" to a noncommissioned officer; the Yellowstone Park Association butcher who killed a bear without cause; an employee by the name of Rowley (one of those working for E. C. Waters at his Lake shipway) who was expelled for breaking specimens from a number of geysers in Upper Geyser Basin early in the morning when he thought no one was awake; a number of tramps who drifted into the Park from the railroad and were hustled right out again; and a visitor by the name of John Noack who was expelled for writing his name on formations in Upper Geyser Basin. In Noack's case, the offense was aggravated by an attempt to bribe the soldier who apprehended him, so that Captain Harris felt obligated to do more than warn the man. For his part, Mr. Noack felt that he had been abused, and threatened to air the matter in the newspapers—which he did,[41] generating unfair publicity.

A letter to the editor of the *Livingston Enterprise* by a visitor who signed himself "Alexis" but who may have been Mr. Noack is an example of the bad press of that summer.

> In a recent issue in speaking of Uncle Sam's Army which is congregated at this point you convey the impression that the last 15 additions thereto are decidedly tough and worthless. I am glad to bear witness to the fact

that such a reputation does not belong to all of them, as witness the following incident:

Scene—Upper Geyser Basin. Personages—Corporal in the U. S. Army (and one of the immortal 15) and a middleaged lady tourist with a flock of more or less middle aged females under her wing. Bystanders— a few humiliated and depressed tourists and a detachment of soldiers ready to rush to the assistance of the aforesaid Corporal in case he needs it.

Middleaged lady, timidly addressing the Corporal—"Will you please tell us if Old Faithful will probably be in a state of eruption again today?" Corporal (swelling up and striking an attitude)—"I am not here to be talked to death by a lot of women; neither do I propose to answer a thousand and one fool questions." Lady (quietly)—"Well, will you please tell us just what questions we are allowed to ask, and how many of them, so that we may govern ourselves accordingly." Corporal—"It is not any part of my business to answer questions at all, but if you will keep still I will, without being questioned, explain all that is necessary for you to know." Thereupon the ladies assumed various awe stricken positions, and the Corporal delivers a lecture similar to a man who is shooting off a magic lantern.

The foregoing conversation and occurrence are facts, and yet there are people who visit the park not sufficiently civilized to fully appreciate (?) the treatment they receive.[42]

The "Immortal 15" were the fifteen men of the Twenty-second United States Infantry under command of Lieutenant Moody, who arrived in the Upper Geyser Basin on July 22 from Fort Keogh, Montana Territory. They were not in the Park long and the duty was strange to them, so they may not have conducted themselves as well as Captain Harris' more experienced cavalrymen; even so, there was a hero among them. Private John Coyle was on duty at Castle Geyser on August 9 when a young lady from California climbed the wall of its cone to look inside. A shift in the wind enveloped her in steam so she could not see to descend and was in danger of falling into the vent of the geyser. Her terrified shrieks brought Private Coyle, who climbed up, wrapped his blue coat about the young lady and brought her safely down, but not without getting seriously scalded in the face. Orders Number 52, issued at headquarters of the Twenty-second Infantry at Fort Keogh on August 25, 1888, state: "The colonel commanding is pleased to announce to the regiment an act of heroism and gallantry displayed by Private John Coyle, Company B, 22nd Infantry, while on duty in camp at the Old Faithful Geyser, Yellowstone Park." After reciting the circumstances the colonel concluded, "such commendable and exemplary conduct entitles Private Coyle to great praise, and the thanks of the regimental commander are hereby extended to him"[43] Private Coyle later received a silver medal for his courageous act.

A less spectacular side of the army's management of the Park was the concern with establishment of outpost stations and development of effective methods of patrolling in winter. The only place other than Camp Sheridan that was occupied the first winter, it will be remembered, was Soda Butte. Other winter outposts were added as needed, including a detachment in Lower Geyser Basin as early as the winter of 1888-89. The presence of a detachment at that point is known from a sad incident that occurred there.

Across Nez Perce Creek, in the narrow angle between that stream and the Firehole River, stood that primitive hostel built by George W. Marshall in 1884 and variously known as Marshall's hotel or the Marshall House, and, after it passed into the hands of the Yellowstone Park Association in 1886, as the Firehole Hotel. The winter keeper employed to look after the main building and the two wretched annexes added in 1888 was E. C. Culver, whose wife, Mattie, died in childbirth, or soon after, that winter. The men at the nearby soldier station gave Culver what help they could. The ground was too deeply frozen to make a burial at that time, so they brought over two barrels which they set end to end and covered with snow to hold Mrs. Culver's body until a grave could be dug later. Culver's infant daughter was taken by an aunt in Spokane, Washington, and Mr. Culver remained a familiar figure in and around the Park. In later years he had a little grocery store at Gardiner, and was, for a time, the postmaster. A tourist of 1901, who met Mr. Culver when he was a "runner" for the Yellowstone Park Association on the daily train between Livingston and Cinnabar (riding the train for the purpose of interesting visitors in utilizing the association's transportation and hotels in the Park), has this to say of him: "While all know the story of his faded dreams, not even the roughest cow puncher or mountaineer will allude to it in his presence."[44] Mrs. H. W. Child, the wife of an early concessioner in the Park, had Mattie Culver's grave neatly fenced, and saw that it was carefully maintained. The visitor who pauses at the little picnic area near the mouth of Nez Perce Creek may see the small marble headstone with its single rose carved in low relief above the legend: "Mattie S. wife of E. C. Culver died March 2, 1889, aged 30 years"; in the early summer there may be withered flowers at its base, for someone remembers the grave every spring.

Patrolling the Park in winter to protect the wildlife against poachers had its beginning under Captain Moses Harris. An incident involving an elk killing by Frank A. Chatfield at Heart Lake in the fall of 1887, and the presence of poachers like Andrew Page and Thomas

Morrison   *Stitham*   *Holt*

Trip to Fall river 1897

Ski Patrol: Scouts Morrison, Stitham, and Holt, Fall River area, 1897.

Ruin of a poacher's cabin still standing in a secluded hollow on Blacktail Deer Plateau. Photograph by the author.

Garfield, pointed up the need for constant surveillance of remote areas. Open season patrolling was no problem for the cavalry but winter patrolling, when the park interior was blockaded with snow, remained an unknown. So Captain Harris consulted with Scout Edward Wilson (who had been a member of the Haynes winter expedition of the previous year) and they decided to try an extended winter patrol. For his companion on this trip Wilson picked a volunteer from Company M, Sergeant Charles Schroegler. The two men left Camp Sheridan on February 13, 1888, for their "jumping-off place," Yancey's hotel in Pleasant Valley. Carrying their provisions and one blanket each, they proceeded along the crest of Specimen Ridge and Amethyst Mountain, across the Mirror Plateau to Pelican Creek, which they followed down to Lake Yellowstone; from there they followed the Yellowstone River to the Grand Canyon and shelter at the park association's hotel. Resting a day, they returned to Camp Sheridan by way of Norris Geyser Basin, completing a journey of which Captain Harris remarked: "The hardships of an expedition of this character can only be realized by those who are acquainted with the winter aspect of the mountain solitudes into which these brave and hardy men ventured."[45] Wilson made a second ski trip with T. Elwood Hofer across the Central Plateau, between the Yellowstone and Madison river drainages in April. Those successful trips set the pattern of winter patrols for several years.

The scouts and soldiers who patrolled the park interior in winter suffered extreme hardship. Unfortunately they were forced to pass hastily through areas where a protracted search might have discovered a poacher. The poachers had this advantage besides their native hardiness; they could prepare in advance for their winter's work. They often cached food and equipment securely at convenient points within the area they intended to trap or hunt, and usually built snug shelters varying from rude dugouts to comfortable cabins. A rather elaborate example of a poacher's cabin of the mid-1890s is still standing on the Blacktail Deer Plateau. Hidden in a tree-covered maze of outcropping lava rock, the structure was built of large logs, with a fireplace of lava boulders, an earth-covered puncheon roof, and a door of sawn boards. The interior was 7 by 10 feet, with a height of 5 feet at the side wall and 6 feet under the ridge. The door, made of two wide boards, had a glass-covered opening in the upper half to admit daylight. The fireplace, built beside the door at one end of the cabin, had a low, broad throat supported by two iron buggy axles marked "Concord U.S." The indications are that this particular shelter was not used extensively, and that may be why it escaped detection and destruction (such shelters were burned when found).

In order to put his men on an equal footing with determined interlopers and reduce somewhat the hardships of their work, Captain Boutelle requested funds in the fall of 1890 for construction of five or six cabins conveniently located for the winter patrolmen.[46] Construction of six cabins, not to cost more than $100 each, was authorized,[47] and thus the system of snowshoe cabins—so-called from an obsolete terminology that referred to the Norwegian ski as a snowshoe—came into being. A greatly expanded system of cabins remains the basis of present winter patrols in the Park.

Some of the poachers who penetrated the Park in the winter were a nuisance in summer also. Andrew Page was apprehended August 19, 1888, while trapping beaver on the southern edge of the Park. He managed to escape from his captors, leaving his personal property behind, and was never heard from again. Less than a month later, Thomas Garfield, who had been an associate of William James, was caught in the act of trapping beaver on Willow Creek and was expelled from the Park. He then wrote Captain Harris, stating: "As I am ordered out of the park I am determined to go and take up a homestead on the south boundary line, for the purpose of being a nuisance to the park and its officers."[48] That he was deadly serious about making trouble is evident in an excerpt from the report for 1889. Captain Harris mentions that on September 17 the noncommissioned officer of the detachment at Norris Geyser Basin

> discovered a fire in thick timber about four miles from Norris in the direction of Mount Holmes. He, with his detachment, started at once for the scene of the fire, and by hard work succeeded in extinguishing it. He found near the place at which the fire was started the tracks of a man, which, from the character of the imprint, was believed to be Garfield. This belief was confirmed by the arrest of Garfield on the trail leading from Mount Holmes by one of my sergeants stationed at Riverside, on the west side of the park. He was again put out, and after hanging around the western border of the park for a few days disappeared, and has not since been heard of.[49]

Fighting forest fires was an onerous chore in some years. Many of the men of Company M went on the fire line immediately upon their arrival in August of 1886, but the summer of 1887 was an easy one in which not a single green tree was lost. Over one hundred blazes originated in the Park in 1888—some of them from lightning; however, the soldiers were so vigilant and energetic that less than five acres of timber were destroyed.[50] While there were not as many fires during the summer of 1889 (seventy, of which all but three were extinguished by soldiers), conditions must have been more severe, for a large area of forest was lost despite the best efforts of Captain Boutelle and his men. A fire above the Madison Canyon was fought for three weeks before it was brought under control; the difficulties encountered and overcome near the Gibbon River make a story with modern overtones. Of this fire, Captain Boutelle says:

> It took me just an hour to walk around it in making an examination with a view to determining whether it was possible to do anything with it. Concluding that it was worth the trial, I called up all the available men—29 in number—and by night a clearing was made entirely around the fire. All combustible matter was scraped away to the earth. The fire was surrounded and controlled. There was no water on the height, and the only way to do anything was to keep the fire within bounds and let the interior burn out. High winds prevailed almost every afternoon while this fire was burning, and at times the flames would jump the cut-off and get beyond control, but as soon as the winds subsided another cut was made, and at the end of three weeks the fire was out.[51]

Understandably, the soldiers didn't like this part of their work, but to their credit, they did it and they did it well.

The first four years of military administration in Yellowstone National Park accomplished much. The objectives to be served in the management of the area were at last clearly defined: the fauna of the Park was to be protected *absolutely*, not even excepting those animals of "fang and claw," which were beyond the pale in the days of the assistants; the forests were to be protected *absolutely*, even if soldiers had to be metamorphosed into fire fighters to do it, and the thermal features were to be protected *absolutely*, though it meant a constant struggle with name scribblers, pebble tossers, and souvenir pickers. These firm objectives were promoted by the development of a modus operandi that worked despite the failure of Congress to give the area adequate legal machinery. This was nothing more than a discerning use of the only means Congress had ever provided for the protection of the Park—expulsion. Properly used, it proved effective. At the time that Captain Harris' methods of enforcing the rules and regulations were under attack by Montana newspapers, he explained his procedures this way:

> In the exercise of the authority which is devolved upon the office of the Superintendent of this National Park, great care has been taken to keep strictly within the limits sanctioned by law and to avoid all appearance of a harsh and arbitrary exercise of authority. No person has ever been expelled from the Park who had not admitted the commission of the offense for which the penalty was enforced; and whenever there has been reason to believe that the offenses were committed without

A soldier talking with a visitor near the cone of Old Faithful Geyser, 1889. A rare round-format photograph taken with an early Eastman Kodak.

intention or through thoughtlessness, or when a sincere regret was perceived, the persons have been permitted to go unmolested, after suitable instruction and admonition.[52]

How far the military could go in the use of expulsion is evident in the case of the man who attempted an attack upon a chambermaid at the Lake Hotel. The soldiers who apprehended him were ordered to march him to headquarters, which they did, bringing him in afoot ahead of a mounted trooper. The offender, being a tenderfoot, did not stand up well to the march; when he collapsed from exhaustion he was merely revived at the nearest soldier station and herded on toward Mammoth Hot Springs. Though his hearing before the acting military superintendent only resulted in expulsion from the Park, he had already experienced fairly severe punishment. On the other hand, in 1891 Owen Wister witnessed a case of tactful handling of a violator. A soldier on duty in the Upper Geyser Basin had reported to Captain Edwards that a clergyman had broken off a number of specimens which he secreted in his baggage. The captain found him seated in the stagecoach, about to depart, and asked him, "You have taken no specimens of course?" The answer was, "No." "You give me your word as a preacher of the gospel that you have nothing of the sort in that bag?" The minister's answer was "I do." Captain Edwards let him go, and when Owen Wister asked him why he had done so, the officer answered, "I couldn't humiliate a minister in front of the crowd."[53]

No doubt it was the justice used in making expulsions that made this extra-legal proceeding so effective with the visitor. As for local people, its effectiveness had to do with their livelihoods. Most residents in the vicinity at least partially depended upon work within the Park, and it became evident that expulsion could be construed as exclusion. They tended to think a second time, therefore, before offending the military authorities. Even park employees—the highly placed as well as the lowly—came to understand that they were not privileged in the least degree, but were held as strictly accountable as any visitor.

The result of these early years of administration by the army was to halt the destructive trend that would have ended in the dismemberment or revocation of Yellowstone National Park: by introducing order, the basis was laid for eventual improvement of park affairs. Victory was not wholly possible however until war could be waged and won against the railroad monopoly—that bogeyman waiting in the shadow of the wings, just off stage, to press for complete commercialization of Yellowstone National Park.

CHAPTER 13

THE RAILROAD BOGEY

Let poetry have some place here; some one last battlement of rally. The railroads have enough. Spare this one spot of this vast continent. Draw round this one last shrine . . . and declare to man that he is not yet God!

—Joaquin Miller [1]

The opening years of administration by the military set Yellowstone National Park in order and laid the basis for the perfection of its management in the interest of the people. However, before that objective could be realized, a bitter struggle with monopoly interests had to be won. This conflict—appropriately called the first Yellowstone war—was the key factor in Yellowstone's history for more than a decade, and it had to be settled conclusively before the Park was safe enough for the idea it represented to really prosper.

The "bad guys" in this part of the Yellowstone story are the railroads and the commercial enterprises they spawned. Several railroads looked upon Wonderland as a happy hunting ground that would contribute handsomely to their annual revenues. The Northern Pacific, by virtue of its priority upon the scene, was the principal antagonist; its unvarying objective was the one so clearly outlined in a later company office memorandum: "Yellowstone Park must be made a *summer resort*."[2] The methods employed by the railroad company in their approach to that objective were mostly devious and usually camouflaged, so that the corporation's role was more that of a bogey in the shadows than a contestant who could be openly faced.

The influence of the Northern Pacific Railroad Company was not always readily apparent in the commercial affairs of the Park, yet it was always there—sometimes guiding, sometimes cajoling, and sometimes threatening the concessioners to create what the railroad management desired: a summer resort attractive to large numbers of tourists. Tourism was *the* goal of the Northern Pacific (and of several other lines in later years), and interest in the Park lasted just as long as tourism was profitable.

Some of the Northern Pacific Railroad Company's early interest and heavy-handed activities in the Yellowstone region have already been mentioned: the Washburn party's exploration of 1870 was sparked by Jay Cooke, financial agent for the Northern Pacific, through his employee Nathaniel Pitt Langford; the suggestion that was the effective beginning of the movement to establish a Yellowstone National Park came from Judge William Darrah Kelley, a long-time associate of the railroad interests, and found its way to Ferdinand V. Hayden through an officer of J. Cooke & Company; Langford was called to Washington, D.C., by his brother-in-law—Governor William Marshall of Minnesota, a Northern Pacific Railroad promoter—to assist Hayden with his campaign to interest Congress in legislation that would set aside the Yellowstone region; Langford, the first superintendent of the new Park, concerned himself with maintaining the status quo—that is, with preventing the development of strong concession interests in the Park until such time as the Northern Pacific pushed its tracks close enough to dominate the development of visitor facilities; Superintendent Philetus W. Norris was ousted from the superintendency largely because he turned an approving eye toward the northward advance of the Utah and Northern Railroad and was impolitic enough to openly favor that line's proposal to build into the Park from Virginia City; and the Yellowstone Park Improvement Company came into existence under a scheming, mismanaging division superintendent of the Northern Pacific Railroad, who almost immediately became an agitator for railroad development within the Park. Such was the thread of railroad activity connecting the explorers with the exploiters of the Park.

The Northern Pacific had planned to extend its park branch line to several points of interest within the boundaries of the reservation, and preliminary surveys for such a development were completed in the summer of 1882. However, General P. H. Sheridan's junketing in the Park that same summer served the good purpose of making him aware of the difference between the improvement company's plans and the public good. Rightly seeing the Northern Pacific Railroad Company as the real backer of the schemers who nearly had the Park sewed up, the old general opened the first Yellowstone war by inducing the secretary of the interior to forbid the building of any railroads within the Park.

The Northern Pacific had a multi-million dollar investment in the park branch line, however, and they had to think in terms of dollars and the percentages thereon (the percentage they must pay on the borrowed money and the percentage earned beyond the operating costs), hoping each year to finish in the black and well aware of the penalty for any prolonged failure to do so. In other words, the park branch line was constructed for the mundane purpose of making a profit, in this case by hauling tourists; but there had to be some place to haul them to, hotels where they could be fed and lodged, and facilities for their transportation between points of interest (particularly important since the railroad was proscribed from extending its lines into the area). Wary of direct involvement in such an unfamiliar enterprise and the problem of raising investment funds, the railroad arranged that the necessary business of handling tourist travel within the Park should be placed in loyal but entirely independent hands. The anointed were Carroll T. Hobart, one of the railroad's division superintendents and thus presumed loyal, and Henry F. Douglas, the post trader of Fort Yates in Dakota Territory, whose Washington connections were a distinct asset. With Douglas' Washington influence and the railroad's backing, these men easily arrived at an agreement with acting Assistant Secretary of the Interior M. L. Joslyn on September 1, 1882,[3] at which time the secretary, Henry M. Teller, had deliberately absented himself to avoid involvement. Though they did not have a valid lease, the partners were assured a virtual monopoly of the business opportunities in the Park.

Hobart and Douglas believed they had secured a valuable privilege (and it would have proven so except that Congress later took exception to the renting out of the people's property for almost nothing), but they lacked the financial means to exploit their advantage. Between them, they could raise only $6,000 for a venture that would require financing to the extent of several hundred thousand dollars. Thus, they had to go looking for a partner who could supply the money they lacked. They found a man willing to arrange the financing in exchange for the presidency of the company they intended to found and one-third interest in the corporate stock.

He was "Colonel," or "Uncle," Rufus Hatch, a Wall Street broker and former shipping tycoon of a smooth, ruthless type rather common in the nineteenth century. This expansive, determined individual was at his ebullient, jocular best while gobbling up the weak and unwary of the financial world, and he probably saw easy pickings in this partnership.

Much has already been said about the Yellowstone Park Improvement Company created by these sly, cunning men. Although their agreement with Assistant Secretary Joslyn was not a lease, they began construction in the Park, in the fall of 1882, in such a brazen manner that popular condemnation led the Congress to disapprove by means of the Sundry Civil Appropriation Act of 1883, severely limiting the authority of the secretary of the interior in matters of leases and nullifying prior agreements.[4]

Activities of the improvement company were ultimately legitimized by a lease on March 9, 1883, between the secretary of the interior, acting on behalf of the United States, and Messrs. Hobart, Douglas, and Hatch of the company. (This lease was immediately assigned to the Yellowstone National Park Improvement Company by the lessees).[5] Financier Hatch only partially fulfilled his commitment to finance the work in the Park, while General Manager Hobart scandalously mismanaged the resources that were made available. The third partner seems to have contributed nothing but influence. The outcome should have been predictable: an early bankruptcy and a receivership that bumbled along for two seasons, benefiting no one but the shifty general manager.

During this time the traveling public was poorly served in the Park, and the Northern Pacific Railroad Company suffered by association, getting less patronage than had been expected. When the improvement company's remaining assets were at last put up for sale on the order of a Wyoming court in the fall of 1885,[6] the railroad company purchased the property through a bidder working in its interest. The Northern Pacific thus became the real owner of a business they were determined to control but did not want to run—a dilemma the company would maneuver to avoid.

The first Yellowstone war had been touched off when the railroad was forbidden to extend its tracks into the Park. One of the late events of the topsy-turvy summer of 1883 had been the editors' excursion. At the close of the annual meeting of the Western Associated Press, the editors in attendance were invited to be guests of the Northern Pacific Railroad for a tour of Yellowstone National Park. Those who accepted (about thirty-six), left Chicago on the first

of August in three special cars—two sleepers and a diner attached to
the Pacific Express.[7] At the temporary terminus of the park branch
line, near Yankee Jim's toll gate, the party was delivered into the
hands of Wakefield and Hoffman's coachmen for the perilous
evening drive to Mammoth Hot Springs.

The journalists saw the Park in its almost pristine glory. They
returned to the National Hotel bronzed by the sun and wind, grimy
with the dust of the road, and thoroughly fatigued by the stagecoach
mode of travel. At that opportune moment, Manager Hobart of the
improvement company spread them a dinner followed by a speech in
which he unfolded the company's plan to push for a railway in the
Park. The editor of the *Livingston Enterprise*, in commenting on this
dinner and the other promotional activities of the summer, said:

> The host of influential persons, great and small who have visited the
> Park this summer were not induced to come merely to advertise the
> Park. Other plans are in process of development, and a railway in the
> Park is one of them . . . and when the time comes for its denouement,
> there will be plenty of advocates, both within the halls of Congress
> as well as throughout the country.[8]

Carroll T. Hobart spent the winter of 1883-84 in Washington,
D.C., lobbying for a railroad through the Park to Cooke City. Early
in January the word was out that J. Cooke and U.S. Railroad
Commissioner Armstrong (who had been deliberately involved in the
Clarks Fork mining development in order to secure his support) were
advocating construction of a narrow gauge line through the Park
from Cinnabar to Cooke City, and the articles of incorporation for a
Bullion Railroad Company to be capitalized at $1 million for the
purpose of building and operating the line, were soon filed.[9] The
advocates of this extension disclaimed any connection with the
Northern Pacific Railroad Company, pointing out that its odd-gauge
track would be of no use to the larger railroad—a specious argument
considering the relative ease with which track gauge could be
changed. In fact, a Northern Pacific attorney, George Haldorn, was
known to be concerned in the organization of the new line.[10]

The incorporation of the Bullion Railroad Company was
followed immediately by attempts to obtain a charter from Congress.
On January 29, Delegate Maginnis of Montana Territory introduced
a bill—H.R. 4363—authorizing a Cinnabar & Clarks Fork Railroad;
and on February 4, Senator McMillan of Minnesota introduced S.
1373 for the same purpose. The house committee for railroads
reported a substitute measure—H.R. 6083—on March 18, but it was
not acted upon. The Senate measure was reported favorably on

The National Hotel at Mammoth Hot Springs as seen from the Liberty Cap (cone of an extinct hot spring), probably in the late 1880s.

James C. McCartney's primitive "hotel" which the National replaced in 1883. *From an F.J. Haynes photograph, 1885.*

February 27 and was debated at length on May 27.[11] This debate developed considerable opposition to the railroad scheme, an outcome that surprised the friends of the Park as much as it disconcerted the railroad interests. Several senators (Conger, Garland, Call, and Voorhees) had feelings akin to those of Senator Harrison who "did not like to see the park thus invaded"; but it was Senators Logan and Vest who were the Park's real defenders. Logan characterized the Clarks Fork mines as "a mere cover" and offered his opinion that the real object was to give the Northern Pacific Railroad a branch through the Park. In his words, it was "a gobble by the railway." He created a sensation by stating that an official of the Department of the Interior "in the pay of the railroad" (Assistant Secretary Joslyn, who so nearly delivered Yellowstone Park to the monopolists of the improvement company in 1882) had lobbied persistently in behalf of the project. For his part, Senator Vest expressed a concern for the precedent that would be established. In his opinion, allowing any railroad to enter "would end in the destruction of the Park."[12]

At this time Senator Vest was shepherding legislation he had introduced at the opening of the Forty-eighth Congress. It was intended to improve the Yellowstone Park Act by adding provisions to secure benefits of the Sundry Civil Bill of 1883, at the same time providing protection under the laws of Montana Territory and eliminating the Idaho and Montana strips and the Clarks Fork mining region from the Park, extending the boundaries eastward and southward as General Sheridan had previously recommended.[13] After the failure of their own legislation, the railroad monopolists were content to watch the steady progress of the Vest bill, knowing that its segregation of the Montana strip was a step in their direction. From the Senate, S.221 went to the House where it was favorably reported on by the House Committee on Territories, January 24, 1885. On February 13, the House debated, amended, and passed the bill, and conference committees were appointed in the House and Senate that same day. There was every expectation that a compromise satisfactory to both houses would soon be reached, solving many of the Park's longstanding problems; and it was with just such expectation that certain friends of the monopolists laid claim to the lands in the Montana strip. As we have seen, their action was premature; there was no meeting of minds between the two Congressional committees. Though the principal result of the chicanery of Superintendent Robert E. Carpenter was his own downfall, the railroad monopolists also took a setback where they had hoped to make clear gain.

The immediate result of the furor created by the Carpenter scandal was the appointment on March 3 of a special committee of the House, consisting of Representatives Holman, Hatch, Peel, Cannon, and Ryan to investigate, among other things, affairs in Yellowstone National Park.[14] Blame for the Carpenter scandal and miscarriage of other monopolist affairs was soon attributed to Carroll T. Hobart, who "seems to have the remarkable luck of throwing a shadow over whatever he puts his hand to. The Northern Pacific Company, with which he was formerly connected thinks so; Rufus Hatch and other members of the Park Improvement Company think so; and the friends of the Cinnabar & Cooke Railway have the same opinion."[15] The full import of what the monopolists had done to their cause is seen in a conversation reported to have taken place between a Livingston man and Representative O'Neil.

> "Mr. O'Neil," said one of our citizens . . . "have you given any thought to the railway that our people want to get extended to Cooke City?"
> "Yes, I should say that I have given it attention. I have been almost talked to death on that subject ever since I have been in the country. Look at me! I am a total wreck just from listening to this railway talk. And I tell you right now there will never be a d____d inch of that park cut off. I want to see it enlarged instead of cut down. Your bill came nearer passing last winter than it ever will again. Just on information and belief that it had passed just about half the population of this country got fresh and went out and plastered the park with mineral location notices. That settled it. It looked a good deal as if the land was of more importance than the railway . . . I met a man who impressed it upon my mind, or tried to, that all his past life and future prospects were intombed in that northern strip of the park like a toad in the trunk of a tree . . . This nation has only got one park and I want to see it left alone."[16]

The special committee of the House that investigated affairs in Yellowstone National Park during the summer of 1885 was not heard from until March 16, 1886. They had listened to considerable testimony and were not in agreement as to their findings, but they did make a significant contribution by providing a statement of policy that is as valid today as it was then. (See Vol. I, page 323.)

The Senate had already received a report of another investigation of park matters. Special Agent W. Hallet Phillips of the Department of the Interior had been in the Park during the summer of 1885 and his report was available February 1, 1886.[17] While the Phillips report dealt mainly with matters of administration and justice, the issues of railroad penetration and segregation of park lands were not ignored. Predictably, Phillips was against construction of a railway in the Park, but he opposed removal of the Montana strip from the Park because it formed an essential part of the wildlife refuge. This viewpoint, though not yet fully accepted, was sufficient warning to the railroad monopolists that they could probably expect little or nothing favorable to their cause from segregation; so they turned once again to advocating direct railroad legislation.

Delegate Toole of Montana and Senator McMillan of Minnesota both introduced railroad bills. On February 23, a House committee reported a substitute for Toole's legislation, and on March 6, the Senate Committee on Railroads reported a substitute measure for McMillan's bill. The latter was debated in the Senate on June 21, with Vest speaking strongly against it.

> He denied that the road was intended in good faith to reach mining property. Why had not at least a preliminary survey been made? He would not appeal to men who thought that the Mammoth Cave and Niagara Falls should be transferred to commercial use, or that the great geysers should be devoted to laundry purposes and dished out to Chinamen for dirty linen. But he would appeal to Senators to preserve at least one spot of beauty from the rack and roar of commerce and the greed and avarice of selfish men.[18]

Those powerful sentiments prevented the bill from being called up and the railroad people were again defeated.

Senator Vest's vigorous opposition had only begun. On December 8, 1885, the senator introduced a bill to replace S. 221, which had failed so narrowly in the Forty-eighth Congress. This new try (S. 101) was reported from committee as S. 2436 on May 17, 1886, and, when Vest attempted to get it before the Senate on July 12, Senator McMillan blocked him despite the reminder that with the repeal of Wyoming law "this park is entirely without a form of Government."[19] The fate of those legislative attempts by McMillan and Vest in 1886 epitomizes the struggle during the next several years: whatever the "railroad gang" proposed, Senator Vest and his park supporters countered; likewise, the legislation so badly needed for better management of the Park was consistently blocked by the monopolists.

There were interesting variations to this game. For example, when Senator Vest's bill S. 2436 at last cleared the Senate and was sent to the House near the end of January 1887, the railroaders proceeded to amend the measure to their own purpose. As *Forest and Stream* pointed out,

> Judge Payson of Illinois is still their leader, and as he is a member of the Public Lands Committee he has a fine opportunity for helping his co-conspirators, and for injuring the national park. Such an oppor-

tunity he is not going to let pass . . . Judge Payson is no such man. Although he has been in the national park, knows what it needs, and knows that the public demands that it shall be protected, he cares little for park or public when the question of the dollar comes up."[20]

The man into whose hands Senator Vest's bill had fallen was Judge Louis E. Payson, representative from Illinois, the very man whose abuse by Justice of the Peace Hall at the Lower Geyser Basin in 1885 had been the cause célèbre that precipitated the end of early civilian administration of the Park; Payson may,consequently, have been interested in revenge as well as dollars.[21] In this instance, Judge Payson earned his money by amending Vest's legislation so that the northern boundary of Yellowstone National Park would coincide with the Yellowstone River-Lamar River-Soda Butte Creek line, which would have opened the way for a railroad on lands taken from the Park. The editor of *Forest and Stream* also noted, "the railroad gang showed their usual shrewdness in using the bill advocated by the friends of the Park as a cat's paw to draw out their own chestnuts. It is the old cry, 'if you don't give us our railroad we'll bust the park.' "

Senator Vest introduced legislation for the benefit of Yellowstone National Park in the Fiftieth Congress, but the action taken in regard to it was almost a replay of the maneuvers that defeated his previous try. In this case, S. 283 (introduced on December 27, 1887) was favorably reported on February 20, and considered and passed by the Senate on March 29. In the House, it was reported on July 26, but again, with an amendment that authorized a Cinnabar & Cooke City Railroad. In that form, the bill was called up for consideration by the House on October 8, but the announced intention of Representative David B. Henderson (brother of former Assistant Superintendent George L. Henderson) to defeat the measure prevented any action being taken on it by the House. Thereupon Senator Vest sent S. 283 back to the Senate, where it was properly purged then returned to the House. An attempt by Representative Holman to secure the immediate passage of the purified bill was prevented by Representative Payson, ending the struggle in that Congress.

Again, in the Fifty-first Congress, Senator Vest introduced legislation for the benefit of Yellowstone National Park; this bill was passed by the Senate on February 21, 1890. It was favorably reported in the House by Representative Payson on April 15, though with two recommendations: that the army be retained in the Park in place of the civilian police force Senator Vest had proposed, and that a right-of-way be provided for a Montana Mineral Railroad. Representative Stockdale then proceeded to insert a right-of-way proposal into the bill. Of this, Representative Dunnell of Minnesota said, "If this bill provides for the building of a railroad in any part of the national park, I enter my objection."[22] About his stand on this point, Representative Dunnell later said privately, "I was the father of the national park bill and still have a paternal interest in that Wonderland. I am opposed to granting any railway the right-of-way through the park because the first would only force the precedent for many which would follow."[23]

The railroad monopolists tried yet another approach in 1891. Senator Turpie of Indiana introduced a bill to grant a right-of-way to a Montana & Wyoming Railroad Company, which was to cross the Crow Indian Reservation to the Clarks Fork mines. When this bill came up for consideration by the Senate on February 12, Senator Manderson was able to add to it an amendment that would prevent the railway from coming nearer than one mile to Yellowstone National Park; in that form it passed, but apparently it was no longer of interest to its originators and was not even considered in the House.

The struggle reached its climax in the Fifty-second Congress. Senator Vest started the action by introducing yet another bill intended to revise the Yellowstone Park Act, and Senator Sanders of Montana introduced a measure to alter the boundaries of the Park, as did Senator Warren of Wyoming. No action was taken on either of these bills. Then Representative Stockdale of Mississippi teamed up with Senator Carlisle of Kentucky to introduce companion measures that would grant a right-of-way through the Park to the Montana Mineral Railroad Company. In his opposition to this latest effort of the railroad monopolists, Senator Vest referred to "the aggressive action of a lobby that for years have been endeavoring to put a railroad into the park in order to sell it for a large sum to the Northern Pacific," and he added somewhat bitterly, "the fact remains that no legislation can be had for the park until the demands of these people are conceded."[24] Senator Vest's disclosure that the charter of the Montana Mineral Railroad Company had already been put upon the market for sale prevented the Stockdale-Carlisle measure from getting out of committee. However, a bill introduced by Senator Warren of Wyoming on February 26, 1892, for the avowed purpose of eliminating the railroad and mine controversy from park affairs, was harder to deal with. This measure (S. 2373) returned to the old Yellowstone River-Lamar River-Soda Butte line for the northern boundary and proposed eliminating the remainder of the Montana and Idaho strips. It was particularly difficult for Senator Vest to deal with because he felt an obligation not to interfere with Senator Warren's proposal, remarking that he submitted to it "because I cannot help myself not because my judgment approves it."[25] With Vest unable to oppose this measure effectively, it passed the Senate; fortunately, it did not do so well in the House.

Senator Warren's bill was the high-water mark of the railroad monopolists, but not the end of their efforts. Representative Stockdale attempted to repeal the Yellowstone Park Act (H.R. 7693), and some bitter, sarcastic things were said; but the important comment was the quiet testimony of Thomas F. Oakes, president of the Northern Pacific Railroad Company, as the year was closing, that "his company had thoroughly examined the mines at Cooke City and the various routes to them, and that under no circumstances would his company build a road to them."[26] That decision ended the serious efforts to build a railroad into the mining region, but it did not end the struggle, which persisted into the Fifty-third Congress.

In its last ditch efforts, the segregationists found little comfort in a statement by Chairman McRae of the House committee inquiring into northern park boundary changes. He said:

> Your committee has finally come to the conclusion after a thorough examination of the arguments of both sides that the Yellowstone Park should remain undisturbed so far as its boundaries are concerned, although they do not wish to exclude such additions as may from time to time be made to the present area of the reservation. Your committee think the public interest and the public sentiment call upon Congress not to recede from this wise policy by which this park was dedicated for the benefit and enjoyment of the entire country.[27]

The railroaders, for their part, made one more try; they proposed an electric railway within the Park, dwelling upon the convenience and cleanliness of such a mode of transportation, and upon the fact that it could be operated by power generated at the Falls of the Yellowstone River. This approach, which was supported by some cagey pamphleteering, was a clever last try on the part of the Northern Pacific Railroad Company—though they did not openly admit it.[28] The principal effect of 1893 legislative efforts was to delay passage of measures long needed for good management of the Park.

Such were the aspects of monopoly that might have affected the integrity of Yellowstone National Park. There was more to monopoly than that, however. Monopoly existed within the Park in the organization and management of its concession businesses—persistent monopoly which, again, had its roots in the Northern Pacific Railroad Company.

The railroad's interest in the Park, which stemmed from concern for its large investment in the park branch line, led to its sub rosa support of the Yellowstone Park Improvement Company. The railroad became directly involved in 1885, when their agent purchased the property of the defunct concern. The Northern Pacific's executives, mindful that the railroad's Minnesota charter forbade operation of subsidiary businesses, preferred to entrust management of its park properties to others, however.

To that end, the Yellowstone Park Association was incorporated on April 15, 1886, by Charles Gibson, a St. Louis hotel man, and Nelson C. Thrall and John C. Bullitt, both of Philadelphia. The concern was capitalized for $300,000,[29] and its officers— elected at a meeting of the board of directors held two days later in the offices of the Northern Pacific Railroad Company in St. Paul—were Charles Gibson, president; Theodore B. Casey, vice president, and Preston Gibson, secretary and treasurer.[30] This company was insufficiently financed, however, and accomplished little more than its predecessor.

In the summer of 1887 the Northern Pacific took steps to assure the association sufficient operating funds by proposing to purchase 250 shares of the association's stock for cash, at par, and to sell the Yellowstone Park properties and their related franchise to the association for an additional 750 shares of stock. This proposal was acted upon favorably at the meeting of the directors of the Yellowstone Park Association on June 2, 1887.[31] As a corollary of the agreement, Gibson was required to reduce the rates charged at the hotels in the Park by about twenty percent, a matter that became the subject of a law suit at a later date on the grounds that the new rates were unreasonable and did not allow the association to operate profitably.

Thus financed, the Yellowstone Park Association was able to buy out the Cottage Hotel Association established by the Henderson family at Mammoth in 1886, and having a satisfactory working arrangement with Wakefield and Hoffman concerning the transportation of visitors within the area, the concern was in essential control of the park business and could turn its energies toward the building of much needed facilities in the geyser basins, at the Grand Canyon, and at the outlet of Yellowstone Lake. Concerning the Northern Pacific Railroad's active intervention in the business affairs of the Park, a local editor noted "that the authorities look upon this solution of the problem with relief," adding, "for that seems to be the only way by which tourists could be certain of finding good accommodations, and government be sure of securing adequate facilities for sight-seers."[32]

Sir Charles Gibson, president of the Yellowstone Park Association. *Portrait by Guerin, St. Louis.*

In spite of assistance from the Northern Pacific Railroad Company, the Yellowstone Park Association's operations in the Park remained unsatisfactory and were soon the object of severe criticism by *Forest and Stream*, which thought that the Northern Pacific could well afford to operate at a loss in the Park. The Northern Pacific did undertake the burden of deficit financing in 1889. In the minutes of a meeting of the board of directors of the Yellowstone Park Assosciation held in New York on October 22 is the statement:

> The president of the Association is hereby authorized to enter into any agreement he may see fit on behalf of this association with the N. P. Railroad Company, fixing for 20 years the rates for the carriage by said company of all persons into the employ of the Association, of all property belonging to or intended for it, providing for the erection of new hotels, and the operation of same; and generally as to the transaction of all business of the Association, and obtaining at the same time from the railroad company an agreement insuring to the Association a fixed net annual income during the period of the existence of the agreement, amounting to $30,000 per annum.

The records of the association show that it was firmly controlled by the Northern Pacific. Charles Gibson remained the president, but railroad officials held the other executive positions: Theodore B. Casey was the vice president, W. B. Pierce was the treasurer, and N. C. Thrall was the secretary. The distribution of the association's stock is also interesting. Out of 1,000 shares, 610 shares can be identified as held by railroad officials (a device used to camouflage the Northern Pacific's financial interest in the association): 100 shares each were held by Frederick Billings, Charles B. Wright, Miles D. Carrington, Theodore B. Casey, Thomas F. Oakes, and Henry Villard, and 10 shares by James Dean.[33]

An obvious and beneficial effect of the Northern Pacific's increasing involvement in park concession affairs was completion of the Canyon Hotel, for which the railroad advanced $25,000. A less acceptable result was the Yellowstone Transportation Company, a concern organized by Charles Gibson and Thomas Oakes under cover of the association's transportation privileges. This privilege had been exercised by George W. Wakefield of Bozeman, who had lacked capital to operate on an adequate scale. Wakefield was retained as general manager of the new company, which supplied him with horses and equipment in return for $7,500 per year rental.[34] The new transportation arrangement was destined to be short lived.

George W. Wakefield, pioneer stagecoach operator in the Park. *Portrait by Potter, Livingston, Mont.*

At that time the road from the geyser basins to Lake and Grand Canyon went by way of Nez Perce Creek, Mary Mountain, and Hayden Valley; the portion of the route from Nez Perce Creek to the top of Mary Mountain was a difficult climb for loaded stagecoaches and was facetiously called the Devil's Stairway. It had been customary to ask the passengers to walk up the grade, as they were asked to do at several other steep pitches on park roads. In late July 1890, Guy R. Pelton, a 64-year-old former representative from New York state, descended from the coach along with other passengers and began the hot, dusty tramp up the Devil's Stairway behind the slow-moving stagecoach. Mr. Pelton had a weak heart, however, and the climb was too much for him; he collapsed and died by the side of the road.[35] Mr. Pelton's death was publicized in the newspapers of the national capital by Judge Lambert Tree, the former United States minister to Belgium and Russia, who happened to be in the Park at that time. According to Judge Tree, "travellers are treated more like cattle than civilized people," and he damned the hotels and stage line for their rapacity, noting that there was need for investigation.[36] The *Washington Star* soon took up the cry, charging that the manager of the park transportation company made visitors walk to spare his horses (which was and always had been true, although it did not look so good in print), and there was a request that Secretary John W. Noble send a special agent to investigate the matter.

As a result the secretary of the interior cancelled Yellowstone Park Association transportation privileges on November 11, 1891.[37] G. L. Henderson, who had become a lobbyist for the association as a condition of the sale of his Cottage Hotel enterprise in 1889, confided to William Pearce, general purchasing agent of the Northern Pacific Railroad, that the "object of investigation of Yellowstone Park affairs is to make political capital."[38] The manner in which that was to be done would soon be made clear.

With George Wakefield (a Montana Democrat) out of the way, Secretary Noble proceeded to grant a lease to a company organized by Silas H. Huntley (a Montana Republican and personal friend of Russell Harrison, son of the president). The Yellowstone National Park Transportation Company was incorporated May 20, 1892, by Aaron Hershfield, L. H. Hershfield, Harry W. Child, Silas Huntley, and E. W. Bach, with a capitalization of $250,000.[39] The Yellowstone Park Association fought back by seeking a congressional charter (S. 1963) that would allow them to keep the transportation rights and also permit the construction of an electric railroad in the Park, to be operated with power generated by the Falls of the Yellowstone River.

Fortunately, nothing came of this sly attempt to gather two birds with one cast of the net (had it succeeded, the association would have retained its transportation privilege and the Northern Pacific Railroad would have gotten its tracks into the Park as it had long tried to do); nor did any of the succession of electric railway bills that followed make any progress.

Perhaps the adherents of the Yellowstone Park Association were a little too eager to succeed. It seems that E. C. Waters encouraged Charles Gibson to issue 100 shares of association stock in Russell Harrison's name with the evident intention of embarrassing him politically. Harrison did not take the bait, however, and made an issue of the fact that the association was attempting to discredit him.[40] It was a bad move, and not the only disservice Waters had rendered to the association.

Charles Gibson may have been deliberately duped by Waters; certainly Gibson should have known better than to trust him, for Waters was removed from his position as general manager of the association in 1890 on the direct order of Vice President Thomas Oakes when it became evident that Waters was using his position to extort considerable sums of money from a meat contractor.[41] A man of Mr. Waters' unforgiving nature should never have been trusted by the president of the company that had fired him; beyond that, it is quite possible he acted in the interest of the foes of the association, for Mr. Waters was rewarded with a lease allowing him to operate his boat business on Yellowstone Lake free of the Yellowstone Park Association (under whose transportation privilege he had previously done business).

The association had trouble of another sort. Construction of hotels and facilities by the association was directed by Superintendent of Construction R. R. Cummins, whose management of the work at Canyon Hotel (completed in 1889) was far from satisfactory. It was at first thought that much of the difficulty was due to the meddling of E. C. Waters; after the removal of that individual there was no real improvement, however. Further, work on the Lake and Fountain hotels in 1891 proved so expensive that the Northern Pacific Railroad had to advance an additional $60,000 to meet costs. When a labor strike developed as a further byproduct of mismanagement, Mr. Cummins was let go.

At this time, management of the association itself was little better. The agreement whereby the Northern Pacific Railroad Company guaranteed the association an annual net income of $30,000 put no premium on efficient operation, and Charles Gibson's regime just limped along until 1895, when he was forced to resign from the presidency.[42] At nearly the same time, the Northern Pacific Railroad Company went into receivership for the second time, and its stock in the Yellowstone Park Association, valued at $372,550, passed into the control of an entirely new management on September 1, 1896. A listing of assets at the time of the transfer shows that the gross passenger receipts from the Yellowstone Park business had averaged $92,357 annually between 1890 and 1896.[43]

The new management was at first inclined to liquidate the park investment. Word that the Union Pacific Railroad intended to build a line to the west entrance prompted President Mellen to inform James Dean (by then head of the Yellowstone Park Association): "I want to dispose of the interest if we can do it."[44] Perhaps the fact that the railroad was then being sued by Charles Gibson and his group of St. Louis investors contributed to that decision, and certainly, the balance sheet for the park operation was not encouraging. The association's business during 1897 showed an income of $89,387.30, with expenses totaling $85,182.72, leaving a net profit of only $4,205.48—all of which was used up in shingling the roofs of hotels that fall. The only bright spot as far as the railroad was concerned was the fact that the park branch line contributed $18,000 in net earnings.[45]

Charles Gibson's suit against the railroad charged that the Northern Pacific held down prices in the Park to an uneconomical level, that the railroad required too long an operating season, and that its de facto control of the Yellowstone Park Association was illegal. The merit of his claims was never decided as the case was settled out of court. A notable result was that Gibson sold his stock (705 shares) to the Northern Pacific on April 25, 1898. As sole owner then of the association, the railroad sold its stock to the Northwest Improvement Company in June, appearing to have disposed of its business interests in the Park. This was subterfuge, however, for the Northwest Improvement Company was a Northern Pacific subsidiary, a holding company designed for a variety of purposes not entirely in keeping with the railroad's principal business interest; it was wholly railroad owned, its officers were railroad men, and its policies and objectives were those of the parent concern. Even so, there remained some sentiment for a genuine abandonment of the park business. This feeling, cautiously expressed, led Harry W. Child, a stockholder of the Park Transportation Company, to indicate an interest in buying the Yellowstone Park Association, though he lacked the financial means to swing the deal. E. C. Waters was also interested, getting as far as a discussion of terms. On May 18, 1898, President Mellen offered Waters the following proposition: $50,000 cash, five notes of

$21,278 each at five percent interest, and security (5,213 shares of association stock, seventy-five percent of the stock of the Wylie Camp Company, and seventy-five percent of the stock of the Yellowstone Lake Boat Company.[46] Waters responded by stating, "deal will be closed as soon as I can return."[47] Waters was probably unable to raise the cash, for he did not close the deal, and on June 14 President Mellen made a second offer reducing the amount of the cash payment to $20,000. Waters stalled, and when he attempted to resume negotiations late in July, President Mellen informed him, "propositions made you were for acceptance within reasonable time . . . do not care to pursue." To an official of the railroad he confided he was indifferent as to whether Waters carried out the agreement or not, as he had in any case misrepresented, adding, "everyone here and west who knows Waters represents him utterly unreliable."[48] The Northern Pacific had by this time decided to dispose of the Yellowstone Park Association to the group of men who controlled the transportation company.

The transfer of the Yellowstone Park Association's stock to Harry W. Child, Edward W. Bach, and Silas S. Huntley was at first opposed by the Department of the Interior. The opposition was thought to have originated with Frank J. Haynes, proprietor of the Monida & Yellowstone Stage Company operating into the Park through the western entrance, who had feared his passengers would be unfairly treated at hotels controlled by a rival company. It soon developed that the opposition was the work of E. C. Waters, who raised the issue of monopoly in the Park. In 1901 the monopoly issue was resolved and transfer of the Yellowstone Park Association's stock from the Northwest Improvement Company to Child, Bach, and Huntley, in the amount of one-third to each, was accomplished by April 4.[49]

One reason the Northern Pacific Railroad Company sold its interests in the Yellowstone Park Association was to avoid investment in a new hotel in the Upper Geyser Basin. A combination of the break-even hotel business with the always profitable transportation business, on the other hand, should, they thought, provide the needed revenue. It did not work out quite that way. The year following the merger, Silas S. Huntley died and his one-third interest in both the association and the transportation companies passed into the hands of the Northwest Improvement Company. Edmund Bach disposed of his share of both businesses to the railroad's holding company, which thus controlled two-thirds of the merged enterprise. Mr. Child, though the nominal president of both companies, lacked the money to go ahead with the Upper Geyser Basin hotel and went to the

Northern Pacific to finance the project. Thus the railroad was right
where it had not wanted to be: principal stockholder in two park
operations, rather than one, and more deeply involved financially
than ever.

The Northwest Improvement Company, which is to say the
Northern Pacific Railroad, was tempted to partially disengage itself
from park business operations in 1903 by selling one-half of its stock
in both the Yellowstone Park Association and the Yellowstone
National Park Transportation Company to what were called the
Carter and Hershfield interests, leaving the Northwest Improvement
Company holding only one-third of the stock of each company.
Rather complicated readjustments of the stock resulted, by 1905, in
Harry Child and the Northwest Improvement Company becoming
equal partners in the combined hotel-transportation business. It was
a profitable enterprise at this time due to a $6,600 railroad advertising
campaign promoting park travel and sending two tally-ho coaches on
tour, to California and the World's Fair, prior to the tourist season.
Northern Pacific records indicate that traffic on the park branch line
grossed more than $166,000 that year, while dividends from the hotel
and transportation investments in the Park brought the railroad
$52,130 and $63,550, respectively. In a letter to Harry Child at the
close of the 1905 season, President Elliott of the Northern Pacific
mentioned his delight at the profitable turn taken by business in the
Park, but added that he was "afraid we disappointed . . . in the service
we gave . . . [and] made some enemies."[50]

At this point, when park business had at last been brought to a
profitable state, E. C. Waters once again raised the cry of monopoly.
In expectation of an investigation, the Northern Pacific sold its stock
(held by the Northwest Improvement Company) to Harry Child,
taking his note for $225,000. Mr. Child's indebtedness to the
Northwest Improvement Company at this time (1907) was
$372,711.98.[51]

E. C. Waters' Yellowstone Lake Boat Company was in financial
difficulty after the turn of the century because of his unscrupulous
activities. He had alienated the concessioners, the government
authorities, and even the employees in the Park, and had made an
unwise investment in a larger boat, the *E. C. Waters*. His boat
concession was canceled in 1907 for a multitude of reasons that added
up to sufficient cause, and the privilege was given to T. E. Hofer, the
old-time guide and friend of the Park. But "Uncle Billy" Hofer did not
have the necessary capital to launch such an enterprise and had to
borrow from Warren Delano to begin operations. The following
year, Harry Child provided $50,000 to buy out E. C. Waters, with the

The Gardiner, Mont., depot of the Northern Pacific Railroad's park branch line, under construction in 1903. The architect, Robert C. Reamer, also designed Old Faithful Inn and Canyon Hotel.

A group of stagecoach drivers.

understanding that the money would be repaid soon, but the T. E. Hofer Boat Company did not prosper, becoming, upon its failure in 1910, another enterprise for which Mr. Child had to go to the Northern Pacific for financial assistance. This new enterprise was incorporated at Helena, Montana, on May 27, 1911, as the Yellowstone Lake Boat Company, jointly owned by Harry Child, Warren Delano, and the Northwest Improvement Company.

Park business was no longer going well for Mr. Child. He was engaged in the construction of the large Canyon Hotel, for which he had obtained a $100,000 loan from the Northern Pacific in 1901 and a similar loan in 1911, just at a time when competition was reducing the profit from his operations in the Park. The squeeze began after the Union Pacific Railroad completed its branch line to the west entrance in 1907. Determined to get a share of the park business, the Union Pacific backed Frank J. Haynes' efforts to get hotel privileges from the enterprise Harry Child was running. Such trafficking with a competitor was bound to put Mr. Child in a perilous position and he recognized it. In a letter to an official of the Northern Pacific, he saw himself as "so involved that I cannot get from under but can easily be bankrupted by cutting up the available business," and he was greatly worried that he would be crushed between the two railroad systems.[52] A settlement for Mr. Haynes' application for hotel privileges was effected by Secretary of the Interior Ballinger, who arranged for Haynes to drop the idea of entering the hotel business in the Park in return for a share in the Wylie Permanent Camping Company profits. Of this cartel scheme, Child wrote that he could not afford to have such an arrangement come to the attention of the general public.[53]

Mr. Child seems to have remained skeptical of the possibility of operating successfully between two giant railroad systems, each of which was eager to control the park business for its own advantage. Thus, he was anxious to sell out if he could get his price, $3 million. He began negotiating with the Harriman interests (then controlling the Union Pacific system), and that alarmed the Northern Pacific, which had loans totaling $565,000 at stake, in addition to its traffic into the area. The attitude of the Department of the Interior was, by that time, so clearcut that the Northwest Improvement Company could no longer step in as a direct owner; therefore, the Northern Pacific attempted to arrange a combination whereby they, with the Union Pacific, the Burlington, and the Milwaukee systems, would jointly support the park operation and jointly profit from it.

Such an agreement was nearly consummated in May 1913 when three lines (Northern Pacific, Union Pacific, and Burlington) agreed to finance a loan of $1,250,000 to the park companies in the proportion of forty percent each to the two larger railroads and twenty percent to the Burlington. At that critical moment, the secretary of the interior cancelled the Haynes lease, which caused the Union Pacific to back out of the agreement. As a result, the million dollar hotel that had been planned for construction at West Yellowstone was not built.[54]

In 1914, Mr. Child came to the Northern Pacific for a $385,000 loan in March and for a $50,000 loan in July; business was so poor that he was unable to pay the interest on the loans at the end of the year. The railroad took a quick look at its books, saw that the traffic to the Park had grossed them nearly $238,000, and decided to support Mr. Child a little longer. His request for an extension of time on the interest payments was granted. The amount owed the Northwest Improvement Company by the park hotel and transportation companies had risen, by 1915, to $1,065,000. Of this massive support of the park business, which was always so close to monopolistic control, the president of the Northern Pacific Railroad Company later said: "With our experience I question if we would duplicate this action voluntarily."[55] That admission also marked the end of the Northern Pacific Railroad Company's attempt to monopolize park business. In 1917, that railroad joined with the Union Pacific and the Chicago, Burlington & Quincy in the first of those cooperative agreements whereby the major railroads (this soon included the Milwaukee line) continued to provide financial assistance to the park businesses, but without the outright ownership or domination that had been a feature of earlier railroad assistance. The railroads continued to be interested in Yellowstone National Park and its tourist business for another three decades, that is, until the automobile effectively ended the "carriage trade" after World War II; but railroad activities never again assumed monopoly proportions after the close of the period of army administration in the Park.

CHAPTER 14

THE YELLOWSTONE CRUSADE

*If the Yellowstone National Park is to be reserved
and preserved from despoilation . . . then the grass-
subsisting, inoffensive game which may be found
therein, or can by any means be induced to take up
its abode there, should be sacredly preserved from
wanton destruction.*

—Bozeman Avant Courier
Jan. 11, 1883

The *Avant Courier's* editorial statement amounted to endorsement of the first move toward a new policy of absolute
protection of the Park's wildlife. It appeared upon receipt
of word that Senator George Graham Vest had introduced legislation
to amend the Yellowstone Park Act,[1] which would, among its several
provisions, prohibit the killing of all those animals classed as
"game"—antelope, deer, elk, moose, and buffalo, with some fur-
bearers and all birds. It also limited fishing to that which could be
done with hook and line. A crusade was thus opened that has been
both a blessing and a curse for the Park, solving some problems while
creating others. In the larger view of wildlife conservation, the
protection policy has been mostly gain, establishing our national
responsibility to save representative samples of the wilderness fauna
in a wilderness setting. Out of the long struggle to protect the Park's
wildlife has come the principle of maintaining primeval ecological
relationships which is central to park wildlife management.

The Yellowstone crusade began to take form in 1883; but the wildlife problems it dealt with had existed since the creation of the Park, and park administrators have been struggling with them ever since. The men who wrote the organic act seem to have had the English game preserve in mind. And what other model could they have looked to? The preservation rationale that is now an integral part of the wilderness park idea had been only tentatively suggested by George Catlin and Henry Thoreau, nor was there yet any particular public concern for endangered species.

Colonial America, after 1740, showed some interest in its deer, but only in a regulatory sense, to insure sufficient game for hunters. This attitude prevailed in the states and territories until 1870, although some concern for species was evidenced in a Massachusetts act of 1818 prohibiting the killing of robins in the spring, and an act of 1864 in Idaho Territory setting a season for buffalo hunting. Until the year 1870, when the California legislature established a small refuge for water birds, there was no example of absolute protection of wildlife; even that beginning seems to have been unknown to the framers of the Yellowstone legislation.

The English game preserve concept, with which the Park's founders were more familiar, allowed gentlemanly hunting; indeed, such recreation was the principal reason for maintaining preserves. It was hunting that was the real object of preservation, rather than the wildlife. Yellowstone's organic act was therefore concerned with providing "against the wanton destruction of the fish and game found within said Park, and against their capture and destruction for the purposes of merchandise or profit."[2] It was thought that restrained fishing and hunting, either for sport or for food, was a proper activity in the national park, a viewpoint that failed to recognize that neither the visitor nor the resident could distinguish at what point sport and meat-hunting became "wanton."

Early in the first decade of the Park's existence the large animals disappeared from the frequented areas and traveled routes, a fact observed by William Strong in the summer and fall of 1875 (see Vol. I, pages 207-8). It was Strong's opinion that with protection hunting for sport in the Park could be reserved "for those who shoot in season and in a proper manner."[3]

Others testified to the carnage that was so rapidly depleting the Park's wildlife. Philetus W. Norris, estimating "from the unquestioned fact that over 2,000 hides of the huge Rocky Mountain elk, nearly as many each of the big horn, deer and antelope, and scores if not hundreds of moose and bison were taken out in the spring of 1875," thought the slaughter had claimed as many as 7,000 animals.[4]

He pointed out that few were used for food; usually the tongue and hide were taken and the carcass poisoned with strychnine to serve as wolf or wolverine bait.

Captain William Ludlow, also in the Park in the summer of 1875, noted that "hunters have for years devoted themselves to the slaughter of game," and he suggested that hunting should be prohibited entirely there, and that the military should police the area.[5] Such testimony, bearing the stamp of official credibility, fostered an assumption that the graminivorous herds and flocks of Yellowstone Park—its so-called game animals—were close to extinction. This belief was pointed up vividly, if somewhat inaccurately, in 1878, by a New York magazine, which showed on its cover a mounted hunter with smoking rifle, sitting his horse in front of the Lower Falls of the Yellowstone River, surrounded by acres of dead and dying "elk"—all bearing the palmate antlers of moose.[6]

Locally, there had been an attempt, which grew out of the first federal law enforcement in the Yellowstone region, to stop hide hunters from operating in the Park. In the fall of 1875, Jack Baronett was deputized by the United States marshal at Bozeman, Montana, to break up the traffic in stolen horses carried on between Montana and Idaho by persons familiar with the trails across the Park. His party of soldiers and citizens chased part of the gang into Jackson Hole, where they shot a horse thief and recovered fifty animals. The episode is recorded in the *Bozeman Avant Courier* of November 26, where it is also stated that Jack was then engaged in "preventing slaughter of game in the National Park." His activity in this regard seems to have displeased some local people who were in sympathy with the hide hunters of the Yellowstone Valley; on December 31 the editor reminded his readers: "Jack Baronette, a live, wide-awake U.S. Marshal, is at present in charge of same, but we do not think his duties extend to ordering people off the Park, unless they come there for unlawful purposes. He is there to see that the laws governing the Park are not violated."

Such gratuitous policing should have pleased Superintendent Langford, but that it did not is all too evident in the following reply to James C. McCartney's letter sounding him out on the subject:

> I have made no appointment of any one as custodian of the Park, except that of yourself and Harry Horr, made in the summer of 1874.
>
> If Mr. Baronett has been appointed Deputy U. S. Marshall, he doubtless has all the authority that U. S. Marshalls have in removing all trespassers from Government reservations, pursuant to law. I have given no one authority to remove trespassers.

THE DAILY GRAPHIC

AN ILLUSTRATED EVENING NEWSPAPER.

39 & 41 PARK PLACE.

VOL. XVII. | All the News. Four Editions Daily. | NEW YORK, THURSDAY, JULY 11, 1878. | $15 Per Year in Advance. Single Copies, Five Cents. | NO. 1655.

THE NIMROD OF THE YELLOWSTONE.

Reports of wanton killing of game animals in the Park prompted this propaganda sketch of a hunter killing elk near Yellowstone Falls. Note the palmate moose antlers on the dead "elk."

Publication of that negatively phrased letter in the *Avant Courier* on February 18, 1876, seems to have ended the well-meant attempt of Bozeman people to control the worst abuse of the national park, the slaughter of its herds of ungulates by mercenary hide hunters.

The secretary of the interior was swept along in the rising tide of opinion that the larger Yellowstone fauna were endangered species. In his report for 1880 Carl Schurz recommended that the Academy of Sciences be invited to designate a qualified person to make observations of the Park's phenomena, analyze its waters, and report upon the destruction of its game. Moved by reports of the wholesale slaughter of wildlife, he deemed it proper under the law to make regulations "to prohibit the hunting and killing of game in it altogether; while fishing, except with nets and seines, is to be left free."[7] For some unexplained reason, no attempt was made that year to put such a regulation into effect; instead, the employment of a gamekeeper was allowed, in order to implement Superintendent Norris' plan to save representative herds of the Park's ungulates by semidomestication on a game preserve in the northwest corner. The first gamekeeper, Harry Yount (see Chapter 9), did all one man could possibly do under the circumstances and resigned in the fall of 1881, recommending an entirely different approach to the problem, protection by an adequate police force.

An attempt to replace Yount with a naturalist came to nothing:

> In 1882 [Spencer F.] Baird conceived the idea that a naturalist might well be attached to the staff . . . of the Yellowstone Park for the purpose of scientifically observing the elk, bear, beaver and other wild animals. He therefore asked me [David Starr Jordan] to suggest a good man, and I proposed Meek, then one of my advanced students in Zoology. But this stirred up our representative in Congress, Columbus C. Matson, who insisted on the right to nominate if anyone from his district were to be put in office. Matson's first candidate, however, was a man who could not possibly accept, being confined at the time in the Monroe County jail to expiate the social error of larceny. His second choice received the telegram announcing his appointment on Sunday morning when he was trying to ride a serious, remonstrant horse through the door of a Martinsville [Indiana] saloon! This fellow sobered up sufficiently to reach the Park, but soon died of alcoholism at Mammoth Hot Springs, and Baird's excellent plan came to nothing.[8]

The name of the worthless and short-lived occupant of the position of gamekeeper does not appear in the scant record of the day; he was succeeded by Cassius M. Conger, the son of Superintendent Conger, and his performance was in no way distinguishable from that of the force of park police facetiously termed rabbit catchers.

After General Philip H. Sheridan traveled through the Park in the summer of 1882 he reported that "last winter in and around the edges of the Park, there were as many as 2,000 of these grand animals [elk] killed," and he believed that the boundaries should be extended eastward forty miles and southward ten miles in order to create a larger game preserve. The general appealed to all American sportsmen to press for enlargement of the Park and offered to provide troops for its protection.[9] Both Senator Vest's attempt to legislate against hunting in the Park, and Secretary H. M. Teller's order of January 15, 1883, extending protection to nearly all the Park's wildlife,[10] came directly from Sheridan's interest.

A local editor recognized the inherent weakness of the secretary's order when he stated:

> probably a few years after the wild game shall have become extinct our national law makers will have become impressed with the idea that some additional enactment other than the Park "Rules and Regulations" was necessary to preserve the animals and prevent wanton destruction.[11]

How right he was in distrusting unsupported rules and regulations was soon proven by the rabbit catchers (see Chapter 11). However, the army succeeded in establishing a de facto basis for all the orders that the secretary of the interior had provided for management of the Park (see Chapter 12).

General Sheridan's crusade was largely the product of subjective thinking—the surfacing of a vague, persistent feeling that the Park's large animals were doomed to be swept away utterly, just as their kind had so generally been removed from most of the American scene. (Henry Thoreau called it, "civilized off the face of the earth.") The emphasis was upon numbers only, with little or no regard for the habitat. Both the military officers within the Park and the residents surrounding it saw the park fauna as individual species— some useful and some obnoxious—rather than as an assemblage of species delicately balanced in their environment. They did not understand the complex relationships of the ecosystem, nor even suspect the dangers inherent in tampering with it.

The subjective nature of most thinking directed to Yellowstone's wildlife problems during the period of army administration is apparent in the estimates of the numbers of buffalo and elk taken from the annual reports of the superintendents for the period from 1877 through 1915 (see Table V, Appendix C). It is at once obvious that the buffalo did not show an alarming decline in numbers until the latter half of the period, and the elk, instead of decreasing, showed a strong tendency to increase throughout. Obviously, the degree of protection given the Park's wildlife was more than adequate to maintain the elk and probably all the ungulates except the buffalo (which were subjected to the inroads of scalp hunters).

And yet, the trend of those official estimates was ignored in favor of the preconceived idea of diminution. Not only was de jure enforcement of the rules and regulations sought in place of the de facto enforcement established by the military (with this there can be no quarrel, since it served a broad and necessary purpose), but such measures as predator control, winter feeding, and restriction of movement were undertaken for the specific purpose of increasing the numbers of animals (buffalo excepted) which were already quite numerous in terms of available winter range. The existence of a credibility gap between the official statements and the local viewpoint is indicated by this fragment of verse from a local newspaper.

> Ananias Anderson is Captain of the Guard,
> He patrols the National Reserve, he guards the U.S. yard;
> And 'neath his magnifying eyes and multiplying tongue,
> The increased herds of game are more than when the
>   World was young.[12]

Let it be added that such comments did not bother Captain George S. Anderson; rather, he gloried in them, proudly forwarding derogatory excerpts to his superiors and to the secretary of the interior.

It fell to a mere poacher of the type known as a head hunter to complete the protection of the herds and much more. By his ruthless slaughter of a few buffalo for their scalps (which could be sold to taxidermists for up to $300 each), Edgar Howell of Cooke City converted the de facto protection established by the military authorities into de jure form, ended the power of the monopolists over the Park, and involved the area in activities that were soon recognizable as wildlife management. A scoundrel seldom accomplishes so much.

There had been some trouble with individuals eager to speculate in park buffalo prior to the depredations of Ed Howell. Upon taking charge of the Park in February 1891, Captain Anderson learned that three or four buffalo heads (probably obtained within the northern boundary) had been mounted by a Livingston taxidermist, and E. E. Van Dyck, a Cooke City resident and the principal hunter for that settlement, was under suspicion of providing them. Three patrols were sent into the northeast corner of the Park, where Van Dyck was in the habit of meat-hunting, before he was finally apprehended on the Lamar River "with beaver traps and other evidences of his trade in his possession."[13] There was then no law under which he could be brought to trial, but he was held in the Fort Yellowstone guardhouse

Officers of the Sixth Cavalry posing with confiscated buffalo "scalps"—probably those taken from poacher Ed Howell in March 1894.

for over a month and his personal property was confiscated, which treatment became the basis of a vigorous complaint intended to break down the army's extralegal procedures. Though he had the support of Montana congressmen, Van Dyck was unsuccessful and his effort had the opposite effect of strengthening military control. In speaking of poaching in general, Captain Anderson thought that "one or two more examples like that of Van Dyck will put an end to it."[14]

In June 1892, Charles Pendelton, "a butcher and poacher from Cooke City," captured two buffalo calves on Specimen Ridge and took them north of the Park, where they died. He was arrested but all that could be done was to restrict his movement within the area to the Cooke City-Gardiner road—a condition he immediately violated by roaming at will. The result was similar to that in the Van Dyck case: a brief confinement in the guardhouse and confiscation of personal property. Captain Anderson was forced to concede that "Every bit of property found on such men is at once claimed by their partners and confederates, on real or fraudulent bills of sale, and confiscation if made hurts the transgressors very little."[15]

Those incidents and some activity along the western boundary by the Henrys Lake gang (particularly the Courtney brothers and Dick Rock) were minor, so that the superintendent could confidently report, prior to the winter of 1893-94, of the Park's four hundred buffalo: "Their perpetuity within the park is thoroughly assured, and a steady and gradual increase may be looked for."[16]

Early that winter, Ed Howell and an unidentified partner moved supplies and equipment into the Park from Cooke City on a hand sledge. A camp was established on Astringent Creek, which drains to Yellowstone Lake by Pelican Creek, and there they settled with the intention of killing all the buffalo wintering in the meadows on the latter stream, skinning out the heads, and hanging the scalps safely in trees to await the spring, when they intended to take the trophies out on packhorses and realize from $100 to $300 apiece for their trouble. But Howell quarreled with his partner and drove him out of camp, remaining alone in his winter-bound tipi to accomplish his "base and ignoble purpose."[17]

In February a scouting party went into the country on the east side of the Yellowstone River to report on buffalo in the Pelican Valley and came across a sledge trail too old to be followed but which appeared to be going toward Cooke City. This tied in nicely with an earlier report of a similar trail made by Ed Howell, who had passed the Soda Butte outpost in the night, thereby arousing the suspicions of the detail stationed there. It was decided to send a second party into the Pelican drainage to find out what was going on.[18]

Accordingly, a detachment under Captain G. L. Scott went to Lake Hotel and, on the morning of March 12, Scout Felix Burgess (a tough veteran of the Indian wars) and Sergeant Troike of Troop D, Sixth United States Cavalry, crossed over into the snowy wilderness east of the Yellowstone River. Their snowshoe trip turned into an adventure summarized by Captain Anderson:

> On the morning of the 13th, very soon after starting, they came across some old snowshoe tracks which they could scarcely follow, but by continuing . . . they soon came across a cache of six bison scalps suspended above the ground, in the limbs of a tree. Securing these trophies, the party continued down Astringent Creek to its mouth and then turned down Pelican. They soon came across a newly-erected lodge, with evidences of occupation, and numerous tracks in the vicinity. Soon after this they were attracted by the sight of a man pursuing a herd of bison in the valley below them, followed by several shots from a rifle. After completing the killing, the culprit was seen to proceed with the removal of the scalps. While thus occupied with the first one my scouting patrol ran upon him and made the capture.[19]

The capture was a braver act than one might expect, for Burgess had to cross two hundred yards of open snow to get within pistol range of a man who was not only armed with a rifle, but had a dog to warn him. However, the scout was favored by a high wind and managed to get the drop on Howell. The poacher coolly remarked to his captors that they could not have taken him if he had seen them first, and they understood him very well when he tried to kill the dog that had let him down.

As the soldiers were escorting Ed Howell to the Fort Yellowstone guardhouse, they unexpectedly met another party that was greatly interested in Yellowstone's wildlife. This was the Yellowstone National Park Game Expedition, sponsored by the New York weekly magazine *Forest and Stream*. It included Emerson Hough, field correspondent of the magazine, photographer Frank J. Haynes and T. E. "Billy" Hofer, who was a competent guide and an able skier with ten years' experience carrying mail between snowbound Colorado mining camps.[20]

Hough was an ardent conservationist and, being a journalist, recognized a scoop when he saw it. He wrote a dispatch on the spot and sent it to Fort Yellowstone with Howell's captors (for the telephone wires were down between Norris and headquarters); from there that fateful account was telegraphed east. George Bird Grinnell, then editor of *Forest and Stream*, was not satisfied with mere publication of Hough's story. He and some influential friends went to the national capital where they presented their facts so adroitly that a bill (H.R. 6442) drawn "To protect the birds and animals in Yellowstone National Park, and to punish crimes in said park, and for other purposes," could be introduced by Representative Lacey of Iowa, on March 26—a mere thirteen days after Ed Howell fired the shots that brought down those five buffalo in the valley of Pelican Creek. The Lacey Act passed the House and Senate on a wave of public indignation and was signed into law on May 7, 1894.

The principal effect of the Lacey Act was to provide for enforcement of those laws classed as misdemeanors (actions defined locally as offenses, though not universally recognizable as such; hence the numerous but less serious minor infractions for which the penalty is strictly limited by statute). Felonies (those offenses that are morally reprehensible in our society, such as murder, rape, arson and robbery) could be dealt with under existing federal laws, though not always conveniently, and several persons charged with serious crimes in the Park were successfully prosecuted prior to passage of the Lacey Act. In this regard, there is a tendency to overlook the fact that John W. Meldrum (first U.S. commissioner for the Park under the Lacey Act) had predecessors.

As a result of a fourth of July brawl at Mammoth Hot Springs in 1879, James McCawley attempted to ambush and kill one of Superintendent Norris' men. McCawley was captured and taken to Bozeman for trial, but the Montana authorities were so unsure of their jurisdiction in the matter that they released the culprit. Norris thereupon requested the appointment of N. D. Johnson as a United States commissioner for the territorial court of Wyoming and C. M. Stephens as a deputy United States marshal. The legal machinery Norris hoped would control crime within park boundaries went awry, however, when the Wyoming court failed to designate a commissioner. (Stephens was made a deputy under the marshal of Wyoming Territory.)

Lawlessness reached such proportions early in the tenure of Superintendent P. H. Conger that he, also, sought appointment of a U. S. commissioner for the Park. On January 31, 1884, he wrote to the secretary of the interior that the Wyoming federal judge had promised to make the appointment at the February term of the territorial court but had not done so, perhaps because of the decision to use the laws of Wyoming in the Park. The effect of this ill-considered decision was to substitute military management for the discredited civil administration.

The new regime was satisfied to handle misdemeanors in an extralegal fashion and rely upon the federal district court at Cheyenne for punishment of criminals prior to admission of

Wyoming as a state in 1890. The act of Congress conferring statehood also placed Yellowstone Park under "exclusive control and jurisdiction" of the United States, and that seems to have raised a hope that legal machinery could at last be established within the area. Captain F. A. Boutelle corresponded with Wyoming's Senator Joseph M. Carey, who made arrangements for appointment of a commissioner that fall. In a letter written November 10, 1890, Senator Carey asked the acting superintendent:

> Have you a good man in view, an actual resident of the park, who you desire appointed United States Commissioner, if so, please name him.
> Judge Riner would like to appoint the Commissioner before the adjournment of his court. Any honest man who is not holding a position under the State or is not a commissioned officer of the United States will be competent to fill the place.

The appointment was finally secured in the spring of 1891; Acting Assistant Surgeon Samuel S. Turner, stationed at Camp Sheridan, took the oath of office on June 26. Turner was not a commissioned officer of the army, only a contract doctor; therefore he was eligible to hold the office. He performed the necessary functions satisfactorily at the only hearing during his brief tenure: the case of Henry Bentson, a bellboy at the Mammoth Hot Springs hotel, who was charged with "taking and carrying away personal property with intent to steal and purloin same," and who was subsequently found guilty in the U.S. District Court at Cheyenne, Wyoming, and confined in the Laramie County jail for seven months.

The appointment of Dr. Turner as U.S. commissioner, with the concurrent appointment of Scout Felix Burgess as a deputy marshal, gave the Park legal machinery that was only partially effective, for lack of statutory authority over misdemeanors. Captain George S. Anderson emphasized this defect in a letter to the secretary of the interior, written September 1, 1891:

> I trust that the secretary will lay special stress in his annual report, on the need of a special act for the protection of the park, with penalties for such offenses as poaching, trapping, defacing the formations, carrying off specimens, not extinguishing fires, etc. Without it protection of the buffalo and the fur-bearing animals will be exceedingly difficult.

A further difficulty with the arrangement, and one not mentioned in the acting superintendent's letter, was its impermanence. Dr. Turner soon left the Park and the authorities were put to the trouble of obtaining a second commissioner, Ellery C. Culver, who took the oath of office on April 12, 1892. Culver was an employee of the park transportation company and lasted longer than his prede-

Judge John W. Meldrum, fourth U.S. commissioner for Yellowstone Park (the first to be appointed under the Lacey Act of 1894). *Portrait by Hartsook.*

cessor. Passage of the Lacey Act, with its provision of authority over all types of offenses, specification of jurisdiction and penalties, and establishment of a full-time position of United States commissioner for the Park, was the adequate solution needed for so many years. Judge John W. Meldrum was appointed commissioner June 20, 1894, and held the position more than forty-one years—to July 2, 1935— becoming affectionately known as the "grand old man of the Yellowstone."

The windfall of laws and legal machinery that resulted from Howell's action was called by Captain Anderson "the most fortunate thing that ever happened to the Park." The legislation enacted with such ease did cure a congenital defect that had troubled our first national park from its birth, but it did more than that. It meant ultimate defeat for the monopolists and segregationists who had been attempting to turn the Park to their own advantage, a result that did not stem from any provision of the Lacey Act but only from its existence. With passage of that legislation, opponents of the Park lost the leverage that had been their only hope: the ability to deny what was so desperately needed.

Howell's action was of importance in yet another way, for it was the open sesame to beginnings in wildlife management.

Ed Howell could not be tried, for there was yet no law suited to the purpose; but Captain Anderson did the next best thing by putting him in the guardhouse for a little more than a month, after which he was "removed from the Park, and directed never again to return without proper permission." However, such directness was not plain enough for Ed, of whom the superintendent soon had to report:

> On the evening of July 28 I found him coolly sitting in the barber's chair in the hotel at this point. I instantly arrested him and re-confined him in the guardhouse, had him reported to the U. S. attorney for this district, and on the evening of August 8 he received the first conviction under the law which he was instrumental in having passed. He was convicted before the U. S. Commissioner of returning after expulsion, in violation of the tenth of the Park regulations, and sentenced for one month and to a fine of $50.[21]

Ed Howell, through some peculiar quirk of his nature, was always proud of his part in bringing bona fide law into Yellowstone Park, and, when employed later as a special detective in solving the second stagecoach holdup, he did a good job.

Sergeant Troike and Scout Burgess both received written commendations for their part in the apprehension of Howell. In addition, Burgess' bravery was acknowledged by the Boone and

Crockett Club, which presented him with a fine field glass.[22] The club also defrayed $118 in expenses which Captain Anderson had incurred in connection with the incident, but which the Department of the Interior had declined to honor.

Emerson Hough's winter expedition prowled about Hayden Valley, where tracks and the burrowing of scavengers led them to the carcasses of a number of buffalo under six to eight feet of snow. Captain Anderson seems to have considered their death a result of the particularly hard winter, but "Uncle Billy" Hofer maintained the animals were killed by head hunters. According to him, "There were three of them and the weather had been bad after they killed the buffalo and when they was about to go back after the heads Howell was captured and they never went back."[23]

Hofer's comments on the poachers operating from the country west of the Park (the Henrys Lake gang) are also interesting. He says:

> We ran onto Ed Staley on one of our trips. He would take in and cache his rifle and ammunition in the fall. Then when the snow fell he'd go for the buffalo. If he was seen he had an excuse. The time I saw him . . . he went to the station at the Lower Basin, telling he'd never seen a buffalo—wanted to see one—so they sent a soldier with him.[24]

In concluding that letter, Hofer added: "All those hunters earned all they got on their trips. Hard work and exposure."

Both the official and the unofficial information that reached Washington, D.C., in the Spring of 1894 agreed that the herd of wild buffalo in Yellowstone National Park (the last such herd in the United States) was doomed unless measures were taken to safeguard the remaining animals. At that point, the Smithsonian Institution proposed building an enclosure for the retention of wild animals native to the Park, and Captain Anderson was asked to suggest a site and estimate the cost of construction. However, the amount required was beyond the means then available.[25]

The project was revived a year later, when Professor Langley provided $3,000 for building the enclosure and feeding such buffalo as could be driven into it. Captain Anderson seems to have expressed the hope of most conservationists when he wrote: "If this plan succeeds we will be able to retain a small herd and keep them nearly in a state of nature."[26]

The enclosure was constructed by Hofer on Alum Creek in the fall of 1895. A stout fence of poles encompassing a considerable area was arranged to follow the higher, windswept ground, and openings were left on the east and west sides for a buffalo trail that passed directly across the area. A stack of wild hay inside the fence was the bait that was expected to attract any buffalo visiting Hayden Valley, and it was arranged for soldiers to watch the enclosure and shut the herd up when the time came. The plan was a total failure. A few buffalo visited the enclosure early in the winter, but it was left open in the hope that others would be attracted there. The snowfall was light that year, however, and the animals soon scattered beyond reach. Segments of that fence still stand, three-quarters of a century later, as a reminder of the first attempt to save the buffalo.

In the spring of 1896, when it had become apparent the attempt to trap the Hayden Valley buffalo was unsuccessful, a man who probably had followed that operation with great interest went to Washington with a plan of his own. He was C. J. Jones, better known as Buffalo Jones for his success in capturing calves from a remnant herd of two or three thousand buffalo in southeastern Colorado. From those calves he established a small herd of semidomesticated animals at Garden City, Kansas, where he had managed to crossbreed buffalo and domestic cattle. The proposition that Jones took to Secretary of the Interior Hoke Smith and on to President Cleveland's private secretary was an offer to corral the Yellowstone buffalo for a wage of "$200 per month and actual expenses," or, in case of failure to corral the animals, he was willing to accept $500 as compensation for his efforts and a report.[27]

Nothing came of that, or a somewhat similar proposition Jones advanced in April 1897, when it came to his attention that $5,000 was available for the protection of the Park's buffalo. At that point, biographer Henry Inman made himself ridiculous as a prophet by stating: "Unfortunately, no action was ever taken by the Department upon these propositions, and the United States lost forever its greatest race of native animals."[28] How that statement must have haunted Colonel Inman, for neither Buffalo Jones nor the American bison was finished in Yellowstone Park.

The great interest in making Yellowstone Park the place of the buffalo's salvation promoted two very different approaches to the problem. While the enclosure on Alum Creek was being built, Captain Anderson was arranging to halt the incursion of poachers and head hunters from west of the Park. He says:

> I at once organized three parties for operations against the merciless freebooters of the Henrys Lake country. One party consisted of two men acting as detectives among the suspected element; another party, also of two men, operated near the Idaho line, and often outside the park; the third party was under the personal charge of Lieutenant Lindsley. The ground covered by the buffalo in their summer range was most

thoroughly gone over. Carcasses, or at least a portion of about ten buffaloes were found, all of which had been killed within three or four months. One party of poachers was encountered, but they escaped by flight in the darkness. Unfortunately they were not discovered until near dusk and pursuit had to be soon discontinued. Soon after this I obtained information that certain parties from that region were offering buffalo scalps for sale in the city of Butte. I had a careful watch kept, and finally arrested James Courtney, who had in his possession the scalps of four buffaloes. He was brought to this place and had his trial before the United States commissioner. Possession of the trophies was *prima facie* evidence of his guilt, but no one saw the killing done, and hence no one could swear positively that it was done within the limits of the park. He testified for himself, and his brother, his father-in-law, and a partner in crime testified most positively that the killing was done in Idaho, and without the park. With this positive but untruthful evidence before him the commissioner felt obliged to acquit, but there is not, nor has there been, any doubt in my mind of Courtney's guilt. The trial,however, proved so expensive to the marauder that its effect upon his neighbors has been excellent.[29]

Even that summary fails to fully explain Lieutenant Lindsley's campaign. Aided by inside information furnished by such honest old-timers as "Beaver Dick" Leigh, the lieutenant succeeded in spreading a mood of dismay all the way from the little Idaho town where a Mormon bishop served as a "fence," to Butte, Montana, where a culpable taxidermist made the mistake of ignoring a subpoena to appear at James Courtney's hearing. (The taxidermist was arrested by a U.S. marshal and taken to Cheyenne, Wyoming, where he was treated far more severely than a poacher would have been!) Express shipments were watched and often inspected and some of the notorious poachers were interrogated so often they abandoned their old haunts. An aged Idahoan, who resided near the southwest corner of the Park in those days, recently recalled how two of his neighbors were picked up by soldiers in the Bechler Meadows (he didn't know for what), were taken to Mammoth Hots Springs, fined, and put out of the Park by the north entrance just as the weather turned bitter. They were two weeks making their way home by the Madison Valley and Monida Pass and nearly died enroute. "The blizzard caught 'em and they stayed in camp with their horses tied to a tree in two and three feet of snow, two and three days at a time."[30] Though Captain Anderson had been very pessimistic about his chances of saving those few buffalo which he saw as "struggling against an almost certain fate," his protective measures were effective.

Another, less helpful result of the interest in saving the buffalo was E. C. Waters' scheme to put buffalo and other animals on an island in

Yellowstone Lake as an attraction for his boat business. A zoological garden in connection with steamboat service on Yellowstone Lake had been proposed by Superintendent Norris but was not feasible before 1892. The rerouting of stagecoach traffic over the new road from Upper Geyser Basin to the outlet of Lake Yellowstone put the Yellowstone Lake Boat Company into the business of transporting tourists between the lunch station on Thumb Bay and the Lake Hotel as an "extra" item costing $2.50. As it was optional, the lake trip required some selling; the public's interest in buffalo after 1894 suggested that a zoological garden on an island near the steamer's route would be a worthwhile come on.

Such a proposal was advanced by Mr. Waters in 1896, and since what he had in mind was not much different from the attempt to fence in the Hayden Valley herd, he was given oral permission to put a few animals on an island in Lake Yellowstone[31] provided they were obtained outside the Park. Four buffalo (two cows and two bulls) were purchased from Charles Goodnight of Goodnight, Texas, and loaded into a boxcar on June 21, 1896, for shipment in care of a cowboy named William Timmons. It was a fourteen-day journey by way of Fond du Lac, Wisconsin—where a bull was left and a cow was picked up—to the terminus of the Northern Pacific's park branch line at Cinnabar. From there the buffalo were hauled into the Park on four wagons and moved across the lake to Dot Island on a barge towed by the steamboat *Zillah*. Timmons stayed with the animals for a month to make certain they had adapted to their new home.[32]

By then it was doubtful that corraling the Hayden Valley buffalo herd was feasible. Colonel S. B. M. Young, who had taken over the superintendency from Captain Anderson, expressed the new viewpoint this way:

> I have consulted with Dr. Frank Baker, Superintendent of the National Zoological Park at Washington, as to the advisability of corraling the remaining buffalo in the Park with a vew to their preservation and increase, and our concurrent conclusion is that it has been the experience of most persons engaged in the capture and domestication of wild animals that while the young of two classes to which the buffalo belong may be caught and confined with usually successful results, it is otherwise with adult animals, a large proportion of which fail to adapt themselves to even slight restraint, and die in consequence ... Even were the advisability of the project free from doubt, the difficulties in the way of its successful accomplishment appear to be impossible.[33]

His statement provided the basis for future efforts to save the Yellowstone bison. No further attempt was made to entrap the Hayden Valley herd; instead, funds were sought to purchase semidomesticated buffalo suitable for establishing a captive herd—which could be augmented with calves caught from the wild herd in the spring.

Soon after Captain John Pitcher became superintendent in 1901 he submitted an estimate of $30,000 for purchasing thirty to sixty buffalo and establishing them in a suitable enclosure; Congress made half that amount available for the fiscal year beginning July 1, 1902. Charles J. Jones had evidently kept himself informed concerning the Yellowstone buffalo, for he immediately sought and received a commission as game warden for the Park.[34]

Buffalo Jones was more than fifty-eight years old when he arrived at Mammoth Hot Springs on July 16, 1902. In his appearance, he probably differed very little from the description provided by a reporter of the *Kansas City Star* in 1897: "a slenderly built man, with piercing gray eyes, a firm jaw and a slouching gait, as if he had spent much of his time on horseback." He was then serving as sergeant-at-arms for the Kansas legislature, having lost a considerable fortune and his herd of domesticated buffalo through some unwise speculation in Kansas lands. The reporter noted that he wore an antique coat with a collar cut from a buffalo robe, remarking, "When that collar is worn out, Jones' last buffalo relic will have disappeared." But he misjudged the old frontiersman, for Buffalo Jones made a comeback in the buffalo business.

Following his arrival at the Park, the new game warden helped Major Pitcher select a site for an enclosure, which was constructed one mile south of Fort Yellowstone. The area contained a small stream and a grove of trees, and was fenced with Page woven wire; a log house was erected nearby. Fifteen cows were purchased from the Allard herd in northwestern Montana and three bulls from the Goodnight herd in Texas. Howard Eaton of Medora, North Dakota, delivered the Allard cows in good condition early in October, and Jones returned from Texas at the end of the month with three bulls that he had personally selected. A small corral was also built in the valley of Pelican Creek for use in holding calves that were to be captured from the wild herd in the spring.[35] Pitcher later admitted that Jones did very good work during this period of establishing the new herd, but adds adamantly, "here his usefulness in the park ended absolutely."[36]

Buffalo Jones was a man of puritanical morals, whose statement that he "never used tobacco, never drank whiskey . . . [and] steered clear of poker" was undoubtedly true. Such righteous ways in a frontiersman might have been overlooked in view of his ability as an animal handler had he not been intolerant of others. The Park's game warden was not a tolerant man. When in February 1903 Major Pitcher put Jones in charge of the scouts assigned to capture calves from the wild herd, he proceeded to lecture those men as "habitual drunkards and gamblers" and openly questioned their honesty. The scouts took violent exception to his remarks; one resigned and the others were so uncooperative the major had to terminate Jones' supervision.[37]

But Jones did not allow his trouble with the scouts to end there. On May 6, he left Fort Yellowstone with Scouts Morrison and Holt, intending to ski to Pelican Creek and begin capturing the buffalo calves. They carried no blankets, as they intended to stop at outpost stations each night (the first being Norris, twenty-one miles away). Scout Morrison had been out late the night before and took some "medicine" along for his hangover. At the seven-mile post he proceeded to take a nap in a grove of pine trees by the road. Jones and Holt pushed on slowly, thinking the laggard would eventually catch up, which he did late in the afternoon, but five hours had been lost and there was no hope of reaching Norris; instead, they had to shelter in a wretched cabin at Crystal Springs, without bedding and unable to keep up a fire because the stovepipe lacked four inches of reaching the roof.

On their return to headquarters, Jones reported Morrison's dereliction, whereupon Major Pitcher gave the scout a severe reprimand. The result was that Morrison would no longer speak to Jones, and later conspired with Scout Waagner to explode a large cannon firecracker under the game warden during the fourth of July celebration at Mammoth Hot Springs. Buffalo Jones thought they intended "to either do me bodily harm, intimidate, or show contempt for my methods of doing business," and he demanded that Major Pitcher fire both scouts.[38] But the major, having had about enough of his crotchety game warden, ignored him.

Thereafter, relations between Buffalo Jones and Major Pitcher deteriorated rapidly. The game warden continued to tend the herd of captive buffalo, discipline the bears at the hotel garbage dumps, and hunt predators with his pack of hounds (he once ran a cougar into an abandoned coal mine on Mount Everts, tied the big cat up, and brought it back behind his saddle); but he became more and more a loner whose inability to get along with others became so serious he was at last forbidden even to make suggestions to the soldiers.[39]

Many years ago, Judge Meldrum (the U. S. commissioner for the Park during the years Buffalo Jones was its game warden) was asked for his recollections of Jones and his part in establishing the captive herd. He paid tribute to Jones' knowledge of wild animals and his ability to handle them, but he also mentioned that "his balance wheels weren't working," and he illustrated his point with an anecdote from the park visit of President Theodore Roosevelt:

> Roosevelt, Jones and I [Meldrum] were delegates to the same convention in 1884. It was the convention at which Blaine was nominated. This seemed to be sufficient excuse to Jones to consider Roosevelt as an old "buddy" and when he learned of Roosevelt's coming to the park, he came to me and said, "Judge, now that the President is going to come into the park, I think we ought to get together and talk over old times." I replied, "Well, I don't make a habit of bothering Presidents of the United States." Jones said, "Aren't you going out in the park with him?" And I told him that I wouldn't unless I was asked and I had not been asked yet but I hoped he enjoyed it. Well the long and the short of it was that when Roosevelt came into the park he left all of his aides and secretary at headquarters and gave orders to Pitcher that he would be accompanied only by Pitcher, Burroughs and the smallest number of men necessary to take care of camp. When the cavalcade started out Jones took his hounds and went along in the hope that he might tree a mountain lion and thus provide a little entertainment for the President. The first evening in camp Roosevelt called Pitcher to him and told him to send the hounds and their owner back stating that he did not want them. This word was given Jones and he suggested that Scout McBride take the hounds back, but the result of it all was that Jones and his hounds returned to Mammoth. I met him down at the Post Office shortly after he came in and said, "Hello Jones, I thought you were out with the President," Jones was so mad that he never said a word.[40]

Buffalo Jones finally resorted to politicking in his struggle with Major Pitcher, writing critical letters and publishing uncomplimentary items concerning the administration of the Park. He must have felt triumphant when the secretary of the interior informed Major Pitcher,

> I deem it best that you should be no longer burdened with the details of the preservation of game in the reservation, and hereafter this work will be delegated to the Game Warden who will be held to strict accountability for the care, preservation and management of the game within the Yellowstone National Park.[41]

Jones soon found his authority meaningless, however, without the cooperation of park personnel. He had backed himself into a corner and finally tendered his resignation, which took effect September 15, 1905.[42]

Thus ended Buffalo Jones' association with Yellowstone Park and the bison herd he helped to establish. Though a colorful individual, he does not deserve the credit occasionally given him for "saving" the American bison; nor can he be credited with preservation of the Yellowstone herd. Since the wild herd survived both the poachers who killed adult animals for their scalps and the occasional kidnapping of calves in the spring, there is reason to suspect the bison would have survived without establishment of a captive herd. Here, where the Yellowstone crusade appears at its best, it may well have been groundless.

Two years after Jones resigned and left the Park the captive herd outgrew the enclosure at Mammoth Hot Springs, so some of the animals were moved to a corral at Rose Creek in the Lamar Valley.[43] That establishment, on the site of Buckskin Jim Cutler's homestead of earlier years, finally became known as the Buffalo Ranch. A semidomesticated herd was managed there until 1952, but interbreeding with the wild herd on the summer range eventually produced hybrids differing from both their plains and mountain progenitors.

The Park ultimately gained possession of the animals that had been brought in by the Yellowstone Lake Boat Company. Between 1896 and 1907 the "game show" maintained by Mr. Waters on Dot Island provoked no adverse comment and it is presumed that the animals were reasonably well cared for. Each fall the corraled buffalo and elk were brought back to the boat company's establishment adjacent to the Lake Hotel and wintered on hay cut in Hayden Valley, near the Mud Volcano. As Mr. Waters' fortunes declined, however, he neglected his animals. The first complaint was made in a letter signed jointly by the manager and the transportation agent at Lake Hotel. On June 12, 1907, they wrote concerning the nearby pens:

> The condition of these yards is most deplorable. Mud and filth is knee deep; no shelter to speak of and absolutely nothing dry for the buffalo and elk to lie on. Among the herd are two elk fawns and one buffalo calf and it is with difficulty that they wallow through this filth, and owing to limited feeding they are in very poor condition . . . it is plainly a case of cruelty to animals and we are positive that this information will be appreciated.[44]

The pens were cleaned up at Superintendent Young's demand and the miserable animals were returned to Dot Island, but their lot there was not much better. On August 2 Mr. Waters was advised to remove his animals from the Park not later than October; he did not bother to reply and was notified on August 7 that "at the close of the present tourist season you must at once remove from the park all buffalo and elk now confined on Dot Island." This second letter was delivered to Mr. Waters by an officer.[45]

Before the superintendent's wrath had cooled, a number of complaints came to him from members of the National Association of Game and Fish Wardens and Commissioners, who were in the Park to hold their annual meeting. (This organization had come into existence July 21, 1902, at a conference of state game wardens held at Mammoth Hot Springs on the invitation of Mr. W. F. Scott, game warden for Montana, and Major John Pitcher.) A feature of the 1907 convention was a boat trip on Yellowstone Lake, including a stop at Dot Island. The game wardens were horrified by what they saw there; W. F. Scott, their president, wrote:

> I was one of the last to land, and, while going down the gang plank, my attention was attracted by a nauseating and sour smell. Upon looking around I saw a deck hand following me, carrying two bucketts of the vilest smelling slop or swill. Upon being asked what the same was used for he replied that it was to feed the elk.
>
> When we reached the corral this repugnant mess was poured out into a trough where these poor emaciated creatures, driven to desperation by hunger, fought for an opportunity to eat at the trough, where, for the first time in my life, I saw elk eat flesh.
>
> The condition of these animals on this Island is pitiful . . . not alone are the elk suffering, but the buffalo confined there are in almost as bad shape.
>
> When I reflect upon the repulsive conditions that were witnessed by our party of Game wardens, and the further fact that this inhuman sight is witnessed daily by hundreds of tourists from all over the world, I am impelled to make this protest in the name of humanity.[46]

Superintendent Young was thus constrained to reiterate his earlier stand: the animals were to be removed from the Park.

E. C. Waters closed his business on September 22 without making any but his usual preparations for winter; evidently, he did not intend to remove his animals as ordered. He was requested by letter the following day to inform the superintendent of his intentions, as it would be necessary to turn the animals loose if they were not removed. On September 26, Mr. Waters replied, spelling out what was already obvious, that he intended to winter his animals in the pens near Lake Hotel, just as he had always done.[47]

On October 15 the corral fences at Lake Hotel were pulled down under the personal direction of the superintendent, and the animals (eight buffalo and seven elk) were released to fend for themselves. Mr. Waters had notified his attorney, I. L. Bullock of Washington, D.C., of his late decision to offer to sell four buffalo cows and seven elk to the Park for $6,000. The offer was not mailed until the fourteenth, reaching the Park three days after the release of the animals. Regardless, the price was exorbitant and would not have been accepted.[48]

Superintendent Young had intended to drive the released animals entirely out of the Park because they were infected with mange. It is unlikely that was done, however, for one old buffalo bull was running loose near the outlet of the lake in June of 1908, "disturbing traffic and endangering the lives of tourists by frightening horses, etc., along the stage road." Scout Sam Graham and the soldiers finally managed to drive the old bull across the outlet to the Pelican Creek meadows,[49] where he probably lived a solitary life without contact with the wild herd farther up the drainage. There is no hint of the fate of his former companions.

The Yellowstone Lake Boat Company soon went the way of its zoological garden. The secretary of the interior was at last convinced the company's franchise should not be renewed. Because he ignored the orders of the superintendent, Mr. Waters was barred from entering the Park and a legal action was begun to terminate his business there. The matter was settled out of court by the sale of Waters' assets to the new T.E. Hofer Boat Company.

While the Yellowstone crusade was preoccupied with preserving the American bison, the elk, or wapiti, were increasing in the area. The extent of this problem should have been evident before the turn of the century, but it wasn't until 1912 that sportsman-conservationist Teddy Roosevelt defined the problem and suggested an answer. He noted that "elk are hardy and prolific," with the ability to "double in numbers every four years." He also recognized that "where natural checks are removed" they increase to the limit of the food supply, so that "either disease or starvation must come." Remarking that "from time to time well meaning people propose that the difficulty shall be met by feeding the elk hay in winter or by increasing the size of the wintering grounds," he offered his opinion that neither approach was "of the slightest use." Instead, he thought "hunting them should be permitted right up to the point of killing each year on an average what would amount to the whole increase."[50]

This wise counsel fell largely on deaf ears, probably because very few people believed him. Within the Park, hunting was ruled out, of course, as a means of controlling the proliferation of the elk—the policy of absolute protection established by the Lacey Act had settled that; yet, hunting might have helped the situation if allowed to operate to maximum effect outside park boundaries. There were forces at work at that very time, however, that had just the opposite effect.

Although the elk were so numerous in the winter of 1910-11 that they drifted down the Yellowstone Valley into Montana in their efforts to find forage, doing "much damage to haystacks, fields, and fences on the ranches near the park," the Montana legislature set aside a strip several miles wide, from the Yellowstone River west to the northwest corner of the Park and then southward along the western boundary for seven miles, as a game preserve, which was expected to "be of great assistance in protecting the game in the park."[51] Wyoming followed suit by also setting aside game preserves adjacent to the Park, and, the following winter, both Wyoming and the federal government provided money for feeding elk in Jackson Hole (many of these animals were from the Park's "southern herd").

The Biological Survey and the U.S. Forest Service cooperated in a study of elk wintering grounds adjacent to the Park, and met with the park superintendent on September 9, 1912, to formulate the following policy:

> 1. That the whole elk problem should be handled as a unit.
>
> 2. That for the present the elk herd of about 50,000, which includes the park herd, the Jackson Hole herd, and those that range in the forest reserves just outside the park, should be maintained at its present size, of which the northern herd should not exceed 35,000.
>
> 3. That under present conditions the annual crop from the herd (killed under game laws of the adjoining States, shipped, etc.) should not exceed 7,500 or 8,000.[52]

Presumably, the annual crop figure was to apply to the entire management unit of 50,000 elk, and thus offset a sixteen percent increase in the herd. That is slightly below the rate of increase established by a later study[53] and would not have stabilized the herd size; as for reduction, it seems not to have been considered necessary then. Instead of a serious attempt to bring the elk population within the carrying capacity of the winter range, the emphasis was placed upon a reduction of domestic livestock grazing on National Forest lands used by the elk.

This was all intended to maintain a status quo, to preserve the elk in their then existing numbers; and although it recognized an upper limit for the northern herd and provided a partial mechanism for staying within it, it was not effective. Beyond the normal hunting kill and winter loss (probably minimal because of the very mild winters from 1913 to 1916), the northern herd was reduced only by trapping and live shipment of limited numbers of elk to those areas desiring animals for stocking purposes. Such shipments accounted for 137 animals in the winter of 1911-12; 538 in 1912-13; 99 in 1913-14 (far below the limit of 800 animals within any one fiscal year which was set December 3, 1913);[54] 375 in 1914-15, and 618 in 1915-16. An estimate of the total number of animals removed by man (that is, by live shipment, legal hunting, and poaching) in 1915-16 is only 1,875, a figure probably representative of such loss during the preceding four seasons, which were all relatively mild. Thus, about five percent of the annual increase in the herd was being removed by man, only one-third of the ceiling set in 1912.

Certainly, there were warning signs that the elk population was building up. It is said that as many as 7,000 elk could be seen at one time below the town of Gardiner during the winter of 1915-16; the attraction led the Northern Pacific to run several "game excursions" on its park branch line.[55] During the second decade of this century, the elk responded to the decrease in hunting pressure (a result of the establishment of game preserves adjacent to the Park and improved law enforcement) and to the increase in forage resulting from amelioration of weather and competition by breeding up to the food supply, increasing by nearly ten thousand animals between the reports for 1912 and 1915. (If the more conservative figure appearing in the 1916 report is used the increase was only two thousand.) Regardless of which figure is used, the validity of Roosevelt's prognosis was about to be demonstrated.

The winter of 1916-17 was a hard one for the elk. Temperatures were not severe but the snowfall was heavy (150 percent of normal), with two feet of snow on the ground from December through February, three feet in March, and two in April.[56] The elk were unable to reach much of their new winter range and had difficulty getting forage on their old wintering grounds. They starved, and though it is not possible to say with any accuracy how seriously the northern herd was depleted, the loss was sufficient to raise the old, subjective fears of extinction of the species. Thus alarmed, and forgetful that the Yellowstone elk had survived a similar catastrophe at the turn of the century (and had rebounded quickly from others before that), the park administration immediately advocated measures that Roosevelt had mentioned were of no real value: the feeding of hay and the extension of wintering grounds. The result of these efforts to maintain a large elk herd will be discussed later.

The elk problem, which was so dramatically exposed during the winter of 1916-17, had deep roots in the warfare that had been waged against the Park's predators. Predation provides a desirable natural check upon the growth of an ungulate population. By pulling down and devouring the weak and the sick, predators eliminate the less hardy individuals and the total number is adjusted toward equivalence with the food supply; with that attained, healthy and well-nourished animals become a more difficult prey, so that the predators, in turn, suffer from having overrun their food supply. Such fluctuations in the numbers of the eaten and the eaters form a cyclic basis for an ecological balance that is self-adjusting—except where tampered with by man.

In the Yellowstone, tampering with this delicate balance of nature is nearly as old as the Park. Hide-hunting in the 1870s decimated the herds gathered on wintering grounds in the northern valleys. Philetus Norris indicated that between two thousand and five thousand animals were slaughtered for their hides and tongues in one season; the only other use made of the carcasses was to poison them with strychnine to kill wolves and wolverines. All that can be said to the credit of this combined hide-hunting and wolfing is that it was less disturbing to the ecosystem than either alone would have been.

The secretary's order of January 15, 1883, which prohibited the hunting of most park animals, was interpreted as not applying to the predators because it did not name those beasts of "fang and claw." Thus, coyotes, wolves, cougars, wolverines, and bears were shot on sight by employees and visitors, prior to the era of army management. An item that appeared in the *Livingston Enterprise* ("Bear Hunting in the National Park")[57] describes a two-month hunt made by H. A. Pearson of San Francisco. His bag was three grizzly bears, two black bears, and a cougar "of fine proportions." He was so pleased with this second hunting excursion in Wonderland that he planned to return in September with some wealthy Californians who were also anxious to kill bears, cougars, and wolves. Mr. Pearson even contemplated building a clubhouse at Henrys Lake as a headquarters for bear hunters.

Captain Moses Harris, the first military superintendent, recognized the impropriety of allowing visitors to hunt even the noxious animals. It was his opinion "that at the present time more injury would result to the game from the use of firearms or traps in the Park than from any ravages which may be feared from carnivorous animals."[58] This gave the predators a respite.

Though they were not molested again for a decade, the predators were not really safe. In 1889, Captain Boutelle mentioned the carnivora as having, "in common with other animals," increased to the point where he considered "something should be done for their extermination," and in the following year he attributed a scarcity of elk and buffalo calves to the mischief of bears and cougars. He recommended control of the predators by persons working under his direction.[59]

The first deliberate control measure was instituted in the winter of 1895-96. Captain Anderson thought the coyotes were becoming too numerous in the vicinity of Fort Yellowstone and ordered the destruction of some (a seemingly illogical action in the light of his accompanying statement that he found "the young of all the ruminants especially numerous and in good condition").[60] The work was entrusted to one of the scouts, but was questioned "by a few of the friends of the park" on the grounds that extermination of the coyote would lead to destruction of the winter range by gophers. Regardless, Captain Anderson remained an advocate of coyote reduction.[61]

The superintendent's report for 1898 indicates a continuation of the poison campaign against the coyotes (because they were presumed to be destructive of young deer and antelope), and this was routine thereafter. Other species were soon marked for control. Cougars were then numerous, particularly on Mount Everts, so they were hunted there in 1899 and several were killed, merely because they were thought to "destroy much game." The following year, gray wolves and wildcats were included among the proscribed.[62]

Early in 1903 the Park received a pack of eight lion hounds, which arrived in two lots from Aledo, Texas.[63] They were the hounds Buffalo Jones attempted to take on President Roosevelt's outing in the Park. A later comment by T.R. explains why he sent the hounds back: "As the elk were evidently too numerous for the feed, I do not think the cougars were doing any damage." He also observed that the coyotes were plentiful at the time of his visit, with the elk showing "no dread of them."[64] Despite that realistic appraisal, reduction of the numbers of coyotes and cougars continued.

The superintendent's report for 1905 noted that as the cougars and coyotes were destructive of the game and "also a pest to stockmen of the surrounding country, they are destroyed." That summer three hunters (John B. Goff, W. B. Wells, and Jack Fry), who had just guided President Roosevelt on a bear-hunting trip in Colorado, brought their lion hounds to the Park for the purpose of clearing it of cougars. It is said that the job came to them through the president,[65] but, as yet, that remains unconfirmed. The effect of their efforts, together with those of Buffalo Jones, was to rid the Park of at least sixty-five cougars prior to the fall of 1906, when the big cats were reported as "almost exterminated." In due time, that came to Roosevelt's attention and he wrote Superintendent Young as follows:

> I do not think any more cougars (mountain lions) should be killed in the park. Game is abundant. We want to profit by what has happened in the English preserves, where it proved bad for the grouse itself to kill off all the peregrine falcons and all the other birds of prey. It may be advisable, in case the ranks of the deer and antelope right around the Springs should be too heavily killed out, to kill some of the cougars there, but in the rest of the park I certainly would not kill any of them. On the contrary, they ought to be let alone.[66]

The advice was accepted and the government lion hounds, purchased in 1903, were sold to the highest bidder.

Thereafter, the cougars were not molested for five years, until the winter of 1913-14, when the effort to eradicate them was continued. With the help of Steve Elkins and his hounds, forty-six more animals were killed, bringing the total destroyed over two decades to at least 111.[67]

Although wolves were marked for elimination in 1900, there is no evidence any were killed before the winter of 1914-15; in fact, it was stated in 1912 that "there is no absolute proof that they exist within the limits of the reservation."[68] Proof seems to have been found two years later when they were reported as traveling in packs of up to ten animals. The reaction was predictable: "They are very destructive of game, and efforts will be made to kill them." By the fall of 1918, at least forty-five wolves were destroyed.

Meanwhile, the coyotes were taking their lumps with the resilience characteristic of the species. By the fall of 1918, control measures—poison, trapping, and shooting—had accounted for 1,600 (as with the cougar, the figure could be greater), yet they still appeared to be numerous. But appearances are not the whole story. The considerable loss suffered by the predators had impaired their effectiveness as a check upon the ungulate population; so those other checks—starvation and disease—were left to operate with greater severity than should have been the case.

Another factor on the negative side, though of less importance than those just mentioned, was the feeding of hay to certain of the ungulates in winter. This activity developed out of a concern for the antelope and deer that congregated near the north entrance of the Park. The settlement of Yellowstone Valley in the vicinity of the town of Gardiner had greatly accelerated near the turn of the century, so that the customary wintering range of the antelope was drastically curtailed. The acting superintendent reported in 1899 that the animals, estimated to number 700 or 800, were "constantly trying to get across the line and outside the park limits, where there are numerous hunters watching for an opportunity to shoot them."[69] He found it necessary to keep a scout and two soldiers constantly on the boundary line "to drive them back." The solution he suggested was construction of four miles of fence to retain the animals, which led to recognition of "scarcity of feed" as the root of the problem.

The state of Montana passed a law in 1901 prohibiting the killing of antelope for an indefinite period, and the prediction that "they will probably increase very rapidly in the future" was quite accurate. By 1903, the number estimated as wintering in the vicinity of the northern entrance was 1,000, and the acting superintendent was advocating supplemental feeding of both the antelope and the bighorn sheep, though he readily admitted the impracticality of feeding "all of the large game" (an idea which had evidently been raised by that time).[70]

Following construction of the great arch at the northern entrance, the boundary fence proposed earlier was erected and had the effect of keeping loose stock belonging to persons in and around Gardiner from consuming the forage on the flat facing the town; but of even greater importance to the antelope was the irrigation of that field with water from the Gardner River (made available through the ditch intended to supply the plantings with which the arch was landscaped) and the sowing of alfalfa seed there. The acting superintendent had already concluded that the ungulates

> should be treated in the same way that cattlemen handle their range stock; in other words, in case of a very bad winter or a spring when the snow falls very deep and a crust forms over it, we should have a number of haystacks scattered about the range, so that the greater part of the game could be fed just a sufficient amount to carry them over the dangerous period, which in most cases would not continue for more than a week or two.[71]

Some experimental feeding of hay to deer on the parade ground at Fort Yellowstone had already been tried, and it was hoped that the fifty-acre field at Gardiner would yield 100 to 200 tons of hay which could be stacked in anticipation of a hard winter.

The effects of these several measures—better protection, exclusion of domestic stock, and feeding—were soon obvious. The antelope, deer, and bighorn sheep became "exceedingly tame," seeming to recognize man as their friend, and there was an obvious betterment in the physical condition of all the animals, particularly the females about to bear young. The result was an increase in the number of antelope to an estimated 1,500 in 1905,[72] a doubling in five years. The deer and bighorn sheep prospered also, subjecting the limited winter range to the demands of ever increasing numbers of animals. These demands would eventually prove to be destructive.

By 1916 the antelope, deer and bighorn sheep being fed at the Gardiner hayfield were consuming 200 tons of hay, only slightly more than the amount raised; and by 1918, the amount of hay fed (elk were also feeding) was up to 350 tons. The winter-feeding of ungulates would become a much larger operation before the truth of Roosevelt's appraisal became evident and this policy was repudiated.

A feeding problem of a different type had already developed from the familiarity with which bears were treated at the park hostels. The bears had become such a nuisance by 1898—so "destructive to the stores of the detachments on station, lunch stations and campers"—that the acting superintendent was led to suggest some means would have to be taken "to rid the park of the yearly increase."[73] However, prior to 1902 the bears were subjected to no more control than the killing of an occasional rogue.

By that time the inroads of bears had become nearly intolerable; they were guilty not only of breaking into storerooms and kitchens (see Chapter 15), but also of becoming over-friendly with chance acquaintances (such as tourists out for an evening stroll) and of raising the very devil with the property and subsistence of campers.

A visitor of that day tells of two men who were traveling through the Park in a single-seated buggy, camping and sleeping under their vehicle. After retiring, one (a German) was awakened by a noise overhead and, by the time he got out of his blankets, a bear was standing upright in the bright moonlight, chewing on a ham taken from their grub box. The German later told our informant,

> Och, I vas so mad, I say I go mit club and kill dat bear, but mine pardner, he vas old bear man; he say, "No Fritz, dat bear have got hog's ham. You go mit a stick for him, he got your ham." So I leaved dat d____ bear sit on him tail and chew, vile I cuss him till daylight comes.[74]

More often, bruin's effrontery was met by a spontaneous rallying of sagebrushers, likened to "a midnight sally to route the neighbor's cow from one's garden patch." Such affairs were generally begun with the use of loud, indelicate language, were prosecuted with whips, clubs, and stones, and only ended upon the clumsy retreat of the culprit.

Upon his arrival in the Park, Major Pitcher found the situation so bad that it seemed but a matter of time until someone was seriously injured; so he had circulars placed in all the hotels and permanent camps forbidding the molestation or feeding of bears. However,

Feeding hotel garbage to bears, probably at the Grand Canyon.

tourists continued to frequent garbage dumps to watch the animals feed. Finally, and despite the warning, Mr. R. E. Southwick of Hart, Michigan, was badly injured at such a "show" in 1902. After that, all dumps were provided with fencing to protect the tourists and signs to explain the danger.[75] Pitcher's recommendation that the gist of his circular on bears be incorporated into the rules and regulations, in order that violators "may be promptly brought before the United States Commissioner," was put into effect the following season. A vigorous program of enforcement was begun, but contrary to the major's expectations, it was not "all that is needed to render the bear in the park perfectly harmless." After the passage of nearly three-quarters of a century, the problem remains.

The grizzly ordinarily prefers not to become directly involved with people, but when he does meet them, the danger is far greater than in any similar confrontation with a black bear. In fact, a grizzly bent on camp raiding caused the first death of a person attributable to a park bear. The grizzly involved in the incident was a tremendous animal which may have been forced into an untypical way of life through development of an infirmity, such as worn teeth or arthritic joints. The grizzly came into the camp of Ned Frost, Sr., a Wyoming guide who had stopped with his party at Indian Pond,[76] several miles east of present Fishing Bridge in mid-August 1916, and proceeded to drag a man out of a sleeping bag by the shoulder. When Mr. Frost intervened to halt the attack, he was bitten in the thigh and nearly bled to death before medical assistance could be obtained from Lake Hotel.[77] A search party went out prepared to kill the bear but failed to find him.

On the evening of September 7, the same bear appeared about seven miles farther east, where teamster Frank Welch of the Army Quartermaster Corps had camped by the road with the wagonload of hay he was hauling to a road camp near Sylvan Pass. Welch was sleeping under the wagon, while two young men—laborers, who were hitchhiking a ride to the camp—were bedded down on top of the load. It appears that the teamster attempted to defend his outfit, was mauled, and then dragged some distance before his companions were able to rescue him. They put the injured teamster on top of the loaded wagon and one man stayed there, armed with an axe, to protect him while the other rode a team horse to the outlet of Lake Yellowstone for help. But Welch died after reaching the Fort Yellowstone hospital.

Again the bear eluded a search party, but this time he did not hide out; instead, he raided the road camp the next evening. That very day a small terrier, lost or abandoned in the Park, had wandered into

Fred Muse's camp, and the foreman, who had no use for dogs, left that forlorn little creature out in the cold. When the bear moved into camp, the terrier raised a racket that brought out the crew, armed with whatever came to hand, to drive him off. No one was hurt, thanks to the dog, because every time the bear turned to charge, his heels were nipped and he had to face the terrier. The bear was finally driven into the woods, but the men suspected he would return and prepared accordingly. A barrel baited with garbage was placed on its side with a charge of dynamite at the opening. The old raider did return that same night and the boys blew him up; as one said later, they "raised that bear up maybe four or five feet ... broke every bone in his body."[78]

The dead grizzly was a huge creature with a skull measuring eighteen inches across the brow. He had evidently had some experience with traps, for he was missing some toes from a hind foot, and the story has persisted that he had left a trail of depredations across the Shoshone National Forest. For his bravery, the little terrier gained a home; in fact, Fred Muse would not take a job unless the dog could go along. So the terrier lived many years in the Park.[79]

That particular bear is said to have inspired Ernest Thompson Seton to write the story of Wahb, the grizzly. Seton brought Wahb to a melodramatic end with a bear version of euthanasia at Death Gulch. The place is real and grizzlies have died there, but there is no reason to believe those deaths were other than accidental. The locality was discovered in the summer of 1888 by Frank H. Knowlton and Walter H. Weed of the United States Geological Survey. Weed noted:

> The gulch ends, or rather begins, in a scoop or basin about two hundred and fifty feet above Cache Creek, and just below this was found the fresh body of a large bear, a silver-tip grizzly, with the remains of a companion in an advanced stage of decomposition above him. Near by were the skeletons of four more bears, with the bones of an elk a yard or two above, while in the bottom of the pocket were the fresh remains of several squirrels, rock hares, and other small animals, besides numerous dead butterflies and insects.[80]

The deaths were attributed to asphyxiation by irrespirable gas, probably carbonic-acid gas resulting from the action of acid waters on the underlying limestone. In applying the name Death Gulch to this V-shaped rent in the canyon wall on the east bank of Cache Creek, Knowlton and Weed were figuratively linking it to the ancient fable of the Death Valley of Java. In that tale there was, in the center of the island, a valley dominated by a deadly *upas* tree which poisoned everything within a radius of ten miles. According to the Dutch surgeon, Foersch, its virulence was so great "there was no fish in the waters, nor any rat, mouse, or other vermin to be seen there, and when birds fly so near this tree that the effluvia reaches them, they fall a sacrifice to the effects of the poison." Investigation by Junghuhn proved those claims to be gross exaggerations; the lethal vale was only a saucerlike depression about one hundred feet in diameter and fifteen feet deep—a mere sump collecting carbonic-acid gas emanations.[81] This gas is the agent that kills small birds and mammals in the Stygian Cave at Mammoth Hot Springs, and its presence in the Devils Kitchen led to discontinuance of guided trips that once gave visitors a glimpse into the labyrinth underlying the hot spring formation.

The beginning of management of the park fishery was a parallel event to the Yellowstone crusade. The explorers of the Yellowstone region found that fish were plentiful in some of its waters and entirely absent from others. As early as 1868, Lake Yellowstone was known as a place where "elegant fish can be 'forked up' by the boat load,"[82] and that statement, though couched in exaggerated terms, does indicate the abundance from which Cornelius Hedges was able to take forty-one fish, weighing two pounds each, while fishing from the beach in front of the Washburn party's camp of September 12, 1870. The abundance was also typical of the Yellowstone River and all its tributaries except the Gardner River and Tower Creek.

On the other hand, the explorers of 1869 found the Lower Geyser Basin barren of fish, a condition they were inclined to attribute to some noxious effects of the locality,[83] and the subsequent discovery that the drainage of the Gibbon River was likewise uninhabited by fish led to a belief that there was not much to be hoped for—fish-wise—in streams that were warmed by hot springs and chemically impregnated. Indeed, this empirical view of the barren waters in the western half of the Park persisted even after it should have been obvious that the absence of fish was the result of the obstruction of stream channels by waterfalls.

There were few scientific studies related to the park fishery in the early years of the Park, and those were limited to the taxonomic interest of the zoologists attached to the Hayden Survey and some investigation of the parasites found in the trout of Yellowstone Lake and its outlet stream down to the falls. This condition of the trout (not found in fish taken below the great falls or in the crowded waters of Trout Lake and Lake Abundance) was first noted by A. Bart Henderson, but his comment on the Yellowstone Lake trout ("We found a few of them wormy from some unknown cause"[84]) hardly does justice to the revulsion with which the ordinary fisherman viewed his catch when it proved to be full of long, white worms. Quite naturally, scientific inquiry was, at first, directed almost exclusively toward that problem.

Professor Joseph Leidy was soon able to identify the parasite,[85] a larval worm with the formidable name of *Diphyllobothrium cordiceps* (also entirely harmless to man), but the other half of the question—how it got there—was not so easily answered. Subsequent research indicated that one stage in the life cycle of the parasite was passed in the intestines of fishing birds, but it was nearly fifty years before the alternate host was identified as the pelican.

The Park's barren waters attracted no attention until 1889, when Captain F. A. Boutelle, who was an enthusiastic angler, initiated a program of stocking the barren streams and lakes. He reported:

> In passing through the Park I noticed with surprise the barrenness of most of the water of the Park. Besides the beautiful Shoshone and other smaller lakes there are hundreds of miles of as fine streams as any in existence without a fish of any kind. I have written Col. Marshall McDonald, U.S. Fish Commission, upon the subject, and have received letters from him manifesting a great interest. I hope through him to see all these waters so stocked that the pleasure-seeker in the Park can enjoy fine fishing within a few rods of any hotel or camp.[86]

Colonel McDonald's interest in Boutelle's proposal stemmed from his fledgling organization's need of a proper outdoor laboratory in which to exercise its science. Thus, Yellowstone's barren waters represented an opportunity to broaden the commission's activities from a preoccupation with the price of shad (greatly lowered through improved culture) to the development of a sport fishery in what was then the only area of wild land under federal management.

Although he was in poor health, McDonald visited the Park that summer and decided upon a rudimentary program. This called for the immediate stocking of some streams (brook trout for Glen Creek and the Gardner River above its falls, rainbow trout for the Gibbon River above Virginia Cascades, Loch Leven trout for the Firehole River above Kepler Cascades, mountain white fish for Twin Lakes and the Yellowstone River between the lake and the falls, and blackspotted or "native" trout for Lava Creek above its falls), and for a reconnaissance by David Starr Jordan as a basis for all future fish-planting activity.

The plants made during August and September of 1889 were not entirely satisfactory. Due to an error in identification, there was an unintended switch, with brook trout going into the Firehole drainage and Loch Leven into the Gardner River. The rainbow trout seem to

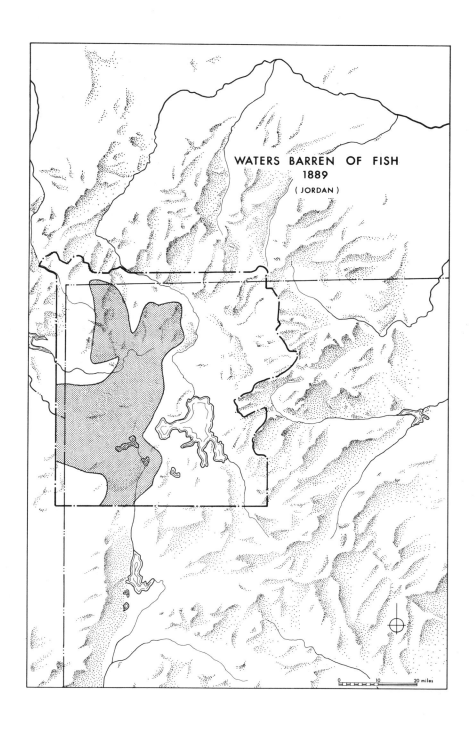

WATERS BARREN OF FISH
1889
(JORDAN)

0   10   20 miles

have passed over Gibbon Falls into the Madison River, and the whitefish failed to establish.[87] Jordan's work was far more comprehensive than might be expected in a study based on only two weeks' fieldwork (September 27 to October 11, 1889). His report catalogued the native fishes and where they were found, described the lakes and streams, listed the barren waters, and advised as to which were suitable for planting.[88]

Despite the planning, the fish-planting activities of the 1890s were not well coordinated and much that was done now appears ill-considered, if not promiscuous—particularly the introduction of exotics at the expense of native species (an impairment that must now be corrected through selective fishing). Although it was the Fish Commission's announced policy to keep the different species separate by reserving a distinct drainage or section of river for each, no account was taken of the facility with which fish pass over obstructions such as waterfalls and cascades with the resulting mixing of incompatible species. Perhaps this danger was not clearly understood in that day, but some idea of the problems created can be seen in a single example.

The native species of the Madison River below Madison Junction were blackspotted trout, mountain whitefish, and grayling; but by 1900, there were also rainbow trout (which came over Gibbon Fall after 1889), brook trout (from the Firehole drainage after 1889), and brown trout (also from the Firehole after 1890). The complications are these: the blackspotted trout hybridize with the rainbows to produce fish of very low fertility (genetic suicide, in a way), while the brown are extremely predacious and the brookies are competitors of the blackspotted "natives" for food. According to recent lists, the blackspotted trout is no longer present in the upper reaches of the Madison River—though formerly listed as a native of those waters.[89] The introduction of brown trout into the Snake River drainage has had a similarly adverse effect upon the blackspotted trout.

Perhaps it is fortunate that not every attempt to introduce exotic species succeeded. Whitefish placed above the Falls of Yellowstone River and land-locked salmon placed in Yellowstone Lake failed to establish and left those waters unsullied; the failure of early efforts to plant black bass in certain lakes saved the expense of eradicating an undesirable species at a later date (as had to be done with the yellow perch planted in Feather and Goose lakes by unknown persons).[90] In 1891, and again in 1893, Captain George Anderson suggested the introduction of black bass as a game fish, but this species was not introduced until the fall of 1894. The first shipment of fingerling was started to the Lower Geyser Basin in very cold weather and, as they appeared to be dead by the time they reached Norris, they were dumped into the Gibbon River at that place. Another shipment of bass the following summer reached its destination but did not survive.

While the barren waters of the Park were being stocked, more or less appropriately, with fish which generally prospered (multiplying "inconceivably" in some cases), members of the Fish Commission sought answers to several intriguing problems. Chief among these was just how the blackspotted trout of Pacific slope waters crossed over the Continental Divide into the Yellowstone River headwaters. Of course, there was Jim Bridger's Two Ocean River, a hydrographic connection verified by the Jones Expedition in 1873; but the question remained, could fish really cross from Pacific to Atlantic waters by that route? An old trapper, who had written of "fish crossing mountains," already had the answer,[91] but as he was unknown to science, Barton W. Evermann was sent to Two Ocean Pass in the summer of 1891 to check its illogical hydrography. He took trout from each of the streams (Atlantic and Pacific creeks) at points where they could easily have exchanged positions. He noted that "Jim Bridger is vindicated."[92]

Another puzzle of the Yellowstone region drew the attention of the Fish Commission. Stephen Forbes and Professor Edwin Linton were on Shoshone Lake one bright, still morning in the summer of 1891 when they first heard those "mysterious aerial sounds for which this region is noted." Forbes says:

> It put me in mind of the vibrating clang of a harp lightly and rapidly touched high up above the tree-tops, or the sound of many telegraph wires swinging regularly and rapidly in the wind, or, more rarely, of faintly heard voices answering each other overhead. It begins softly in the remote distance, draws rapidly near with louder and louder throbs of sound, and dies away in the opposite distance; or it may seem to wander irregularly about, the whole passage lasting from a few seconds to half a minute or more. We heard it repeatedly and very distinctly here and at Yellowstone Lake, most frequently at the latter place.[93]

He concluded that the sounds were aerial echoes, a belief shared by later observers.

A fish hatchery was suggested for the Park by Captain J. B. Erwin in 1898, but nothing was done about it until 1902, when a fish egg collection station was authorized for Thumb. The station was put into operation the following year, greatly facilitating the taking of trout eggs which had been started at that place in 1901 (the eggs were taken to Spearfish, South Dakota, for hatching). By 1909, the Thumb station was recognized as the most successful collecting point for blackspotted trout eggs in the United States.

The following year (1910), the Bozeman, Montana, hatchery began egg collection at Trout Lake, near Soda Butte in the northeast corner of the Park,[94] and the entire operation in the Park was turned over to that more convenient hatchery the next season. From then on the fishery activity in the Park increased rapidly: the Thumb station was enlarged and three boats were put into operation in 1912; a hatchery was constructed near Lake Hotel and a collecting station at Clear Creek in 1913; a third collecting station was put into operation at Columbine Creek in 1914.

Eggs taken from the spawning trout of Yellowstone Lake served to stock streams throughout the United States and Europe (and some within the Park), but they were lost to the waters from which they had been taken. The continual drain began to show up in a serious decline in sport fishing on Yellowstone Lake. In 1914 it therefore became policy to return "a large number of blackspotted trout eggs or fry to the Yellowstone Lake waters each year following the egg collecting.[95] By 1917 it was necessary to restrict the fishing operation of the Yellowstone Park Hotel Company, which employed men to catch trout for its dining rooms; that drain (amounting to as much as 7,500 pounds of fish per season in those latter years) was stopped entirely after 1919.[96]

Other restrictions upon fishing had developed gradually over the years. In 1896 the acting superintendent sought a limit on the size of fish that might be legally retained by fishermen, suggesting five or six inches as the minimum length, and such a regulation appeared in the Instructions to Persons Traveling Through Yellowstone National Park at the beginning of the 1897 season. The minimum length of "keepers" was thus set at six inches, and all fish of lesser size were to be "returned to the water, with the least damage possible to the fish." The number of fish that could be taken was not to exceed what was needed for food.[97] The legal catch was limited to twenty fish in 1908, and the minimum length for fish retained was raised to eight inches in 1911. In addition to the foregoing general regulations, a special regulation appeared in 1907 with the closing of Glen Creek because most of the fish caught after August 1 "were under size and were thrown back more or less injured," while Sportsman Lake was closed entirely to stop the illegal fishing that had been going on there.[98] In these regulations, the essential pattern of the future was established.

The reservation of forest lands as permanent federal holdings was an offshoot of the Yellowstone crusade. Indeed, it is in its influence on the establishment of those early forest reserves, which were the percursors of our national forests, that this movement accomplished most.

The continental landholdings of the U.S. (excluding Alaska) total 1,442,200,320 acres, a birthright of natural wealth called "greater than that of any other nation on earth."[99] It was long our national policy to dispose of this public domain to private ownership as rapidly as possible to extend settlement and development; reservation of any considerable portion for the use of the people as a whole was a concept contrary to our tradition. The first step in that direction was the federal government's assumption of title to 3,348 square miles of western real estate for a park upon the headwaters of the Yellowstone River. The reservation of Yellowstone National Park was the extent of federal stewardship prior to General P. H. Sheridan's junket through Wonderland in 1882.

General Sheridan's visit led him to suggest that the Park should be enlarged by adding to it those unoccupied forest lands extending forty miles to the east and ten miles to the south. Senator George Graham Vest introduced legislation that would have accomplished that, but his bill (S. 2317) lacked the necessary support. As a local editor remarked in calling upon Delegate Maginnis of Montana to remonstrate with the backers of the legislation: "The Park is already too huge a joke for them to comprehend,"[100] which was probably the prevailing opinion in the neighboring territories.

Sheridan's proposal ultimately found friends in the East, however. The American Forestry Association, after its merger with the American Forest Congress in 1882, initiated a national campaign for reservation of timbered portions of the public domain as watershed areas, and though not immediately successful,[101] this organization's efforts during the 1880s laid the basis for later success. Formation of the Boone and Crockett Club in 1887, at the instigation of Theodore Roosevelt, added a group of vigorous enthusiasts to the burgeoning conservation movement. The group had a definite objective: the preservation of Yellowstone Park's "game" animals. The influential members of this first broad-gauge sportsman's organization had the backing of George Bird Grinnell's *Forest and Stream,* and had no difficulty working with the watershed-conscious membership of the American Forestry Association. (This was an instinctive recognition of the "multiple use" concept.)

The partners in this working combination of wildlife and forestry interests had each suffered defeat in attempts to effect their purpose by direct legislation (the Vest and Edmunds measures); so they resorted to slyer politics. Concentrating their efforts upon obtaining a broad congressional authorization that would allow the president to set aside forest lands as "public reservations" by executive order, the conservationists managed to get a rider with that effect attached to the Sundry Civil Service Appropriation Act of March 3, 1891.[102]

Evidence that the game-preservationists were primed to use that amendment appeared within the month, with President Benjamin Harrison's proclamation of March 30, 1891, setting aside "for a public forest reservation" a large tract of land bordering Yellowstone National Park on the east and south.[103] As the map of original forest reserves shows, General Sheridan's proposal was reduced somewhat to the north and east to eliminate the mining region on the headwaters of Clarks Fork and most of the settlement on the branches of the Shoshone River, but to the south, where no such complications existed, it was accepted. This block of reserved forest land (the first of the areas that would later be called national forests) was known for more than a decade as the Yellowstone Park Timber Land Reserve, but it is of interest here for more than its name, or its origin as an offshoot of the Yellowstone crusade. The secretary of the interior, who was responsible for the reserved lands until 1905, had no organization for their protection until July 1, 1902, so he did as he had with Yellowstone Park: he asked the military to pinch hit.

It cannot be said that the army undertook this additional task cheerfully. Captain Anderson's reaction was expressed this way:

> The Park, with the timber reserve, contains an area greater than the State of Connecticut. This is to be protected from fires, from the vandalism of specimen hunters, and from depredations of poachers, by two small companies of troops, who at the same time are required to perform all of their ordinary military duties. I have but one citizen scout to aid in this work. I had a citizen packer who was useful as an assistant, but by orders from superior authority have recently been obliged to discharge him.[104]

The influence of the cavalry beyond the boundaries of Yellowstone Park proper was negligible, amounting to no more than the passage of an occasional mounted patrol. If the Yellowstone Park Timber Land Reserve received little attention, it was a larger measure of protection, however, than was given to most of the early forest reserves; indeed, it has been said that these precursors of our national forests were only saved "from the wrath of the West" because there was no enforcement of the unrealistic regulations that their sponsors had insisted on.[105] However, the situation could not continue.

Appointment of a commission from the membership of the National Academy of Sciences was provided by an act of Congress in

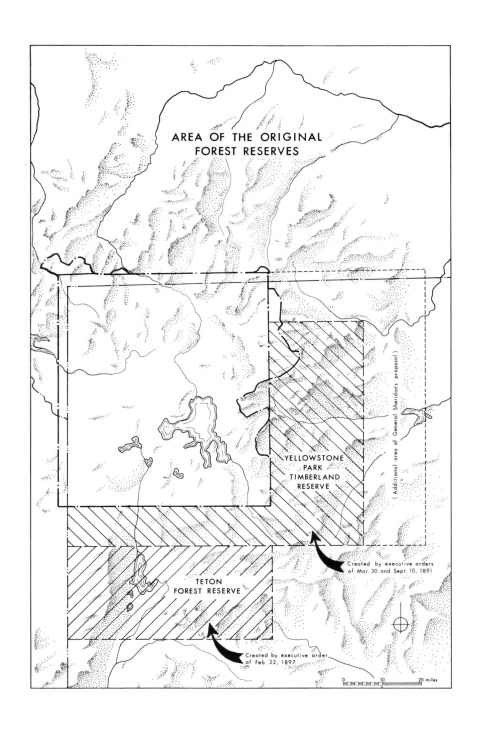

AREA OF THE ORIGINAL
FOREST RESERVES

YELLOWSTONE
PARK
TIMBERLAND
RESERVE

(Additional area of General Sheridan's proposal)

TETON
FOREST RESERVE

Created by executive orders
of Mar. 30 and Sept. 10, 1891

Created by executive order
of Feb. 22, 1897

0   10   20 miles

1896 to formulate plans for a national forestry system. President Grover Cleveland commented favorably on this development in his message of December 7, 1896,[106] and he followed the commission's recommendation by increasing the area of reserved lands. His additions included the Teton Forest Reserve, created by public proclamation February 22, 1897; thus the reserved lands south of the Park were extended to engulf the northern end of Jackson Hole, including most of the area from which Grand Teton National Park was later created. Cleveland's enlargement of the reserved lands (by 21 million acres) was followed by passage of an act of Congress on June 4, 1897, providing for the administration and protection of the forest reserves.[107]

Again, the military detachment in Yellowstone Park drew the chore of managing the two adjacent reserves (a combined area nearly equal to that of Yellowstone Park), but they did have some fiscal means. The appropriation provided under the foregoing act was $6,737.74 (nearly twice that amount became available the following year), which was used mainly for hiring extra scouts to patrol the reserves. On the whole, these men served well. They dampened the illegal hunting and discouraged trespass in a wild area where (as in the early years of Yellowstone Park) there was no penalty for violating the rules and regulations beyond eviction of the culprit, prosecution for trespass, or civil action for damages. As Captain James B. Erwin remarked, in requesting legislation to extend the provisions of the Lacey Act to the forest reserves, the punishment "does not form a sufficient safeguard for the protection of the reserve and its game."[108] He also thought the forest reserve lying south of Yellowstone Park should be incorporated into the Park because it was "unquestionably a game country," but he opposed inclusion of the reserved lands to the east since the reports of his officers indicated it was not a wildlife habitat of any importance.[109]

The park superintendent reminded the secretary of the interior the following year that where the forest reserves were concerned "the superintendent has no authority to prevent hunting." He might well have added that an average annual appropriation of $5,000 for administration and protection was a very lean budget for fighting forest fires and evicting sheepmen as well—particularly since frequent replacements of personnel in the Yellowstone detachment concurrent with the Spanish-American War and the insurrection in the Philippines had materially decreased the efficiency of the park forces.

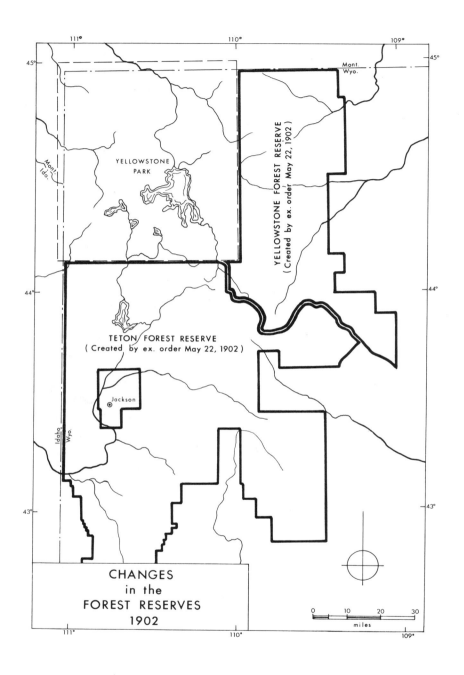

YELLOWSTONE
PARK

Mont.
Ida.

Mont.
Wyo.

YELLOWSTONE FOREST RESERVE
(Created by ex. order May 22, 1902)

TETON FOREST RESERVE
(Created by ex. order May 22, 1902)

Jackson

Idaho
Wyo.

CHANGES
in the
FOREST RESERVES
1902

0   10   20   30
miles

But a change was coming. By 1901 President Roosevelt had imbued the conservation movement with enthusiasm. Typically, a Wyoming friend of the president, a rancher named A. A. Anderson, who lived on the edge of the forest reserve, objected to out-of-state sheepmen moving their bands across the public forest leaving a trail of fires by accident or by design. Anderson went to the national capital early in 1902 and induced the president to enlarge the reserves and give them a civilian administration, which was done by executive order on May 22, 1902.[110] The areas abutting on Yellowstone Park— the Yellowstone and the Teton Forest reserves (see map showing changes in forest reserves)—were considerably larger than the old reserves. Also, each was assigned a supervisor and a corps of rangers designated in military style as lieutenants, sergeants, and privates.

Anderson headed the Yellowstone Forest Reserve from his log-cabin headquarters at Wapiti on the north fork of the Shoshone River.[111] He was under the secretary of the interior until February 1, 1905, when President Roosevelt signed the act transferring the forest reserves from the Interior to the Agriculture Department, and his organization was always independent of the military in Yellowstone Park. Major Pitcher probably felt only relief at having no further responsibilities for the forest reserves; in any case he bowed the army out with the comment, "It is to be hoped that every possible support will be given Supt. A. A. Anderson."[112] In that manner, a system of national forests was launched as the finest achievement of the Yellowstone crusade.

CHAPTER 15

ON THE
GRAND TOUR

*A land of contradictions, a spectacular pageant, a
world incomprehensible . . . a wonderful gift to men
from a benign God—all this and more.*
                              —Olin D. Wheeler [1]

U pper-class families of Victorian England sent their sons on
extended tours of continental Europe as a useful and
pleasant way of finishing off the years of formal
education. These grand tours made accomplished travelers of
cultured Britons and undoubtedly promoted the seasonal migrations
of England's leisure class—to the spas, the beaches, the Alps, the
races—which were imitated by wealthy Americans in the latter part of
the nineteenth century.

The gadabouts who took the waters at Saratoga Springs,
promenaded at Newport Beach, "roughed it" at elegant resorts in the
Appalachian Mountains, or summered comfortably atop the Cat-
skills were moneyed people of the old, established families and the
upstart nouveaux riches, all able to go first class. This "carriage
trade" dominated the Yellowstone scene from the building of the
railroad to the entry of private automobiles—a thirty-two-year
period during which most visitors came to the Park by railroad,
stayed at its hotels, and toured in its stagecoaches. They were people
accustomed to ease and luxury, experiencing a wilderness where very
little luxury had been created.

The visitors were properly called "tourists," either from having purchased coupons that made a specified park tour a part of their railroad fare, or from having arranged with Cook and Sons, Raymond Excursions, or some group of a mercantile, fraternal, or religious sort to conduct them through Wonderland. The Raymond excursionists and the members of the tour groups sponsored by newspapers, fraternal orders, ministerial associations, and conventions tended to be rather plebian, with characteristics their genteel traveling companions often found offensive (a native expertise at the dinner table, an ability to elbow their way into the best seats, and a garrulous, sometimes ignorant, enthusiasm); also, they were poor tippers, and were thus relegated to the lower echelon of the carriage trade by the park employees as well. Whether a tourist was of high or low caste he was still a "dude" in park parlance (the term carried no particular opprobrium, as used[2]) and was thereby distinguishable from the "sagebrusher," who went through the area in his own (or a hired) conveyance, camping by the way instead of patronizing the hotels.

The tourist of the stagecoach era was familiar with a phraseology quite as expressive as anything heard at the present time. Accordingly, the person who proceeded on his own responsibility did so "on his own hook," and whatever was remarkably good was a "stunner," with the very best being a "regular stunner." When requested to pay a bill, he was being asked to "stand Sam," which was done by "stumping up," when he had the "tin," "the needful," "the rhino," or "the ready"; if he didn't have it, he was "hard up." A savage dog, or a man of similar disposition, was an "ugly customer" and had to be met with "pluck," or otherwise our tourist might be "taken down a peg or two," or be "made to sing small." To him, the sensible man was a "chap who was up to snuff" and the eccentric was a "rummy old cove." There was little talk of home, but our tourist did have a place where he "hung out," and when he went anywhere, he "bolted," "sloped," "mizzled," "made himself scarce," "cut his stick," "walked his chalk," "made tracks," or was "fired out"—from which one can divine something of the manner of going. This man, who was careful to tip his "tile" to a lady, could also "blow up" on occasions, and he often found himself "used up" at the end of a long day; but if he stood it well, he could be complimented by calling him a "regular brick."[3]

A familiarity with such slang—though for polite reasons he might refrain from using it—enabled the tourist to understand a few terms peculiar to Yellowstone Park. He soon found that the stagecoach drivers were "savages" (a term later generalized to include all employees of the park concessioners), the horses were "tackies," and the hostlers were "barn dogs." At the hotels, there were "bell hops" and "heavers" (waitresses) and, by some strange twist, the lady he had always thought of as his wife had suddenly become a "dude heaver." The ever-present soldiers were "swaddies" (a term borrowed from the British-Indian army's "swattie") and love in the moonlight (known in that day as "spooning") was "rotten-logging" in the Park.[4] The foregoing does not exhaust the list of usages peculiar to the area but it is representative of the average tourist's understanding of its jargon.

The railroads delivered tourists to the Park by three routes during the stagecoach era: by the Northern Pacific and its park branch line to the Cinnabar terminus (to Gardiner after 1903); by Utah & Northern narrow gauge to Beaver Canyon or Monida, from where they were staged into the Park from the west until 1908 when the Union Pacific system extended its Oregon short line to the west entrance; and toward the end of the period, by the Burlington line to Cody, Wyoming, for delivery to the Park by motor bus through the east entrance—a precursor of the general motorization of the transportation facilities in 1917.

The Northern Pacific Railroad served the Park longer than the other lines, in fact, throughout the stagecoach era; hence, it was by way of its rails, from the east over the grasslands and badlands of Minnesota, Dakota, and Montana, where a vast loneliness was only infrequently interrupted by little towns drawn up along the right of way like Falstaff's company, or from the west over the equally lonely, but less naked mountain ranges of western Montana, Idaho, and Washington, that most tourists reached the Park. But whether they came from the East or the West, they left the main line at Livingston, Montana, which Rudyard Kipling noted was

> a town of 2,000 people and a junction for the little sideline that takes you to the Yellowstone National Park. It lies in a fold of the prairie and behind it is the Yellowstone River and the Gate of the Mountains through which the river flows. There is one street in the town where the cowboy's pony, and the little foal of the brood mare in the buggy, rest contentedly in the blinding sunshine while the cowboy gets himself shaved at the only barber shop and swaps lies at the bar.[5]

Kipling also remarked that he exhausted the town "including the saloons" in ten minutes, but he seems to have missed the live cougar chained in front of the taxidermist's shop, nor did he know that the cowboy had once used his pistols to instruct a dude in exhibition dancing on the station platform.

In its earlier years, the park branch line operated in a highly informal manner. A passenger has recorded that the "train stopped for ten minutes in one place to leave a box of merchandise in the

Tallyho stagecoaches loading at the Gardiner Depot for the five-mile drive to the hotel at Mammoth Hot Springs (1903-15).

A "Yellowstone Wagon" loading at the National Hotel, Mammoth Hot Springs, for the trip to the Upper Geyser Basin. *From Detroit Photographic Company's no. 018192, c. 1905.*

middle of a field," and at another point to allow passengers and crew to dispose of a bucket of buttermilk a little girl brought down to the track. Shortly afterward, there was yet another stop while the engineer, with revolver in hand, pursued two prairie chickens he had sighted. One was bagged, and "the train stubbornly proceeded to its destination."[6] Later, the operation of the daily train to the Park was more in keeping with the spirit of the Northern Pacific's current motto: "That's the way to run a railroad!"

The Cinnabar terminus was even less imposing than Livingston: saloons, store, blacksmith shop, livery stable, and a hotel of sorts (patronized mainly by freighters) were arrayed opposite the station platform, where tourists alighted to be exhorted by vendors of souvenirs and jostled by "independents" with various propositions for transporting them through the Park. But coupon holders who had paid an extra $40 for the five-day side trip through the Park (a package deal that included all transportation, lodging, and meals) were hustled into the stagecoaches of the regular transportation company[7] for the eight-mile drive to the National Hotel at Mammoth Hot Springs.

Upon being decanted into that shoving, howling crowd, Kipling asked a driver: "What means this eager, anxious throng?" and he was told, "You've struck one of Raymond's excursion parties, that's all." Being one of Cook and Son's genteel tourists, Kipling obviously thought poorly of the American enterprise.

> He [Raymond] collects masses of downeasters from the New England states and elsewhere and hurls them across the continent and into Yellowstone Park on tour. A breakload of Cook's Continental tourists trapezing through Paris (I've seen them) are angels of light compared to the Raymond trippers. It is not the ghastly vulgarity, the oozing, rampant, Bessemer steel self-sufficiency and ignorance of the men that revolts me as much as the display of the same quality in the women folk. I saw a new type in the coach and all my dreams of a better and more perfect East died away. "Are these, umh, persons here any sort of persons in their own places?" I asked a shepherd who appeared to be herding them. "Why certainly, they include very many prominent and representative citizens from seven states of the Union and most of them are wealthy. Yes, sir, representative and prominent!"[8]

The Cinnabar terminal is notable also for one of the souvenir vendors who did business there. He was called Specimen Shultz, and one day he put up a sign on the station platform which read, "For Sale—Specimens From Out of the Park." His advertising came to the attention of the park superintendent, Captain George S. Anderson, a large, florid man with red hair and temper to match. Shultz' wording brought out the mad bull in Captain Anderson, and he had his "striker"hitch the team to his buggy and was off in a cloud of dust, bound for the Cinnabar Station. When he arrived there, his naturally ruddy complexion was a flush that extended down into his collar, and he laced into Shultz without preliminaries. The old German took some stiff abuse before he had his opportunity for a rebuttal. "Captain, I vas careful mid dot sign; you see it says 'specimens from *out* of the Park,' nod from *in* the Park."[9]

The passengers who alighted from the stagecoaches at the National Hotel and trooped into the lobby in linen dusters and shaker bonnets became part of a strange mélange. There were business men vacationing in black coats and top hats, smartly dressed ladies, young men in tennis flannels and others in mail-order suits, several ladies in low-cut dresses with flowers in their hair (they were summer boarders, not transients), and a few men in the rough garb of the frontier; "every description of tourist and traveler, in every sort of 'get up.'"[10] The local scene contributed some tip-conscious oversolicitous hotel employees, a few stage drivers, and several uniformed officers from the nearby garrison (among them Captain Anderson) who were apt to wander over to the hotel at stage time. The scene of the nineties changed in the following decade: visitors became the "sturdy, golf-skirted American girl with her Kodak" and the "Eastern youth turned suddenly Western, with oddly worn sombrero and spurs."[11] There was, in sum, a lessening of formality.

The tourists had come to see the wonders of the Yellowstone, and as their arrival at Mammoth Hot Springs left them most of the afternoon, they were soon about their pleasure. An old gentleman, accompanied by his stenographer, settled himself on the veranda to dictate an account of what he had seen, and a youth with a fine pair of field glasses was soon pointing out the marvelous sights he could see from that vantage point. Others were content to visit the nearby store for souvenir spoons ("which will help convince the friends at home that no wonder has been missed")[12] or the Haynes studio, behind its elk-horn fence in the middle of the parade ground, for a stereopticon view or postcards handsomely printed in Germany.

The more inquisitive and venturesome tourists made a tour of the hot spring terraces, usually with a hotel porter who doubled as a guide. There they were sure to meet some of the "boys in blue" (in khaki after the turn of the century), whose badge of authority was the pistol and cartridge belt. Though Kipling thought they were accoutered "with loaded six-shooters in order that the tourists may not bring up fence rails and sink them in a pool, or chip the fretted treasury of the formations,"[13] the situation was not that serious. There were vandals then, as now, but they were mostly furtive in their mischief and it was only rarely that one had to be marched to headquarters for some enlightenment. As for the souvenir collectors, the mere presence of a soldier was sufficient to limit their activity to the filching of such bits and pieces as could be secreted in recesses of clothing. A visitor from England thought it very amusing that the appearance of a soldier caused some tourists to "instinctively put their hands behind their backs, or guiltily move in an opposite direction."[14]

The soldiers, on the other hand, were genuinely helpful, so that many tourists and sagebrushers could thank one of the Park's guardians for an opportunity to sit in "Arthur's seat" and view the hotel plateau as the president had in 1883, or for a peek at the dead birds in the Stygian Cave. But whether gratuitously guided by a soldier boy whose remuneration was some pleasant chitchat with folks like those at home or by a hotel porter whose uppermost thought was always of the elusive tip, the tourist was sure to see most of the terrace sights, from the Liberty Cap at the bottom to the Devils Kitchen at the top—and obtain but precious little real information about them. Kipling's admiration of a pretty little basin "which some lurid hotel keeper had christened Cleopatra's Pitcher or Mark Anthony's Whiskey Jug, or something equally poetical" indicates that he had probably perused a copy of the newspaper-like guide published and sold by G. L. Henderson,[15] manager of the Cottage Hotel Association and godfather to a great many features with classical names.

There were other, and easier, ways of "doing" the terraces than tramping over them; one could hire a surrey and drive or rent a horse and ride. It was a favorite sport to bring some particularly ornery cayuse up to the main entrance for an unsuspecting dude, who was promptly put a-sprawl in the dust for all that little world to see. Often it came out that way, but not always. Four Germans ordered horses one morning and "four vicious looking cayuses were brought in front of the hotel, and when the word was passed that those were the animals the 'Dutchmen' were going to ride, a crowd quickly gathered on the veranda." The Germans appeared, positioned themselves, and one gave three words of command, at which they "vaulted into their saddles from over the hindquarters of the astonished ponies and in a moment were galloping away," leaving the onlookers to reflect on how they had been taken in. The foreign dudes were German cavalry officers and very accomplished equestrians.[16]

Among the diversions available to tourists at the Mammoth Hot Springs was bathing at Bath Lake above the terraces. Bathing suits being scarce in that day, the pool was monopolized by males bathing strictly in the buff, but an English couple touring the Park somehow innocently missed that fact. So they took their bathing togs, went to Bath Lake (fortunately then deserted), and had a delightful swim. Later, at meal time, the lady was extolling the virtues of their swimming hole when she noticed the horrified glances of their table companions. Reference to a guidebook enlightened her concerning the faux pas she had committed, for it stated: "Ladies, alas, cannot even see it [Bath Lake], owing to the male bathers that occupy it exclusively." She adds that the audience vanished before she was able to retrieve her character.[17] The ladies did eventually gain some swimming rights. In a later day, there was a polite agreement between the boys and girls working for the hotel company that the boys would have the use of the pool at certain hours and the girls during others. Occasionally the boys were hogs, whereupon the girls would stone them from an adjacent hillock.

The grand tour began in earnest on the morning of the second day. While the tourists were at breakfast the coaches lined up along the veranda which extended entirely along the front of the hotel at just the proper height to serve as a loading platform. Then the names of the passengers who were to occupy each numbered coach were read off (this assignment generally was permanent; that is, a driver had the same coach-load all the way around the loop—which could be either good or bad!). The loaded coaches were dispatched at intervals intended to keep them about 500 feet apart to lessen the dust nuisance; and so, with a pop of the whip and some endearments, such as "Gid-ap! you Pirates!" the lumbering Yellowstone Wagons took their places in the slow moving procession[18]—every tourist filled with a nameless exhilaration, everything especially beautiful, especially marvelous.

The drivers of the four-horse, eleven-passenger rigs used in the Park were mainly young cowboys and ranchmen who took such summer employment in order to be part of the gay, carefree life there, or to supplement a marginal income. They were weather-beaten and tobacco-stained beyond their years, and friendly and loquacious. Those who had been around long enough to be appraised by their peers were generally known by picturesque "handles," as: Society Red (who took in every dance he could get to); Cryin' Jack (from his features); Big Fred (a 320-pound behemoth of a man); Scattering Jesus (a particularly flighty kid); White Mountain Smith (from his

New Hampshire origin); and Geyser Bob (a teller of tall tales). There were many more colorful characters among the drivers who "tooled" Yellowstone stagecoaches, men who had two things in common— they were accomplished reinsmen, and they had a strong aversion to being called Jehu.[19]

A former stagecoach driver, describing the beginning of a park tour, says that the first question asked by his dudes was sure to be,

"Driver, how long before we will see a geyser?" or, "What is the first thing we will see?"

Next the person who is on the seat with the driver will discover that one of the lead lines runs through a ring at the side of a "wheeler's" head, while the other one goes through a ring between the other horse's ears. And the question: "Driver, why does one line go on the side of this horse's head and the other one over that horse?" On being told that the near, or left-hand line, goes through what is known as a drop ring so as to keep from pulling the horse's bridle off, while the ring on the top of the other horse's head is a line ring to sight through, so you can see if your horses are in line with each other and know you are keeping in the road, the one who asked the question will then turn around and proceed to tell the people in the back seats what he has found out about the use of the two rings. By this time you have come to the first mile post, and someone will ask:

"Driver, are there mile posts all through the Park?" On being told that there are, he will then want to know how far apart are the mile posts. On being told that they are one mile apart, he will reply, "I might have known that." You next come to a sign on a steel post set about four feet above the ground, at which someone will want to know if there are sign posts all along the road. On being told that there are sign posts at all places of interest, someone will ask: "Well, driver, how long before we come to the next sign post, and what will be on it?" Following your reply that you think it is Golden Gate, and about a mile distant, someone will ask: "How long before we get there?" The answer: "About twenty minutes." Then comes the question, "What will we see when we get there?" and "you be sure and tell us, so we won't miss it!"[20]

Yes, he told them: how Lieutenant Dan Kingman built a wooden trestle to carry his road around the wall of the narrow gorge called the Golden Gate (from its profusion of yellow lichens); and the tourists marveled as the horses passed the pillarlike sentinel rock at the lower end and clip-clopped along the precarious roadway. Then there was Rustic Falls, Swan Lake Flat, the crossing of the Gardner River, and the long drive through Willow Park to Apollinaris Spring, and the driver answered questions and offered comments the whole way. Some did well by their dudes, some did poorly, and others shamelessly substituted rubbish and wild tales for the facts they didn't know. These are samples: "The flowers are all wild, but harmless," and, "If you want to see a mountain lion, just look off in the distance and you can most always see a mountain lyin' somewhere in sight."[21]

The stagecoaches stopped at Apollinaris Spring to enable the passengers to stretch their legs and drink the water so like that from the namesake spring in Germany. Almost everyone was thirsty—at times, even the driver (depending upon where he had been the night before and how much he had been "geising" to his dudes); but, since a driver was not allowed to leave his rig, and seldom liked spring water anyhow, he had to find another way to slake his thirst. An old surrey driver (Doc Wilson) would roll souvenir bottles of "Old Yellowstone" whiskey (then fifteen cents each) in the side curtains of his vehicle for use in such an emergency. On one trip, he was taking a nip from that hiding place when a lady tourist, who had not walked up to the spring, stepped around the rig and caught him at it. He later confided to another driver, "Herb, I was so embarrassed!"[22] Actually, the transportation company had a strong antipathy toward drinking drivers (for very good reasons) and its control of the supply of liquor within the Park was so effective that its employees were known to rummage tourist baggage at lunch stops in the hope of discovering a bottle of something or other. Such a frisk could be slyly accomplished under the pretext of rearranging the "boot"—that leather-covered hamper at the rear of the coach where all hand luggage was carried.

With the passengers back in the coach, the journey continued: southward past Obsidian Cliff, where the driver was sure to say something about Indians having used it as an arrowhead quarry; past Roaring Mountain, which deserved a name more in keeping with the satanic nomenclature then in vogue (but had somehow escaped that fate), and on to the Devil's Frying Pan (now Frying Pan Spring),[23] which did have a devilish denomination but didn't deserve it. Yet the use of that name is understandable, for gas bubbles break through a skim of water creating an appearance similar to hot grease popping and sizzling on a griddle. The illusion is so realistic one has to test the water with his finger to understand it is really cold. But did the driver tell his dudes that? Probably not. More likely, they got a cock-and-bull story about how the birds in that locality drank so much hot water they all laid hard-boiled eggs, and anybody who didn't believe it could look in the woods roundabout, where the trees were full of nests containing just such eggs. Any skeptics were reminded their coach was nearly late for the lunch stop at Larry's,[24] more than a mile away, so there wasn't time to verify the driver's un-natural history.

The descent to the Gibbon River, at Norris, has been described as "a desperate, dusty slope," down which the coach plunged, "brakes shrieking on the wheels, the hooves clicking among unseen rocks," to cross a little timber bridge and pull up before the Norris Lunch Station. The appearance of the station varied considerably over the years. It could have been a group of white tents, a board shack, or a frame hotel, depending on the year—for, of all the hostels in the Park, the Norris Lunch Station was the one most plagued by fires. The fine Norris Hotel erected by the Yellowstone Park Association in the fall of 1886 had just opened its doors to the public the following spring when it was destroyed. (Someone connected a stove to a chimney left unfinished in the attic.) After that, the public was served in tents, which were succeeded by a rough frame building, and then by tents again. At the turn of the century, a second hotel was built overlooking the Norris Geyser Basin and closer to the thermal features. It was razed in 1927, after motorization of park transportation had ended its usefulness.

The Norris Lunch Station housed in tents was managed by a genial Irishman who had made it Larry's.[25] Of all the managers who have played host to the traveling public in Yellowstone Park, Lawrence Francis Mathews remains the incomparable peer. He came from the Ould Sod, and doubtless kissed the Blarney Stone before he left, for Larry had a glib tongue as the working end of a ready wit. He met each passenger alighting from the coach with some such salutation as "Good morning, Governor," "Welcome, Judge." A tourist says, "I shall never forget his approach to a line of weary, dusty, elderly ladies in Shaker bonnets and linen cloaks, just alighted from a fifty-mile ride . . . he grasped one by one their reluctant hands: 'Shake, ladies, shake.'"[26]

According to Kipling,

> Larry enveloped us all in the golden glamor of his speech ere we had descended and the tent with the rude trestle table became a palace, the rough fare delicacies of Delmonico's, and we, the abashed recipients of Larry's imperial bounty. It was only later that I discovered that I had paid eight shillings for tinned beef, biscuits, and beer but on the other hand, Larry had said, "Will I go out and kill a buffalo?" And I felt that for me, and for me alone, he would have done it. Everybody else felt that way. Good luck go with Larry.[27]

Another who ate at Larry's board noted that "dinner was a regular circus. Everyone was jolly and hungry . . . a funny Irishman & the general manager, kept everyone in a [good mood]. It is fun to get away from the conventional big hotel."[28]

"Larry" Mathews (leaning against a post), the genial host of Norris Lunch Station.

"Larry" serving guests in the dining tent at Norris.

There was another side to Larry: he had some snob in his make-up, preferring to serve only the carriage trade, and his strong dislike of the "great unwashed" occasionally surfaced violently. Mr. C. S. Batterman complained that his wagon party was abused by Larry on the afternoon of August 2, 1893, when they stopped at the Norris Lunch Station to buy some cool milk. It appears that the proprietor sized up the three couples as just another load of sagebrushers, and so did not bother to be pleasant when the men entered his establishment. Mr. Batterman asked for milk and was told there was none for sale, but that they could buy beer. Declining that, he carried some water to the ladies waiting in the wagon. When he returned the water glasses, Larry produced a pitcher of milk, offering it at 25 cents a glass. As that was an extortionate price, the milk was refused, whereupon Larry proceeded to charge them 25 cents for each glass of water. Along with the tab came "a torrent of vile language" and an order to get out. Batterman and the other men of the party did just that, but were followed to their wagon by the angry Irishman, who "informed us and the ladies that no pricks were allowed in his house, but that it was exclusively for gentlemen and that if we dared set foot in his place he would send for the soldiers and have us driven out of the park."[29] Mr. Batterman's complaint developed the fact that although he did not rate as a gentleman at Norris Lunch Station he was prominent enough to get the support of several senators.

Larry's treatment of the Batterman party was a reflection of hotel and transportation company attitudes in the Park. Dislike of all visitors who did not belong to the carriage trade was often manifested by denying independents and sagebrushers hotel accommodations, forage for their stock, essential blacksmithing work, and even provisions. Democracy, later introduced with the private automobile, was unknown in the Park of the stagecoach era.

After lunch at Larry's the tourists trouped across the Norris Geyser Basin on a boardwalk under the guidance of a hotel porter. One early interpreter has described the routine:

> The guide took visitors down from the hotel to Constant Geyser, then past the Black Growler, to the Bathtub; [then by] a path through the woods to the New Crater Geyser, ending at the loading platform near Minute Man Geyser. The guide gave a 15 or 20 minute talk (as factual as the information allowed—Bunsen's theory, some history and geology). Some guides and drivers "spoofed" the tourists; they just didn't know... Tips were good—a fine class of people—they could afford to spend money on travel.[30]

At the loading platform, which had bench seats sheltered by a canopy, the sightseers were loaded into their coaches for the afternoon ride to the Lower Geyser Basin. Kipling, who made his round of the Park in company with an elderly couple from Chicago, notes that the visible horrors of the Norris Geyser Basin caused the lady to say, "Good Lord!" at thirty-second intervals for some time after their departure, while the old man muttered about the "drefful waste of steam power." When the driver cursed the near wheeler for stumbling, the old lady—still under the influence of meditations theological—shrieked, "and what I say more after having seen all that is that the Lord has ordained a hell for such as disbelieve his gracious works." Her comment was a direct hit; the driver flinched visibly and later confided to Kipling: "I drive blame curious kind of folk through this place. Blame curious. Seems a pity that they should a come so far just to liken Norris to hell. Guess Chicago would have served them, speakin' in comparison, just as good."[31]

Profanity was a natural attribute of the teamster and stagecoach driver. It was honed and polished into an occupational form that was smooth, perfect, and astounding, yet this art (for such it was), being so impersonal, seemed less vile than common cursing. Doubtless the average stagecoach driver was inhibited by the presence of women among his passengers; it must have been a real pleasure to haul a coachload of men around the Park. Dave Johnson, an old-timer best described as a tobacco-chewing, dried-out little wisp of a man, had such an opportunity in 1894 when he drove for a party of journalists including the artist-writer, John T. McCutcheon, and Ed Hardeen of the *Chicago Tribune*. These men were so impressed by Dave's use of his specialized version of the English language that they thought he ought to have a medal. So they had one made up by Spaulding's (Chicago's equivalent of Tiffany's) and sent it to him. It was of sterling silver, inscribed on one side, "To Dave Johnson, Champion Cusser of the Pacific Slope," and on the reverse, "From His Admiring Friends, Hardeen and McCutcheon, Chicago, '94." It hung by a ribbon from a pin-bar covered with shorthand characters which probably went unnoticed by Dave. It seems that he wore his medal proudly for a long time—until about 1908, when E. O. McCormick, an official of the Union Pacific Railroad and an old friend of McCutcheon, chanced to be in his coach. He asked Dave if he knew what the shorthand meant, and was told, "Oh, jest ornyment, I reckon."

But McCormick wasn't content with that. It seems he took it to several hotel stenographers who hesitated and then professed to be unable to read it. Then he found a male clerk to whom the language was more familiar, and who read it off without hesitation, but not without considerable surprise.

The message hidden in the Pitman characters was: "Giddap there, you Goddam, ornery, pisellum, scenery-lovin' sons o'bitches!"

That much of the story appeared in 1950 as a part of McCutcheon's reminiscences.[32] A friend of Jack Ellis Haynes called his attention to the anecdote as an interesting bit of Yellowstoniana, and Jack realized immediately that *he* owned that very medal. How had it come into his possession? Jack had found it in a pigeon-hole of his father's old rolltop desk. Possibly, Dave hesitated to wear the medal after he knew what was on it, and so left it in the care of his employer—F. Jay Haynes, Jack's father.[33] That part of the story is likely to remain uncertain. Dave Johnson's medal was lost for a number of years but has been found and transferred to the Montana Historical Society with other items displayed by Jack Haynes in his private museum in Bozeman, Montana.

Beyond Norris Geyser Basin the road crossed Elk Park and Gibbon Meadows much as it does now, but part way down the Gibbon Canyon it climbed out on the left bank and passed over the ridge east of Gibbon Falls. There was no view of the waterfall from the road, so those who wished to see this feature were given an opportunity to scramble down a wickedly steep trail to a viewing place. If the descent was bad, the return to the waiting coach was worse—a slip and slide proposition which would have led to disaster without the handholds afforded by bushes and saplings. Most tourists wondered if the view was worth the bruises and perspiration.

The remainder of the day's travel was through a seemingly endless forest of lodgepole pine, a hot, dusty, monotonous ride with nothing of interest until the road broke into the Lower Geyser Basin. (This route was later abandoned in favor of several less direct but more scenic alignments until it was finally stabilized as now used.) The heat of the afternoon and the fatigue of their climb at the Gibbon Falls induced the tourists to refresh themselves with bottled water and beer brought along from Larry's. This resulted in what the driver termed "dead soldiers"—empty bottles strewn along the old stage-coach routes in testimony "to the thirst and timidity of the traveling public."[34] The hotel people deliberately discouraged the use of park waters for drinking, offering their mineral water and Lager beer "at fifty cents a bottle" instead. The tourists, willing to believe almost anything told them in Yellowstone Park, accepted this imposition

Visitors wading in the warm water overflowing from Great Fountain Geyser, prior to 1915.

Visitors at Handkerchief Pool, Upper Geyser Basin, 1909. *From a stereoptican slide in the lecture series of Mrs. Ogden W. Dean.*

better than most to which they were subjected, for the idea that the waters of the Yellowstone Plateau were noxious was in accord with the evidence of their own senses. (There was an everpresent, all-pervading stench of rotten eggs about the thermal areas, and a loathsome potage of pools and rivulets on every hand.) So they drank bottled waters and littered the roadside.

Prior to 1892, the overnight stop in the Lower Geyser Basin was made at the Firehole Hotel, which the Yellowstone Park Association had purchased from the successors of George W. Marshall,[35] whose Marshall House it originally was. The only improvement made at that place for the accommodation of the increased number of tourists was the addition of

> two cheap wooden structures, two-stories high and each divided into four rooms on each floor by placing partitions at right angles. The staircases being on the outside of the building. The partitions afford but little privacy for guests.[36]

Captain Harris' comment concerning the lack of privacy at the Firehole Hotel was an understatement. A description of the accomodations by a lady who stopped there indicates the rooms were "about six feet square, sufficiently filled with two beds," but lacked a table or closet. The walls were stretched over with canvas, and the door "declined to shut." She adds: "It could not be described as luxurious, and every snore was audible."[37] Unfortunately, worse things than snores were sometimes heard, as another lady complained after having to listen until midnight to the bawdy stories exchanged by two gentlemen in an adjoining room.

The accommodations available to tourists in the geyser basins were much better after the Yellowstone Park Association opened the Fountain Hotel in 1891. Built at a cost of $100,000 to accommodate 350 guests, the hotel had steam heat, electric lights, and hot spring water in the baths (one of the unique features). Its location was also superior to that of the old Firehole Hotel; the Fountain geyser area one-half mile to the south contained an interesting complex of thermal features, including outstanding pools and paint pots, while other hot areas in the Lower Geyser Basin could be reached by surrey.

But the Fountain Hotel had more to offer. It had a social life which featured frequent "balls"; in fact, prior to the turn of the century, it was the only place beyond Mammoth Hot Springs where a lady might need a silk dress, or a gentleman something better than his traveling clothes. The troop of U.S. Cavalry stationed at the summer encampment on Nez Perce Creek seems to have promoted those gala affairs, for both officers and enlisted men liked to waltz and to swing the girls in The Lancers.

Another diversion that made its debut at the Fountain Hotel was not only popular but also the beginning of similar "shows" throughout the Park—bear-feeding. The kitchen garbage was dumped each evening about six o'clock at a point one hundred yards behind the hotel, and a tourist of 1897 noted that from ten to sixteen bears came there for their supper, "quietly munching the bones and fruit peelings, while a dozen or two of the hotel guests look on ten yards away."[38] Particularly bold persons even fed the bears "apples out of the hand." This ill-considered entertainment soon matured into a bear problem.

Only a year later, the editor of a Wyoming newspaper commented:

> There is one phase of Park protection that needs revision. The black and brown bears are becoming so numerous as to be an actual nuisance if not dangerous. All hotels are nightly invaded by from six to eight of them. The slop bones and waste materials furnish all the food they need. They have become too indolent to hunt for themselves. But the Malthusian law that mouths tend to multiply faster than food seems to hold good in the bruin family as well as the human. When the ash pile fails to supply food for eight or ten of those monsters . . . they naturally use what intellect and strength they possess to increase the supply.[39]

How true! In that day of almost no refrigeration, the hotels in the Park were supplied with meat from a beef herd kept on the headwaters of the Gardner River. Animals were slaughtered, as needed, at the "meat ranch" on Indian Creek, and a special wagon was used to transport the meat at night to the hotel that had ordered. In this instance, Richard Cox arrived at Fountain Hotel in the early morning hours with the beef and a bag of U.S. mail. He put up his team and, considering the meat and mail safe enough (it was locked in a vehicle made of two-inch plank) Dick went to bed. At about the same time, the bears went to work, assailing the meat wagon "with tooth and claw until a hole was cut . . . sufficiently large for the insertion of a forearm." They got the meat *and* the mail, thereby becoming mail robbers—possibly another "first" for the record. The mail was recovered with only minor damage to the sack; the same could not be said for the meat.

The Fountain Hotel was also the locus of an inscrutable mystery. On the evening of July 30, 1900, a tourist by the name of L. R. Piper—cashier of the First National Bank of St. Marys, Ohio, and a man of influence and means—ate his dinner, bought a cigar at the stand in the lobby, and stepped out into the night, where he vanished utterly. Detachments of cavalry searched for a month, a reward of $1,000 was offered for his body, and a brother-in-law came to the Park to conduct a personal search (even sleeping out in the nearby hills

$1,000 REWARD!

MR. L. R. PIPER, Cashier of the First National Bank of St. Marys, Ohio, arrived at the Fountain Hotel, in the Yellowstone National Park, as a tourist, on the 29th day of July, 1900, and disappeared from the hotel on the evening of the 30th, and has not been seen or heard from since that time.

DESCRIPTION:

Age, 36; Height. 5 feet 9 inches; Weight, 130 pounds; Complexion, sandy; Color of Hair, light, inclined to reddish tinge, Nose, slightly crooked; smooth-shaven face. Wore blue suit with dark check about one inch wide; no vest; soft-bosomed white shirt, with initials "L. R. P." at bottom of bosom, embroidered in red. Black patent leather lace shoes, laces much broken. Two diamond rings, one Knight Templar emblem, a Shriner's button in lapel of coat. Dark Derby hat.

The First National Bank of St. Marys, O., wires me as follows:

"MRS. L. R. PIPER offers a reward of ONE THOUSAND DOLLARS for the finding of Piper, or his body, if dead.

"Signed, FIRST NATIONAL BANK."

Aug. 10, 1900. Address,

J. H. DEAN,

Supt. Y. P. A., M. H. Springs, Wyoming.

Notice of reward offered for finding a visitor who disappeared from the Fountain Hotel. *From the author's collection.*

through most of September in the hope that the howling of coyotes would lead him to the lost man's remains).[40] It was all to no avail; Piper had vanished without a trace. Nor was there the hint of a reason for such a disappearance. Other tourists had died in the Park—of heart attacks, of hot pool burns, and of injuries sustained in accidents—but only Piper *vanished*. It seems somehow indecent never to know his fate.

Until 1904, when the Old Faithful Inn was built, the Fountain Hotel was an important stopping place—the one hostel where the tourist ordinarily spent two nights. This was necessary because the visit to the Upper Geyser Basin, on the third day, was handled as a side trip from the lower basin. This practice began in the days when the stage road went up Nez Perce Creek and over Mary Mountain to a junction in Hayden Valley with the road connecting the Grand Canyon with the outlet of Yellowstone Lake. After Lieutenant Hiram Chittenden built the road connecting the Upper Geyser Basin with the lake's outlet in 1891, the stagecoaches took the new route; however, the principal hotel facilities were maintained in the Lower Geyser Basin, requiring a "doubling," or retracement of a part of the route (between the geyser basins) as the tour continued on the fourth day. The location of the hostel in the Lower Geyser Basin was dictated by the distance a stage horse could travel in a day, and Mammoth Hot Springs to the Fountain Hotel was the uttermost stretch.

This, perhaps, raises the question, Why was the Old Faithful Inn ever built? Toward the turn of the century, the growing volume of tourist traffic into the Park from the west entrance (brought in by the Monida & Yellowstone Stage Company) made a good hotel in the Upper Geyser Basin economically feasible. Also, it had become expedient to build there because several upstart operations were in a fair way to get the whole business in that end of the Park. F. Jay Haynes' company, carrying from the Union Pacific system lines west of the Park, was a serious competitor, both for the Yellowstone Park Association and its silent partner, the Northern Pacific Railroad. It was such a competitor as is better placated than opposed; better to build a hotel to serve both concerns than to let the opposition build their own and take over entirely. In addition, a large hotel in the Upper Geyser Basin was considered the best counter to the irritating "Wylie Way" operation. Finally, a good hotel in the upper basin would help to soften that greatest of all tourist complaints: the inadequate stopover arrangements of the association.

Old Faithful Inn was an unusual structure, called the largest log building in the world[41] (though no evidence has been presented in proof of that statement). It was designed by Robert C. Reamer, a Seattle architect of outstanding ability. As constructed in 1903-04 the Inn was described as "a remarkably beautiful and comfortable establishment," with all of the modern conveniences and "a great improvement on the tents."[42] Its 140 rooms would accommodate 316 guests. The lobby was the focus of Mr. Reamer's rustic effect. It is a great, balconied cavern, open to the roof, with all supporting beams and braces exposed to view like the skeleton of some enormous mammal seen from within. In one corner is a mighty fireplace with its chimney exposed to the point where it passes through the ridge 85 feet above the floor (another 20 feet projects above the roof), containing, in all, 500 tons of stone taken from a quarry site five miles to the east. The fireplace chimney is faced with a giant clock hammered out by a blacksmith named Colpitts, who also made the distinctive hardware.[43]

The original building was enlarged in 1913 by the addition of an east wing (100 rooms) and in 1928 was brought to its present dimensions with completion of the west wing (150 rooms). An exterior feature of considerable interest was the powerful searchlight installed in 1904 on a platform on the roof, intended for the illumination of evening eruptions of Old Faithful Geyser (a purpose it served until World War II) and for pointing out deer and elk in the meadow in front of the hotel, the bear sniffing about the garbage cans, and occasional couples "rotten-logging."

In the days before Old Faithful Inn, tourists were transported from the hotel in the lower basin to the Upper Geyser Basin, where they had one-half day for sightseeing before returning to their hotel of the previous night. This was a "once over lightly" treatment that left too much unseen. The obvious answer was a stopover in the Upper Geyser Basin for those who wished to see more of its wonders. That was theoretically possible—the tour agents said so, and it was allowed by the fine print on the tourist's coupon; however, such a practice was discouraged by the transportation company, which did not like empty seats in its coaches. (They would allow a stopover if the entire coachload agreed to it; but how do you get eleven people to want the same "extra" at the same time when it costs more?) The lack of a liberal policy in regard to stopovers was the most common complaint of tourists during the early years.

Some tourists insisted upon their right to stop where they wished as long as they desired, and then took their chances of finding a seat in a coach when ready to move on; thus, the lunch station near Old Faithful Geyser doubled as a hotel of sorts. The shabby structure erected by the Hobarts in 1884 burned down ten years later and was replaced by a rambling structure of unhewn logs, picturesquely located in a grove. Upon asking for lodging, a tourist laying over for a few days was

> shown a long tent ostentatiously marked No. 1. A hallway down the center formed of canvas divides it. At the end of the hall a small wood stove looks pitifully inconspicuous when compared with the size of the tent. The rooms are canvas, formed with a flap for a door. A deal bed, small table, and a wash-bowl, with a four by six looking-glass furnish the accommodations. Scrupulous cleanliness prevails. . . . lunch is served by a squat-figured, black-eyed "Bossy Brander" of Montana and spoiled by an officious landlord with great whiskers, hollow chest, and hollower cough, who takes the first opportunity to tell us that four years ago he was dying of consumption but now, thanks to the climate . . . [44]

The principal sport of those who stayed at the hotel was "geyser watching," and Owen Wister, who was a guest there, mentions that they had help in this from a young lad who "would be called a bell-hop today; in that day no bell was there, but the boy hopped a great deal." This teenager, whose voice was in the process of changing, talked in a deep bass until excitement caught him up, then he "cracked into a wild treble." Picture, then, this scene:

> We would be sitting tilted back, reading our mail, the tourists would have ceased talking and be lounging drowsily, the boy would be at the door, motionless as a set steel trap. Suddenly the trap would spring, the boy would catapault into the door, and in his piping treble scream out: "Beehive's a-goin off!" at which every tourist instantly started from his chair, and a leaping crowd gushed out of the hotel and sprinted down over the formation to catch the Beehive at it. Beehive finally quiescent, they returned slowly, sank into chairs in exhausted silence; you could have heard a mosquito. . . . and again the silence was pierced: "There goes Old Faithful!" Up and out they flew once more, watched Old Faithful and came back to their chairs and silence, more exhausted. [45]

Surrey parties were often arranged by tourists who were anxious to explore the farther reaches of the Upper Geyser Basin. In that way, it was possible to see the beautiful Lone Star Geyser in its wooded setting, several miles south of Old Faithful; visit the Black Sand Basin, where one could try that diminutive laundry, Handkerchief Pool, and marvel at the greenish depth of Emerald Pool; chase after such really big geysers as Giant and Grand; and see the peculiar formation of the Biscuit Basin. Equally important was an opportunity to hear some more of those stories drivers liked to tell: of the Chinaman Spring (see Chapter 12) or the Englishman who went over

The Fountain Hotel in the Lower Geyser Basin.

Old Faithful Inn, Upper Geyser Basin, built in 1903.

on Geyser Hill to watch for an eruption of the Lioness Geyser. He sat down on one of the Cubs to wait, but failed to identify the source of the preliminary growlings—and was blown from his seat! (An English tourist remarked, "It would have been an American in England, I suppose."[46]) It was even possible, in that day, to be served up a legend by its creator, as was the lady who asked a driver known as Geyser Bob (he was really John Edgar) how he got his picturesque name. "Well," said the old stage driver, "I clum up on Old Faithful one day and got too near the crater and fell in." "How interesting!" commented the lady. "What happened?" "Why," said Bob, pointing to the Beehive Geyser across the Firehole River, "I came out of the Beehive—over there." "Well! Well! How long did it take?" "Oh," said Bob, "if I had come straight through it would have taken about ten minutes, but I stopped on the way for a haircut and a shave!"[47] Another, and more expansive, version claims that "many years ago he fell into Old Faithful and emerged nineteen months later in the mud geyser, away across the mountains and the woodlands."[48]

Sightseeing in the Upper Geyser Basin (whether it was a quick look on a regular tour or the leisurely poking about possible on a stopover) was followed by a return to the lower basin. Prior to 1892 the stage route went by way of Nez Perce Creek, Mary Mountain, and Hayden Valley to the Grand Canyon, where the fourth and last night in the Park was spent, and on the last day, the tourist traveled across the Cutoff to Norris and back to Mammoth Hot Springs over the same road used on the outward journey. After construction of a road from the Upper Geyser Basin to the outlet of Lake Yellowstone, tourists were hauled that way, which added an overnight stop at the Lake Hotel and increased the length of the park tour by one day, raising the cost to $50.

After 1891 stagecoaches were routed to the Grand Canyon over the new road to Thumb Bay and the outlet of Lake Yellowstone. Accordingly, on their fourth day in the Park the tourists retraced their journey of the previous day to the Upper Geyser Basin; beyond Old Faithful the route was new to them although not particularly novel. The road followed the Firehole River to Spring Creek, a short distance from Lone Star Geyser, then turned up the narrow, twisting canyon of that minor drainage, past the Turtle Rock (scene of a holdup) to a crossing of the Continental Divide at Craig Pass. (The pass got its name from the maiden name of Mrs. Ida Craig Wilcox, the first lady to go through it on the road built by Lieutenant Chittenden in 1891. The name of Isa Lake, a beautiful little pond within the pass, was concocted from the given name of Miss Isabel Jelke.)

Corkscrew Bridge, on the east entrance road (later replaced by a concrete structure).

The original Fishing Bridge at the outlet of Yellowstone Lake.

East of Craig Pass the road descended into the drainage of DeLacy Creek by a steep and twisting grade called the Corkscrew Hill, which local wits maintained was "so crooked that you pass one place three times before you get by it." It was considered the most dangerous hill in the Park and was the scene of a number of wrecks. Driver Del Jenkins remembers a nerve-wracking experience he had there with a four-horse, eleven-passenger rig—2,000 pounds of coach and nearly an equal weight in passengers and baggage. Brakes alone would not hold such a load on that hill; the wheelers (two larger horses hitched directly to the wagon tongue) were depended upon to hold back on the down grades. In this case, an obstreperous wheeler kicked a leg over a tug soon after starting down and took fright. Jenkins almost had more than he could manage fighting that team to a stop with the brake and reins. When the coach was halted, a young man got down and carefully unhooked the tug and took it from between the legs of the horse. Jenkins was fortunate to get off without a bad wreck.[49]

Another driver recalls that his exhibition of driving on that awful grade failed to get the approval he thought it deserved. Among his passengers was an elderly lady who was disappointed with the walking gait of the stage horses and kept after him to show her some of the western driving she had heard about. The other passengers laid over at the Upper Geyser Basin leaving the old lady to continue on, so, when they came to Corkscrew Hill, the driver decided to show her how he could drive. It was a wild ride, just on the edge of recklessness, and the driver thought that would certainly satisfy his passenger; but when he pulled up at DeLacy Creek and looked back, the seats were empty. His passenger was on the floor, scared speechless. She refused to ride another mile with him but waited right there for the next stagecoach.[50]

That was rough sport, but occasionally passengers were rough on drivers, in their own way. A group of gay young ladies embarrassed Jenkins so much he hadn't forgotten after sixty-four years. He got his chance to drive in the Park in 1897, when the Christian Endeavor groups returning from their San Francisco convention swamped the Park. In an effort to handle the traffic, the transportation facilities put on every old stagecoach, team, and driver that could be found. Among the extra drivers was Del, who made the circuit with a load of vacationing school marms. He said:

> These women was always askin' all kinds of questions. . . . They asked me where I was born and raised and I told them Utah, and they started a-kiddin me about Brigham Young and the Mormons, and finally they wrote on a cardboard, "Brigham Young and his family," and tacked it on my old stagecoach. Yeah! that was somethin' I didn't like."[51]

From the foot of the Corkscrew Hill the road climbed to Shoshone Point (scene of another of the Park's stagecoach holdups), then ascended Dry Creek to a second crossing of the Continental Divide and down to the lunch station, called a tea-and-coffee geyser (now West Thumb). It was a terrible drive for the horses, twenty-eight miles, much of it on soft road which made the coach pull hard. It kept the driver in a sweat, pushing on the lines as if he could assist his laboring team that way. Also, the drive was monotonous for the dudes—too many pine trees and too few vistas, with much dust and a driver preoccupied with tired horses.

The drivers knew there were nineteen miles of sandy road around Yellowstone Lake to the hotel near the outlet, so they were eager to "boat"as many of their dudes as possible at Thumb. As the coach rolled down that last grade toward the blue waters of Thumb Bay, where the steamer *Zillah* lay toylike at its dock, the driver began a softsell to get as many of his passengers aboard as possible. This boat ride was not a part of the regular tour, but an extra, costing an additional $2.50, so it was necessary to play up the advantages of the short cruise compared to the land route: absence of dust, freedom to walk about and stretch cramped legs, marvelous views of forested shores and islets backgrounded by magnificent, snow-capped mountains, and the stop at Dot Island to see live buffalo and elk close up. All those features were paraded before the tired dudes. And for every one put aboard the boat, the driver got fifty cents, or $5.50 for a coachload, which was a respectable bonus for a man whose wage was $50 per month.[52]

But, as all good things come at last to an end, there came a day when Captain Waters, the boat concessioner, thought he could no longer afford to pay that fifty cents a head to the drivers. His decision was a mistake, for they boycotted him. It worked this way: when a coach came in sight of the boat dock, some tourist would be sure to ask about the steamer, whereupon the driver would mutter, "Oh, they got it back up again!" Of course he would be asked to explain and would enlarge upon the unseaworthiness of the *Zillah*.[53] The tourists would want to know what they would miss if they didn't take the boat. "Well, you'll miss a swell drive—Arnica Creek, the knotty pines and the natural bridge," they were told. So they stayed with the coach. One old driver said: "It was a shame. We'd get 'em on that hill (between Arnica and Bridge creeks) and they'd have to get out and walk to relieve the ponies."

The quiet little war waged by the drivers was a large factor in the ruination of E. C. Waters and his boat business; but there were other factors. In 1905, Captain Waters launched a second and larger steamboat: the *E. C. Waters*. This wooden vessel had a length of 125 feet, with a beam of 26, and was thought adequate for transporting 500 persons.[54] However, the authorities refused to license the vessel for that number and Captain Waters refused to settle for less; so his fine steamer was an idle investment, lying unused at its anchorage on the east side of Stevenson Island. Also, the captain was never completely honest with his trade. At the store he operated near the Lake Hotel, and in the business of renting rowboats to fishermen, he constantly misrepresented and overcharged in a way that fattened the file of complaints against him. One tourist who was charged $12 for his evening of lake fishing in one of the captain's boats commented, "a piece of highway robbery, and the only satisfaction I had was in telling him that I now knew why Christ walked on the water, that in the face of such charges anybody else would walk that was able to."[55]

Whether the tourist sailed across Lake Yellowstone or coached along its shore, his destination was Lake Hotel. Construction of a permanent hostel to replace the little used tent camp near the outlet of the lake was begun in 1889, but work progressed so slowly that when guests were admitted in 1891 only one wing had been completed. Captain Anderson thought it was "all that will be needed until the tide of travel sets more in that direction."[56] Though he considered Lake Hotel the most desirable place in the Park for a prolonged stay and deserving of better patronage, it remained a small establishment (only 80 guest rooms) until 1903. An addition in that year doubled the capacity, and further work in 1904 raised the number of rooms to 210, enough to house 446 guests.

The Lake Hotel had become an imposing structure with a suggestion of classic beauty. Well situated, fronting upon the lake, its four-storied, 300-foot broadside was painted a soft yellow, with white trim and a porte cochere ornamented with Ionic columns 50 feet high. It enjoyed a brief distinction as the Park's largest hotel, with "all the modern conveniences including suites of rooms, with baths attached."[57]

Guests at Lake Hotel found a serenity absent elsewhere in Wonderland. After a good dinner, well served by waitresses instead of by waiters as at other large hotels in the Park, there were only quiet things to do. Whether one slipped through dim woods behind the hotel, hopeful of seeing bears feeding at the dump, walked the lakeshore, or merely sat and watched the backdrop of wooded hills and rugged peaks far across the water dissolve into the night, the mood was one of restfulness. What a blessing after four days of staging—of sun, wind, dust, and mosquitoes!

"Yellowstone wagons" loading at Lake Hotel, 1909. *From a print made by the Detroit Photographic Co.*

Canyon Hotel (the last structure, built in 1910-1911).

The fifth day of the park tour was also easier. There was a relaxed half-day ride down the Yellowstone River from the outlet of its lake, past the Mud Volcano (which more than one tourist thought was the Park's "most repulsive and terrifying sight"[58]) and through the lush meadows of Hayden Valley to the Grand Canyon of the Yellowstone River. Near the northern extremity of Hayden Valley the stage crossed Alum Creek, where the driver was sure to tell one of those awful tales extolling the ability of its waters to shrink practically anything. One stock yarn claims that a "man came along driving four very large horses and a big wagon. He forded the creek and when he came out on the other side he found the alum had shrunk his outfit to four Shetland ponies and a basket phaeton;" another tale concerns a lady in Chicago who wore number eight shoes. She heard about the remarkable qualities of the water and so came to the Park, waded the stream, and went home wearing number twos. It seems that the second story soon fell into disuse because of the unfortunate experience of a driver who had a lady from Chicago among his passengers. Upon hearing that story she suggested that if the waters were so good for shrinking things he should try bathing his head in Alum Creek![59]

The Canyon Hotel, to which tourists were delivered in time for their noon meal, was a hostel whose character varied with time. The Yellowstone Park Improvement Company established one of its tent camps there in 1883 and the association replaced that, in 1886, with a prefabricated building intended to serve for the summer only but which remained in use until 1891.[60] Both the tent hotel and the barracks-like temporary structure that replaced it were near the Upper Falls, on the site now occupied by the parking area; but the permanent hotels were on an open hillside above the Lower Falls.

Even before the 250-room structure erected at the latter site was completed, it was discovered that its foundations were insecure and by 1896 it was necessary to replaster. The foundations required extensive repairs in 1901, when an additional 24 rooms were added; yet, despite such clear evidence that the site was unstable, a much larger hotel was built there in 1910-11.[61] Foundation damage was later to contribute to its destruction.

The hotel that served the traveling public from 1890 to 1911— which Captain F. A. Boutelle considered in such "bad taste," though he admitted it would be "a most comfortable and commodious house"[62]—featured a grizzly bear cub chained to a pole near the back door, and a brass band which tooted much of the time. One tourist described the noise as execrable, adding: "There is no such thing as

A group of young ladies employed at Canyon Hotel, photographed on the rim of the Grand Canyon.

bad music, it is either music or it is noise." He was willing to admit the beds were clean and soft, the table fair, and the attendance quite good.[63]

Arrival time at the Grand Canyon left tourists an entire afternoon for "doing" the sights along the rim and about the falls. Most rode horseback on an eight-mile jaunt described in a letter home:

> The Grand Canon of the Yellowstone is the grandest, most sublime sight I have ever seen— That is the truth & you know how much of the sublime in nature I have seen. If only you cd. see it for yourself for no description of mine will give any idea. I don't know any figures but we rode on narrow, steep bridle paths, part of the time through pines, part on the edge of the top of cliffs, way, way above the Yellowstone river. It seemed almost as far down as from Bel Alp hotel to the valley. At Lookout Pt. we seemed to be up in the air & up the valley saw the Lower Falls, over twice as high as Niagara, with a great vol. of water but not as wide. Below us, on both sides, were *Painted Cliffs*. They are immense in height, solid rock from base to summit & of loveliest, softest shades of yellow, pink, light browns, reds. They all blend beautifully & here & there a few pines stick to the sides. Far below us on a crag, an eagle had its nest & we heard the young ones scream.[64]

For the more active, there was climbing in the canyon. This could be either a guided trip or an impromptu scramble. "Uncle Tom" Richardson was the guide prior to the building of the Chittenden Bridge,[65] and after that time, certain of the versatile hotel porters performed the service until Uncle Tom's Trail was equipped with wooden stairways and railings which made it safe for the general public. During Uncle Tom's day, the trip to the bottom of the Lower Fall was an adventure that began with a boat trip across the Yellowstone River where it flows slowly just above the site of Chittenden Bridge; then there was a walk through unspoiled woods to the gully down which a descent was made, on wooden ladders and with the help of ropes, to the edge of the river below the great fall. This allowed the tourist to stand in a misty realm overawed by thundering waters and everpresent rainbows. Uncle Tom added a perfect finish serving a campfire supper in a sylvan setting before boating his guests back across the river.

A season's business usually netted Uncle Tom about one thousand dollars, and that, with what he earned from the Wylie Permanent Camping Company in spring and fall, should have kept him comfortably through the winter; but he liked cards too well and rarely had much money left after scrupulously paying for his pleasure of the previous winter. On completion of the Chittenden Bridge in

Uncle Tom Richardson, builder of the trail to the foot of the Lower Falls of Yellowstone River, probably before 1903.

1903, Uncle Tom's permit to guide visitors to the foot of the Lower Fall was revoked. Several years of vain efforts to regain his lost business ended with his death at Bozeman.

Those who scrambled the canyon walls unaided are typified by Owen Wister, whose diary for the year 1887 states: "Monday, August 29. West, George Norman, and I are having a hell of a time trying to get down to the bottom of the Canon with ropes. . . .I am at present sitting about nowhere, halfway . . . George is above, undecided whether he'll untie the rope from the last tree, or not." We also know from Wister's own postscript, added forty-nine years later, that they got to the bottom and back—safely—somewhere between Inspiration Point and the Lower Fall, and we have his recollection of "West's remarks at various stages of our descent . . . (1) that he would give ten dollars not to have started, (2) that he would give fifty, (3) that he hadn't enough cash in the world to give what he'd like to."[66] Such were the principal sports at the Grand Canyon.

Tourists spent their last day in the Park returning from the Grand Canyon to the railroad by way of Norris Junction and Mammoth Hot Springs. The only new features seen on the Cutoff (that monotonous, eleven-mile shortcut built in 1886) were the Virginia Cascades (named for the wife of Charles Gibson, president of the Yellowstone Park Association) and the Devil's Elbow, a meet-yourself-coming-back sort of curve in the road below the cascades. Incidentally, the early road followed the stream to the foot of Virginia Cascades, then climbed steeply out of the canyon alongside the dashing waters. This pitch was a terrible one for the freight wagons bound for the Grand Canyon and outlet of the lake (they nearly always had to double-team), but it was no obstacle to the stage-coaches since they only descended over that route.

There was lunch again at Larry's before continuing toward Mammoth Hot Springs by the familiar track. Along that road, where loaded coaches and other rigs were frequently met, it was the custom to exchange pleasantries, or "yell the state they were from,"[67] and, as these tourists had seen the sights, they often settled down to singing popular airs as they rode along. Dinner was served them at the National Hotel, then there was a short stagecoach ride to their train, waiting at the terminus of the park branch line—and, suddenly, the Yellowstone adventure was over.

The foregoing is more or less typical of how visitors toured the Park in the yellow coaches of the Yellowstone National Park Transportation Company (1891-98) and the Yellowstone Park Transportation Company (1898-1936).[68] It is typical, too, of the

touring of those who rode in the red coaches of the Monida &
Yellowstone Stage Company (1898-1913) and the Yellowstone-
Western Stage Company (1913-17), except that patrons of these
latter two were brought in through the western entrance and did not
ordinarily go to Mammoth Hot Springs on their tour. Whether they
entered the Park from the north in yellow coaches, or from the west in
red ones, these tourists patronized the hotels and were the carriage
trade.

Another type of tourist enjoyed a different way of seeing the
Park: by the permanent camps system, or Wylie Way, as it is often
called from its originator. The Wylie Way substituted tent camps for
hotels, thus avoiding a large investment in fixed installations and
reducing operating costs. It was a development fraught with controversy and innovation, yet was successful.

The idea of housing tourists in tent camps was as old as the
concession business. The Yellowstone Park Improvement Company
had tent camps at Norris, Upper Geyser Basin, and Grand Canyon,
and the Yellowstone Park Association operated similar establishments at Norris, Upper Geyser Basin, and Lake. These were no more
than interim developments, however, intended to provide accommodations until permanent hotels could be built. It remained for
William Wallace Wylie, a public school superintendent from Bozeman Montana, to comprehend that such tent camps might be
organized into a system that could provide low-cost accommodations
satisfactory to a considerable percentage of park tourists.

Mr. Wylie became acquainted with Yellowstone Park in the
summer of 1880, when he conducted his first visitor through
Wonderland—a young jeweler from Bozeman named Jackson, who
paid a dollar a day for that service, which included board.[69] Wylie
returned to the Park later that summer with a wagon party which he
claimed was the first group to go from Mammoth Hot Springs to the
geyser basins with a wheeled vehicle over the Norris Road. An
extended visit in 1881 with the Bozeman photographer, Henry Bird
Calfee, led Mr. Wylie to give a short-lived, and unsuccessful,
illustrated lecture tour the following winter.[70] A notable result of the
tour, however, was publication of a guidebook that made Mr. Wylie
an "authority" on the Park.[71]

As a result, Wylie was often asked to conduct parties (generally
groups of teachers) through the Park. Thus he became an "independent," taking small parties through the Park with his own
equipment in the style of sagebrushers, that is, camping by the
wayside wherever night found them. He says that "it was at least ten

Tourists waiting for their coaches at a Wylie permanent camp, 1912. Their linen dusters were provided for protection of their clothing.

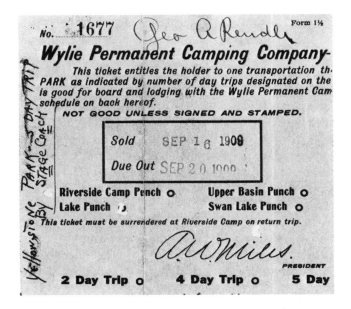

A ticket used by a Wylie-way tourist who made a five-day tour of the Park in 1909. *From the author's collection.*

years after this work began, before Mrs. Wylie and I realized that we were drifting into a tourist business."[72] With that realization came the inspiration to establish permanent tent camps to serve as hostels at convenient points, and he went to Washington, D.C., in 1893 to promote the idea. Wylie secured a two-year lease for a number of sites suited to his purpose, and organized his Wylie Camping Company.

This new business represented a threat to the Yellowstone Park Association; indeed, it would not have managed a foothold except that the association was then in disfavor for its inept handling of the transportation privilege. (See Chapter 13 for events leading to formation of the Yellowstone National Park Transportation Company.) Thus, the Wylie Camping Company owed its existence to a transient sentiment in the Department of the Interior for breaking the power of the railroad-sponsored association; but almost before he could get his new business into operation, Mr. Wylie found he had powerful foes.

The immediate reaction of the park superintendent to Mr. Wylie's operation was to foresee a shanty-like development of the permanent camps, a "desecration of the Park" which he thought should not be allowed.[73] The competition (this included the hotel and transportation companies and the Northern Pacific Railroad) was neither so direct nor so honest, preferring to work through their lobbyists at the national capital to discredit the new and threatening enterprise. As a result, Wylie was never able to obtain a franchise for his business, but had to make-do on annual permits which were only reluctantly given.

For his part, Wylie fought back by taking his case "to the people," both with his pen and by speaking to groups at his camps and elsewhere. By gaining the support of some prominent persons (among them Representatives John Fletcher Lacey and Mark Hanna), he managed to promote his Wylie Way successfully. However, it became increasingly apparent that he would never be given a franchise, and so, at the close of the 1905 season, Wylie sold his venture to Arthur W. Miles, a Livingston merchant who was immediately given a ten-year lease for the reorganized Wylie Permanent Camping Company.

The contributions of the Wylie Way to the stagecoach era were several. Foremost among the advantages was economy. A Wylie tour of seven days (this allowed two days each in the Upper Geyser Basin and at the Grand Canyon) cost $35, while the association's six-day tour was priced at $50. Thus, the Park was opened to people of lesser means. And there were attractions other than economy. Many persons enjoyed the informality of the Wylie Way. A surprising

number of these were Victorians of ample means who could afford
hotel prices but were disenchanted with the tip-conscious bowing and
scraping of hotel professionals. From the beginning, Wylie recruited
a different type of help; he employed school teachers and college
students, bringing a fresh genuineness to what had been a rather
hackneyed service. In that, he established a pattern that persists in the
operation of park concessions in Yellowstone and elsewhere.

There was always entertainment at the Wylie camps. This seems
to have developed spontaneously among the enthusiastic young
people employed there, taking the form of campfire songfests and
impromptu entertainments which guests considered great fun. This,
too, set a pattern that has persisted in the entertainment programs of
later concessioners and in the campfire programs of the National
Park Service. The wholehearted acceptance of this feature of the
Wylie Way is illustrated by a story about the camp in the Upper
Geyser Basin, located south of Daisy Geyser, which had a piano in
the reception tent. It is said that a college professor who was a guest
there wandered into the tent, and seeing a sign which announced,
"Daisy Will Play _____ ," with the time chalked in, sat down and
waited a long time in the expectation that a young lady would appear
to perform on the piano. Of course, the performer was the Daisy
Geyser, less than a hundred feet away.[74]

A further advantage of the Wylie Way was the effort made to
supply guests with accurate, interesting information about the Park.
The hotel company had made an early start in that direction, but its
efforts never got beyond the part-time activity of lively young
porters. Mr. Wylie, from his school-teaching experience, understood
the value of such "interpretation." He employed guides whose
principal duty was to conduct tourists about the thermal areas, and
guiding in the thermal basins attained a stature it had never
previously enjoyed. The hotel company's people were thus encouraged to do better, and one of them, Milton P. Skinner, became
the effective advocate of a government educational service. How he
accomplished it will be shown in Chapter 19.

The performance of the early guides, regardless of the company
they served, was seldom entirely adequate. They were too bold in
passing the hat after a tour of the sights, for example, (an aggressive
young man could make up to twenty dollars on a good day),[75] and
that put a premium on "facts" with audience appeal. And inevitably, a
strain of malarkey persisted in the talks these men gave.

Jack Haynes was greatly impressed by one of the Wylie guides,
Ralph T. Knight, a medical student who served also as first-aid man.

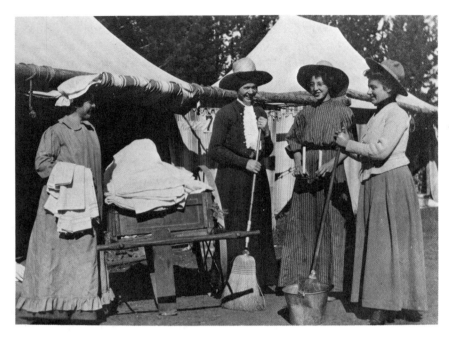

Maids employed at a Wylie permanent camp, 1908.

A Wylie Permanent Camping Company store tent. *From the Hall family album (author's collection).*

A Wylie Permanent Camping Co. information tent at the Cinnabar terminus of the Northern Pacific Railroad's park branch line. (Uncle Tom Richardson is talking with a uniformed guide.)

A Wylie Permanent Camping Company reception tent. *From the Hall family album (author's collection).*

"Doc" Knight was a good lecturer, but he stood out in Jack's memory for an entirely different kind of educational activity, one that was directly related to the animosity existing between the Wylie concern and the older companies. During the summer of 1910 the Monida & Yellowstone Stage Company (operated by Jack's father) employed two rather fractious drivers, Bill Flyn and "Pinky," who had formerly been pugilists. While on a binge, they decided to go over to the Wylie camp, at Riverside, and wreck the place and had just begun their raid when the screams of the young ladies employed in the dining hall brought Doc Knight on the run from his tent. Drunk enough to be sure of themselves, the two troublemakers took on Doc Knight, who proceeded to K.O. both of them. At that moment the manure wagon, with a load of barn cleanings, happened to be passing; both losers were tossed in and taken to the dump to sober up.

Jack was closing up the studio (which he ran for his father in addition to serving as transportation agent at that point) when Doc Knight came around to report the fate of the two drivers—a decent thing for Doc to do, since it gave Jack a chance to gather in his two wayward drivers and sober them up for the workday just ahead. When Bill Flyn drove up to the hotel to pick up his dudes the following morning, Jack said: "Say, Bill, that horse nearly got you, didn't he?" Bill grunted a sheepish "Yeah," and Jack proceeded to give the passengers a line about the driver getting caught in a stall with a mean horse. With his bruised appearance thus explained, the driver became a hero in the eyes of his passengers. "Pinky" got the same treatment, and both drivers later reported their tips on that trip around the Park were the largest they had ever received.[76]

The Wylie Permanent Camping Company had troubles other than those concocted by the opposition. By the very nature of the camps, housed as they were in flimsy canvas, they were constantly harassed by bears. Ed Moorman was "camp man" at Willow Park in 1899, which meant he had to get up at 4:30 A.M. to build a fire in the kitchen range, milk four to six cows, start warming fires in the dude tents, pack hot water to them for washing, brush the flies (immobilized by the chill of night) off the canvas walls of the dining tent, carry the tourist baggage to the loading platform, haul the day's water up from the creek, saw and split the wood, rake the grounds, and prepare the campfire circle for the next evening, and other things that needed doing, for which he was paid $20 per month and board. His bed was placed in the commissary tent so that he could keep the bears out, and that was the rough part of the job.

He had brought a dog with him but the bears finally killed it. He "had to drive the bears away 8 or 10 times each night," and remembered one instance when he was tempted to quit. That night

> after I had been up many times, Mr. Wylie came to my tent and said I must keep the bears away. He was in his nightshirt and throwing sticks of wood at the bears on top of the kitchen roof, tearing up the slabs.[77]

The bears were so bold that Ed was seldom able to get all the way to the garbage pit with the kitchen swill; usually they met him enroute and took over the bucket without formalities. The camp personnel did what they could to reduce the bear population by feeding them broken glass in meat, for example, or an old sponge fried in kitchen grease. More often than not such practices went undetected and unpunished, but in one instance, where the bear's demise was entirely accidental, the camp manager was brought to task. A small bear that had been bothering the camp at Upper Geyser Basin climbed a tree, and one of the drivers attempted to pull him down with a lasso. In the process, the bear fell from a limb and hanged himself with the snarled rope. The manager thought it was a shame to waste a bear skin, so he salvaged the hide. His action came to the attention of the soldiers, who hailed him before the U.S. commissioner, and he was fined for killing a bear.[78]

The dire predictions concerning the Wylie Way did not materialize; the permanent camps did not become shanty towns. Instead, the candy-striped tents set in woodsy places were neat and gay. The traveling public was generally pleased and Mr. Wylie's idea soon burgeoned in the form of a similar enterprise by the Shaw and Powell Camping Company, which established permanent camps in 1913. The business of both concerns increased rapidly until the end of the stagecoach era, causing the president of the hotel company to complain: "The Camp people are like Banco's [Banquo's] ghost, they will not down."[79]

A tourist's view of the Park as seen on the Grand Round would be incomplete without mentioning stagecoach wrecks (seldom publicized) and stagecoach holdups (well publicized). The reluctance of the transportation people to say much about the accidents that occurred in the Park is understandable; they felt that notoriety would be hard on business. However, one former driver thought otherwise: it was his observation that "the wilder the team acted, the more people wanted to ride with 'em."[80] He also mentioned that stagecoach wrecks did as much damage as automobile accidents do today, which is certainly an understatement if statistics have any validity. According

Interior of a Wylie permanent camp dining tent, 1912.

to figures published by Paul M. Johnson, state highway engineer for Montana, the incidence of fatalities in 1909 was 30 for each 100 million horse-traveled miles against only 5.6 for the same number of automobile-traveled miles in 1966.[81]

Travel in horse-drawn vehicles was dangerous, but perhaps the driver was right: people were so habituated to the danger that it held no terrors for them. Even so, there was another cogent reason for a close-mouthed attitude about stagecoach wrecks. Few concerns carried liability insurance in that day (definitely not those doing business in the Park), and they did not want their chances for a quick, easy settlement compromised by publicity. Records of the Yellowstone Park Transportation Company show that they often managed to quiet an injured passenger by offering fifty dollars in addition to paying the medical expenses (and sometimes board and room for others of a party).

The reminiscences of former drivers and the few published accounts indicate that then, as now, a fair proportion of the accidents could be laid to drunken, reckless, or inept drivers, or to other stupid people, passengers not excluded. Other causes varied from the sudden fright of team horses to mechanical failure of equipment and geological instability. Thus, there was a reasonable coverage of possible causes, from human fallibility to acts of God. Geological instability sounds like a strange cause for a stagecoach accident, and yet, how else can we classify the death of the woman who was struck by a rock that bounded down the wall of the Gardner River Canyon and into the open coach where she was riding?[82] And when the roadbed collapsed under a coach passing through the Hoodoos above Mammoth Hot Springs, dropping the vehicle into an unsuspected cavern, instability was certainly the cause; in that mishap the passengers fared better than the team and coach.

The tendency of stage horses to take fright and run away, or bolt over an embankment, led to many wrecks. A ridiculous happening of this sort occurred at Mammoth Hot Springs. "Big Fred" Schultz had just unloaded his dudes at the veranda of the National Hotel when one of the ladies popped her parasol open to shake out the dampness. The team bolted instantly, heading for the transportation barns near the lower end of the present esplanade, with Fred still on the box and powerless to stop his animals. One witness remembers that the coach hit a lawn hydrant in front of the Weather Bureau office and careened along on two wheels for fifty feet before righting itself. At the barn, Fred had some luck; in attempting a tight turn around the end of the building, several horses went down, piling up the rig. If that hadn't happened, the frightened horses undoubtedly would have run through the open stable door, plastering all 325 pounds of Big Fred on the overhead.[83]

That accident furnished some bunkhouse merriment, but it usually wasn't funny when a team bolted. Wally Walker was trotting his six bays along the road in the Gardner River canyon when a fisherman stepped out of the willows, frightening his team. The leaders turned back, jack-knifing the big tally-ho, and injuring seventeen passengers. The animals were injured so badly they had to be disposed of. A similar accident occurred near the Lake Hotel when a deer ran across the road, but only one passenger was injured there.[84]

Occasionally an accident could be fairly ascribed to mechanical failure, according to testimony.

August 14, 1908, Frank Davis, of lawful age, being first duly sworn, deposes and says: My permanent address is Butte, Montana. . . . I am forty years old and this is my seventh consecutive season as a driver of a four-horse, eleven passenger coach for the Yellowstone Park Transportation Company, and the sixth consecutive season that I have driven Abbot-Downing, eleven passenger coach No. 15, concerned in the accident which occurred on Jupiter Terrace hill about 3:30, Thursday afternoon, August 13th, 1908. This is the first accident that I have ever been concerned in during that time and the first injury to any passengers riding in my coach . . .

The company's regulations require that the brake blocks on each coach shall be shod before leaving the Canyon for Mammoth Hot Springs. . . . I securely and properly shod both brake blocks in the regulation manner and with the usual and regulation brake shoes [cottonwood]. The brakes worked perfectly and the weather was fair and normal until we reached a point about fourteen miles from Mammoth Hot Springs, when it began to rain. The last four miles of the drive into Mammoth Hot Springs is down hill and an even grade, requiring constant use of the brakes. The rain had increased to a heavy downpour during these last four miles and . . . when about three quarters of a mile from Mammoth Hot Springs Hotel on the grade south from Jupiter Terrace, the brake failed to hold the coach off the horses even though I exerted myself to the utmost to apply the brakes and make them hold the wagon off of the team. This they failed to do and the coach struck the lead team, and the team became unmanageable and ran. I turned the team up Capitol Hill and left the regular road as soon as I saw the conditions, as it would have been disastrous to have continued on the regular road down the hill.

The team after leaving the regular road ran up the side of the hill for a distance of about seventy-five yards and I had almost brought them to a stand still, when on a sloping piece of ground the coach turned over . . .

A loaded Tallyho stagecoach in the Gardner River Canyon, bound for Mammoth Hot Springs. The driver is John McPherson. *From a photograph by Berry's Studio, Livingston, Mont.*

the front wheels became uncoupled from the rest of the wagon and the team thus became disconnected from the coach. Neither the coach nor any of the passengers were dragged at all.[85]

Only one of the six passengers was seriously injured, a young man who broke a leg jumping from the coach; all were cut or bruised to some extent.

In another accident at nearly the same place, the driver had successfully halted his runaway team and was having his passengers unload before he attempted to recover a dropped line. A passenger, Mr. C. W. Smith, started toward the leaders, saying to the driver, "I will get the line for you." The driver warned him to stay back, as the team was nervous and would bolt. But the stubborn young man grabbed for the bit of a leader anyhow, thinking he could hold the team; instead he frightened the animals into bolting up an embankment and the coach overturned before the last two passengers were out. Both were injured, and Mr. Smith was trampled by the team he failed to hold.

An accident in which Mrs. Jenny V. Cowdry of St. Louis was injured was the driver's fault, according to Mrs. Cowdry's testimony at the trial of a subsequent suit for damages.

Question: "How were the roads?"

Answer: "The roads were good, they are government roads. It was uphill all the way and we went very slowly, trotting gently most of the time until we reached a spring where passengers always alight to get a drink [Apollinaris Spring]. Before we left the coach, they told us to be sure and remember our number. I remembered mine by the song, *Dwelt a Miner, Forty-Niner*. Before I reached the coach coming back from the spring, I heard them calling for the people to come . . . and a man said, "*Here is your coach, get in quickly as we are behind*."

Question: "Who was this man who asked you to get in?"

Answer: "I think he was a representative of the company, he seemed to have charge of the coaches at the spring. He put people in where they belonged. When I came up there were only two seats left, one on the outside with the driver and one on the inside. Glancing at the top seat and seeing that it would be cut just under one's shoulder blades, I knew I was stronger than Miss Sloane, and I said, *Jump in the inside seat Miss Sloane*, then I went on the seat with the driver. The same gentleman who sat on the inside with me before we reached the spring, was sitting with me on the driver's seat."

Question: "Who were the other people in the coach with you?"

Answer: "I had a full list of the names in my purse but it mysteriously disappeared. I do not know whether through accident or not. After the accident, when we were on the train going to Livingston, the conductor handled my purse."

Question: "When did you notice anything wrong with the wheel?"

Answer: "Before we got to the spring the right-hand back wheel of the coach creaked terribly, like a wheel was dry, and I called to the driver, *Driver, do you hear that wheel creak?* He said, *Yes*, and did not pay any attention. We went quite a little while and then I said again, *Do you know that wheel is going dry. Don't you hear it creak?* He said he heard it and then it stopped."

Question: "How long had you been gone from the hotel?"

Answer: "We were about halfway to the spring. We had been out probably a couple of hours."

Question: "Where did you go after you left the spring?"

Answer: "We left the springs, I on the outside, over the wheel that went off. The man who sat with me was a geologist [mining engineer, for whom the town of Aldridge, Montana, was later named], a naturalist, and kept calling my attention to the formation of the rock. When we came to a little bluff on the side of the road with very high rocks behind, he said, *You see, here is the same sort of formation on this bluff.* As we were driving, I had to turn my eyes back a little, and he said, *You see the formation flows down over that and forms this little soft formation on the ground*, which caused me to turn my eyes to the ground. As I did so, I saw that wheel had just commenced to wobble, and I said immediately to the driver, *Your wheel is loosened! It is coming off, take your reins quickly!* Then I looked down again to watch the wheel. It had loosened considerably, so that I could see it slant. I did not feel the least fear in the world because I had utter confidence in the stage driver and had no idea but what he would check the horses. If I had felt the least fear, I would have warned the other passengers. When I saw that he did not check his horses, I said again, *Driver, your wheel is going off!* And the next thing I knew, I was landed on the ground and felt people being dragged over me."

Question: "Did he make any reply when you spoke to him?"

Answer: "In the first instance he did not speak. When I spoke the second time, I think he drew his horses quickly, which meant to a stage horse, the bound."

Question: "Could he see the wheels himself?"

Answer: "No."

Question: "Do you think that he could have stopped his horses after you first told him that the wheel was going off?"

Answer: "A first class driver, from the time I spoke, and when spoken to again, could have stopped his horses."

Question: "What was the distance required for him to stop his team after the accident?"

Answer: "I do not know. I did not hear anyone say."

Question: "How old did the driver seem?"

Answer: "He looked about 18."

Question: "When he started out on this trip did he seem an experienced driver?"

Answer: "He did not strike me so. He said to my seat companion just a little while before the accident, *This is a good day to sleep.* Mr. Aldridge said, *Are you sleepy?* And he said *Yes, I did not go to bed until after 2:00 a.m.* My companion turned around sharply and said, *Does the company work you like that?* And the boy said, *No, I was at Livingston having a good time last night.* A little while after, I looked and he had his eyes shut. He was very sleepy and apparently everything was going right. Our horses were not fractious and he was sitting there in a half-dazed condition."

Question: "Was there a brake on the coach?"

Answer: "Yes."

Question: "Did he use it when you called to him?"

Answer: "I don't know. He did not speak to his horses when I told him. I think he doubted my word. I suppose he thought, here is a woman who thinks there is something wrong when there isn't."

Question: "Did anyone hear you speak to the driver?"

Answer: "The man with me heard all of this."

Question: "Did you fall where it was rocky?"

Answer: "No, I fell by the side of the road. I felt Miss Sloane being dragged over me and recognized her dress just after she passed over me. I felt something very heavy being dragged over me; I thought at the time that it was the wheel of the coach, but I think now that it must have been another passenger."

Question: "Were all the people in the coach thrown out?"

Answer: "Yes, the coach was on its side being dragged; so they told me. When our coach overturned the horses hauling the coach behind frightened and ran away. They were so close to us that they felt they could not avoid running over us. I was in a direct line of the four horses and coach, but they had an excellent driver and he swerved them just enough to escape me."

Question: "What became of this companion of yours when the coach pitched?"

Answer: "He was the first one to me."

Question: "Was he hurt?"

Answer: "Yes. This gentleman came to me and put his arms under me and tried to lift me up. When he saw I could not be lifted, he settled me back on the ground and said, *Do you know where you are hurt?* I said, *I think my hips are broken. I am crushed through the hips.* Then I looked down and saw my foot and said, *My leg is broken.* My face was cut and the flesh was hanging from my cheek; beyond that I could not tell what was the matter. I asked him if he was injured and he said, No. But I found out afterwards that he was. He said, *No one was seriously injured but you.* A coach came by and they put the passengers out and took us to Norris."[86]

Though Mrs. Cowdry received medical attention at Norris, her tribulations were far from over. Her journey by army ambulance and train to a hospital at Livingston, Montana, was particularly painful, and there she was held a virtual prisoner for a time because of her refusal to talk settlement with a representative of the transportation company. Out of that mistreatment arose the lawsuit that provides such a vivid picture of a stagecoach wreck.

That other hazard of travel in the Park—the stagecoach holdup—was a far less common happening. There were, in all, five holdups in the Park, and of those three were related to the Grand Tour.

It appears that when Hiram M. Chittenden was preparing his last revision of *The Yellowstone National Park*, he corresponded with Olin D. Wheeler, the Northern Pacific Railroad's eminent historian, concerning the insertion of a chapter on the Yellowstone holdups, and was bluntly told:

> Of course you probably understand as well as I do that the railroad company would not look with any particular favor upon that proposition. That is one of the phases of Park travel which transportation companies naturally do not care to exploit and publicize very much. From the historical standpoint, which, of course, is yours, it is doubtful whether it could be entirely ignored. I hope, however, that in handling it you can make this feature as innocuous as possible and I have no doubt you will, for you undoubtedly appreciate the fact that treated in one way it would have a tendency to diminish travel.[87]

Fortunately, Chittenden ignored expediency and reported the holdups he was familiar with in a manner that agrees closely with the facts. Later, Jack Ellis Haynes added satisfactory accounts of the last two holdups.[88] The following is drawn from both sources.

A holdup took place on August 24, 1908, in Spring Creek Canyon, at a point four and one-half miles from the Upper Geyser Basin on the road toward West Thumb. Considering the number of vehicles (17) and passengers (174), this probably *was* the greatest stagecoach robbery of the twentieth century, as the victims claimed. In terms of the loot taken it was nothing to brag about: $1,363.95 in money and $730.25 in jewelry, or a total value of $2,094.20, hardly enough to excite a "Black Bart."

The procession that left the Old Faithful area that morning consisted of twenty-five vehicles escorted by a single cavalryman. Immediately behind the trooper, spaced about one hundred yards to avoid some of the dust, were sixteen coaches belonging to the Yellowstone National Park Transportation Company and the Monida & Yellowstone Stage Company. All these had loaded at the Old Faithful Inn. A considerable distance behind the coaches was a group of nine spring wagons and surreys of the Wylie Permanent Camping Company with passengers taken aboard at that company's camp near Daisy Geyser.

The vehicles moved slowly up the Firehole River and turned up Spring Creek toward the Continental Divide. Near a feature known then as Turtle Rock the driver of the lead coach—Jim Connell— noticed a man idling beside the road, but he thought no more of it than the trooper had. This man, who was undoubtedly the robber, had shrewdly picked a place where the visibility in the direction from which the coaches were coming was limited by the sharp elbow where the road passed around the rock, and where the roadway was too narrow for a driver to turn around after he saw what was happening. The robber, being a careful man, allowed the first eight coaches to pass by unmolested, thus putting more than one-half mile between himself and the escorting trooper before he stepped into the road at 8:30 A.M. and halted the coach driven by Charles Morgan of Powder River, Wyoming.

The highwayman, who had disguised his features by putting on a sack with holes cut for mouth and eyes ("like a fisherman in Santa Claus garb," according to one tourist) held his Winchester rifle on the three men on the front seat and commanded them to "Get down from there and be damned quick about it!" Morgan started to twist his lines around the brake handle when the robber remarked, "I don't mean you, I mean that Son-of-a-bitch in the middle. If you drivers have got anything, you keep it, for you have to work for your money."

The young man so roughly designated was P. H. Gaskin of Orlando, Florida, who was given a sack, and was told he would be the "bag-man"—with a strong hint to "dig up" if he had anything. Mr. Gaskin started things off with a contribution of $20.75 and his watch, and his traveling companion, Mr. Benjamin Drew, also from Orlando, added $160.00. The robber then said to the remaining occupants of the coach, "If you have got any money, hurry up and put it in here," pointing to the sack, and when all had contributed, he told the driver, "If you drive on before I tell you, I'll kill this fellow," referring to his unwilling assistant.

Meanwhile, the next coach in line had pulled up, and the dudes asked their driver (Charles J. Smith, who was known as White Mountain Smith) what the trouble was. He said, "It's a holdup and you'd better give him your money or someone will get shot!" As Smith later told it,[89] there was a young "smart aleck" on the box with him, and that lad took his bill fold from an inner pocket, extracted a ten-dollar bill and put the rest of his money away. "When the holdup man got to our stage, this man came up with this ten-dollar bill and threw it in the sack as though he were making a donation." The robber growled at him, "Is that all the money you've got?" "Yes," the dude said, "That's all I've got." "You dirty liar," was the reply, "get down off that stage. I'm going to search you, and if you've got any more, I'm going to shoot you right here in the road!" The man nearly fell off the coach in his haste to comply, and the robber, who was holding the rifle with his right hand, with the hammer cocked, frisked the dude with his left hand. He found the hidden wallet, shook some more bills into the sack and said, "I ought to shoot you like I said I would, but if I catch anyone else holding out on me I will!" Then he hit the young man on the head with the barrel of his rifle, which discharged at the same time. The terrorized lad took off on the run, but the robber's harsh "Come back here!" stopped him as if he were on the end of a string.

Vehicles continued to arrive at the scene of the holdup, and, while awaiting the attention of the robber, passengers had a chance to hide money and valuables. The passengers of the fourth coach were ordered to throw the lap robes on the ground and the robber shook them to see if anything was hidden in their folds. He left one on the ground, at which Fred Irvin, the driver, remarked, "I wish you would put that blanket in, I might need it later on." The robber tossed the robe into the coach and moved on to the next rig.

At the order to "shell out and be quick about it," a lady said to her husband, in German, "Give him all you got as he might shoot us." To her surprise, the robber added in that language, "Yes, and be damned quick about it!" Several passengers were less willing to contribute; one had to be poked in the ribs several times with the gun muzzle before he would shell out. A young lady told the robber she didn't have any money, and he answered, "Oh yes you have! I guess you got it stuck down in your stocking." Apparently fearful that he might continue his quest along the line suggested, she said, "Here it is," and threw her purse into the bag.

As he attended to the last of the coaches, the robber told his victims, "Well, you know that every little bit added to what you got makes just a little bit more," and he did a little dance step in sheer joy. The man who had been "holding the bag" for him was then told to get into the coach and the eight vehicles he had robbed were sent on their way with a "Good bye, I'll see you all in Heaven." But that was not the end of the day's work.

Instead of fleeing, the highwayman lay in wait for the Wylie contingent to enrich himself further at their expense. One of these rigs carried five girls, one of whom was sitting by the driver with a box of candy on her lap. The robber asked, "What have you got in that box?" On being told it was chocolate candy, he said, "Well give me some," and proceeded to take two pieces. He also asked another girl for a stick-pin she was wearing, and was told, "Oh, you don't want that, it only cost 19 cents." But he did want it, "for luck"; and lucky it must have been, for he was never caught. The entire robbery had taken only fifty minutes and had gone off very smoothly.

Upon being told he could proceed, Charles Morgan drove as fast as possible to a maintenance building two miles farther up Spring Creek and telephoned the alarm. Cavalrymen were soon galloping to the scene from Old Faithful, but all they were able to find were empty wallets and papers, which were returned to their owners before they left the Park. Some of the loot was recovered four years later by a trooper looking for lost horses northwest of Shoshone Lake. He found three gold watches and a silver-handled knife (all known to have been taken by the robber) on a small knoll in the forest. Unlikely as it would seem, the watches ran when wound.

It is said that the despoiled tourists were so unnerved upon their arrival at Thumb lunch station that their noon meal was a near-comic affair, highlighted by ridiculous actions and inane statements. The true feelings of these people were probably expressed quite accurately by one man, who said:

> Now, of course, I might have jumped on him. I might have gotten him but he might have gotten me. It is well enough for people to criticise and say what they would have said or done; but generally the man who blows the loudest gets his hands up the highest when the time comes. We have no apologies to make. We think we got off cheap and would not sell our experience, if we could, for what it cost us.[90]

That night, at Lake Hotel, the "victims of the greatest stagecoach holdup and highway robbery of the twentieth century," held a meeting presided over by Benjamin Drew. Out of it came the printing of a list of the victims and their losses (of interest later as a souvenir). The meeting also called for an investigation by the "Hon. James A. Garfield, Secretary of the Interior," ending with approval of the following resolution:

That whereas the military authorities in charge of the Park have proven themselves incompetant to protect the tourists visiting the Park . . . we urge congress to provide funds with which to thoroughly police the Park and to guard against a simular occurance.[91]

This was undoubtedly a blow to Superintendent S.B.M. Young, who had already taken abuse over a previous stagecoach robbery.

Who was the robber? He may have been William Binkley, a fugitive from justice who had escaped from the Fort Yellowstone guardhouse where he was serving a sentence for poaching. The description of the highwayman as "40 years of age, 150 to 160 lbs., stockily built, sandy complexion, raspy voice, trace of gray in the hair," and the fact that he spoke German, all fit Binkley; also, he was known to have remarked at one time, while under confinement, "that it would be an easy matter to hold up the coaches and that he would 'show them' when he got out." On those grounds, a reward of $1,300 was offered for his apprehension, but nothing was ever heard of him.

The robber who held up fifteen stagecoaches at Shoshone Point, on the same road, on the morning of July 29, 1914, was not as clever as the presumed Binkley, which is to say, he was caught. If ever a man was "hoisted by his own petard" it was Edward B. Trafton. The stagecoaches always stopped at Shoshone Point, about midway between the Upper Geyser Basin and Lake Yellowstone, in order for passengers to enjoy the view of Shoshone Lake and the distant Teton Range; the first coach to arrive there on the morning of the robbery did so. Among the passengers was a Mr. W. I. Allinder, who climbed the bank above the road in search of a vantage point for photographing the scene. He had just snapped a picture when someone in the woods asked him what he was doing, and he turned around to find himself looking into the muzzle of a rifle. The robber ordered the coach around the point, out of sight, and assembled the passengers in a little opening beside the road.[92]

In that sheltered place, the robber spread a blanket on the ground and ordered the dudes to line up and walk past him, telling them to "drop your valuables in this blanket! And don't you hide none!" Mr. Allinder had pushed his wallet into the dirt while sliding down the bank to the coach, and when it came his turn, he was able to show empty pockets, whereupon the robber asked him what he was traveling on. When properly fleeced, the dudes were told to "just sit around and be comfortable . . . none of you are goin' to get hurt if you act like good little boys and girls!"[93] They were warned "not to make any false moves because my partner in the timber has you covered," but this subterfuge was unnecessary, for these victims were stunned by the sheer nerve of the man behind the black kerchief.

The procedure was repeated as other coaches came up. It is said that the robber occasionally exhibited gallant impulses, although that description hardly fits his character. One such incident involved an elderly lady from the second coach. In her frantic effort to secrete her valuables, she dropped them on the ground, whereupon the robber is said to have handed them back to her, saying: "There, Madame, you keep these. You look as if you need them more than I do." Even harder to believe is the robber's reported behavior toward two pretty girls from the fifth coach. They were crying hysterically over the prospect of losing their watches and jewelry, and he is reported to have said, "Don't cry. You gals are too pretty to be robbed anyway, an' I won't take yer things. Where would ye have hid'em if I wasn't lookin'?" At that hint, the girls proceeded to tuck the trinkets in their stockings, while the robber assured them, "I can't look the other way, but I'll look over yer heads."[94]

Evidently, the robber did joke with his victims as he forced them to come across, which earned him billing as a merry bandit, but he did not do as well as the highwayman of six years before. The newspapers tended to credit him with a larger haul than he actually made, mentioning amounts from $5,000 to $10,000; the loss was actually $915.35 in money and jewelry valued at $130. That averaged out as $6.35 each for the 165 passengers robbed, which was only half as much as taken in 1908. This robber was also less discreet. He was photographed by several tourists: Miss Ethel Slater of Fairfield, Iowa, took his picture standing by the loot-covered blanket, while Miss Estelle Hammond of London, Miss Anna L. Squire of Chicago, and, of course, our Mr. Allinder, all took his picture sorting the loot.[95] A Rev. John D. Bostwick is even credited with doing a rough pencil sketch and noting down details of the robber's clothing, and none of these activities, so fraught with danger to himself, drew a rebuke.

No more coaches arrived after the fifteenth was robbed, simply because driver Billie Frazier caught a glimpse of the proceedings and turned his rig around. On the way back to Old Faithful to report the holdup he warned other stagecoach drivers and thus stopped the movement of vehicles toward West Thumb. The robber waited for some time, meanwhile sorting the valuable part of his loot into a gunny sack; then he swung the bag over his shoulder and backed cautiously into the woods.

Highwayman Ed Trafton sorting his loot after the 1914 holdup, as photographed by a tourist he had robbed. *From a snapshot given to Judge Meldrum.*

In time, soldiers arrived, and with them were Scouts James McBride and Raymond Little. They soon found the tracks of two horses about one-half mile south of Shoshone Point, and far to the west they came upon the tracks of a man traveling on foot. They followed both. The horse trail passed out of the Park through Winegar Hole, across Squirrel Meadows to Conant Creek and on to the vicinity of Driggs, Idaho, while the man-made tracks led directly to a cabin on Conant Creek, eleven miles south of the southwest corner of the Park. No one was in the cabin but it was known to belong to Charles Erpenbach, a half-wild trapper and hunter who lived there with his niece. The peculiarities of this man (he always traveled afoot as rapidly as a man on horseback, and was always armed and accompanied by vicious dogs) made him a likely suspect. The cabin was staked out for eleven days before Erpenbach returned and could be taken into custody. Though he disclaimed any knowledge of the holdup, he was charged with it and required to post bail.

Actually, it was the horses that led to the apprehension of the true robber, though not at once. Because the left hind foot of one animal was unshod, it was easy to backtrack them. The trail made prior to the robbery led back to the camp of a Mexican sheepherder, Jesus Martinez. He remembered the horses, and the man who was with them, for a very good reason; he, too, had been robbed. The man with the horses had come into his camp on the evening of July 23, had spent the night there, and then had repaid that hospitality the next morning by taking half the sheepherder's food, a pack saddle, and his fine riding saddle, at gunpoint.

From the camp the scouts backtracked the horses into Jackson Hole, where it was found they had been stolen on the night of July 22 from a party of Idaho men camped near the outlet of Jackson Lake. The simultaneous disappearance of one Ed Harrington, who had been staying at Ben Sheffield's place nearby, developed another likely suspect.

Ed Harrington was an alias for Edward B. Trafton, a member of the old Conant gang of poachers who had troubled the southern marches of the Park for many years. He may have been in that country as early as 1880,[96] and it is certain that he knew it well. Trafton was born in Missouri's Ozark Mountains about 1853, and an early inclination toward petty theft kept him in constant trouble up to the time he attempted to imitate the James and Younger boys, only to find that train robbery is sometimes expiated in the penitentiary. Thereafter, he stayed out of serious trouble until 1909, when he undertook to rob his mother-in-law of $10,000 in Denver, Colorado.

That crime was both despicable and stupidly engineered and brought him a five-year sentence at Canon City (his wife got three years for her part), and he was still a parolee when he held up the Yellowstone stages.

When he reached Driggs, Idaho, after the holdup, Trafton sent some money to his wife so she could join him, and together they went to Denver, where he stole an expensive automobile. On their return to Idaho, Trafton heard of the arrest of Erpenbach on suspicion of being the Yellowstone Park robber, and decided to clear himself at the trapper's expense. He prepared a suicide note in which Erpenbach supposedly admitted the park robbery, and with that in his pocket sneaked back to the cabin on Conant Creek, intending to kill that innocent man and plant the note on him. But Erpenbach, a naturally suspicious man, having been taken once by surprise was not sleeping in his cabin but in the woods outside. He saw Trafton first, got the drop on him, and found the suicide note.

Erpenbach's first inclination was to shoot Trafton and "plant him out in the yard where he could keep track of him," but the would-be murderer pleaded so eloquently for his life that he allowed him to go. However, the web Trafton had spun was fast enmeshing him. He got a job on an Idaho ranch but paid too much attention to the rancher's wife and had to leave, selling the two stolen horses at an auction as he went. The horses were bought by the neighbor of the man they had been stolen from in Jackson Hole, and Trafton was thereby linked to several crimes. His wife, angered by the attempted infidelity, gave evidence against him, and Erpenbach came forward with information he had wrung out of Trafton in the course of their heart-to-heart talk in the moonlight.

It only remained for Special Agent James Melrose of the Department of Justice to add these revelations to the fragmentary information he already had to complete the case against Trafton. Federal officers arrested him at Rupert, Idaho, on May 22, 1915. he was tried in the federal district court at Cheyenne, Wyoming, and sentenced on December 14, 1915, to serve five years in Leavenworth penitentiary. The charge against Erpenbach was dropped.

There is an interesting sequel to this story. Trafton served his sentence, then returned to the Jackson Hole country where he prowled around for a time in the hope of revenging himself on Charles Erpenbach and Scout Raymond Little. Failing in that, he went to California, where he dropped dead of apoplexy on a Los Angeles street August 16, 1922. In its notice of his death, the *Los Angeles Times* quoted the following from a letter found in his pocket:

"This will introduce Edwin B. Trafton, better known as Ed Harrington. Mr. Trafton was the man from whom Owen Wister modeled the character of the Virginian."[97]

As to the truth of that claim, it can only be said that Owen Wister was once asked if he knew the Virginian, and his answer was, "As well, I hope, as a father should know his son." That statement seems to say that the famous prototype of all the cowboy heroes was a creation of Wister's imagination rather than a flesh-and-blood person. But one does find, in Wister's book, some grounds for concluding that Trafton may have been the model for Trampas; even their names sound similar.

The last stagecoach robbery in the Park, and perhaps the last in this country, took place July 9, 1915, approximately one mile south of Madison Junction. Compared with the holdups of 1908 and 1914, this one was anticlimactic.

One coach was allowed to pass unmolested, then five were halted and passengers robbed of about $200. The highwayman might have done better (the procession of coaches on the road that morning extended nearly twelve miles) except that F. Jay Haynes, president of the Yellowstone Western Stage Company, was near the head of the column in his light buggy. He saw what was happening and was able to turn around and drive back to the road camp at Madison Junction to telephone an alarm to the soldiers. Meanwhile, a Mr. Rice jumped out of a coach and ran back along the road warning all passengers. The robber fired one shot at him, decided the game was up, and fled into the woods. Tracks were found leading from the scene of the robbery to the nearby road camp, but the culprit was not apprehended. Bernard Baruch, who was one of the victims of the last robbery, commented, "It was the best $50 I ever spent."[98]

In retrospect, what meaning did the Yellowstone experience, whatever its nature, have for the thousands who rode and tramped "all in ceaseless course, around the Park"? Of course they had fun, made acquaintances, and were involved in adventures, but what deep meaning did it hold for them? One tourist wrote: "I have just completed the six days' circular journey by stage through the Yellowstone National Park. I am moved to admiration, but still more to awe,"[99] while another visitor felt that

> while admitting that there is a great deal of interest to attract in the Yellowstone Park, and conceding to it its well merited nickname of Wonderland, I reserve to myself the privilege of expressing disappointment. My expectations were not realized. This may arise from the fact of having heard so much of its splendor and wonder before my

visit. I believe this to be the opinion of most who came here, but they do not express it as it is considered bad taste to do aught else but admire and praise.[100]

We also have the opinion of the cowboy artist, J. M. Moore, who firmly believed some visitors could appreciate the Yellowstone and some could not. As he bluntly put it, "No man that's a narrow-minded, big-headed damn fool can grasp it!"[101]

What did it mean? Perhaps Olin D. Wheeler came as close to an answer as anyone will when he wrote: "It may, indeed, be all things to all men inasmuch as every type of humanity, every individual, may place his own interpretation upon what he finds here."[102]

CHAPTER 16

FORT YELLOWSTONE IDYLL

I can't get 'em up, I can't get 'em up,
I can't get 'em up in the morning;
I can't get 'em up, I can't get 'em up,
I can't get 'em up at all.
The corporal's worse than the private,
He won't obey the call;
The sergeant's worse than the corporal
And the captain's worse than all.[1]

L
ong before Irving Berlin turned that army doggerel into his hit tune of World War I ("Oh! How I Hate to Get Up in the Morning") tradition had established it as the bugle's message at reveille. It was that nearly forgotten nonsense from his soldiering days that surfaced in the mind of Carl E. Schmide as the clear bugle notes rang across the parade ground on the crisp morning air. Having had quite enough of his uncomfortable attic room (all the desk clerk had to offer him at his late arrival the evening before), he arose, dressed, and was standing at the window contemplating the stately buildings of officers' row when a troop of cavalry trotted into view, the white stable coveralls of the men blending with their white mounts. Another day was beginning at Fort Yellowstone.

Fort Yellowstone from Capitol Hill about 1903. The salute cannon is at left. *From a stereo view by Underwood & Underwood, New York.*

The fort was established May 11, 1891, in accordance with General Orders No. 45, Headquarters of the Army.[2] It provided permanent facilities for the troops detailed to the administration of Yellowstone National Park, replacing the temporary structures of Camp Sheridan after the decision was reached to retain the army in the management of the Park (the use of the military for that purpose had originally been looked upon as a temporary expedient). The "new post," as the soldiers called it for many years, soon came to be known as a comfortable place, perhaps as much for its pleasant surroundings and relaxed discipline as for the good facilities provided there. Duty at Fort Yellowstone was always a welcome relief from hard soldiering on the hot and sultry plains, or in the equally hot and dusty Southwest. For many officers and enlisted men, Fort Yellowstone provided the idyllic moment of a military career.

Soon after Captain George S. Anderson took over management of the Park in February 1891 he was asked to report upon the site tentatively selected by his predecessor for the new buildings. This location, on the eastern edge of the Hotel Terrace, met with his approval and was adopted, allowing construction to start that summer. Though the initial work provided for only one troop, the plans were drawn to allow for eventual expansion into a two-troop post.[3] Twelve buildings were completed and put to use that fall. These were a guardhouse with a capacity of fifteen prisoners, an administration building containing three offices, a pair of duplex quarters for officers, a troop barracks for sixty men, commissary, quartermaster storehouse, granary, bakery, stable, and two quarters for noncommissioned officers (see numbers 1-12 on the plan of Fort Yellowstone, 1894).[4]

The quarters for noncommissioned officers were known, collectively, as "soap-suds row" because the wives of those men usually supplemented inadequate army pay by taking in washing or doing ironing. Many of the women were former laundresses whose official status with the army was ended by an order of June 18, 1878, but who had remained by marrying soldiers. They were hard-working, respectable women who raised good families.[5]

The one-troop establishment was completed in 1893 by the addition of a ten-bed hospital, quarters for the hospital sergeant, and a hay shed capable of storing 150 tons of feed. The post was supplied with water taken from Clematis Creek, above the McCartney cabin, and a small sewerage system served the troop barracks (all the residences had earth-closets in the backyard in that day). Overall, the appearance was somewhat austere; the white-painted buildings with

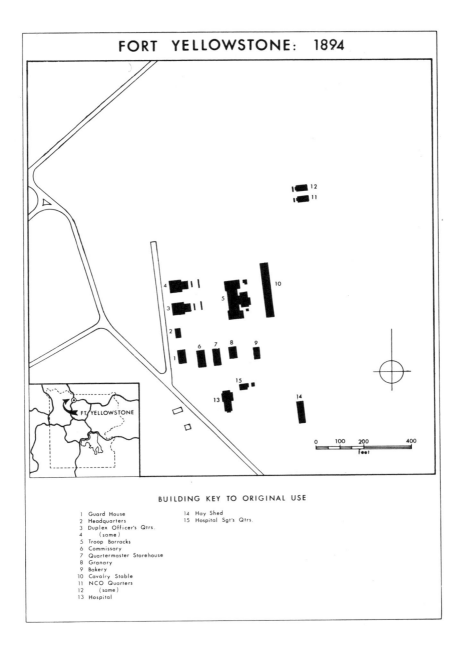

FORT YELLOWSTONE: 1894

BUILDING KEY TO ORIGINAL USE

1 Guard House
2 Headquarters
3 Duplex Officer's Qtrs.
4   (same)
5 Troop Barracks
6 Commissary
7 Quartermaster Storehouse
8 Granary
9 Bakery
10 Cavalry Stable
11 NCO Quarters
12   (same)
13 Hospital

14 Hay Shed
15 Hospital Sgt's Qtrs.

FORT YELLOWSTONE: 1904

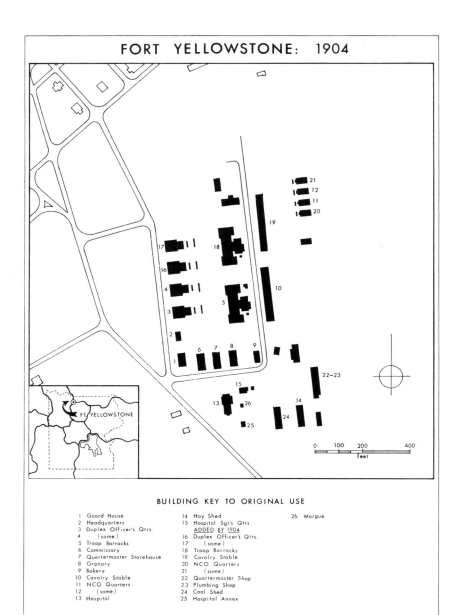

BUILDING KEY TO ORIGINAL USE

1 Guard House	14 Hay Shed
2 Headquarters	15 Hospital Sgt's Qtrs.
3 Duplex Officer's Qtrs.	ADDED BY 1904
4 (same)	16 Duplex Officer's Qtrs.
5 Troop Barracks	17 (same)
6 Commissary	18 Troop Barracks
7 Quartermaster Storehouse	19 Cavalry Stable
8 Granary	20 NCO Quarters
9 Bakery	21 (same)
10 Cavalry Stable	22 Quartermaster Shop
11 NCO Quarters	23 Plumbing Shop
12 (same)	24 Coal Shed
13 Hospital	25 Hospital Annex

26 Morgue

their red tin roofs[6] stood nakedly in a wasteland of disintegrating hot spring formation. The streets were au naturel, paralleled by board-walks only where absolutely necessary, while landscaping was a thing of the future.

Funds were made available in 1897 for increasing the size of Fort Yellowstone to accommodate two troops. Another pair of duplex officers' quarters, a second troop barracks, stable, and two more noncommissioned officers' quarters were added which, with the addition of several service structures and a post exchange, brought the facilities to the stage shown on the plan of Fort Yellowstone, 1904.

The construction of an adequate water system by the Corps of Engineers in 1902-03 had several beneficial effects. The old water system, with its 100,000-gallon covered reservoir in Clematis Gulch, barely met the demand for potable water, so that lawn watering was out of the question; but the new supply, taken from Glen Creek and the Gardner River, was adequate for all of the domestic needs of the fort and the concessioners, with water to spare for irrigation and power generation. Thus, landscaping and electric lighting was at last a possibility.

Control of the dust nuisance from the parade ground—that "attractive bit of open sand, several acres in extent"—was accomplished by hauling enough topsoil from the hill north of the fort to spread a one-half-foot layer over the entire parade ground; that was covered with stable manure, seeded, and watered by a system of irrigation ditches fed from a circular fountain located in front of the U.S. commissioner's residence.[7] In time, Major Pitcher could report "a fair crop of grass and clover . . . where it is hoped that we will eventually produce . . . lawn." It was an improvement of which the editor of the *Gardiner Wonderland* remarked: "The change that has been wrought in the face of nature on the old 'formation' at Mammoth Hot Springs is truly remarkable."[8]

Meanwhile crews of the Corps of Engineers (Captain Chitten-den's men) had laid out formal streets and provided concrete sidewalks (each totaling nearly two miles in length). These much-needed improvements were augmented by a landscaping plan furnished gratuitously by Mr. Warren H. Manning of Boston. Some of Mr. Manning's plan was never carried out, and that is perhaps as well, for neither his extensive groves nor the semiformal walks to scenic points would have been more than an intrusion upon the naturally open scene.[9]

The settlement was also provided with series street lights, energized from a hydroelectric plant located about 500 feet west of the present plant (which replaced it in 1909). The first powerhouse was a two-story frame building with two 50 kw Pelton-driven generators below and quarters for the operators above. The output also provided electricity for lighting the buildings of the fort, and an act of Congress, approved March 3, 1903, allowed the sale of surplus power to private users at cost, plus a small depreciation charge.[10]

In 1905, the small building that had housed the post exchange was replaced by a fine structure that also contained a gymnasium (building number 28), and two years later, when the cavalry stable built in 1897 was destroyed by fire, a larger frame stable was erected on the site (building number 29). Another complex of buildings came into being between 1903 and 1908 with construction of a stable, wagon sheds, and a bunkhouse for the Quartermaster Department. They were located southeast of Capitol Hill and were always referred to as the wagon-train outfit.

It was the work completed in 1909 that gave Fort Yellowstone its characteristic appearance. Seven stone buildings were added: a three-story, two-troop barracks (the present administration building), a BOQ or bachelor officers' quarters (now the park museum), a duplex to house two captains, a field officers' quarters (presently the residence of the park superintendent, two large cavalry stables, and a combined blacksmith shop and stable guard. These structures are, respectively, numbers 32, 36, 35, 34, 30, 31, and 33 on the plan of Fort Yellowstone, 1914.

The stonework for the 1909 buildings was done by Scottish masons using sandstone quarried from the hillside between the Gardner River and the present campground. Sixty years of exposure to sun, wind, and rain have given those walls the same gray-and-tan coloration as the cliffs of nearby Mount Everts; otherwise, time seems hardly to have touched them. Even the severe earthquake of August 17, 1959, did no serious damage to the stone buildings of Fort Yellowstone, very likely because of the caution of the builders.

One of the men on that project was Herb French, of Gardiner, a teamster who was employed hauling building materials from the railhead. His first load was cement—120 sacks, on a wagon and trailer pulled by six big horses. At the fort he was told to unload where the carpenters were preparing forms for the foundations of the big barracks, but, as he was driving around the northeast corner of the staked site, a front wheel of the trailer broke through the formation, exposing a large cavern which proved to be one of the solution caves and passages by which Clematis and Primrose creeks pass under the Hotel Terrace. Forewarned by that fortunate accident, the engineer in charge of the work was able to fill the cavern beneath that corner of the building, and as a further precaution the footings for all the stone

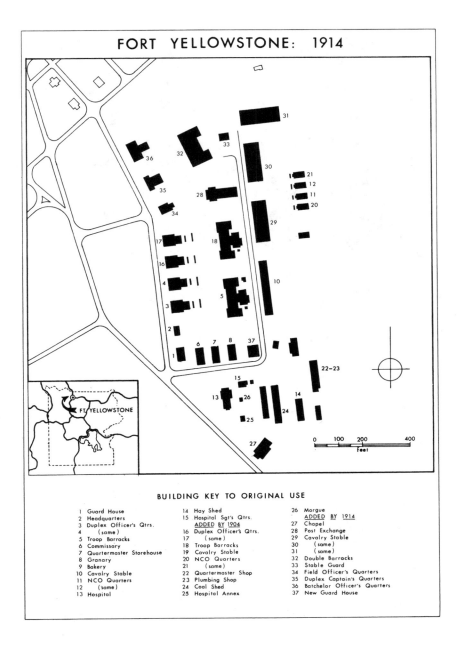

FORT YELLOWSTONE: 1914

BUILDING KEY TO ORIGINAL USE

1 Guard House	14 Hay Shed	26 Morgue
2 Headquarters	15 Hospital Sgt's Qtrs.	ADDED BY 1914
3 Duplex Officer's Qtrs.	ADDED BY 1904	27 Chapel
4 (same)	16 Duplex Officer's Qtrs.	28 Post Exchange
5 Troop Barracks	17 (same)	29 Cavalry Stable
6 Commissary	18 Troop Barracks	30 (same)
7 Quartermaster Storehouse	19 Cavalry Stable	31 (same)
8 Granary	20 NCO Quarters	32 Double Barracks
9 Bakery	21 (same)	33 Stable Guard
10 Cavalry Stable	22 Quartermaster Shop	34 Field Officer's Quarters
11 NCO Quarters	23 Plumbing Shop	35 Duplex Captain's Quarters
12 (same)	24 Coal Shed	36 Batchelor Officer's Quarters
13 Hospital	25 Hospital Annex	37 New Guard House

Interior of the Fort Yellowstone post exchange, probably in 1901.

Soldiers on outpost duty at Norris Station in 1917. *From Corps of Engineers Photograph no. 7G la.*

structures were enlarged and reinforced.[11] Thus, they were strong enough to stand the stresses of the Park's great earthquake.

The only structures of importance erected during the last nine years of the fort's existence were the "new" guardhouse (now the jail), the "new" hospital, both completed in 1911, and a hospital annex and post chapel in 1913. The chapel was the last building constructed by the army at Fort Yellowstone, and it remains both in its architectural features and its setting the most beautiful structure in the Park. The fort was complete.

At the end of the army period, Fort Yellowstone consisted of three groups of structures: the main post with a capacity of four troops of cavalry, the buildings southeast of Capitol Hill which housed the wagon train, and the old Camp Sheridan buildings, home of the packtrain after 1909. The permanent buildings of the post (this excludes Camp Sheridan) represented an investment of nearly $552,000; add to that $75,000 for utilities and a like amount for the improvement of the parade ground, sidewalks, roads, and street lighting, and the total expended by the War Department in the construction of this facility for the administration of Yellowstone National Park was about $700,000.[12] To the physical plant described for the fort proper must be added a post cemetery somewhat south of the Camp Sheridan site, a post garden two miles north of the fort on the Gardner River, and a target range near the north entrance to the Park.

The garrison of Fort Yellowstone consisted of from one to four troops of United States Cavalry. The outfits detailed for service in the Park from 1890 to 1918 were the First, Third, Fourth, Fifth, Sixth, Seventh, Eighth, Eleventh, Thirteenth, and that odd hybrid, the Yellowstone Park Detachment. (See Appendix C, Table IV, for a listing of units by years.) These were mostly proud regiments of "regulars"—the First had memories going back to March 2, 1833, when it was organized as the Regiment of Dragoons for service on the high plains, while all the regiments through the Sixth had seen service in the Civil War. The Seventh and Eighth were organized July 28, 1866, specifically for service in the West, and the Eleventh and Thirteenth (organized February 2, 1901, for service in the Philippine Islands) were an outgrowth of the war with Spain.[13] The Yellowstone Park Detachment was an experimental unit composed of men selected from the old cavalry regiments on the basis of their individual qualifications for service in Yellowstone Park. From it came many of the men who made up the first ranger force under National Park Service administration.

Fort Yellowstone was established as a one-troop post, yet it functioned on a two-troop basis until 1897 through the continued use of the temporary facilities at Camp Sheridan. Captain Anderson's Troop I (Sixth Cavalry) occupied the new post the year around, while Captain Scott's Troop D spent the summer season in a tent encampment at Nez Perce Creek in the Lower Geyser Basin, nearer to the scene of any emergencies in the interior of the Park, and were quartered in the old Camp Sheridan buildings from early October to early June. For a few years after the enlargement of Fort Yellowstone in 1897, the two troops stationed in the Park could winter together in the new facilities; but in 1904 and 1905, when the park command was increased to four troops, the Camp Sheridan buildings were again put in use as winter quarters (one of the extra troops summered at the outlet of Yellowstone Lake while the other was scattered throughout the Park in small details at the various outposts). However, that was an unsatisfactory arrangement, and Fort Yellowstone was returned to a two-troop basis until 1910 (in fact, one troop in 1906). With the increased facilities made available through the construction of the stone buildings in 1909, Fort Yellowstone functioned as a four-troop post until its abandonment, with the Camp Sheridan buildings given over entirely to the use of the packtrain.

The officers and men who made up the famous cavalry regiments were Old Army—something that has been aptly described as "a strange mixture of Minnesota farm boys and New Jersey clerks, toughs and drunkards, teachers and lawyers."[14] They differed from today's soldiers in their motivation; it was not the necessity of service that brought the trooper of that period into the ranks, but the tug of adventure, the urge to escape, and the desire for security. The typical enlisted man of the Old Army was the eager lad from Maine whose head was addled by the echoes of that Civil War refrain, "If you want to have a good time, jine the cavalry!"; the moonfaced German who left home and an unfaithful wife for the solace of hard, isolated duty, and the tough old regular with the hash marks of his reenlistments from cuff to elbow, for whom there never had been any life but soldiering. A sergeant who served with the First Cavalry in the Park wrote:

> Thirteen dollars a month was not much inducement, but the cavalry branch of the service was very popular in the early days with the daring and the romantic. And may I say we were exceedingly proud of our personnel.[15]

The standard adhered to by recruiting officers when enlisting men for the cavalry arm of the service indicates the lean, wiry type was preferred: five feet five to five feet ten, less than 150 pounds in weight, and from eighteen to thirty-five years old.[16] These men came to the Park as "boys in blue," wearing the post Civil War uniform. Rudyard Kipling, that Boswell of the British soldier, met two on patrol on the Mammoth terraces when he visited the Park in 1889. He described them as "in a very slovenly uniform, dark blue blouse and light blue trousers, unstrapped, cut spoon-shape over the boot, cartridge belt, revolver, peaked cap and worsted gloves. . . .By the mercy of Allah!" Later on he met a mounted trooper in dusty blouse and grey campaign hat, whose whalebone poise convinced Kipling the American cavalryman could ride even though he "keeps his accouterments pig, and his horse, cow fashion."[17] During the years the cavalry patrolled the Park, the all-blue uniform was replaced by the blue blouse and khaki breeches of the Spanish-American War period, and that was supplanted in turn by the olive drab uniform of World War I, with its high-collared blouse, wraparound leggings, and campaign hat.

The officers of the cavalry regiments prior to the war with Spain were of two types: battle-wise veterans of the Civil War who, as often as not, had risen from the ranks to captain or major or colonel and then had accepted a lesser commission in the token postwar establishment; and bright, young "shave-tails" fresh from West Point. Later, after retirement had removed the old veterans, the regular officers were all academy-trained professionals—a tight and competent brotherhood. Officers had to subsist themselves and even furnish their own uniform, arms, horse, and equipment out of meager pay, and where there was a family to support, austerity often became genteel poverty. The Park was fortunate that the officers who sought service in the cavalry were adventurous, bright spirits, and it was twice favored in those who were selected as acting superintendents. Of eleven officers who had charge of affairs in the Park, five were superior administrators, and it is hardly a surprise to find that five were decorated heroes (three received the Congressional Medal of Honor) and six attained general rank in the course of their military careers; indeed, one (S.B.M. Young) reached the pinnacle as chief of staff of the army.[18]

Administrative ability at the top was important, but no more so than the relationship between company officers and their men. Kipling remarked on it after talking with a captain he met at Mammoth Hot Springs. He says:

> He began to talk of his troop as I have heard his brethren in India talk. Such a troop, built up carefully and watched lovingly, "not a man that

I would wish to exchange and I believe, not a man that would wish to leave on his own account. We're different, I believe, from the English. Your officers value the horses, we set store on the men. We train them more than we do the horses."[19]

A private soldier said it another way in his letter to the editor of his hometown newspaper: "Capt. G. L. Scott is our troop commander and is beloved of all his men. Our lieutenants . . . are both strict in military affairs and hold the respect of their troop."[20] That sentiment was sincere.

The routine at Fort Yellowstone was often easygoing, and necessarily so. The effective strength of the troop at headquarters (sixty men, if none were in the hospital, the guardhouse, or "over-the-hill") was reduced in summer by from fifteen to twenty men assigned to outposts in the interior of the Park; thus, with the kitchen crew, the farrier, company clerk, and stable detail deducted, there was only half a troop to mount guard and patrol the terraces. Understandably, there was little drill during "the season" and a minimum of the ceremonies dear to the heart of the military. Even the necessity for turning out an occasional honor guard to welcome a V.I.P. required difficult readjustments.

But protection of the terraces did not suffer. Captain Moses Harris established the army's unvarying policy toward visitors in 1886 by requiring his men to "conduct themselves in a courteous and polite, but firm and decided manner" when engaged in the enforcement of their orders.[21] That they were courteous and polite is frequently attested: "The soldier who escorted us was very polite, but would not permit us to carry away a bit of clay." "The collection of specimens in the Park is beset with difficulties, as the soldiers are ever watchful, and you are politely informed that you must not take anything." "It depresses one to be constantly under the watchful eyes of the soldiers. They always treat you courteously enough, but for all that . . . " (This last witness needed watching, by the evidence of his own diary, so he had no real basis for complaint.) James B. Wasden, who was a subforeman on a park road crew in 1896, liked to tell how the "firm and decided" part of the policy was once applied. The culprit was an Englishman of royal blood, who was determined to have a souvenir from the terrace formation. According to the story,

The soldier on duty had warned him once. Even a second time the soldier asked him to desist. The third time, he collared the Englishman and started for the guardhouse. "I'll say old boy, you can't do this to me," objected the Englishman, "I'm a Count, I'm a Count." "I don't give a damn," said the soldier, "you only count one here."[22]

Guard-mount ceremony at Fort Yellowstone, 1910. The officer of the day (far left) is 2nd Lieut. Jonathan M. Wainright, later World War II hero. *From a photograph provided by G. W. Petrach.*

A less serious moment on the Fort Yellowstone parade ground—a footrace at the Fourth of July celebration in 1917. Compare the rebuilt hotel in background with original construction in the photograph above.

The shorthandedness typical of the summer season at Fort Yellowstone made guard duty more onerous than it should have been. As one of his arguments for the assignment of an extra troop of cavalry or a company of infantry to the Park, Acting Superintendent S.B.M. Young stated: "It is necessary to require all extra and daily duty men to do regular guard duty in order that all may have two or three nights in bed.[23] The guard detail had to be large enough to provide proper relief for the sentries posted at several places about the fort. Thus, a soldier "walked post" only a part of his twenty-four-hour tour of guard duty, spending the off hours lounging at the guardhouse (which was also the lockup for any malefactors—soldier or civilian— who might be under detention).

Prior to 1911 the Fort Yellowstone guardhouse was the south-ernmost building of "officers' row" (the buildings fronting on the parade ground). It was perfectly situated to control traffic into the Park from the north, for the road did not enter the Mammoth Hot Springs area as it does now but made a wider sweep around the tree-covered base of the Hotel Terrace, entering the fort from the south at the eastern base of Capitol Hill. This made it possible for one of the men at the guardhouse to contact each incoming party, stagecoaches included. The name of the driver and passengers (with stagecoaches, only the number of passengers was required), type of rig, destination, and firearms carried was entered in a large leather-covered ledger. Guns were either held at the guardhouse (when the party intended to return by that route) or were sealed with the kind of red tape then commonly used to bind packets of government documents (the knot was secured with a sealing wax). Since this method was not tamper-proof, persons carrying guns through the Park had to stop at each outpost enroute so that the noncommissioned officer in charge could examine the seal, and a form, signed at each checkpoint, had to be turned in at the exit station.

Captain Anderson found even that elaborate procedure in-sufficient, stating in his report for 1897:

> The custom of carrying firearms through the park has been almost universal among those who live in the neighboring states and travel in their own conveyances or on saddle animals accompanied by pack animals. During the first half of the season it was found that many firearms, fastened with red tape and sealing wax at the point of entry, had broken seals at the point of exit. In many cases it was evident that the seals were broken by accident; others showed signs of having been broken and resealed. To remedy this a new system of sealing has been adopted similar to that used by express companies, and the practice of using red tape and sealing wax has been discontinued.[24]

This was the origin of the practice of sealing firearms with wire secured by lead seals—a technique passed on to the National Park Service.

The guardhouse was the setting for one of Jack Haynes' stories of his boyhood at Mammoth Hot Springs. His father's photographic studio in the center of the parade ground, facing the National Hotel, was Jack's home each summer season, and, boy-like, he was all over the place. A favorite spot was the brow of Capitol Hill, where the cannon stood which was used to fire the sunrise and sunset salutes. This also overlooked the guardhouse and was so close Jack came to the conclusion that his father's trapgun could flip a pebble onto its tin roof. So it became a favorite sport to slip up there, emplace the trap gun in the cover of tall grass, and direct a harassing fire upon the building below him. The puzzlement of the sentry walking his post before the guardhouse, and of an occasional relief man, made it a delightful sport—until the day when Jack was "taken from the rear" and hustled off to face Captain Anderson.

During the slack season in the Park, the troop of cavalry that summered at Nez Perce Creek returned to Fort Yellowstone. Then there were men enough for the daily routine and some drill also. Private Walsh says:

> Our drilling instruction consists of marching on foot, also mounted, saber exercise and carbine manual. We also go through the same drill on horseback as an infantryman does on foot. Our horses are good, all-around animals, good jumpers, runners and drillers. Each horse understands the trumpet calls, all as well as we do and some much better.[25]

There was also mounted pistol practice, usually on the little flat east of the present automobile campground, and target practice on the rifle range.[26] Beyond that, no small part of a trooper's day was devoted to the care of his mount.

The trooper went to the stable at 5:30 A.M. to grain his horse. (The sixty horses of a troop were stalled there by twos, with a kicking bar between each pair.) At 7 A.M. the cavalryman was back to water his mount, and a half hour later he curried and inspected, and then either saddled up for patrolling, practice marching, or mounted drill as was prescribed in the orders of the day or turned his animal into the corral behind the stable. If it was a day of drill, the morning period ended at 11 A.M., at which time the trooper took his mount to the picket line— a shoulder-high rope stretched behind the stable—where one-half hour was spent in a thorough grooming prior to feeding and watering. The cavalryman's day concluded with another stint at the stable, caring for his mount and accouterments, a chore done regardless of his personal fatigue.

Soldiering was not all of life at Fort Yellowstone. The soldiers were organized in a fire brigade, just as government employees at Mammoth Hot Springs are today. Scout Ray Little recalled one turnout in response to a fire call from the Cottage Hotel, which was then (1910) used only as a dormitory during the summer season. The fire brigade responded promptly and managed to suppress the fire (a small blaze in the attic) with a maximum of confusion. As Ray told it, the eager "swaddies" were busy carrying mattresses down the stairs and throwing chairs and china washbasins down from the second-story balcony when there was a diversion that temporarily stopped the show. A young lady known as "Tweet-tweet," who worked a night shift at the National Hotel, was asleep in one of the upper rooms in a state of undress, and the racket raised by the fire crew frightened her onto the street without thought of apparel. She was quickly supplied with a blanket so the business of fire suppression could go on. The fire fighters were rewarded with a round of beer, but privately the president of the hotel company expressed disappointment that the old log structure had been saved.

The stone barracks constructed in 1909 (the present park headquarters building) was also saved by the prompt action of the army fire brigade. The fire, which originated in the north end of the attic at 11:30 A.M. on July 18, 1911, was not nearly as serious as reported in the *Livingston Enterprise*, which described the building as "gutted." Actually, damage was limited to the charring of a few rafters, but a soldier was seriously injured at the height of the excitement by falling three stories.

An enlisted man's free time could be spent in a variety of ways. There was a day room for reading, letter-writing, and friendly games of pool. (A bowling alley was available in the latter days of the fort.) The post exchange, built in 1905, provided a gymnasium as well as the usual canteen functions: sale of sundries and beer, and a place to play cards (for beer chits, not money; the serious gambling had to be done on the q.t.), and, as early as 1903, moving pictures were shown on Thursday evenings. Attendance was good because, as one man said, "Most any kind of an entertainment is interesting these long winter nights.."[27]

Among other diversions on the post were the occasional dances arranged by the social circle. These could be gotten up to honor almost any date or event, such as the transfer of "Sgt. Jones ('Dobbie') and Pvt. Davis of Troop B." In 1895, the troop quartered

Soldiers fighting roof fire in the north wing of the barracks at Fort Yellowstone, July 18, 1911.

An anonymous employee's impression of the latter years of the Cottage Hotel— another structure saved by the Fort Yellowstone fire brigade. *From the author's collection.*

in the old Camp Sheridan buildings constructed a fine dancing pavilion, and it was "crowded with tourists and campers," to the great delight of the soldiers. Of this amusement, one lad wrote

> Our music was the finest. . . . On one occasion we had the ladies' orchestra from Butte, Mont. We also had the Boy Band from the same place. At other times our troop soldiers furnished whatever music was needed. We have some very fine talent in the troop. . . . Our officers at different times added to the enjoyment of the occasion by appearing with their wives.[28]

After the turn of the century, religious services were held at Fort Yellowstone on Sundays when a minister was available. An Episcopalian missionary—John F. Pritchard, who was known as Whiskey Ike in the upper Yellowstone Valley—served as unofficial chaplain of the post for the last eighteen years the army was there. This was a remarkable accomplishment, for Reverend Pritchard served all the towns upriver from his ranch near present Emigrant, Montana. He was well known at Horr, Aldridge, Cinnabar, Gardiner, and Jardine, as well as Fort Yellowstone, and, though he would take a drink whenever one was offered, he would also go any place in any weather on the Lord's work, and travel in any manner, walking included. He did a great work and was respected for it, despite the sobriquet; in fact, a more perfect shepherd might not have done so well with such sheep as made up his flock. In the early days of this ministry, before construction of that beautiful chapel erected "not only for the soldiers, but for everyone in the Park,"[29] services were held evenings in a troop mess hall, the post exchange, or a private residence.

In season, there were other diversions, such as "rotten-logging" with the young ladies who worked for the hotel company; however, a soldier, or "swaddie," with a monthly pay of only $13 was badly outclassed by "savages" (stagecoach drivers) making from $35 to $75 and their tips. But for those who were unlucky at love there was fishing in the Gardner River, swimming at Bath Lake, and baseball.

Oh, those ball games! Jack Haynes recalled one Fourth of July when the soldiers' team played the concessioners' team. All went well to the fourth inning, when there was an altercation at second base involving the drummer from the hotel orchestra. Three soldiers set upon him, one after the other, and each was rendered hors de combat in his turn, for the second baseman had been a professional prize fighter in Chicago before he drummed in Yellowstone Park. The game was stopped, but isolated contests flared all afternoon. Colonel Lloyd Brett, dining at the residence of the photographic concessioner that evening, was heard to complain that the guardhouse wasn't big enough to hold all the combatants who should have been confined that day.

Of course, liquor may have contributed to the excitement (it was because of just such brawling that the sale of beer to soldiers at the Cottage Hotel had to be stopped), but generally the only place hard liquor could be obtained was the town of Gardiner, where a "collection of groggeries" had crowded so close to the Park that the boardwalk was on the boundary line and the main street was entirely inside. A soldier could get roaring drunk in Gardiner, he could gamble there, and he could patronize the "house" that was reputed to have figured in Calamity Jane's old-age assistance plan.[30]

After the fun, there was always the five-mile hike back to the post, a particularly grim business for some celebrants. A reminder of their misery is a seepage called Whiskey Spring that oozes from a clump of willows near the foot of Soap Hill. For two troopers the hike was a death march: Private Andren Preiber, Troop I, Sixth Cavalry, died of exposure a short distance from town on March 14, 1893, and Private Frank F. Monaghan, Troop H, First Cavalry, disappeared on the evening of November 22, 1910, after starting for Fort Yellowstone in an intoxicated condition. He was listed as a deserter in December, but the recovery of his body from the Gardner River a mile from town cleared up the mystery. Both were buried in the army cemetery a mile south of the fort, facing Jupiter Terrace.

From October 1, 1888, when Private Thomas Horton, Company C, Twenty-second Infantry, was laid to rest in that burying ground, until the army abandoned Fort Yellowstone, fifty-five burials were made there, including thirteen soldiers from detachments stationed in the Park and civilian employees or dependents. Others who died in the area were buried elsewhere. It is interesting to note that accidents caused most of the deaths among soldiers. Of nineteen known to have died in the Park, the cause is recorded for fifteen:[31] exposure (five), drowning (four), snowslides (two), horses (two), gunshot (one), and illness (one), though it is likely this last category should include some of those deaths for which no cause was listed.

Runaways, a cave-in, lightning, pneumonia, cancer, circulatory diseases, typhoid fever, chronic alcoholism, suicide, senility, and a grizzly bear took their toll on the civilian employees; yet those burials, however they remind one of the vicissitudes of life in a rough environment, have not the emotional impact of the disproportionate number of burials of the very young. The families of Fort Yellowstone left their children in that plot of ground: the slight depression in the southeast corner is the grave of an "unknown baby;" a fenced grave is marked tenderly with a pair of worn shoes carved in stone. There was Celia, the daughter of Hospital Steward Veneinan, and Harry, the son of Commissary Sergeant Wilson; scarlet fever took Ralph David Korn, and little Frank Schmidt died of pneumonia. Nor was rank or profession any bulwark against death, for the infants of a lieutenant, a chaplain, and a surgeon were buried there also. One is glad to climb back over the sturdy pipe railing that surrounds the old cemetery and walk away through the tall grass.

Despite the hardships, life at Fort Yellowstone—particularly family life—was normal enough. There was marrying as well as burying, and all the trials and joys in between. A park marriage was usually a private ceremony at the home of a friend, and often had to be repeated north of the Wyoming-Montana line because the license had been obtained in Park County, Montana;[32] however, there was one notable military wedding at the fort.

On September 19, 1914, Kathrine Piercy Edmunds and Captain Albert Ady King, First U.S. Cavalry, were married in the new chapel. The little building was austerely furnished, but its barrenness was hidden with flags and bunting, and by a lavish display of yellowed boughs of aspen along the walls, while the lack of candelabra was offset by placing the candles on stacks of books. Reverend Pritchard, the Episcopalian missionary, officiated at the first wedding in the Yellowstone Park chapel. The distance he had to come (by train from present Emigrant, Montana) made it necessary for him to stay overnight at Fort Yellowstone, so Lieutenant Haserkamp, who was to be the best man, was given the additional chore of looking after the minister. His orders were as unusual as they were necessary: "No drinks until the reception."[33]

Mrs. King found life pleasant at Fort Yellowstone. During the tourist season no leave was granted but there was much company: visitors and friends as house guests. These contacts, and the outdoorsiness of life—carriage rides and picnics during the better months, and sleigh rides and snow sports in winter—softened the isolation of garrison life remote from towns of any consequence. There was also much socializing. Luncheons and dinners were common and no particular strain for families who had domestic help (the Kings had a Chinese cook and a Filipino houseboy, both picked up by the captain while soldiering in the Philippine Islands), but it could be grim business for the overworked wife of a lieutenant. For the officers, there were evenings of poker.

Emerson Hough was intrigued with winter life at Fort Yellowstone, which he thought the "most beleaguered of all the army garrisons." He noted that, with the first snows of winter, everyone turned to skis to get about—the soldiers, the officers, the wives, and the children. He says, "We saw skis and heard ski talk and pondered on stories of ski adventure. . . . The officer who is blessed with children buys skis just as he does shoes, and the porches of the officers' quarters were decorated with graduated collections of skis."[34] Inevitably, there were casualties, including a death that can be attributed to recreational skiing. The victim was Lieutenant Joseph E. McDonald, who triggered a snowslide while skiing off the terraces at the mouth of Clematis Gulch.

The Christmas season took on special importance in such an isolated situation. The following description of a community Christmas party, as George L. Henderson recorded it long ago, doesn't sound so different from similar occasions in recent years. He says:

> The ladies of Fort Yellowstone united in making Christmas a joyful occasion for the Sunday School children. The Christmas tree was brilliantly illuminated and bore an abundance of that fruit which children most desire. Captain Brown made one of the jolliest Saints that ever distributed dolls to the outstretched arms of baby-mothers, so eager to kiss and embrace them. The boys were in raptures over their horns, tin horses, soldiers and locomotives. All were sweetened up to the highest degree ever indicated by any saccarimeters, boys and girls being most accurate ones. When the tree was cleared of its fruit the jolly Saint informed his patrons that there were millions more expecting to see him that night and that he must bid them farewell. "Have you far to go?" enquired a sweet little girl in a voice that indicated both affection and pity for the good, hard-working Saint. This Mother Eve curiosity and sympathy brought the house down with laughter and applause, alike from citizen and soldier. The hoary-headed Saint vanished, surrounded by a halo of glory in the minds of the children, and that he was no mere illusion was evident from the fact that arms and pockets were full of dolls, candies and many other good things. Mrs. W. E. Wilder, although suffering from a sprained ankle, was present and furnished the music to which the school children marched and sang in joyful concert. Mrs. Wilder is very much loved and respected by the children. That night she looked radiant, having had a telegram from Col. Wilder that he was alive and well at Manila."[35]

Summertime brought other pleasures for the children, among them release from school. Though always a tenuous thing and hard to finance, there was usually school. If there was a soldier in the garrison who was qualified to teach, a school could be organized at no more expense than the cost of books and paper; but when there was no enlisted man who could be detailed as teacher, it was necessary for the families to chip in and hire one. A young lady by the name of Anna

Trischman taught school before she became Mrs. Anna K. Pryor, of Pryor Stores, and Mrs. Brandon, who was the wife of a plumber, taught school in the old Camp Sheridan building known as the Beehive. Clarence Scoyen remembers that no teacher could be found in 1910, so most of the children had to be sent away. He went to relatives near Spokane, Washington, for the winter.

Jack Haynes has recalled some of the highlights of summertime in those days. At the foot of Capitol Hill, directly behind his father's photographic studio (in fact, almost upon the site of the Haynes Picture Shop of recent years), was Clark's livery stable, an exciting place to play. There were "rigs" of every sort, strange people, rough talk, and the grimy fascination of blacksmithing. Also, there was a hay-lift (an arrangement of tackle used to put hay into the loft), which was ideal for elevating small passengers heavenward; and there was the watering trough. One of Jack's playmates was Ellen Dean Child, who as the wife of William M. Nichols would later be the Grand Dame of the Yellowstone Park Company; in those days she was an agreeable "buggy horse" in their imaginative play. Properly reined with string, Ellen was "driven" down to the livery stable—until the day Jack tried to make his "horse" drink out of the watering trough.

Another fun place for the children was the Devils Kitchen, atop the Mammoth Hot Springs terraces. Porters from the hotel took parties of tourists into the cavern by a rickety wooden ladder in those days (a practice later discontinued because of the danger of suffocation by carbonic-acid gas), which was scary enough; but Jack had found that it took only a few scraps of lighted paper dropped down behind a party to stir up the bats and create a near-panic among the ladies in that gloomy hole.[36]

Fort Yellowstone was the headquarters for a series of outposts which were collectively the army's means of administering the Park. The outpost system established in the fall of 1886, when Captain Moses Harris sent small detachments to occupy the buildings vacated by assistant superintendents at Norris, Nez Perce Creek, Old Faithful, Riverside on the Madison, Grand Canyon, and Soda Butte on the Cooke City road, was expanded during the following thirty years to keep pace with the development of the Park. By the end of the army period, detachments were stationed at sixteen places in the Park (several were occupied only seasonally), where they were housed in buildings that became the ranger stations of the opening years of National Park Service administration. The pattern thus established has not changed materially through the years.

1. Soda Butte (1886)
2. Grand Canyon (1886)
3. Norris (1886)
4 Riverside (1886)
5. Lower Geyser Basin, or
   Fountain (1886)
6. Upper Geyser Basin, or
   Old Faithful (1886)

SOLDIER STATIONS
Yellowstone Park

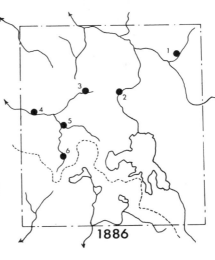

1886

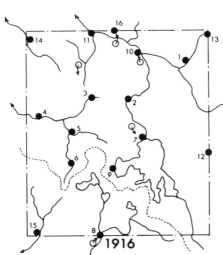

1916

7. Lake Outlet (1887)
8. Snake River (1892 & 1902)
9. Thumb Bay (1897)
10. Tower Fall (1901 & 1907)
11. Gardiner (1903)
12. Sylvan Pass (1904)
13. Cooke City (1904)
14. Gallatin (1908)
15. Bechler (1911)
16. Crevice (1901 & 1912)

The detachments at the "soldiers stations," as the outpost establishments were called, varied in size from as few as two men to as many as fifteen (though the larger number appears to have been used only once, at Old Faithful in the summer of 1888). Ordinarily, a detachment consisted of at least four men, under a noncommissioned officer, during the winter season, with as many more enlisted men in summer as the particular station required. The number of men employed depended somewhat on the number available; hence, in years when Fort Yellowstone was a one-troop post (sixty men), the outposts were minimal—both in the number of detachments and in their strength.

Did the soldiers like the demanding, and often isolated, rugged, even dangerous service so different from the life most of them had known? According to Captain Anderson, the freedom and ease of such a life made outpost duty popular, and he states: "I have no difficulty in obtaining from the best of men applications for this service."[37] Frederic Remington, who got acquainted with the Park's snowshoe cavalry while gathering information for his article, "Policing the Yellowstone," found that the enlisted men liked their rough life in the "remote recesses of the savage mountains," and that they freely applied for such detached service.[38]

Although Captain Harris established six outposts upon taking over the administration of the Park (see upper right, map of soldier stations), only one was maintained throughout the first winter that the army spent in the area. A small detachment remained at Soda Butte, on the road to the Cooke City mines, occupying the frame building that had been used on a year-round basis by assistant superintendents stationed there. The structure taken over by the soldiers stood west of the present road, directly opposite the limestone formation for which the nearby stream is named, and, though constructed of rough-cut lumber, it proved satisfactory during the months of savage cold and deep snows—altogether one of the worst winters ever experienced in the northern Rocky Mountains. The original station was replaced soon after the turn of the century by another identical to the one built at the east entrance in 1904 (the present ranger station at that point).

The poaching activities of William James and his confederates, which came to light early in 1887 (see Chapter 12), pointed up the need for continuous occupancy of the stations at the Grand Canyon and Norris Geyser Basin. Just how the flimsy frame structures at those points were made comfortable for winter use (they had never been considered so by the assistant superintendents) is not known, but detachments were stationed in each the following winter.

The original station at Norris was replaced by a one-and-a-half-story log building in the fall of 1897; after the accidental destruction of the second structure on February 15, 1908, the present one-story, T-shaped log building was erected on the same site.[39] The original station at the Grand Canyon (labeled a "shack" in 1892) stood well back from the west bank of the Yellowstone midway between the Upper Fall and the cascade where Chittenden bridged the river. It was replaced by a log building on the site later occupied by the Haynes Picture Shop (about 500 feet below the Upper Fall), soon after the spur road was constructed to the new hotel site above Lower Fall.

The date of the building of the Riverside soldier station is also uncertain; however, correspondence between W. H. Bassett of Bassett Brothers (operators of a small stage line into the Park from Beaver Canyon on the Utah & Northern Railroad) indicates that the army took over the old Riverside mail station entirely during the summer of 1888, probably in preparation for construction there.[40] The log building that was erected stood 4.0 miles east of the park boundary and somewhat south of the present west entrance road. This location had the advantage of being at the fork in the road (many visitors still preferred the Madison Plateau road built by Superintendent Norris) and was close to a good fording place on the Madison River—an important consideration for patroling the country northward.

The presence of soldiers at the Fountain station in the Lower Geyser Basin in the winter of 1888-89 is known from the assistance rendered to E. C. Culver at the time of his wife's death; so it is probable the log station near the mouth of Nez Perce Creek was built in the fall of 1888, coincident with construction of Riverside station. The Fountain station was erected one-half mile northwest of the site of the station built for the assistant superintendents and occupied by military detachments in 1886 and 1887, on a slight bench and about 200 feet east of the northern junction of the Fountain Freight Road and the main road through the Lower Geyser Basin.

The soldier station in the Upper Geyser Basin was a log structure located on the west bank of the Firehole River opposite the Lion group of geysers. It was close to the site of the Norris cabin (the first building in that part of the Park) and probably on the same site as the frame station built for the assistant superintendents.

Other soldier stations were established as it became necessary to place detachments at other points. A frame building had been erected near the outlet of Yellowstone Lake in the days of the assistant superintendents, but it was used only as a summer station by the army and was replaced by a log station built on the edge of the meadow, opposite the present Lake Lodge—probably in 1891, when the road was constructed from Old Faithful to Lake Hotel by way of Thumb Bay. The new station was not occupied in winter from 1895 to 1898, the detachment occupying, instead, a building known as Mud Geyser station, located on the west bank of the Yellowstone River above the Nez Perce ford (a location that facilitated the patrol of the country east of the river and put the soldiers nearer to the enclosure built in Hayden Valley for trapping the buffalo wintering there). After that project was abandoned there was no real need for a winter station there and the detachment was kept at Lake on a year-round basis.

In 1892 a soldier station was established south of the Park, where Polecat Creek enters the Snake River, to protect the southern part of the Yellowstone National Park Timberland Reserve and to control traffic coming from Jackson Hole (which had been opened up to the people of Wyoming by the construction of the Washakie Military Road). A wagon road roughed out southward from the Thumb into the forest reserve soon linked the Snake River detachment with the Park. After the forest reserve lands were removed from the supervision of the military personnel in Yellowstone Park, there was no need to maintain a soldier station at Polecat Creek; the building there was torn down and its logs hauled to the point where the south boundary of the Park crosses the Snake River. Reassembled there, the building served the detachment stationed at the south entrance until destroyed by fire August 7, 1914. The T-shaped station completed by the end of September served to the end of the army era and was replaced by a two-story, duplex ranger station in the twenties.

The road connecting that outpost with the interior of the Park was sufficiently improved by 1895 to require some control at the point where it joined the belt line at the Thumb, and a detachment was stationed there in tents from 1897 until 1904, when a frame building was erected at that point.

Construction of the last major portion of the belt line (the road between the Grand Canyon and Tower Fall) led to the establishment of an outpost north of the Overhanging Cliff at a point about 500 feet west of the Calcite Springs overlook. This rude log cabin was unsatisfactory and was abandoned in 1907 when the detachment was moved to a frame station built near the junction of the Cooke City road and the belt line. Much of this second soldier station remains in use in the present Tower Junction ranger station.

Development of a formal entrance into the Park at the town of Gardiner, Montana, in 1903, with the attendant investment in landscaping, fencing, ditches, and hay meadow made it desirable to

The original Tower Falls soldier station near Calcite Springs overlook, 1905. This site was abandoned in 1907 when a new station was built at Tower Junction.

Later outpost stations were more pretentious and comfortable. *Photograph by the author.*

station a detachment at that point; a soldier station was built there near the site of the present ranger station. In that year two soldier stations were established on the east boundary of the Park: on Middle Creek, where the new road from Cody, Wyoming, entered the Park, and on Soda Butte Creek, where the Cooke City road left the Park near the northeast corner. The former was called the Sylvan Pass soldier station, although it was not in Sylvan Pass but more than seven miles east of it on the park boundary. The frame station built there in 1904 still serves as the ranger station at that point; however, it is 200 feet north of the original site. The soldier station at the northeast entrance was a log building on the other side of Soda Butte Creek from the present entrance development.

Road construction in the northwest corner of the Park led to the construction of the Gallatin soldier station in 1908; it was destroyed by fire at the very end of the army period and never rebuilt. This building was similar to the soldier station built on Wyoming Creek, in the southwest corner of the Park, in 1911. The latter remains in use as the Bechler ranger station, with altered interior arrangements.

The last soldier station built in the Park was constructed just within the north boundary on Crevice Mountain in 1912. This station provided seasonal quarters for a detachment that had been stationed intermittently at Knowles' cabin at the mouth of Crevice Creek from 1901 on. Soldiers were needed in that area to control local persons interested in reopening the old placer claims there and in poaching within that portion of the Park cut off by the Yellowstone River. With Crevice station the number of outposts had been increased from six in 1886 to sixteen at the end of the army era. Thus perfected, the system of outpost stations became the principal ranger stations of the National Park Service administration which succeeded the army.

The summer encampment at Nez Perce Creek was an essential adjunct of the outpost system in Yellowstone Park. There, on the south bank of the stream, west of the crossing of the present main road, was a tent camp occupied by a troop of cavalry during the busy summer season to provide available manpower in that part of the Park for fighting forest fires. After the construction of the Fountain Hotel in 1890 and the consequent abandonment of the old hotel development near the mouth of Nez Perce Creek (at the site of the Marshall House), the unneeded facilities were turned over to the military and the summer encampment was organized around them. In those years when the Park was garrisoned by only one troop of cavalry, the summer encampment on Nez Perce Creek was not used; when there were more than two troops in the Park, an extra encampment was established near the outlet of Lake Yellowstone.

Supervision of these widely separated detachments was left to the immediate officers, who were required to be almost constantly on the go during the summer season making rounds of the occupied stations. Before the turn of the century, an officer had to share the quarters of the detachment where he happened to be at night; in fact, he might not be that lucky. Captain King used to carry a bedding roll, a frying pan, a pot for coffee, a few supplies, and a fine little fishing rod which separated into one-foot sections. One evening when he had stopped short of the Snake River station, he had just begun to settle himself for the night when a lone rider came along. There were greetings, and as the other man had no camping equipment, King invited him to stop for the night. When assured that his guest was a fisherman he handed him the fishing rod and pointed him toward Snake River to catch something for supper. The man returned with a good string of fish and they had supper; they then shared the captain's bedroll for the night. This incident was typical of the time and the place; until they parted the following morning neither man had bothered to identify himself to the other, and the captain was surprised to find that his guest was Nathaniel S. Thomas, the Episcopal bishop of Wyoming.[41]

The lives of the wandering officers were made a little more comfortable after 1904 by small structures known as "officers' dog houses," furnished to serve as guest quarters for officers and other traveling personnel who might be authorized to use them.[42] It would appear that other than the prescribed use was occasionally made of such facilities, for in 1906 an order was issued specifying that the furnishings were not to be removed from the officers' quarters, nor were they to be used by unauthorized persons.[43]

The men on outpost duty were supplied the regular army ration from the commissary at Fort Yellowstone and were allowed a replacement in kind for any rations they supplied to officers, scouts, teamsters, or other employees entitled to army food while traveling in the Park. The soldiers supplemented their plain army fare by fishing, by charging twenty-five cents per meal to certain civilian employees, and by accepting contributed groceries or purchased items from unauthorized persons who might share their rations. Also, the officers bought young pigs with troop funds and took them to the stations, where the soldiers raised them until ready to be butchered. Then the animals, which had generally become pets, were carried along to adjacent stations for butchering so that the soldiers were spared killing or eating the animals they had raised.[44]

The hospitality of the troopers appears to have been unstinting. One visitor who was traveling through the Park on horseback was caught in a summer downpour as he neared the Norris soldier station. Making for shelter at a gallop, he received a hearty welcome:

> I slipped into the kitchen as one of the soldiers hurried Chub to shelter. A short distance beyond was Norris Geyser lunch station, but I stayed to supper with the soldiers who had the meal already spread on clean oil cloth. The fragrance of bacon, fresh baked bread, jam, fried potatoes and coffee made me hungry as a wolf. This food they gave cheerfully and urged the storm bound stranger to remain the night, longer if he chose. Such was the hospitality proffered. While smoking on the veranda I gave meager news of the outside world and when the rain ceased we all strolled toward the little lunch station where I was to remain for the night at the edge of Norris Geyser Basin.[45]

This incident was by no means singular, and one senses from the tone of a circular of instruction ("no woman will be permitted to enter any station, at any time") that hospitality was sometimes carried too far. As the only exception to that rule, noncommissioned officers could "permit tourists to visit or go through their quarters or stations at any time between the hours of four P.M. and six P.M.[46]

Fort Yellowstone issued a pocket manual to each trooper containing park regulations and instructions for dealing with parties traveling through the Park and spelling out responsibilities of officers, enlisted men, and scouts on duty in the Park.[47] This booklet covered such matters as patroling in summer and winter; relations with the traveling public; care of quarters and government property; and administrative details, particularly reporting. The frequency and extent of the required patroling and the manner of keeping records and reporting left very little to chance; and perhaps necessarily so since there were problems, difficulties, and dangers to which those men were generally strangers. Whether patroling the road, standing bear guard at the hotel garbage dump, or taking a turn at cooking and housekeeping for the detachment, the trooper had guidance. He was told how to make an arrest, what to do with stray stock, how to put out a fire left burning by an overnight camper, when not to use his firearms, and the particular limitations of his authority. As a result, these men did a reasonably good job with very little complaint against them or their activities.

During the busy summer season, morale on the outposts was good. The men were occupied with routine duties and contacts with visitors and other park employees, and were kept on their toes by frequent inspections. Daily contact with neighboring stations in the course of patroling, and the coming and going of teamsters and other government employees, kept these men in touch with their own little world. There was a conviviality that went with summertime and such scenes as this at the Norris Lunch Station:

> Within the homely hostelry all was animation. Cooks, maids, stablemen and porters were dancing a quadrille to the music of a mouth organ, played by a fat, young Irish lad, who sat at the edge of a writing table and stamped time with his heavy boots. The dancers with their ruddy, healthy faces, their hearty laughter, and their gay raiment made a merry scene. Here the soldier found friends and joined in the dance.[48]

In the winter, morale sagged. After the quartermaster's wagon had come with its load of rations, heavy clothing, and skis and had left to come no more that season; when the paymaster's buggy could no longer break a track through the ever-deepening snow; and officers ceased their visits, a curtain of isolation was drawn securely around each outpost, to be broken only by occasional messages over the slender strand of iron wire connecting them by telephone with Fort Yellowstone or by the occasional mail handed along from station to station. In that different world of winter, life sometimes seemed unduly hard, and cabin fever was an ever-present threat.

Winter life at an outpost was a combination of activity and inactivity, of long patrols on skis in bitter weather, and of storm-bound days with nothing to do but read or play cards, of too little mail and too much of the same faces. It is amazing that these men, isolated for months in small groups, managed as well as they did.

The detachments were maintained through the winter to prevent incursions by poachers. While the men on patrol usually did their best, they could seldom equal the frontiersmen in woodsmanship or native craftiness. As Captain Anderson saw it, "My great trouble is to get noncommissioned officers to put in charge of them who are able and disposed to cope with the class of men who form the poaching population.[49] The solution, insofar as there was one, lay in the use of civilian scouts (men who were the equal of the poachers in woodcraft and ability to travel and survive under any winter conditions) to instruct the soldiers, visit them in winter, and lead them on difficult patrols. The scouts passed along the lore of their way of life, the use of skis, how to dress and what to carry on patrols, where to travel and what to look for, and, occasionally, how to get out of a tight scrape. In the process, they developed a nucleus of rangers for the civilian National Park Service when it took over administration from the army.

The men stationed at winter outposts usually wore old woolen breeches and shirts, and were armored against the cold with woolen underwear, blanket coats, fur caps with ear flaps, and woolen mittens.

Soldiers on ski patrol at the Grand Canyon, 1910.

In that day before ski boots, their feet were covered with bulky felt overshoes in which coarse German socks were worn on top of regulation wool socks. Their overshoes were accommodated to the ski by means of a leather housing, which was slipper-like and attached firmly to the ski only under the ball of the foot. Thus, the heel could raise, much as it does when fastened with a modern ski binding set for cross-country travel. The ski, or Norwegian snowshoe, as it was often called, resembled an elongated sled runner.

> It is from eight to ten feet long, about an inch thick at the middle, which is the thickest part, tapering thence front and back. The front end pointed and turned up like that of a Turkish slipper, usually with a slight attempt at ornamentation. At the front end it may be a quarter of an inch thick, but at the heel it runs down to an eighth of an inch except at the center rib or back bone, which is left midway to give it strength. The ski is about three and three quarters inches wide just back of the curved front and runs back in gradual taper to the heel, where it is a trifle less than three and a half inches in width. In the middle or at the balancing point there is a flat place left of full thickness, where the foot rests . . . a foot piece of tin or rubber is usually placed here. Underneath the ski blade and running its full length a shallow groove is cut opposite the rib on top, the groove being meant to give the shoe a better side bite on the snow.[50]

The skis were made of ash, hickory, or pine, ash generally being preferred because it was both tough and light; hickory was heavy and pine was brittle. Regardless of the kind of wood, it was necessary to treat the bottom of the ski with wax or grease which was usually smoothed with a hot flatiron.

The skier used a single, long, hardwood pole, often with a can lid attached near each end. With this held in hand like the balancing pole of a tight-wire artist, he was able to run rapidly down slopes and make turns by setting one end or the other of the pole in the snow and pivoting about that point. On level terrain, the skier progressed by sliding his feet forward alternately, which led some individuals, when they had sledges to pull, to cover all or part of the bottom of the ski with elk hide with the hair pointing backward. This gave better purchase on the snow (it operated very much as the sealskin climbers used by present-day cross-country skiers). On steep slopes, it was necessary either to corduroy up (a slow process of side stepping) or place a clog made of rope or burlap around the ski just behind the foot to prevent the skier from sliding backward. Crude as this sounds, it was a good way to cover the country. The average day's journey was from twelve to twenty miles, and as much as forty miles distance was occasionally made in a day and a night. When conditions were right, that is, with a good downhill course and a crusted surface, speeds of thirty miles an hour could be obtained, and it was not considered uncommon to come down the three-and-one-half miles from the Golden Gate to Mammoth Hot Springs in ten minutes. No wonder one soldier called his skis his "only chance for enjoyment during the winter months."

Patroling the interior of the Park in wintertime would have been too hazardous without the system of shelters (snowshoe cabins) initiated by Captain Boutelle in 1890 (see Chapter 12). During the nineties, the original layout of six cabins was expanded to nineteen, located as follows: on Gneiss Creek, nearly due north of Riverside soldier station; on the Gallatin River, northwest of Crowfoot Ridge; at Gallatin Lake, nearly at the head of the Gallatin River; in Christmas Tree Park, south of Mount Holmes; at Crystal Springs, near Obsidian Cliff on the road between Mammoth Hot Springs and Norris; in a saddle west of Observation Peak in the Washburn Range; on the head of Geode Creek; on Hellroaring Creek, close to the north boundary; on Slough Creek, above what is now called the "transfer"; on the Lamar River below the mouth of Willow Creek; on Astringent Creek, somewhat above the junction with Pelican; at Park Point on Lake Yellowstone; at the mouth of Trappers Creek in the valley of the upper Yellowstone River; on the west shore of Heart Lake; on the Lewis River below the mouth of Aster Creek and probably very near where the Lewis River road camp used to stand; at the "Pot Hole" or Rocky Ford on the Bechler River; near Buffalo Lake on the western boundary; at Shoshone Geyser Basin; and near Mary Lake.[51] The cabins provided shelter and the makings of a fire, and usually a tin-lined grub box with matches, candles, and a few staples; sometimes blankets were provided. Snowshoe cabins were usually spaced out about ten miles, which was considered a day's travel.

One would think that patroling the Park would lead to violent collisions with poachers; however, only one such incident is recorded over nearly thirty years. Jim McBride, an early scout and later chief ranger, told of his narrowest escape.

> It was when I made my second arrest. Two of us found a fellow near Snake River, whom we suspected of possessing furs. I started up to him and he shot at me. I dropped on the ground and lay behind a rock while he fired seven times. When he had emptied his rifle I knock him off his horse with the butt of my gun. We thought he was dead and were debating whether to bury him, bring his body to headquarters or throw it in the Snake River—we had decided upon the latter and were stooping over to pick him up, when he suddenly came to. That meant that we had to bring him to headquarters and we did. For a long time we could not find his traps, but eventually we found them hidden in his flour sack.[52]

Despite a reminiscence to the effect that a soldier patroling out of Riverside station was shot in the back by poachers and not found until the following spring, no lives were lost that way in the Park. What Charley Marble recorded was a badly garbled version of the death of Private David J. Mathews, who froze to death on a mail trip. In his version, Charley says:

> A few days later I saw Sergeant Burns and two soldiers, that Captain Anderson had stationed at Riverside for the winter. They told me that scout Matthews had been killed by some poachers. They sent out ten soldiers from Fort Yellowstone, Mammoth Hot Springs, to search for him. They searched for a week and gave it up. This was about the 15th of February, and on May 10th they found him lying face down on his skis, as he fell forward, shot through the back. His left ear was eaten off and so was the point of his nose. Outside of this he was in perfect condition.[53]

The facts are somewhat different—sadder and less romantic. Of this occurrence, Captain Anderson says:

> In my last report, I noted the death of Private Mathews, of Troop B, Sixth Cav. while on detached service from the Riverside station to the Lower Basin for the mail. A most thorough search for his remains was continued for almost six months after his disappearance. His body was found early in June of this year on the south side of the Gibbon River about three miles from its junction with the Firehole. It was evident that he became lost, and while in that condition became crazed and perished from cold.[54]

As a result of the death of Private Mathews, men traveling in winter were required to go in pairs, and yet, despite that wise precaution, another mail carrier shortly gave up his life quite needlessly. The circumstances were these:

The stations occupied during the winter of 1897-98 (Lower Geyser Basin, Riverside, Soda Butte, Norris, Mud Geyser, and Snake River) were isolated earlier than usual by severe weather that began early in November. The men at the outposts were soon dependent upon the telephone wire and their twice-monthly mail trips for contact with the outside world. The detachments at Mud Geyser and Snake River had an agreement to meet on the fifteenth and thirtieth of each month at a cabin on the shore of Thumb Bay to exchange reports and mail, and the two men from Mud Geyser station— Private John W. H. Davis and another whose name is not known— left on the thirteenth of December in weather that was deceptively mild. They went lightly clad, depending mainly on the exertion of skiing to keep warm. While they slept at the Lake Hotel, where they stayed overnight with the winter keeper, the weather changed and the temperature fell to several degrees below zero before they pushed on at eight o'clock the following morning.

The distance from Lake Hotel to the cabin where they were to meet the men from Snake River was nineteen miles and exertion of travel under the frigid conditions soon drained away the body heat of the skiers. Less than half-way to the cabin, Davis' comrade turned back to Lake Hotel (a violation of the very strict order issued by the commanding officer that no one should travel alone, and that if one man had to turn back, or stop, the other should stay with him). He did not reach its shelter until the following day, arriving with frosted fingers, ears, and toes after spending a night in a cabin on the shore of Bridge Bay. A report was immediately made by telephone to Captain Erwin, the commanding officer at Fort Yellowstone. He did not seem particularly concerned about Davis at the outset, undoubtedly sharing the common opinion that there was plenty of dry wood along the route and the man would surely have matches.

But the failure of Davis to return, coupled with declining temperature on the sixteenth (at seven A.M. it read minus nineteen degrees F. at Mammoth and minus thirty-five F. at Norris), finally led to a search. At 11:45 P.M., Sergeant Max R. Welch, in charge at Norris, received orders from Fort Yellowstone to assist, and he left his station with two men within the hour. They traveled on skis to the Canyon Hotel, twelve miles distant, where they arrived at 7:30 A.M. on the seventeenth. Though the temperature was minus six degrees F. that morning, they continued on to the station at Mud Geyser, which was reached at 11:45 A.M.. Dropping off Private Hemstead at that point, Sergeant Welch left at 1:45 P.M. with Private Akers for the Lake Hotel. They made it that far by 4:30 P.M., which was twenty-nine miles traveled in sixteen hours (from their home station).

On the morning of the eighteenth, the sergeant left Lake Hotel at 8:20 A.M. and pushed down the road toward West Thumb with Private Akers. Ten miles out, near a small bridge, they found the body of Davis where he had frozen to death in the road. The corpse could not be moved, so they returned to Lake Hotel, arriving at 4:25 P.M., to make their report. The sergeant then began construction of a sledge, using a pair of skis for runners while the soldier went back to the Mud Geyser station for assistance and horses. Sergeant Simmons of that station brought the animals forward that night, and he, with Welch and Akers, went out on the morning of the nineteenth to recover the body of Davis. At the same time, scouts George Whittaker and James Morrisson left Fort Yellowstone in a sleigh with a driver and four-mule team to bring in the body. It took eight men and another four-mule team to get them through Snow Pass, but once out on Swan Lake Flat they did better. The weariness of the mules made it necessary for them to stop at the Crystal Springs cabin the first night and at Canyon Hotel the second. The scouts reached Mud Geyser station at noon on the twenty-first and found the canvas-wrapped body there, ready for the trip back to the fort. Though it was snowing and the temperature remained sub-zero, the six-man party started back with their cargo at 1:00 P.M..

The return trip was the same slow pull for the straining, steaming mules. They stopped overnight at Canyon Hotel, then pushed on for Norris through snow up to four feet deep. Private Hemstead was left there while Sergeant Welch and Sergeant Simmons (who came back in place of Private Akers) skied on with the sleigh to Crystal Springs cabin. The body of Private Davis was delivered to the general orderly at Fort Yellowstone at noon on the twenty-third. The unfortunate soldier was buried at the post cemetery that same afternoon in grave number 12.

Sergeant Welch returned to his station, completing 132 miles on skis in eight days, most of it in sub-zero temperature conditions. There is nothing to indicate that either he or any of the other men received even the most perfunctory recognition for what they did, but perhaps that was part of the code. One is inclined to agree with "Uncle Billy" Hofer's comment that it seemed almost impossible for a man to lose his life in such a way in that country, "as there is any quantity of dry wood and timber all along the road. He could not have been so careless as to be without matches."[55]

Tragedy had a way of setting ambushes for the careless in the Yellowstone country. The men at the Gallatin soldier station had been told by Lou Bart, an old prospector living at the Apex mine nearby, never to pass close to the foot of the mountain that descends steeply to the Gallatin River about one-half mile south of the station (which was then on Specimen Creek). One day early in 1904, two corporals of Troop C, Third Cavalry (Christ H. Martin and Charles Nelson) started southward on skis intending to travel to the Riverside station. Heedless of Bart's warning, they veered over to the west side of the valley and were caught by a thunderous avalanche. Corporal Nelson, who was some distance behind Martin, was not entirely engulfed and managed to free himself and go to Jim Trail's cabin for help. Jim and Ed Moorman, who was staying with him that winter, immediately went to the slide area and searched for Martin, but with no success. Five men shoveled for ten days before the body was recovered.[56]

Illness at a winter-bound station could be as deadly as accidents while on patrol. Scout Raymond G. Little tells of helping to bury a soldier who died at the Snake River station. This man had not appeared to be dangerously ill, so his buddies left him well supplied with split wood and whatever else he might need and went on a routine patrol. When they returned they found him frozen to death in the kitchen where he had been trying to make a fire.[57] He was probably Private Richard R. Hurley who is listed in the record of interments at Fort Yellowstone as dying on May 3, 1904, "at Thumb emergency cabin." However that may be, he is of interest for an entirely different reason: the moving of his body to Fort Yellowstone for burial furnished the substance for an enduring Yellowstone legend.

This tale is usually related as occurring at Norris station at the time Ranger Phillip's body was transported from Old Faithful to West Yellowstone; however, old-timers such as Harry Liek, Scotty Bauman, and Bill Wiggins, all agree that it happened earlier, and that the body, which was placed at a cabin window and dealt a hand of cards, was that of the soldier (Hurley) who died at the Snake River. Bill tells the story this way:

> I remember Harry [Liek] tellin' about the dead soldier. Brought him from Snake River—got as far as Fountain ranger station, and the soldiers had just come back from West Yellowstone with a bottle of whiskey, so the guys got in a big poker game, played poker all night—so, Harry says, "we better let old Joe"—the dead soldier lying there—"play a hand." So they stood him up by the window, so he could watch them play poker; they played poker until ten o'clock the next day and it was on the south side of the building. The sun came out and he started to thaw out and wiggle a little bit, and Harry says, "wait a minute Joe, I'll be right out and open her up"; [laughter] that was the coffin.[58]

The early scouts were a rough bunch, so it might have happened that way.

We are on safer ground in telling how the soldiers of the detachment stationed at Old Faithful set the winter keeper's leg. Howard O'Connor, who overwintered in the Upper Geyser Basin to look after the hotel company's property there, went up on the roof of Old Faithful Inn one day in April 1912 to relieve the strain on the timbers by chopping away the ice and pushing off the snow. But he slid off with a large mass of snow, was injured, and barely managed to crawl into the building and call the soldier station by telephone. The boys got Howard to his quarters and, on examining him, found he had a fracture of the left leg between the ankle and the knee. There was no possibility of getting a doctor in over forty-three miles of snow-blocked roads, and none of the men in the detachment knew anything about setting broken bones.

The corporal in charge called Fort Yellowstone on the telephone and explained the problem to the post surgeon, who instructed him in the care of the injured man, and also warned that if a swelling developed on either side of the leg, the bone would have to be set. The swelling did appear, so the soldiers practiced bone setting according to instructions they had from the post surgeon and went over to the winter keeper's quarters prepared to set his leg in spite of his loud protestations. After the leg had been gently removed from the crude frame that held it, two men gripped the injured man by his shoulders, and another held him down, while the corporal took hold of the ankle of the broken leg and pulled. It seemed to him that the leg stretched a foot or more, but he noted: "we succeeded in resetting the bone, although the yelling of the patient must have been heard in Salt Lake City. He accused us of attempting to murder him, and every time we came near him he let out a yell."

The post surgeon was kept informed of the patient's progress until May 15, when an ambulance got through from Fort Yellowstone, after much shoveling to pass the worst snowdrifts. In due time O'Connor was delivered to the post hospital where the surgeon was surprised to find the leg properly set and knitting well. The winter keeper was so pleased that he sent the men of the Old Faithful detachment a check, with a note not to return it.[59]

There was another and more insidious danger in the isolated life in the interior of the Park: cabin fever. One soldier described it:

> When the winter starts to drag and the playing cards are worn to rags; when the reading matter that has done years of service gets still older, and, as the lights in the cabin are extinguished for the night, and the coyotes assemble and yelp, that is when "old grouch" affects each man. Every morning a fellow gets up, looks at the same faces, eats, puts on his skis, goes out for his patrol, comes back, eats, and lies down, to do the same thing the next day.[60]

Cabin fever could vary from a mild case, where a man went a bit "queer," to a very serious malady. In the case of Private Engle, who was reported from Soda Butte station as walking up and down the room with his hands behind his back and talking to himself as if he were out of his head,[61] a transfer to Fort Yellowstone was enough; his affliction was nothing like the madness that overwhelmed the detachment at Sylvan Pass station.

The outpost, which was not at Sylvan Pass but east of it, cut off from the Park by the rugged Absaroka Range, was taken over on July 3, 1911, by Sergeant C. A. Brittain and four privates (Carol, Mutch, May and Cunningham) of Troop E, First U.S. Cavalry. Unfortunately, two of these men had divergent personalities; Sergeant Brittain was unimaginative and taciturn while Private Cunningham was a fair example of that type known in the army as a "guardhouse lawyer." Cunningham questioned every order the sergeant gave and was evidently bent on running the station himself, while the sergeant's uncommunicative nature gradually alienated him from the other privates. Thus, a virulent hatred developed between these two, who represented authorized leadership on the one hand and natural leadership on the other.

Cunningham's influence with the three privates of the detachment was increased quite by chance early that fall. Private May became lost while on patrol up Jones Creek and it was Cunningham who found him during the ensuing search. Thereafter, the four privates were solidly arrayed against their sergeant, so that life at the Sylvan Pass station alternated between snarling arguments and morose unsociability.

The station log gives some idea of the dangerous nature of Private Cunningham. Early in January he went to Cody, Wyoming, on pass and while there got drunk and shot up the Irma Hotel, for which he was fined $50 and costs. Unable to raise that amount, Cunningham lay in the Cody jail for the rest of the month, returning to duty February 3, 1912. This probably further hardened Sergeant Brittain's attitude toward his troublesome subordinate, and the cleavage that had developed within the detachment is evident from the fact that the privates patrolled in pairs but the sergeant always patrolled alone.

Such was the state of affairs at the Sylvan Pass station on a day in the first week of April when Sergeant Brittain started on a ski patrol, armed as usual with his Colt .38 service revolver. Before he had gone one hundred yards he broke his ski pole and turned back to the station to secure another. Carrying a broken piece of ski pole like a fifteen-inch club, he entered the station where the privates, who had not expected him to return, were talking about him in rather disparaging terms.

When he opened the door of the cabin and stood there with club in hand, Cunningham asked him gruffly what he was going to do with it, whereupon the sergeant told him it was none of his business. Cunningham then told him if he did not drop the club he would drop him, at the same time advancing toward the sergeant. The latter immediately pulled out his pistol and fired, the bullet striking Cunningham between the eyes, killing him instantly. Another private, named Carol, advanced behind Cunningham, and the sergeant fired at him, the bullet penetrating the left arm and nearly severing the large vein. As no other man advanced, the sergeant ordered one of the remaining privates, who had previously been in the hospital corps, to put a tourniquet on Carol's arm, which no doubt saved his life.[62]

A sledge was improvised to haul the wounded Carol and the body of Cunningham to the Cody road, from where transportation was secured into town. There, they were met by a detail from Fort Yellowstone. Sergeant Brittain and Private Mutch were taken back to the fort under arrest, while Private May went back to the Sylvan Pass station temporarily with Corporal Wisdom and Private Gibson. Sergeant Brittain was tried by a court-martial held in the post exchange building at Fort Yellowstone and was found not guilty of homicide on the grounds that he was justified in defending himself. The three surviving privates were subsequently tried for mutiny and found guilty; Carol, whose arm was permanently disabled, received a three-year sentence and the other two received two years each. So ended the most serious case of cabin fever in the Park.

Liquor was seldom a problem at the outposts because it was rarely available. However, a classic brawl did develop from the sale of whiskey to soldiers at Norris station. Mr. and Mrs. Robertson, the winter keepers at Norris lunch station in the fall of 1912, made the stock of liquor at that establishment available to the soldiers after the tourist season. This arrangement blew up one day when three privates—Joseph Peters, Ephriam Nelson, and Ernest Combs—went over to the lunch station to drink and play cards. All had been drinking, Private Peters considerably, and, when Nelson caught him cheating at cards, there was a rough-and-tumble fight. This led to Peters' going back to the soldier station to get a gun to shoot the others, but Corporal Schultz, who was in charge of the detachment but in no way involved in the fracas, prevented the drunken man from carrying out his intention. His report led Colonel Brett to demand the immediate removal of the winter keeper and the entire stock of liquor.[63]

That the clandestine sale of liquor to soldiers did not meet with the disapproval of the officials of the hotel company, however much they might disavow it where the practice backfired, is evident from a letter written by manager James Dean to the president of the Northern Pacific Railroad. In remarking that Captain Brown had summarily halted the sale of liquor to soldiers at the Cottage Hotel, Dean lamented the fact that the prohibition would have the effect of decreasing the revenue of that establishment about $50 to $60 a week.[64] Such liquor sales, unlike the activity of the "peddlers" who frequented the Park in summertime, were easily dealt with.

An example of the less formal traffic carried on by local residents is found in the case of John Daugherty of Gardiner, who was arrested at the outlet of Lake Yellowstone August 19, 1915, "on suspicion of selling whisky without authority." Daugherty was apprehended on the information of Private Charles Shilling, Troop Two, Yellowstone Park Detachment, who purchased a quart bottle of whiskey from the peddler. This man, who had eleven quarts of liquor, most of it in soda-water bottles without labels, was ordered to Fort Yellowstone under guard. However, while they were stopped for the night at the Norris station, Daugherty escaped with his team, leaving his wagon and stock of liquor behind, and was never seen again.[65]

Occasionally, liquor was responsible for the failure of a soldier to properly perform his duty, as in the case of Sergeant Dennis Driscole, Troop H, Fourth U.S. Cavalry. At the time of the stagecoach holdup on Solfatara Plateau, August 14, 1897, Sergeant Driscole proceeded from his station at Norris to the Grand Canyon, where he made a number of unwarranted arrests and interfered with the functioning of the detachment stationed there. Sergeant Max R. Welch, in charge of the Canyon station, made this statement in his report on the incident: "I firmly believe Sgt. Driscole to have been so far under the influence of liquor as to place him beyond the use of any judgment in the actions he took.[66]

Sergeant Driscole was immediately removed from Norris station, but his actions were not the whole of the army's embarrassment. The 1897 holdup was particularly galling to the military authorities because one of the vehicles involved was an army ambulance carrying a number of officers who were not spared by the robbers. Perhaps this explains the particular energy with which the incident was investigated.

The robbery took place four miles from Canyon Hotel on the road to Norris. The army ambulance and fifteen stagecoaches were stopped just before noon by two armed men—one tall, one short— who had blackened their faces and hands, wore masks, and had their feet wrapped with gunny sacks. It was also noticed that one of the men spoke with a German accent and that one of the pistols used (each man had a rifle and a pistol) had a piece of russet leather sewn around the muzzle.

These men stopped the vehicles in turn as they came up. The first vehicle was driven by Louie and carried seven passengers. While one robber watched from the edge of the road with his Winchester at the ready, the other ordered the men to alight and then frisked each one. The pocket book of Mr. David Meade Massie of Chillicothe, Ohio, yielded a one-hundred-dollar bill which so delighted the highwayman that he stuck his pistol under the tourist's nose and inquired whether he had any other valentines of that kind about him. In order to be rid of his tormentor, Mr. Massie handed him a small purse containing a few coins and the tips of his fishing rod. Upon completion of this shakedown the men were ordered back into the coach and the driver was told to move on a short distance and then stop until he received a signal to go on, being also warned that his leaders would be shot if he disobeyed.

The government ambulance soon came up and its passengers— General Hawkins, his son-in-law Lieutenant Reynolds, their wives, and Doctor Godfrey—were also despoiled. However, the general saw what was about to happen and managed to conceal most of his money by dropping his pocketbook by a bush when he alighted. Doctor Godfrey told the robber that all the money he had was $17 he had made the night before by riding from the Canyon Hotel to the Lower Geyser Basin and back to attend a sick visitor, to which the robber replied that the money had been made so easily he shouldn't be allowed to keep it. In all, the highwaymen obtained $630. They took no watches, being interested mainly in cash.

The holdup was reported when the stagecoaches arrived at Norris soldier station (the erratic behavior of Sergeant Driscole then followed); the gradual buildup of circumstantial evidence during the following days led to the apprehension of the highwaymen. The morning following the holdup (early on Sunday) two men leading saddle horses passed through the horse camp of Charles B. Scott of Gardiner. They ordinarily would not have been noticed except that they were obviously anxious to avoid meeting anyone and were very reluctant to talk. This information reached the superintendent of the Yellowstone Park Transportation Company, who passed it on to the military, and in due time the two suspicious individuals were visited by a detail of soldiers at their camp about four miles northwest of Gardiner. They turned out to be Gus Smitzer and George Reeb, two local men who claimed they had been out prospecting. They were not taken into custody at that time for lack of evidence, though the evidence would soon be forthcoming.

General S.B.M. Young in dress uniform. He was the only officer to serve the Park both as acting military superintendent and full superintendent.

Immediately upon hearing of the robbery, Colonel S.B.M. Young had put all the roads leading out of the Park under surveillance, while Elmer Lindsley and a party of soldiers scoured the valley toward Yancey's, and Scout James Morrisson, who was also a deputy U.S. marshal, went directly to the scene of the holdup. Lieutenant Lindsley, swinging in a wide arc, came out on Pelican Creek where he met a party guided by J. N. "Pretty Dick" Randall, and the robbery might have been solved right there if one of Randall's employees had told what he knew. Al Golif had previously been approached by Reeb and Smitzer, who wanted him to join them in a holdup job, but he had refused to have anything to do with it. Morrisson's search of the holdup scene was more rewarding; he discovered two cuds of chewing tobacco that retained their cubical shape. This led him to suspect that George Reeb had been there, for Reeb was known to use plug tobacco in just that way—by pouching it in his cheek and sucking on it rather than chewing.

But these developments did not satisfy Colonel Young, and on the suggestion of Frank J. Haynes, Ed Howell, "who knew all the bad men and poachers around the park," was temporarily employed as a scout to search for the highwaymen. The manner in which Howell was recruited is rather amusing. Colonel Young asked Judge Meldrum to drive to Aldridge, Montana, to solicit Howell's aid, which the judge did. Howell was agreeable and proposed that he ride up to Mammoth Hot Springs with him. "You will not," the judge told him. "I can't afford to be seen riding with you." Howell was duly employed and his work merited the confidence that had been placed in him, though he had to work as a loner because Lieutenant Lindsley and Scout Morrisson both refused to have anything to do with him.

A great deal of patient tracking and sleuthing in the area immediately north of the holdup scene led to the discovery, five days after the holdup, of horse tracks near Observation Peak, and that in turn led Lieutenant Lindsley and Scout Frank Scott to an abandoned campsite north of Grebe Lake. At this camp the investigators found a piece of leather from a man's belt that had been sewn to enclose the muzzle of a pistol and recovered the distinctive labels from two milk cans, a piece torn from a blanket, two .38 caliber pistol shells, four rifle shells and, most important, two fishing rod tips. From that camp they were able to follow the trail left by horsemen (one mount being shod in a peculiar manner) almost to the road leading from Mammoth Hot Springs to Yancey's.

Ed Howell identified the horse track as having been made by an animal owned by George Reeb. An inescapable net of circumstantial evidence was rapidly woven about the two holdup men enabling the authorities to order their arrest on August 30. They were placed in the guardhouse at Fort Yellowstone for a hearing before U.S. Commissioner John Meldrum on September 10.

The preliminary hearing, which Judge Meldrum called "the most interesting case I ever saw in court," was held in the billiard room of the old National Hotel at Mammoth Hot Springs. The circumstantial evidence presented by Lieutenant Lindsley was devastating. The piece of russet leather that had been observed by a robbery victim as covering the muzzle of a holdup man's pistol, and which had been recovered from the campsite north of Grebe Lake, was shown to fit exactly onto the cut end of Reeb's belt; the condensed milk cans, an odd brand called St. Charles Cream, were shown to have been purchased on credit by Reeb at the W. A. Hall Store at Gardiner prior to the holdup, and yet, immediately after the holdup Reeb was able to send a money order to a Billings merchant in payment for a revolver purchased before the robbery. The pistol shells were shown to have come from ammunition which Reeb had purchased from a soldier. Also, the firing pin of Reeb's gun had left distinctive marks on the brass shell cases. The evidence was sufficiently conclusive to warrant holding Reeb and Smitzer, and the *Livingston Enterprise* of September 17, 1897, duly noted: "Morphine Charley and Gus Smitzer are held to await action of the grand jury in the United States court in Cheyenne."

George Reeb was indeed addicted to morphine, so much so that a few days of confinement in the Fort Yellowstone guardhouse left him in a state of near collapse. He and "little Gus" (Smitzer's alias) were tried in the U.S. District Court at Cheyenne in May 1898, found guilty and given sentences of two and one-half years in a federal penitentiary. The sequel is stranger than one might expect: after serving their sentences both men returned to the Park, Reeb to thank Judge Meldrum because his incarceration had broken the drug habit responsible for his nickname, and Smitzer to seek the judge's help in getting a job. Judge Meldrum found him one, as an irrigator at the Buffalo Ranch on Rose Creek, where he was a faithful employee for many years.

Because he had been a poacher (Chapter 14), Ed Howell's part in solving the case was bitterly denounced by Theodore Roosevelt on behalf of the Boone and Crockett Club. Nevertheless, Howell received half of the reward money—$150, which Judge Meldrum sent to him at Manila, Philippine Islands, where he had established himself in the restaurant business. (Lieutenant Lindsley was offered the other half of the reward but refused it.) However it is viewed, the 1897 holdup generated an investigation as unusual in its painstaking thoroughness as it was in its ultimate success.[67]

This holdup, like the one ten years earlier, was the source of a tale that is entirely without foundation. According to this version, Ed Howell tracked the horse with the odd shoe to Smitzer's cabin near Cinnabar Creek (present Mol Heron Creek), and as he approached he saw Smitzer out in the sagebrush digging a hole. Suspecting that the robber was engaged in burying his share of the loot, he supposedly allowed him to finish the job before riding up and arresting him. According to this story, Ed went back to the cabin after the trial and conviction of the robbers and dug up the loot, stated to be approximately $4,000, then went to Livingston and bought a ticket to the Philippine Islands.[68] This story does not agree with the fact that only $630 was obtained in the robbery.

The Fort Yellowstone idyll came to an end October 26, 1916, when the management of the Park was turned over to the newly organized National Park Service. It would have been well if the era of the army in the Park had ended there, where it could be said: "Many officers and men look back upon their service here with the keenest pleasure. Their duties have been well and creditably performed, and the 30 years of military control will be memorable ones in the history of the Yellowstone National Park."[69]

Instead, the legislature of Montana, responding to the local feeling that never favored the withdrawal of a military force or the abandonment of an installation that could benefit the local economy, by a joint memorial of both houses in March 1917 importuned as follows: "Resolved, that the Congress of the United States is hereby petitioned to again police the Yellowstone National Park with officers and soldiers of the regular army to the end that it shall be well protected from fire, as well as from vandals who would destroy its beauty."[70] Congress listened to that counsel and the National Park Service was denied the funds needed for its organization in the Park. Thus, troops were put back into the Park in 1917 for the protection of the area.

The last cavalry outfit in Yellowstone Park only managed to smirch the reputation for generally good management that the army had earned during its many years protecting the people's park. The wartime levies that made up most of the strength of the Eleventh Cavalry at that time lacked the soldierly pride of the old army men. In short order the commanding officer was court-martialed, a sergeant and soldier were arrested for stealing tires from automobiles passing through the Park and selling them in the town of Gardiner, while individual soldiers did a shabby and ineffective job throughout the area. At last, on November 1, 1918, Acting Superintendent Lindsley could telegraph the director of the National Park Service that Fort Yellowstone had been formally abandoned by the military as of October 31.

Some years later "Uncle Billy" Hofer visited the old barracks in Key West, Florida. At the office he asked the ordnance sergeant in charge for a drink of water, and was told: "There's some in the bucket behind the door." Hofer then asked the sergeant what branch of the service he had been in previously and the answer was the First Cavalry. M Troop of the First had been stationed where he lived in Yellowstone Park, "Uncle Billy" told him, and the sergeant asked if he knew Jimmy Dugan, the bugler. Hofer said he did and turned toward the water bucket, but the sergeant yelled at him, "Hey! Don't drink that water!" Gone was the casual treatment; "Uncle Billy" was taken about the post, met several other old soldiers who had served at Fort Ellis and in the Park, and was treated royally. He says: "They were all homesick and to meet anyone from their old stamping ground was to meet an old friend; they could not do too much."[71] The Yellowstone experience *was* their idyll.

CHAPTER 17

THE WORK
OF THE CORPS

*. . . the balance of the sum appropriated to be
expended in the construction and improvement of
suitable roads and bridges within said park, under
supervision and direction of an engineer officer
detailed by the Secretary of War for that purpose.*

—Sundry Civil Appropriations Act, *March 3, 1883* [1]

The succession of officers of the army's Corps of Engineers
detailed to Yellowstone National Park to supervise construction and maintenance of roads and bridges in accordance with the foregoing act were well-trained professionals of their
day. More important for the Park, their technical competence was so
leavened by one man's vision and sensitivity that more than a good
road system was eventually created.

Captain William Ludlow was the first to point out that the
planning as well as the construction and maintenance of roads and
bridges should be supervised by an engineer officer of the army.[2] His
suggestion evidently made a favorable impression on General Philip
H. Sheridan, as it reappeared in the official report of the general's
visit to the Park in the summer of 1881.[3] General Sheridan returned to
the Park the following season accompanied by Senator George
Graham Vest, whom he easily convinced of the necessity for
legislation beneficial to the Park and that the Park's engineering

The road at Trout Creek in Hayden Valley, July 1909.

problems should be placed in the hands of the Corps of Engineers. The senator's attempt to get legislation for the Park was blocked, but he did manage to salvage something by incorporating some of his measures into the Sundry Civil Appropriation Act passed March 3, 1883. In that manner, the responsibility for the construction and maintenance of the Park's roads and bridges passed from the superintendent to an engineer officer to be detailed by the secretary of war.

There was some local dissatisfaction with the inevitable delay in securing the services of an engineer officer. The fact that Superintendent Conger was not authorized to incur any expense toward the opening of park roads was considered as "placing a faithful servant . . . and an honorable gentlemen in an unenviable and embarrassing position."[4] However, it was not easy to get just the right officer for the position.

> Several weeks ago General Sheridan made application to the War Department for the detail of Lieutenant Dan C. Kingman, United States Engineer, to make a survey of the roads and superintend the disbursement of the money voted by Congress for the improvements of the Yellowstone Park, under the charge of the Secretary of War. Last week Lieut. Kingman received notification that he had been ordered to West Point. It has since transpired that by the personal request of General Sheridan the order will be revoked and that Lieut. Kingman will be directed to prosecute the work in the National Park as it was originally designed by General Sheridan.[5]

Lieutenant Kingman arrived at the Park on August 13, rather late for accomplishing much that season. He made a thorough reconnaissance of existing roads in the Park and evolved a plan of operation that had for its immediate objective rebuilding the road from the north entrance to Mammoth Hot Springs and constructing an entirely new road from the Springs to Swan Lake Flat by way of the Golden Gate. The difficult and at times nearly impossible grade over the hot spring terraces and through Snow Pass (then called Hell Gate) could thus be avoided entirely—an improvement that met with immediate and enthusiastic response locally. The new engineer also had a larger and grander plan in mind. He proposed to construct a double-track wagon road entirely around the Park from Mammoth Hot Springs by way of Norris to the Upper Geyser Basin, then to Yellowstone Lake and on to the Grand Canyon, and from there across to Norris, where he would tie into the road from Mammoth Hot Springs. For this work, which encompassed much of what would later become the figure-eight road system of the Park, he estimated $140,000 as sufficient for construction and asked for $30,000 for the 1884 season.[6]

Lieut. Dan Kingman near Mammoth Hot Springs in 1885.

Lieutenant Kingman was eager to use the funds that remained unexpended because of his late arrival in the Park, so he organized a crew of twenty laborers under Oscar S. Swanson and began to build a road through the limestone Hoodoos toward Golden Gate. His crew of Swedes, working with a few mule teams, plows, scrapers, and much giant powder, accomplished in two months what the editor of the *Livingston Enterprise* considered a feat for 150 men, comparing the road to the Roman Appian Way, to which it probably bore not the least resemblance. The work was pushed to the portal of the Golden Gate before winter storms forced a halt in mid-January.

Meanwhile Lieutenant Kingman had purchased a portable sawmill powered by a thirty-horsepower steam engine and had begun sawing planks for bridges and lumber for camps. Working under the direction of E. J. Lamartine, the sawmill crew had 400,000 board feet of material on hand by the time work was suspended.[7] The cost of the first piece of good road built in Yellowstone Park was $14,000, or about $2,800 per mile.

The gales that stopped the road work were the forerunners of a mean winter during which Swanson's crew of hardworking and hard-drinking ex-railroaders had nothing to do for several months. The saloons in Gardiner naturally attracted them, and seven were returning from town one evening in a sled, perhaps a little worse for their fun, and were about halfway to the Springs when a snowslide swept down upon them carrying sled, men and team 100 yards below the road and burying them under snow. Fortunately, James Wrist saw the accident and went to their assistance. He succeeded in getting four of them out immediately, after which he went back to Gardiner for help. Nearly all of the townsmen turned out and found the remaining three men; one of them, a Finlander named Jacob Hess, was dead.[8]

During the 1884 working season, Swanson's crew pushed their road through the gorge of Glen Creek, blasting 15,000 cubic yards of stone out of the canyon wall at one place, and at another building a wooden trestle on which the roadway was carried around the face of a cliff. A feature of this trestle was a detached pillar of rock which created the illusion of a portal at the lower end. This pillar, though moved several times during the intervening years, remains as an ornament of the present concrete viaduct.

A second road crew was put to work that summer under foreman Lamartine on the construction of a new road up the Gardner River. This road, which required bridges at the Eagle Nest Rock and a short distance below the Boiling River, was completed in the early summer

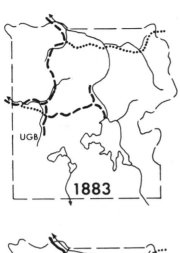

1883

1886

1892

1903

1905

Construction
of
PARK ROADS
1883-1918

of 1885 and became known as the Lamartine Road. It was a great improvement over the road Norris had built (approximately on the line of the present high road between Gardiner and Mammoth Hot Springs).

Lieutenant Kingman was able to put a total of seventy-five men to work during the summer of 1885, organized in three crews of twenty-five under Oscar Swanson, Lamartine, and James Blanding. Swanson's crew put the finishing touches on the road from the Golden Gate across Swan Lake Flat to the Gardner River, then graded the old Norris road through to the Lower Geyser Basin where they began work on an entirely new route from the Marshall House, at the mouth of Nez Perce Creek, to the Midway Geyser Basin. This road, which had a relatively straight alignment, was known then as Park Avenue; in more recent times it has been called the Fountain Freight Road.

Blanding's crew spent much of the summer bridging the Gibbon River. In late summer they returned to Norris to begin construction of a road intended to improve upon Norris' route between that point and Obsidian Cliff. At the same time, Lamartine's crew started work on the north end of this road, and by the joint efforts of both crews a road approximately on the alignment used today was built that fall, eliminating a bad hill between Beaver Lake and Lake of the Woods.

As a grand windup for the season's work, the crews of Swanson and Blanding joined forces in pioneering a road from Norris toward the Grand Canyon, a project that Blanding finished in the spring of 1886. A grade on this Norris Cutoff was known as Blanding Hill until the reconstruction of the 1950s eliminated it from the traveled route.

The effect of the work done by Lieutenant Kingman's crews was great. Improvement of the road from Gardiner through to the Lower Geyser Basin reduced the cost of freight hauled into the interior of the Park by fifty cents per hundred weight,[9] and tourists were now able to see the Park in thirty miles' less travel and one day's less time.[10]

Lieutenant Kingman's road building met with the whole-hearted approval of all who traveled through the Park, but his attempt to regulate the use of those roads drew the ire of those who freighted into the area. It was soon apparent that the iron tires of freight wagons were damaging the roads, particularly when wet, and in the spring of 1886 Kingman proposed that freighting be limited to wagons with tires at least four inches wide. The secretary of the interior concurred in this, [11] but the regulation was so unpopular that it had to be revoked.

An amusing by-product of this regulation was its effect in scaring an early bicyclist out of the Park. The young man (unfortunately he cannot be named) had entered the Park from the west. On his arrival at the Lower Geyser Basin he met Montana's famous frontier marshal John Xelpho Beidler, who was quite a jokester in his way. Beidler convinced the cyclist that if he tried to go to Mammoth with a vehicle equipped with tires of less than regulation width, he was liable to be arrested and fined. Properly discouraged, that hero of the high wheel terminated his park tour by scooting back out the west entrance.

Dan Kingman's successors apparently accomplished less. In four seasons Kingman had provided a passable road from Gardiner to the Upper Geyser Basin and from Norris to the Grand Canyon, at a cost of about $75,000, but much remained to be done. Captain Clinton B. Sears, who succeeded Kingman in 1887, thought the project could be completed most efficiently by a well-organized effort during the 1889 fiscal year, and he requested $130,000 for the purpose.[12] Congress, far from allowing any such amount, appropriated only $25,000, which was made available so late that nothing at all could be done from the first of July through September, 1888. This lack of maintenance during the busy season generated considerable criticism, though it was not the fault of Sears or Major Charles J. Allen, who took over responsibility for work in the Park in May.

However, the new officer was made the scapegoat, not openly, but by subordinating him to Major William A. Jones, apparently in the belief that Jones, from his headquarters at St. Louis, could successfully cope with the vagaries of funding. But Jones could do no better, as was evident when Congress was again tardy in providing an appropriation. Funds for the 1891 fiscal year should have been available July 1, 1890, but as Major Jones noted in his report:

> On the thirtieth of June, 1890, Congress was still in session, but had not acted on the Sundry Civil Bill, which carries the appropriation for this work. Under the operation of the law, no funds could be carried beyond that date for the care and maintenance of the roads and public property on hand. Consequently, on that date all employees had to be discharged and the public property, for which I was personally responsible and the loss of any part of which had to be made good from my private resources, had to be left to the mercy of chance until I became officially aware of the appropriaton, which was passed August 30, 1890.[13]

Thus, the better part of another working season was lost, though Lieutenant William E. Craighill, who represented Major Jones in the Park after November 14, 1889, did all he could once the funds were available.

Activity in the Park in the fall of 1890 included a reconnaissance intended to further the major's proposal "during the coming year to carry forward the project for opening new . . . roads with the utmost vigor." The plan called for a road between Upper Geyser Basin and the Thumb of Lake Yellowstone, but Lieutenant Craighill soon discovered that the country along the direct line between the proposed terminals was "of the roughest description." He decided upon a route that would extend the road up the Firehole River and into the Shoshone Geyser Basin by a low gap (Grants Pass, named for M. G. Grant of the Northern Pacific Railroad survey of 1882), and from there around the south shore of Shoshone Lake to its outlet and across low, forested country to Thumb Bay. This devious route plan, however practical it may otherwise have been, did not gain the approval of Congress, so that the appropriation act of March 3, 1891, which provided funds for the building of the road from Old Faithful to West Thumb, also stipulated that it should be built along the "shortest practicable line between these points."[14]

As things stood in the spring of 1891, four years of piecemeal maintenance had not materially advanced either the condition or the extent of Kingman's roads, though $100,000 of additional funds had gone into them. The only real progress Lieutenant Craighill had made toward beginning new construction was in getting a forty-foot steam launch hauled into the Park for use on Lake Yellowstone (where it would serve to supply the crew that was to begin work on the east end of the road).[15] At that stage of the project, Craighill was replaced by Lieutenant Hiram M. Chittenden on June 5, 1891.

The lieutenant was returning from Europe, where he had gone to recover his health, and on reporting to the chief of engineers was told he was slated for the Yellowstone National Park. Chittenden then went on to St. Paul and reported to Major Jones, of whom he notes:

> The Major was a peculiar character, not over scrupulous in matters of official work and I don't think that he particularly welcomed my entrance upon the scene. He took a great deal of pains to impress upon me that his civil assistant in the Park, Lamartine, by name, was absolutely indispensable to the work, and that I must rely very largely upon his judgment. He pressed the point so far that I became a little suspicious and determined to reserve my judgment.[16]

Chittenden arrived in Yellowstone Park with Major Jones during one of those inclement periods typical of early summer, and he appeared so frail and sickly that the new military superintendent, Captain Anderson, thought he might last "just about two weeks." But he plunged directly into the work and soon discovered that foreman Lamartine was not nearly as competent as he had been made out to be. After a quick look around the interior of the Park, Major Jones returned to St. Paul, leaving Chittenden in charge of the work—though only nominally, as the supervisor saw it.

> And now my troubles began. Here were practically $150,000 available; very important roads to build, not a sign of a survey or even reconnaissance, or even a passage of anybody over the route to afford us a guide as to where to begin or where to go. Very fortunately, there were two excellent foremen and it was decided to organize a large party under each of these and have one begin at one end of the work and the other at the other, although nobody knew where these ends were. But it would take several days to get the parties out in the field and in the meanwhile I wasn't idle in informing myself about the situation. Lamartine was very greatly surprised when he found that I was going to take active charge in the field and his displeasure was manifest enough. Nevertheless he learned it was useless to argue.[17]

Chittenden found that Lamartine was locally considered a rather notorious crook, so was on his guard concerning the man. Lamartine immediately went to Livingston and bought a handsome fishing outfit as a present for the new engineer, but Chittenden would have none of that and only accepted the outfit on condition that he could reimburse Lamartine for the cost—though he could "ill spare the money at the time." The relationship between Chittenden and his assistant engineer gradually worsened until fall when the construction work had to be shut down for lack of funds due to Lamartine's failure to keep an adequate accounting. At that point Chittenden solved his difficulties by firing Mr. Lamartine.

To begin construction of the road across that chaotic wilderness between Old Faithful and West Thumb, Chittenden accompanied the crew that went to West Thumb on the little steamer, while Lamartine accompanied the other crew to the Upper Geyser Basin to work from the west end. The two crews were to work toward each other while Chittenden found the best location across the intervening terrain. Upon reaching Lamartine's party Chittenden was disappointed to find that they had been following the old Norris trail. "That was Mr. Lamartine's idea of locating a road—to follow a trail with all its irregularities and excesses of gradients, regardless of what improvements could be made by something of a survey." Chittenden found it necessary to do the locating himself, working alternately at the two ends of the line with a hand level, a five-foot staff, and the assistance of two laborers. East of Craig Pass, at the top of what would become known as the Corkscrew Hill, Chittenden had one of his helpers climb a tall tree and securely fasten a large piece of white cloth to serve as a signal. This mark could be seen plainly from Shoshone Point and helped to keep the locaters on their course. Chittenden says that when he returned to the Park seven years later the cloth was still waving in the breeze at the top of that tree.

When all was going well on the Old Faithful to Thumb section, Chittenden turned his attention to locating a road around the north side of Lake Yellowstone to connect with the end of the existing road near Lake Hotel. He was laboring there when Captain Anderson precipitated a clash with Major Jones. In his annual report Anderson innocently complimented Chittenden, which caused the crochety major to write him on September 17:

> My dear Anderson
>
> I quote as follows from your annual report: "Lieut. Chittenden, U.S. Engineers, in charge of work, is zealous, untiring, and remarkably efficient in its prosecution and will certainly make a fine showing by the end of the year."
>
> Don't you think, old fellow, that giving away all the glory to a subordinate at the expense of the Boss is calculated to stir up the latter's feelings?
>
> I know very well you have not intended to do me an injustice, but how would you feel were I to officially report that your 1st Sergeant was entitled to all the credit for all the beautiful discipline of your company? I don't ask you to glorify me, nor do I ask you not to glorify Chittenden. He has done very well. Only, do it so as not to throw an odious light on Yours very truly [signed] W. A. Jones.

In his endorsement of the letter, Anderson noted at the bottom, "Complains of want of reference to him in annual report. *(Rot)*".[18]

One way or another, the road was roughed through from the Upper Geyser Basin to the Lake Hotel before financial disaster struck the operation. Chittenden says: "I do not know to what extent I was intentionally made a victim in the affair, or to what extent it was purely accidental." However, he was able to escape any serious consequences through the kindness of local merchants who were willing to delay requesting payment for a considerable quantity of supplies.

The most serious aspect of overspending the account was the effect on the opening of the park roads in the spring of 1892. Silas S. Huntley and Captain Anderson decided to make a preliminary round of the Park prior to the opening of the tourist season, and "they simply had an awful time. Every bridge in Spring Creek Canyon was washed out and in one place the coach sank down on its side and water rushed over and came pretty nearly drowning the inmates." The new road was obviously in no condition to be used; a call for help went over the wires to St. Paul and Lieutenant Chittenden was sent to the Park to see what he could do. After a quick look, Chittenden decided that if Captain Anderson could spare him $500 and a few enlisted men, with supplies and wagons, and if the transportation company and F. J. Haynes could each add as much, he could get together a work party that would make the road passable in fifteen days. He got what he needed and a "motley party" was organized and put to work, and, with Chittenden personally showing some of his men how to shovel or how to chop, the road was opened on time. It was because of the initiative shown in that emergency that Chittenden was returned to the Park for some glorious accomplishment in 1899, but before that happened the road improvement program nearly foundered.

In the spring of 1893, Chittenden was detailed to Louisville, Kentucky, a change that Captain Anderson called "a most serious blow to road building here."[19] His place was taken by overseer Burns, one of those civilian assistants for whom Major Jones had such a marked preference.

Captain Anderson was frankly critical of this new arrangement, stating in his annual report, "At the opening of the season this year we were again confronted with a lack of funds for road repairs. This is one of the great evils of leaving the distribution of the money to one who resides so far from the work."[20] For his part, Major Jones made slighting remarks about Captain Anderson's engineering experience, which was actually considerable despite his lack of professional training. The result was that Captain Anderson officially recommended "the acting superintendent of the Park be given the control of the work, and that an officer of the Corps of Engineers be detailed to report to him to superintend it, make the detailed plans, and disburse the appropriations." This brought Major Jones' supervision of construction and maintenance of roads and bridges in the Park to an end on August 29, 1894, putting that responsibility in the hands of Captain Anderson—but without the assistance of an officer of the Corps of Engineers, as he had requested.

Upon his assumption of responsibility for engineering activities in the Park, Captain Anderson inherited several problems. One of these concerned construction of a bridge at the Grand Canyon, the one called the Canyon Bridge, which spans a dry ravine a short distance above the Upper Fall. His predecessor had lavished nearly half the appropriation of the preceding fiscal year upon construction of an elaborate bridge, where a $2,000 structure would have sufficed, and yet had left the span uncompleted and the road interrupted at that point.[21] Completion of that bridge was pushed vigorously in order to have it ready for use during the next tourist season.

Another project over which Major Jones' men had been dallying for two years was the projected road from the Thumb of Lake Yellowstone to the south entrance and on to the boundary line of the forest reserve. Captain Anderson put a locating party on that section in the summer of 1895 and had the road roughed out and usable by the end of the following season.[22] A location survey was also completed for a road intended to connect the Grand Canyon with Yancey's, by way of the summit of Mount Washburn, "enabling tourists to view from the summit . . . some of the grandest mountain scenery in the world."

Captain Anderson was particularly active in opening side roads to points of interest along the belt line. He constructed a loop driveway from the Fountain Hotel by way of Black Warrior Springs and the Great Fountain Geyser; opened the road to the Lone Star Geyser and another to the Natural Bridge; built a full-width, graded road down the Grand Canyon to Inspiration Point and a driveway from Yancey's to the two standing petrified trees nearby.[23] He also toyed with the idea of bridging the Yellowstone River above the Upper Falls in order to make points of interest on the east side of the Canyon accessible to tourists. Such a project had been considered by Superintendent Norris and by Chittenden in 1892. The latter, aware that the situation was "one of magnificent scenery," would not consider a cheap bridge, trussed with wood or iron, at that point; rather, he planned a rustic masonry arch, but found the cost to be prohibitive and laid the idea aside. Captain Anderson did not have the same sensitivity to esthetic considerations and went ahead with plans for an iron bridge. The chief engineer of the Northern Pacific Railroad assisted him by having the computations made in his office, and the resulting plan (which is still in existence) was exactly what one would expect: a utilitarian structure with a strong resemblance to every bridge on the Northern Pacific main line. Fortunately, it was never built.

Captain Anderson's standards were not those of the Corps of Engineers, but he was not lacking in energy. In addition to routine maintenance and new construction he undertook some unique improvements. One of these was the marking of the Park boundaries, which he regarded as "the most important bit of work yet to be accomplished." The fieldwork was carried out under the immediate direction of Lieutenant Bromwell of the Corps of Engineers, who placed reference monuments of cut stone at the most easterly and

southerly points of Yellowstone Lake and at the westerly point of
Shoshone Lake, in order that the east, south, and west boundaries
could be run on the ground as described in the Organic Act. Similarly,
Captain Anderson placed a granite monument at the point in front of
the present Lake Lodge where the U.S. Coast and Geodetic Survey
had established the latitude and longitude. Both the geographic
coordinates and the elevation, as determined by running a line of
levels from the end of the Northern Pacific Railroad at Cinnabar,
Montana, were graved upon the stone. Later work has proven the
elevation to be considerably in error, a fact which occasionally
embarrasses engineers concerned with projects in that vicinity.

Captain Anderson's successor, Colonel S. B. M. Young, was not
so interested in the engineering aspects of his assignment to
Yellowstone Park; in fact, it would seem that he was alarmed at the
responsibility he had to shoulder in that regard. Evidently he did not
feel qualified to guide the development of the road system then taking
form. Whether he was concerned for the scenic values involved or
merely seeking to buffer administrative pressures, he made the
following recommendation in his supplemental report for 1897:

> It is due to the public that a commission, composed of a member of the
> Geological Survey, an officer of the Engineer Corps, United States
> Army, and a gentleman from civil life, be appointed to advise with the
> acting superintendent on the location of new roads and saddle trails,
> in order that all the beauties, wonders, and grand scenery may be made
> accessible to visitors.[24]

Colonel Young had other progressive ideas. He believed that all the
main traveled roads should be macadamized, that dangerous places
should be protected by guard rails, and that the wooden viaduct built
by Kingman at the Golden Gate should be replaced by a masonry or
steel structure, "the former preferable." This, with Chittenden's
concern for a sightly bridge across the Yellowstone River above the
Upper Fall, marked an awakening to the need for considering
esthetics in park construction.

The last of the officers charged with managing the Park and
improving it was Captain James B. Erwin. He subscribed to the idea
that "nature cannot be improved upon,"[25] and was content to
maintain roads and bridges already constructed. Upon Captain
Erwin's transfer from the Park on March 15, 1899, Silas S. Huntley,
head of the transportation company, remembered the enthusiasm
and efficiency of Hiram M. Chittenden and decided he would make a
good acting superintendent. So, Huntley and Senator Carter urged
the chief of engineers to return Chittenden to the Park as its acting

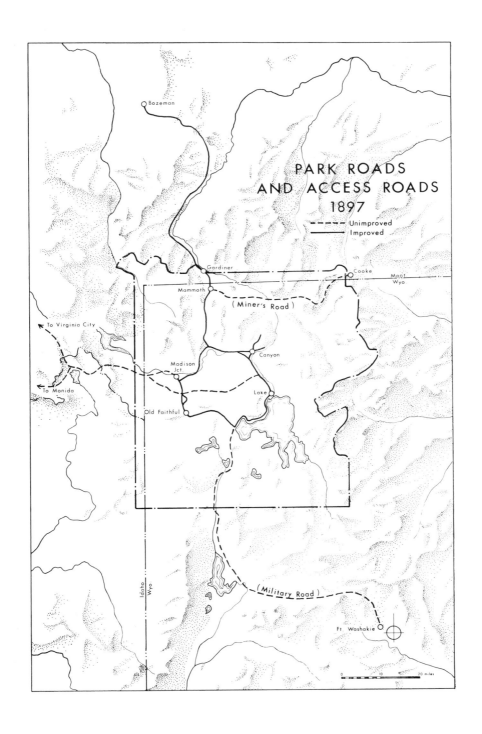

PARK ROADS
AND ACCESS ROADS
1897

- - - - Unimproved
——— Improved

Bozeman

Gardiner

Cooke

Mont
Wyo

Mammoth

(Miner's Road)

To Virginia City

Canyon

Madison
Jct.

To Monida

Lake

Old Faithful

Idaho
Wyo

(Military Road)

Ft. Washakie

0   10   20 miles

superintendent. When General John M. Wilson asked Chittenden (by that time a Captain) if he would take full charge of the Park, he replied "no superintendency," and returned in a technical capacity only.[26]

Chittenden entirely rebuilt the road from Mammoth Hot Springs to the Golden Gate by taking it directly through the limestone Hoodoos (where a little fragment of his work remains in that bit of scenic road called the Silver Gate). In that manner Chittenden began a series of engineering works that have been a continuing credit to himself and the Park.

As the park road system stood at the close of 1899, the belt line— that internal loop designed to provide a circuit of the area—was completed to a reasonable standard except for the portion intended to connect the Grand Canyon with Mammoth Hot Springs by way of Tower Fall. Of the four entrances proposed for the Park, only the northern was completed, while the eastern remained unopened. The side roads and the miners' road to Cooke City were single-track, dirt roads. Chittenden believed, as Captain Sears had, that the completion of the park road system could be done more efficiently as a single, massive project undertaken in one year, and he prepared an estimate that proposed to accomplish the entire job at a cost of $300,000. As he said, "only once in the history of the work has it been possible to make any really rapid progress toward its completion; that was in the season of 1891, when two appropriations, aggregating $150,000, were available."[27] This monumental proposal was not entirely ignored, for the appropriation made available under the act of June 6, 1900, was $55,000—an increase of $21,000. Though less than he wished, Chittenden made good use of these funds.

The two important projects of the season of 1900 were the rebuilding of Kingman's viaduct at the Golden Gate and the beginning of construction of the east entrance road. The timber trestle erected by Dan Kingman had become somewhat rickety, and though still considered safe it was a matter of such concern to tourists who were hauled over it that it was felt necessary to replace the old structure with a more secure one. The old Snow Pass road was prepared as a temporary route and the wooden viaduct was closed to traffic on the sixth of August; then the timber trestle was torn out and forms were built for erecting a concrete structure carried on arches spaced eighteen feet apart and rising from firm rock below. Despite difficulty in finding good sand for the concrete work, and rugged working conditions because of the constant wind, the new viaduct was opened to traffic in four weeks. The distinctive rock pillar at the

Captain Hiram M. Chittenden, Corps of Engineers, about 1903.

Moving the rock pillar to widen the road at the lower portal to the Golden Gate in 1903, when Kingman's wooden trestle was replaced by Chittenden's concrete viaduct.

lower end of the old trestle, which weighed approximately twenty-three tons, was broken off, lifted six feet to the new grade, and moved equal distances down the road and outward, where it was placed upon a concrete pedestal. The foundation was then covered to hide its artificial nature.

Chittenden's concrete viaduct was replaced by the present structure in the mid-1930s, not because of any lack of stoutness but to gain additional width required for modern vehicular traffic. The one-half mile of roadway from the viaduct onto Swan Lake Flat was also widened at that time, thus removing the last section of dangerous, one-way road between Mammoth Hot Springs and Norris.

The other noteworthy project initiated in 1900 was the east entrance road. Work started on July 1, as soon as the appropriation was available. Much work went into preparing approaches for the piling bridges to be built over the Yellowstone River and Pelican Creek; for this, the clearing and grading crews were transported along the lake shore by means of the little steam launch. An indirect result of the project, which was to have its eastern terminus on what had previously been known as the North Fork of the Stinkingwater River, was the renaming of that beautiful mountain stream. Concerning this change Chittenden says:

> This stream has heretofore been known as the Stinking Water River. It was so named in 1807 by its discoverer, John Colter, who came upon it where there is a large tar spring near the junction of the two forks and gave it the name on account of the impression received at this particular point. The name was wholly inappropriate as the stream is one of the finest in the mountains, both in the purity of its water and the character of its scenery. Local usage has succeeded in changing it to "Shoshone," but this change has never received official recognition. As the valley of the river will soon be followed by a tourist route from upward of 50 miles, it was considered important that an appropriate name be adopted, and acting upon a recommendation from this office to the Governor of Wyoming, the legislature of that state passed an act (February 14, 1901) changing the name to Shoshone. The stream will hereafter appear in the official reports and maps of the Park under its new name.[28]

The work on the east entrance road was continued in 1902, with completion of the two piling bridges and six smaller structures over lesser streams. The bridge over the Yellowstone River was 360 feet long, carried on piling bents 16 feet apart. This first bridge (which in 1914 would be called Fishing Bridge) differed from the present structure both in location and appearance. It used the same western abutment, but crossed the river diagonally upstream (that is, toward the lake), and its center was elevated in "camel-back" fashion to allow the passage of row boats beneath. It was entirely rebuilt in 1919. When the present structure was built in 1937, walkways were added for fishermen and others crossing on foot.

Two other important bridges were planned for construction during the summer of 1902: a steel structure to replace the aged Baronett Bridge at a point approximately one-half mile upstream, and a bridge over the Gardner River above its junction with Lava Creek. The wooden false work had been put in place for these structures, but the American Bridge Company, under contract to provide the steel, was unable to fufill its commitment that season because of a strike. Thus the tired old Baronett Bridge, a government structure since 1894, had to be used for another season.[29] Materials were on hand that summer for three fine steel bridges in the Gardner Canyon below Mammoth Hot Springs; much of that road was relocated behind a massive dry masonry wall on the west side of the river.

The year 1902 marks the beginning of efforts to end the dust nuisance so aggravating to early-day tourists. Captain Chittenden proposed an oil treatment for the park roads similar to that used successfully on roads in the Bakersfield, California, area. As he saw it, "the experiment of the use of oil in the Park is worth trying, and if the next appropriation will justify it I recommend that it be made.[30] While it was to be some years before the Park had any oil-surfaced roads, he did lay the dust fairly effectively that summer on four miles of road from Mammoth Hot Springs to Swan Lake Flat—with water hauled in a tank wagon. The sprinkling was considered a distinct success, particularly by the public.

An engineer involved with the complex and multitudinous details of constructing and maintaining a road system of the magnitude of Yellowstone Park's might have had no time for extracurricular activities; but that was not so in Chittenden's case. His strong interest in history led him to mark the route taken across the Park by Nez Perce Indians and pursuing troops under General Oliver O. Howard in 1877. To assure accurate identification of sites Chittenden had Colonel W. F. Spurgin of the Fourth Infantry detailed to the Park, and arranged for George F. Cowan and James C. McCartney to accompany a party to trace out the route. Chittenden's explanatory signs placed at points where notable events took place have all been lost during the intervening years.[31]

Of most importance to park development that year was the appropriation in the Sundry Civil Act of June 28, 1902. Through it, in "hardly a dozen words," the Park received $250,000 and an authorization for $500,000 more in the next two years. With that guarantee of a continuing appropriation, Captain Chittenden was able to lay out and execute projects that would systematically and rapidly complete the park road system—a result he had hardly dared to hope for. Actually, Chittenden and the Park were beholden to "Uncle Joe" Cannon, chairman of the House Appropriations Committee, for that fortunate outcome.

The previous summer (1901) Uncle Joe had visited the Park while resting from his arduous duties as watchdog of the U.S. Treasury. While he was in the area Captain Chittenden had conducted him about the Park, with the result that the crusty old representative from Illinois developed a keen appreciation of what Chittenden had accomplished and planned to do. How much of an impression had been made became apparent the following spring when E. W. Bach and H. W. Child, of the Yellowstone Park Association, appeared before the House Committee on Appropriations to beg additional funds for improvement of park roads. When they stepped upon the red carpet of the committee room, they found the veteran chairman reposing in a sunny corner and perfectly aware of the purpose of their visit, for he said: "Boys, how are ye? Its no use saying a word. Go right back to the West and leave it all to me."[32] The result was that munificent appropriation, for which, in Captain Chittenden's words, the Park owes Mr. Cannon "a debt of gratitude which it would be difficult to repay."

With such a chest of funds at his disposal, Captain Chittenden grandly finished his work in the Park, which brings us to that banner year—1903. The year opened with a presidential visit and closed with completion of three projects that provide enduring evidence of Chittenden's engineering genius.

Spring came to the Yellowstone country early that year. Even before the arrival of the presidential party, crews were at work preparing foundations for the great archway of basaltic stone to face upon the site of the Northern Pacific Railroad depot on the outskirts of Gardiner. The idea for such a structure was Chittenden's and the design had been worked up from his notes by Robert C. Reamer, architect of the Old Faithful and Canyon hotels. The plan called for a structure fifty feet high, pierced by an opening twenty feet wide and thirty feet high, with wing walls twelve feet high running out fifty feet on either side. Above the keystone of the arch a concrete tablet would bear the inscription, "For the Benefit and Enjoyment of the People," in letters large enough to be read from the depot. Smaller tablets to the left and right of the passageway were to read "Yellowstone

National Park" and "Created by Act of Congress, March 1, 1872."
This imposing entrance was designed to offset the uninteresting
character of the surrounding country. In Chittenden's words, "the
first impression of visitors upon entering the Park was very
unfavorable."[33]

President Roosevelt's visit culminated in the laying of the cornerstone of the arch on April 24, 1903. The president arrived at the
Cinnabar terminus of the park branch line on April 8; his train was
parked on a siding there since the newly laid track to Gardiner was not
yet ready for use. Leaving Secretary William Loeb, Jr., to handle
affairs of state from his rolling white house (the railway car Elysian),
the president mounted a horse provided by Troop B. Third Cavalry,
and cantered off with Major Pitcher toward Fort Yellowstone, where
he was to be the major's guest that night.[34]

On the eight-mile ride to Mammoth Hot Springs the president
was shown the animals wintering in the vicinity. He was particularly
impressed by the tameness of the antelope, considering it "extraordinary
to find them showing such familiarity almost literally in the streets of
a frontier town [Gardiner, Montana]."[35] Major Pitcher was an old
friend of Roosevelt's and knew where his keenest interest lay; indeed,
the president probably saw much to admire in the major, who was like
himself an advocate of the strenuous outdoor life, a marksman, and
horseman, and reputed to be able to lick any man in the army at
catch-as-catch-can or knock-down-and-draw-out fighting, all abilities
which the president greatly admired. Concerning the horse ridden by
Roosevelt while in the Park, there are photographs showing the
president in khaki breeches, puttees, dark coat, and Stetson hat
astride his large, surefooted grey mount, but none at all of the earnest
secret service agent who was up before dawn to make sure that the
horse assigned to the president was gentle. Had Teddy known that his
mount had been so carefully checked out in advance he would
probably have been angry, but that would not have altered the
situation except that the secret service "might have become a little
more secretive."[36]

The following day the president and his traveling companion,
John Burroughs (whom he called Oom John because of his flowing
white whiskers), left for a camping trip into the country at the
junction of the Yellowstone and Lamar rivers. Major Pitcher had
provided a supply wagon to carry the two Sibley tents and one wall
tent to house the party and had sent along two orderlies, two cooks,
and a small force of cavalrymen to serve as escort and handle the
stock. Precautions were taken (by sealing off the area in which the

President Theodore Roosevelt and Major John Pitcher at the Liberty Cap, Mammoth Hot Springs, 1903.

President Theodore Roosevelt in rough attire at Tower Falls, 1903. *Photo taken by Wilbur A. Hunt, a surveyor for the Corps of Engineers (from the author's collection).*

John Burroughs, Roosevelt's companion on the 1903 visit to Yellowstone Pa* *From the author's collection.*

president was vacationing with the cavalry) to protect the president from the idle curious and the news hawks who had swarmed into the town of Gardiner.

One newsman was not so easily discouraged. He informed himself concerning the country up-river by talking with various townsmen at Gardiner, obtained a dog (just why he thought that was a necessity is not clear), and set off to spy upon the president. He did not get far before he was intercepted by a cavalry patrol that proceeded to shoot the dog and take the newsman back to Gardiner, where he was put out of the Park and told not to reenter.

This vacation was apparently everything the president had hoped it might be. He saw large numbers of elk, and once was able to round up a band of them "so that John Burroughs could look at them," but he adds, "I do not think, however, that he cared to see them as much as I did."[37] Naturalist Burroughs was more interested in birds.

While camped near the old Tower Fall soldier station, about 500 feet west of the Calcite Springs overlook, Roosevelt was busy shaving when word was brought in that a band of mountain sheep across the Yellowstone River were disporting themselves on the rim above the prominent columnar basalt formation of the east wall. The president sprinted to a viewpoint "without hat or coat and with his face covered with lather." A legend has developed to the effect that Roosevelt's camp was on the site of the present Roosevelt Lodge, under the shelter of the huge Douglas fir that still stands there,[38] but Jack Haynes always maintained the story was a fabrication of Howard Hays, who found it useful to popularize his Roosevelt Lodge established at that point.

The presidential party returned to Fort Yellowstone on April 15 and left the next day for the interior of the Park in sleighs provided by Harry W. Child, president of the Yellowstone Park Association. Soon after Roosevelt's arrival at Norris Hotel, a shadow fell over the trip. One of the teamsters, George Marvin, a heavy man who had worked in the Park for twenty years, died from the strain on his heart of managing his four-horse team. Nevertheless Roosevelt and Burroughs continued the excursion; both tried skis at Norris and soon piled up in the snow—an event gleefully reported in the newspapers. The expedition continued to the Upper Geyser Basin, and on the return a side trip was made to the Grand Canyon. As the president wanted to see some bears, Scout James Morrisson called to the winter keeper at the Lake Hotel—a young man by the name of Bill Scales—in the hope that some bears might have broken hibernation there. Actually, they had. But Scales was a peculiar fellow; he had no use for Theodore Roosevelt and said there were no bears out. The presidential party turned back to Fort Yellowstone. Scales later explained his behavior this way: "I did not want to build fires, and clean up the mess that crowd would make."[39]

Roosevelt's party was back at Fort Yellowstone on April 22. There, he was allowed a little rest before making a public appearance in the National Hotel on the evening of April 23, at a dinner that became the occasion of a nostalgic reunion. One of the first persons the president inquired for on his arrival at Cinnabar was an old crony of his cattle ranching days in North Dakota. This man, who was probably Patrick McKeone (born in West Meath, Ireland, in 1850), had been the sheriff of Billings County, North Dakota, from 1892 to 1896, and it was there that Roosevelt met him. Of their association, and this reunion, Roosevelt wrote:

> In addition to my private duties, I sometimes served as deputy sheriff for the northern end of our county. The sheriff and I criss-crossed in our public and private relations. He often worked for me as a hired hand at the same time that I was his deputy. His name, or at least the name he went by, was Bill Jones, and as there were in the neighborhood several Bill Jones'—37 Bill Jones, Texas Bill Jones, and the like—the sheriff was known as Hellroaring Bill Jones. He was a thorough frontiersman, excellent in all kinds of emergencies, and a very game man. I became much attached to him. He was a thoroughly good citizen when sober, but he was a little wild when drunk. Unfortunately, toward the end of his life he got to drinking very heavily. When, in 1903 John Burroughs and I visited the Yellowstone Park, poor Bill Jones, very down in the world, was driving a team in Gardiner outside the Park. I had looked forward to seeing him, and he was equally anxious to see me. He kept telling his cronies of our intimacy and what we were going to do together, and then got drinking; and the result was that by the time I reached Gardiner he had to be carried out and left in the sagebrush. When I came out of the Park, I sent on in advance to tell them to be sure to keep him sober, and they did so.[40]

Johnny MacPherson and some of the Gardiner townsmen took Bill Jones over to Hall's Store and bought him a suit of clothes, then had him tubbed and shaved at the barber shop and sent him up to Mammoth Hot Springs in a surrey, for he was "beyond the years of bronco riding." According to the newspaper account, the president recognized his old friend immediately and said: "Bill, I'd give a hundred dollars for a half-hour's talk over old times; but we'll have to try it later."[41]

That may or may not be the way it was, for there is another version current locally. One of the men who shepherded Bill Jones to that dinner, at which there were more than two hundred invited guests, says they were late in getting there but that T. R. had held up the proceedings waiting for his friend. Our informant claims that Roosevelt wanted Bill Jones to sit beside him, but that Bill said he "wasn't goin' to eat with all those dressed up sons-of-bitches." So, he was served in another room.[42]

There is a sequel to this episode in the life of Hellroaring Bill Jones, who lasted only a short while after that. One stormy, winter day he was returning to his shack at a sawmill near the town of Jardine, when he stopped in at the Davis place to inquire the way. This was considered odd, since he was well acquainted with the locality, but he was given careful directions and went back into the storm. Later, his team was found tied at the gate where he had left them when he walked up to the house to make his inquiry, and, for the remainder of the winter, no trace of him could be found. The following spring a fisherman found him lying in the water of Bear Creek about one-half mile above Jardine, and that is where his grave is.

On the last day of his visit, the president took part in the ceremony dedicating the north entrance arch, which gave it the name of the Roosevelt Arch. The work being at just the proper stage for a cornerstone-laying at the time of the president's visit, Charles W. Miller, manager of the park hotels, had suggested that the president dedicate the arch, under Masonic auspices. Judge Meldrum communicated this idea to Major Pitcher, who replied on April 14:

Dear Judge: The President directs me to say that it will give him great pleasure to comply with the request of your committee concerning the laying of cornerstone at the entrance gate to the Yellowstone National Park, on April 24, 1903.

Captain Chittenden will see you tomorrow evening and will arrange the details for the ceremony.[43]

On the afternoon of the dedication, several thousand persons were on hand at Gardiner (four special trains had been run up from Livingston that day). Shortly after three o'clock a line of Masons formed on the main street and marched and counter-marched for some time accompanied by the Livingston band; then two troops of cavalry appeared from Fort Yellowstone, followed by Major Pitcher and the president of the United States. Promptly at four o'clock the ceremony was begun with the laying of the cornerstone, which was placed over a recess containing "a record of the proceedings of the last

President Theodore Roosevelt dedicates the north entrance arch, 1903. Capt. Chittenden is standing at the president's left ; John Burroughs (with white beard) is seated at his right.

meeting of the Grand Lodge, its code of laws, several coins, a Bible, several articles written several years ago by Cornelius Hedges of Helena advocating the creation of Yellowstone Park, some park views, a photo of President Roosevelt, the *Livingston Enterprise* and *Post* and a copy of the first and latest issues of *Wonderland*."[44] With the block of stone securely seated on mortar troweled into place by the president himself, the crowd was treated to one of Roosevelt's impromptu speeches.

The local newspaper reported the president was introduced by "Mayor" McCartney in "a very appropriate manner," but one who was present that day says that Jim froze up and was only able to mutter "Ladies and gentlemen, President Roosevelt."[45]

The president was more loquacious. He began by thanking the people of Montana, the soldiers, and the employees of the Park, "for my very enjoyable two-week holiday." Then he launched into a rambling speech on the uniqueness of the Park, the prospects for its management, the future of forest and water conservation, his hopes for the successful crossbreeding of buffalo with common cattle and his pleasure at again being in "this great western country." His closing line, which from any other politician would have been a platitude, seemed to ring true: "I like the country but above all I like the men and women." It was typical of Teddy and it went over big.

Following the ceremonies President Roosevelt was escorted to his railway car. Among those who conferred with the president during the hour before his departure was a Mr. Burns, park representative of President Mellen of the Northern Pacific Railroad. The *Wonderland* had noted on April 23 that "press dispatches last week made the statement that Captain Chittenden had been ordered to Manila, to take charge of some important work there. It is about the first time that an order in military circles has occasioned a storm of protest here, and regret is universally expressed and it is sincerely to be hoped that it may yet be rescinded." In local eyes the captain was considered to be "the hardest worker in the whole department." Burns explained to Roosevelt that Chittenden's plans were so fully made, and the work so well in hand, that it would be little short of a national calamity if he were not allowed to complete his current projects. The president agreed, and immediately dictated a letter to Secretary Root asking that the order transferring Chittenden be rescinded.

Burns brought that information to Captain Chittenden at once, but the engineer did not consider it good news. He went to the president's car and in private conversation explained that the change in assignment would put him in a bad light with the war department. The president agreed to withdraw his letter to the secretary of war. Nevertheless, President Mellen of the Northern Pacific Railroad later put a stop to Chittenden's transfer, so that in mid-June word was received from headquarters: "Orders will issue in two days revoking your orders to the Philippines against your protest."[46]

In the crowd at the dedication of the north entrance arch was "Uncle John" Yancey, who "came in to hear the president talk, as he has a warm spot in his heart for him." But Uncle John contracted a cold there that soon became pneumonia, and the old Kentuckian was carried away at two o'clock on the afternoon of May 7, 1903.[47] In his passing, the Park lost one of its most colorful characters—a man who was a personal friend not only of President Roosevelt but also of senators and congressmen, for he had an unusual faculty for making and holding friends. Uncle John is buried in the Gardiner cemetery.

This "goat-bearded, shrewd-eyed, lank, Uncle Sam type" (Owen Wister's description of Uncle John) came to Pleasant Valley in 1882. His first station, built on the Cooke City road for the accommodation of teamsters freighting to the mines, was a rock-walled, earth-roofed cavity in the toe of a rock slide. Upon receiving a lease in March 1884, allowing him the use of ten acres of land, Yancey began construction of a two-story log hotel, twenty by forty-three feet with a kitchen addition, which was completed prior to 1887. A log saloon was erected fifty feet east of the hotel some time between 1887 and 1893, and a large barn and cattle-feeding shed was added about the same time. A stage station for the convenience of the mail contractor on the Cooke City route was built after 1893 at a point 200 feet south of the saloon.

The principal building was known as Yancey's Pleasant Valley Hotel, though it was really more of a wayside inn for miners and freighters passing between Cinnabar and Cooke City. Frankly, it was a primitive establishment which Captain George Anderson thought was "not kept at a standard which would attract guests," yet Uncle John did have the patronage of a considerable number of outsiders who stopped there to enjoy the superb fishing on the Yellowstone River at that place now called Yancey's Hole. Thus, his unlikely hostel repeatedly sheltered such notables as Owen Wister, Ernest Thompson Seton, and Senators Boies Penrose and George Graham Vest.

Carl E. Schmide, who stayed at Yancey's hotel in 1901, describes it in his book, *A Western Trip*.

Uncle John F. Yancey, *from a studio portrait by Finn, Livingston, Mont.*

PLEASANT VALLEY HOTEL,

YELLOWSTONE NATIONAL PARK.

The prettiest place in the Rocky Mountains, and justly cele-
brated for excellent Trout Fishing in close proximity.

Excellent Accommodations for Tourists and Travelers.

The Petrified Forest and Tower Falls, two of the most inter-
esting features of the Park, within walking distance.

J. F. YANCEY, Proprietor.

Advertisement for John Yancey's Pleasant Valley Hotel near Tower Junction (prior to 1903). *From the author's collection.*

Yancey's Pleasant Valley Hotel. "Uncle" John is standing with his dog in front of the saloon building. *An F.J. Haynes photograph.*

We asked to be shown to our rooms. A pink cheeked little maid [daughter of the housekeeper-cook] leads the way up a stairway of creaking, rough boards and when we reach the top announces that the lady and her husband, meaning me and my daughter, can take Room No. 1. The little hallway in which we are standing is formed by un-dressed boards and the doors leading from it have large numbers marked upon them in chalk from one to five. An inspection of the bedrooms prove them to be large enough for a single bedstead with a box on which are washbowl, pitcher and part of a crash towel. Of the four window lights at least one was broken in every room. The cracks in the wall are pasted up with strips of newspaper. No. 1, being the bridal chamber, was distinguished from the others by a four by six looking glass. The beds showed they were changed at least twice, once in the spring and once in the fall of the year. A little bribe on the side and a promise to keep the act of criminality a secret from Uncle John induces the maid to provide us with clean sheets.[48]

Mr. Schmide adds that when he retired for the night in Room No. 2, the chill night air seeping in through a broken window caused him to forget that the blankets were "black with use," and he pulled them snugly about himself.

The cuisine was drab and repetitious, invariably organized around bacon and eggs—or fish fried in rancid butter, if someone had been to the river. The only relief from the frontier plainness of the "grub-pile" came with the slices of raw Bermuda onion which Uncle John often urged on his guests at breakfast, as "good for the narvs." The unpalatable menu was the principal complaint of the few outsiders who stopped at Yancey's, and it was that which caused Major John Pitcher to write the proprietor on May 31, 1902, with this advice:

I am aware of the fact that it is not an easy matter for you to run a first class restaurant or table at your hotel, on account of your isolated position and distance from the railroad, but you certainly can improve on your arrangements of last summer. You have an attractive place, and in your own interests I should suggest that you make some changes and improvements in the fare which you offer travellers and tourists.[49]

Yancey's hotel was said to accommodate twenty guests, but how that was done with only five rooms is a mystery. The charge for accommodations was $2 per day including meals, or $10 per week.

A unique feature of Yancey's establishment was the saloon building. On the second floor, reached by a steep, angled stairway, Uncle John slept on the floor with his two hound dogs, according to local gossip. The plain furniture of the saloon included a stove, a chair, a pair of up-ended barrels supporting boards which formed the bar, and on it, a whiskey keg, tin measure, and three glasses described as unwashed "since the day they had left the shelves of the crockery store." Mr. Schmide, author of that comment, adds that the whiskey was good, "perhaps because of Yancey's assurance that he received it direct from 'Old Kaintuck.' " Owen Wister had another explanation: Uncle John spiked the Bourbon with "some sort of fermented stuff made from oranges he obtained from California."

Uncle John was always short of change. The customer who handed him a quarter for a ten-cent drink could have two more drinks, or forego the drinks and the change, just as he chose. There seems to have been one man who did get his change. As Mrs. Lena Potter of Gardiner tells the story, a tourist proffered a $100 bill in payment for a drink and received 99 silver dollars in change. Herb French, a former stagecoach driver, tells a more specific version:

> There was a fellow named Bob Whitson that used to live on the Stillwater, and he was up here workin' on the Mount Washburn road—workin' under Kelly—and, at that time, the paymaster'd come around to give you your check. . . . They give this guy his check and so he quit and came down to Uncle John's. All he had was his check. So he had supper, lodging, and breakfast, and he sprung the check on Uncle John. Uncle John said, "you thought I didn't have money enough to cash it didn't ya?" Whatever is was—50 or 60 dollars—he give 'im all dollars, y'see, and this guy was walkin' from there—all dollars![50]

Upon John Yancey's death the Pleasant Valley hotel passed into the hands of a nephew, Dan Yancey of Livingston, Montana. About three years later, on April 16, 1906, the hotel building burned to the ground. Thereafter, Dan lost interest in the place and neglected to pay the annual rental on the lease. The secretary of the interior notified him on November 11, 1907, that his privilege was cancelled. Dan Yancey was later paid one thousand dollars for the other structures, thus terminating any property rights he might have retained.

Even as the foundations were being prepared for the north entrance arch, the gray sandstone for another notable structure was arriving at the railhead. This material had been prefinished at a Minnesota quarry and was shipped marked for reassembling into a headquarters building for the U.S. engineers in the Park. It was a distinctive structure—truly a show piece—when completed. The coursed Ashlar masonry of its exterior walls, the green-glazed tiles of its pagoda-like roof and the rich oak finish of its interior gave Chittenden's new office a solid dignity which remains to this day.

Toward the end of the summer season, Chittenden was ready to begin the work that remains his best memorial: the Chittenden Bridge at Grand Canyon. He had already decided the bridge should be built above the Upper Fall of the Yellowstone River, just at the head of the rapid, where projecting buttresses of volcanic rock compressed the flow so that it could be bridged by a span of 120 feet. He had also decided that some form of arch or suspension bridge would be more suitable than the ordinary steel truss contemplated by Captain Anderson a decade earlier. He recognized that a masonry structure would be excessively expensive, so was pleased when he came upon a description of a steel-reinforced concrete arch bridge designed by an engineer named Melan, which would be a compromise between beauty and economy. He obtained use of this patented design, and materials for construction were assembled at Canyon early in the summer.

Construction began with placement of a falsework timber frame supported on two abutments and a large, rock-filled pier of green timber sunk in the center of the stream. This part of the work was completed August 1. The bridge built upon the falsework would have a length of 160 feet and a width of 18½ feet. At the top of the arch, where the surface of the roadway was to be 2½ feet higher than at either end of the bridge, the thickness was 24 inches. Strength was derived from ten arched steel girders enclosed by a monolithic pour of concrete; that is, the bridge was to be one continuous mass of material without joints at any point, and with no filling of earth or rubble in its 900-cubic-yard bulk.

In the days before large mixing machines, preparation had to be made with great care to insure continuity in the work of pouring such a large mass of concrete. Since the crewmen would do the mixing on a single twenty-five-foot mortar board, the materials were stockpiled close to them. The mixing was done in this manner: material was wheeled to the board, mixed three times dry, turned three times as water was added, and then turned three times more before it was shoveled into wheelbarrows and pushed to the bridge. The method allowed a mixing rate of ten cubic yards per hour. One hundred-fifty men worked in three shifts of eight hours each. The job was scheduled so the night shift would have the advantage of a full moon to supplement the electric lights powered by a portable dynamo borrowed from the hotel company. The work of pouring the concrete began at seven A.M. on August 10, beginning at each abutment of the structure and proceeding to completion at the center of the arch—a junction effected after seventy-two hours at 10 A.M. on August 13.

The falsework was removed on September 8, twenty-eight days after completion of the pour, and careful measurements of the structure showed that it had settled only one-tenth of an inch after the supports were removed. With its balustrade in place, the completed bridge was a uniquely beautiful structure exactly fitting the site.[51]

By 1960, the action of frost and weathering had made such inroads on the original Chittenden Bridge that a reconstruction of the span was indicated. (It was also too narrow for modern vehicular traffic, as well as somewhat dangerous because the low positioning of drivers in present-day automobiles made it difficult for them to see over the raised center.) Thus, Chittenden's masterpiece was replaced in 1962, after fifty-nine years of service, by a similar appearing structure built upon the same site, and appropriately designated the Chittenden Memorial Bridge.

In the same banner year of 1903, the east entrance road was opened to traffic on July 10, although much work remained to be done. (The project was not completed until 1905, when the spiral east of Sylvan Pass was finished.) Considerable progress was also made in closing the last gap in the Park's belt line—the section between the Grand Canyon and Tower Junction. But this proved more difficult than expected because of the large amount of rock work required, and neither the Dunraven Pass road nor the scenic loop over the top of Mount Washburn were usable until 1905. Thus, it was at the conclusion of the 1905 working season that the project upon which Chittenden had labored so long and so well could be considered complete. The cost of all construction and maintenance work on roads and bridges in the Park was then reckoned at $1,830,359.42. The expenditure had produced the first road system of any extent in the United States built according to definite, uniform specifications. For a time, it was a unique and inspiring model.

Major Hiram M. Chittenden, the man whose genius brought the Yellowstone Park road system to completion, was transferred to other duties early in 1906. The officers who succeeded him only had to maintain the system and make minor improvements at points of interest. Among the latter was one project that involved the removal of rock from around one of the petrified trees at the end of the spur road built earlier from Yancey's. The standing, stony trunk was then enclosed with a wrought iron fence set in concrete to thwart the vandalism of specimen pickers. It was noted that "a second stump in the immediate vicinity should be similarly protected,"[52] but it wasn't and has since disappeared. Similar protection was given the small pile of rock on top of Mount Washburn which was all that remained of

Visitors at the petrified tree near Yancey's hotel. In 1907, this thirty-foot stump was fenced to protect it from specimen collectors, who removed every trace of the other tree in background.

the original summit of the mountain. (That, too, is now gone; it was turned into parking area at some later date.) But concern only with such relatively minor things did not last long, for there was a pressure swelling up around the Park that would soon sweep it into another grand construction program.

Early in 1904, a committee of citizens of Bozeman, Montana, wrote to Senator Paris Gibson asking him to press for construction of a road from the West Fork of the Gallatin River into the Park by way of Bighorn Pass. A survey of the proposed route was finally made by Lieutenant Ernest Peek in 1907, and, while he found that a crude road could be built for $32,055, or a more adequate one for approximately $100,000, he came to the conclusion that the burden of maintenance would be very great "without any corresponding benefit to the general public."[53] That particular proposal was easily relegated to limbo, but the force that generated it (the growing number of automobiles in the immediate vicinity of the Park) was not at all lessened. In May 1910 the county commissioners of Gallatin County, Montana, obtained permission to survey and build a road through the northwest corner of the Park in order to provide a more direct route between Bozeman and the new settlement at the west entrance to the Park (present West Yellowstone). The 31.1 miles of county road built within the Park under this agreement shortened the distance between Bozeman and the west entrance to seventy-five miles, half of what it had previously been.[54]

At the same time, automobiles were becoming common enough in the immediate vicinity of the Park for the organization of clubs devoted to the particular interests of automobilists. A Bannock County Automobile Club appeared at Pocatello, Idaho, in the summer of 1911, and a Gallatin Valley Automobile Association was organized at Bozeman at about the same time. These fledgling organizations tried to arrange with Utah automobilists for a grand tour by two hundred vehicles from Salt Lake City, Ogden, and Denver, about September 15, as part of a movement to force revocation of the rule excluding automobiles from Yellowstone National Park. While this grandiose plan failed of its promise, which was "to be the opening wedge whereby the Park will be open to autoists after this year,"[55] the efforts of these clubs, backed by the American Automobile Association and by the work of those groups interested in the so-called park-to-park highway (a proposed route to link Yellowstone and Glacier National Parks) and the Yellowstone highway, between the Park and Minnesota's twin cities, inevitably bore some fruit. Senate Resolution No. 275, April 2, 1912, called upon the War Department to submit an estimate "of the cost of new roads or changes in the present roads in the Yellowstone National Park in order to permit of the use of automobiles and motorcycles therein without interfering with the present mode of travel in vehicles drawn by horses or other animals."[56]

In response to that request, Captain C. H. Knight, the engineer officer in charge of work in the Park, estimated the cost of putting the existing stagecoach roads in a condition suitable for automobiles to be approximately $2,265,000. Large as the amount was, it did not deter the Congress from including in the Sundry Civil Bill approved August 24, 1912, an item for $77,000 with which to begin the work of widening and improving the road surfaces, and for reconstructing bridges and culverts in order to make the park roads "suitable and safe for animal-drawn and motor-propelled vehicles."[57] With the passage of that legislation, preparation began for the eventual entry of the automobile, despite the fact that the secretary of the interior had not yet made his historic decision to admit such vehicles into all national parks.[58]

It must be noted that the automobile gained a foothold in Yellowstone Park only a month after its precedent-setting victory at Yosemite. A memorandum of May 31, 1913, states:

> Automobiles will be allowed to travel over the wagon road between Gallatin Station, Yellowstone National Park, and the town of Yellowstone, Montana, of which road about 17 miles lies wholly within the park. This authority granted upon condition that extraordinary care be exercised not to jeopardize life or limb of persons using road with animal-drawn vehicles; that speed limit does not exceed 15 miles per hour; that rules and regulations of the park be strictly observed; and with further understanding that additional regulations and toll charges may be exacted later by the Department if found desirable.[59]

The secretary of the interior, Franklin K. Lane, visited Yellowstone National Park from July 30 to August 3, 1913. He was impressed with the excellence of the system of roads and bridges which Hiram M. Chittenden had laid out in the Park, and particularly the road to the top of Mount Washburn, which he decided should be known as Chittenden Road. So, he "directed the acting superintendent to make that fact of record and cause suitable sign posts to be erected."[60] Despite the secretary's good opinion of the road system, there had been considerable deterioration under Chittenden's successors. From 1906 to 1912, the annual appropriations for maintenance of roads and bridges were far too small for such an extensive system, and Captain Knight mentioned the cumulative result of deferred maintenance in the "worn out bridges, which, in their present condition, are a positive menace to the lives of travellers," and also in the fact that the entire road surface was in a "poor and worn out condition."[61] Funding was better after 1912, yet the roads were never made satisfactory for automobile traffic during the remaining tenure of the army engineers in the Park. In the latter days, the Corps of Engineers struggled endlessly against the great slide that endangered the road through the Gardner Canyon in 1911. Elaborate masonry revetments failed to hold it; a steam shovel was unable to bucket away the debris rapidly enough; and hydraulic sluicing only worsened the problem. The road finally had to be moved back to the east side of the Gardner River where it had been in Lamartine's day. This was all frustrating, inconvenient, and expensive, as well as hard on the reputations of certain engineer officers. Yet, some progress was made during those years. The oiling of park roads was begun in 1915, and motorization of the maintenance operation was initiated the following year with the purchase of two dump trucks.

To this point, little has been said of the host of workingmen who built and maintained the Park's roads and bridges in a day of pick and shovel and giant powder, of horse-drawn slip and pull grader and primitive tent camps; likewise, the young men who did the clerical work and served as survey assistants have been largely anonymous, with little said to mark their hard but fruitful lives.

Road work, being a seasonal business in the early days, was accomplished mainly with crews hired on the spot when needed. A few local men could be picked up to serve as foremen and subforemen, and others were hired with their teams to handle the railroad plows for breaking the earth, the slips, scrapers, and dump wagons to move the earth, and freight rigs to haul supplies and forage for the crews. The bulk of the working force, however, was made up of pick and shovel laborers (husky young lads from nearby ranches or transient workingmen hired on the street at Gardiner). The itinerants, some of them mere tramps, appeared in the spring as regularly as the swallows of Capistrano, sheltering as best they could, odd-jobbing, begging a little, even stealing at times, while they waited for work to open up in the Park. Mrs. Potter remembers how, from the old bridge below town

> clear up to where the checking station is now, along the Yellowstone and along the Gardner, was just one man after another with a roll of bedding, waiting for the Park to open so they could get a job . . . . One year Congress didn't vote the money in very early, and really, it was a

menace to the town . . . those men didn't have any money and if there was any place they thought they could break in, they broke in. And one time we had to apply to the government to come down and move them.[62]

The foremen and the assistant engineers and overseers hired what men they needed from that labor pool, signing them on at the going rate of $1.75 per day and food. The paperwork was negligible, and the men could be dropped if they proved lazy or inept. Al McLaughlin, later a famous driver of a six-horse tally-ho, recalled how he went to work on a road crew at the age of sixteen. He was raised on a ranch below Gardiner, of which he says, "we didn't have much on it," and, being the oldest, he decided to get out and find a job. So he went up to the Park and applied to foreman John Spiker for work. The necessary personnel actions were handled in this manner: "Well, son, you can drive a team, can't you?" "Yes, sir." "Alright," Spiker said, "roll your bedding in that tent over there, and you'll drive a team, but listen, you're not to hold the plow and you're not to hold the scraper—a boy as young as you are." Al never forgot that genuine concern.

For several summers, the same foreman had a black cook named Bill Brumington, who was a genius at converting the government ration (long on bacon, beans, and biscuit) into something tastier. He would trade staples for vegetables brought in by sagebrushers making the circuit of the Park in their farm wagons, and he knew how to make good doughnuts. Bill often put in long days feeding up to one hundred men with only one "cookee" to flunkie for him. One evening Bill sent the flunkie around to the tents, where the men were smoking and chatting, with a big bowl of doughnuts, one for each man before going to bed. The remainder he left covered on the table in the mess tent to be served at breakfast. In the morning not a doughnut was left. Thinking the men had stolen them, Bill was so mad that he wouldn't talk to anyone. The crew was perplexed, not knowing what the trouble was, and Bill kept up his silence until camp was moved. Then, when the floor boards of the kitchen tent were taken up, there were all the doughnuts stored underneath, where a pack rat had put them away. Bill said: "Well, you boys are free now; I thought you stole the doughnuts."[63]

Living conditions were hard. The tent camps were moved often to keep them near the work, and no more effort was expended upon them than was required (for example, when establishing camp, the foreman "will see that tents are arranged in as regular order as the accidents of the ground will permit."[64]) The work was also hard, but

The tent of a road worker's family in a Corps of Engineers camp, 1913.

One of Capt. Chittenden's road crews in camp. *Photograph courtesy of Doris Whithorn, Livingston, Mont.*

the pay was relatively good. James B. Wasden, who went to work in the spring of 1892 as a subforeman, thought his pay of $75 per month large compared to the $40 he had been getting for skinning a freight team. The food was also as good as could be managed: solid and plentiful. In the days before refrigeration, fresh beef was obtained from meat contractors who drove their animals in on the hoof and slaughtered them as needed. A sample menu from the foreman's instruction booklet suggested the bill-of-fare for Wednesday, for example, as follows: For breakfast: oatmeal, hot bread, beef steak, baked potatoes, and coffee. For dinner: soup, corned beef and cabbage, boiled potatoes, onions, bread and butter, dessert, and coffee. For supper: hash, hot bread, fruit, and tea. Such predetermined menus merely helped the cook to work with the limitations of the supplies furnished to him.

In addition to the pay and the food, "sock and tobacco" were available from the timekeeper; so that life in those tent camps, which might be situated in mosquito-plagued marshes along Snake River, in the windy throat of Sylvan Pass or amid snowbanks a mere 800 feet below the summit of Mount Washburn, was not so bad for men who worked hard enough to sleep well at night.

There was another reason for the high morale that seems to have existed continuously within these crews: the men knew their efforts were appreciated. When the Chittenden Bridge was built, the daily wage was raised two bits (to $2 a shift) for the extra effort, and one of the workmen notes: "We were real proud of that job." Also, when President Roosevelt dedicated the north entrance arch, he asked all the park employees to line up, the horny-handed laborers of the road crew along with the others, and shook their hands and wished them well. Captain Chittenden, too, never forgot his men were people (though he had as many as 800 men and 240 teams at work in the Park at one time).[65]

Chittenden's recommendations for the maintenance force reveal the extent of operations in the Park. He thought the office should be staffed by a clerk, a copyist, two assistants, a receiver of materials, a team hirer, and a timekeeper for the laborers. As overhead for the field work he recommended an overseer, two assistant engineers, and a messenger; the actual work was to be accomplished by four crews, each consisting of a foreman, a subforeman, a cook, two cookees, a blacksmith, a water carrier, forty-five laborers and fifteen teams. There was to be a combined sawmill and bridge crew under a foreman and two subforemen, with the necessary skilled help, common laborers, and teams. Construction projects were to be carried on by as many more organized crews as the work at hand required.[66]

After completion of the park road system in 1905, the maintenance organization was placed on a different basis. Small crews were established at points about ten miles apart, and these units, of from thirteen to fifteen men under a foreman, included a cook, eight or ten laborers, and two drivers of sprinkling wagons. Thus, it was possible to lay the dust for five miles each way from the camp with the horse-drawn sprinkling wagons, while the crew accomplished whatever maintenance work was needed within the sector. As soon as satisfactory locations were determined for the camps, small permanent buildings were constructed to house supplies and kitchen, and mangers were built for feeding the teams.[67] Such semipermanent camps, which Chittenden likened to the section-gang system on railroads, were the forerunners of the road camps of a later day.

Work at Corps of Engineers headquarters is revealed to us today through the eyes of a young clerk who kept a diary while employed by Captain Chittenden at Mammoth Hot Springs in the summer of 1902.[68] Albert L. Noyes, twenty, was a civil service appointee from St. Paul, Minnesota. He arrived at the Cinnabar terminus on the fourth of July, and, having his "wheel" in the baggage car, he tried to ride to Mammoth Hot Springs, an experience which got him "wet, cold & muddy." Fortunately, he was picked up halfway by a government rig and delivered to Mammoth Hot Springs "very, very tired." He started to work in the office the following day, and on the sixth, a Sunday, found time to rig up a proper bed in his tent, unpack his trunk, and settle down. Two days later he notes that he had "hustled lamp for tent, two chairs, washbasin, pail, cup & made wash stand. Very cold for this time of yr."

His entry for July 13 states: "Hot A.M. not much work . . . clear evening played ball, cards P.M." and two days later, "bot. lemons . . . paid 40 cents for 8. Drank so much lemonaid got sick . . . wind blowing like sam hill very dusty & out of the wind hot oh so hot. Tent blew full of pulverized manure off formation covering." Noyes was there just at the time when the parade ground and the area around the buildings had been covered with topsoil hauled from the hill to the north, and a lawn had not yet established; nor were the permanent buildings of the engineer headquarters yet built, so everything was housed under canvas except the stores, which were in three small frame buildings.

So it went that summer: there was swimming at "boiling river" and Bath Lake; the laundry was sent to Sam Toy, the Chinese who had set up business in the old McCartney cabin in Clematis Gulch; and souvenirs were coated in mineral waters of the hot springs. There was berry picking and shooting at jack rabbits with sling shots, and days when it was just "work, work," for which Noyes received $50 per month. Inevitably there came the day when he confided to his diary, "I begin to tire of the monotony. Say won't take another office job."

In mid-September the young man was allowed to make a tour of the Park with Paymaster Oakley G. Haines, who had to take the prepared payroll sheets to each of the crews to get signatures of the workers; then their checks were drawn and the men were paid. This gave Noyes an eight-day tour of the Park before he left for home.

Captain Chittenden's consideration for his young men stands out in another instance. Neil Clark rented a mountain surrey and a team from the transportation company in order to take Miss Borden, Captain Chittenden's stenographer, for a drive. All went well and Neil delivered Miss Borden to her quarters and drove to the trough to water the horses before taking the rig back to the barn. There he made a mistake; he got out of the surrey to get a drink for himself, the horses took fright and were off for the barn in a moment. On arriving there both horses tried to go through the door at the same time. The harness and surrey were a wreck, the pole broken, wheels awry, axles bent, and poor Neil in almost as bad condition from fear of what it would cost him. Through the good offices of Captain Chittenden, the transportation company let the young man off with a token payment of $50. The incident was ever after referred to as "Neil's $50 buggy ride."

Much more could be said of the Corps of Engineers, which built and maintained the Park's roads and bridges over a period of thirty-five years until July 1, 1918, when Major G. E. Verrill turned over the business of the Corps of Engineers in Yellowstone Park to Chief Engineer George E. Goodwin of the National Park Service. With that transfer went something more than the responsibility for 278.8 miles of main road, 24.8 miles of secondary road, and 106.5 miles of approach road in the forest reserves; and something more was transferred than a road crew totaling 150 men and 70 teams, with all its tools, equipment and buildings. Also handed along was an idea—the idea of park-standard roads—roads with the least detrimental effect on the landscape. Long ago, Chittenden wrote:

> The selection of roads in the national park should obviously proceed on different principals than obtain in the selection of roads for ordinary traffic. The former are emphatically *park* roads. Their use is principally for tourist traffic, secondarily only for the hauling of freight. As recommended by Major Allen in his report for 1889, "all roads in the park should be well contructed not only with a view to permanency but also

Construction of the road through Firehole Canyon, 1917.

A bridge over the Firehole River built by the Corps of Engineers. This structure remains serviceable after sixty-five years of heavy use. *Photograph by the author.*

to appearance." In their selection the shortest distance between the terminal points should not be the object of first importance. While the road ought not to be unnecessarily lengthened, it should be selected with a view of securing easy grades and proximity to as many as possible of the features of interest near which it passes. In short, everything should be done to reduce to a minimum the irksomeness of the long drives that separate the principal points of interest in the park.[69]

In speaking of the road between Norris and the Grand Canyon, the eleven miles called Norris Cutoff, Chittenden noted,

> The road bed is here as good as any in the park, and yet the subject of constant criticism on the part of tourists. The reason is that there are many miles where the road follows nearly a straight line with little attempt to avoid the hills, and where the view ahead is one continuous succession of ups and downs visible along the narrow roadway cut through the woods. . . . It goes without saying that if this road had been made more winding, following the valleys and avoiding the hills, thus by its short views ahead giving the tourists the continual sense of expectancy, instead of treating him to the long perspective of a monotonous roadway ahead of him, the whole effect would have been better. The importance of securing these features may not be very apparent at the time the road is being built, but it is fully appreciated by those who subsequently use it.[70]

The work of the corps, and its contribution to Yellowstone National Park, to our national park system, and to the park idea everywhere, should perhaps have its memorial. If we were to propose one it would be upon the southern shoulder of Mount Washburn, a few steps from Chittenden Road, built by the Park's greatest engineer; for there, behind a clump of alpine fir, stands a rusty railroad plow where the teamster unhitched it at the conclusion of his work. There it remains, a nostalgic relic of a great era, with the far-flung panorama of half the Park spread out below.

CHAPTER 18

THE COMING OF
THE AUTO

*If Adam had known what harm the serpent
was going to work, he would have tried to
prevent him from finding lodgment in
Eden; and if you were to realize what the
result of the automobile will be . . . you will
keep it out.*

—Lord James Bryce, 1912

The British ambassador uttered those prescient words at a banquet of the American Civic Association in Baltimore just as the campaign of American automobilists to get their noisy, smelly, somewhat unreliable vehicles into the Yosemite Valley was reaching a victorious climax.[1] Though he referred to the Yosemite, his words applied equally well to Yellowstone Park, where a similar struggle was taking place; and there, also, the automobilists were victorious, so that the Park has never been the same since.

But it is not our purpose to dwell on the consequences of the admission of private automobiles—certainly a mixed blessing, in which a most desirable democratization of the Park has been largely negated by the destructive impact upon the environment; rather, we are concerned here only with the change and how it was accomplished.

The Yellowstone story has always been concomittant with the development of transportation facilities. The founders presumed the wonderful region they were setting aside soon would be made available to large numbers of tourists through the construction of the Northern Pacific Railroad, and that the traffic thus generated would be served within the Park by concessioners willing to pay large fees for their privileges (incidentally relieving the government from any expense in the operation of the people's playground). But that is not what happened.

A decade of adversity for the railroad was reflected within the Park by a corresponding period of stagnation and penury, and, when development at last began, in consequence of the extension of tracks into the vicinity, it was development that subserved the railroad's interests—though not exactly what the monopolists had sought. The result was the shaping of the park business into a form of operation in which tourists were delivered to the area by rail, hauled through it in horse-drawn stagecoaches, and accommodated at large hotels while within the bounds.

This system was oriented toward the first-class trade, catering to those of more than average means, and it had the effect of turning the Park into a semi-exclusive haunt of middle- and upper-class vacationers. It was always operated in a manner to discourage "sage-brushers" (visitors who came in their own rigs and camped by the wayside) and "independents" (outsiders who conducted visitors through the Park in a similar manner), and the success of the methods employed to exclude such unremunerative use (from the concessioner's viewpoint) is evident from available records. The graph shows the increasing percentage of visitation transported by regular carriers operating within the Park (from 50 percent in 1893 to slightly more than 82 percent in 1915). The prominent sag in 1897 was due to the franchised company's inability to fully serve a large number of Christian Endeavor tourists who visited the Park. Independents were encouraged to pick up the slack and, once they had a piece of the business, they tended to hang on to it for a time.

Actually, the transportation service in the Park (despite its monopoly character) was a remarkably efficient operation that annually handled thousands of visitors on reliable schedules. Some idea of the magnitude of the problem can be had from a listing of the vehicles and stock used by the three transportation companies in 1909. There were 6 large Concord coaches of the six-horse, 29-passenger type known locally as a tally-ho; 165 four-horse Concord

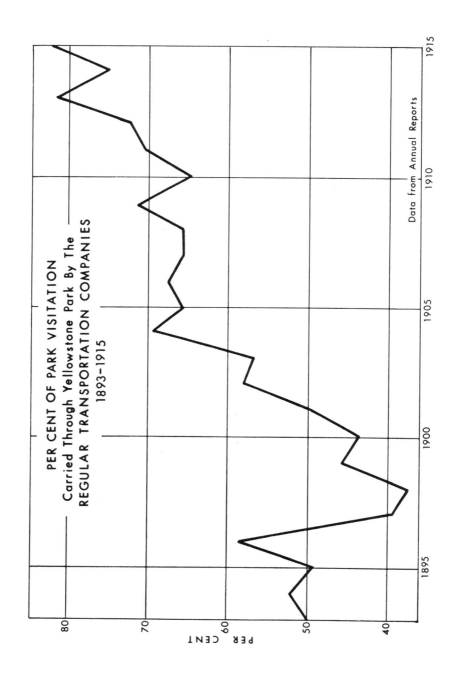

PER CENT OF PARK VISITATION
Carried Through Yellowstone Park By The
REGULAR TRANSPORTATION COMPANIES
1893–1915

Data from Annual Reports

PER CENT

coaches seating 11 passengers; 79 two-horse surreys; 14 "formation wagons," and 129 mountain spring-wagons—the total drawn by 1,372 horses.[2]

The passenger-carrying vehicles of one company required the services of 83 drivers for the entire summer, supplemented by 155 temporaries during the peak of the travel. They worked directly under a transportation superintendent and the agents who represented him at the hotels. In addition, there was a stable foreman, 8 stablemen, 2 day-herders, 1 night-herder, 3 blacksmiths, a wagon maker, a coach painter, a coach washer, and a varying number of freighters engaged in hauling tons of hay and oats for the use of the teams on the passenger rigs.

From the yellow, red, or brown coaches (the color identified the company) with their sleek, snorty teams to the colorful drivers, and on down through the backup organization to the washers, who kept the rigs clean and pretty, it was a smooth-functioning outfit—the perfection of a century of American business know-how; and it must have seemed incredible that a "rickety, ugly, and still unreliable mechanical contraption" could make the coaches obsolete in a few years.[3]

The automobile owes much, in its appearance upon the American scene, to the bicycle. This vehicle became practical in 1871 with the introduction of the "ordinary," which had a front wheel 40 to 60 inches in diameter, driven by pedals, and connected from its steering fork to a small trailing wheel by means of a curved back bone. But they were dangerous to ride, requiring peculiar balancing skill, and although the large front wheel gave a smooth ride, "headers" were frequent. The early machines were heavy, but the use of tubing in the frame, and development of the tangentially-spoked wire wheel in 1874, reduced the weight to less than 50 pounds. The ordinaries were strictly men's bicycles, of interest here because a few of them got into the Park very early.

The first of the ungainly wheels to make an appearance anywhere near the Park was a source of amusement to onlookers in the town of Bozeman, Montana, in October of 1881.[4] Similar machines were used by three members of a Laramie, Wyoming, bicycle club on a tour of the Park two years later.

The group—William O. Owens, Charles S. Greenbaum, and Walter K. Sinclair—boarded a Union Pacific train at Laramie with their wheels and equipment and rode the cars to Beaver Canyon station on the Utah & Northern narrow gauge line. There they hired a team, light wagon, and driver to haul their camp outfit and left at 9

A.M. on September 19 for the Park by the dirt road that passed over
the Camas prairie to Henrys Fork of the Snake River. They reached
Rea's ranch at the river crossing fifty-five miles from their starting
point at 6 o'clock that evening. The following day they covered the
remaining forty-eight miles to Marshall's Hotel in the Lower Geyser
Basin, and from the twenty-first to the twenty-ninth they toured all
the points in the Park that could then be reached by road. Their dusty,
sweaty tour of the Park was comfortable compared to the return to
Beaver Canyon, made entirely in rain, sleet, and snow.[5] At least one
other ordinary was ridden into the Park in the eighties (see Chapter
17); however it took a further development of the bicycle to make it
generally usable.

The modern bicycle had its origin in the "safety bicycle" of H. J.
Lawson, which appeared in the United States in 1885 as the Rover
safety. In four years the Rover was dominant. The development of the
pneumatic tire by John Boyd Dunlop in 1888 greatly increased the
comfort of bicycling. By 1890 United States industry was building
safe, comfortable, and practical machines. By 1893 there were more
than one million bicycles in use in this country and the bicycle craze of
the nineties was well under way. In Yellowstone Park, a trio of cyclists
went through the area on safety bicycles in 1897; by this time bicycles
had become sufficiently numerous in the Park to require regulating
them.[6]

The three young men who alighted from the train at Cinnabar
station "unshorn, unshaven and unkempt" from their four days of
travel by chair car could understand why the ladies held back their
skirts. Retrieving their wheels from the baggage man, they attached
their blanket rolls and fishing rods to handle bars, stowed utensils and
provisions in small school satchels and valises behind their seats, and
moved out with such odd items as a coffee pot and canteen tied on
here and there. And therein lay a great virtue of the safety bicycle:
unlike their predecessors who toured the Park on the ungainly
ordinaries, these boys needed no escort wagon to carry their camp
outfit. Otherwise, the going was not any easier for they too found the
upgrade to be "miles of toil for us, pushing our heavily laden wheels . . .
right hard, solid work."[7]

Beyond the Golden Gate riding was easier and they were able to
camp for the night near Apollinaris Spring, with a blanket tent for
shelter and a huge supper of bacon, potatoes, bread, and coffee. It
was a comfortable place within sight of other campfires, from one of
which came the tinkle of a banjo and a girl's voice singing familiar
songs.

They proceeded the following day along a smooth road they considered a "cyclist's dream," going around the features at Norris Geyser Basin and on to Nez Perce Creek, where evening found them near the summer encampment of the U.S. cavalry detachment in the Lower Geyser Basin. There they established rapport with the swaddies, who not only steered them to an abandoned cabin for the night but invited them into the mess tent for food. They slept another night in a grove of trees "with the song of the geysers as our lullaby," and struggled through sand which seemed bottomless and endless as they crossed the Continental Divide toward Yellowstone Lake. At the Thumb they were happy to trundle their wheels aboard the little steamer *Zillah* for an easy crossing of Yellowstone Lake to a camp by the soldier station near the outlet.

They spent the evening with the soldiers, singing to the accompaniment of a guitar and listening to tales of poachers and wild chases after highwaymen. The next morning there was time for good fishing before they pedaled on toward the Grand Canyon. Their campsite that night was the most memorable of all, on the brink of the "jumping-off place" of the fairy tales, where they could contemplate the shadows in the fathomless gulf of the canyon below them. That, like their whole tour, was such a rich adventure it is no wonder the return to Cinnabar and the railway was tinged with regret at having to re-enter "commonplace civilization."

Young men enjoying an economical vacation were not the only cyclists in those days. Frequently a wagon party would bring along a bicycle on which everyone could ride by turns, including the ladies. The most unusual group of cyclists to go through the Park was a military detachment from Fort Missoula, Montana. This "infantry bicycle corps," which was the inspiration of Lieutenant James A. Moss, consisted of 23 men who toured the Park in the course of an 800-mile training march in the summer of 1896.[8] Lieutenant Moss had hoped to develop the bicycle into a substitute for the cavalry horse, but his hopes were dashed by the rapid development of the automobile.

A further example of bicycling in the Yellowstone shows the prestige of those wheelmen of yesterday. In 1892, R. O. Vandercook, a newspaperman of Evanston, Wyoming, and Professor C. S. Cook of Northwestern University toured Wyoming and Yellowstone Park with a high-wheeled bicycle and a horse-drawn wagon. They took turns riding the bicycle or put it in the wagon if the going was too rough, which it frequently was because they entered the Park from Cooke City over the miner's road. Vandercook was on the bicycle after they left Yancey's on their way toward Mammoth Hot Springs, and he decided to ride ahead and see if there was any mail waiting for them at the hotel. He described his experience thus:

> It started to rain and the clay roads turned to mud and I got soaking wet. Several miles from the Springs, I approached the top of a hill and there below in the valley, I could see the hotel. The clear atmosphere of the west makes it possible to see great distances. There were quite a few people on the veranda of the hotel and some of them were peering through binoculars. They soon discovered my high wheel, silhouetted against the mountains.
>
> Being young, I felt the need of making a dramatic entrance. It was a steep, downhill grade and although the road was muddy, I went down as fast as the wheels would turn, mud spurting all over. I rode up to the stage landing with a flourish, jumped off the bike, and swaggered into the hotel lobby with water squirting out of my moccasins at every step. I carried a gun and a sheathed hunting knife in my belt; my face was covered with several weeks growth of beard. Of course, the guests of the hotel all stared. It was a big moment. I strode up to the desk and registered—R. O. Vandercook of the Evanston Press and Chicago Herald. Then I pulled my knife from my belt and called to a colored bellboy standing near, "Come and help me scrape off this mud." He followed me to the washroom and between us we cleaned off as much mud as possible.
>
> While standing at the desk a whiff of food came from the dining room, and I experienced the ravenous hunger which comes from a hard day's bicycle ride. Almost every one in the dining room was in evening clothes but I had money in my pocket and was too hungry to worry about social barriers, so in I went. Every time my sleeve contacted the immaculate tablecloth, it left a wet mark, but in spite of the fact that I knew I was not presentable, I never enjoyed a meal more than I did that one. I had been eating the usual camp fare for some weeks and the hotel food tasted like the famed "nectar and ambrosia." The manager of the hotel came up to me as I left the dining room and said, "I am always glad to meet the gentlemen of your profession. May I give you a courtesy card for all the hotels in the park?[9]

The bold wheelsmen had influence even in the Yellowstone country; also, they belonged to the future, not the past, as one of their favorite tunes proclaimed: "You've been a good old wagon but you've done broke down."[10]

The effect of the bicycle on the development of the automobile is traceable in such features as the indispensable pneumatic tire and the method of constructing light, strong wheels. It is in other ways however that the gas buggy profited most from its little predecessor. The bicycle (or rather, the bicycle craze) was a phenomenon that touched the American people as nothing had before. During the half-dozen years when bicycling was a national fever, Americans became used to a personal mobility they had never before known and would never give up. As a result, the hemlines of ladies' dresses went up and women became used to healthful exercise. There was an irresistible public demand for the improvement of roads, which had been execrable outside of cities, and Americans learned how to organize in clubs and groups to get what they wanted.

The first automobile that Henry Ford road tested in 1893,[11] was to profit greatly from the efforts of the bicycle fadists, who numbered more than thirty million by the end of the nineteenth century and had organized themselves as the League of American Wheelmen. Meeting in local and national congresses, the wheelmen had pioneered the marking of roads and preparation of road maps and guide books; had organized tours and bedeviled local and national authorities into doing something about the roads. A direct result was the establishment of the National League for Good Roads in 1892, a group that pressed for federal action and got it the following year in the form of an act of Congress establishing the Office of Road Inquiry. The wheelmen also fought out a succession of legal battles of tremendous importance to later automobilists. Through court actions in several eastern states they established the right of vehicles to use the public roads regardless of their motive power, that is, with other than horse power. While this may sound trivial in our time, it was a hurdle of the first magnitude in a day when many people (and most farmers) were vociferously against anything that scared horses.

With all that the wheelsmen accomplished, and it was much, the automobile had a rough beginning. It was ten years after Henry Ford rolled his first test model onto the street that a gasoline propelled vehicle crossed the North American continent—and the Winton required 63 days for a journey of approximately 6,000 miles.[12] Its average of 95 miles per day was nearly as good as the 103 miles per day logged by an ocean-to-ocean automobile party eight years later (4,371 miles in 46 days).[13] Something was obviously blocking progress.

Meanwhile, another early Winton became the first automobile to enter Yellowstone National Park. This 1897 model, which had bicycle wheels, an engine under the seat, and tiller steering, was owned by Henry G. Merry, the general manager of the Montana Coal and Coke Company at Horr (now Electric), Montana, who had purchased it because he was allergic to horse dander. Merry's son has this to say about the first trip into the Park:

When the Winton car arrived it was the conversation piece of the time. The word reached the commandant at the fort, along with the information that the noise it made was terrifying to horses. Very wisely, he issued an order prohibiting this machine and others like it from the confines of the Yellowstone Park.[14] My father knew of this order but thought he would pilot the car to the fort and talk things over with the commandant. In the interim, two troopers had been stationed at the entrance to prevent any such violation of his [the commandant's] order. As related in father's diary, on June 2nd, 1902, he and my mother took off. When the north entrance was reached, he opened up the speed to about 25 mph, and the troopers mounts acted up so that they could not block the passage and the machine was well on its way before they got their horses quieted down and started after the car, which was rapidly widening the distance between them. All went well as long as the road was level but, as you know, that was not for long. As the grade became steeper, the speed was reduced and soon the car came to a stop. The troopers arrived at a hard gallop. Fortunately, each one had a lariat and between the two horses they managed to pull the car to the commandant's office and gave him a report of how things happened. He was quite pleasant and took time to explain to father, who already knew, that the noise of his conveyance posed a threat to the lives of all tourists who were visiting the park in horse-drawn vehicles. Then he became quite stern and reminded him that he was still under arrest and would have to pay a penalty to be released. When my father asked what the penalty would be, the officer very seriously replied, "You will have to take me for a ride in this contraption." He got his ride and then assigned a detail to escort father to the gate through which they entered.[15]

Later, when Mr. Merry's Winton blew out a tire the casing was stuffed with sawdust and sewed up, by way of makeshift, until another could be obtained from the East.

By about 1910 the automobile was probably reliable enough for cross-country touring, but the roads were generally not up to it. In settled areas rural American roads were mainly unimproved dirt tracks; however passable they might be in good weather, they were utterly unserviceable for motor vehicles in wet seasons. These roads were unmarked except where they had had the attention of the cyclists of some nearby community. In the arid and mountainous West where there were few, if any, farmers to maintain roads in the time-honored manner of working out their taxes, thoroughfares were mainly natural routes, often without bridges and having a confusing multiplicity of wheel tracks. Thus the automobile's very real potential could not be realized until the automobilists, like the wheelmen, combined into effective pressure groups to get the highways they needed.

Local groups modeled after the national American Automobile Association had appeared here and there by 1910, and one group had come into existence in the Gallatin Valley. For them, it was not enough that automobiles were allowed to pass through the northwest corner of the Park on the county road connecting Bozeman with the new townsite at the west entrance of the Park; the group proceeded to lobby for admission of private automobiles into Yellowstone Park proper. This move, which was debated at length at a convention of park superintendents and concessioners at the Canyon Hotel on September 11, 1911, asked the secretary of war, through a Senate resolution of April 2, 1912, to estimate the cost of new road construction or of necessary changes in existing roads for the use of automobiles and motorcycles in the Park. The estimate submitted by Lieutenant Ernest Peek was high, yet Congress made funds available for the gradual improvement of the road system toward that day when automobiles could be admitted (see Chapter 17).

Even before those preparations were begun in the Park, steps had been taken to develop touring routes connecting the Park with eastern cities and with its neighbor to the north, Glacier National Park. A "pathfinder crew," sent out by the Minnesota Automobile Association, arrived at Bozeman, Montana, on May 25, 1911, having worked out a practicable route from the Twin Cities along a line recognizable as present U.S. 10 (see the map of the Yellowstone Trail). The group shipped their automobiles back to St. Paul on flatcars, took a quick look at Yellowstone Park, and returned home by rail.[16] The route from the East eventually became the Yellowstone Trail, a rambling patchwork of county and rural roads identified by orange symbols the size of a pie plate painted on rocks, telephone poles, barns, and anywhere else that would serve as a landmark along that primitive route. The following month a local newspaper reported that the "park-to-park highway" (a Montana project) would soon be ready for use, with grading proceeding on the last six miles of the route connecting Yellowstone with Glacier.[17]

Automobiles were getting into Yellowstone Park meanwhile one way or another. Following the episode of Mr. Merry's Winton, a car of unknown make was brought to Fort Yellowstone by a surgeon assigned to the post. It is said that he kept his car in one of the horse corrals behind the cavalry stables and used to exercise it evenings by driving around the compound.[18] A party of automobilists arrived at the Snake River station in 1908 unaware they could not drive through

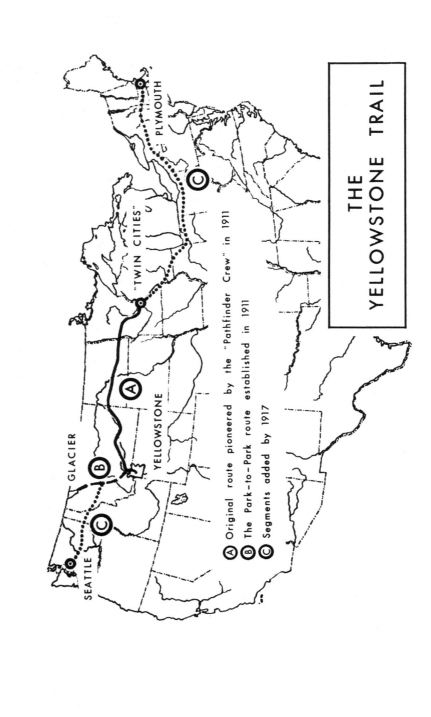

THE
YELLOWSTONE TRAIL

PLYMOUTH

TWIN CITIES

GLACIER

SEATTLE

YELLOWSTONE

Ⓐ Original route pioneered by the "Pathfinder Crew" in 1911
Ⓑ The Park-to-Park route established in 1911
Ⓒ Segments added by 1917

the Park. Not wishing to go back over the Washakie military road (a primitive wagon track they had negotiated with difficulty), they asked permission to pull their vehicle through the Park with a team. Superintendent Young would not agree to that, but he did allow them to haul it to the western entrance on a wagon.[19] Mr. Huntley Child, the son of a park concessioner, brought his White touring car from Gardiner to Mammoth Hot Springs on a freight wagon on November 20, 1914, to have it repainted at the transportation company's carriage shop. By then, automobilists were exerting such pressure to get their machines admitted to the Park that Colonel Brett could not allow a vehicle to come in for any purpose; so he ordered the White hauled back to Gardiner immediately.

Such were the passenger vehicles that gained entry more or less by accident. The Park did authorize a chain-drive, hard-rubber-tired Vulcan truck to haul ore and supplies for several years on the Cooke City road for Mr. McKay, a Cooke City mine operator. The special permit required McKay to maintain the road (a route seldom used by visitors at that time), since his truck broke down many of the bridges and culverts.[20] The ponderous, four-wheeled trailer once pulled by the ore truck now stands beside the main street in Cooke City, Montana, as an interesting relic of the freighting venture through the Park. There was some traffic through the Gallatin corner of the Park after May 31, 1913.[21]

Word was received at park headquarters on April 21, 1915, that Secretary of the Interior Franklin K. Lane had authorized the admission of private automobiles beginning on August 1.[22] As Colonel Brett was skeptical of the ability of motor vehicles to negotiate the park roads, he decided on a test as soon as conditions would allow. Accordingly, the personal cars of Harry W. Child, president of the Yellowstone Park Hotel and Transportation Companies, and Mr. Van Dyck of the Van Dyck & Deever Meat Packing Company of Gardiner, were brought up to Mammoth Hot Springs on June 5, in preparation for the trip. The vehicles, a Franklin and a Buick, made the trip around the loop in two days with an official party, fully satisfying Colonel Brett that automobiles could handle the grades in the Park. Upon the return of the party, the colonel recieved a letter from D. E. Burley, then general passenger agent of the Union Pacific Railroad at Salt Lake City, inquiring about the trip and providing some information on an interesting might-have-been: Mr. Burley, who had been an automobile owner and driver for a number of years, had once persuaded Secretary James R. Garfield (head of the interior department January 15, 1907

An automobile in the trial trip around the Park prior to admission of private autos in 1915. Officer is Col. Lloyd Brett. *A Haynes photograph, used with permission of the Haynes Foundation.*

to March 5, 1909) to allow an automobile trip around the Park during hours of darkness; just at that time the superintendent of Yosemite Park permitted a friend to try out an automobile in that area with the result that a six-horse stagecoach was rammed from behind, the team ran away, and five or six passengers were seriously injured. Mr. Burley added, "That killed my project."[23]

The last use of park roads by motor vehicles prior to the official opening occurred on July 4, 1915, when a party of congressmen and officials of the U.S. Reclamation Service were brought to Lake Hotel by motor car over the east entrance road. Regulations governing admission of automobiles in the first season were published on July 7.[24] They specified that a "ticket of passage must be secured and paid for at the checking station where the automobile enters the Park," and the fees ("payable in cash only") were set as follows: single-seated cars, $5.00; five-passenger cars $7.50, and seven-passenger cars $10.00. Speeds were limited to 12 miles per hour when ascending and 10 miles per hour descending, and to 8 miles per hour when approaching sharp curves, and not to exceed 20 miles per hour at any time. Speeding was to be controlled by comparing the elapsed time between check points with the approved minimum time of passage, and penalties were provided for those who were under the minimum elapsed time (that is, those who drove too fast). The regulations also covered such matters as the mechanical condition of the vehicle and its performance characteristics and set up rigid time schedules for use of various sections of the park road system.

The regulations were to go into effect on the morning of August 1, but the superintendent attempted to lessen the anticipated congestion by issuing seven permits on July 31, a day early. Permit number 1 was issued to Mr. K. R. Seiler of Redwing, Minnesota, at 7:30 P.M. He paid a fee of $5 for his single-seated Ford (license, Minnesota 60236) and gave the Shaw and Powell camp at Willow Park as his destination for that evening. The car later left the Park by way of the east entrance. Five of the first seven vehicles to officially enter the Park were Fords; the others were a Buick and a Haynes.[25]

An amusing aftermath of the official opening was a publicity release by the White Motor Company claiming that a vehicle of their manufacture had been the first admitted officially. Their claim referred to the White touring car of the president of the Yellowstone Park Association, which had led the procession into the Park on August 1. The editor of *Motor Age*, having already been informed that a Ford was first, fired off this telegram to Colonel Brett: "White Company states first car to enter Park was Child's White car. Your

The first automobile to enter the Park—an 1897 Winton driven to Mammoth Hot Springs by Henry G. Merry, June 14, 1902.

wire of August 3 said Ford was first. Please wire us collect which is correct." The colonel's reply confirmed his original statement that Seiler's Ford runabout was first.[26]

On opening day, August 1, only 50 cars carrying 171 persons entered the Park, as heavy rains throughout the West had put the roads in such condition that few vehicles were moving. Total park entries for the season were 958 vehicles carrying 3,513 persons; 365 permits were issued at the north entrance, 392 were issued at the west entrance (though the first was not sold until August 2), at the east entrance 193 were issued, and the south entrance issued only 8. Permit number 13 was refused and had to be cancelled—doubtless a superstitious driver.

Once within the Park the tourists were very much on their own. Gasoline could be purchased at park stores, where it was transferred from barrels with gallon measures, but mechanical services and parts were unobtainable in the area, which accounts for the rigid inspection of vehicles upon entering the Park. Besides showing adequate supplies of gasoline, oil, and spare tires, drivers were required to skid their machines to demonstrate their brakes.

A visitor of 1916 recalls a breakdown that occurred near the outlet of Lake Yellowstone about the time a grizzly bear killed teamster Frank Welch on the east entrance road. Near Pelican Creek our informant passed a Buick touring car being pulled by a fine span of army mules. The driver of that strange arrangement said that his vehicle had broken a rear axle and the soldiers at the Lake station had provided him with the mules to help him get his family out of the Park. The driver had heard of the attacks by the monstrous grizzly (perhaps hearing more than was true) and had disconnected his brakes in the hope of getting out of the Park a little faster. In just a few miles, unable to hold his vehicle back, he had lacerated the hocks of those fine mules. The visitor insisted upon reconnecting the brakes out of a humane feeling for those mules, and offered to take the man's wife and five-year-old daughter as far as the east entrance soldier station in his car. The child went with him but the wife demurred stating, "I'll stay with my husband." Our informant adds, "I wonder how this fellow fared when he delivered this wonderful span of large mules, with cut-up hocks, as they were, when he checked out at the east entrance."[27]

The soldiers stationed in the Park were called upon to rescue many of these early automobilists, including Jack Haynes. He was returning from Jackson Hole in late October 1917, after a photographic junket south of the Park, when a bitter storm caught him near the

Automobilists of the 1920s lunching in the parking area of Mount Washburn.

A baggage sticker of the 1920s displayed the silhouette of an early White bus against a yellow background. *From the author's collection.*

south entrance soldier station. There one of the soldiers helped Jack remove part of the floor board of his car in order to get engine heat into the driver's compartment and loaned him a blanket to wrap his legs in. Before Jack could return the blanket, the trooper was transferred out of the Park with the Seventh Cavalry, and was left short one blanket for about six weeks.[28]

The immediate effect of admission of the automobile to Yellowstone National Park was the motorization of the Park's public transportation and a reorientation of all development in the area. Within a year it was obvious that transportation on park roads had to be either horse-drawn or motor-propelled, not both. Thus, the motorization of the transportation business, which had been suggested by William Wallace Wiley before the turn of the century,[29] was at last a necessity.

In the fall of 1916 Director Stephen T. Mather of the newly organized National Park Service called all the Yellowstone concessionnaires to Washington, D.C., for a conference to reorganize the businesses in the Park. This meeting resulted in the following decisions: (1) The Yellowstone Park Transportation Company was given the exclusive privilege of operating the public transportation facilities, which were to be motorized before the next season. (2) The Yellowstone Park Hotel Company was to continue with the operation of the hotels. (3) Frank J. Haynes was to dispose of all his business interests in the Park except the photographic business. (4) The Wiley Permanent Camping Company and the Shaw and Powell Camping Company were to abandon their individual enterprises and merge into a single permanent camps business in which A. W. Miles would own fifty-one percent of the stock and the Shaw and Powell people would own forty-nine percent.[30]

The several companies doing transportation business in the Park then proceeded to dispose of their horses, rolling stock, harness, and related equipment, while the Yellowstone Park Transportation Company contracted with the White Motor Company for purchase of 116 motor buses, with tires and spare parts, for $427, 104.67.[31] The consolidation of competing interests and motorization of park transportation elminated the need for many of the intermediate stopping places and led to abandonment of a number of facilities in the Park. Among these were the Wylie camps at Swan Lake, Old Faithful and Canyon, and Wylie lunch stations on the Gibbon River. at the Thumb of the Lake, and at Riverside, near the west entrance to the Park; the Shaw and Powell camps at Willow Park and Bridge Bay were likewise closed. The Yellowstone Park Hotel Company's hotel on the Porcelain Terrace near Norris Junction was closed, as was the Shaw and Powell hotel at present West Yellowstone, Montana. All park transportation facilities operated by F. J. Haynes were abandoned (the Yellowstone-Western Stage Company and the Park's first line of motor stages, the Cody-Sylvan Pass Motor Company, which had operated into the Park from the east during the summer of 1916). A further casualty of the reorganization was the boat operation on Lake Yellowstone; transportation across the lake was rendered unprofitable by the automobile.

The permanent camping business in the Park was simplified into a single system with installations at five points: a new camp at Mammoth Hot Springs (south of Capitol hill, where Mammoth Lodge developed later), a camp on the old Shaw and Powell site near Old Faithful, one on the old Wylie site (the present lodge area) at Lake, another on the old Shaw and Powell site on the Artist Point spur road at Canyon, and a camp on the Wylie site near Tower Junction (present Camp Roosevelt). The new system used the Wylie Permanent Camping Company name for a time.

These changes were far-reaching and unsettling to park business. They might have been managed with little difficulty if the nation had not become involved in World War I just at the time they were undertaken. Motorizing the park transportation company exhausted the finances of the concerns headed by Harry W. Child, and he was forced to ask the Northern Pacific Railroad for funds to maintain operation.[32] Deepening financial difficulty led Mr. Child to suggest turning over the recently purchased automotive equipment to an equipment trust to be founded and administered by the several railroads interested in the park operation.[33] Just such a solution was arranged in June 1917; the Northern Pacific, the Union Pacific, and the Chicago, Burlington, and Quincy each underwrote shares of a mortgage covering the cost of the equipment purchased.[34] Even this assistance came perilously close to being too little, for the loss of operating revenues during the war period put Mr. Child's businesses in such bad financial condition that he considered disposing of the least profitable part—his hotels—in 1918. He attempted to dispose of them to the Northern Pacific Railroad, which was disenchanted but not disinterested, and to the National Park Service, which was eager but not able to deal. Unable to come to a satisfactory arrangement with either, Mr. Child held on and the stormy period of adjustment to the new form of transportation was finally weathered. At last the Park was set upon that course of democratization which would make it truly *for the benefit and enjoyment of the people.*

An event that occurred in the last days of the army's administration of Yellowstone National Park may be prologue to a future in park transportation that is yet unclear. In October 1917 two army officers, a Captain Smith and a Lieutenant Blanton, landed their stick-and-string Jenny on the flat northwest of the old Fountain Hotel. They had almost rolled to a stop when a wheel hit a soft place and the airplane nosed over. No harm was done, and with some help to get the nose up, the plane was operational again and was flown out of the Park.[35]

IV
A PARK COMES OF AGE

The withdrawal of the military units from the Yellowstone National Park in 1916 marked a major development of the National Park Idea. Henceforth the direction of the nation's parks would be in civilian hands and future development would be civilian development.

—Harold Duane Hampton,
Conservation and Cavalry *(1965)*

Superintendent Horace M. Albright speaking at the Park's semicentennial celebration at Madison Junction.

CHAPTER 19

ENTER THE RANGERS

"Hunt—Fish—Trap—Live in a cabin. Be a ranger!"
—A sarcasm of the 1930s

There was a time when a Yellowstone ranger could smother disappointment by declaiming lines frequently used in pulp magazine advertising of the late twenties and early thirties. Such proposals, with their subtle hint that the correspondence course being hawked was the entrée to a federal job, were a means of mulcting gullible boys out of a few dollars; they were also an indication of the romantic connotation of the word "ranger"—an aura noted two centuries earlier by the poet who said, "The rangers in the wild just God design'd."[1]

The word "ranger" as resurrected by Americans in the twentieth century comes from an archaic British use designating wardens who patrolled the deer parks and forests of England, and is unrelated to the American use of the word in such titles as Roger's Rangers or the Texas Rangers.[2] As it first appeared in colonial America, "ranger" designated an officer responsible for gathering estrays and returning them to their rightful owners, and evolved to include mounted men organized to protect outlying settlements from Indian attacks. Ranger companies were included in the Continental Army during the Revolutionary War and were used thereafter in states and territories troubled by Indians and outlaws.[3] Most ranger organizations disappeared with the frontier conditions that spawned them, so that the word was no longer current—except in a few localities—in the last decade of the nineteenth century. When it did come into use again, it was used in its original sense, and to whom we are indebted for this convenient resurrection remains unknown. How the forest rangers became established, however, is no mystery.

In 1897 Congress finally provided for the administration and protection of the lands that had been set aside from the public domain as forest reserves. On July 1, 1898, $75,000 became available for implementing the provision of the Forest Reserve Act authorizing the secretary of the interior to "establish such service as will insure the objects of such reservations,"[4] and the commissioner of the General Land Office proceeded to develop an organization. The plan adopted provided each reserve (except those adjacent to Yellowstone National Park) with a "forest supervisor," who had under his charge "forest rangers" assigned to districts. The first forest rangers were twenty men appointed July 30, 1898, by Colonel B. F. Allen for protection of reserved lands in the state of California. The exclusion of the Yellowstone National Park Timberland Reserve and the original Teton Forest Reserve from the general plan was dictated by the stringent financing allowed the new forest organization; with so few dollars available for management, the commissioner of the General Land Office was satisfied to leave a portion of his problem to the army, which operated in its accustomed manner (even imparting its methods to the first civilian administration of the neighboring reserves).

Events took an opposite course in California. The army's influence in the three parks established in 1890 (Yosemite, Sequoia, and General Grant) was only seasonal, and, with United States involvement in war with Spain, no soldiers were available. Inspector J. W. Zevely of the General Land Office was instructed to protect the areas, which he did by recruiting a force of "special forest agents" for the summer of 1898. Troops were again available that fall, but they needed guides; so two men of the special agent force, Archie C. Leonard of Wawona and Charles A. Leidig of Yosemite Valley, were temporarily employed with funds appropriated for the adjoining Sequoia Forest Reserve, necessitating use of the title "forest rangers" for these men. Their employment was subsequently extended, so the Yosemite had forest rangers until 1905, when transfer of the forest reserves to the Department of Agriculture made a different title necessary, and the term "park ranger" was adopted.[5]

Park rangers soon appeared in all parks except Yellowstone. There, the first civilian employees to have that title came on duty July 26, 1915, nearly a decade after the position was authorized. This lag was an indirect result of a peculiar poverty that afflicted Yellowstone Park throughout the army era. Because of congressional failure to provide an appropriation for the administration and protection (A & P) of the Park in 1886, management of the area had depended on War Department funds. The small appropriations available for A & P from 1894 on were intended for the establishment and maintenance of a buffalo herd, although barely sufficient for that purpose (see Appendix C, Table III). Consequently, except for the buffalo keepers and their assistants, the only way the army could employ civilians for protection purposes was as scouts.

In those days the table of organization allowed the employment of one scout for each company of soldiers, so that the number of permanent scouts varied with the strength of the Fort Yellowstone garrison: only one when it was a one-troop post, two to three after 1895, and always three after September 1911. There is an interesting marginal note on a letter of instruction written by some person in the interior department to Captain George Anderson at the time he took over management of the Park. He was advised: "Strive with all your might before you leave [Washington, D.C.] to allow you to employ two scouts—one is allowed now. Two are really indispensable to the scouting that has to be done."[6] From 1895 on, the force of permanent scouts was augmented by "extra" scouts employed to patrol the Park boundaries and the adjacent forest reserves (for which some funds became available under the Forest Reserve Act in 1898 and subsequent years). These men were not empowered to do more than report illegal activities.

The pay of the Yellowstone scouts was $75.00 per month, which was slightly less than the monthly pay of the early park rangers ($83.33 per month) and considerably less than the $100.00 per month received by four seasonal rangers employed to check automobiles in 1915. In fact, their pay was the same as that received by Jim McBride when he was made chief scout in May 1914. How a unified ranger force was finally fashioned from such diverse elements—scouts, rangers, and soldiers—can be understood by looking at events during the last decade of the army's management of the Park.

Use of soldiers for policing Yellowstone Park, though necessary in the beginning, had certain drawbacks that finally outweighed the advantages. In general, the men who served in the Park were not

A group of Yellowstone scouts: left to right, Peter Holt, Wells (an unknown), Jim McBride, and R.A. Waagner (familiarly called "the Duke of Hell Roaring").

woodsmen, which limited their usefulness; they were poorly paid, which does not encourage initiative; and service interfered with their training in military matters. Also, the system was unduly expensive.

These facts came to the attention of President Roosevelt prior to 1907 (possibly through C. J. "Buffalo" Jones, whose differences with the military led him to advocate a return to civilian administration of the Park). However it was that Roosevelt became aware of the faults in the system of army management, his reaction was to ask Superintendent S.B.M. Young to look into the possibility of forming a "civil guard" for Yellowstone Park.

Superintendent Young replied that he thought the cost of administering and protecting the Park could be cut from $150,000 to about $50,000 by substituting a civilian organization for the military detachment then serving as its guardian, and he advanced a plan for a suitable force.[7] Briefly, his proposal called for establishment of a Yellowstone National Park Guard of twenty men, serving under an assistant inspector.

In his annual report to the secretary of the interior, Young emphasized:

> Such details [as duty in the Park] are injurious to the Army in that regimental and squadron organizations are not only disturbed, but the troop organization is largely demoralized by subdividing the men into small parties far separated for indefinite periods of time without the personal supervision of an officer. . . . Proper and necessary military instruction and training can not be carried on and thorough discipline can not be maintained.[8]

Young further recognized an injustice to the Park in that "the enlisted men of the Army are not selected with special reference to the duties required of them," which could only lead to inferior results, in his opinion.

For some obscure reason, President Roosevelt changed his mind at this point, whereupon the secretary of the interior decided not to ask Congress for money for such a changeover. For a time, the attitudes of the two departments most concerned with the management of the Park remained contradictory, the secretary of the interior advocating military control and the secretary of war opposing it. Events were to bring them to a common point of view by 1914.

President Roosevelt called his Conservation Conference of Governors in 1908, a meeting at which the nation's parks received little notice. Among the few who spoke up in their defense was J. Horace McFarland, who, aware of the developing battle for Yosemite's Hetch Hetchy Valley, stated: "The national parks, all too few in number and extent, ought to be absolutely inviolate."[9] As head of the American Civic Association, McFarland thereafter labored unceasingly to get the national parks and all their affairs in the hands of a single government bureau. He encouraged Secretary of the Interior Richard A. Ballinger to suggest "a bureau of national parks and resorts, under the supervision of a competent commissioner, with a suitable force of superintendents," which was subsequently recommended in the annual report for 1910. That report led to a "six-day conference of all national park superintendents to meet at the Yellowstone National Park, beginning September 10, [1911], to make a thorough study of the national park problem and incidentally to launch a movement for the establishment of a bureau of national parks."[10]

The conference endorsed the idea of a unifying organization for all the park areas, each of which, to that time, was a direct and separate responsibility of the secretary of the interior. The movement had the support of President Taft, who said in a special message to Congress February 2, 1912:

> I earnestly recommend the establishment of a bureau of National Parks. Such legislation is essential to the proper management of those wonderful manifestations of nature, so startling and so beautiful that everyone recognizes the obligations of the government to preserve them for the edification and recreation of the people. The Yellowstone Park, the Yosemite, the Grand Canyon of the Colorado, the Glacier National Park, and the Mount Rainier National Park and others furnish appropriate instances. In only one case have we made anything like adequate preparation for the use of a park by the public. That case is the Yellowstone. . . . Every consideration of patriotism and the love of nature and of beauty and of art requires us to expend money enough to bring all these natural wonders within easy reach of our people. The first step in that direction is the establishment of a responsible bureau, which shall take upon itself the burden of supervising the parks and making recommendations as to the best method of improving their accessibility and usefulness.[11]

The Congress ignored Taft's recommendation (legislation sponsored by Representative John E. Raker, California, and Senator Reed Smoot, Utah, was not enacted), but the Department of the Interior did establish a quasi-national park service in 1913: park matters were put in the hands of a busy attorney in the secretary's office, assisted by the clerk best able to spare time from a full schedule. Such organizational looseness was tightened considerably when Adolph C. Miller designated Mark Daniels (a San Francisco landscape architect whose enduring contribution is the National Park

Service uniform) as General Superintendent and Landscape Engineer of National Parks. The rudimentary organization thus brought into being had the virtue of closeness to the parks and their problems, and was just effective enough to point out the need for something better.

Stephen T. Mather, who took over Miller's position as first assistant to the secretary of the interior in January 1915, opened a many-faceted campaign to get a bona fide service established. He began with a mid-March conference of park superintendents and officials of the interior and war departments, concessioners, boosters, conservationists, and congressmen on the campus of Stanford University at Berkeley, California; from that start, he proceeded to cultivate influential people and build favorable public opinion. A trip into the high park country of California's Sierras was arranged for a select group; a *National Parks Portfolio*, prepared by Robert Sterling Yard (who was retained as a publicity man), was distributed free to 250,000 persons, publicity of national scope was provided by popular writers of the *Saturday Evening Post* and *National Geographic Magazine*, and support was obtained from such effective organizations as the National Civic Association and the Sierra Club.[12]

In the political arena, Representative William Kent, a dedicated conservationist who enjoyed better standing in Congress than Raker had, sponsored the new park act. The result of his efforts, backed by the endless legwork of Mather's young assistant, Horace M. Albright, was passage of the National Park Service Act, signed into law by President Woodrow Wilson on August 25, 1916.[13]

The victory was not quite complete, however. Congress did not at once provide the funds necessary for its translation into organizational form. Fortunately, Mather had established the interim organization in Washington, D.C., under Robert B. Marshall, who was borrowed from the Geological Survey and appointed superintendent of national parks on December 11, 1915. Consequently, when funds were made available by Congress through a deficiency appropriation act of April 17, 1917,[14] the skeletal organization was able to prepare the way for establishing an effective bureau, the National Park Service.

In Yellowstone Park, a change in the army's manner of handling its stewardship gave the area a headstart toward management by a civilian organization. From 1908 on, the secretary of war favored withdrawal of the military from the Park and the duty that he could only consider as disruptive of the discipline and training of the units involved. The movement in the Park toward civilian park service had gained such ground by 1914 that the secretary suggested a special unit be formed for the park detail. The Yellowstone Park Detachment was to consist of two troops with particular aptitude for park work. They were to be drawn from nine cavalry regiments, none of which would be impaired functionally—an advantage for the army. The competence of experienced men was bound to result in better service in the Park; furthermore, this corps could be handed over to a civilian agency as a sort of "instant Park Service."[15]

It was a good idea, and was accepted. The Yellowstone Park Detachment, consisting of Troops 1 and 2, each of 100 men, was formed in time to take over the guardianship of the Park from the First United States Cavalry (Troops E, F, G, and H) on July 3, 1914.[16] The men who volunteered for this service were told they would soon be turned over en masse to the Department of the Interior, which would employ them as park rangers. The plan, had it carried through, would have shortened the army's stay in Yellowstone Park by several years.

An attempt to fund the change in 1915 was defeated by Representative J. J. Fitzgerald of New York, chairman of the House Committee on Appropriations, who took the view that Congress had placed Yellowstone Park under protection of the military and intended, in his opinion, for it to remain that way. In this he was influenced by a belief that civilian management would cost more, despite assurance from both departments that it would be about half the $194,193.59 appropriated for the army's use in the Park during the fiscal year ending June 30, 1915.[17]

The reaction of the military men, following Mather's decision on April 21, 1915, to allow the entry of private automobiles into Yellowstone Park in August, was to question the legality of using soldiers for any duty other than strict protection. This attitude, in which they were later supported by an opinion of the judge advocate general, made it necessary for the Department of the Interior to hire four park rangers to work at the entrance stations.

The first Yellowstone rangers were John Delmar and Stephen M. Kilpatrick from California, Leo E. Huston from Minnesota, and George T. Dustman, who came from Franklin County, Ohio. Dustman's employment record shows that he was on duty at the east entrance from July 26 to September 15, 1915, under a temporary appointment as a "1st Class Ranger" at $1,200 per annum. He was a rather typical seasonal: twenty-one years old, with a year and a half of college, and working experience over an equal period. He could drive an automobile and had noted on his form, "I have had experience in camping and can ride a horse."[18]

That fall the Park employed two temporary rangers of a different type. They were Donald Stevenson and Cruse Black, both westerners of limited schooling but considerable experience in the particular work they were hired for, to kill coyotes, wolves, and cougars. Cruse is an interesting individual. He was employed first as a buffalo herder at the ranch in Lamar Valley in 1912, but soon dropped back to assistant buffalo keeper (a decrease in salary from $900 to $720 per annum). He gave up that position in 1913 to go to Alaska, returning to the Park and his former work toward the end of the year, and from that he went to predator control work on a ranger appointment— again at $900 per annum. He never did stay put, but gravitated to guiding and cooking for dude outfits in and around the Park. The six men mentioned were the only park rangers employed in Yellowstone prior to the Park's return to civilian management.

Serious negotiations toward formation of the first ranger force were begun in March 1915, in the railway car carrying Steve Mather and his party to the conference of park superintendents at Berkeley, California. Mather and Major General Hugh L. Scott, then chief of staff of the army, chanced to meet, and agreeing on the undesirability of keeping troops in Yellowstone Park, discussed ways and means of removing them. The principal obstacle was lack of funds available to the secretary of the interior for employment of a force of rangers or for maintenance of buildings and equipment. It was thought however that there would be sufficient park revenues by late summer of 1916 to make the changeover possible.[19]

The hope of financing a civilian administration from park revenues was based on the proviso of the organic act whereby the secretary of the interior was authorized to expend "all of the proceeds of said leases, and all other revenues that may be derived from any source connected with the park," for management of the area.[20] A desire to increase the revenues undoubtedly was a factor in Mather's decision of April 21, 1915, to admit private automobiles to the Park in August.

Continuing in the words of Mr. Albright, who was Mather's personal secretary and legal advisor on legislative problems:

> When General Scott left us, he agreed to meet Mr. Mather again in Washington in the autumn. and in the meantime I was to confer with Army officers assigned by General Scott to find just what would be involved in the proposed transfer. The acting superintendent of the Yellowstone at the time was Colonel Lloyd M. Brett [who was] to attend the Berkeley and San Francisco national park conference. He did attend, and Mr. Mather and other Interior Department men,

On Mount Washburn summit, 1915: Col. L.M. Brett, in uniform, hand on elk antler; Steve Mather, later National Park Service director, at Brett's left, and Horace Albright, last man on Brett's left.

including Attorney W. B. Acker, and myself, discussed the proposed transfer.

In September, 1915, Mr. Mather and I visited the Yellowstone and further discussed the troop withdrawal plan with Colonel Brett and his associates. On returning to Washington, we had a further talk with General Scott . . . .

During the winter, Mr. Mather and General Scott conferred from time to time about the withdrawal of the troops from Yellowstone, and I was concerned with some of the details of the transfer of property. The plan contemplated the release of a number of sergeants and corporals who had had such experience in leadership and had shown real interest in Yellowstone Park, these men to be appointed park rangers. Other rangers were to be recruited from stage drivers, scouts who were on duty to help the soldiers (there were only four or five of them) etc. Fort Yellowstone with all its buildings, including a fully-equipped hospital, many horses, wagons, etc. were to be transferred. All this program was to be carried out in the autumn of 1916.[21]

Passage of the National Park Service Act (an uncertain outcome up to the last moment) did not disturb the arrangement for ending the military management of the Park. On September 30, 1916, twenty-two enlisted men were discharged from the army. All of them were to be employed as park rangers. The other soldiers discharged at that time were to form the nucleus of a maintenance force.[22]

A report forwarded to the superintendent of national parks by Acting Supervisor Chester A. Lindsley (the title was changed from acting superintendent on March 28, 1916), named the men who made up the first ranger force.[23] This was the organization that took over protection of Yellowstone Park, "by arrangement with the War Department, and with its hearty cooperation," beginning October 1, 1916.[24] The last soldiers entrained on October 25; the Fort improvements and moveable property were formally transferred to the National Park Service a month later.

The resumption of civilian management did not please everyone. The people of Gardiner, Montana, reacted in a manner typical of a frontier community faced with abandonment of a military installation profitable to the local economy: they protested loudly. Word of their protest reached Senator Thomas H. Walsh while attending the 1916 Democratic national convention in Chicago. Being mindful of his constituents and the coming elections, the senator demanded that the secretary of the interior delay abandonment of Fort Yellowstone until January 1, 1917. When he was informed that the order had already been given, he sought a postponement, first through the secretary of war and then through the president; but he was too late:

the troops were already leaving. This so angered the Montana delegation that they took the matter to Congress, backed by a joint memorial in which the Legislative Assembly of Montana petitioned Congress to "again police the Yellowstone National Park with officers and soldiers of the regular army to the end that it shall be well protected."[25]

None of this escaped the baleful eyes of Representative John Fitzgerald, whose hostility to the civilian changeover had already been evident. His power in appropriation matters was such that he was able to deny funds to the civilian force for the fiscal year beginning July 1, 1917, and to require return of a detachment of troops to the Park. As a result of this low blow (a manuever particularly galling to an army involved in a foreign war) the first ranger force was disbanded June 30, 1917, and the protection of the Park fell to the Seventh U.S. Cavalry (450 soldiers to replace 50 rangers).

Fortunately, the army's return to the Park was brief, for military management was no longer what it once had been. The wartime levies, more often than not, were inefficient; sometimes they were arrogant and drunken, and occasionally they proved dishonest; that, combined with the too-frequent changes in the units, and public disapproval of such nonmilitary use of troops when the nation was at war created dissatisfactions that even a stubborn Congress could not overlook. Fitzgerald's restrictive clause did not appear in the Sundry Civil Bill that provided funds for Yellowstone Park for the fiscal year beginning July 1, 1918. The way was open for reconstituting the ranger force.

A number of men had been salvaged from the first ranger force and carried on the army's rolls as scouts (needed more than ever after the 1915 ruling of the judge advocate general limiting the use of soldiers in the Park to those activities spelled out in the Sundry Civil Bill for 1883—see Appendix B, Part II). Four men (McBride, Trischman, Little, and Brooks) were on the rolls as permanent scouts, and six others (Lacombe, Dewing, Lawson, C. Smith, Pound, and Anderson), were employed as "temporaries." The ten, with several other former rangers who returned to the Park, formed a cadre to which new men were rapidly added. By November 1, 1918, when Acting Supervisor Lindsley was able to telegraph the Washington office the good news that Fort Yellowstone had been "formally abandoned" by the army on the previous day, the ranger force had been increased to twenty-one permanents.[26] There should have been twenty-three on the list, but one appointee, Peter A. Iverson, died enroute to the Park from his home in Alaska; Scout Raymond G. Little was serving with the army at the time the ranger force was reconstituted and did not become a member until May 24, 1919. In addition to the listed permanents, several seasonal rangers who had checked automobiles at the entrance stations during the summer were still on duty in the late fall of 1918.

The early park rangers can be typified as practical men, with less education and more experience than their present-day counterparts. They varied from the gentlemanly, tea-drinking Brooks to the rough-cut Lacombe, whose toughness had considerable depth, but they shared an esprit de corps that was a Yellowstone trait. It came in part from the scouts and their dependence on personal competence, appearing in the ranger force as pride in an ability to do whatever was required, whether to track a horse or build a cabin; and in part from those old soldiers whose military service had habituated them to discipline and neatness. Snappy, capable, and dedicated, the Yellowstone rangers made an immediate good impression, as the public press was quick to note.

Calling the new protection force the "spread-eagle men," from the central device of the park ranger badge, a newsman wrote:

> Nearly all carried away favorable impressions of the men who did so much to make their Park travel safe, and on bitter nights last winter, around many a hearth, there was thought for the lonely spread-eagle men on ski patrol. Sliding the boundary trails from station to snowshoe cabin and back again that poachers might be kept out and game protected against another playtime. ... The National Park Service is the youngest of the governmental agencies, having been uniformed for the first time last summer, when it finally succeeded the regular army in policing our national playgrounds, yet it inherits from the scout organization upon which it was founded, traditions of veteran bravery, annals of sacrifice for game protection. Patterned somewhat after the Northwest mounted police of Canada, taking example from the Texas Rangers of the Rio Grande, but with an individuality of its own beyond the use of skis and motorcycles, the service, with the months is taking form that promises to make it as powerful an arm of the law as either of the older bodies. In its territorial scope, it is as national as the Parks themselves. ... Mt. McKinley National Park will draw the forest-green uniform north, and half-way across the Pacific, Hawaii is calling.[27]

The prophecy was accurate, for Yellowstone men have spread out through an expanding park system, carrying with them something of their training in the first of all national parks. Harry Liek and Ted Ogston, for example, went north to Mount McKinley;

The park ranger force at Mammoth Hot Springs early in the 1920s.

A ranger on ski patrol in the Bechler Meadows in 1940.
Photograph by the author.

Frank Oberhansley and Fred Johnston went to Hawaii. The experience and training of such men were part of a transfusion that has reached into every unit, old or new, under the management of the National Park Service. Their usefulness was a result of service that included far more than just "sliding the boundary trails," for a Yellowstone ranger's life fifty years ago was a richly varied experience.

The ranger force was headed by Jim McBride, who had been chief scout during the latter park days of the army. He was a tough, capable frontiersman, but a crotchety "loner" who was not liked by everyone. He was unable to accommodate fully to the automobile or to the changes it brought about. Jack Haynes recalled once giving McBride a lift from Mammoth Hot Springs to Gardiner in his Buick touring car. It was a trip made memorable by his passenger's frantic attempts to slow their descent of Soap Hill by pushing on the floor boards to the tune of "Whoa! Whoa!" Strangely, Jim had come to terms with the motorcycle, and his side-car-equipped machine was a familiar sight as he made inspection rounds in the Park. At the start, Mather had some doubt about McBride's ability to handle the complex problems that had devolved upon the new protection organization and delayed a year before naming him chief ranger in October 1919. That decision turned out to be a mistake and it was necessary to reassign McBride to wildlife management two years later. From then until his retirement December 31, 1928, Jim McBride handled the captive herd of buffalo in the Lamar Valley and the fish-planting operations.[28]

Samuel T. Woodring succeeded McBride as chief ranger. He was a former army packmaster (a veteran of the Spanish American War who remained with the army, campaigning in the Philippine Islands with such Yellowstone old-timers as Bob Lacombe and Joe Douglas). He had been a park ranger only a year at the time of his promotion on January 16, 1922, yet Sam had already demonstrated that he was an organizer and a natural leader, qualities responsible for his appointment as first superintendent for Grand Teton National Park upon its establishment in 1929. A visitor to the Park in 1921 who later came to know Woodring quite well as a fellow employee, has this to say of their first meeting:

> I was fishing the Yellowstone River across from Canyon Station. I had some fish of questionable length and my heart went up in my throat as I saw this ranger riding toward me along the trail. I saw visions of fine and imprisonment, perhaps both, but the ranger spoke to me in a quiet voice, remarking something about the weather, and passed on. I

remember how he looked as he went on down the trail, moving easily with the swinging of his horse. There was something about his face, kindly, yet with a certain grim determination, that I have always remembered.[29]

It was determination, coupled with an affable nature, that created a crack organization out of Yellowstone's twenty to thirty permanent, and nearly twice as many seasonal rangers, a force Woodring was described as handling "with the efficiency and calmness of a Field Marshal." Though ordinarily the unflappable type, Sam could do his share of bellowing when properly moved.

At the beginning of the National Park Service era, Yellowstone Park was divided into three ranger districts (north, west, and south) each supervised by one of the assistant chief rangers. The important stations within a district were in the charge of first-class rangers, who had park rangers (both seasonal and permanent) under them. This pattern, which stressed the line-of-authority of a military organization, was modified during the 1930s by turning the three districts into nine more closely identified with distinct areas of the Park (Mammoth, Tower Fall, Lamar River, West, Old Faithful, Canyon, Lake, Bechler, and Snake River), each supervised by a district ranger (a category that replaced the former first-class ranger). This new arrangement eliminated the supervisory duties of the three assistant chief rangers so that they could take over functional duties related to wildlife management, forestry, fire control, and relations with the concessioners. A complete reorganization of protection activities under Mission 66 (a ten-year program of improvement intended to revitalize the Park by 1966) resurrected the earlier pattern.

In the initial organization, the northern district, which included the Norris and Canyon areas, was under Harry Trischman, a former army scout who grew up in the Park as the son of the Fort Yellowstone post carpenter. Harry Trischman supervised the northern district until it was reorganized in 1935, at which time he became the chief buffalo keeper, serving in that capacity until his resignation July 2, 1940. He was a man of tremendous physical endurance and a fine sense of humor. That humor of his provided an amusing story that made the rounds of the force during the 1930s, when the practical rangers had been mostly replaced by college-educated men.

Harry had been down to the Thorofare corner of the Park, and while there had climbed onto the 11,000-foot Trident Plateau. On his return to headquarters he mentioned the ascent to George Baggley, the first chief ranger who was a college man, and was asked: "Harry, when you were up there, what did you see?" With a straight face, and mindful of where George's alma mater was, Harry replied: "Well, I looked away down south and I saw the smoke of that ranger factory at Fort Collins!" Thereafter, Colorado Agricultural and Mechanical College was the "ranger factory" in park parlance; and perhaps that was appropriate, considering the number of its graduates among the rangers.

The western district was supervised at first by Charles J. "White Mountain" Smith, who was every bit as colorful as the handle suggests. He was a Connecticut boy who had learned how to manage stage horses hauling tourists to resorts in the White Mountains of New Hampshire and at the Ormond-Daytona Beach resorts in Florida, before he began his nine seasons as a stagecoach driver in Yellowstone. Near the end of the army era, White Mountain was employed as an "extra" scout, which qualified him for a position on the first ranger force. He took over the western district on October 1, 1918, supervising it until his transfer to Grand Canyon National Park in January 1921.[30] From his departure until the reorganization in the mid-thirties, Eivind T. Scoyen, and then Joseph O. Douglas, supervised the western district.

The southern district was supervised initially by James P. Brooks, of whom nothing is known except that he was a thoroughly nice guy (the verdict of his contemporaries). On his transfer to Glacier National Park October 13, 1920, the district was handled successively by George T. Dustman, Forest L. Carter, Harry J. Liek, and Edward E. Ogston.

The number of rangers on the force during the summer months varied from twenty-four to twenty-seven permanents and forty-one to fifty-three seasonals, but the organization as it stood at the opening of the 1930 season is typical of the early period. There were two permanents working out of headquarters on special assignments (assisting with fisheries work and the geophysical study conducted by the Carnegie Institute); the northern district was staffed with nine permanent park rangers, ten seasonal park rangers and a motorcycle messenger; the western district was assigned six permanents and twelve seasonals, and the southern district had seven permanents and nineteen seasonals. Thus, the force at that time was seventy-one men, including the chief ranger and four assistants.

From the beginning, it was intended that the permanent ranger force would be composed of men who qualified under the Civil Service rules,[31] but such selection was not fully effective until 1925. There is an amusing story concerning the special examination by which the men gained their permanent status. The Department of the Interior sent Assistant Secretary Ballou to the Park to make arrangements for the examinations, and Superintendent Albright gave Ted Ogston the chore of shepherding Ballou about the area as he gathered information. Later, when all the rangers were called into headquarters to take the test, Ted, who felt he had the inside track through his assistance to Ballou, told Guy McCarty: "I'll bet you twenty-five dollars I pass the examination higher than you do." But he lost, for Guy passed at 96.4 and Ted scored only 87.6.[32]

Selection of seasonal rangers was made in an entirely different manner, by appointment. Some were secretarial appointees (the superintendent had little or no say concerning their selection), while others were picked locally. The position of park ranger had been so completely glamorized by the end of the 1920s that many young men sought such summer work with no real conception of a ranger's life. The superintendent therefore found it necessary to caution applicants in these words:

> It has been our experience that young men often apply for a place on the park ranger force with the impression or understanding that the ranger has a sort of sinecure with nothing resembling hard work to perform, and that a ranger's position offers an opportunity to pass a pleasant vacation amid the beauties and wonders of Yellowstone Park, with very frequent trips about the park and innumerable dances and other diversions to occupy one's leisure hours.
>
> Again, young men very often apply for ranger positions with the feeling that the duties of the place require no special training or experience and that any man with a reasonably good education can perform these duties regardless of whether he has a pleasing or poor personality or whether he has or has not experience in outdoor activities.
>
> Also, many young men apply for ranger positions in the hope of making and saving considerable money to aid them in continuing their college work.[33]

The reality was something entirely different. A seasonal ranger worked under the supervision of one of the permanents, performing one or more routine duties, such as: checking cars at an entrance station, providing information at a ranger station, patroling afoot or horseback at a point of heavy visitor use, cleanup of quarters and grounds, controlling traffic (motorcycles were used then), fighting forest fires, investigating accidents, rendering first aid, handling bear problems, checking automobile campgrounds, and doing such paperwork as the situation required. Nor were those responsibilities limited to an eight-hour day; instead, the seasonal ranger was considered to be on duty from the time he arose ("at 6:00 A.M.") until he retired ("not later than 11:00 P.M.") under a system of semimilitary discipline that recognized no overtime and allowed no leave, except in the direst emergency.

This was a service that required more than ability. The considerable amount of contact with the public, occasionally even including lecturing, guiding large parties, and conducting VIPs, called for a pleasing personality (tactful, diplomatic, and courteous) and the patience to endure much plain drudgery. Despite careful screening of applicants, enough misfits turned up every season to keep the expression "ninety-day wonder" alive, even though it was a fair description in only a few cases.

Nor was such employment particularly lucrative. A seasonal ranger had to buy a uniform at a cost of $75.00, transport himself to the Park, and then pay $5.00 per month for his quarters and $1.20 per day for board at a government mess, all out of a salary of $140.00 per month. Thus, were he the very soul of frugality, one month's pay out of a season of work would be about all he could expect to take home. Despite the demanding nature of seasonal employment, morale was good.

After 1919, park rangers, whether permanent or seasonal, were handsomely uniformed. Other employees also wore the uniform until 1935, when it was decided only field personnel in administration, protection, and interpretation should wear it. In the beginning, the uniform consisted of pegged breeches and a Norfolk jacket, both of forest-green serge, worn with a white shirt, black tie, cordovan leather riding boots, and a grey Stetson hat (without the leather band). An air of authority was created by the silver-finished NPS collar ornaments, bronze buttons (the only feature that has remained unchanged over the years) and a nickel-plated badge.[34] The ranger badge, which came into use in 1920, was worn by all protection personnel the first year; after that the chief ranger and his four assistants wore a gold-plated version, and the superintendent wore a round, silver badge.

The uniform has undergone many changes during its first half-century. Sleeve insignia, worn on the right sleeve between shoulder and elbow, to show the rank and activity of the wearer, were added in 1922. The chief, assistant, and base grades were indicated by three, two, and one oak leaves: with acorns for administration, an inkwell for clerical, a transit for engineering, and crossed lightnings for electrical. That same year, the women's uniform appeared, with galluses to hold up the skirt! (though that would not have been apparent, since all uniformed employees were strictly enjoined to keep the jacket buttoned at all times). To that point, evolution of the uniform was toward a distinctive appearance; subsequent alterations have been refinements tending toward greater utility or comfort.

The early collar ornaments were replaced by gold-finished US NPS letters in 1926, and the colored shirt (steel grey) and green tie, along with a more practical whipcord fabric, were introduced two years later. At the same time, a cap and black leather puttees were approved for motorcycle patrolmen, and the round badges worn by the superintendent and his assistant were differentiated by gold-plating the superintendent's badge. The leather hat band appeared in 1930 and length-of-service insignia were added to the lower left sleeve in 1933 (hash-marks for single years and stars for multiples of five). Two years later, at the time of the general revision that took facilitating personnel out of uniform, the material was changed to wool elastique and the hat to a grey-brown color. A field jacket, trousers, and bag-over ski pants (with white spats) were used as a winter uniform at the Park's early ski area on the slopes of Mount Washburn prior to World War II.

On the eve of the war, a developing shortage of good leather prompted a far broader change in the uniform. In 1940 breeches and boots were replaced with trousers and shoes, a change not fully accomplished until 1947. Following that "new look," alterations were minor for more than a decade: an arrowhead shoulder patch in 1951 and a nametag over the right jacket or shirt pocket in 1958. There was, however, a relaxing of traditionally severe regulations concerning the wearing of the uniform, so that rangers could appear before the public in shirt sleeves when the weather was appropriate.

The decade of the sixties brought agitation for further change; what remains of the original ranger appearance teeters in the balance, at which point these words have the ring of an admonishment: "The National Park Service uniform can and does build morale in the man who wears it, and prestige in the eyes of the public."[35] Without further comment on the value of conservatism in this regard, we can go back to the first men who wore the uniform in such a proud way that a real esprit de corps developed in the Park. Occasionally, a young man was inclined to wear the uniform inappropriately, that is, to town on a day off or as an accessory to his courting. The recent change whereby the spread-eagle badge design was dropped for one more symbolic, recalls that when the old badge design was yet new, young rangers "lost" badges much too often—until a policy of requiring a $5 deposit was instituted by administrators who were more concerned with accountability than with romance.

What, exactly, did the rangers do? In Yellowstone Park the routines of rangering have always been sharply differentiated between a short summer season, with problems created by a massive visitation, and a long "off" season (much of it winter) in which the protection of the Park and its wildlife is the principal occupation.[36] Since facilitating and controlling visitor use of the Park in summer is the dominant reason for existence of a ranger force, it is that aspect of ranger life we shall describe first (making no particular differentiation between activities of permanent and seasonal rangers, except occasionally, because they have always been rather similar in all but the supervisory responsibilities of the permanents). For this purpose one could not make a better start than at a park gate, the point where the visitor first contacts the uniformed force, perhaps forming lasting impressions.

Checking automobiles at the several entrances was largely the work of seasonals, supervised by a permanent ranger or a designated senior. In the beginning, a fearsome amount of information was recorded in the issuing of a permit: the driver's name and hometown, the license number of the vehicle, with its make and number of seats, the number of passengers, and answers to a query concerning guns and dogs, all entered on the form and in a ledger. By the end of the 1930s name and license number only were required, and now merely the license number. The gate ranger also had to make change (accurately, since any till shortages came out of his pocket) and hand out an information booklet (later a fold-map) and windshield sticker. While that was going on, driver and passengers were likely popping questions which had to be answered as faithfully and cheerfully as though they had never been asked before.

The gate ranger's routine was repeated umpteen times each day and seldom with any more variety than an occasional gun to seal (with wire, secured by a lead slug pressed on with a plier-like tool) or the spotting of a license number on the "message" list, usually to inform a traveler of trouble at home. There was always a feeling of accomplishment in identifying one car out of a flow of hundreds or even thousands if the notice had been posted for some time, but no ranger liked to stand by while a visitor called headquarters to receive tidings of illness, death, or disaster at home. All too often it meant the end of a once-in-a-lifetime vacation.

The first checking stations were small buildings set at the shoulder of the road, mere shelters from which a gate ranger could step to register a vehicle. This was not too inconvenient when cars were few and drivers were on the right-hand side, but such facilities soon became entirely inadequate and were replaced by structures centered in the roadway at all entrances except the north. There, the awkward stone gatehouse remained in use until after World War II.[37] Located as it was on the right of the inbound lane, the ranger at the window had to talk with the passenger or past him to the driver, while the man checking exits had to walk to the center of the road (which could be dangerous on a busy day). Even the better arranged, rustic checking stations built at the east and west gates in 1922 eventually becme unhandy as the lower silhouette of modern automobiles left the ranger in a good position to talk with the top of the vehicle instead of its driver. Incidentally, ladies were employed quite early as checkers at the north entrance. Miss Francis Pound, daughter of the permanent park ranger at that gate, was hired as a uniformed seasonal during the summers of 1926 to 1929, and her sister Virginia was similarly employed in 1927.[38]

At the other end of the scale from the monotonous life of the gate rangers was the exciting life of the highway patrolmen. In the beginning, these jaunty fellows—certainly the most envied men on the force—were bike riders. Mounted on six Harley-Davidsons purchased in 1919,[39] they made endless war on speeders, who were a problem on the narrow, gravel-surfaced roads, providing the U.S. commissioner's court with considerable business. This was law enforcement of a dangerous type and patrolmen were occasionally thrown off their cycles by being crowded off the road or by skidding on a turn. Fortunately, no lives were lost, but there were some serious injuries. (Joe Douglas was out of circulation most of the summer from such an injury, incurred on Swan Lake Flat late in June 1925.)

The motorcycle era came to a close in 1936 with the purchase of four patrol cars.[40] They were V-8 Ford convertibles, each with a rumble seat and a nickel-plated siren on the left running board; they were sporty and capable of speeds of ninety miles per hour, but not with safety because of their mechanical brakes. One patrolman, while chasing a fast-moving Buick across Hayden Valley, hit his brakes too hard and went into an end-swapping skid, straight down the blacktop. The only serious consequence was to his morale; he went back to headquarters and resigned!

Chasing speeders was not the whole day's work. Early-day patrolmen kept in touch with headquarters by checking in routinely by telephone from roadside emergency boxes located five to ten miles apart. They could thus be dispatched to the scene of an accident, injury, bear problem, or traffic congestion, a system that worked

The author as a highway patrolman in 1940.

Motorcycle patrolman Mathew (a seasonal ranger), 1923.

remarkably well in the days before two-way radio communication. With time the patrolman's lot has become a safer one. Overcrowding of the park roads has made speeding less common, while better equipment and development of mobile radios has reduced the patrolman's dependence on his own guts and driving skill to corner such violaters.[41] The job has also lost much of the glamour of those early, dangerous days.

The Park's highway patrolmen were more than jaunty hot rodders of an earlier day, as a visitor who wrote to Judge T. Paul Wilcox testified:

> Perhaps it is not the custom for persons sentenced in your court to write and thank you for it but the whole occasion was so unusual that I cannot but do it. In the first place, I appreciated your advice thoroughly on the subject of speeding in the Park and am quite in sympathy with what you said. In regard to the fine, I think I quite deserved it. Ever since, I have been cautioning people going Parkward that the signs regarding 45 miles an hour should be read with great care and heeded equally well.
>
> The high point for us in the whole affair was making the acquaintance of the Ranger, Lee Coleman. He drove me down from the Ranger Station and back again and I don't think I have spent as enjoyable a day in recent years. It took some time for him to thaw out but I found him to be the deep river that runs so smoothly. You made a casual remark as we left court that he didn't talk much—I found it quite the reverse—he regaled me with the natural history of the Park in all its forms; geologically, the fauna, the flora, Indian lore, a myriad of subjects and he was remarkably well informed.[42]

The gate rangers and patrolmen were not the whole force. Other rangers were assigned to stations scattered throughout the Park, performing duties that varied greatly from place to place. Service at a principal point on the visitor-thronged Grand Loop was demanding but not uninteresting (especially for the socially inclined), while a summer at a backcountry station could be an idyllic experience for some.

Old Faithful was always the busiest place on the loop. A ranger assigned there was certain to spend most of his time between the information desk and uniformed patrol in the geyser basin. At the desk he must repeatedly answer such queries as "When will she spout?" (meaning Old Faithful geyser, across the road), although there were refreshing variations, such as this one quoted from the station log of 1939: "In the winter does the water from Old Faithful freeze on the way up or the way down?" Besides keeping track of the major geysers, the ranger on the desk must counsel the fisherman and the photographer, suggest an afternoon hike in the geyser basin or a two-day tour of the Park, direct a worried driver to a filling station or a small boy to the comfort station; he had to identify the plucked flower, yet tactfully make the point that flower-picking deprived others of beauty, and as tactfully suggest that the visitor had seen an osprey at the Canyon, not a bald eagle, and, most difficult of all, he was occasionally called upon to explain the operation of the model geyser installed by the station door.[43]

Duty in the geyser basin, performed as it was in a buttoned-up wool uniform, was something of a test of endurance. Often it consisted of random patroling intended to inhibit such thoughtless vandalism as name-writing on the margins of colorful pools, sounding the depth of hot springs with poles, and the soaping of geysers, but there were also guided walks with explanations of interesting features for the benefit of visitors. Such a tour once provided a seasonal ranger with an opportunity to make a fool of himself. He was conducting a group around Geyser Hill, across the Firehole River from Old Faithful, when an elderly gentlemen said: "I was here before you were born and helped to name all of these springs." A few moments later the old man heard the ranger confiding to another visitor that he had just met "the biggest liar who ever visited the park," which brought forth the remark: "Young man, if you had drunk the waters of the upper Yellowstone as many years as I have, you would be a liar too." The speaker was Joseph Edsall Mushbach, an assistant topographer with the Hayden Survey, who had mapped those very springs one-half century earlier.[44]

Giving the "cone talk," that three- to five-minute rundown to enlighten the crowd assembled before Old Faithful Geyser prior to each eruption, was a duty shared by the rangers stationed in the Upper Geyser Basin. Some did it well, others not so well; regardless, they were performing an interpretive service that went back to 1887 (see Chapter 12). Unfortunately, the talk had to be discontinued in recent years.

Involvement of rangers in interpretive activities developed out of the Mather-Albright concept of rangers as more than protectors, a viewpoint that led to lecturing, information services, museum development, guided tours, and eventually to a distinct educational service. At this point our concern is with the versatile park rangers of the formative period.[45]

Since there was, initially, an "official fear lest suggestion of lessons and study would keep people away from the Parks," the interpretive approach was low-keyed and entertaining, centering on an entirely new type of facility: a ranger station with an attached "community room." This rustic hall, adorned with elk antlers, sheep horns, and bison skulls, served an information purpose by day: a place where visitors could get their bearings and any other help they might need. In the evening it became the scene of a folksy gathering by a log fire. There, visitors could listen to a "lecturer" talk about the Park and join in group singing. It was a personalized experience with great appeal.

Three such structures were built from plans drawn in 1920: two, Old Faithful and Canyon, were completed by August of the following year; the third, at Lake, was not finished until June 18, 1923.[46] The first of the early lecturers was Mrs. Isabel Bassett Wasson, a graduate of Wellesley College and Columbia University. While a visitor to the Park in 1919, she lectured on the hot springs and geysers, making such a good impression on Superintendent Albright that he offered her a position at Old Faithful, where she was to "act as a ranger in guiding people about the geyser formations while performing the duties relating to protecting of those formations." She was also expected to give an evening lecture, obtain museum specimens, and prepare information bulletins, all of which she did very satisfactorily during the summer of 1920. While Mrs. Wasson was unable to return to the Park for the 1921 season, she continued to provide advice for several years.[47]

Among the rangers who lectured at Old Faithful was Walter P. Martindale, who became prominent through his "Sermon on a Mount," a talk delivered from horseback at the bear-feeding ground east of the old auto camp. There, the visitors sat on rude benches behind a flimsy wire barricade while Martindale talked about the bears foraging a pile of hotel garbage; that is, until one evening when a big black bear chased a little black bear through the wire *and* the spectators, effectively closing down the bear show at Old Faithful. Martindale was not above "stuffin' dudes" at times. A tale attributed to him concerns a ski trip on which he was supposedly treed by a moose. As he told it, he got to the very top of the lodgepole pine before he realized he hadn't taken his skis off!

Bear feeding, as a public attraction, was finally restricted to the Canyon area, where in the 1930s an elaborate feeding place was built on Otter Creek. Seating was arranged behind a chain link fence on a hillside overlooking a concrete platform where fifty or more bears, many of them grizzlies, would congregate each summer evening to forage the hotel garbage.

Visitors waiting for the evening show at Old Faithful bear feeding ground, early in the 1920s.

Cars waiting to enter the parking area at Canyon bear feeding ground on Otter Creek, in 1935. *Photograph by Earl E. Evans.*

The principal scheduled activities at Canyon were operation of the bear grounds (requiring several men in the adjacent parking area as well as armed guards within the enclosure); duty on the information desk at the ranger station, and traffic control at Chittenden Bridge.[48] Unscheduled activities included rescuing persons who were unable to ascend the colorful, steeply sloped wall of the Grand Canyon after slithering down to the river one-quarter mile below. A long, stout rope was kept coiled in a back room of the ranger station for such emergencies.

Ted Ogston, the ranger who lectured at Canyon for several seasons during the 1920s, has recalled his vain attempt to straighten out a seasonal who was addicted to telling highly imaginative tales. The young man was mortally afraid of bears, and as Ted tells it,

> He was always coming up with these weird stories about a grizzly attacking him while he was coming home [from courting a girl at the lodge, across the river from the ranger station] . . . and I said, "Well, I'll give that fellow something to talk about," so one evening I took a pair of woolly chaps, that I used to ride in when it was cold, and walked over to Chittenden Bridge. I got down right by the edge and kneeled there for a long time, until I heard him coming. I reared up and wrapped those woolly chaps over his head and you never heard such an unGodly scream out of a man as he lit out for the ranger station.[49]

Ted slipped into the station by the back door to find the seasonal telling another of his fantastic tales.

Lake Ranger Station was headquarters for what was always the largest district in the Park, a vast area of water and wilderness devoted mainly to fishing, boating, and enjoying the backcountry. The rangers at Fishing Bridge developed a knack for extracting fish hooks from ears and noses (a first-aid problem created by the elbow-to-elbow fishing on the famous bridge), and those at Lake became boatmen quite early.[50] But it was the isolated Thorofare Station that was the prize assignment. There, twenty-five miles from the nearest road, in that broad, willow-covered valley dominated by 11,000-foot peaks, a ranger was pleasantly on his own, concerned mainly with cutting logs out of the trails and keeping the telephone line up, packing supplies and cutting cabin wood, and checking horse parties and riding the boundary. There he could know, for a season, something of that life the word "ranger" connotes.

In such remote and peaceful surroundings as the Thorofare, one would hardly expect any rascality worse than a marauding bear in the oat bin, but it was there that Ranger Ray Little lost his horses to "Horse Thief" Kelly, who was hiding out in that general area in 1920. (This was a low blow in Ray's estimation because the horses were his own; permanent rangers had to furnish their own mounts in those days. Also, he had his bride with him, and she had to walk out too.) And then, Frank Kowski had trouble with a cabin-pilfering "phantom" in the summer and fall of 1938, which should remind us to expect snakes even in Eden! Another piece of horse country, where the rangering was almost synonymous with buffalo ranching, predator control, and backcountry tripping with VIP parties, was on the north side of the Park, along the Lamar River.

The educational work of the early park rangers underwent a transition over the years from random activities to a coordinated program operated by an educational service, namely the naturalist department. As noted in Chapter 12, interpretation had its faint beginning in the "cone talks" made by those soldiers of the Twenty-second Infantry who were stationed in the Upper Geyser Basin in 1888, and educational work of a sort was carried on throughout the stagecoach era by porters of the Yellowstone Park Association and the part-time guides of the Wylie Camping Company. The efforts of these interpreters were seldom adequate, however; the soldiers lacked reliable information and the guides tended to develop a repertoire of stories to inspire generous tipping.

Milton P. Skinner, who came to the Park in 1896 as a college student employed by the Yellowstone Park Association, has described the situation at Old Faithful:

> At that time the tourists were guided over the formation and given lectures by a young chap from Aurora, Ill., employed by the hotel company. He did good work but deplored the fact that he had no special training for the work, that he had no time to study, then, anyway. I often substituted for this guide, and so began my first work as a guide and lecturer. Every year after that, I was in close contact with the guides on all the formations.[51]

Later, in 1910, while working as an overseer for the Corps of Engineers on road work in the Park, Skinner heard of a proposal to build a small government museum at Mammoth and thought it was such a good idea he became its active advocate.

Skinner says he "talked with everyone at Yellowstone from the Superintendent of the Park and the President of the Hotel Company down," and, in the winter of 1913-14, went to Washington, D.C., in the hope of interesting the secretary of the interior in establishing an educational service in the Park. He was able to generate interest in an official service that would include guiding, lecturing, information bureaus, and a museum, but found there was no money for such a development. He returned to the Park with only the first park information circular to show for his efforts.

Skinner had made a lasting impression, however. This became evident in June 1919 when Horace M. Albright made it one of his first official acts as superintendent of Yellowstone National Park to ask Skinner to organize an educational program. Skinner accepted an appointment as a park ranger on October 1, 1919, on the understanding that his position would be changed to park naturalist as soon as possible, which it was, on April 1, 1920.

Skinner's first move was to open an information office in the former bachelor officers' quarters at Fort Yellowstone,[52] where he began displaying a few specimens on the walls as they became available. The response of visitors was so enthusiastic that he decided to enlarge the exhibit space, which he did the following winter. The 1,500 square feet of floor space available that season proved too small and a room behind the information office was given over to museum use in 1922. By the time Skinner resigned in September (he was unhappy with the lack of time for research and writing), the collection exhibited there included 47 pieces of igneous rock, 43 pieces of geyserite, 41 pieces of petrified wood, 2 mounted animal heads, 1 mounted eagle, 4 pieces of wood cut by beaver, 1 contorted tree trunk, 2 mineral specimens, and pressed flowers representing 80 species.[53] He had also begun editing "Yellowstone Letters," which preceded *Nature Notes*, and had set up a summer program utilizing the services of five rangers.

After Milton P. Skinner left, the educational work was handled differently. Dr. Frank E. Thone directed the program on an acting basis during the 1923 season, and the position of park naturalist was not filled on a permanent basis until March 1924, when Edmund J. Sawyer, an artist-ornithologist, took over the duties. After August 27 of that year he was counseled by Jack E. Haynes, who served as acting director of the museum on a gratuitous basis during the four years Sawyer was in the Park.[54] While the arrangement was makeshift, it served well enough for a period in which the objectives and methods of educational work were being developed for the National Park Service as a whole.

In 1923, Ansell F. Hall was designated chief naturalist and placed in charge of educational programs in all the parks, and the following year Director Mather secured the services of Dr. Frank R. Oastler of New York as consultant to prepare a general policy for such activity. Secretary Hubert Work's milestone announcement, in 1925, equating education with recreation as a National Park Service objective, had such immediately beneficial results as the establishment of a headquarters for the service's educational activities

An evening lecture in the courtyard of the Old Faithful Museum, about 1931.

at Berkeley, California, and the Yosemite School of Field Natural History for the training of naturalists. The importance of education and enrichment of the spirit as primary objectives of park management was confirmed in 1927 by an advisory committee headed by Dr. John C. Merriam. This was all prologue to further expansion of Yellowstone's educational program.

Construction of a modern, fire-resistant museum building at Yosemite Park, begun in 1924 by the American Museum Association (with a grant from the Laura Spelman Rockefeller Memorial) encouraged Superintendent Horace M. Albright to seek funds for a similar Yellowstone facility.[55] However, his efforts were unavailing until 1928, when the American Museum Association undertook the development of a series of trailside museums in the Park. This entirely new approach was financed by a grant of $118,000 provided by the Laura Spelman Rockefeller Memorial "for the development of educational activities in Yellowstone National Park."

Dorr G. Yeager, a Yosemite-trained naturalist who took over the direction of the Yellowstone educational program April 10, 1928, immediately began planning, jointly with Herbert Maier, the first of those beautiful structures that formed a unique museum system. The proposal for Norris Museum was submitted on September 3, and the rustic structure, complete with exhibits intended to give one "a splendid short course in rocks and their formation," was opened to the public July 5, 1930. At that time, two other museums were nearing completion, a small one at Madison Junction and a larger museum-office at Old Faithful, and construction of a fourth, at Fishing Bridge, was just getting underway. These trailside museums were intended to provide a "hook-up between an object or spectacle charged with dynamic information and a mind that is receptive to informational impulses."[56] Thus, two (Norris and Old Faithful) were associated with thermal geology, one (Madison Junction) with the Park's history, and the fourth (Fishing Bridge) with the ecology of the Yellowstone Lake area.

The trailside museums were not only effective interpretive facilities, but also pleasing examples of that rustic, stone-log architecture which, for a time, became synonymous with national park structures. Unfortunately the National Park Service has since abandoned the distinctive style it pioneered with such success, resorting to less appropriate and less durable construction.

The trailside museums served the Park adequately for one-quarter century. A force of thirty naturalists provided activities that included, in addition to the museum services already mentioned, evening campfire talks illustrated with lantern slides, nature walks conducted by naturalists, "game stalks" (automobile caravans intended to get visitors to those areas where elk and moose customarily fed at evening time), self-guiding nature trails, roadside exhibits, and "game shows" (the several bear-feeding grounds, a zoological garden, and the buffalo show corral). Some of those activities have been curtailed in recent years in accordance with policy changes, yet the educational program remains similar today.

It is not uncommon for a summer visitor to ask the man in the forest-green uniform, "What do you do in the *winter*?"—implying that he curls up by a hot stove during the season of storms, like a bear in his den; or, "Do you stay here *all* winter?" in which is revealed a belief that rangers, like elk, should annually succumb to a migratory instinct intended to lead them to a better wintering-ground. Neither is a true view of the off-season in Yellowstone Park; even with the visitors gone, there is enough to do, and whatever is lacking in people-pressure is made up by the pressure of the hostile environment in which the ranger works to protect the Park and its wildlife.

Off-season activities have always been of three types: "housekeeping" chores, wildlife management, and protective patroling. The first, which included rationing of patrol cabins, cutting fuel wood, making necessary repairs to cabins and fences, maintaining trails, bridges, and telephone lines, and clean-up of trash was usually accomplished routinely by personnel of the district; in the case of larger projects, like building a pasture fence or raising a cabin, a large part of the force might be assembled as a crew. These were jolly get-togethers where spare time was given over to poker playing, barbering (Earl Bowman would say: "I used to be a damned good barber, and if any of you fellows need a shave or haircut, I'm the guy can give you one!"), horseplay, and drinking (if anyone had the necessary moonshine, or "alky").[57]

In the off-season the rangers managed the elk and buffalo in the northern part of the Park. They cut hay in the meadow at Yancey's (Pleasant Valley, near Tower Junction), on Slough Creek, and on the bottom lands along the Lamar River at the Buffalo Ranch, stacking from 500 to 800 tons for the park horse herd and for feeding elk and buffalo during the worst part of the winter. The hope was to prevent large loss of elk and buffalo by holding them in the Park during very hard winters. The ranching operations were handled by a chief buffalo keeper, who had an assistant, one or two herders and an irrigator, and the help of rangers for feeding and for such big operations as slaughtering excess animals, castrating, and innoculating calves.[58]

Work at the Buffalo Ranch was hard and dangerous. Beginning early in January, picked men scoured the slopes adjacent to the Lamar Valley as far as Miller Creek, driving in the little bands of buffalo through snow that was sometimes belly-deep to their horses. The buffalo were herded into a large corral and were moved from there in small groups to the corrals where they were tallied and grouped for castration or innoculation. Bob Lacombe, buffalo keeper in the twenties, was a fearless, rough man, and an excellent horseman. He preferred men who were tough and would do instantly what he wanted, and his attitude was well known. Thus, it was with some misgiving that Ted Ogston reported for work at the ranch.

The first morning Ted asked deferentially, "Bob, what would you like me to do?" and LaCombe said: "Well, I tell you, we're goin' in this upper corral and we'll run down a bunch of buffaloes; you cut-off about 15 head and then send the rest of them back," and with that Bob Lacombe, Sam Woodring, and Harry Trischman rode off after the buffalo, leaving the greenhorn to manage the big gate to the inner corral. Down came the buffalo, and when Ted had his fifteen animals, in something less than the time it would take to count them, he waded out among those hooves, heads, and horns expecting to wave the remainder back and close the gate. But there was no stemming that wild-eyed, shaggy tide the horsemen were forcing out of the large corral, and Ted had to take refuge atop one of the gateposts. He says the herders "just about fell off their horses laughing."[59] The victim of their little joke didn't think it was that funny.

Just how dangerous it was is evident from a close call Bob Lacombe had in the corral one day. He had dismounted and was walking toward the gate when a big buffalo bull made a pass at him from close ahead. With no room to dodge, Bob grabbed both horns and was flung onto the fence with one lift of the bull's great head; miraculously he was not hurt. Pete Schultz, a laborer, was wheeling manure out of the barn to a pile where a nasty-tempered old bull was eating phosphates. The bull had shown no animosity to Pete and his wheelbarrow until, suddenly, he decided he really didn't like the man. Pete got the message in time to make a dash for the corral fence and was starting up when a horn ripped his pants open from thigh to belt—an inch short of a serious, if not fatal, wound.

No men were seriously injured feeding and handling buffalo at the ranch, but the horses were not always so lucky. A visitor to the Buffalo Ranch in 1924 has recalled his shock at coming upon a horse standing miserably in a corral with a great, raw wound ripped through hide and flesh to the bone, at the shoulder, reminiscent of "the sort of sickening wound common in the bull ring, where blindfolded horses are urged on to the horns of frantic, maddened bulls."[60] In this case, a "tame" bull had turned on a rider and the horse had borne the brunt of the attack.

Predator control by rangers was a corollary of the effort to propagate elk and buffalo until prohibited by the director's order of November 12, 1934. This warfare, which accounted for an average of 183 coyotes each year over the dozen years prior to cessation of such control, was based on the idea that predators hanging on the flank of the ungulate herds were killing a significant proportion of the calf crop, which was probably never true.[61] But from the ranger's viewpoint these "little wolves" were enemies—to be shot on sight, trapped, or poisoned.

Putting out poisoned bait for coyotes came near ending the career of one Yellowstone ranger. Sam Woodring, Scotty Bauman, Bill Wiggins, and Harry Liek stopped for the night at the Lower Blacktail cabin, and in the morning Sam, who had been an army packer in the Philippines and was pretty much a jack-of-all-trades, set about to cook some hot cakes. Harry Liek tied into the first stack, but one bite was enough. He spat out his mouthful with the comment: "Sam, you can have 'em!" A closer look at the baking powder can showed that someone had scratched on the back, "Stricknine for Coyotes." Nick Carter had been using the cabin while poisoning coyotes in that area and had left the can in the cupboard.[62]

Another facet of off-season ranger life was boundary line patrol. Beginning with the opening of the Montana hunting season in the fall, a ranger was posted on the north line, between the town of Gardiner and Hellroaring Creek, to prevent hunters in the Gardiner-Jardine area from trespassing on the Park. The man assigned this duty worked out of the Crevice ranger station, which stood in utter loneliness on the side of a mountain midway along that twelve-mile span of boundary (more like twenty miles to travel by the up-and-down, zigzag trail).

Something of the life on boundary line patrol is evident in the diary of James Dupuis, a French Indian from the Flathead country who was one of the early rangers. Jimmy's diary opens November 1, 1918;[63] by the twenty-fourth the temperature was sinking as low as ten below zero at night. On December 5 Jimmy noted "Patrol from Crevice to seven miles post in Cottonwood Basin. Miles made 18, time seven hours. Cloudy, cold." One can picture him, his sheepskin collar rimed from his breath and his legs gone stiff under his chaps, dismounting clumsily to walk awhile ahead of his horse to stir up his circulation.

After a lonely Christmas at Crevice (which was so isolated his family had to remain at the town of Gardiner), Jimmy's entry showed "Patrols both ways from Station. Miles 8 seen 150 elk," and on January 3, 1919, after a layover in Gardiner, he "Patroled Park line to Crevice on foot 10 miles." That could only mean the snow and cold had conspired to make travel on horseback an impossibility. Except for days when he remained at the station to cut wood, bake bread, or do his laundry, Jimmy was out on the boundary line, making certain no hunters crossed into the Park to molest the elk, and to drive migrating animals back into the sanctuary of the Park whenever an opportunity appeared.

There were other lonesome winter stations in those days: Sylvan Pass, where Tex Wisdom held forth, entirely separated from the Park proper by the Absaroka Range; the Bechler corner, where Ray Little remained with his wife and baby behind a barricade of snow (up to six feet on the level) which prevented any frequent contact with the nearest ranch five miles down the road toward Ashton, Idaho. There was also the south entrance, a beleaguered outpost of two families, and Riverside, the old ranger station 1.2 miles inside the west entrance at The Barns, a place notable for the fact that the bitter cold once drove the mercury of the official thermometer below the calibrations on the tube.[64] Before the road was kept open to Bozeman in the winter (1936), the nearby town of West Yellowstone was as isolated as the ranger station; only a few residents remained there over winter (to shovel snow off the roofs and play cards in the rear of Slopansky's store). The ranger stationed at the northeast entrance was similarly situated, except that the town of Cooke City was even more snowbound and isolated than West Yellowstone prior to the opening of a weekly mail route in the thirties.

The most isolated of all the stations occupied in winter were those in the remote interior of the Park, Old Faithful and Lake. Ranger Charles Phillips was assigned to remain in the Upper Geyser Basin during the winter of 1926-27 to make wildlife and thermal observations. This was no novel assignment; rangers had overwintered at Old Faithful before, as had several generations of hotel winter keepers, and no one imagined a tragedy shaping up. All went well enough into April. Phillips was in frequent contact with headquarters by telephone, and he was visited by Chief Ranger Woodring and Harry Liek, who skied around the loop in early

January; also, Phillips was not entirely alone as he had the company of the hotel winter keepers, Mr. and Mrs. Bauer.

On the evening of April 11, Mr. Bauer brought Phillips some plants he had found growing in a warm rivulet near his headquarters and asked the ranger to identify them. It was decided that they belonged to a species of wild parsnip which has an edible root, whereupon they determined to try some for dinner. The meal was eaten about 8 o'clock and Phillips returned to his quarters at 11:15 P.M. Both the winter keeper and his wife were taken violently ill about two in the morning, suffering from waves of nausea and vomiting which made them so weak they remained indoors until the evening of the twelfth.

Having heard nothing from Phillips, Mr. Bauer finally put on his webs and crossed the several hundred yards of snow to the ranger station. He found the building dark and cold, with the ranger dead on the kitchen floor. The plant they had eaten turned out to be the deadly Water Hemlock.[65]

In the 1920s Lake ranger station was occupied in winter by four or five men under an assistant chief ranger and was the hub of far-ranging ski patrols. Traveling in pairs, these men covered nearly one-third of the Park, everything from the head of the Lamar River, south along the Absaroka Range to the Thorofare corner, and eastward to the Snake River. After winter had set the surface of Lake Yellowstone solidly, they took shortcuts across the ice whenever they could to shorten their route. Going from Lake to Thorofare they traveled on ice for about ten miles (Lake to Stevenson Island to Park Point), and on the trip from Lake to West Thumb, crossed Bridge and Thumb bays on the ice. Though more direct, such crossings posed some hazards.

Harry Liek once came back alone from West Thumb and was caught by darkness before he made that last crossing over the Bridge Bay ice from Gull Point to the Lake ranger station. He should have stayed on the road and passed around the bay, but, confident that the prevailing southwest wind he had had at his back all day would serve as sufficient guide, he launched out on the trackless ice of the lake. Unknown to Harry, his southwest wind had shifted to the northwest quarter, and the land he at last came upon was Stevenson Island. But Harry didn't know that, and spent most of the night circling the island, looking for some familiar landmark to tell him he was near Lake ranger station. He was rescued near morning, when the boys at the station, worried by his absence, built a bonfire on the shore to serve as a beacon.[66]

In later years such misadventures were duly celebrated at the ranger conference, held at headquarters each spring, in a brief ceremony termed "joining the club." During some convenient interlude not noted on the agenda, those unfortunates who had spent a night under a spruce tree while on patrol the previous winter were herded out on the lawn to demonstrate their proficiency at fire-starting with a match and a few sticks. There were always some "alumni" standing by to offer encouragement and advice.

On the longer crossings of the lake that were a part of the Thorofare trip, skiers could stop on Stevenson Island to warm up in the shelter of the abandoned steamboat, *E. C. Waters*.[67] The hulk had lain aground in the cove on the east side of the island throughout the twenties; its engine and boilers had been removed through a gaping hole which left the boat a useless derelict. Beyond the shelter it gave skiers, the *E. C. Waters* was useful as a prop for Jack Croney's fish-fry business and as a retreat for brawls fueled with moonshine. On the other hand, the hulk was an eyesore, and, since the rangers were under pressure to clean up the debris of more than fifty years of indiscriminate use of the Park, the boys at Lake decided to do something about the boat—burn it!

So, in the spring of 1930 a little party consisting of Albert Elliot and Skeet Dart, both rangers, with winter keeper "Boots" Chenard, skied over to Stevenson Island, poured a can of kerosene on the bow of the boat and torched it. Assistant Chief Ranger Ogston, who was in charge of Lake District but was not present when the boat was burned, was called into headquarters some weeks later, charged with destroying the boat company's property, and told to make restitution in the amount of $500. Unwilling to clear himself at the expense of the men who had innocently committed the vandalism, Ted paid up.[68]

The men who patroled a frigid Yellowstone in a day before snowmobiles, helicopters, and two-way radios, knew, as they set out upon a circuit of snowshoe cabins, that they were dependent on their own bag of tricks for survival. Such ski patroling (50- to 100-mile trips, which kept a pair of rangers out a week or two at a time) is largely a thing of the past. The first long patrol of the winter ordinarily was a trip to the Thorofare corner soon after Christmas. If the roads were yet passable, someone would take the skiers as far as a pickup could go with the assistance of chains and occasional shoving and shoveling. An open season might allow a vehicle to get as far as Lake ranger station, while an early, hard winter might block the road below Golden Gate; whatever the case, from the time the patrolmen mounted their "boards" they were on their own and largely beyond help.

The early snow was always too dry and powdery to hold a man up well, so those extra-wide, extra-long skis, Yellowstone Specials made by Strand, were generally used for the first trips. Even so, it was not uncommon to ski all day and see only the tips of the skis when they were deliberately lifted out of the snow. Such cross-country travel called for a regular rotation of the lead position, usually at fifteen-minute intervals, to allow one man to "ride the buggy" while the other was breaking trail. This conserved energy, so that a speed of two to three miles per hour could be maintained. With the odds so very much against survival in case of a serious accident, there was little inclination to *schuss* the slopes; rather, steep descents were made by "riding the sticks": the skier put the doubled ski poles between his legs, crouching upon them with his left hand on the poles behind him just above the rings. In this three-point position he could control the speed of a descent, or stop completely, by forcing the ends of the ski poles down with his left hand.

Even habitual caution did not always suffice. Jerry Yetter was feeling his way across the up-and-down terrain of Hayden Valley in a white-out (a condition occurring in cloudy weather, where the lack of shadows leaves the eye no basis for estimating relief on a snow-covered surface) and had the misfortune to pitch over a ten- to twelve-foot snow cornice. His skis stuck point-first in the snow of a gulley and he fetched-up with such a shock that the lacings tore out of his boots. He wasn't hurt, but some ingenuity was required to patch his footgear sufficiently for a five-mile haul into Canyon ranger station.

Like the mountainmen of an earlier day, each ranger carried a "possibles sack" into which he could dip in such emergencies. Extra toe straps, a length of boot lacing, a few feet of stovepipe wire, copper rivets, bicycle pliers, and a Boy Scout knife (the type with screw driver and leather punch) made a minimum repair kit. Just such an outfit sufficed to repair the ski Art Jacobson split with his Hudson Bay ax while felling a tree to use as a foot log over the open water of Cascade Creek. With his shattered ski bound with wire and thongs, he was able to limp back to Bechler ranger station in the track made by his partner.

Many streams in the Park received enough runoff from the hot springs to prevent them from freezing over in the winter. To get at this open water the rangers carried an unusual drinking vessel, made of a used milk can fitted with a bail and a cord by which it could be suspended from a ski pole when dipping up a drink. The skiers carried this device handily on the outside of the pack; without it, they had no safe way of reaching the water running so invitingly below a three- to eight-foot verge of snow.

The patrolman's pack was never heavy, but it did contain a few indispensable items in addition to his possibles sack: extra mitten liners and socks, matches and a candle stub, map and compass, and sun glasses, medical tape (for covering heel blisters) and zinc oxide (for protecting sunburned skin). The cautious souls included an emergency ration such as oatmeal mixed with raisins or a can of corned beef, and of course tea and sugar. Thus, rangers who had to overnight along the trail in a hole stomped in the snow beneath some thick-branched old spruce tree could manage with little discomfort. They could make a fire with twigs and the lower dead limbs of their sheltering tree and sit out the night with their backs to the trunk, melting snow in their drinking cups for tea. While not the best way to spend a sub-zero night, it was not the worst, and no Yellowstone men ever suffered serious consequences from such a camp-out.

Ordinarily, a day's run on skis (ten to twenty miles) ended at a snug log cabin. These had a large porch overhang to shelter the doorway, and a rick of split wood; also, a snow shovel was hung under the peak, where it could be reached to dig out the door and relieve the roof of some of its burden. With that done, and the coffee-can cover removed from the stovepipe, the patrolmen could retire into their 10 by 14-foot shelter, light a lantern, and build a fire in the sheet-iron stove.

When the glacial chill was at last vanquished and the cots were made up with blankets that had been suspended from the ceiling beyond the reach of mice; when the big, zinc-covered box that served as a mouseproof cupboard for dishes and dry goods was opened; and cans of food were brought up out of the cellar hole below the floor; and particularly when the smell of coffee, biscuits, and sizzling ham began to vie with the odor of socks and mitten liners drying in the rafters; and with the tang of beeswax being ironed onto the bottom of a pair of skis—when rangering had been reduced to these terms, it was a good life, however cold the day may have been.

Perhaps it was just such a feeling that prompted Harry Trischman to write the simple, eloquent note he left on the washstand at Crevice ranger station as he finished his last day of duty on December 31, 1945, bringing to a close thirty-four years of service as an army scout and park ranger.[69] He wrote, "They won't let me sleep in their cabins any more." It was the statement of a man who loved the Park and his job, and helped to make both great.

CHAPTER 20

GREATER YELLOWSTONE

It is no longer an argument whether Yellowstone Park should logically increase its territory and rectify its borders, it has come to be an argument whether conservation itself shall be hampered, or, even more, done away with.
—Struthers Burt, 1926.[1]

The Greater Yellowstone movement originated in an attempt to give substance to an old dream of the Park's friends, a dream of expansion that never materialized. That early out-thrusting of the conservation spirit shaped the future of the Jackson Hole region instead, an area as large as Yellowstone Park, adding another park to our national system and furthering the preservation aspect of American conservation. Although Yellowtone Park itself was left but little greater by the movement, the accomplishment was worth the effort, for the thread of creation was woven into these events.

Conception of the movement can be traced to the early fall of 1917,[2] but it had its antecedents. The recommendation advanced by Secretary of the Interior Franklin K. Lane at that time, involving the addition to Yellowstone Park of 1,200 square miles of national forest land lying south of it, was a far-off echoing of General Sheridan's suggestion of 1882 for doubling the area of the Park in order to make it a better game sanctuary. The progress of that idea has been traced (Chapter 14) from the original suggestion through the unsuccessful efforts of Senator George Graham Vest to give it a legislative form, to quasi-fulfillment under the presidential authority to reserve forest lands. Subsequently, the idea reappeared in the annual reports of Colonel S.B.M. Young and Captain J. B. Erwin, both advancing strong arguments for adding the reserved lands to Yellowstone Park; even the organization of the adjacent reserves into national forests administered by the Department of Agriculture did not quash this persistent notion.[3]

The Greater Yellowstone movement received its apt label from the pen of Emerson Hough.[4] Much effort could have been saved and the general good would have been better served if more Wyoming citizens had understood what Hough was trying to tell them when he wrote of their state, "Give her Greater Yellowstone and she will inevitably become Greater Wyoming." Out of a failure to understand him came the Jackson Hole controversy, which raged for three decades before the truth of Hough's statement was at last too clear to be denied.

The addition proposed in the opening years of the National Park Service era was defined by a line that began on the eastern boundary of Yellowstone Park near Eagle Peak, traversed the crest of the Absaroka Range southward around the headwaters of Monument Creek, Thorofare Creek, and the Yellowstone River to the Buffalo Plateau, and then passed westward down the Buffalo Fork of the Snake River to the outlet of Jackson Lake. From there it zigzagged southwesterly around the lake nearly to the foot of the Teton Mountains, skirted their foothills southerly to a point about three miles north of Menors Ferry over the Snake River, and then climbed westward to the summit of the mountains. Continuing northward along the divide to the head of Boone Creek, the line descended the creek to the Idaho-Wyoming line and followed it northward to its crossing of the south boundary of Yellowstone Park (see the map of proposed boundary changes, 1918).[5] This area of 1,265 square miles included Jackson, Leigh, and Jenny lakes and the great peaks of the Teton Range, those shark-toothed elevations that an eastern editor considered "from their nature a component part of the Yellowstone Park whose gamut of majestic scenery they complete."[6] The lands involved were almost entirely national forest that had been set aside from the public domain so early that there were few entrymen on them. The attitude of the local people was expressed this way in the *Jackson Hole Courier:*

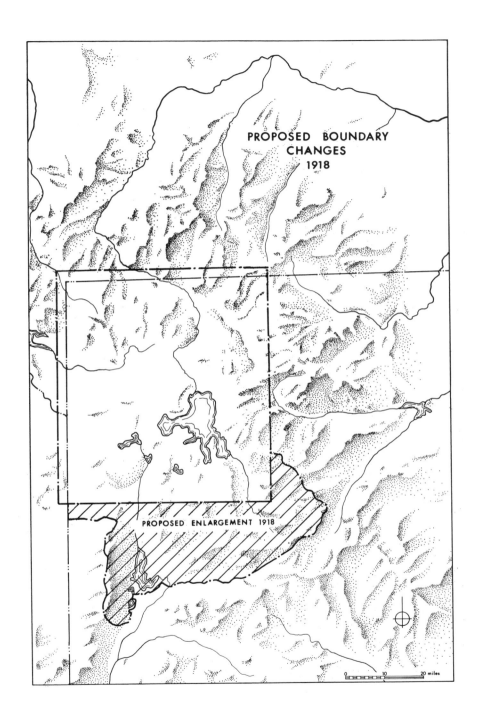

PROPOSED BOUNDARY
CHANGES
1918

PROPOSED ENLARGEMENT 1918

0   10   20 miles

When the extension was first talked of, some very bitter opposition was manifested in this valley, but this has gradually given way until many who were bitterly opposed are now heartily in favor of such a move, if, the extension will not interfere with the grazing of Jackson Hole cattle. The united effort should be made here to have this bill introduced.[7]

Generally, that was the original feeling: a tongue-in-cheek acceptance.

Congressman Frank W. Mondell, Wyoming's sole representative, introduced a bill in the House, and a supporting measure was sponsored in the Senate by John B. Kendrick, also of the Wyoming delegation. These had the approval of Governor Carey and the interior and agriculture departments, suggesting a prompt enactment by Congress. The House bill was quickly passed, and, as there was no particular feeling against it, the Senate's approval was expected that session. The measure was so far down on the Senate calendar, however, that unanimous consent was required for its advancement to a place where it could be considered before adjournment. Denial of such consent by Senator Nugent of Idaho ended the progress of park extension legislation in 1918; though disappointing, that outcome caused no concern as it was believed passage could easily be obtained in the next session.

While this was transpiring in Congress, the land concerned was withdrawn from settlement on July 8, 1918, by presidential order, as an aid to the pending legistlation.[8] This action seems to have given grave concern to Jackson Hole cattlemen, who were accustomed to ranging their stock on the national forest lands. By the time Congressman Mondell reintroduced his bill in 1919, the Jackson Hole Livestock Association had raised formidable oppostion. The association's work on behalf of the cattlemen had results: the extension proposal was soon "antagonized by every little association in Wyoming."[9] And worse was to come.

Unfortunately, a Mr. I. H. Larom, who is described as "a Princeton graduate, just discharged from the Army, a big game hunter, and a friend of Wyoming, who was intending to situate in this state,"[10] happened to be passing through Cheyenne. He knew what was happening in Washington, and being unsympathetic to the idea of extending the boundaries of Yellowstone Park, proceeded to stir up a similar antipathy among the Wyoming legislators. He drafted a memorial that was passed the same day and forwarded to Congress, where Representative Mondell was taken completely by surprise. It was a counterattack he was incapable of meeting, since it came from the legislature of his own state; thus, the congressman had to abandon his bill.

Other friends of the park extension measure were unwilling to quit the fight. Senator Kendrick, Land Commissioner Tallman, and Superintendent Horace M. Albright of Yellowstone National Park arranged an open meeting at the town of Jackson on August 25, 1919, in the hope of reasoning with the local people and inducing them to withdraw their opposition. The meeting was a disaster. The speakers were "hooted off the platform by the enraged citizens."[11] Even some friends of the Park became less than helpful: just at that ebb point, Horace W. Lorimer, editor of the *Saturday Evening Post* and a recent visitor to Yellowstone Park with Emerson Hough, became critical of the extension plan. The National Park Service had announced that a new road would be built through the addition from a point near the outlet of Jackson Lake to a connection with the park road system on the east shore of Yellowstone Lake. This route up Pacific Creek, over Two Ocean Pass and down the valley of the Upper Yellowstone River would give the Jackson Hole community a second entrance into the Yellowstone country—an attractive proposal. Mr. Lorimer, a preservationist, came out strongly against the road and hotels within the addition, and consequently against the extension idea.

The ruckus raised by Lorimer's stand against commercial development brought out another powerful opponent of park extension in the person of Maxwell Struthers Burt, an author, traveler, and rancher who corresponded publicly with Congressman Mondell at that time.[12] As a result of accumulating antagonism, park extension was nearly a dead issue by the end of the year. At least one Wyoming resident lamented the outcome, noting:

> The scenery of this proposed extension added to the Park's geysers, would put it in a class by itself, not only in this country, but also probably upon the face of the whole globe. But what are these considerations compared to the imperious demands of a few stockmen?[13]

The year 1920 opened with the chief forester of the United States, H. L. Graves, giving proponents of park extension some encouragement by advancing the thought that it would aid in solving the elk problem in the area south of Yellowstone Park (presumably by making more range available to elk by excluding cattle). However, anything gained after the inevitable backlash of local cattle interests was offset by damaging opinions and rumors developing north of the Park. There, the editor of a Livingston newspaper, while admitting that his town and Park County would "receive nothing but benefit from this exploitation," felt obliged to comment on public opinion of a national scope "which is powerful enough and which overlooks local interests to such an extent that the park authorities can appeal to the nation and obtain results which will work hardships on communities close to the park." Reasoning from there, he advised his readers:

> What can we do to meet this national sentiment and the power to develop it so far as park extension on the north side of the park is concerned? First of all Park County can formulate some plan for a SMALL elk reserve and aid the park authorities to establish it. In this way we can forestall any extension which would forever close Jardine and other mining property near the park.[14]

The community of Red Lodge, Montana, near the northeast corner of Yellowstone Park, was disturbed by a rumor that the major portion of the Beartooth Forest Reserve was to be added to Yellowstone Park in order to bring the Grasshopper Glacier within its boundaries. The town's newspaper, while expressing a hope that the information was no more than rumor, hastened to express its disapproval of any such move.

The Greater Yellowstone movement gained a powerful adherent in 1921. He was the noted author, Henry Van Dyke, who had come to Jackson Hole "to taste the rude delights of the wild West before it vanishes." In other words he was one of those "dude ranch" guests who were housed in log cabins, fed on hearty fare, and turned loose on cow ponies to roam the pine-scented forests. Such folk were not supposed to see farther than a clear trout stream or a sun-dappled trail. Van Dyke however saw the Jackson Hole controversy through the eyes of a newcomer, noting the supremacy of the area's recreational values over its limited usefulness as a cattle barony, divining, also, that no one need lose anything in the changeover. Even where private land holdings were concerned, he thought the adjustment could be fairly made by buying out the owners.[15] This idea would not be overlooked by proponents of park extension.

The movement wobbled indecisively until the end of 1922, with the extensionists stressing the rugged grandeur of the Teton mountain range and the enticements of Jackson Hole, while their opponents dwelt upon the obligations of the National Park Service to improve Yellowstone Park before looking for other places to develop (not neglecting to mention a supposed moral obligation to leave neighbors alone if they wanted it that way). This state of affairs came to an end with what can be called the Albright forecast.

During December of 1922, articles appeared in a number of influential Wyoming newspapers quoting Yellowstone Park Superintendent Albright to the effect that "men backing the extension movement have revised their lines and may shortly ask that the cream of the scenery be incorporated into Yellowstone, leaving the grazing lands to the stockmen."[16] It was an astute move. By limiting their objectives to the headwaters of the Yellowstone River and the main mass of the Teton Mountains, the expansionists destroyed much of the opposition they had previously faced. Many adherents were gained in the Jackson Hole area, particularly among the dude ranchers, while the people of the state as a whole were divided into two camps—some for and some against this new proposition. Among the dude ranchers who were thus won over was Struthers Burt and that same Mr. Larom who was so influential in defeating Representative Mondell's measure.

If the Greater Yellowstone movement had gained friends, it had also gained no less an enemy than the U.S. Forest Service. Officials of the forest service apparently felt that the new proposal left them holding the bag. Recognizing that the 1918 order withdrawing the reserved lands was not likely to be rescinded by a president on record as favoring park extension, as President Harding was, they did not look forward to denying to cattlemen the grazing use of forest lands under their management. The difference of opinion between the forest service and the park service at last reached such proportions that it came to the attention of President Harding, who took steps to end it by the appointment of a President's Coordinating Commission.

The commission appointed in 1925 was composed of the Honorable H. W. Temple, congressman from Pennsylvania, who served as chairman; Doctor Barrington Moore of New York; Major W. A. Welch, general manager of Palisades Interstate Park, New York; Colonel W. B. Greeley, chief of the U.S. Forest Service, and Stephen T. Mather, director of the National Park Service. The commissioners were to have the assistance of Colonel B. F. Cheatham of the President's Outdoor Recreation Council and Arthur Ringland (who was to serve as secretary).[17] The commissioners were to gather in Yellowstone Park about August 10 for a conducted tour of the disputed territory. On the thirteenth the party departed on horseback from a base camp established at the mouth of Beaverdam Creek, on the Southeast Arm of Yellowstone Lake, for the upper Yellowstone country and a hasty inspection of the vast area lying between the Yellowstone headwaters and the outlet of Jackson Lake. Their five-day ride was followed by a public hearing held at Moran on the night of August 19 and by an inspection of the Teton Mountains as seen from the Jackson Hole side. A second hearing was held at Jackson on the night of the twenty-first, and an executive session met there the following day to decide upon recommendations.

The commissioners came to a unanimous decision on several matters. They agreed that the headwaters of the Yellowstone River

President Warren G. Harding views the Grand Canyon of the Yellowstone, 1923. He used his influence to prevent exploitation of park waters by irrigation and power interests.

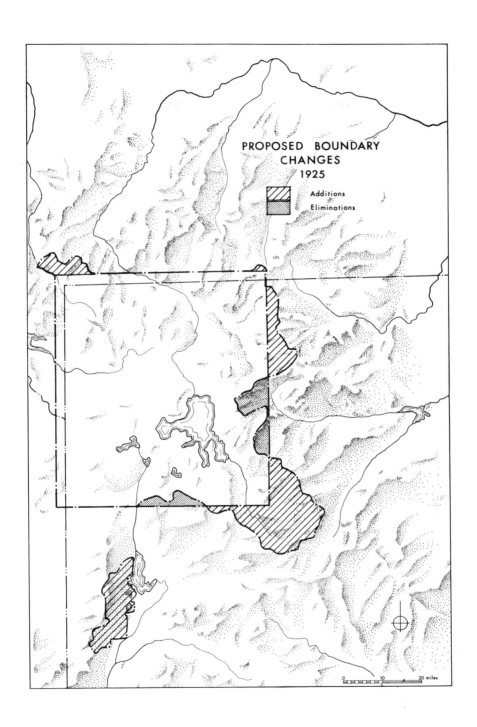

PROPOSED BOUNDARY
CHANGES
1925

Additions

Eliminations

0   10   20 miles

should be included in the Park and that the Teton Mountains should form a separated annex. Reference to the map of the adjustments proposed by this commission shows that these men were also concerned with certain changes in the boundary of Yellowstone Park which were intended to make it administratively more manageable. They thought the south boundary should be altered to eliminate the country lying south of the Snake River, which would put the entire south boundary, eastward from the south entrance, on easily defined topographic features, that is, the Snake River and the Continental Divide. On the east boundary, they proposed elimination of the heads of two drainages that belong to the North Fork of the Shoshone River and addition of the extreme headwaters of the Lamar River. The north boundary was to be changed by addition of the headwaters of Pebble Creek, a small, mountain-walled basin entirely cut off from the surrounding national forest land, and by addition of a sizeable fragment of the Gallatin Range at the northwest corner of the Park, where the boundary could be placed along a hydrographic divide and also include an area of petrified forest.

Recommendations of the President's Coordinating Commission resolved the difference that had developed between the two federal services, but did little to abate what Struthers Burt was beginning to call "the battle of Jackson's Hole." As he saw it, efforts of the conservationists to add sizeable areas to Yellowstone Park were warranted not just for the scenic value of those areas or their wildlife refuge potential but also as a means of meeting the growing need for recreational lands. He thought scenery alone was not enough in a world that was "becoming hourly more noisy and hasty and destructive."[18] There was certainly prophecy in that view.

Skirmishing during 1927 and 1928 revolved about the proposal of Senator Tom Cooper that the people of Wyoming should receive from the public domain the equivalent of the lands put beyond the use of Wyoming citizens by relegation to park status. Specifically, he asked that three million acres of public domain land be transferred to the state of Wyoming to provide income to the school system and that sheep grazing permits be allowed on national forest lands to the south and west of Jackson.[19] Later, Senator Cooper's "deal" was advanced on the premise that park extension ignored the rights of a sovereign state and a free people, implying that something was being taken away from the state of Wyoming. Not all his fellow citizens held that view; a Wyoming editor looked at it this way:

> Wyoming people have finally realized just what the Park means to the state and as a consequence we are spending more time there ourselves

and are telling the world that Yellowstone Park is almost entirely within our borders and is truly a "Wyoming Park."

Superintendent Albright is certainly the "right man in the right place." He has worked untiringly in an effort to make Yellowstone Park the national playground of the United States.[20]

With a note of regret, the editor commented that "while Montana was capitalizing on it, we, as a whole, were doing our utmost to discredit it."

The son of a former Wyoming Governor, while arguing for settlement of the controversy along the lines proposed by the President's Coordinating Commission, managed to look beyond the narrow issues of the moment when he stated "the value of this proposed extension cannot be judged by monetary consideration, nor can the value be realized until generations to come."[21]

The states rights sentiment developing in Wyoming during this controversy reached the point where the Wyoming legislature memorialized Congress to cede to the state a part of the Teton National Forest for a state park to include the Teton Mountains. This effort to counter the southward extension of Yellowstone Park was dissipated early in August of 1928, when President Calvin Coolidge expressed himself as favoring extension, a stand he refused to take following his park visit of the previous summer. His crucial support of the Greater Yellowstone movement encouraged a flurry of legislative activity. Senator Gerald P. Nye (North Dakota), chairman of the Committee on Public Lands and Surveys, introduced a measure on December 6, 1928, to create a separate Grand Teton National Park in the Jackson Hole country and to revise the boundaries of Yellowstone Park.[22] Opponents of Yellowstone extension hailed this move as a checkmate to the plans of Yellowstone officials, and in that guise the effort to establish a separate park rapidly gained adherents. There was some speculation that the new park would be named Kendrick National Park for Senator John B. Kendrick of Wyoming, who had been involved with Representative Mondell in that earliest attempt to add the Teton Mountains to Yellowstone National Park.[23]

At this point (the opening days of 1929) the legislative effort took on a somewhat different form. Senator Nye's measure, which would have created a Grand Teton National Park and revised the Yellowstone Park boundaries by one act, was laid aside, and its place was taken by two separate proposals. Senator Kendrick introduced "a bill to establish the Grand Teton National Park in the State of Wyoming, and for other purposes," on January 24, 1929. His bill (S.5543) was worded to prohibit the construction of new roads, and to prevent operation of the Federal Water Power Act within the new park.[24] The other measure (S.3001, Senator Norbeck) differed from Nye's measure in regard to boundary revisions by leaving out of the proposed Yellowstone Park addition the area at the headwaters of the Yellowstone River. This omission, which was reported out of the Senate Committee on Public Lands on January 22, was a concession to guides operating in the vicinity of Cody, Wyoming, who had resisted all Yellowstone Park boundary revisions so long as the Thorofare addition remained a part of the proposal. The guides had made enough headway in organizing their opposition to force the Park's supporters to drop the contested area from the current measure. Director Horace M. Albright commented, "It was absolutely impossible to get this country included so I decided to take at this time what we could get."[25]

Separation of the proposed legislation into two measures was a wise move. By divorcing the Grand Teton Park issue from the problems involved in the revision of the Yellowstone Park boundaries, support of the Idaho delegation in Congress was gained and S.5543 passed easily through both houses. The bill creating Grand Teton National Park was signed into law by President Coolidge on February 26, 1929, one of the last bills to receive his approval. The pen used by the president was sent to Director Albright, who knew that Senator Kendrick wanted the pen to go to the Wyoming State Historical Library and forwarded it to him for presentation at Cheyenne.[26]

Wyoming's new park was satisfactory to most people of the state, but not to all. Sheepmen, who had hoped to gain grazing privileges on a considerable area of national forest east and south of Jackson Hole under the earlier proposal of Senator Tom Cooper, made one more effort to get what they wanted. Their Lundy memorial to the Wyoming legislature, asking that the southern part of Jackson Hole and the adjacent national forest lands be opened to sheep grazing, was recognized for what it was: an opening wedge for a takeover by the sheep industry. The editor of the *Jackson Hole Courier* rejected the move with the comment, "Jackson's Hole as is, is on the highway to prosperity."[27]

The other piece of legislation waiting action at that time, Senator Norbeck's bill S.3001, for the revision of the Yellowstone Park boundaries, was facilitated by the passage of an act of Congress authorizing the president to appoint a Yellowstone National Park boundary commission.[28] This move to break the deadlock between the National Park Service and interests in Wyoming and Idaho originated in Senate Joint Resolution No. 206, introduced by Senator Gerald P. Nye, and was designed to settle the southern boundary issues—the proposed addition at the headwaters of the Yellowstone River, so repugnant to the Cody hunting guides, and the reservoir sites in the Falls River Basin, so dear to the irrigation interests of Idaho. With removal of these issues from the boundary revision proposal, Senator Norbeck's legislation was cleared for consideration. On March 1, 1929, President Herbert Hoover signed into law the first revision of the original boundaries of Yellowstone National Park.[29] By this act approximately 159 square miles of national forest land were placed within the boundary of the Park, and 81 square miles inside the old east boundary were returned to the forest service; the net gain was 78 square miles, raising the total area within the new boundaries to 3,426 square miles.[30]

The revision accomplished some desirable purposes: the boundary on the northwest corner and at the head of Pebble Creek near the northeast corner and along much of the eastern edge of the Park was placed on easily identifiable hydrographic lines; a considerable area of petrified forest was added to the Park with the Gallatin addition; and an important section of summer range for park bison was added by including the headwaters of the Lamar River. These advantages were not apparent to everyone, however. A pure conservationist by the name of Willard G. Van Name circulated a paper entitled "Raid on Yellowstone National Park," in which he criticized cession of the 81 square miles at the head of Jones and Middle creeks (tributaries of the North Fork of the Shoshone River, and east of the summit of the Absaroka Range). The area was returned to the forest service because it lacked national park features and was so cut off from the remainder of the Park as to be unmanageable. Stung by the bitter attack of Van Name and others, Director Albright complained: "Why cannot they look at the great areas added . . . instead of the insignificant, and utterly unimportant areas that were thrown out? Nobody is fighting harder to extend the Park lands than I."[31]

Boundary revisions accomplished by the act of March 1, 1929, were not to be the only alterations of original park lines; another "addition" was then coming into being. An act of three years before (May 26, 1926) that originated in a measure introduced by Senator Burton K. Wheeler for funding the new highway through Yankee Jim Canyon, provided for addition of some 7,600 acres of private land extending north and west from Gardiner, Montana, as a rough triangle on the west bank of the Yellowstone River. According to this legislation,

The President of the United States is hereby authorized to add by executive procedure to Yellowstone National Park any or all of the lands within a certain territory or tract in Township 9 South, Ranges 7 and 8 East, Montana Principal Meridian, to wit: beginning at a point on the north line of said Yellowstone National Park where said line crosses the divide between Reese Creek and Mol Heron Creek, thence northeasterly along said divide to the junction of said divide with the branch divide north and west of Reese Creek; thence along said branch divide in a northeasterly and easterly direction around the drainage of Reese Creek to the Yellowstone River; thence southerly and easterly along the west bank of the Yellowstone River to the line marking the western limits of the town of Gardiner, Montana; thence south on said town limits to the north boundary of Yellowstone National Park, thence west along the north boundary of Yellowstone National Park to the point of beginning.[32]

The authorization was intended to acquire winter range for park antelope, but was not utilized at once due to lack of federal funds. In October 1928 a game preservation company, organized in New York City under A. G. Wingren, donated $14,000 to park officials for acquiring lands within the proposed Gardiner addition. During the following four years the Gallatin Game Preservation Company acquired all the private holdings except two, between Gardiner and Reese Creek. Upon transfer of the deeds to the United States, President Herbert Hoover attached the described area to Yellowstone National Park by proclamation on October 20, 1932.[33] The tract has been known since that time as the Game Ranch.

As a sidelight to the story of boundary changes, an interesting anomaly was discovered in 1929. In their effort to tax Yellowstone Park Transportation Company property erected within the park boundary at Gardiner, the officials of Park County found that the legislation that created Park County out of Gallatin County in 1887 was defective. It described the southern limits of the county as the north boundary of Yellowstone National Park, rather than the Wyoming-Montana state line some two miles to the south. This oversight left a thin strip of Gallatin County, resembling the handle of a hockey stick, within the north boundary of the Park. The defect, which was soon remedied by the Montana legislature, was of no consequence except that "many marriages performed on or near the line are held technically to be invalidated" because the ceremony was not performed in the county which had issued the license. However, the authorities were quick to add that "without remarriage, there would be legal resort of considering the announcement of marriage to at least comply with 'common law' marriage regulation."[34] Echoes of this denouement are occasionally heard in skepticism toward the validity of any marriage ceremony performed within the boundaries of Yellowstone National Park, but this is unfounded, for park marriages are as binding as any when performed within that portion of the Park lying within the described bounds of the county that issued the marriage license.

The Yellowstone National Park Boundary Commission, established in 1929 to consider the problems of the south boundary, was composed of five members whose expenses were to be paid from the appropriation for Yellowstone National Park and who were to report to Congress on or before January 1, 1931. The commissioners were Doctor E. E. Brownell of San Francisco, chairman; Arthur Morgan, president of Antioch College; Doctor T. Gilbert Pearson, president of the National Association of Audubon Societies; C. H. Ramsdell of Minneapolis, and Arthur Ringland of Washington, D.C., member and secretary.[35] In this committee, which was certainly conservation-minded, reposed the hope that Director Albright had expressed when he wrote: "The southeastern corner is not entirely lost."[36]

Members of the boundary commission gathered at Cody, Wyoming, on August 15, 1929, for a public meeting with the town's citizens, then motored through the Park and crossed Lake Yellowstone on the nineteenth to begin a horseback trip through the forest area lying south of the boundary. For eight days they investigated the headwaters of Thorofare Creek and the Upper Yellowstone River and Two Ocean Pass, crossed the Continental Divide to Fox Creek and Big Game Ridge, and descended Wolverine and Coulter Creeks to Snake River ranger station. Spending the twenty-eighth and twenty-ninth in Jackson Hole, they reached the southwest corner of Yellowstone Park on the last day of July, and left the Park by way of Ashton, Idaho, and the Union Pacific Railroad on August 3. Results of this visit, and the commission's deliberations, were published in a 184-page report transmitted to the Congress of the United States by President Herbert Hoover on January 5, 1931.[37]

Prior to the appearance of the commission's report, Representative Addison T. Smith of Idaho voiced fears that the document was intended to show the Bechler River area as scenic in order to influence Congress against the proposed legislation that would have Bechler Meadows turned into a storage reservoir for irrigation water (see Chapter 21). Actually, the commission was careful to protect the integrity of the Park. Not only did they see no "demonstrated public necessity" for the storage of irrigation water in the southwest corner, they also recommended against the detachment of the portions of the original park lying between the south boundary and the Snake River; on the other hand, they endorsed the addition to the Park of the headwaters of the upper Yellowstone River—the area generally known as the Thorofare. As Senator Norbeck commented to Director Albright: "The report is large; the commission took themselves seriously; they went into various fields; they are irrigation experts; from a park standpoint the report is harmless; I rejoice with you."[38] It appeared that the way was at last open for adding the headwaters of the upper Yellowstone River to Yellowstone National Park; but it was not to be. The continuing opposition of Wyoming people interested in hunting areas at the eastern end of the line, combined with the equally determined irrigation interests of Idaho, prevented the change.

Meanwhile, a development in the Jackson Hole area turned the park extension movement away from Yellowstone. The establishment of Grand Teton National Park early in 1929 was followed by a campaign to purchase private lands lying east of the new park in order that they could be deeded to the United States as part of a much larger park. These purchases, intended to eliminate hot dog stands from the area, were made by the Snake River Land Company, a corporation financed by John D. Rockefeller, Jr., who provided more than two million dollars for buying up private lands during the five years following establishment of Grand Teton National Park. The foes of this effort to extend the Teton park induced the Senate Committee on Public Lands to investigate the purchases; the committee was quick to give its full approval to both the motives and the methods used, finding no evidence of personal gain in any of the transactions. Rather, they found that the program of quietly buying up properties for the completion of what was then "only half a park" was in the public interest.[39] Thus legitimized, the transfer of the Rockefeller lands to Grand Teton National Park seemed so certain that Governor Lessly A. Miller of Wyoming requested a delay in legislation until a method could be worked out for compensating local schools for the loss in revenue. Senator Robert B. Carey of Wyoming introduced legislation to reimburse Teton County for its loss in taxes, whereupon Senator O'Mahoney indicated his approval of the transfer of Rockefeller lands to Grand Teton National Park, stating: "The National Park Service has given the state assurance that there will be no further Park extensions proposed in Wyoming. This is the end of National Park extension in our state."[40]

Senator Carey's efforts were unsuccessful, however. The controversy flared again in 1938 for much the same reason: a fear of federal park extension and the concurrent loss of local taxes. As the editor of the *Jackson Hole Courier* saw it:

> The State of Wyoming will lose title to 337 square miles of territory if a bill drafted by the Department of the Interior and soon to be introduced into Congress becomes law. The bill would add around 216,000 acres of land to Grand Teton National Park. Inasmuch as the Federal Government already owns 60 percent or more of the area of the State, citizens of northwestern Wyoming are indignant at this latest "grab" which would permanently remove another large section from the tax rolls as well as from private development. . . . In this particular matter, however, Wyoming is the only state vitally interested and it would be most difficult for our two senators and one congressman to rally enough support to defeat the proposed bill. Their hands will be strengthened if they can show the citizens of the state are solidly opposed to park extension.[41]

A Senate subcommittee held a hearing on the extension bill at Jackson in August 1938. The hearing was highlighted by the offer of a Cody attorney, Milward Simpson (who represented a group of Jackson Hole landowners) to abide by the results of a plebiscite of the people of Wyoming. The senators were there to listen; they were told the movement to enlarge Grand Teton National Park had been kept alive only by purchase of improved lands by the Snake River Land Company, and that removal of those lands from the tax rolls of Teton County would be an irreparable loss.[42] Again, Senator O'Mahoney came forward with a statement to the effect that the extension could be made "if the Federal Government would agree not to ask further extension later."[43] Despite the hopes raised among advocates of the Teton extension measure, it came to nothing.

The deadlock was at last broken during the war years when President Franklin D. Roosevelt set aside 221,000 acres adjacent to Grand Teton National Park by proclamation on March 15, 1943. The fate of this Jackson Hole National Monument hung in the balance for a time, but local demand for its abolishment was countered by such men as Struthers Burt, whose careful analysis of the battle he had been engaged in for nearly thirty years left no doubt of the issues involved. He summed up the controversy this way:

> Anyone who knows anything of conservation, knows it is not a partisan matter. It is a nationwide movement, conceived for the benefit of the nation as a whole, and for the benefit of the majority as opposed to the minority, and for the protection of the average citizen against his more powerful and, in some cases, ruthless neighbor. Conservation is no more partisan than religion, and anyone who tries to make it so, does a dire thing.[44]

The Rockefeller lands were donated to the United States in 1949, and Grand Teton National Park was enlarged in 1950 by addition of the monument lands.[45] The fruits of that act, which could be called fulfillment of the Greater Yellowstone movement, bore little resemblance to General Sheridan's initial suggestion or to the first proposal of National Park Service officials. However, the result was grand, even if Yellowstone Park did get left out.

CHAPTER 21

WORDS OVER WATER

Thousands will always believe that prospective water power, not those disproved irrigation claims, was the real purpose behind the Yellowstone Lake bills which conservation organizations fought four years in Congress.

— *Robert Sterling Yard* [1]

It is ironical that two men who were as concerned for Yellowstone Park as any who have had a hand in the making of its history were involved in events that came near to destroying the Park after their time. Out of the well-meaning actions of Captain Hiram M. Chittenden and President Theodore Roosevelt came what has been called the second Yellowstone war. Though it was but a war of words, Yellowstone Park stood in grave jeopardy, and with it the integrity of the entire national park system; however, it was a fight in which the Park found staunch allies who saved the day.

The first rumblings of conflict over water and power appeared toward the end of the earlier struggle with monopolistic railroad interests (Chapter 14). An alternative proposed by the "railroad gang," when it became evident they could not get a steam railroad into Yellowstone Park, was a proposal for building an electrified line inside the Park. Accordingly, Senator Shoup of Idaho introduced S.884 in the Senate on September 9, 1893. This bill to authorize an electric railroad in Yellowstone Park had a companion measure in H.R. 59, introduced into the House by Representative Doolittle of Washington. The measure also proposed to grant two waterfalls for manufacturing electric power to operate the railway. Fortunately, that firm friend of the Park, Representative John Lacey of Iowa, reported adversely on the House bill, quoting a statement of the acting superintendent, Captain George S. Anderson, who called this measure "unneeded, undesirable, vicious." Thereafter, no action was taken on either the Senate or House versions of the bill.[2]

That first attempt to develop Yellowstone's waterpower resources found no support outside the efforts of the railroad monopolists. Soon the basis was established, however, for a firmer effort. In 1897, Captain Chittenden was alotted $5,000 to study possibilities for storage of irrigation water in the states of Wyoming and Colorado. On completing his investigation the following year, he strongly recommended government aid for irrigation work, particularly in construction of water storage facilities; his report was very popular in the West.[3] While Chittenden's work did not result in reservoir construction, it did point out how the federal government could aid in the development of the arid west, and thus was a direct forerunner of the establishment of the United States Reclamation Service on June 17, 1902.

Next there was a local controversy involving the town of Gardiner, which had once been supplied with water by a man named Billy Shrope, who made his living hauling barrels from the river up to the dry bench on which the town was located and selling the water at 50 cents a barrel. Albert Spiker operated the town's hotel then and his daughter says, "We used that water until it was pretty thick, and the bill would be something terrible."[4] Hoping to reduce his costs, Mr. Spiker obtained permission from the acting superintendent of Yellowstone Park to take water from the Gardner River and pump it up to the town. The enterprise matured into the Gardiner Electric Light and Water Company, which by 1902 represented an investment of about $2,000, owned jointly by Albert Spiker and J. C. McCartney. Power was produced with overflow from the government ditch used to water hay fields inside the park boundary. Piping the surplus water down the bank to the river provided enough energy to light a few electric bulbs in the hotel and several other buildings in town; but it was far from adequate.

Prior to the ceremony dedicating the north entrance arch on April 24, 1903, a delegation of Gardiner townspeople called upon President Roosevelt, seeking his influence and intercession to obtain a better water supply from within the Park. In particular they sought reversal of the secretary of the interior's refusal the previous year to allow an expansion of this commercial operation. The president, with his usual sympathy for westerners and their problems, immediately agreed to their request without consulting anyone. The matter was placed in Chittenden's hands and he followed up with this letter to the secretary of the interior:

> Sir: The President presents his compliments and directs me to inform you that he desires you to grant the petition of the Gardiner Electric Light and Water Company to take water from the Gardiner River in the Yellowstone Park for municipal purposes. Reference is made to your communication of the 14th instant to the above company denying their petition.
>
> The water is to be taken at the park boundary from a ditch which the government is building in connection with the road work. The privilege is not an appropriation in the ordinary sense and will not involve private control of any portion of the ditch on the reservation. The topographical situation of the town of Gardiner is such that it has no other practicable source of supply.[5]

Captain Chittenden was in no position to protest this arbitrary action of the president's because the government had just completed construction of a hydroelectric plant at Fort Yellowstone as the result of a recommendation made by Captain John Pitcher in 1901.[6] He undoubtedly had some misgivings concerning the arrangement to supply water to the Gardiner Electric Light and Water Company. In a letter to Major Pitcher nearly a year later he says:

> My Dear Major: Thinking further about the Gardiner ditch, it looks to me rather inexpedient to authorize or recommend it. I assume that authority from the department should be asked. You remember the unqualified refusal of the Secretary last spring. Although the President said he would overrule it, his decision has not, so far as I know, taken any official form further than a promise . . . and the present status of the case is that the Gardiner people are without authority to take out a ditch on the reservation. They are using the overflow from a ditch belonging to the government, and no precedent is thus established for private parties to take out ditches on the reservation.

He concluded the letter with the statement, "a precedent of this kind ought to be considered pretty carefully. The matter struck me more favorably when I first looked into it."[7]

Captain Chittenden's concern over precedent was certainly not unfounded in this case, for time confirmed the right to take water from the Gardner River through a ditch originating at the mouth of the Gardner canyon and paralleling the north entrance road for more than one-half mile. The ditch remained nearly to this day, long after any essential need, as unsightly evidence of commercialization of park waters.

Evidence of future trends was soon to appear very near the Park. In 1904 Congress authorized construction of a dam near Cody, Wyoming, with the dual objectives of storing the waters of the Shoshone River for irrigation, and production of hydroelectric power. The Shoshone Dam (since renamed the Buffalo Bill Dam), constructed in a narrow gorge between Cedar and Rattlesnake mountains, was 328 feet high and only 200 feet wide at the top. By 1911, when the work was essentially completed, a reservoir capable of holding 439,850 acre feet of water had been created, along with a generating capacity of 5,600 kw. While this project in itself posed no particular threat to the Park, it did whet the appetite of the water-starved area surrounding Yellowstone Park.[8]

Significant events were taking place at this time in California. In 1901 the city of San Francisco, feeling the pinch of a water shortage, had applied to the secretary of the interior for the right to use the Hetch Hetchy Valley in Yosemite National Park as the source of a municipal water supply. There were other sources from which the water could have been obtained, but the city seems to have been influenced in its choice by the fact that a dam at the mouth of that beautiful valley could also provide cheap hydroelectric power. Hetch Hetchy Valley was a favorite of the great naturalist, John Muir, who called the attention of the secretary of the interior to its superlative beauty, second only to the Yosemite. The secretary then denied San Francisco the desired permit and the city, unwilling to accept that decision, took the matter higher. The fight that developed became a contest between "conservationists" (those who held to the idea of the highest and best use of the land whatever that might be) and "preservationists," who would save our rare scenic treasures by locking them up for the future. Gifford Pinchot of the U.S. Forest Service and President Theodore Roosevelt were on the conservationists' side; "T. R." overruled the secretary's decision and authorized construction of the dam. But John Muir was not through; he took the fight into Congress, where the people's will eventually appeared to be in favor of the dam, and the go-ahead was given in 1913. John Muir was crushed. Of the lost fight for his beautiful Hetch Hetchy Valley on the Tuolumne River, he made this bitter comment:

> These temple destroyers, devotees of ravaging commercialization, seem to have a perfect contempt for nature, and, instead of lifting their eyes to the God of the Mountains, lift them to the almighty dollar. Dam Hetch

Hetchy! As well dam for water tanks the peoples' cathedrals and churches, for no holier temple has ever been consecrated by the heart of man.[9]

The congressional act signed into law by President Woodrow Wilson actually camouflaged a scheme to gain control of suitable federal sites, regardless of their other superlative characteristics, for the purpose of power generation. The camouflage was not sufficient however to blind the public to what was going on. The Hetch Hetchy became a rallying cry for defenders of wilderness values. Because of the flagrant misrepresentation of that grab, future proposals for development of waterpower on federal lands were looked at with a suspicious eye.[10]

The victory gained by conservationists and the waterpower interests at Hetch Hetchy did not establish the precedent they had desired. On the contrary, it had the effect of stirring up a powerful opposition, and it was well that it did. On the southern doorstep of Yellowstone National Park the U.S. Reclamation Service was engaged in its Minidoka Project, which began as an irrigation venture for the particular benefit of potato farmers in the vicinity of Burley, Idaho. Necessity for additional water storage capacity for the Minidoka Dam led to construction of the Jackson Lake Dam from 1913 to 1916. The 70-foot high, 4,920-foot long dam changed the appearance of the beautiful lake that lay almost at the feet of the Teton range.[11]

There is no better testimony of the change than Owen Wister's:

> . . . that disgusting dam. There is more beauty in Jackson's Hole than even such a beastly thing could kill; but it has destroyed the august serenity of the lake's outlet forever; and has defaced and degraded the shores of the lake where once the pines grew green and dark. They stand now white skeletons, drowned by the rising level of the water.[12]

He might also have mentioned the effect of the fluctuating water level, which turns the beautiful Jackson Lake of June into broad mud flats and cut stumps after the summer draw-down of irrigation water.

Increased demands on agriculture during World War I led to cultivation of submarginal lands on the Snake River plains southwest of Yellowstone Park; available irrigation water was utilized to the limit and soon there was need for more. Most Idahoans believed the resulting postwar hardships could be ended if they only had access to the waters of Yellowstone National Park. At the moment of desperation, the Sixty-sixth Congress passed the Federal Power Bill, giving the people of Idaho some reason to think they could satisfy their needs with park waters. As it turned out, they were very nearly right.

The measure had slipped quietly through the Senate and into the House before it was discovered that the bill authorized a commission to lease public waters, including those within the national parks, for the generation of power. Friends of the Park immediately organized in defense of park waters and the secretary of the interior, John Barton Payne, laid the situation before President Wilson, who refused to sign the Federal Power Bill into law until leaders of the Senate and the House promised to put through legislation at the next session of Congress to exempt national parks from its provision.[13]

During the summer and fall of 1920, elements of the public press favoring the water interests pushed a concerted attack on the national park system. Presidential candidate Warren G. Harding came out strongly in defense of national parks just before the election, and Congress made good its promise to amend the Federal Power Act, in the Jones-Esch Bill. However, the bill had been amended to leave *future* national parks within the scope of the Federal Power Commission's operation. The Jones-Esch Bill, with its objectionable Pierce amendment, was signed into law by President Wilson on the last night of the Sixty-sixth Congress.[14]

A direct attack on Yellowstone National Park had already begun. In that same congress Representative Addison T. Smith of Idaho had introduced H.R. 12466, which sought to obtain reservoir sites in the basins of Falls and Bechler rivers, within the Park. This first attempt to break into the area on behalf of local water-using groups would have authorized the construction of ditches, roads, buildings,and telephone lines necessary to maintain a system of storage reservoirs for impounding irrigation water.[15] The primitive character of that corner of the Park might have been entirely destroyed had there not been strong voices to speak in its defense.

One of these defenders was George Bird Grinnell, whose letter to the *Sun and New York Herald* pointed out that there would "always be well meaning utilitarians who cannot see 'the primrose by the river brim,' " men who could only see waterfalls as so much power for commerical uses. He noted that the reservoirs would threaten the integrity of Yellowstone Park and would establish a dangerous precedent. In his opinion, the Smith bill was a "finger on the public pulse to test . . . opinion." Plans had already been drawn for utilization of Yellowstone Lake, he said, and propagandists were in readiness to create a favorable atmosphere in areas around the Park for passage of legislation even then being prepared.[16]

Meanwhile, the National Parks Association was active. Robert Sterling Yard lambasted "this project upon which the combined interests are depending for a national parks precedent," and warned that the "granting of even one irrigation privilege in any national park will mark the beginning of a swift end."[17] Action of a different sort was being taken by another member of the association, William C. Gregg of New Jersey, who explored the little-known Falls River Basin to inform the public as to its true character. The Gregg party "found more falls and cascades than in all known parts of the park," and far from finding the Bechler meadows a useless area of swamp land, they thought it a camper's paradise, with good fishing and an abundance of wildlife. They considered the area essential for a future access road from Idaho to the geyser basins by way of Bechler River. The most important thing to come out of Gregg's exploration of the Cascade Corner was his clear statement of essential guidelines:

1. National parks are created for . . . the whole public.
2. No commercial project—for private advantage—must be permitted.
3. Park extensions should be advocated only after careful and unprejudiced study of the reasons for and against them.
4. The motives of plausible persons who express great devotion for the parks they wish to exploit are always to be suspected.
5. Persons living near a national park who feel themselves harmed by their situation must bear their burden cheerfully.[18]

Thereafter, as the true character of the Cascade Corner became known, the Smith bill, which had fared poorly in Congress, died of popular condemnation.

It was inevitable that a strong interest in Yellowstone Park waters would develop in Montana; evidence of it appeared in 1920 in the annual report of the Montana Irrigation Commission. Included among the proposals that had the commission's blessing was one "to divert the Yellowstone River by a dam in Yankee Jim Canyon near Sphinx, to irrigate 20,000 acres in Paradise Valley," of which the commission noted: "This project is now held up pending the outcome of the campaign now under way to control the flood waters of the Yellowstone Lake."[19]

The report was referring to an undercover movement that broke into the open in May 1920 as the Walsh bill (S.4529, Sixty-sixth Congress) and proposed to allow the state of Montana to dam the Yellowstone River within three miles of the outlet of its lake.[20] Senator Walsh tried surprise hearings in Washington, D.C., on February 21 and 24, 1921, but the Department of the Interior irrigation experts were on hand to prove decisively that damming of Yellowstone Lake would not increase the supply of available water or influence flood control.[21] The proposal, which was called "another

Hetch Hetchy" by *The Outlook* magazine,[22] made no progress in that Congress.

In the Sixty-seventh Congress, Senator Walsh attempted to promote his legislation by presenting biased facts, but he was unsuccessful and changed his course by introducing a different bill February 15, 1922. The second Walsh bill proposed to allow the U.S. Reclamation Service, rather than the state of Montana, to dam Yellowstone Lake; the bill might have fared better than its prototype if Secretary of the Interior Albert B. Fall had stayed out of the picture. On July 9, 1932, Secretary Fall, who had previously gone on record against National Park Service preservation while reporting on the Walsh bill, called defenders of Yellowstone Park "meddlers interfering with the sworn duty of the Secretary of the Interior," and he threatened to take the Yellowstone Lake dam into politics. In his view, "the people around the Park have the votes."[23] The Montana primary elections held in August 1922 were a resounding defeat for the Walsh forces. The senator stumped the state for support but was denied it because of his identification with the discredited Fall. Among the tactics tried by Walsh was an appeal to the people of Montana to subscribe to a private fund for re-survey of the water storage potential of Yellowstone Lake, but he could not raise even a small sum.[24]

At the seasonal opening of Yellowstone National Park on June 20, 1923, Dr. John Wesley Hill spoke for President Harding when he said: "It is at last the established policy of the government that our national parks must and forever shall be maintained in absolute, unimpaired form, not only for the present, but for all time to come." That should have been a clue to Senator Walsh that he had lost his fight to dam Yellowstone Lake, yet he continued the struggle by introducing two more bills in the Sixty-eighth Congress.[25] On May 23, 1924, Secretary of the Interior Hubert Work took a stand against the Walsh legislation, stating that "absolute preservation should be the unwavering policy of Yellowstone administration," adding, "this bill for Yellowstone National Park, if adopted, will in practice become a dangerous precedent for similar industrial uses of other national parks."[26]

That strong statement did not end the attempt of the water interests to enter the Park. On April 18, 1926, Representative Smith of Idaho reopened the assault on the southwest corner by taking advantage of an administration-sponsored bill intended to improve the boundaries of the Park: he proposed to amend the legislation to eliminate the Bechler River Basin entirely. His proposal ran into trouble immediately and he took it to the Senate Committee on Public Lands, headed by Senator Robert Stanfield. This second attempt of the water and power interest to gain a foothold in the southwest corner of the Park brought forth a vigorous protest from *The Outlook*. Beginning with the statement "Idaho is trying to loot Yellowstone," the editor pointed out that Idahoans were willing to destroy the scenic beauty of the Bechler meadows to make a million dollars a year out of its twelve square miles, and the opinion was offered that "no state has a right to do it, no special interest has any business there."[27]

In order that it might not be accused of being one-sided, *The Outlook* opened its pages to an article by Representative Smith entitled, "Wanted—A Reservoir," following that with a rebuttal by Dr. Henry Van Dyke, "A Meadow That Belongs to the People."[28] In this exchange Addison Smith maintained his earlier arguments that the reservoir sites that could be developed in the Falls River Basin were absolutely essential to the economy of Idaho, and the area itself was relatively useless for park purposes, while Henry Van Dyke concentrated upon the line that "year after year land speculators and power promoters come up to the assault upon park lands, proposing to dam a river here, to destroy a forest there," all of which, he pointed out, belonged to the people and to their children "by a sacred entail". Van Dyke concluded by warning the power interests that there were other sites that would serve their purpose, and, though they might cost a little more to develop, they would "keep your souls cleaner."

The Stanfield committee held hearings at St. Anthony, Idaho, in August 1926 and managed to generate considerable local enthusiasm, but early in 1927 it became enmeshed in charges of refusing to give information. As a result, the bill to reorganize the boundaries of Yellowstone National Park died with the Sixty-ninth Congress, and with it, the work of the committee.[29] The entire matter of boundary revision became the subject of an investigation by a Yellowstone National Park Boundary Commission, which had this to say about continued agitation for removal of 17,280 acres from the Bechler corner of the Park for storage reservoir sites: "In the absence of a demonstrated public necessity, the commission finds that it is unnecessary and undesirable to break into the integrity of Yellowstone National Park by the elimination of the Bechler River meadows from its boundaries."[30]

Even that considered decision did not stop the Idahoans in their drive to obtain water from the Park; the pinch of the Great Depression set in motion further rationalizing with regard to it.

Beginning almost wishfully,[31] advocates of a scheme to take Lake Yellowstone water through a diversion tunnel to Shoshone Lake, and then in similar manner to the North Fork of the Snake River, promoted the idea into a Kosanke plan.[32] Not wishing to be outdone, the Montana water interests pressed for congressional action to allow the states of Montana and Wyoming to "negotiate and enter into a compact or agreement for the division of the waters of the Yellowstone River."[33] Eventually, the Idahoans returned to their old dream of a storage reservoir in the Bechler meadows. Among the virtues extolled in connection with the diversion project, they mentioned that "by controlling the amount of water in the lake, the roughness of the shoreline which is now exposed in low water will be done away with."[34] The dreams of yesteryear also reappeared in Montana, where a dam at the Little Gate of the Mountains, near Livingston, with a diversion tunnel to carry the water into the Gallatin Valley, was proposed as a public works project.[35]

Before either scheme became a real threat, there was a "falling out among friends" which soon put an end to the whole idea of tapping Yellowstone Lake. First Wyoming balked, refusing to negotiate with Montana over waters originating in Yellowstone National Park[36] and opposing the Idaho plan;[37] then Montana showed its teeth to Idaho.[38] At that point Robert Sterling Yard reminded the conservation groups that "The Rocky Mountain tunnel could have been killed if resolutely opposed. . . . Let us not permit the same blunder to be repeated."[39] Thanks to the American Society for the Advancement of Science, the National Wilderness Association, the National Parks Association, the Sierra Club, and many like-minded people, it wasn't repeated. Instead, Idaho irrigation interests accepted an alternative solution that added two storage dams to the Minidoka Project in 1935, one of them the Grassy Lake Dam (118 feet high and 1,170 feet long),[40] at the head of Cascade Creek just outside the south boundary of Yellowstone Park.

For the moment, the Park is safe. Given the right set of economic circumstances, however, the old need for irrigation water (so like the drunkard's thirst) could again generate schemes inimical to the purposes for which the area was set aside. The companion issue, of power generation, which so often masqueraded in the popular guise of irrigation, grows less dangerous as we incline toward other sources of power. Yet, should Yellowstone National Park ever be brought again under attack by the water *or* power interests, may it find just such staunch defenders as those who rallied to its defense during the second Yellowstone war.

CHAPTER 22

ASPHALT
AND CABINS

Every man is rich and poor according to the degree in which he can afford to enjoy the necessaries, conveniences and amusements of human life.
—Adam Smith, Wealth of Nations, *1776*

The American became richer with the passage of the first "flivver" through the great, basaltic arch at the Park's northern entrance. It is a beautiful irony that the automobile, characterized in 1906 by the then president of Princeton University, Woodrow Wilson, as a "picture of the arrogance of wealth," should be the means of democratizing Wonderland. The little single-seated Model T with the brass trim on its radiator, which entered Yellowstone Park on the evening of July 31, 1915, and the procession of motorcars to follow were to overwhelm the "carriage trade" way of life. They brought a new type of visitor, and a bold new era.

The re-orientation of park management to meet the needs of the casually attired, self-reliant automobilist who dominated the years between the great wars came out of Steve Mather's firm conviction that the national parks belonged to everyone. This left the newly created National Park Service only one direction to go: "We've got to do what we can to see that nobody stays away because he can't afford it."[1] The Park was opened to all, though some have preferred to call it handing over the Park to the "great unwashed."[2] In the light of what happened in and to the Park during one-quarter century of burgeoning use, it is well to ponder another Mather dictum: "We can pick up the tin cans. It's a cheap way to make better citizens."

The automobile era in the Park was opened by a Ford from Minnesota. The "poor man's Cadillac," the Model T, was three times more numerous than any other make of vehicle on the Park's roads during the early years[3] and typifies automobile touring of that era. A Model T, for example, was driven on a vacation trip into the Park by a family named Van de Water, from Brooklyn, New York, in the summer of 1926.

Deciding that a western tour could be made "with as much comfort and ease as any one who rides in a Ford has a right to expect," they loaded what were presumed to be the necessities of life-on-the-open-road into their particular miracle from Detroit (fondly known as "Issachar"[4]) and were off. It was part of the esprit de corps of Ford owners that they accepted their ungainly vehicles humorously, even lovingly, often flaunting their attachment with a painted-on name or witticism (seldom original), as: "Lizzie," "Rolls Rough," "Four Wheels - No Brakes," "No Top, We're Covered By the Mortgage" and, of course, "A Tin You Love to Touch." Occasionally Model T owners were capable of a more vulgar note, as in the case of the driver who hung a pair of coconuts beneath his car with the succinct legend: "This Ain't No Lady."

On the other hand, there were those who knew the dark side of life with a Model T, as hinted by a paraphrase of the Twenty-third Psalm beginning "The Ford is my chariot, I shall not want another," and ending, "Surely, if Lizzie follow me all the days of my life, I shall dwell in the house of the nuts forever."[5]

Once they were on the road, the advantages of technology were apparent to the Van de Waters. Their machine, costing new about the same as a good buggy horse, was able to average 175 miles a day (something the horse could never have done) while transporting a family of four, their clothing, bedding, utensils, provisions, tent, and such accessories as a spare tire, shovel, axe, and a runningboard rack holding containers of gasoline, oil, and water. It was a serviceable piece of transportation with only one serious fault: difficulty in negotiating long, steep grades. Climbing, a Model T was prone to overheating; descending, it was in mortal danger of burning out its drive and brake bands. Mr. Van de Water describes the tricky business of a downhill run:

The Ford charioteer behaves like an unfortunate smitten by the Charleston. He steps on the low speed pedal. When he fears this is beginning to heat, he tramps on the reverse or else applies the emergency brake until it begins to scream like a damned soul. Then he pushes down on the low speed pedal and begins all over again.[6]

Of course, the Van de Waters intended to camp each night, as was the fashion with "tin can tourists," but there were few opportunities to do so in the thickly settled East; there, where even the "tourist cabin" was nearly unknown, they had to watch for an occasional sign displayed in the window of a private home, offering to take in the dusty tourists for a price. As they proceeded beyond the Allegheny Mountains, camping places became increasingly common. In the trans-Mississippi West, they found fenced tenting grounds providing water, privies, and usually showers and a community kitchen. These stopping places varied from very good to very poor, and charged a standard fifty cents per night. (The charge was made, they were often told, only to keep out automobile tramps.) Many such camps were sponsored by towns as a form of advertising, while others developed as profitable adjuncts to stores and filling stations.

Beyond Chicago, our "tourists" (by then the term included far-ranging automobilists) were on that segment of the Yellowstone Trail once described by the *Christian Science Monitor* in these words: "No transcontinental highway in America offers greater inducement to the tourist, and sightseer, than that which in its main division begins at the Mississippi and ends at the Yellowstone";[7] but they found the fabled route rich in dust and gravel rarely mentioned by its ardent boosters.

Somewhere along that road, in a little town with a triumphal arch spanning its one street, the Van de Waters received a silver dollar in change and were in the West. Their further progress was measured by the increasing loneliness of the sun-drenched landscape and the frequency with which gophers darted under their wheels.

The Yellowstone Trail of the mid-twenties was already blurred by an accretion of feeders and alternate routes; by one of these the heavily laden Model T crossed the Wyoming Basin and fetched up at the town of Cody, opposite the eastern portal of Yellowstone Park. There, the Van de Waters stopped for the night in a motor camp "filled to the fence" with tents and cars, and overflowing with rumors. The windshields of many vehicles bore the octagonal buffalo sticker[8] indicating successful passage through the Park, and the occupants of several were serving as "eager prophets of gloom." One veteran of the roads beyond the east entrance described his descent of Sylvan Pass this way:

> We started out from the park this morning. I never seen such grades in all my life. Steep as a barn roof. Burned out my foot-brake right off and then, by gosh, we wore out the emergency brake, too. Had to pull over to the roadside and put in new brake shoes. We was lucky to have 'em along, else we'd be stranded up there yet.[9]

There were some who growled about the prices in the Park, claiming they were so high only a millionaire could afford to stay there (they *were* high by outside standards, but were not that bad);[10] others pictured frightful conditions in the campgrounds, calling them dirty and overcrowded. That this, too, was but a half-truth was unknown to the miserable pilgrims waiting at Cody for the light of another day and entrance into Wonderland.

As the Van de Waters left Cody, they passed the DeMaris Springs—feeble remnants of the "Hell" visited by John Colter in 1807. The sulphur-laden waters discharging into the nearby Shoshone River were responsible for its earlier designation as the Stinkingwater. Seven and a half miles west of town there was a much more prominent, though manmade, wonder: the dam blocking the narrow gorge by which the river broke out of the mountains. The structure stood like a wedge of concrete driven between Rattlesnake and Cedar mountains. Eighty feet wide at the bottom and 200 at the top, standing 328 feet above the stream bed, the Buffalo Bill Dam was hardly more remarkable than the grade by which the road climbed the canyon wall to the level of the impounded waters. The road was cut out of the rock of Rattlesnake Mountain, with several tunnels to add charm, and was so steep that in later years it became a serious obstacle to house trailers moving into the Park. It was reconstructed following World War II.

Beyond the artificial lake filling much of the basin where the two branches of the Shoshone mingled their waters, the approach to the Park became increasingly scenic as our travelers progressed up the north fork. Development of that route was begun in 1890, the road was opened to traffic in 1903, and was completed several years later. The portion within present Shoshone National Forest was originally constructed by the Corps of Engineers as a part of the project to give access to the park road system from the east, via Sylvan Pass;[11] it was maintained by National Park Service crews until after World War II.

The road through the east forest was a good one by standards of that day, providing a pleasant drive through a lodgepole pine forest broken with groves of quaking aspen and little meadows by the clear stream, the whole valley overlooked by weirdly sculptured canyon walls suggesting various forms to a lively imagination. There were features likened to a goose, a holy city, wooden shoe, Thor's anvil, a mutilated hand, and a chimney—even a point dedicated to Henry Ford! Although the C. B. & Q Railroad (the Burlington Route) took an interest in this eastern approach to the Park at the turn of the century,[12] its attractions remained nearly unknown until discovered by the automobilists.

By the mid-twenties there were a number of small camp and lodge developments catering to tourists along the North Fork of the Shoshone River. The principal one was established by W. F. Cody (Buffalo Bill) at a spot three miles east of the park boundary where he had once brought deluxe hunting parties. Its name, Pahaska Tepee, after the affectionate title given to Colonel Cody by the Sioux Indians, could be translated "Long-Hair's Camp."[13] The entrance fee of $7.50 was collected by the young man in forest green uniform on duty at the checking station near the former site of the Sylvan Pass soldier station. The old station (moved to the north side of the road) had been replaced by a rustic lodge used for the lunch stop by Burlington Railroad passengers bussed from Cody to Lake Hotel and a connection with the regular park tour.[14]

Once within the park boundary, the road pitched steeply up toward Sylvan Pass, where it did not cling to the mountainside as it does now but followed up the drainage of Middle Creek, gaining elevation at the steepest place, just below Sylvan Pass, by a cleverly engineered structure called the Corkscrew Bridge, actually an overpass by which the ascending road crossed itself in the narrow confines of the valley. Here the Van de Waters witnessed an accident involving three girls from Oregon. A road crew had parked a pull-grader at the side of the road and were eating lunch when an unmanageable Model T rammed their equipment. When the foreman asked the driver, "Why didn't you girls put on your brake?" the answer was: "Oh, there isn't any brake. It's all wore out."[15] The crew disengaged the Ford and got the innocents safely down the grade.

At Fishing Bridge, the Van de Waters began a gypsy-like existence that introduced them to the major automobile campgrounds of the Park. They were quick to recognize that whatever was wrong with those campgrounds, the fault lay in lack of funds to make them "duplicates of the best tourist parks"—a Park Service objective difficult to achieve without charging for campground use. Like most campers of that day, the tourists had their share of bizarre experiences, such as being awakened from a sound sleep by a noise likened to "the sack of Troy." The racket came from a neighboring campsite where a bear had invaded the tent of a family who had taken their eatables to bed with them. Bruin was driven off by papa, mama, and the kids, aided by other fun-loving campers, and the neophytes were shown how to hoist their commissary to a safe height above ground by throwing a rope over the limb of a pine tree.[16]

Also on the debit side was the unexpected evening downpour, the quarter-inch of ice in the water bucket at dawn, and the mosquitoes, horse flies, and buffalo gnats. But there were credits on the ledger: the smell of sizzling bacon, frying potatoes, and strong coffee drifting through the trees with wood smoke, the relaxing game of horseshoes with the retired real estate man from Los Angeles, and songs by firelight. It was a life without slavery to a timetable, without contrary bus drivers, without fussy concern for conventionalities of dress, khaki being the cloth and knickers the cut regardless of how they brought out the differences in people. Besides, it was a life of low expenses and a high amount of fun.[17]

These "rubber stiffs" (as good a name as any for those latter-day sagebrushers) arrived in open touring cars over narrow, dusty roads to dusty campgrounds where they set up Baker tents alongside their heavily laden vehicles. They came in such numbers that the developed part of the Park had to be remade to serve them. Facilities available to the public in Yellowstone Park at the time the National Park Service assumed its stewardship were almost entirely intended to serve the carriage trade. "Almost" covers the work of army engineers in preparing roads for the eventual entry of the automobile (described in Chapters 17 and 18) and the work of a small crew burying trash and digging new holes for the privies in the informal campgrounds—the only kind the Park had. Otherwise, both sagebrusher and the automobilist who followed him were left to their own devices.

All that was to change. Horace M. Albright, appointed superintendent in 1919, came to his office "with absolute power to develop the property along his own lines under the general policy laid down by the Department."[18] Albright had definite ideas as to how that should be accomplished. Sharing Mather's viewpoint that the Park should be open to everyone regardless of means, and recognizing the potential of the automobile to effect such a democratization, he proceeded to redesign park facilities to meet the needs of the new era. In a complete face-lifting, he upgraded the roads and provided automobile campgrounds and bathhouses, tourist

Horace M. Albright, first Yellowstone superintendent under the National Park Service. During his tenure—1919-1929—the Park was reorganized to accommodate automobilists.

cabins and lodge developments, cafeterias and delicatessens, service stations and garages, and an educational program (described in Chapter 19).

A picture of this revolution begins with the roads. The Van de Waters could as well have followed the Yellowstone Trail proper and entered the Park from the north, at the town of Gardiner, after traveling up the west bank of the Yellowstone River on a narrow, gravel road (the present county road), essentially the pioneer road with a little ballast added. Yankee Jim's toll road, through the canyon that now bears his name, was taken over by the county commissioners in 1914, just prior to admission of automobiles to the Park,[19] and graveling of the fifteen miles northward from Gardiner was accomplished in 1920 as a joint venture of the county and the Gardiner townspeople.[20] The highway on the east side of the Yellowstone River was completed in 1926, partly with federal aid obtained by Senator Walsh of Montana, and the segment between Pine Creek and Pray is said to have been the first oiled highway in Park County. This alignment was the Park's northern approach road for thirty-five years, except that the original bridge over the Yellowstone River at the outskirts of Gardiner was replaced by the present concrete bridge in 1929 (the bridge was rebuilt in the course of widening the road through Gardiner in 1975). Construction during the past decade has put the highway back on the west side of the Yellowstone up to Point of Rocks, and the work accomplished through Yankee Jim Canyon has made that section much safer, though with a loss of much of its former charm.

The western approach to the Park was multiple. The town of West Yellowstone,[21] which sprang up in 1908 where the Union Pacific's rails reached the park boundary, funneled traffic from Utah and Idaho, as well as Montana, into the Park, and visitors leaving by the west gate could go southward, over Targhee Pass into Idaho, and on to Salt Lake City or Boise, or westward (roughly speaking) down the Madison River and on to Virginia City, Helena, or Butte; lastly, they could go northward to Bozeman by way of a mediocre road down the West Fork of the Gallatin River.

The southern approach, out of Jackson Hole, remained essentially a wagon road (though it received a thin oil surfacing in the 1930s) until it was entirely rebuilt following World War II, while the Park's fifth approach, the scenic Red Lodge Highway across the 12,000-foot Beartooth Plateau, was a creation of the twenties and thirties. A visitor who passed over the almost completed road in 1933 in a 1927-model touring car remarks that it took two hours to negotiate eight miles; even so, the fenders were abraded by projecting rocks at several places. Two years later the same driver found the road so good that he was led to speak wonderingly of the change.[22]

However the visitor reached the Park, the roads within were mainly gravel surfaced up into the Depression years. Upgrading of the system of roads inherited from the Corps of Engineers fell, at first, to George E. Goodwin, a road builder borrowed from the army in 1916 to coordinate roadwork in all the National Park Service areas. Goodwin's office at Portland, Oregon, designed roads that were economical to build and saving of the landscape, but not adequate for the automobile. Therefore, when Director Mather went to the Bureau of Public Roads to design Glacier Park's difficult Going-to-the-Sun Highway, Goodwin was piqued and left the National Park Service. Since that time, major road construction in Yellowstone Park, as in all areas administered by the National Park Service, has been planned and supervised by the bureau under an interagency agreement dating from 1925.[23]

That agreement opened the way to building roads of higher standards in Yellowstone Park, which, through the efforts of the landscape architects, who represented the National Park Service's preservation instincts from the beginning,[24] are also more attractive. The restorative effect of the new construction has been described in these words:

> When the grades, alignment, and surface of the roads were adjusted for automobiles, the roadside debris was cleared, borrow pits were erased, the sprinkling-system tanks carried off, and the telephone lines set back out of sight. The roads no longer throw up a fine white powdery dust, and roadside vegetation is now green. The meadows once more are lush, and wild animals may again be seen browsing in them.[25]

Further benefit resulted from adaptation of park roads to the automobile: with much longer drives now possible for visitors, two hotels (Norris and Fountain) and twelve camps and lunch stations of the horse era could be abandoned and the sites cleaned up; dairy and beef herds in the Park were no longer necessary. The automobile eliminated the need for hundreds of draft animals. In 1909 licensed transportation in the Park had required 1,734 horses,[26] which were grazed at least part of the time in the meadows, while the 1,600 horses used by the "sagebrushers" who entered in their own rigs that summer were grazed an average of twelve days each.

Modernization of park roads was not the work of a season, but a tedious process requiring most of two decades. The original objective was merely to turn the narrow stagecoach roads into two-lane, gravel roads on grades a Model T could negotiate safely. Those early Fords, incidentally, were durable despite their appearance of frailty. One old-timer told me how he came most of the way down from Dunraven Pass, on the Tower Fall side of Mount Washburn, without brakes—by putting his wheels in the inside ditch and deliberatly scraping along the bank to slow his speed. It was the need for brake bands at Tower Fall that put Jack E. Haynes in business there. The Yellowstone Park Transportation Company was asked to arrange for the sale of items needed by autoists at that point but refused to undertake such a "nuisance" operation; Jack volunteered to provide the service, which ultimately developed into his profitable Tower Fall Picture Shop.

The first three-year program of road improvement, begun in 1925, included oiling the park roads to alleviate dust. The sprinkling of the Grand Loop road with water wagons ended in 1927, and asphalt paving soon began. The last section of the loop to be paved, between Old Faithful and Craig Pass, was completed after World War II.

In a related development of the 1920s, Superintendent Albright looked for a better way to open the roads in the spring. This had always been a joint venture, by the thaw and gangs of shovelers, a slow process and bad for the softened roadbed, which was cut up badly unless given time to dry out. Shoveling was an expensive method, too, which could not be relied on to get the roads open and usable by the announced official opening date, June 20. What Albright came up with was a tractor-mounted snowplow. The plow, fabricated of ¾-inch steel plates and shaped like the cow-catcher of a steam locomotive, stood five feet high. It was attached to a 75-horsepower Caterpillar tractor borrowed from the Corps of Engineers, making a juggernaut capable of bashing its way through snow up to five feet deep (deeper drifts had to be shoveled down to that level). This equipment proved its worth in the spring of 1920, when it opened the loop on schedule despite an unusual depth of snow remaining from a hard winter.[27] The fifty years that have passed since the first mechanical plow was put to work have brought a succession of improvements, from blade plows through SnoGos to the giant, diesel-powered Snowblast machines which seem capable of vanquishing any blockading drifts.

Yet, machinery occasionally meets its match. A few older employees of the road crew have bitter memories of such an instance, a tragedy involving considerable heroism. From the time the Red Lodge-Cooke City road was completed until very recently, park crews were responsible for opening and maintaining the high and scenic approach to the northeast entrance. In 1947, the work of plowing was completed on June 12 and the road was in good enough condition to be opened to the public the following week. A severe storm swept over the 11,000-foot Beartooth Plateau on the evening of June 20, stranding a number of visitors on the exposed summit before steps could be taken to close the road. Among the vehicles caught on the heights was a government truck with a load of Red Lodge coal for the Park. This vehicle had chains on and was able to make slow but steady progress through the storm, gathering a train of passenger vehicles as it came upon stalled cars.

As soon as the maintenance foreman at the Beartooth Camp (situated on the Cooke City side of the summit) was aware of the severity of the storm, he closed his end of the road and dispatched a crew to check the high country for stranded cars. As the coal truck was breaking a way through deepening drifts, leading its caravan of cars across the exposed plateau, a three-auger SnoGo (ponderous, but capable of gnawing a hole through any snowdrift) and its attendant pickup truck were moving slowly up out of the valley of Clarks Fork. Just below the first summit, the plow operator came upon a trailer house stuck in a snow-filled cut, and in attempting to work around it, the plow slipped into the ditch where it was hopelessly high-centered. The five-man crew worked the remainder of that windy, frigid night trying to get the stalled plow back on the road, as it was blocking the progress of the coal truck and its train of cars. Exhaustion at last forced the men to give up their efforts, the automobilists were packed into a few of the cars for mutual warmth, and the road crew men got in the truck and pickup to await relief. When it arrived the next day (another SnoGo had to be trundled out of the Park) all the vehicles were buried in drifted snow. The people huddled in the passenger cars were all right, as were the three men in the truck; but those in the cab of the pickup (Vernon E. Kaiser, John P. Baker, and Richard N. Ruckels) were dead.[28]

The change from dusty, one-lane stagecoach roads to paved, two-lane highways testifies to the magnitude of the overall change wrought by the automobile and to its importance for the Park. Corollaries of that change were the facilities developed to serve the automobilists who used the better roads. Service stations and garages took on nearly as much importance as the roads. The first automobilists were enjoined to carry tires, oil, and gasoline with them, though a limited supply of gas was available at the general stores, where it was kept in drums and measured out at a dollar per gallon.[29] Gasoline, oil, and repair services were made available at the

Filling station at Mammoth Hot Springs, 1917.

A modern service station at Canyon Village.

depots of the Yellowstone Park Transportation Company in 1919, and the first true filling station in the Park was built on the site of the present installation at Mammoth Hot Springs in the fall of that year. Another, near Whittaker's store at Canyon, was ready for use in 1920, by which time gasoline prices were down to a more reasonable forty cents per gallon at park headquarters and forty-five cents elsewhere.[30] Mr. C. A. Hamilton built a filling station near his lower store at Old Faithful in 1927, and at Lake, Fishing Bridge, and West Thumb filling stations were adjuncts of the stores.

Free auto camps built at Mammoth Hot Springs, Old Faithful, Lake, and Canyon, in 1916, were probably the earliest attempt to provide for the needs of the new visitor, the autoist. In addition to pit toilets and tap water, facilities at each camp included a twelve-stall, open shed to shelter vehicles. The auto camp at Mammoth was enlarged the following year, yet the demand for space there grew so rapidly that the old quartermaster corps stable area below Capitol Hill had to be used temporarily in 1919. Superintendent Albright proposed that fall to build forty-six public auto camps as part of the plan to make Yellowstone Park "a motorist's paradise." Each was to be equipped with modern "bathhouses, toilets, washrooms, cooking spits, and other comforts."[31] The extensive development was necessary: two-thirds of those who came to the Park that summer came prepared to camp out. Two units of the new system of campgrounds (Old Faithful and Canyon) were put into service in July 1920; those at Lake and Fishing Bridge were opened a year later.

The camp at Canyon was to become the prototype of the modern automobile campground. In 1921 Sanitary Engineer H. B. Homman was detailed to Yellowstone to study the problem of the possible spread of communicable diseases among the large number of persons congregating in the Park under nomadic conditions. Mr. Homman's observations led to the rebuilding of Canyon campground in 1923. By that year, of 91,224 persons visiting the Park in 27,259 cars, 85,000 used the campgrounds, justifying the Public Health Service's concern. As opened to the public on July 26, 1924, Canyon campground covered thirty acres and was novel in that day: sites were equipped with table and fireplace; there were four comfort stations with flush toilets; and there was provision for garbage collection and disposal.[32] During the 52 days the campground was operated that season, it was used by 14,923 persons who arrived in 4,495 cars; it was a success. The major campgrounds built since that time have all conformed to the pattern established at Canyon (with restrictions on parking in more recent developments, in order to protect the vegetation).

Automobile campers at Mammoth Hot Springs in the mid-1920s.

Other automobilists "roughed it" pleasantly at the tent camps of the Yellowstone Camping Company.

Yellowstone Park's automobile campgrounds have served the public well. They have been used by uncounted thousands of visitors, many of whom would not otherwise have been able to remain overnight in the Park. Tent campers predominated prior to World War II, yet there have always been those who preferred more elaborate living arrangements. Vehicles altered into rolling homes appeared early in the 1920s. Some of them were made by tarping over the stake-rack of a farm truck, or by securing a sheep-wagon body on such a vehicle, but others showed both ingenuity and craftsmanship. Photographs of the time show several types: a trailer with a canvas, fold-out top (1922); a boxy, self-propelled motor home (1923)—there were many of these, including a custom-built "Owen's Car-house" (1930); a neat conversion of a hearse (1923); and a pickup house built in sheep-wagon style (1929). The true trailer-house was the innovation of the following decade.[33] Tenting, however, remained the most popular camping style between the wars.

The automobilists were soon catered to in many ways, for the sheer number of these gypsy-like visitors was an enticement to the Park's lesser concessioners. Stores (often called delicatessens when intended to serve the auto campgrounds) appeared at Old Faithful and Fishing Bridge in 1920 and at the Mammoth auto camp in 1924, while lunch counters were installed in the existing stores at Canyon and Lake (they were conveniently located). Provision of eating facilities for autoists became established policy in 1925,[34] and cafeterias were put into operation at Canyon and Fishing Bridge in 1926, at Mammoth Auto Camp in 1927, and at Old Faithful and West Thumb in 1928. These were run by Vernon Goodwin's Yellowstone Park Camps Company, as were the housekeeping cabins they were associated with, until the fall of 1928, when operation of such facilities passed into the hands of H. W. Child (as the Yellowstone Park Lodge & Camps Company, a precursor of the Yellowstone Park Company).

Housekeeping cabins were established adjacent to the automobile campgrounds in 1926, except at West Thumb, where the Gratiot camp (which had operated unsuccessfully at Lewis Lake for one season) was relocated in 1928. These cabins were designed as economical shelter for automobilists who did not care to sleep on the ground or cook over an open fire. They were furnished in a Spartan manner; in fact, they could be rented with or without bedding. The occupant furnished the fuel for the sheet-iron heater, a distinctive appliance resembling a nail keg turned on its side, with the upper surface flattened to hold coffee pot or frying pan. Outside tap water and a central washhouse were available.

Even plainer shelter was provided at Old Faithful in the "tent-tops," which had board floors and differed from the cabins mainly in rental, which was more reasonable. Although popular up to World War II, tent-tops were discontinued after the war due to wartime deterioration of tentage, according to the Yellowstone Park Company. In general, such low-cost services did not prosper under the company's management and were gradually eliminated at most points.

Bathhouse and laundry facilities were made available to automobilists. At Old Faithful, H.P. Brothers opened a bathhouse in the auto campground (in addition to his plunge) and the Yellowstone Park Lodge & Camps Company added bathhouses at Fishing Bridge and Mammoth, but these were unprofitable during the Depression and were abandoned. Beginning in 1929, the Yellowstone Park Fuel Company launched another venture to serve the automobilists: dry split wood for the little sheet-iron heaters installed in the cabins. (Anyone familiar with the chill of a summer night in the Park's interior will understand the need for such fuel.) Campers who had not arrived early enough or did not wish to forage far enough to find down, dry wood in the adjacent forest were customers of the "wood yards." A visitor could buy for a quarter a bundle of split wood (about an armful), which came with a package of kerosene-impregnated sawdust called "dope," sufficient fuel to cook a meal or take the chill out of a cabin. Wood-cutting operations along the Park's roads to supply the demand proved to be both unsightly and destructive, however, and the service was halted after World War II.

The system of lodges in the Park developed during the 1920s and '30s from roots in the stagecoach era. The lodges were successors to those permanent camps operated by the Wylie and the Shaw and Powell companies and were heirs to the unique tradition of housing guests under canvas and hauling them around the Park in company conveyances. In 1916 the lodge development lost the transportation privilege its predecessors had enjoyed[35] and became oriented to the automobile, maintaining its services and prices midway between housekeeping cabins and the hotels.

The lodges of that era in the Park offered features commonly found in today's large motels. Cabins were heated and the early ones at least chamber-pot equipped, while later developments included modern plumbing. Units were grouped conveniently near a central complex, the "lodge," where the visitor found a comfortable lobby, dining room, gift shop, barber and beauty shops, and recreational facilities such as a dance hall and cocktail lounge. It was a successful pattern during that period.

Bathhouse and plunge operated by Henry P. Brothers at Old Faithful, 1915-51.

Madison Junction Museum, one of several rustic "trailside" museums built as focal points for the National Park Service interpretive programs which developed out of the 1920s.

Behind the loss of transportation privileges by the lodges lies a merger development of importance to the Park. Director Mather was a strong believer in the efficacy of a regulated monopoly, which he presumed would be advantageous to both the public and the operator, the regulatory power of the government protecting the visitor while exclusion of competition protected the concessioner. The latter days of the stagecoach era had been rife with commercial wrangling, leading to duplication of services and facilities which was expensive to the visitor and damaging to the Park. Mather proposed to end that unproductive, ruinous competition through a series of mergers that would put the principal businesses under one management.[36]

The first merger reformed the hotel and transportation enterprises in the Park under management of Harry W. Child, a former Helena banker who entered the concession business to safeguard his own invested money when Silas S. Huntley died in 1901. Mr. Child was a capable manager (efficiency was his fetish) who had the confidence of the Northern Pacific Railroad officials and an ability to get along with his associates, and he held the controlling interest in three concerns: the Yellowstone Park hotel, and the transportation and boat companies. One phase of the merger allowed Mr. Child to take over the large transportation businesses of Frank J. Haynes (Yellowstone-Western Stage Company), the Wylie Permanent Camping Company, and the Shaw and Powell Camping Company, thus consolidating all public transportation in the Yellowstone Park Transportation Company. The price Mr. Child had to pay, beyond the money laid out to purchase the facilities of his competitors, was agreement to motorize park transportation, which was effected in 1917.[37]

The advantage to Mr. Child was great, since he gained complete control of transportation, which had a good record as a profit maker while the hotels were nearly always losers. Director Mather had thought to manage the park business by balancing the profits from transportation against the inevitable losses from the hotels. The loss of their transportation privileges was a mortal blow to the two permanent camping companies, and they were brought to accept the consolidation only by the threat of losing their franchises, which were up for renewal. The same leverage was effective against Frank J. Haynes, but loss of his transportation business was not so serious since he had no other enterprise dependent on his stages.

A second merger was arranged to consolidate the permanent camping, resulting in the formation of the Yellowstone Park

Camping Company, which went through a series of changes (see Note 35) orienting it toward the automobilist for its survival. As lodge developments had come into the hands of Mr. Child in 1928, the business inherited by his successor, William M. Nichols,[38] in 1931 was an amalgam of five enterprises organized as hotel, transportation, boat, lodge, and fuel companies. These were the elements formed into the Yellowstone Park Company on June 6, 1936, without any substantial change in the management.

The general stores were not involved in the process of consolidation begun with the 1916 mergers (probably because these were highly individual enterprises of localized importance); however, these businesses gravitated naturally toward monopoly. At the opening of this period (1916), the mercantile arrangement in the Park was as follows: At Mammoth Hot Springs, a general store and post office was operated by George Whittaker; there was also a curio store and soda fountain for which Pryor & Trischman (Mesdames Anna K. Pryor and Elizabeth Trischman) held a permit, and a picture shop covered by the contract held by Frank J. Haynes. At the Upper Geyser Basin Charles A. Hamilton operated a general store purchased in 1914 from the widow of Henry E. Klamer, and there was a picture shop there. At Lake, Hamilton operated a general store through a lease with the successors to E. C. Waters' boat enterprise (Waters had maintained a store adjacent to the hotel as a convenience to fishermen); at Canyon there was a picture shop of the Haynes chain.

George Whittaker established a general store at Canyon the following year (1917), occupying the log building abandoned by the Holm Transportation Company.[39] He rebuilt on that site in 1921, as did Hamilton at Lake (the store there having been purchased from the boat company). Hamilton enlarged the old (lower) store in the Upper Geyser Basin in 1923 and established a small one in the auto campground and similar small stores in the auto camps at Fishing Bridge and West Thumb the following year. It was also in 1924 that George Whittaker and Anna Pryor began the joint operation of a small store at the Mammoth auto camp, and Pryor started the unique refreshment stand on the upper terraces called the Devil's Kitchenette. Pryor & Trischman bought out George Whittaker in 1932, and they, in turn sold to C. A. Hamilton in 1953. With the recent purchase of the Haynes' interests by Hamilton's heirs[40] (Trevor and Ellie Povah), the process of consolidation of park stores is complete; all are now under management of Hamilton Stores, Inc.

The Boy's Forest and Trail Camp, operated in conjunction with the Camp Roosevelt development fom 1921 through 1923, was a bold attempt to expand the educational value of the Yellowstone experience. Professor Alvin Whitney of the New York State School of Forestry at Syracuse University conceived the idea of a summer school for boys, where they would be "trained in woodcraft and other branches of education."[41] Unfortunately, he was unable to bring out enough boys to make the project a financial success and after three seasons, during which the Yellowstone Park Camps Company lost $4,000, the venture was terminated.

A retrospective view of the period between the great wars leaves one with the feeling that it should have ended better. The tremendous enthusiasm with which it was begun, the drive that prepared the Park for its new type of visitor, the automobilist, was somehow lost among the doldrums of the Great Depression. In the beginning, Stephen T. Mather's belief that the Park should be open to everyone, regardless of means, was implemented in a most imaginative and constructive manner. The twofold thrust of the 1920s provided interpretation of the Park's features (see Chapter 19) and the development of visitor-use facilities. The campgrounds, cafeterias, and cabins strung on the asphalt ribbon of a system of park-type roads democratized the area, bringing it very close to what it was intended to be, the people's playground.

Had there been no enervating depression years to dry up the means for renewal of those facilities and had there been no wartime hiatus to worsen the obsolescence—in short, had the realistic progress we have been speaking of been maintained—the problems facing the Park since World War II probably would be less serious.

CHAPTER 23

THROUGH A GLASS, DARKLY

Surely our people do not understand even yet the rich heritage that is theirs. There can be nothing in the world more beautiful than the Yosemite, the groves of giant sequoias and redwoods, the Canyon of the Colorado, the Canyon of the Yellowstone, the three Tetons; and our people should see to it that they are preserved for their children forever, with their majestic beauty all unmarred.

—Theodore Roosevelt [1]

Yellowstone National Park enjoyed a respite during the war years. The visitation in 1942 was but one-third of the previous year (which had set an all-time record at 581,761 people), and the available facilities and services were also very much curtailed. Lake Hotel and all the lodges remained closed, and, though the yellow buses ran on schedule, there were no sightseeing trips and the whole operation was terminated two weeks earlier than usual. From 1943 through 1945, the rationing of gasoline and tires effectively restricted travel to the occasional visits of local people (mainly fishermen) and a very few cross-country travelers who were allowed to use their automobiles for business purposes or while changing residences; thus, there was need for only a few cabins at Old Faithful and Fishing Bridge to shelter travelers stranded in the Park.

Meals were available at the Hamilton Stores at those points, and at the Pryor Store at Mammoth Hot Springs. The entire visitation during the four years of World War II was less than the figure for 1941.

Of course, the government's activities in the area were also greatly reduced—practically to a caretaker status—both as an economy measure and because military service made recruitment of seasonal employees extremely difficult (one-third of the Park's permanent personnel was eventually drawn off also). The Park was allowed only twenty-two seasonal rangers and no seasonal naturalists during that period and all project construction was closed down for the duration of the emergency. The two principal projects thus interrupted were the road from Old Faithful to Craig Pass, which had not received its final oil mat, and the rebuilding of roads in the Canyon area in conjunction with development of a new visitor-use site at that point. The latter project was well into the construction stage, with the new grade roughed out and a large, earthen fill already in place at the crossing of Cascade Creek. All this work deteriorated badly during the long hiatus before the project was resumed.

Concessioners made no effort to improve their facilities during the war years. Beyond the minimal operations already mentioned, they were content to protect the fleet of buses, the silent hotels, and other equipment from weather damage and theft.

It had been presumed that the return to normalcy after the war would be a gradual one, but that was not the character of the Park's awakening. Weary from military service or war work and with money to spend (from high wages, bonds, and bonuses), the American public wanted a change of scene, and the national parks were among the places they traveled to, looking for it. The wave of visitors that inundated Yellowstone Park in the summer of 1946 was nearly one and one-half times greater than the peak visitation before the war, and that load was put upon obsolete, neglected facilities while labor and materials shortages were as severe as they had been during the war. The following excerpt from the superintendent's annual report describes the situation:

> Plans were made during the winter to have all operations underway in the park for the 1946 season on a pre-war basis. However, all of the hotels and lodges and a number of other facilities having been closed throughout the war and considerable repair and maintenance work necessary, it was not possible to have all operations opened on schedule because of the scarcity of materials and the general attitude of labor expecting to receive high wages with little work. Positions were difficult

to fill and food supplies were hard to obtain. The numerous OPA, building, and other restrictions further prevented the concessioners from getting everything in readiness for the 1946 visitors. The various park concessioners started opening their operations for the summer during the month of May, and by June 20 all facilities which were to become available had been opened. Lake Hotel did not open for the summer and by the end of June the Haynes Picture Shop, cafeteria, and general store in the Mammoth campground were not operated. While Camp Roosevelt was opened on June 20, as scheduled, it was necessary to close it before the end of the month due to a labor shortage. Employees who had been engaged there were moved to other operations in the Park. Only about 75% of the accommodations ordinarily available were open to handle the 1946 crowds and all sleeping accommodations were taxed to capacity each night. Many visitors were obliged to seek accommodations outside the park or sleep in their cars. Conditions were very much the same outside. Never before have eating and sleeping establishments, curio shops, grocery stores, and other merchants done such a land-office business. New and inexperienced help greatly retarded the proper handling of visitors, resulting in numerous complaints and dissatisfied tourists.[2]

The National Park Service shared the difficulties of the postwar period. Authority to raise the number of seasonal rangers to fifty-two (five above the prewar level) and to reconstitute the force of seasonal naturalists at twenty-six, also above the prewar level, was received prior to the 1946 season; yet, it was not possible to fill those positions adequately. It was even more difficult to reestablish adequate maintenance and get the stalled construction program moving again. The surfacing required to complete the road between Old Faithful and Craig Pass was finished in October of 1946, but bids on the Canyon job were rejected twice as excessive, and a satisfactory bidder was not found until the fall of 1948. Two years later the road realignment was practically completed.

The road work was a necessary preliminary to further progress on a development project begun before the war: the construction of an entirely new Canyon Village, which was to replace the old facilities scattered around the Falls of the Yellowstone. The planning and initial surveys for the Canyon project had been completed prior to the war and construction of a water system was begun with Emergency Conservation Works Program labor. That, with the road work, was a considerable start to which additional utilities surveys were added in 1946-47. Such early progress laid the basis for subsequent rapid development of Canyon Village under Mission 66.

Another project that moved into the planning stage in the immediate postwar period was relocation of the West Thumb complex at a distance from the thermal features. Topographical surveys, started south of the old area in 1947, were extended eastward around Thumb Bay, providing data on the site later developed as Grant Village. In general, planning was then far ahead of the National Park Service's ability to construct, and development of that site was out of the question until the late 1950s.

The government's postwar construction program did not actually get rolling until 1952. Contracts for building roads and utilities (water and sewer) for the new Canyon area were let that summer, and work on a campground was started the following year. All the preliminary work was finished by the summer of 1955; the main roads had been aligned, including the eastern end of the Norris Cutoff; the access roads, plaza, and parking areas for the village proper were completed, and the water and sewerage systems were useable. The new site was ready for the buildings that would transform it into Canyon Village.

The second phase of the Canyon development involved construction of entirely new visitor facilities by the concessioners—an involvement the Yellowstone Park Company was not really prepared for. The financial condition of the concern, if not unsound, was at least shaky through the loss of a longtime ally, and a reorientation of its business methods and objectives was the great need of the moment; certainly, a massive investment in new facilities for an old-style operation was not the answer.

The problems faced by the Yellowstone Park Company in 1955 came out of the past. The concern brought into being through the consolidation of June 6, 1936, continued to walk the financial tightrope trod by its predecessors. To an indebtedness of $186,800 remaining from the amount borrowed in 1928 under a joint mortgage arrangement among the four railroads interested in park tourism[3] (the Northern Pacific, Burlington, Union Pacific, and Milwaukee systems—their cooperation in support of park transportation and hotel concessions is explained in Chapter 13), an additional $500,000 (to be retired at $50,000 per year) was added January 29, 1937. More than one-quarter million dollars of the total obligations remained unsatisfied at the end of the 1941 season ($72,805 owed to the Northern Pacific), and business was so poor during the summer of 1942 that the Yellowstone Park Company was forced to ask for a suspension of further repayment. Even the interest went unpaid until November 22, 1944, when President William M. Nichols sold his

Gallatin Gateway ranch to raise the money.[4] That desperate measure carried the company through until the resumption of operations in 1946 furnished revenue with which to continue liquidation of the outstanding indebtedness. Most of the earnings of the postwar years were thus absorbed, and the Yellowstone Park Company was not free of its financial obligation to the railroads until March 25, 1955.[5]

It would seem that the Yellowstone Park Company had done well to clear itself of that longstanding obligation, but it was a gain made at a fearful cost. The construction of additional facilities to handle the postwar visitor load (over the million mark in 1948 and double the prewar record by 1951) was entirely neglected and maintenance of the existing, obsolete facilities was held to a bare minimum. The failure to modernize and provide services expected by postwar visitors led to many, often quite justified, complaints concerning the parsimonious operation by which the company struggled toward financial solvency.

The public's discontent with conditions in the Park finally became too great to be entirely ignored. In its justification for rate increases in the summer of 1951, the Yellowstone Park Company announced its intention to launch a program that was expected "to provide additional and more comfortable accommodations for visitors and employees." This effort, calling for an expenditure of more than one-half million dollars, included the following:[6]

116 cottages at Lake Hotel location	$100,000
Rearrangement of cabins and other improvements	75,000
Girl's dormitory at Lake	20,000
Repairing 80 rooms at Lake Hotel, bathing facilities and employees quarters at Fishing Bridge	38,000
Multiple unit at Fishing Bridge	50,000
Boat Docks	5,000
Public baths, etc., at Old Faithful tourist cabins	20,000
Cabins at Old Faithful Lodge	30,000
Renovation of Canyon Lodge cabins	60,000
Remodelingof Canyon Hotel kitchen	100,000
Laundry at Mammoth (including $7,000 for a sprinkler system)	29,000
	$527,000

Less than half the amount listed was earmarked for truly new construction; the program was no more than lip service to the idea of modernization.

The only other effort to modernize during the decade following World War II was one-quarter million dollars spent for equipment and construction in 1955 by way of replacement of the $100,000 loss suffered in the fire that destroyed the tourist cabin office and dormitory at Old Faithful on June 29 of that year. On the other hand, enough obsolete facilities, such as the old lodge development at Mammoth Hot Springs and the tent tops at Old Faithful, were eliminated to materially reduce the number of "pillows" available in the Park; and that, coming when an increase was so badly needed, was hardly tolerable.

The financial weakness behind the Yellowstone Park Company's failure to modernize, or even maintain its investment in the Park, was complicated by the loss of that source of credit drawn upon for financing all the major improvements made prior to World War II— the railroad loans. Following the war, the Northern Pacific Railroad found Yellowstone Park tourism less profitable than it had been in earlier times and soon decided to give up its postwar effort to reestablish the former pattern of passenger traffic to the Park. Thus, the hauling of tourists to Gardiner by rail ended with the 1948 season, after which the service to the northern entrance of the Park was supplied by buses. The same course was eventually taken by the other lines: the Burlington abandoned its rail service to Cody, Wyoming, and its famous Burlington Inn, in 1956; both the Union Pacific and the Milwaukee gave up their passenger business into the Park (via West Yellowstone and Gallatin Gateway, respectively) in 1961. As the railroads abandoned their traditional interest in Yellowstone they also became reluctant to act as a financial partner of the Yellowstone Park Company.

This change in attitude was a serious threat to a business that was essentially an extension of the carriage trade of earlier days: it was dependent upon rail carriers to funnel-in those tourists who rode the yellow buses and stayed at the hotels. The withdrawal of the carriers should have been sufficient warning to the company to reorient its operations almost entirely toward the automobile traffic which, by then, was bringing 98.5 percent of the visitors into the Park. Instead of making such a logical adjustment, the Yellowstone Park Company clung to the outmoded procedures of the past.

The failure of the management of the major concession to reorient in accord with the needs of most visitors was the result of an infatuation with another form of transportation. The hope that air service could be substituted for rail service as a prime carrier for a continuing tourist traffic into the Park was raised in 1951 when

National Park Service, the Civil Aeronautics Administration, and Western Airlines officials met at West Yellowstone to consider establishment of a commercial airport to serve the Park. Translation of that idea into a reality a decade later proved to be no answer to the Yellowstone Park Company's malaise, for before the airport became operational the company was doomed by a series of events which, once activated, had fatal consequences.

A travel study initiated by the Wyoming State Highway Department in August 1950 to determine the value of park traffic to the local economy revealed that an estimated $18,994,301 worth of business was generated in the immediate vicinity (with other, nationwide benefits assessed at $121 million). Viewed in that light, the management of the Park—and particularly of its concessions— became a matter of considerable interest in Wyoming.

The awareness of the Park's recreational business potential created by the 1951 survey led directly to the formation of the Yellowstone-Teton Development Association on August 8, 1953, at Mammoth Hot Springs Hotel,[7] and that generated a proposal that the state of Wyoming should purchase and operate the concessions in Yellowstone Park. The Yellowstone Park Company did not object when the idea was enacted into law by the Wyoming legislature (House Bill 228) on February 14, 1955, but the vigorous opposition of Wyoming's neighbors prevented any further action.[8]

Such a scheme of management, pregnant as it was with possibilities for a collision between state and federal authorities, would have been unacceptable in any event, but particularly so in the light of the plan the National Park Service was just then maturing. The ambitious proposal being put into final form by a steering committee headed by Chief of Conservation Lemuel A. Garrison envisioned a ten-year, service-wide effort which was to put the national parks in condition to adequately serve the visiting public by the year 1966; from that objective the program took its name: Mission 66.

The broad program was related to Yellowstone Park in November 1955 with the completion of a prospectus that identified the problem in these words:

> Three things are necessary in order for Yellowstone to yield the benefits of which it is capable: an adequate road and trail system giving access to important and significant features of the Park; adequate facilities for visitor comfort, welfare and subsistence; and effective presentation, interpretation, and protection of the resources of Yellowstone by a management staff.[9]

The desired result—the accomodation of thousands of visitors without damage to the Park—was to be obtained through the improvement of facilities and management. The construction phase of the program called for an expenditure of $70 million for new facilities within the Park during the ten-year period. Of that total, the government was to spend $55 million ($36 million for roads and trails, $11 million for buildings and $7.5 million for utilities), to be complemented by a private investment of $15 million in new concession facilities. The management phase required increased staffing, changes in protection and interpretation, and the dispersion of visitor use in order to lessen the impact on particular areas.

Modernization of the road system was the key to the program. The general pattern of the system was satisfactory but many segments required upgrading, and fourteen bridges were obsolete, creating bottlenecks by impeding traffic flow and limiting freight loads. Also, the lack of parking areas and turnouts limited the ability of visitors to stop at will while traveling through the Park.

Under Mission 66, the west entrance road was rebuilt to Madison Junction, providing easy ingress from the most heavily used entrance, and a new road was constructed southward from Madison Junction, bypassing the difficult Firehole Canyon and allowing an unrestricted flow of traffic into the geyser basins from the north. Reconstruction of part of the lakeshore road between West Thumb and the outlet of Yellowstone Lake made possible an increased recreational use of that enticing locality, while completion of the western end of the Norris-Canyon road greatly increased the usefulness of the cut-off.

But it was in the matter of bridges that most was accomplished. The original Chittenden Bridge at Canyon, a structure that was both too narrow and too camel-backed to be safely used by modern automobiles, was replaced in 1962 by the Chittenden Memorial Bridge, a similarly beautiful creation on the same site. This replacement conforms to present-day standards for vehicular use, making it easier and safer for visitors to go to Artist Point on the east rim of the Grand Canyon of the Yellowstone. Only a little less important was the replacement, in 1963, of the old Yellowstone River bridge near Tower Junction by a handsome concrete and steel structure with approaches that eliminated a hazardous situation and unfettered the northeastern approach road.

The Lewis River bridge on the south entrance road was rebuilt, and that, with the replacement of a number of smaller structures that had been little more than traffic nuisances for years, brought the bridging up to the general standard of the road system.

The new construction included turnouts that would allow visitors to stop and enjoy the scenery or picnic or fish. In two instances (at Virginia Cascades on the old Norris Cutoff, and Firehole Canyon south of Madison Junction) sections of old road were turned into scenic loops.

The need for buildings and utilities had its basis in the obsolescence of existing facilities (most of which were built in the 1920s and '30s when the largest visitation that could be foreseen was a few hundred thousand people each season) and in the desirability of regrouping the administrative and concession facilities at better locations. The idea of relocation as a means of conserving scenic, geological, and recreational values went back to 1935, when work was begun on a new site for the various facilities scattered about the Falls and Grand Canyon of the Yellowstone. Mission 66 proposed the completion of that project (Canyon Village) and the beginning of a similar development on the shore of West Thumb Bay (Grant Village). A third complex called Firehole Village, intended to replace facilities at Old Faithful, was suggested for Lower Geyser Basin. Lesser developments at other points (Mammoth Hot Springs, Norris and Madison Junctions, Bridge Bay, Lake, Fishing Bridge, and Tower Junction) with extensive improvement of the public campgrounds were intended to complement the major sites, so that the Park would be able to accommodate the more than two million visitors expected by 1966.

The role of the park concessioners in this vast modernization was largely the replacement of older cabin accommodations with enough modern, motel-type units to increase the overnight accommodations from 8,500 to 14,500 persons. The plan called for a corresponding increase in service facilities such as stores, filling stations and eating establishments, but foresaw no change in hotels; thus, Mission 66 was mainly concerned with serving those automobilists who, by 1956, made up 98.7 percent of the Park's visitors.

Expansion and reorientation of protective, interpretive, and maintenance activities called for under the plan was expected to increase the cost of park operation to the taxpayer from $1,470,000 to $2,226,000 by the year 1966. The increase was presumed necessary to reach an adequate level of visitor service and safeguard the park features.

In its broad outline the plan was a joint venture through which the government and private concessioners could expect to overcome two decades of obsolescence in half that time through their joint efforts. The Yellowstone Park Company entered into this partnership with the greatest reluctance, for its means were insufficient and the management was in a mood to sell out; however, the National Park Service had a most compelling leverage: the company's franchise was up for renewal, and without a new contract its business in the Park was not salable. So the company reluctantly agreed to cooperate in the Mission 66 development.[10]

The program on which the National Park Service and the concessioners had embarked was formalized with the ground-breaking ceremony at the Canyon Village site on May 25, 1956. Its real beginning was three months earlier, when the Yellowstone Park Company made arrangements with eastern bankers for a loan of $2.5 million and retained the firm of Welton-Becket and Associates to plan and supervise construction of the new facilities. The contract went to the McNeil Construction Company, which immediately began prefabricating 300 motel-type units. These were to be arranged adjacent to a lodge building facing a large parking plaza, opposite the government visitor center, while the third side of the plaza was to be closed by a picture shop housing the Haynes business, and a general store to be built and operated by C. A. Hamilton.

The Hamilton Store operation had expanded into the Canyon area years earlier, when "Ham" finally consolidated the entire general store business in the Park under his management.[11] His is a success story without parallel in the Yellowstone, an astounding rise from a clerkship in the purchasing department of the old Yellowstone Park Association to control of the Park's most profitable business, and it is interesting to note that it was done by catering assiduously to the needs of the automobilists.

Because of the planning and preliminary work that had been accomplished at the Canyon Village site during the two previous decades, the first Mission 66 project in the Park moved along rapidly. Enough so, in fact, that a portion of the concessioner's facilities could be opened to the public July 1, 1957. The public-use portion of government construction (visitor center, amphitheatre, and campground) was completed by the end of the summer, so that the conference of national park superintendents held in Yellowstone Park that fall could be hosted at Canyon Village beginning on September 10.

The planning on which this development was based called for removal of all the old concession facilities at Canyon, except the hotel, as soon as equivalent units became available at the new site. Rapid construction progress allowed abandonment of the old Canyon Lodge (on the east rim, opposite the Upper Fall) after the 1956 season, but that shift led to an entirely unexpected change in patronage.

It had been assumed that the motel-type units at Canyon Village would serve visitors who had patronized the lodge; however, during the 1957 season, the old Canyon Hotel filled to the roof nearly every night (something that had not happened for years) while much of the capacity of the Village went begging. The change in preference was the direct result of the substantially higher rates charged for lodgings in the new development (a necessary increase, since Canyon Village had been built with borrowed money and had proved far more expensive to construct than was anticipated). The trend continued through the 1958 season and was so inimical to that precarious financing on which Canyon Village was based that the Yellowstone Park Company decided to abandon the hotel in order that the Canyon Village units might be filled and the investment there made to pay its way.[12] Accordingly Canyon Hotel, with all its furnishings and appurtenances, was sold in August 1959 to wreckers, who paid $25 for it. Salvaging the vast structure, which was a mile around its foundation wall, went on through the winter of 1959-60, and the remaining hulk was destroyed by an accidental fire the following summer.

But even that massive sacrifice was insufficient. The cost of the Canyon Village development was more than the Yellowstone Park Company could bear; just a hair's-breadth short of bankruptcy its affairs were placed under the management of a board representing the mortgage holders.

After the construction of Canyon Village, commercial power lines were extended into the Park, replacing power generated by small government diesel plants in the area. The changeover followed the Yellowstone Park Company's favorable experience with the service extended to Mammoth Hot Springs by the Montana Power Company in June 1951. A study made for the company by Eugene W. Schilling of Montana State University in August 1954 indicated that the power line could be extended into the interior to provide cheaper, more reliable service than that available from local power plants. As extended by Montana Power in 1958-59, the line roughly paralleled the road from Mammoth Hot Springs to Norris Junction, where it branched, one spur running to the Upper Geyser Basin by way of Madison Junction, the other crossing to Canyon along the old Norris Cutoff, then passing southward to the Lake-Fishing Bridge area and around the north shore of Lake Yellowstone to West Thumb and Grant Village.

The commercial power installation proved less advantageous than expected because the electrical demand did not reach a level that would yield the anticipated rate reduction (largely a result of a curtailment of the Mission 66 program); also, the open-ended system suffered outages from its vulnerability to windfall along many miles of right-of-way opened through forest.

Telephone service in the Park was taken over entirely by Mountain States Telephone and Telegraph Company on May 31, 1958. Prior to that date, the National Park Service and the Yellowstone Park Company had maintained separate systems (though their wires were strung on the same poles). These antique installations, so typical of an earlier time, were replaced by a single, modern system. Overhead wires gave way to buried cables, the switchboard (and the operator's cheery "Number, please!") to a room full of clicking relays, and the hand-cranked phones to business-like dial models. The new system was more efficient, as all will agree who have strained their ears to make out a message between static crashes induced by summer lightning, but there was a cost beyond the fee charged for the service. Gone were the helpful operators whose switchboard was the Park's message center and whose voices doubled as town crier for the headquarters settlement; also, a switching relay doesn't crack a joke or show any interest in a sick youngster!

When the Canyon Village project was completed, the proposed development on the south shore of Thumb Bay was begun. This new area, called Grant Village for President Ulysses S. Grant, who signed Yellowstone's organic act into law on March 1, 1872, was intended to entirely replace the old West Thumb development, which had crowded upon important thermal features. The construction started in 1961 by the National Park Service has provided roads, utilities (water and sewer), campgrounds, comfort stations, a marina, and a visitor center, all usable by 1966. However, the Park's major concessioner, or rather its successor,[13] not wishing to become involved in another venture as expensive as Canyon Village, has not provided overnight or eating facilities at the new site but continues to do business at the old West Thumb location, where the Hamilton Store also remains. In this case, the Mission 66 plan was largely vitiated by the failure of concessioners to complement the government's investment.

The third relocation project proposed under Mission 66, Firehole Village, was never undertaken, which was fortunate in the light of the experience at Grant Village. However, the lesser developments scheduled for other points of interest around the Park were mostly accomplished according to plan. Except at Bridge Bay, the west entrance, and Tower Junction the concessioners were not involved; rather, these were campground or administrative developments connected with the new pattern of National Park Service management.

The new management pattern was decentralized by creating three super-districts similar in extent to those prior to 1936 but embracing all government activities—interpretive and maintenance as well as protective, with all three branches under the supervision of a district manager who was, in effect, a "little superintendent." The pattern called for the development of two entirely new district headquarters (the northern district was to be managed from existing facilities at park headquarters) and for changes in staffing. A headquarters for the southern district was adapted from buildings vacated by the Fish and Wildlife Service (Bureau of Fisheries) at the old Lake fish hatchery site; a residential and utility development was added at what had formerly been the Civilian Conservation Corps camp for that area.[14] A similar headquarters for the western district was established in a temporary building erected adjacent to the Old Faithful Museum; a residential-utility complex for that area was built on the site of the former Old Faithful CCC camp.

The new districts were staffed to handle all problems locally, the presumption being that such autonomy would be more responsive to current needs than the former departmental organization operating on a park-wide basis. This concept had some advantages, particularly in buildings and utilities maintenance, where sending crews from headquarters often meant excessive travel; what was gained in that respect however was mostly lost in the lower efficiency of the small district crews. Also, autonomy brought an insularity hitherto unknown.

Among the changes intended to improve the Park's administration was a shift of the superintendent's office from the building inherited from the Corps of Engineers (that pagoda-like, sandstone structure with the green tile roof known to several generations of Yellowstone employees as the Temple of Truth) to the three-story, stone barracks that once housed two troops of the Fort Yellowstone cavalry. This move allowed grouping of the department heads close to the superintendent, creating a functional unity unknown when staff members were scattered among several buildings. The old superintendent's office was thus made available as a north district ranger station, a function for which is was ideally situated. Perfection of a park-wide FM radio communication system working through a repeater station on Bunsen Peak (later shifted to Mount Washburn for better coverage) gave the instant communication necessary in emergencies.

Another target of the Mission 66 effort was the improvement of employee facilities. Much of the year round housing available to government employees were old buildings inherited from the army past, unsuited to modern living and uneconomical to heat and maintain. The seasonal quarters, particularly the road-crew bunk-houses and mess halls scattered throughout the Park, were flimsy, hardly satisfactory for pre- and post-season use when opening and closing roads or for limited winter use in keeping some roads open to the public around the year. Also, increased staffing proposed under Mission 66 meant additional quarters for both permanent and seasonal employees.

The need was met in two ways: by building new quarters and by providing modern trailer-court facilities. At park headquarters a residential development begun before World War II, near the powerhouse, was extended eastward into the area formerly occupied by tourist cabins. A school for the lower grades (all students above the sixth were bussed to the Gardiner school) and a modern clinic were built in 1963. A trailer court for the area was developed on the site of the Mammoth CCC camp.

A residential and trailer-court development for government employees as an adjunct of the Canyon Village project allowed abandonment of the old ranger station site near the Upper Falls and the old road camp and utility area site west of Chittenden Bridge. The new quarters at Canyon were mainly multiple-dwelling units, with provision for winter use whenever necessary.

Similar residential developments were a part of the project work at Lake and Madison Junction, and some improvement of facilities was accomplished everywhere except at Old Faithful. All develop-ment there was held in abeyance in the hope that the proposed relocation in the Lower Geyser Basin (Firehole Village) could be undertaken.

The Mission 66 program as described to this point has been essentially developmental, intending to improve access to the Park, services rendered to visitors, and the administration of the area generally; in all this it furthered use of park resources by preparing the area for an increased visitor load. Fortunately, there was another side to this program: a concern for the preservation aspect of park management, apparent in the steps taken to protect ecological relationships and maintain "naturalness," in the effort to disperse visitor use and thereby lessen its impact on the park environment, and in better orientation of the visitor-user to the wilderness.

A concern for naturalness, and its concomitant recognition of the complex interrelationships of the ecological system, was not new. Adolph Murie's study of the ecology of the coyote during the late thirties set the pattern.[15] Not only was the idea of predator control entirely discredited, but this and similar research established the return of a philosophy of noninterference with the ecological system.

Accordingly, the feeding of hotel garbage to bears at Canyon as a public spectacle was discontinued (1941) as were the exhibiting of wild buffalo in the "show" corral at Antelope Creek (1942) and the feeding of hay to buffalo at the ranch in Lamar Valley (1946). The longstanding policy of stocking park waters for fishermen was reversed in 1958; the artificial propagation of fish at the Lake hatchery was halted and the catch limited to a figure within the natural regenerative powers of the species. "Fishing for Fun" was promoted: a concept of sport fishing using barbless hooks and returning all uninjured fish to the water to lessen depletion of the resource. However, few fishermen keep their sport that pure and regulations are required to prevent anglers from depopulating the Park's waters.

The chronic elk problem also became a major concern at this time. The program initiated in 1951 to reduce the northern elk herd to a size commensurate with the carrying capacity of the available winter range, through live-trapping and shipment of the excess animals to other areas, failed to check increase of the species. It was believed that further delay in effecting a reduction of the northern herd from its estimated 11,800 animals to the 5,000 the range could support would result in damage of a serious, perhaps even irreparable nature; so during the winter of 1955-56, a total of 6,535 animals were removed from the herd (of that number, 1,974 were killed by rangers as part of a program of direct reduction).[16]

This forthright attempt to restore a natural balance impaired by years of overprotective management of the Yellowstone elk created an uproar in several communities adjacent to the Park. Individuals and organizations interested in the hunting of elk or in the business generated by such hunting chose to consider the reduction a depletion of their resource, despite the fact that hunting outside the Park had failed to provide a sufficient check upon the animals. The park administration was forced to defend its action at a series of meetings and hearings extending over several years; the elk controversy was finally settled on a basis that should prove mutually satisfactory.[17] In any event, another large-scale reduction is unlikely because modern management methods, utilizing the helicopter and portable trap, promise adequate population control on a year-to-year basis.

Another longstanding problem, the begging bears so typical of the Yellowstone roadside throughout the automobile era, was also brought under control. A vigorous campaign to educate park visitors against feeding the bears, combined with removal of troublesome animals while under the influence of a tranquilizing drug, and a return to a better method of garbage disposal (incineration in place of sanitary landfill disposal) are advancing the National Park Service goal: the maintenance of representative populations of grizzly and black bears under natural conditions.[18]

The concern for the Park's environment that developed out of Mission 66 did not stem entirely from its problems as a wildlife habitat; some of the gain in this regard was a response to problems created by visitor use. Some campgrounds were closed in order to halt destructive erosion; road scars were revegetated in an effort to restore the environment, and a campaign was initiated to promote use of the backcountry and thus take some pressure off the narrow strip of terrain adjacent to the roads (the ten percent of the area that received the impact of almost the entire visitation). This last effort probably had little effect, for the Yellowstone wilderness is too big for man afoot and remains true horse country. However, there was a related development of real worth.

Increasing numbers of powerboats on Lake Yellowstone led to a recreational use study of the Lake area in 1959. Chief among the recommendations of the study team was a proposal to ban powerboats from the southern reaches of Lake Yellowstone. This was sought partly to protect fragile beachlines and the nesting grounds of water birds from the damaging wakes of fast-moving boats and partly to provide a sanctuary of quiet naturalness for those wishing the experience of canoeing in a wilderness setting. An attempt to zone the arms of the lake so as to prohibit all but hand-propelled craft was made in 1960 but encountered the opposition of the numerous powerboat enthusiasts.[19] Regulation was effected in 1961, but not in the terms first proposed; instead, a compromise allowed powerboats to use most of the Southeast Arm at reduced speed while entirely banning them from Heart, Lewis, and Shoshone lakes.

The interpretive program developed under Mission 66 was conservation oriented, stressing wilderness values and ecological relationships wherever possible. The message was incorporated into audiovisual presentations and given prominence in the new museums at Canyon and Grant villages.

Overall, Mission 66 was not a success. Most was accomplished in improving access to the Park and in providing administrative and employee facilities; and emphasis on protecting the environment was all to the good. But in the matter of providing visitor accommodations there was no real gain, for the available "pillows" within the Park in 1972 were only 9,000, not much above the 8,500 available at the opening of the program. For the past three years there have been pillows to spare throughout the Park during the summer season, so that one wonders what the result would have been had the Yellowstone Park Company constructed up to the 14,500 capacity called for in the Mission 66 prospectus. Perhaps the Park was saved from unnecessary scarring.

Regardless, Mission 66 passed quietly out of the picture with the secretary of the interior's news release of August 3, 1964, detailing the goals of his "Road to the Future." This evaluation deemphasized construction of facilities, shifting to less specific long-range objectives that have been summarized as:

> Preserving the scenic and scientific grandeur of our Nation, presenting its history, providing healthful outdoor recreation for the enjoyment of our people, working with others to provide the best possible relationships of human beings to their total environment.[20]

Commendable as these goals were, they were vague and did not evoke the enthusiastic response that Mission 66 had. Thus, Yellowstone Park lapsed into an unimaginative struggle to complete those projects already scheduled. The reconstruction of the east entrance road east of Sylvan Pass, relocation of the roads in the Norris Junction area, and the building of a bypass road through the Upper Geyser Basin accounted for most of the construction expenditures. (At park headquarters a few houses were added to the residential development, and a visitor-center complex took the place of the Old Faithful museum.) But this was only tidying up.

Two facts became ever more evident during the post-Mission 66 period: Yellowstone Park was unlikely to receive the funding necessary to keep it abreast of the increasing visitation, and a continuing effort to accommodate all visitors in the traditional manner would eventually be destructive of park values. Fiscal inability in the past has had roots in our national involvement with great and expensive causes such as a foreign war and space exploration, and domestic programs. The thrust of the "Road to the Future," which has been interpreted as a call for more recreational-type areas to be located available to centers of urban population, has left neither money nor manpower for extensive development of old, established parks such as Yellowstone.

Visitor traffic around Old Faithful Geyser during the summer of 1962, as seen from the roof of Old Faithful Inn.

With such limitations in operation, which will probably be in effect for some years to come, the philosophy that has guided the development and use of the Park in the past—essentially one of unrestricted visitor use—will hardly do for a future in which the evermounting pressure of visitor use is unlikely to be matched by funding which will decently accommodate such use (presuming the area could stand the strain without deterioration of its park values). At the same time, an attempt to cope with the present problem in the old manner by providing the roads, public facilities, and administrative developments necessary to unrestricted use would probably be no more successful than in the past and would gnaw at some park values in the name of progress while allowing others to be trampled out.

But there is an alternative. National Park Service management can abandon unrestricted use for one of several forms of regulation that would protect the wilderness and recreational values of the Park by allowing only as much use as is within its "carrying capacity." This is not a new idea; it has been the basis of numerous proposals advanced in the past decade. Regulation, as proposed, would either operate directly by limiting the number of visitors or vehicles allowed to enter the Park on any one day, or indirectly by removing overnight accommodations from within the area or substituting public transportation for private vehicles inside the boundaries.

If we may judge from what happened in the Park during the stagecoach era (a period when public transportation dominated the scene) the exclusion of private vehicles would be the least desirable form of limiting use. It tends to be undemocratic, putting undue emphasis on the ability to pay, and it is certainly inconvenient for the visitor who wants something more than a Greyline tour of the area. Also, it is not a positive approach, for points of interest, and those termini offering accommodations and services, very likely would be overused.

The other method of indirect limitation, doing away with accommodations within the Park (a concept known as "day use"), has several advantages over the foregoing: the visitor retains the flexibility and convenience of private transportation, and the Park is benefitted by a lessening of impact at developed points (through removal of the hotels and cabins, with their tributary installations and employees). However, it is probable that the road system would be burdened even more than under conditions of unrestricted use, which could lead to reconstructions that would be destructive of park values. Also, such a method of control is dependent upon the development of adequate visitor facilities peripheral to the area.

Direct limitations of use by restricting the daily entries on a first-come, first-served basis seems to offer the most advantages. It is democratic, positive in effect, relatively convenient for the visitor, and requires no additional roads or facilities, thus saving the Park from further damaging encroachment upon its wildness.

Regardless of how it is accomplished, regulation of visitor use on the basis of what an area can stand without serious damage is probably the only longterm solution to the dilemma posed by the act of Congress that created the National Park Service and charged it with responsibility for both use *and* preservation of our outstanding natural areas.[21] There is, in that act, the authority (even a mandate) to reconcile these diverse objectives, and restriction is the means for its accomplishment.

It is indeed ironic that a great Park which has pioneered so much that is associated with the national park movement and has triumphed over so many perils during a hundred years of lusty growth should stand stalled upon the threshold of its second century, faced with the grave decision whether to continue in a traditional but outmoded course or change to another course more likely to *serve* and *preserve*. But, in this, Yellowstone National Park is in the same position as our nation, which also stands at a crossroad, faced by fearful decisions.

NOTES

NOTES

CHAPTER 12

1. *Report of the Superintendent of the Yellowstone National Park to the Secretary of the Interior, 1886,* (Washington, D.C.: Govt. Printing Office, 1886), pp. 5 and 6, hereafter cited as *Supt. Report for [year].*

2. Already designated Camp Sheridan for Lieutenant General Philip H. Sheridan, who had personally recommended Captain Harris for the Yellowstone assignment.

3. *Supt. Report for 1886,* p. 7.

4. Ibid., pp. 11, 12.

5. Captain Moses Harris to secretary of the interior, October 4, 1886. Letters Sent, vol. 1, Yellowstone National Park Archives.

6. Phillips to secretary of the interior, October 4, 1886. Letters Received, Department of the Interior, P and M Division, 1885-86, Record Group 48, National Archives, Washington, D.C.

7. Harold Duane Hampton, "Conservation and Cavalry: A Study of the Role of the United States Army in the Development of a National Park System, 1886-1917" (doctoral dissertation, University of Colorado, 1965), p. 163, hereafter cited as "Conservation and Cavalry."

8. "Maintenance Record-book of the Post Quartermaster, 1886-1912." Item no. 167, Yellowstone National Park Archives.

9. Details are taken from Jack Ellis Haynes, "The First Winter Trip Through Yellowstone National Park," *Annals of Wyoming,* vol. 14, no. 2 (April 1942), pp. 89-97; and from G.L. Henderson, "Haynes' Winter Expedition," *Helena* (Mont.) *Independent,* Feb. 6, 1887.

10. Only months before his death in 1892, Lieutenant Schwatka attempted to organize an expedition to explore the environs of Mount Rainier, but that venture also aborted. Evidently, his health was seriously impaired by his arctic adventures.

11. This prefabricated structure, the second such built in the Park, stood near the Upper Falls, almost exactly on the site where the log ranger station was later built.

12. *Supt. Report for 1887,* p. 4.

13. Ibid., p. 25.

14. William James to Captain Moses Harris, August 27, 1887. Box 78 (Undesirables), Yellowstone National Park Archives.

15. J.B. Kirkbride to Captain Moses Harris, November 15, 1887. Box 78, Yellowstone National Park Archives.

16. A pencilled note on stationery of the Yellowstone Park Association. Box 78, Yellowstone National Park Archives.

17. Statement of H.C. Hinkley, October 23, 1887. Box 78, Yellowstone National Park Archives.

18. Statement of Frank Moore, October 23, 1887. Box 78, Yellowstone National Park Archives.

19. Jack Ellis Haynes, "Yellowstone's Stage Holdups," *Brand Book* (Denver, Colo.: Westerners, 1952), p. 3.

20. Told to J.E. Haynes in 1952 during a discussion of his article, "Yellowstone's Stage Holdups," cited in note 19.

21. Captain Moses Harris to secretary of the interior, March 23, 1889. Letters Sent, vol. 2, Yellowstone National Park Archives.

22. Captain Moses Harris to First Assistant Secretary of the Interior H.L. Muldrow, April 11, 1889. Letters Sent, vol. 2, Yellowstone National Park Archives.

23. *Livingston Enterprise,* Sept. 22, 1888.

24. D.G. Stivers to Captain Moses Harris, March 28, 1889. Doc. 514, Box 3, Yellowstone National Park Archives.

25. Assistant Secretary of the Interior Chandler to Captain Moses Harris, April 17, 1889. Doc. 333, box 2, Yellowstone National Park Archives.

26. Acting secretary of the interior to D.G. Stivers, July 20, 1891. Doc. 332, Yellowstone National Park Archives.

27. General Manager E.C. Waters to Cline, Rivers, and Lamartine, September 10, 1888. Docs. 626, 627, Yellowstone National Park Archives.

28. *Livingston Enterprise,* July 28, 1888. While Burdet tells this story with considerable literary license, some similar event did occur, and the naming of the feature called the Chinaman Spring (near Old Faithful Geyser) resulted from it. The year (1885) is established by Arnold Hague in his paper, "Soaping Geysers," read at a meeting of the American Institute of Mining Engineers in New York City, February 1889 (see *Annual Report of the Board of Regents of the Smithsonian Institution. . .July 1892,* p. 153). Hague conducted experiments during the summer of 1885 and found that some geysers, such as the Giantess, do not react to soap or lye; while others, such as the Beehive, are very responsive.

29. Ibid.

30. Yellowstone Park Association records made available by Hugh D. Galusha, Helena, Mont., Record Book no. 383, p. 30.

31. In 1882, General James S. Brisbin was authorized to put a steamboat on Yellowstone Lake, but he failed to do so when it became known that a similar privilege had been given to the Yellowstone Park Improvement Company (which was probably more interested in getting its foot in the door than in providing a service). The renewal of interest in steamboating on Lake Yellowstone is noted by the *Deer Lodge* (Mont.) *New North-West,* Feb. 22, 1889. The franchise granted to the Yellowstone Park Association on April 5, 1889, permitted "a naptha launch on the Yellowstone Lake"; see *Supt. Report for 1889,* p. 5.

32. *Supt. Report for 1890,* p. 11.

33. U.S., 52d Cong., 1st sess., House Rep. 1956, July 20, 1892.

34. Hampton, "Conservation and Cavalry," p. 200.

35. Hiram M. Chittenden, *The Yellowstone National Park* (Cincinnati: Robert Clarke Co., 1895), p. 139.

36. Captain Boutelle to secretary of the interior, July 31, 1889. Letters Sent, vol. 2, Yellowstone National Park Archives.

37. *Supt. Report for 1890,* p. 4.

38. Ibid., pp. 10-11.

39. Secretary of the interior to D.B. May, October 15, 1890. Doc. 405, Yellowstone National Park Archives. Owen Wister later had this to say about the elevator scheme:

Politics was behind it . . . an outrage more abominable than the dam at Jackson Lake. "But why should your refined taste," objected a lover of the multitude to whom I told this, "interfere with the enjoyment of the plain people?" Have the plain people told you or anybody that the one thing they lie sleepless craving for is an elevator to go up and down by those falls the way they do in hotels? "They would like it if it was there." Of course they would. Is that a reason to vulgarize a supreme piece of wild natural beauty for all time? How are the plain people to learn better things than they know if you lower to their level everything?"

See "Old Yellowstone Days," *Harpers Monthly Magazine,* March 1936, p. 476, hereafter cited as "Old Yellowstone."

40. Captain Boutelle to secretary of the interior, August 29, 1890. Letters Sent, vol. 2, pp. 155-67, Yellowstone National Park Archives.

41. *Supt. Report for 1888,* pp. 3-4.

42. "The Immortal 15," *Livingston Enterprise,* Sept. 22, 1888.

43. United States Life Saving Service, *Report of the United States Life Saving Service, for Fiscal Year 1889* (Washington, D.C., 1889), p. 59.

44. Carl E. Schmide, *A Western Trip* (Detroit, Mich.: Herold Press, 1910), p. 11.

45. *Supt. Report for 1888,* p. 5.

46. Captain Boutelle to secretary of the interior, September 11, 1890. Letters Sent, vol. 3, pp. 168-69, Yellowstone National Park Archives.

47. Secretary of the interior to Captain Boutelle, September 24, 1890. Doc. 236, Yellowstone National Park Archives.

48. Thomas Garfield to Captain Harris, September 24, 1888, as quoted by Hampton, "Conservation and Cavalry," pp. 172-73.

49. *Supt. Report for 1889,* p. 4.

50. G.L. Henderson, *Norristown* (Penn.) *Daily Herald,* Jan. 19, 1889. He comments that "the soldiers do not like this new function of preserving a national park; they say that it is not a soldier's work, but Captain Harris has proved that there is a good use to which an army may be put even in time of peace."

51. *Supt. Report for 1890,* p. 4.

52. *Supt. Report for 1888,* p. 3.

53. Wister, "Old Yellowstone," p. 476.

CHAPTER 13

1. *An Illustrated History of the State of Montana* (Chicago: Lewis Publishing Co., 1894), p. 433.

2. Undated memorandum to Mr. Elliott [1904], in file "President, 209A," Northern Pacific Railroad Company, St. Paul, Minn.

3. Patrick J. Curran, "Yellowstone Park Association, 1886-1896," August 23, 1968, manuscript, Minnesota Historical Society, St. Paul, p. 3, hereafter cited as "Park Association."

4. Act of March 3, 1883 (U.S., *Statutes at Large,* vol. 22, p. 626).

5. Letter from secretary of the interior in answer to a Senate resolution of May 28, 1884; U.S., 48th Cong., 1st sess., Senate Ex. Doc. 207, pp. 1-3.

6. Curran, "Park Association," p. 5.

7. "The Editor's Excursion," *Livingston Enterprise,* Aug. 1 and 6, 1883.

8. From the issue of Sept. 3, 1883.

9. *Livingston Enterprise,* Jan. 5 and 18, 1884.

10. Ibid., Jan. 22, 1884.

11. Louis C. Cramton, *Early History of Yellowstone National Park and Its Relation to National Park Policies* (Washington, D.C.: Govt. Printing Office, 1932), p. 43, hereafter cited as *Early History.*

12. *Livingston Enterprise,* May 3 and 31, 1884. Of course, the opposition considered Senator George Graham Vest "a sort of chronic objector, a jack-in-the-box who pops up with a discordant cry on all occasions," yet they could not challenge him directly because his self-constituted guardianship was widely respected for its absolute sincerity and lack of self-interest. Thus, the railroad legislation was laid aside and made no more headway in that Congress.

13. The text of this bill, as passed by the Senate on March 6, 1884, was printed in full by *Forest and Stream,* March 13, 1884. An accompanying letter by Arnold Hague, geologist of the United States Geological Survey, commented on the advantages of Vest's legislation in providing additional area for watershed and wildlife habitat. The exclusion of railways from the Park was recommended, and the limitation of other developments was implied, particularly by this statement: "The park should be kept as a place of recreation and rest for those who can afford sufficient time to enjoy its benefits and reap the advantages of an outdoor life. The country already offers a sufficient number of resorts for grip-sack travelers who like to huddle together in large hotels and move with the crowd."

14. Cramton, *Early History,* pp. 43-44.

15. *Livingston Enterprise,* May 23, 1885.

16. "Congressman O'Neil Talks About the Railway to Cooke," *Livingston Enterprise,* July 11, 1885.

17. Cramton, *Early History,* p. 44.

18. "The Park Railroad Job," *Forest and Stream,* June 24, 1886.

19. Cramton, *Early History,* p. 45.

20. "Can They Hoodwink the House?" in the issue of February 17, 1887.

21. According to an undated clipping on page 48 of scrapbook no. 1, Yellowstone National Park Reference Library, a Livingston, Montana, committee raised $1,500 to support a lobby in Washington, D.C. Of that amount, $600 went to A. Vinnedge of Cooke City, $400 to J.R. King, and $500 to Judge Payson "for his services in behalf of the segregation measure."

22. Cramton, *Early History,* p. 46.

23. *Livingston Post,* Oct. 12, 1890.

24. Cramton, *Early History,* p. 47.

25. Ibid., p. 48.

26. Harold Duane Hampton, "Conservation and Cavalry: A Study of the Role of the United States Army in the Development of a National Park System, 1886-1917" (doctoral dissertation, University of Colorado, 1965), p. 229.

27. Cramton, *Early History,* p. 49.

28. Correspondence in the files of the Northern Pacific show that T.B. Casey suggested this idea to President Thomas F. Oakes in 1891. See Curran, "Park Association," p. 36.

29. From a summary of the development of the Yellowstone Park Hotel Company and Yellowstone Park Transportation Company, prepared by

Auditor E. Askevold, January 30, 1917, in file "President, 209B," Northern Pacific Railroad Company, St. Paul.

30. Minutes of the meeting of April 17, 1886, Yellowstone Park Association, Record Book no. 383, p. 21.

31. Ibid., p. 23.

32. *Livingston Enterprise,* July 7, 1888.

33. Yellowstone Park Association, Record Book no. 383, p. 34.

34. Curran, "Park Association," p. 11.

35. *Washington* (D.C.) *Post,* July 28, 1890.

36. Ibid., Aug. 10 and 27, 1890.

37. Curran, "Park Association," p. 11.

38. Ibid., p. 25.

39. From a copy of the agreement of the incorporation of the Yellowstone National Park Transportation Company, in file "President, 209B," Northern Pacific Railroad Company, St. Paul. Russell Harrison's part in this take-over is explained in the *Butte* (Mont.) *Miner,* Mar. 15, 1891.

40. *Washington Post,* May 8, 1892.

41. Curran, "Park Association," pp. 8 and 15.

42. Ibid., p. 5.

43. "Estimate of Gross Passenger Receipts from Yellowstone Park Business," by fiscal years from June 30, 1890, to June 30, 1896, in file "President, 209B," Northern Pacific Railroad Company, St. Paul.

44. Mellen to Dean, November 29, 1897, in file "President, 209A-1," Northern Pacific Railroad Company, St. Paul.

45. Yellowstone Park Association, balance sheet, July 31, 1897, and related papers, in file "President, 209B," Northern Pacific Railroad Company, St. Paul.

46. Mellen to Waters, May 18, 1899, in file "President, 209A-1," Northern Pacific Railroad Company, St. Paul.

47. Waters to Mellen, May 22, 1899, in file "President, 209A-1," Northern Pacific Railroad Company, St. Paul.

48. Telegrams, Mellen to Waters, July 21, 1899, and Mellen to Lamont, June 26, 1899, in file "President, 209A-1," Northern Pacific Railroad Company, St. Paul.

49. Reed to Mellen, April 4, 1901, in file "President, 209A-1," Northern Pacific Railroad Company, St. Paul.

50. Elliott to Child, September 22, 1905, in file "President, 209B," Northern Pacific Railroad Company, St. Paul.

51. Statement prepared by Auditor Askevold, January 30, 1907, in file "President, 209B," Northern Pacific Railroad Company, St. Paul.

52. Child to Lamar, December 21, 1911, in file "President, 209A," Northern Pacific Railroad Company, St. Paul.

53. Child to Lamar, December 23, 1911, in file "President, 209A," Northern Pacific Railroad Company, St. Paul.

54. Elliott to Child, July 13, 1913, in file "President, 209A," Northern Pacific Railroad Company, St. Paul.

55. Telegram, President J.M. Hannaford of the Northern Pacific to President William Sproule of the Southern Pacific, September 28, 1916, in file "President, 209B," Northern Pacific Railroad Company, St. Paul.

CHAPTER 14

1. U.S., 47th Cong., 2d sess., S. 2317, January 29, 1883. The *Avant Courier* issue quoted is Jan. 11, 1883.

2. U.S., *Statutes at Large,* vol. 17, chap. 24, sec. 1 and 2, p. 33, vol. 32, 33).

3. W.E. Strong, *A Trip to the Yellowstone National Park in July, August, and September, 1875* (Washington, D.C.,1876), pp. 91-92.

4. *Report Upon the Yellowstone National Park, to the Secretary of the Interior, for the Year 1877* (Washington, D.C.: Govt. Printing Office, 1877), p. 842.

5. William Ludlow, *Report of a Reconnaissance from Carroll, Montana Territory, on the Upper Missouri, to the Yellowstone National Park, and Return, Made in the summer of 1875* (Washington, D.C.: Govt. Printing Office, 1876), p. 37.

6. *Daily Graphic,* July 11, 1878.

7. "The Yellowstone National Park," *Bozeman* (Mont.) *Avant Courier,* Dec. 23, 1880.

8. David Starr Jordan, *The Days of a Man,* vol. 1 (New York: World Book Co., 1922), p. 315. Professor Baird was the scientist who established field study as an important method in botany and zoology; he was then secretary of the Smithsonian Institution. The congressman was Representative Courtland Cushing Matson (D) of Indiana.

9. Philip H. Sheridan, J.F. Gregory, and W.H. Forwood, *Report of an Exploration of Wyoming, Idaho, and Montana, in August and September 1882* (Washington, D.C.: Govt. Printing Office, 1882), pp. 17-18.

10. The new regulation was published in the *Bozeman Avant Courier,* Feb. 22, 1883; however, its failure to list those animals of "fang and claw," such as the bear, coyote, cougar, and wolf, was construed as proscription; so they were hunted for several years more.

11. *Bozeman Avant Courier,* Jan. 25, 1883.

12. *Livingston Enterprise,* Feb. 18, 1893. Ananias pretended to sell his lands for the benefit of the Church, but held back a portion (Acts 5:1-10).

13. "Report of Superintendent of Yellowstone National Park," in *Annual Report of the Secretary of the Interior for the Year 1891* (Washington, D.C.: Govt. Printing Office, 1891), p. 645.

14. Ibid., p. 646.

15. *Report of the Superintendent of the Yellowstone National Park to the Secretary of the Interior, 1892* (Washington, D.C.: Govt. Printing Office, 1892), p. 9.

16. Ibid., p. 10.

17. Emerson Hough, "Winter in the Rockies," *Chicago Tribune,* Dec. 23, 1894.

18. *Report of the Acting Superintendent of the Yellowstone National Park to the Secretary of the Interior, 1894* (Washington, D.C.: Govt. Printing Office, 1894), pp. 9-10, hereafter cited as *Acting Supt. Report for [year].*

19. Ibid.

20. For the record, the earliest known use of skis, or Norwegian snowshoes, in the Yellowstone country is the entry in A. Bart Henderson's diary for 1872, in which he mentions a Christmas trip from his ranch at present Stephens Creek to Bozeman "on a pair of 15 foot snowshoes" (p. 108).

21. *Acting Supt. Report for 1894*, p. 10.

22. In a letter to Captain George S. Anderson, January 21, 1895, Theodore Roosevelt writes: "The Club also passed a resolution to give a present to Scout Burgess. It preferred to put this in the form of a rifle or pair of glasses, or something of the kind, at a cost of $30 to $35. Will you tell me what you think Burgess would like? We would like to put his name on the gift." Doc. 1282, Yellowstone National Park Archives.

23. Thomas E. Hofer to Chester A. Lindsley, July 25, 1923; original in Yellowstone National Park Reference Library.

24. Letter to LeRoy Hill, February 5, 1927; original in Yellowstone National Park Reference Library. Ed Staley had bought Gilman Sawtell's ranch at Henrys Lake (now called Staley's Springs).

25. *Acting Supt. Report for 1894*, p. 11.

26. *Acting Supt. Report for 1895*, p. 13.

27. Henry Inman, *Buffalo Jones' Forty Years of Adventure* (Topeka, Kansas: Crane & Co., 1899), p. 263.

28. Ibid., p. 264.

29. *Acting Supt. Report for 1896*, p. 11.

30. Interview with Ernest Murri at Ashton, Idaho, May 5, 1968.

31. This permission assumed a written form in the revision of the Yellowstone Lake Boat Company's lease executed on January 21, 1897. Under Article 5 is the following statement:

> The party of the second part further agrees for the benefit of tourists in the park to place, maintain and exhibit on Dot Island in Yellowstone Lake during the tourist season, such buffalo and other game as it may be able to procure outside of the Yellowstone National Park, and said party of the second part is hereby authorized to range upon Dot Island such animals and the natural increase therefrom, and to winter said animals upon the herein demised tract of land near the Lake Hotel.

32. William Timmons, *Twilight on the Range* (Austin: University of Texas Press, 1962), pp. 66-69.

33. *Acting Supt. Report for 1897*, p. 9.

34. His commission, dated July 8, 1902, specified a salary of "Eighteen Hundred Dollars per Annum," and the accompanying letter from Secretary E.A. Hitchcock informed him: "Immediately upon receipt hereof you will proceed to the Yellowstone National Park and report to Major John Pitcher, U.S.A., Acting Superintendent of that reservation, for duty as Game Warden in the reservation; it is distinctly understood that your employment as warden is to be at the pleasure of the Secretary of the Interior." Letters received, vol. 4, p. 92, Yellowstone National Park Archives.

35. *Acting Supt. Report for 1902*, pp. 9-10.

36. Major John Pitcher to the military secretary, Department of Dakota, November 28, 1906; Letters Received, vol. 7, pp. 25-28, Yellowstone National Park Archives.

37. There were five scouts at that time; three were permanent: James McBride, R.A. Waagner, and James G. Morrison; and two were temporary: Samuel D. Graham and Peter Holt.

38. C.J. Jones to Major John Pitcher, July 5, 1903, Yellowstone National Park Archives.

39. In a letter of August 7, 1904, on this subject, Jones testily informed Major Pitcher that it was, in his opinion, "time to appeal to the American

people to dispense with military affairs in the Park, and turn it over to mounted police, appointed by a president who is so well equipped with good sense as to appoint men eminently fitted for such responsible vocations." Letters Received, vol. 6, pp. 60-64, Yellowstone National Park Archives.

40. Recorded by Newell F. Joyner, August 16, 1930. Copy in Yellowstone National Park Reference Library.

41. Letters Received, vol. 6, pp. 58-59 (July 6, 1905), Yellowstone National Park Archives.

42. Charles J. Jones to secretary of interior, September 5, 1905, with the secretary's reply of September 12. Letters Received, vol. 6, pp. 125, 142-43, Yellowstone National Park Archives.

43. The superintendent's "Journal" for the years 1903-21 indicates the scouts moved twenty-eight animals to the new enclosure on May 18, 1907 (p. 43); hereafter cited as Supt. "Journal."

44. Jas. S. Gibbs and John D. Ripley to Superintendent S.B.M. Young, June 12, 1907, with related telegrams. Box 33, Yellowstone National Park Archives.

45. Superintendent S.B.M. Young to Lieutenant A.B. Cox, Eighth Cavalry, August 7, 1907, with copies of two letters to E.C. Waters. Box 33, Yellowstone National Park Archives.

46. W.F. Scott to Superintendent S.B.M. Young, August 24, 1907 (filed with letters from T.S. Palmer and T. Gilbert Pearson on the same subject). Box 33, Yellowstone National Park Archives.

47. *Supt. Report for 1907,* p. 6.

48. Ibid. For correspondence relative to this subject, see Box 33, Yellowstone National Park Archives.

49. Acting superintendent to the agent of the Yellowstone Lake Boat Company, June 15, 1908; and Captain R. Bigford to acting superintendent, June 17, 1908. Box 33, Yellowstone National Park Archives.

50. Theodore Roosevelt, "Three Capital Books of the Wilderness," *The Outlook,* vol. 102 (November 30, 1912), pp. 712-15.

51. *Acting Supt. Report for 1911,* p. 10.

52. *Acting Supt. Report for 1912,* p. 11.

53. Walter Kittams, "Problem of Surplus Elk in Yellowstone National Park," mimeographed, 1948, in Yellowstone National Park Reference Library, p. 4.

54. *Acting Supt. for 1914,* Appendix A, pp. 24-25.

55. Chester A. Lindsley, "The Chronology of Yellowstone National Park, 1806 to 1939," typescript in Yellowstone National Park Reference Library, pp. 30-33.

56. From a meteorological summary prepared for the United States Weather Bureau station at Mammoth Hot Springs in 1927.

57. Aug. 18, 1885.

58. *Supt. Report for 1887,* p. 14.

59. *Supt. Report for 1889,* p. 22.

60. *Acting Supt. Report for 1896,* p. 12.

61. *Acting Supt. Report for 1897,* p. 9.

62. Henry T. Finck, "Yellowstone Park as a Summer Resort," *The Nation,* vol. 71, no. 1839 (September 27, 1900), p. 249. See also Supt. "Journal"

for 1901-3, November 18, 1901, p. 194. Item 143, Yellowstone National Park Archives.

63. Supt. "Journal," April 1, 1903, p. 248. Item 142, Yellowstone National Park Archives.

64. Theodore Roosevelt, *Outdoor Pastimes of an American Hunter* (New York: Charles Scribner's Sons, 1923), pp. 337-38.

65. Charles A. Heath, *A Trial of A Trail, Notes from the Journal of Charles A. Heath* (Chicago: Franklin Press, 1905), pp. 76-77.

66. President Theodore Roosevelt to Lieutenant General S.B.M. Young, January 22, 1908. Original in Yellowstone National Park Reference Library.

67. That figure was compiled from the annual reports of the superintendents, 1898-1918; since there was no information for the winter of 1915-16, the number killed could be greater.

68. *Acting Supt. Report for 1912*, p. 13.

69. *Acting Supt. Report for 1899*, p. 7.

70. *Acting Supt. Report for 1903*, pp. 5-6.

71. *Acting Supt. Report for 1904*, pp. 6-8.

72. *Acting Supt. Report for 1905*, p. 7.

73. *Acting Supt. Report for 1898*, p. 11.

74. Gardner Stilson Turrill, *A Tale of the Yellowstone; or, in a Wagon Through Western Wyoming and Wonderland* (Jefferson, Ia: G.S. Turrill Pub. Co., 1901), pp. 92-93.

75. *Acting Supt. Report for 1902*, pp. 6-7.

76. The original name of the body of water now called Squaw Lake.

77. From a conversation with Ned Frost, Jr., at Mammoth Hot Springs, June 27, 1968.

78. Herb French, formerly of Gardiner, Montana. His story of this incident was recorded in an interview with Henry Mallon and others at Mammoth Hot Springs, July 5, 1961. Audiotape 61-2, Yellowstone National Park Reference Library. The annual report (1916) submitted by Chester A. Lindsley, acting superintendent, also provides a brief account of the rampages of this bear (pp. 36-37).

79. This does not mean that dogs were particularly welcome in the Park. Dogs had evidently been under some restriction prior to the summer of 1897, when Colonel S.B.M. Young explained his tougher attitude:

> I allow no dogs to run loose on the Park roads because they scare away the wild animals which visitors are eager to see. Campers have been in the habit of putting their dogs in a wagon on passing a guard house, and letting them run as soon as out of sight. I ordered a few of these dogs to be shot, and that had a salutary effect.

Henry T. Finck, "Yellowstone Park in 1897," *The Nation,* (October 7, 1897), p. 277.

80. T.A. Jaager, "Death Gulch A Natural Bear Trap," *Appleton's Popular Science Monthly,* vol. 54 (February 1899), p. 475. He is quoting from an article published in *Science,* February 15, 1889.

81. Frank H. Knowlton, "A Gulch of Death," *Popular Science News* (from an undated clipping in Scrapbook no. 2, Yellowstone National Park Reference Library).

82. "Niagara Eclipsed," *Virginia City* (Mont.) *Tri Weekly Post,* Feb. 4, 1868.

83. Charles W. Cook et al., *The Valley of the Upper Yellowstone*, A.L. Haines, ed. (Norman: University of Oklahoma Press, 1965), p. 44.

84. "Journal of the Yellowstone Expedition of 1866 Under Captain Jeff Standifer . . . ," copy in the Yellowstone National Park Reference Library. See the entry for August 31, 1867 (page 43, as transcribed).

85. F.V. Hayden, *Preliminary Report of the United States Geological Survey of Montana and Portions of Adjacent Territories* (Washington, D.C.: Govt. Printing Office, 1872), pp. 381-82.

86. *Acting Supt. Report for 1889*, pp. 22-23.

87. R.J. Fromm, "An Open History of Fish and Fish Planting in Yellowstone National Park" [1939] manuscript in Yellowstone National Park Reference Library, pp. 8 and 18, hereafter cited as "Open History."

88. David Starr Jordan, *Reconnaissance of the Streams and Lakes of the Yellowstone National Park, Wyoming, in Interests of the United States Fish Commission*, vol. 9 (Washington, D.C.: Govt. Printing Office, 1890), 63 pp.

89. Fromm, "Open History," pp. 10 and 17. Cf. James R. Simon, *Yellowstone Fishes* (Yellowstone Library and Museum Assoc., 1962), pp. 20 and 22-23, hereafter cited as *Fishes*.

90. Simon, *Fishes*, p. 12.

91. Osborne Russell, *Journal of a Trapper*, Aubrey L. Haines, ed. (Lincoln: University of Nebraska Press, 1965), p. 43.

92. "Two Ocean Pass," *Popular Science Monthly*, vol. 47 (June 1895), p. 183.

93. "Mysterious Music in Yellowstone Park," *Literary Digest*, vol. 90, no. 12 (September 18, 1926), p. 26. See also Hugh M. Smith, "Mysterious Acoustic Phenomena in Yellowstone National Park," *Science*, N.S. vol. 63, no. 1641 (June 11, 1926), pp. 586-87.

94. The abundance of fish inhabiting this weedy lake of a few acres extent was noted by an army surgeon in 1880. S. Weir Mitchell was amazed when soldiers of his party's escort were able to take trout weighing five pounds in such numbers as to nearly swamp their raft. See "Through Yellowstone Park to Fort Custer," *Lippincott's Magazine*, vol. 26 (July 1880), p. 34.

95. Fromm, "Open History," p. 16.

96. Ibid., pp. 19-20.

97. *Acting Supt. Report for 1897*, p. 17.

98. *Supt. Report for 1908*, p. 12.

99. James B. Trefethen, *Crusade for Wildlife* (Harrisburg, Pa.: Stockpole Co., 1961), p. 4, hereafter cited as *Crusade*.

100. *Bozeman Avant Courier*, Jan. 11, 1883.

101. Senator George F. Edmunds (Vermont) introduced legislation in 1884 proposing "a forest reserve" in Montana Territory, but he was no more successful than his friend, Senator Vest. See *Livingston Enterprise*, Mar. 4 and June 14, 1884.

102. Trefethen, *Crusade*, p. 48.

103. James D. Richardson, *A Compilation of the Messages and Papers of the Presidents, 1789-1902*, vol. 9 (Bureau of National Literature and Art, 1903), pp. 142-43 and 155-56, hereafter cited as *Compilation*. The second proclamation, September 10, 1891, corrected deficiencies in the description of the tract.

104. *Acting Supt. Report for 1894*, p. 6.

105. Trefethen, *Crusade,* p. 49.

106. Richardson, *Compilation,* p. 735.

107. "The Dawn of Conservation," *American Forests,* vol. 41, no. 9 (September 1935), pp. 446-49. See also *Rules and Regulations Governing Forest Reserves Established Under Section 24 of the Act of March 3, 1901* (Washington, D.C.: Govt. Printing Office, April 4, 1900), 17 pp.

108. *Acting Supt. Report for 1898,* p. 11.

109. Ibid., p. 10.

110. Richardson, *Compilation,* vol. 10, pp. 479-84.

111. A.A. Anderson, *Experiences and Impressions* (New York: Macmillan Co., 1933), pp. 380-81.

112. *Acting Supt. Report for 1903,* p. 5.

CHAPTER 15

1. "Yellowstone's Semi-Centennial," *Western Magazine* 17, no. 2 (February 1, 1921): 29.

2. As first used, the term was no compliment, which the editor of the *Livingston* (Mont.) *Enterprise* indicated when he said: "Names change, but characters do not; the 'dude' is only a second-hand, small-type edition of the serious swell whom Beau Brummell knew and laughed at." (See the issue of October 15, 1883.) An English tourist of 1886 saw the dude as only "the American equivalent for Masher, only 'more so.'" However, time and common usage soon mellowed the term into a mere indication that one was able and inclined to travel first-class, and it is thus used here.

3. From "Slang Words and Phrases," *Livingston Enterprise* Sept. 22, 1883.

4. Charles Van Tassell, *Truthful Lies,* 2d ed. (Bozeman, Mont.: privately published, 1913), pp. 4-5, hereafter cited as *Truthful Lies.*

5. Rudyard Kipling, *From Sea to Sea* (Garden City, N.Y.: Doubleday, Page & Co., 1920), p. 62, hereafter cited as *Sea to Sea.*

6. H.T. Finck, "A Week in Yellowstone Park," *The Nation* 45, no. 1157 (September 11, 1887): 167.

7. During the brief existence of the Yellowstone Park Improvement Company, the transportation business was handled under its franchise by Wakefield and Hoffman. The Yellowstone Park Association, which took over the park hotels in 1886, continued the arrangement with George W. Wakefield, who operated alone and in various partnerships until 1891, when the transportation privilege was taken from the association and given to the "syndicate" formed by Silas S. Huntley and eventually perfected as the Yellowstone Park Transportation Company.

8. Kipling, *Sea to Sea,* p. 75.

9. Told by Jack Ellis Haynes in 1961.

10. Georgina M. Synge, *A Ride through Wonderland* (London: Sampson Low, Marston & Co., 1892), pp. 122-23, hereafter cited as *Ride through Wonderland.*

11. Ray S. Baker, "A Place of Marvels," *Century Magazine* 66, no. 4 (August 1903): 490.

12. Ibid., p. 485.

13. Kipling, *Sea to Sea,* p. 75.

14. Synge, *Ride through Wonderland,* p. 60.

15. *Yellowstone Park Manual and Guide* (Mammoth Hot Springs, Wyo., July 1, 1885), 4 pp.

16. *Livingston Enterprise,* Aug. 1, 1885.

17. Synge, *Ride through Wonderland,* pp. 129-30.

18. The vehicles used on the trip around the loop were designed particularly for sightseeing in Yellowstone Park, having open sides and forward-facing seats; hence the name Yellowstone Wagons. The drivers were required to keep their places in line and to hold their horses to a walk, so that as much as an hour might elapse between the starting of the first and last coach of a string of thirty or forty vehicles.

19. The reckless charioteer of the Bible, mentioned in II Kings 9:20: "and the driving is like the driving of Jehu the son of Nimshi; for he driveth furiously."

20. Van Tassell, *Truthful Lies,* pp. 9-10.

21. Ibid., p. 7.

22. Interview with Henry Mallon and others at Mammoth Hot Springs, July 5, 1961. Audiotape no. 61-2, Yellowstone National Park Reference Library.

23. The practice of naming park thermal features as though they were manifestations of hell or the property of the devil originated with the Washburn expedition of 1870. The idea so fascinated those generations exposed to "hell-fire and brimstone" theology that it was over-used. The devil once had proprietary right to thirty-one features (he has since been divested of all but three—Devils Thumb, Devils Den, and Devils Kitchen), while hell was coupled with five more features.

24. The Norris Lunch Station.

25. The Trout Creek Lunch Station was also known as "Larry's" during his tenure there, and, for a time, the wretched excuse for a hotel that preceded Old Faithful Inn was so-called (though more often known as the Shack Hotel). Larry was the first manager of the Old Faithful Inn (1904). He retired from the Park after that season, possibly because he did not feel he was being paid enough. A letter to the manager of the association stated his case: "I respectfully ask increase of salary for season 1899. I have served YPA 12 years, 1 at Mammoth Hotel, 4 at Trout Creek Station, 1 at Thumb Station, 6 at Norris Station. How I have handled the Business you Sir is the Judge. I am practically speaking devoting my entire time to the service of Co. Hoping you will see to making Salary so I can live on it." Larry Mathews to J.H. Dean, October 1, 1898, Northern Pacific Railroad files, "President, 210A."

26. Henry D. Sedgewick, Jr., "On Horseback through Yellowstone," *World's Work* 6, no. 2 (June 1903): 3575.

27. Kipling, *Sea to Sea,* p. 100.

28. Mary Reeves to her mother, August 2, 1889, p. 2. Manuscript file, Yellowstone National Park Reference Library.

29. C.S. Batterman to Captain Anderson, August 2, 1893. Doc. 681, Yellowstone National Park Archives.

30. Interview with R.M. Shield at Mammoth Hot Springs, August 29, 1962.

31. Kipling, *Sea to Sea,* pp. 83-84.

32. John T. McCutcheon, *Drawn from Memory* (New York: Bobbs-Merrill Co., 1950), pp. 76-77.

33. Information from Jack Ellis Haynes, November 10, 1961.

34. Carter H. Harrison, *A Summer's Outing* (Chicago: Donohue, Henneberry & Co., 1891), p. 70, hereafter cited as *Summer's Outing.*

35. Marshall formed a partnership with George G. Henderson, probably early in 1884, and sold out to him in May 1885. The following month, Henderson entered a partnership with Henry Klamer, son-in-law of George L. Henderson who organized the Cottage Hotel Association. When George G. gave up his interest in the hotel, it passed under the control of the Cottage Hotel Association and was sold to the Yellowstone Park Association in 1889, along with the larger hotel at Mammoth Hot Springs.

36. *Report of the Superintendent of the Yellowstone National Park to the Secretary of the Interior, 1888* (Washington, D.C.: Govt. Printing Office, 1888),p. 11,hereafter cited as *Supt. Report for [year].*

37. O.S.T. Drake, "A Lady's Trip to the Yellowstone Park," *Every Girl's Annual* (London: Hatchard's, 1887), p. 348.

38. H.T. Finck, "Yellowstone Park in 1897," *The Nation* 65, no. 1684 (October 7, 1897): 277.

39. "Uncle Sam's Big Menagerie," *Sundance* (Wyo.) *Gazette,* Nov. 25, 1898.

40. Information from miscellaneous items collected by the author.

41. Horace Sutton, "The Bear Facts," *Saturday Review* 38, no. 28 (July 9, 1955): 29.

42. *Report of the Acting Superintendent of the Yellowstone National Park to the Secretary of the Interior, 1904* (Washington, D.C.: Govt. Printing Office, 1904), p. 9, hereafter cited as *Acting Supt. Report for [year].*

43. Michael Kley, *The Grand Old Gal of Yellowstone.* Yellowstone Park Company leaflet (author's private collection), p. 4.

44. Carl E. Schmide, *A Western Trip* (Detroit, Mich.: Herold Press, 1910), p. 30, hereafter cited as *Western Trip.*

45. Owen Wister, "Old Yellowstone Days," *Harper's Monthly Magazine,* March 1936, p. 474.

46. Synge, *Ride through Wonderland,* p. 62.

47. "Blythe Tells Funny Stories," *Livingston Enterprise,* Sept. 13, 1911.

48. "Dudes Are Amused," *Gardiner* (Mont.) *Wonderland,* Aug. 21, 1902.

49. Henry Del Jenkins, "The Lucky Cowboy," manuscript, pp. 148-49. Audiotape of the manuscript (no. 61-2) is in Yellowstone National Park Reference Library.

50. Interview with Henry Mallon and others at Mammoth Hot Springs, July 5, 1961. Audiotape no. 61-2, Yellowstone National Park Reference Library.

51. Interview with Henry Del Jenkins at Jackson, Wyo., July 3, 1961.

52. Mallon interview.

53. This was a clever play upon the vessel's past. It *had* sunk in Lake Michigan prior to being placed on Yellowstone Lake; thus, it had been raised. During its years on Yellowstone Lake the little vessel performed without mishap.

54. The *Zillah* was 81 feet long and 14 feet in the beam, with a capacity of 120 persons.

55. Schmide, *Western Trip,* p. 43.

56. "Report of Superintendent of Yellowstone National Park," August 15, 1891, in *Annual Report of the Secretary of the Interior for the Year 1891* (Washington, D.C.: Govt. Printing Office, 1891), pp. 642-43.

57. *Supt. Report for 1904*, p. 9.

58. Francis Lynn Turpin, "A Trip through Yellowstone Park, 1895," manuscript, Montana State University Library, Bozeman, p. 32.

59. Louis Miller Henely, *Letters from the Yellowstone* (Grinnell, Ia.: Ray & Frisbie, 1914), p. 15.

60. The annual report issued jointly by D.W. Wear and Captain Moses Harris in 1886 notes that on May 27 of that year "permission was granted Mr. Gibson to erect a temporary building to be used for hotel purposes at the Grand Canon . . . with the understanding that it should be removed on or before the 1st day of August, 1886." It was not removed, and continued in use until 1891, when Captain Anderson could at last report, "The hotel at the Canon is completed; is well and comfortably kept, but is a most unsightly edifice." (*Supt. Report for 1891*, p. 642.)

61. In a fifteen-page booklet entitled *A Miracle in Hotel Building*, published by the Yellowstone Park Hotel Company in 1912 (in author's private collection), J.H. Raftery describes the construction of the large hotel during a Yellowstone winter. It is a story of momumental ingenuity; of the hauling of a mountain of materials and supplies on horse-drawn sleighs from the railhead at Gardiner, of nails being heated on the kitchen ranges for use in frigid temperatures, and of baseball games played on skis for recreation.

62. *Supt. Report for 1890*, p. 10.

63. Harrison, *Summer's Outing*, pp. 80-81.

64. Reeves to mother, pp. 2-3.

65. The statement of H.T. Finck in "Yellowstone Park as a Summer Resort," *The Nation* (September 27, 1900): 249-50, that the trail was an innovation since his last visit in 1897, and Edward Moorman's recollection of helping to rebuild the trail in 1899, would indicate its original establishment was in 1898. See Yellowstone Park Camps History, April 2, 1954, mimeographed, untitled, Yellowstone National Park Reference Library, pp. 4 and 5.

66. Wister, "Old Yellowstone Days," p. 476.

67. Jenkins interview.

68. Despite the difference in names, the two enterprises mentioned here represent a continuous business operation which, though it passed through several reorganizations, was yet under the management of one family, a group best designated as the Silas Huntley—Harry Child—William Nichols interest.

69. William Wallace Wylie, untitled history prepared in 1926. Manuscript, copy provided by Montana State University, Bozeman, pp. 10-14.

70. This venture is mentioned frequently in *Bozeman* (Mont.) *Avant Courier*, Apr. 7, 1881 to Mar. 2, 1882.

71. *Yellowstone National Park; or, The Great American Wonderland* (Kansas City: Ramsey, Millett & Hudson, 1882), 99 pp. See page 19 in the Wylie manuscript (cited in note 69) for the origin of this guidebook, which was *not* the Park's first.

72. Wylie manuscript, p. 20.

73. *Supt. Report for 1893*, pp. 9-10.

74. Henely, *Letters from Yellowstone*, p. 29.

75. M.P. Skinner, Long Beach, Calif., to C.P. Russell, Berkeley, Calif., January 25, 1932. Copy in Yellowstone National Park files.

76. Anecdote related by Jack Ellis Haynes, May 26, 1961.

77. See page 3 of Moorman work cited in note 65.

78. Ibid., p. 7.

79. Ibid., p. 9.

80. Jenkins, "Lucky Cowboy," p. 141.

81. From an item in *Montana Standard,* Sept. 14, 1966, p. 1. The figure for 1968 showed a further improvement, dropping to 5.0.

82. Interview with Raymond G. Little at Gallatin Gateway, Mont., April 12, 1961.

83. Interview with Fred Bonnell at Mammoth Hot Springs, September 1, 1963. Jenkins recalled this incident in the interview cited in note 82, remarking, "All of us fellows laughed about that. You can imagine how that'd be, that team tryin' to make that quick turn there and fallin' down!"

84. Jenkins interview.

85. Yellowstone Park Transportation Company, file A 148. Copy furnished by Hugh Galusha, Helena, Mont., January 3, 1964.

86. Ibid.

87. Wheeler to Chittenden, September 4, 1913. Copy in Yellowstone National Park Reference Library.

88. Jack Ellis Haynes, "Yellowstone's Stage Holdups," *Brand Book* (Denver, Colo.: Westerners, 1952); also presented as *Yellowstone Stage Holdups* (Bozeman, Mont.: Haynes Studios, 1959), 30 pp., illus.

89. From a reminiscence of Charles J. Smith, recorded at Zion National Park, Utah, April 1952.

90. Quoted from Hiram M. Chittenden, "Echoes on Frontier Days—Holdups," manuscript, n.d., Yellowstone National Park Reference Library.

91. From a copy included in *Yellowstone Stage Holdups,* pp. 18-20. The misspellings are in the original.

92. W.L. Allinder to Joseph Joffe, May 3, 1946. Original in Yellowstone National Park files.

93. "Caught! The Lone Highwayman of Yellowstone," *Denver Post,* Jan. 5, 1916.

94. Ibid.

95. "Denver Man Arrested As Park Bandit Who Robbed 15 Stages in Yellowstone," *Denver Post,* May 22, 1915.

96. Mrs. E.A. Stone, *Uinta County, Wyoming: Its Place in History* (Laramie, Wyo.: Laramie Printing Co., 1924), p. 235.

97. Ibid.

98. *Yellowstone Stage Holdups,* p. 27.

99. David M. Steele, *Going Abroad Overland* (New York: G.P. Putnam's Sons, 1917), p. 102.

100. Francis M. Gibson, pocket diary kept on a trip through Yellowstone National Park, August 7 to 27, 1882, original in Yellowstone National Park Reference Library, pp. 44-45.

101. Fred G. Smith, *Impressions* (Minneapolis: Augsburg Publishing House, c. 1925), p. 100.

102. Wheeler, "Yellowstone's Semi-Centennial,", p. 29.

CHAPTER 16

1. Carl E. Schmide, *A Western Trip* (Detroit, Mich.: Herold Press, 1910), p. 16. This account covers a trip through the Park in September, 1901.

2. Records of the United States Army Command (Army Posts), Record Group 98, National Archives, Washington, D.C.

3. "Report of the Superintendent of Yellowstone National Park," August 15, 1891, in *Annual Report of the Secretary of the Interior for 1891* (Washington, D.C.: Govt. Printing Office, 1892), p. 641.

4. "Early Pictures, Government Buildings, 1886 to 1912," an illustrated maintenance record, prepared by the Office of Quartermaster, Fort Yellowstone, March 13, 1909. Item 167, Yellowstone National Park Archives.

5. John L. White, "D.J. 'Kid' O'Malley," *Montana* 17, no. 3 (July 1967), p. 62.

6. C. Hanford Henderson, "Through the Yellowstone on Foot," *Outing* (May 1899), p. 161.

7. Hiram M. Chittenden, "Annual Report Upon the Construction, Repair, and Maintenance of Roads and Bridges in the Yellowstone National Park," Appendix GGG in *Annual Report of the Chief of Engineers for 1903* (Washington, D.C.: Govt. Printing Office, 1903), p. 2887, hereafter cited as "Chittenden Annual Report." An interesting feature of the fountain was a bronze cupid whose upturned mouth was the orifice through which the water was sprayed, and, when the fountain was done away with in the course of construction of a parking area for the coffee shop, the cupid was reinstalled in the small stream beside the powerhouse. It was finally carried off in a scrap metal drive during World War II.

8. *Report of the Acting Superintendent of the Yellowstone National Park to the Secretary of the Interior, 1903* (Washington, D.C.: Govt. Printing Office, 1903), p. 3, hereafter cited as *Acting Supt. Report for [year];* and *Gardiner* (Mont.) *Wonderland,* Aug. 20, 1903.

9. Mr. Manning's report is Appendix A, pp. 2894-98, in "Chittenden Annual Report."

10. "Chittenden Annual Report," p. 2888.

11. Interview with Henry Mallon and others, July 5, 1961, at Mammoth Hot Springs. Audiotape no. 61-2, Yellowstone National Park Reference Library.

12. The original cost of the structures was obtained from the maintenance record of the Post Quartermaster (see note 4); incomplete figures for the utilities show a cost of $56,000 for the water system prior to construction of the Gardner River to Glen Creek ditch (at least a $10,000 project), which would leave only $9,000 for the rudimentary sewage system. No cost figures are available for the grounds work, much of which was accomplished with soldier and prisoner labor, but the subsequent request for $4,000 for annual maintenance would indicate the estimated first cost is reasonable.

13. Francis B. Heitman, *Historical Register and Dictionary of the United States Army,* vol. 1 (Washington, D.C.: Govt. Printing Office, 1903), pp. 65-68.

14. Glen Dines, *Long Knife* (New York: Macmillan Co., 1916), p. 6.

15. Thomas E. Coyne to Assistant Park Naturalist George C. Crowe, Yellowstone National Park, February 2, 1933.

16. Dines, *Long Knife,* p. 10.

17. Rudyard Kipling, *From Sea to Sea* (Garden City, N.Y.: Doubleday, Page & Co., 1920), pp. 75, 82, and 94, hereafter cited as *Sea to Sea.*

18. See Appendix A, Part III, for biographical data on the military superintendents.

19. Kipling, *Sea to Sea,* p. 77.

20. W.H. Walsh, "Bath's Soldier Boy," *Bath* (Maine) *Independent,* Dec. 1895, hereafter cited as "Soldier Boy."

21. *Report of the Superintendent of the Yellowstone National Park to the Secretary of the Interior, 1886* (Washington, D.C.: Govt. Printing Office, 1886), p. 12, hereafter cited as *Supt. Report for [year].*

22. "Lovell Man Recalls Early-Day Work on Yellowstone Park Roads," in Yellowstone National Park Reference Library clipping file, identified only as from the *Billings* (Mont.) *Gazette,* 1956.

23. Letter to the Adjutant General of the Army, July 14, 1897. Letters Sent, vol. 6, pp. 286-87, Yellowstone National Park Archives.

24. *Acting Supt. Report for 1897,* p. 9. The sealing of firearms began at least as early as 1889. See Georgina M. Synge, *A Ride through Wonderland* (London: Sampson, Low, Marston & Co., 1892), p. 35.

25. Walsh, "Soldier Boy."

26. The first rifle range was on Elk Plaza, a mile north of the fort, but it was replaced after 1900 by a more adequate installation at the mouth of the Gardner River. The detachment stationed at the Lower Geyser Basin had a rifle range west of the Firehole River, near the mouth of Sentinel Creek.

27. *Gardiner Wonderland,* Jan. 29, 1903.

28. Walsh, "Soldier Boy."

29. "Many Churches Unite in Dedication of Yellowstone Park Chapel," *Livingston Enterprise,* June 26, 1913. For additional information on the chapel, see *A History of the Yellowstone National Park Chapel, 1913-1963,* prepared by Aubrey L. Haines for the Superintendent's Church Committee on the occasion of the Fiftieth Anniversary, 1963, Yellowstone National Park Reference Library.

30. Less questionable—morally and historically—was Calamity's sale of postcard views of herself in the Park. This was allowed by Special Permit no. 1, issued by order of Colonel S.B.M. Young on July 19, 1897. The permit is recorded, of all places, in a ledger containing a "Record of Property Purchased, Expended" (see item 62, p. 155, Yellowstone National Park Archives).

31. "Record Book of Interments at the Post Cemetery, at Fort Yellowstone, Wyo.," Item 155, pp. 1-5, Yellowstone National Park Archives.

32. There was no easy way to reach a county seat in Wyoming prior to the opening of the east entrance road in 1903. A marriage contracted in the Park, after a Wyoming license has been obtained, is legally binding.

33. Mrs. A.A. King to the author, September 7, 1966.

34. Emerson Hough, "Winter in the Rockies," *Chicago Tribune,* Dec. 23, 1894.

35. "Thoughts of Old," *Livingston Post,* Jan. 11, 1900.

36. Anecdotes told by Jack Ellis Haynes, Apr. 19, 1961.

37. *Acting Supt. Report for 1895,* p. 7.

38. *Harper's Weekly* 39 (January 12, 1895), p. 36.

39. See the historic structures report, *Norris Soldier Station, Yellowstone National Park* (Washington, D.C.: National Park Service, 1969), 47 pp., illus.

40. W.H. Bassett to Captain Harris, July 23, 1888. Doc. 654, Yellowstone National Park Archives.

41. Mrs. A.A. King, letter of September 7, 1966.

42. *Acting Supt. Report for 1904,* p. 13.

43. Circular, issued by the commanding officer, Fort Yellowstone, May 20, 1906, and forwarded to all stations the following day.

44. Mrs. A.A. King to the author, July 20, 1966.

45. Mode Wineman, "Through Yellowstone National Park into Jackson Hole Country," personal journal of a trip in 1908; original in Yellowstone National Park Reference Library, p. 22, hereafter cited as "Through Yellowstone."

46. Issued May 20, 1906.

47. *Rules, Regulations and Instructions, for the information and guidance of officers and enlisted men of the United States Army, and of the scouts doing duty in the Yellowstone National Park* (Washington, D.C.: Govt. Printing Office, 1907), 35 pp.

48. Wineman, "Through Yellowstone," p. 24.

49. *Supt. Report for 1893,* p. 7.

50. Hough, "Winter in the Rockies."

51. *Acting Supt. Report for 1899,* map.

52. Quoted by Dorr G. Yeager in "Some Old Timers of the Yellowstone" (1929), typescript in Yellowstone National Park Reference Library, pp. 4-5.

53. Charles Marble, "Fifty Years in and Around Yellowstone Park, and Miscellaneous Notes" (1932), typescript in Yellowstone National Park Reference Library, p. 6.

54. *Acting Supt. Report for 1895,* p. 7.

55. The sources used here were Elwood Hofer, "Yellowstone Park Notes," *Forest and Stream,* December 19, 1897; *Acting Supt. Report for 1898,* p. 26; and George Whittaker, "Scout's Diary . . . December 19, 1897 to May 29, 1898," original in Yellowstone National Park Archives, pp. 1-5.

56. Information recorded by Moorman. "Yellowstone Park Camps History," typescript dated April 2, 1954, p. 11, in Yellowstone National Park Reference Library; and the author's notes on an interview with Lee L. Coleman at Mammoth Hot Springs, March 20, 1961.

57. Interview with Raymond G. Little at Gallatin Gateway, April 21, 1961.

58. From a tape recorded by Harry Liek, William Wiggins, Herman Biastoch, John Bauman, Rudy Grimm, Bill Wright, and Bob Robinson, at the retirement of Harry Liek, no date. Tape in Yellowstone National Park Reference Library.

59. Thomas M. Connery, "The Winter Tragedy of the Yellowstone," *Wide World Magazine* (June 1919), pp. 145-46, hereafter cited as "Winter Tragedy."

60. Ibid., p. 143.

61. Corporal John Kellner, Troop I, Sixth Cavalry, to Captain George Anderson, Fort Yellowstone, March 29, 1891. Original in Yellowstone National Park Archives.

62. Connery, "Winter Tragedy," p. 147.

63. Colonel L. M. Brett to the secretary of the Yellowstone Park Hotel Company, December 1, 1912. Box 68, Yellowstone National Park Archives. The details of this affair are available in the statements of the soldiers concerned.

64. Dean to Mellen, June 19, 1900, in file "President, 210A," Northern Pacific Railroad Company, St. Paul.

65. Memorandum for United States Commissioner Meldrum, October 15, 1915, Yellowstone National Park Archives.

66. Special Report to the Commanding Officer, Fort Yellowstone, Wyoming, August 16, 1897, Yellowstone National Park Archives (filed with monthly reports, Canyon Station).

67. The following are the sources of information used in compiling the story of the holdup: J.E. Haynes, interview with John W. Meldrum at Mammoth Hot Springs, October 14, 1925; an abstract of Judge Meldrum's record of the preliminary hearing in the case of *United States v. Gus Smitzer, alias Little Gus, and George Reeb, alias Morphine Charley;* and "Holdups in Y. N. Park," and related correspondence. All are in the Yellowstone National Park Reference Library.

68. Jefferson Jones quotes this legend in discussing the article "Yellowstone Stage Holdups" by Jack Ellis Haynes in *Brand Book* (Denver, Colo.: Westerners, 1952). Jones' paper is in the Jack Ellis Haynes Collection, Montana State University Library, Bozeman, Mont.

69. Chester A. Lindsley, "Annual Report of the Supervisor of Yellowstone National Park—1916," typed copy in Yellowstone National Park Reference Library, p. 46.

70. Tom Stout, *Montana, Its Story and Biography,* vol. 1 (Chicago: American Historical Society, 1921), p. 480.

71. T.E. Hofer to H.M. Albright, March 27, 1926, Yellowstone National Park Reference Library.

CHAPTER 17

1. U.S., *Statutes at Large,* vol. 22, p. 626.

2. William Ludlow, *Report of a Reconnaissance from Carroll, Montana Territory, on the Upper Missouri, to the Yellowstone National Park, and Return, Made in the Summer of 1875* (Washington, D.C.: Govt. Printing Office, 1876), p. 38.

3. Philip H. Sheridan et al., *Report of Lieut. General P.H. Sheridan, Dated September 20, 1881, of His Expedition Through the Big Horn Mountains, Yellowstone National Park, etc.* (Washington, D.C.: Govt. Printing Office, 1882), p. 9. General Sheridan's recommendations were evidently available prior to publication of his official report, since the *Bozeman Avant Courier* commented favorably on them in the issue of Dec. 22, 1881.

4. "Park Appropriations and Appointments," *Bozeman Avant Courier,* June 7, 1883.

5. *Livingston Enterprise,* July 26, 1883.

6. Ibid., Jan. 12, 1884.

7. Ibid., Jan. 26, 1884. See also issues of Oct. 3, Nov. 21, and Dec. 5, 1883.

8. "Up-River Mishaps," *Livingston Enterprise,* Feb. 23, 1884. See also issue of Feb. 26.

9. "Doings in Wonderland," *Livingston Enterprise,* June 13, 1885.

10. *Livingston Enterprise,* Sept. 19, 1885.

11. Secretary of interior to Superintendent Wear, May 25, 1886. Doc. 184, Yellowstone National Park Archives.

12. *Report of the Superintendent of the Yellowstone National Park to the Secretary of the Interior, 1887,* (Washington, D.C.: Govt. Printing Office, 1887), p. 15.

13. *Annual Report of the Chief of Engineers for 1891* (Washington, D.C.:

Govt. Printing Office, 1890), Appendix GGG, p. 3934, hereafter cited as *Report of Engineers for [year]*.

14. Ibid.

15. This launch was the second boat placed on Lake Yellowstone by the Corps of Engineers. Foreman Lamartine built a small sailboat named *Pinafore* in 1885, but it was never mentioned again after its trial voyage that year. See *Livingston Enterprise,* Aug. 22, 1885.

16. Hiram M. Chittenden, "The Yellowstone," a manuscript written after 1915 (hereafter cited as "Yellowstone") and published in *H.M. Chittenden, A Western Epic,* Bruce LeRoy, ed. (Tacoma: Washington State Historical Society, 1961), pp. 15-22, hereafter cited as *Chittenden*. The quotation is taken from the typescript in Yellowstone National Park Reference Library, p. 1.

17. Ibid., p. 16.

18. Major W.A. Jones to Captain G.S. Anderson, September 17, 1891. Doc. 1070, Yellowstone National Park Archives.

19. *Report of the Acting Superintendent of the Yellowstone National Park to the Secretary of the Interior, 1893* (Washington, D.C.: Govt. Printing Office, 1893), p. 3, hereafter cited as *Acting Supt. Report for [year]*.

20. Ibid., p. 8.

21. *Acting Supt. Report for 1894*, p. 7.

22. *Acting Supt. Report for 1896*, p. 7.

23. Ibid., p. 4.

24. *Acting Supt. Report for 1897*, p. 24.

25. *Acting Supt. Report for 1898*, p. 13.

26. Chittenden, "Yellowstone," p. 6.

27. *Report of Engineers for 1899*, Appendix EEE, p. 3867.

28. *Report of Engineers for 1901*, Appendix FFF, p. 3781.

29. Aubrey L. Haines, "The Bridge That Jack Built, *Yellowstone Nature Notes* 21, no. 1 (1947), pp. 1-4.

30. *Report of Engineers for 1902*, Appendix FFF, pp. 3038-39.

31. Ibid., pp. 3039-40.

32. "Dudes are Amused," *Gardiner Wonderland,* Aug. 21, 1902.

33. *Report of Engineers for 1903*, Appendix GGG, p. 2889.

34. "Roosevelt's Life in the Wilderness," *New York World,* Apr. 24, 1903.

35. Theodore Roosevelt, *Outdoor Pastimes of an American Hunter* (New York: Charles Scribner's Sons, 1923), p. 328.

36. From a note signed "Scott," sent to Joe Joffe, assistant to the superintendent, February 28, 1929; original in Yellowstone National Park files.

37. Theodore Roosevelt, *An Autobiography* (New York: Charles Scribner's Sons, 1923), p. 321.

38. Louise Miller Henely, *Letters From the Yellowstone* (Grinnell, Ia.: Ray & Frisbie, 1914), p. 12.

39. Bill Scales to the chief ranger, Yellowstone National Park, May 20, 1963; original in Yellowstone National Park Reference Library.

40. Roosevelt, *Autobiography,* p. 115.

41. *New York World,* Apr. 24, 1903.

42. Henry Mallon in an interview at Mammoth Hot Springs, July 5, 1961. Audiotape no. 61-2, Yellowstone National Park Reference Library.

43. "A Great Figure of the Yellowstone—General Hiram M. Chittenden," *Livingston Enterprise,* June 30, 1923.

44. "The Corner Stone Was Laid," *Gardiner Wonderland*, Apr. 30, 1903.

45. Edward H. Moorman, "Yellowstone Park Camps History," typescript dated April 2, 1954, p. 7, Yellowstone National Park Reference Library.

46. *Chittenden*, p. 26.

47. "Uncle John Yancey," *Gardiner Wonderland*, May 5, 1903.

48. Carl E. Schmide, *A Western Trip* (Detroit, Mich.: Herold Press, 1910), pp. 59-60.

49. John Pitcher to John Yancey, May 31, 1902, Letters Sent, vol. 11, p. 396, Yellowstone National Park Archives.

50. Interview with Henry Mallon, Herb French, and others, July 5, 1961, at Mammoth Hot Springs. Audiotape no. 61-2, Yellowstone National Park Reference Library.

51. Details of the construction work have been taken from an account titled "Reinforced Concrete Arch Bridge Over the Yellowstone River, Yellowstone National Park," *Engineering News* 51, no. 2 (January 14, 1904), p. 25.

52. Ernest D. Peek in *Report of Engineers for 1908*, Appendix III, p. 2545.

53. A. Mackenzie, chief of engineers, U.S.A., to secretary of war, January 11, 1908, in U.S., 60th Cong., 1st sess., House Doc. 502, January 15, 1908.

54. *Acting Supt. Report for 1911*, p. 8.

55. "Would Admit Autos to the Y.N. Park," *Livingston Enterprise*, Aug. 9, 1911. See also issue of Aug. 23.

56. *Acting Supt. Report for 1912*, p. 7. See also "New Roads in Yellowstone National Park," U.S., 62d Cong., 2d sess., Senate Doc. 871, July 1, 1912.

57. *Acting Supt. Report for 1912*, p. 8.

58. Richard G. Lillard, "The Siege and Conquest of a National Park," *The American West* 5, no. 1 (January 1968), pp. 28-32 and 67-72.

59. Copy in the Yellowstone National Park Reference Library, pamphlet file.

60. *Acting Supt. Report for 1913*, p. 9.

61. *Report of Engineers for 1911*, Appendix GGG, p. 1116.

62. Interview with Mrs. Lena Potter at Gardiner, Mont., April 20, 1962.

63. Ibid.

64. From the printed *Instructions to Foremen of Working Parties. . . Yellowstone National Park, 1906* (U.S. Engineers Office, April 1, 1906), p. 3.

65. *Gardiner Wonderland*, Aug. 21, 1902.

66. *Report of Engineers for 1892*, Appendix DDD, p. 3448.

67. *Report of Engineers for 1905*, Appendix FFF, p. 2820.

68. Excerpts from the personal diary of Albert L. Noyes, July 4 to October 2, 1902, are used without further citation. Original in Yellowstone National Park Reference Library.

69. *Report of Engineers for 1892*, p. 3449.

70. Ibid.

CHAPTER 18

1. Richard G. Lillard, "The Siege and Conquest of a National Park," *The American West* 5, no. 1 (January 1968), p. 67.

2. *Report of the Acting Superintendent of the Yellowstone National Park to the Secretary of the Interior, 1909* (Washington, D.C.: Govt. Printing Office, 1909), p. 6, hereafter cited as *Acting Supt. Report for [year]*.

3. Frank Kintrea, "When the Coachman was a Millionaire," *American Heritage* 18, no. 6 (October 1967), p. 79.

4. "They Went Bicycle Riding," *Bozeman Avant Courier,* Oct. 27, 1881.

5. William O. Owens, "The First Bicycle Tour of the Yellowstone National Park," typescript dated February 12, 1934, in Yellowstone National Park Reference Library.

6. *Acting Supt. Report for 1897,* p. 17. Appended to the lengthy instructions concerning the manner in which cyclists should pass the teams they met in the Park was a warning: "Riders of bicycles are responsible for all damages caused by failure to properly observe these instructions."

7. Wade Warren Thayer, "Camp and Cycle in Yellowstone Park," *Outing* (April 1898), p. 18.

8. Herbert M. Hart, *Old Forts of the Northwest* (Seattle: Superior Publishing Co., 1963), p. 169.

9. R.O. Vandercook, "A Bicycle 'Odyssey,' " manuscript covering a tour in 1892. Original in Yellowstone National Park Reference Library.

10. A ragtime hit published by Ben R. Harney at Louisville, Kentucky, in 1895.

11. The first gasoline-driven vehicle built in the United States was the one assembled by Charles and Frank Duryea, bicycle designers of Chicopee, Mass., in 1892. It was "barely a success," and Ford's development was more important because of its proliferation and effect.

12. Jay Monaghan , *The Book of the American West* (New York: Julian Messner, 1963), p. 136.

13. R.S. Monihan, "Ocean to Ocean—by Automobile," *American Heritage* 13, no. 3 (April 1962), p. 55.

14. On April 16, 1902, Secretary of the Interior E.A. Hitchcock wrote Superintendent Pitcher informing him there was a possibility an attempt would be made to tour the Park in an automobile during the coming summer (box 21, Yellowstone National Park Archives). The secretary asked Pitcher's opinion on the advisability of automobiles using the Park roads, and the reply of April 23—negative, on the basis of the unsuitable character of the roads and the danger of frightening horses—was approved by the secretary on May 12. This was the prohibition in effect when Mr. Merry drove into the Park. A slightly different version of the trip to Mammoth Hot Springs was given by Chester A. Lindsley (Pitcher's civilian clerk) in a letter he wrote to William M. Nichols, secretary of the Yellowstone Park Association, on May 6, 1914. According to him, Merry drove to Mammoth Hot Springs to attend a dance at the National Hotel and was allowed to drive out of the Park under cover of darkness with the warning "never to try it again" (box 23, Yellowstone National Park Archives).

15. Correspondence with Edward T. Merry, June 8 and Aug. 1, 1966.

16. "Pathfinder Crew Arrives Here from Twin Cities—Send Auto Back Home," *Livingston Enterprise,* May 25, 1911.

17. Ibid., June 29, 1911.

18. Interview with former Scout Raymond G. Little at Gallatin Gateway, April 21, 1961.

19. "Memorandum Relative to First Automobile Entering Yellowstone Park," an undated item in the Yellowstone National Park Reference Library. This incident is also referred to in Chester A. Lindsley's letter of May 6, 1914 (note 14).

20. Interview with Scout Little.

21. The permission granted was of negligible importance since no machines used the road in 1913 and only three were reported in 1914. See letter to the publishers of the *Western Motor Car Company,* dated August 10, 1914, box 43, Yellowstone National Park Archives.

22. "Journal of the Acting Superintendent of the Yellowstone National Park, 1903-1921," item no. 142, p. 73, Yellowstone National Park Archives, hereafter cited as "Acting Supt. Journal."

23. D.E. Burley to Colonel L.M. Brett, June 25, 1915, box 43, Yellowstone National Park Archives.

24. *Acting Supt. Report for 1915,* pp. 7 and 36-39.

25. "Record of Auto Permits—All Gates, 1915," item no. 158, Yellowstone National Park Archives (permits are listed in numerical order by gate of entry). The premature admissions were authorized by the secretary of the interior in an exchange of telegrams that day.

26. See correspondence in box 43, Yellowstone National Park Archives, dated August 3 and 10, 1915.

27. Emil Kopac to David deL. Condon, August 5, 1949.

28. G.L. Norman to the superintendent of Yellowstone Park, June 9, 1967.

29. Henry T. Finck, "Yellowstone Park as a Summer Resort," *The Nation* 71, no. 1839 (September 27, 1900), p. 248.

30. Information recorded by Edward H. Moorman, "Yellowstone Park Camps History," typescript dated April 2, 1954, p. 15, Yellowstone National Park Reference Library.

31. Memorandum to the Northern Pacific Railroad Company, in file "President, 209B," Northern Pacific Railroad Company, St. Paul.

32. Telegram, R.W. Clark to C.A. Clark, February 27, 1917, in file "President 209B," Northern Pacific Railroad Company, St. Paul.

33. Huntley Child to J.M. Hannaford, March 24, 1917, in file "President, 209B," Northern Pacific Railroad Company, St. Paul.

34. Mortgage of June 1, 1917, in file "President, 209B," Northern Pacific Railroad Company, St. Paul.

35. M.K. Musser to the superintendent of Yellowstone Park, October 1, 1935, Yellowstone National Park Reference Library.

CHAPTER 19

1. Quoted from the *Hymnarium* (1721) in *Oxford English Dictionary,* vol. 8, p. 141.

2. In its use as a designation for a forest officer, the term dates at least from 1455, when England had "Almaner and singular Offices of Foresters and Raungers of oure said Forests" (*Rolls of Parliament* V: 318/1).

3. John Henneberger, "To Protect and Preserve: A History of the National Park Ranger," manuscript, October 1965, p. 4.

4. Stated as "protection against destruction by fire and depredations." U.S., *Statutes at Large,* vol. 30, pp. 34-36.

5. Henneberger, "To Protect and Preserve," pp. 16 and 69-71.

6. From an unsigned letter marked "confidential," dated at Washington, D.C., January 26, 1891, Yellowstone National Park Reference Library.

7. Superintendent S.B.M. Young to President Theodore Roosevelt, January 15, 1907, in U.S., 60th Cong., 2d sess., Senate Doc. 752, p. 1. Young's plan for a civilian organization is discussed by Harold Duane Hampton, "Conser-

vation and Cavalry: A Study of the Role of the United States Army in the Development of a National Park System 1886-1917" (doctoral dissertation, University of Colorado, 1965), pp. 336-39, hereafter cited as "Conservation and Cavalry."

8. *Annual Report of the Superintendent of the Yellowstone National Park, to the Secretary of the Interior, 1907,* (Washington, D.C., Govt. Printing Office, 1907), p. 25.

9. Robert Shankland, *Steve Mather of the National Parks* (New York: Alfred A. Knopf, 1951), p. 51.

10. "Will Hold Meet in Yellowstone," *Livingston Enterprise,* Aug. 8, 1911.

11. Shankland, *Steve Mather,* pp. 52-53.

12. Donald C. Swain, "The Founding of the National Park Service," *American West* 6, no. 5 (September 1969), pp. 6-9.

13. U.S., *Statutes at Large,* vol. 39, p. 535.

14. U.S., *Statutes at Large,* vol. 40, p. 20.

15. Hampton, "Conservation and Cavalry," pp. 339-40.

16. "Journal of the Acting Superintendent, 1903-1921," p. 62; item no. 142, Yellowstone National Park Archives.

17. Hampton, "Conservation and Cavalry," pp. 343-44.

18. Information from the General Services Administration, Federal Records Center, St. Louis, Missouri.

19. Horace M. Albright to the author, July 1, 1963, including a seven-page memorandum containing his recollection of the conversations and subsequent events.

20. See Appendix B, Part I, for the full text of The Organic Act.

21. Albright to author, pp. 2-3.

22. They were: Sergeant Rob Roy Wisdom, Troop G, Thirteenth Cavalry; Sergeant John Vosatka, Troop M, Eleventh Cavalry; Sergeant George Winn, Troop B, Twelfth Cavalry; Sergeant Joseph A. Schady, Troop K, Third Cavalry; Sergeant Frank K. Ferris, Troop C, Third Cavalry; Sergeant John D. Fischer, Troop G, Eighth Cavalry; Corporal Frank J. Winess, Troop G, Seventh Cavalry; Corporal Ray V. Stuart, Troop K, Eighth Cavalry; Corporal Michael J. Callahan, Troop M., Third Cavalry; Private Alex Lenhardt, Troop D. Fourteenth Cavalry; Private James Ritchie, Troop F, Fourteenth Cavalry; Private First Class Charles J.T. Schmeker, QMC; Corporal William Wiggins, QMC; Private Roman Mamps, Troop G, First Cavalry; Private Charles G. Johnson, Troop G, First Cavalry; Private Peter L. Benito, Troop H, Sixteenth Cavalry; Private Frank R. Wilson, Troop L, Twelfth Cavalry; Private First Class Coleman Walker, QMC; Private Steven Klenotise, Troop G, Twelfth Cavalry; Private George Adamski, Troop K, Thirteenth Cavalry; Private First Class Abner D. Brown, QMC; Private First Class Hugh L. Bradford.

23. Monthly report for October 1916 (dated November 14, 1916). Box 89, Yellowstone National Park Archives. They were: Chief Scout James McBride; First-Class Park Ranger Harry Trischman promoted from scout October 1; and Scout Raymond G. Little—all old employees. The following new employees were entered on duty in the month of October: First-class Park Rangers Wisdom, Vosatka, Winess, Winn, Schady, Ferris, Fischer, Stuart, Charles J. Smith, Henry Anderson, Schmeker, Brooks, Lawson, Delmar, Pound, and Lacombe; Park Rangers Lenhardt, Ritchie, Fred L. Smith, and Sager.

24. *Report of the Director of the National Park Service to the Secretary of the Interior, 1918* (Washington, D.C.: Govt. Printing Office, 1918), p. 38.

25. This memorial of March 1, 1916, is reprinted by Tom Stout, *Montana, Its Story and Biography,* vol. 1 (Chicago: American Historical Society, 1921), p. 480.

26. From "Status of Employees, November 14, 1918," a list maintained by Assistant to the Superintendent Joseph Joffe. Joffe file, item no. 1 (personnel lists, 1918 to June, 1928, incl.), Yellowstone National Park Archives. The force included: Assistant Chief Rangers James McBride (acting chief), Harry Trischman, James P. Brooks, and Charles J. "White Mountain" Smith; First-class Park Rangers ($1,200 per annum) Burton C. Lacombe, Court B. Dewing, Peter Lawson, Thadeus C. Pound, Henry Anderson, and Rob Roy Wisdom; Park Rangers ($900 per annum) Roy T. Frazier, E. F. Cushman, Joseph O. Douglas, Ford Purdy, Frank J. Winess, J.W. Eline, Laurence Mazzanovich, Albert L. McLaughlin, Fred J. Townsend, James N. Dupuis, and George Winn.

27. "Park Rangers Succeed Cavalry," *Spokane* (Wash.) *Statesman-Review,* June 6, 1919.

28. Henneberger, "To Protect and Preserve," pp. 180 and 182. James McBride died at Chico Hot Springs, Mont., May 3, 1942, and was buried in his National Park Service uniform in the Gardiner cemetery. McBride Lake, in the northeast corner of the Park, is named for him.

29. Dorr G. Yeager, "Some Old Timers of the Yellowstone," (1929), 3 pp., typescript in Yellowstone National Park Reference Library.

30. From reminiscences of Charles J. Smith, recorded at headquarters of Zion and Bryce Canyon National Parks in January and April 1952.

31. In a letter of October 13, 1916, Superintendent of National Parks R.B. Marshall sought the advice of Yellowstone's acting supervisor, Colonel L.M. Brett, concerning the questions that should be asked in examining prospective rangers; however, he noted in a postscript: "This applies more to new appointments than to those you recently approved."

32. Interview with Edward E. "Ted" Ogston at Aspen Creek, Wyo., June 20, 1966, Yellowstone National Park Archives.

33. From an undated form letter signed by Superintendent Roger W. Toll, Yellowstone National Park Archives.

34. As originally adopted, that "spread-eagle badge" (from its central device, an eagle with outspread wings) consisted of two parts (a federal shield and a soldered-on medallion), but later badges were cast in one piece. See Jack R. Williams, et al., "National Park Service Insignia and How the Uniform Grew," mimeographed at Aztec Ruins National Monument, March 1965, p. 2-3.

35. Ibid., p. 5.

36. Winter recreational use, though heartily encouraged, has remained relatively insignificant because of the Park's remoteness from centers of population.

37. The old gatehouse, dating from 1921, was demolished on January 14, 1966, after final service as seasonal quarters.

38. Lemuel A. Garrison, Memorandum to the Chief, Division of Interpretation, relative to a "History of Women's Uniforms in the National Park Service," October 25, 1961, p. 2. A tabulation attached to the copy in the park files shows that the following women were also employed on the gates: Ruby H. Anderson (1928), Irene Wisdom (1929-30), Mrs. Lois Kowski (1942), Mrs. Kathryn Bauman (1942), Mrs. Margaret E. Watson (1942), Mrs. Louise

Chapman (1942), Mrs. Marjorie A. Somerville (1942), Nancy E. Bowers (1944), and Alice L. Hauber (1944-45).

39. Annual Report for 1919 (typed report of the Superintendent of Yellowstone National Park submitted October 19, 1919), p. 75. A bound file of annual reports is available in the Yellowstone National Park Reference Library.

40. Annual Report for 1937 (mimeographed report of the Superintendent of Yellowstone National Park for the 1937 fiscal year), p. 22. One of the old motorcycles was used during the war years as transportation between Canyon ranger station and the fire lookout on Mount Washburn.

41. The first experiments with two-way radios in vehicles were carried out in the Old Faithful area on August 9, 1939, by Assistant Superintendent Emmert and Radio Engineer Hilgedick, but no effective use was made of mobile radios until the establishment of a repeater station on Bunsen Peak linked park headquarters with units operating in other parts of the area.

42. L.R. Kirk, South Bayfield, Mass., to United States Commissioner T. Paul Wilcox, Mammoth Hot Springs, August 23, 1937.

43. This fascinating miniature of Old Faithful was built by Jack Haynes when he was the unofficial director of the Park's educational program. Its eruptions (spaced a few minutes apart) were best explained by comparing the model to a coffee percolator, though that resulted in an over-simplification of geyser action.

44. Robert E. Miller, "Mushbach, Veteran Explorer, Tells of Early Days in Park," *Helena* (Mont.) *Record-Herald,* Dec. 1, 1929.

45. The formative period was from 1919 to 1925. Secretary of the Interior Work opened the way for establishment of a naturalist service by his recognition, in the latter year, of education and recreation as equal objectives of the National Park Service.

46. Two of these ranger stations remain; the one at Old Faithful (among the trees about 500 feet south of the geyser) is now a duplex residence, while the one at Lake still serves a combined ranger station and residence purpose. The old Canyon ranger station fell a victim to progress in 1959.

47. Garrison, Memorandum, p. 1.

48. As the positioning of drivers was lowered in modern cars, the ability to see over the "camel-back" arch of the bridge was reduced. Therefore, it became necessary to keep a ranger on duty at the west end of the bridge, where it opened onto the Grand Loop.

49. Interview with "Ted" Ogston, cited in note 32.

50. A government fleet came into existence in 1938 when two surplus boats were obtained: a small speedboat of the "Gar Wood" type, which had been seized by the Internal Revenue Service on Lake Superior, and an ancient navy eagle-boat, locally dubbed *The Lollypop*. Both served until after World War II, when they were replaced by more modern and serviceable craft.

51. Milton P. Skinner to Carl P. Russell, Berkeley, Calif. , January 25, 1932.

52. This is the present museum building, in which an information service has been rendered to the public for fifty-two years—in the same room!

53. Noted in the museum development file in Yellowstone National Park Reference Library.

54. Annual Report for 1925 (mimeographed report of the Superintendent of Yellowstone National Park for the 1925 fiscal year), p. 34, Yellowstone National Park Reference Library.

55. Horace M. Albright to C.W. Farnham, Stillwater, Minn., July 28, 1924.

56. From "A History of the Educational Department in National Parks," p. 7, undated typescript (c. 1930) in Yellowstone National Park museum files.

57. Such gatherings are described by Ogston in the interview cited in note 32 and by several individuals who contributed to the tape recording made for Harry Liek's retirement. Copy in Yellowstone National Park Reference Library.

58. Up to 100 animals had to be eliminated from the herd each year to keep it at an optimum 800 to 900 (the meat was turned over to local Indian agencies), and all calves were innoculated against hemorrhagic septicemia, to which the buffalo had proven particularly susceptible.

59. From Ogston interview.

60. Wallace Smith, *On the Trail in Yellowstone* (New York: G.P. Putnam's Sons, 1924), p. 23.

61. There was a strong feeling during the 1920s that the elk and buffalo were both endangered species, requiring protection from all destructive influences; while, at the same time, the coyote's role as a scavenger and sanitizer for the herd seems not to have been understood. Also, the onus of contributing to the decimation of the rare trumpeter swans was put upon the coyote in 1929. See Robert Murphy, "Triumph of the Trumpeters," *National Wildlife* 5, no. 4 (June-July 1967), p. 44.

62. From Liek tape recording mentioned in note 57.

63. Manuscript diary of James "Jimmy" Dupuis, November 1, 1918, to September 3, 1922 (held by his granddaughter, Mrs. Eva Ann Meyers of Bozeman, Mont.), 61 pp.

64. Annual Report for 1933 (mimeographed report of the Superintendent of Yellowstone National Park for the 1933 fiscal year), p. 25, Yellowstone National Park Reference Library. The low point was marked and the thermometer was sent to the U.S. Weather Bureau for calibration, and the determined value of the observation of February 9, 1933—66° below zero—stood as the official low for the United States until January 20, 1954.

65. E. J. Sawyer, "Death of Ranger Charles Phillips," *Yellowstone Nature Notes* 4, no. 4 (April 30, 1927), pp. 1-2. See also "Poisonous Plants" in issue no. 5 (May 31, 1927), p. 3.

66. From Liek tape recording.

67. Some ridiculous tales have been told as to how the *E.C. Waters* came to be there; the worst alleged that Mr. Waters was loath to see his fine wooden ship pass into the hands of others and so rammed it high and dry on the island; however, the truth is not so fanciful. The ship was wintered in that cove for many years because it was thought safe from the lake ice, which normally went out with a southwest wind in the spring. But the ice broke up with an easterly wind in 1921, pushing the vessel onto the beach where it remained. The machinery was removed in 1926.

68. From Ogston interview.

69. Harry Trischman, who was surely one of the best of Yellowstone's old-timers, entered government service December 8, 1907. Trischman Knob, on the Continental Divide southwest of Madison Lake, was named for him after his death in 1950.

CHAPTER 20

1. "The Battle of Jackson's Hole," *The Nation* 122 (March 3, 1926), p. 226.

2. "Yellowstone Park May be Enlarged," *Livingston Enterprise,* Oct. 23, 1917. This announcement was evidently a result of Secretary Lane's visit to the Park on October 7-8, 1917.

3. W.S. Franklin, "The Yellowstone," *Science* 37 N.S. (March 21, 1913), p. 447, stated that extension of the Yellowstone Park to the east and south would provide "the most magnificent asylum for wild animals in the whole world," which was exactly what General Sheridan had envisaged thirty years earlier.

4. Emerson Hough, "Greater Yellowstone," *Saturday Evening Post,* December 1, 1917.

5. Prepared from a "Map Showing Proposed Enlargement of Yellowstone National Park and Development of Southern Entrance" (National Park Service, 1918).

6. "Natural Beauty of Yellowstone," *Newark* (N.J.) *Call,* Mar. 31, 1918.

7. "Many Outsiders Interested in Park Extension," in the issue of April 24, 1918.

8. "Annual Report for Yellowstone National Park, 1919," typed copy in the Yellowstone National Park Reference Library, p. 2.

9. W.B. Sheppard, "History of a Bill," *Evening Post* (New York), Sept. 25, 1919.

10. George Taylor Ross, "Yellowstone Park Extension," *Outdoor America* (December 1927), p. 8, hereafter cited as "Extension."

11. Ibid.

12. "Congressman Mondell Writes Jackson Hole Rancher Favoring Park Extension," and "Maxwell Struthers Burt, Author, Traveller, Rancher, Answers Mondell Letter," *Wyoming State Tribune,* Nov. 5, 1919.

13. Sheppard, "History of a Bill."

14. "Appealing to the East," *Livingston Enterprise,* Apr. 30, 1920.

15. Henry Van Dyke, "Rivers, Ranches and Reservations," *New York Times Book Review and Magazine,* Oct. 2, 1921, p. 9.

16. "Renewal of Effort to Incorporate Tetons in Y.N. Park—Albright Forecast," *Jackson Hole Courier,* Dec. 12, 1922 (reprinted from *Wyoming State Tribune*).

17. "Monthly Report of the Superintendent of Yellowstone National Park, for the Month of August, 1925," pp. 12-13, typed copy in Yellowstone National Park Reference Library.

18. Struthers Burt, "The Battle of Jackson's Hole," *The Nation* 122, no. 3165 (March 3, 1926), p. 227.

19. "Senator Tom Cooper Has Plan to Extend Park," *Douglas* (Wyo.) *Budget Review,* Aug. 25, 1927.

20. "Wyoming's Wonderful Asset," *Rawlings* (Wyo.) *Republican,* Sept. 8, 1927.

21. Ross, "Extension," p. 44.

22. "Teton National Park New Proposal for Congress," *Salmon* (Idaho) *Record-Herald,* Aug. 22, 1928.

23. "Teton Measure Before Senate," *Sheridan* (Wyo.) *Post-Enterprise,* Dec. 8, 1928.

24. U.S., 70th Cong., 2d sess., S. 5543.

25. Letter to William C. Gregg, Hackensack, N.J., February 1, 1929.

26. Everett Sanders, presidential secretary, to Horace M. Albright, director of National Park Service, February 26, 1929.

27. "Pertinent Facts—Lundy Memorial," in issue of February 28, 1929.

28. *Public Law* No. 74, 70th Cong., 2d sess. (February 28, 1929).

29. *Public Law* No. 888, 70th Cong., 2d sess. (March 1, 1929).

30. Merrill F. Daum, acting superintendent, to Jack Ellis Haynes, April 4, 1929.

31. Horace M. Albright, director of National Park Service, to Edmund Seymour, New York, September 28, 1929. The critics included Dr. Wm. A. Bruette, editor of *Forest and Stream,* who blasted the National Park Service in January 1930, with an editorial, "Another Raid on the Yellowstone."

32. Act of May 26, 1926 (U.S., *Statutes at Large,* vol. 44, p. 665).

33. The text of this proclamation is given in *Livingston Enterprise,* Nov. 3, 1932. Changes made in the boundary of Yellowstone National Park have had the following effect on its area:

Original area (Act of March 1, 1872)	+	2,165,749.95 acres
Gallatin addition (Act of March 1, 1929	+	27,229.21 acres
Pebble Creek addition	+	2,751.84 acres
Lamar River addition	+	67,279.57 acres
Game Ranch addition (Act of May 26, 1926 and Executive Order of October 20, 1932)	+	6,134.58 acres
Jones Creek deletion (Act of March 1, 1929)	−	31,211.54 acres
Eagle Creek deletion	−	16,161.00 acres
Corrected area (present total)		2,221,777.61 acres

These figures were compiled from official sources by former superintendent Edmund B. Rogers. The total area is nearly seven acres greater than acreage published in the last edition of *Haynes Guide* (Bozeman, Mont.: 1966).

34. "Park County Authorities to Go Before the Legislature with a Plea for Annexation of Land," *Livingston Enterprise,* Jan. 16, 1929.

35. "Yellowstone Boundary Commission Named," *Great Falls* (Mont.) *Tribune,* April 9, 1929.

36. Horace M. Albright, director of National Park Service, to I.H. Larom, Valley Ranch, Wyo., January 24, 1929.

37. *Final Report of the Yellowstone National Park Boundary Commission,* U.S., 71st Cong., 3d sess., House Doc. 710 (Washington, D.C.: Govt. Printing Office, 1931).

38. Senator Peter Norbeck to Horace M. Albright, April 23, 1931.

39. "John D., Jr., Upheld in Teton Park Acts," *New York Times,* May 7, 1934.

40. "Park Extension to Follow 'The Jackson Hole Plan,'" *Jackson Hole* (Wyo.) *Courier,* May 31, 1934.

41. "Why Give It Away?" in issue of January 27, 1938.

42. "Hearing Opens On Teton Park," *Bozeman* (Mont.) *Chronicle,* Aug. 9, 1938.

43. "Park Extension Compromise?" *Jackson Hole Courier,* Sept. 1, 1938.

44. "The Jackson Hole Plan," *Outdoor America,* November-December 1944; from a clipping, Yellowstone National Park Reference Library.

45. The act signed into law on September 14, 1950, appears in *Published Papers of the Presidents, Harry S. Truman, 1950* (Washington, D.C.: Govt. Printing Office, 1965) [248], p. 635.

CHAPTER 21

1. Robert Sterling Yard, *Our Federal Lands* (New York: Charles Scribner's Sons, 1928), p. 178.

2. Louis C. Cramton, *Early History of Yellowstone National Park and Its Relation to National Park Policies* (Washington, D.C.: Govt. Printing Office, 1932), p. 49.

3. This report was published as House Doc. 141, 56th Cong., 2d sess. See also *H.M. Chittenden, A Western Epic,* Bruce LeRoy, ed. (Tacoma: Washington State Historical Society, 1961), pp. 67-75.

4. From an interview with Mrs. Lena Potter, April 20, 1962, at Gardiner, Mont.

5. H.M. Chittenden to Hon. E.A. Hitchcock, April 23, 1903. Copy in the Yellowstone National Park Archives.

6. *Report of the Acting Superintendent of the Yellowstone National Park to the Secretary of the Interior for 1901* (Washington, D.C.:Govt. Printing Office, 1901), p. 7.

7. H.M. Chittenden to Major John Pitcher, April 5, 1904. Copy in the Yellowstone National Park Archives.

8. See Yard, *Our Federal Lands,* p. 167; see also *Livingston Enterprise,* Aug. 1, 1911.

9. For comments of John Muir on the lost fight for Hetch Hetchy, see Raymond F. Dafsman, *The Destruction of California* (New York: Macmillan Co., 1965), pp. 163-64.

10. Sources on the Hetch Hetchy controversy are Yard, *Our Federal Lands,* pp. 178-79, 195, and 266; Roderick Nash, "The American Wilderness in Historical Perspective," *Forest History* 6, no. 4 (Winter 1963), pp. 9-10; and Richard Reinhardt, "The Case of the Hard Nosed Conservationists," *American West* 4, no. 1 (February 1967), pp. 50-54 and 85.

11. Arthur H. Carhart, *Water Or Your Life* (New York: J.B. Lippincott, 1951), p. 238, hereafter cited as *Water.*

12. Owen Wister, "Old Yellowstone Days," *Harper's Monthly Magazine* (March 1936), p. 473.

13. National Parks Association, *Essential Facts of the War on Our National Parks System* (Washington, D.C., October 1927), p. 3., hereafter cited as *Essential Facts.*

14. Ibid., p. 45.

15. U.S., Congress, House, Committee on Public Lands, *Irrigation Easements, Yellowstone National Park: Hearing on H.R. 12466,* 66th Cong., 2d sess., 1920, p. 5.

16. Editorial, "Speak Up Quickly for the Yellowstone, Urges Veteran Naturalist," *The Literary Digest* 65 (June 5, 1920), pp. 90-93.

17. Editorial, "The Fight for the Yellowstone Waters," *The Literary Digest* 67 (October 23, 1920), pp. 90-91.

18. William C. Gregg, "The Cascade Corner of Yellowstone Park," *The Outlook* 129 (November 23, 1921), p. 474.

19. Montana Irrigation Commission, *Annual Report on Irrigation Possibilities in Montana* (Helena, Mont., 1920), pp. 74-75.

20. National Parks Association, *Essential Facts,* p. 3.

21. U.S., Congress, Senate, Committee on Irrigation, *Dam Across the*

Yellowstone River: Hearing on S.4529, 66th Cong., 3d sess., 1921, pp. 3 and 65.

22. In issue of July 7, 1920.

23. National Parks Association, *Essential Facts,* pp. 5-7.

24. Ibid., p. 9.

25. Ibid.

26. Ibid., pp. 10-11.

27. Editorial, "To Looters of Yellowstone Park, Hands Off!" *The Outlook* 144 (October 20, 1926), pp. 229-30.

28. "Yellowstone Park and the Nation," *The Outlook* 145 (January 19, 1927), pp. 77-80.

29. National Parks Association, *Essential Facts,* pp. 13-15.

30. *Final Report of the Yellowstone National Park Boundary Commission,* U.S., 71st Cong., 3d sess., House Doc. 710 (Washington, D.C.: Govt. Printing Office, 1931), pp. 8-9.

31. Editorial, "Idaho Could Use Water From Park," *Jerome* (Idaho) *Northside News,* June 30, 1933.

32. Editorial, "Kosanke Plan," *Pocatello* (Idaho) *Tribune,* June 21, 1933.

33. Editorial, "Ickes Defends National Park," *Detroit Free Press,* June 18, 1933.

34. "Plans Made to Tap Lake," *Idaho Falls Post Register,* Nov. 16, 1934.

35. "Vast Development of Yellowstone and Missouri River Watersheds Proposed to Public Works Body," *Helena* (Mont.) *Record Herald,* Sept. 4, 1935.

36. "Yellowstone Waters Cut from Parley," *Cheyenne* (Wyo.) *Tribune-Leader,* June 18, 1936.

37. "Wyoming Opposes Plan to Divert Water to Idaho," *Rigby* (Idaho) *Sentinel,* Feb. 13, 1937.

38. "First Objective, Hold Water in Montana," *Miles City* (Mont.) *Star,* July 28, 1937.

39. From *Cheyenne Tribune-Leader,* Feb. 18, 1938.

40. Carhart, *Water,* p. 238.

CHAPTER 22

1. Robert Shankland, *Steve Mather of the National Parks* (New York: Alfred A. Knopf, 1951), p. 161, hereafter cited as *Steve Mather.*

2. The cowboy-artist, J.M. Moore, made this comment when asked his impression of the new visitors: "A fellow used to meet people worth knowing in the old days, now he meets a lot of eighth graders and housemaids dressed up to kill and nothing to back it up. A forty-dollar saddle on a five-dollar pony. I wonder if you've got the guts to put this in print." See Fred G. Smith, *Impressions* (Minneapolis: Augsburg Publishing House, c. 1925), p. 101.

3. "Three Times More Flivvers than Any Other of 121 Kinds of Autos Touring the Park," *Livingston Enterprise,* Mar. 17, 1918. The figures for 1917 are typical: Fords, 1,684; Buicks, 499; Dodges, 389; Overlands, 345; Studebakers, 299; Reos, 192; Cadillacs, 192; Hudsons, 189; Maxwells, 122; and Oaklands, 111. All other makes were below 100, with many appearing in single copy.

4. From Genesis 49:14, "Issachar is a strong ass crouching down between two burdens."

5. "The Ford" by Dr. Glenn, *Blackfoot Idaho Republican,* Nov. 18, 1919.

6. Frederic F. Van de Water, *The Family Flivver to Frisco* (New York: D. Appleton and Co., 1927), pp. 19-20, hereafter cited as *Family Flivver.*

7. June 12, 1917. The effort lavished on promotion of the Yellowstone Trail as a cross-country route is almost beyond belief. Chambers of commerce, newspapers, civic groups, and tourist bureaus plugged the route for the same reason that prompted an editor to note, "Lest We Forget: Monday night there were 14 cars in the automobile campgrounds. Right today, with butter worth 5¢ per pound to the rancher and labor conditions poor, the tourists are a splendid blessing to the local business community." From *Livingston Enterprise*, June 8, 1920.

8. The stickers (called "pasters" by some) served as evidence the gate fee had been paid. They were a different color each year, which facilitated handling of re-entry traffic. Originally (1919) they were 5 inches across, but the size was later reduced to 2½ inches in an effort to maintain the driver's visibility (some people accumulated a considerable array of stickers by visiting many parks, and even added some obtained at other places for the ornamental effect). As vehicular speeds increased, windshield stickers became an intolerable safety hazard and were finally outlawed. The National Park Service did not use them after World War II.

9. Van de Water, *Family Flivver,* pp. 184-85.

10. See A.C. McIntosh, "Who Owns Yellowstone Park?" *The American Mercury* 37, no. 148 (April 1936), pp. 493-96. Though he speaks of the Park as being in the hands of "predatory money-changers," his figures only reflect the higher cost of doing business in a place where the haul from the railhead was long, the operating season short, and the loss in held-over merchandise large, factors that had the effect of doubling the price of staple groceries when compared with Pocatello, Idaho.

11. Hiram M. Chittenden, "Annual Report Upon the Construction, Repair, and Maintenance of Roads and Bridges in the Yellowstone National Park," Appendix FFF in *Annual Report of the Chief of Engineers for 1901* (Washington, D.C.: Govt. Printing Office, 1901), pp. 3780-82 and 3793-94.

12. Henry T. Finck, "Yellowstone Park as a Summer Resort," *The Nation* 71, no. 1839 (September 27, 1900), p. 248.

13. David M. Steele, *Going Abroad Overland* (New York: G.P. Putnam's Sons, 1917), p. 118.

14. The first motor bus service into Yellowstone Park was established by the Sylvan Pass Motor Company on this route in 1916. This enterprise of Frank J. Haynes disappeared in the merger that put all public transportation in the Park in the hands of the Yellowstone Park Transportation Company the following year.

15. Van de Water, *Family Flivver,* p. 190.

16. In the 1930s, when open touring cars had given way to coupes and sedans with slat-and-canvas tops, the bears became expert at entering from above when food was cached in a vehicle for safekeeping. Until the advent of the steel cartop, groceries were safest at night when swung from the limb of a tree.

17. "Neighbors for a Night in Yellowstone Park," *The Literary Digest* 82 (August 30, 1924), pp. 44-46.

18. "Californian Appointed Park Director," *Los Angeles Times,* July 6, 1919.

19. Yankee Jim, who was really James George, lived on in his log cabin by the railroad track as a ward of Park County until 1922, when a brother came and took him to California. He died at Los Angeles the following summer. See Jack E. Haynes, "That Man, Yankee Jim," *The Rotospoke* 4 (Bozeman, Mont., December 28, 1954), pp. 2-3.

20. "Cooperation Builds Trail at Gardiner," *Livingston Enterprise*, May 9, 1920.

21. The town was first called Riverside (the post office opened under that name October 23, 1908) but was renamed Yellowstone on November 17 of the following year. When that proved too confusing, the name was altered to its present form, West Yellowstone, on January 7, 1920.

22. Emil Kopac to Chief Park Naturalist David deL. Condon, August 15, 1949. The serious advocacy of this approach began with an item in the *Livingston Enterprise*, Apr. 14, 1920, seeking public subscriptions with which to begin the work; see "Plan Entrances for Cooke Road."

23. Shankland, *Steve Mather*, pp. 157-59.

24. Annual Report for 1919 (typed report of the Superintendent of Yellowstone National Park submitted October 19, 1919), p. 40, notes that Landscape Engineer Punchard was directing the cleanup of roadsides and the hot spring terraces at Mammoth. (A bound file of annual reports is available in the Yellowstone National Park Reference Library.)

25. Shankland, *Steve Mather*, pp. 161-62.

26. Aubrey L. Haines, "Stagecoach Days in the Yellowstone," *Cody* (Wyo.) *Enterprise*, June 14, 1962.

27. "Caterpillar Plow Clears Park Roads," *Livingston Enterprise*, June 2, 1920.

28. Annual Report for 1947 (mimeographed report of the Superintendent of Yellowstone National Park for the 1947 fiscal year), p. 12. Some of the details are from the author's personal recollection.

29. Interview with Mr. Blayne Brooks, Pasadena, Calif., July 7, 1964.

30. Annual Report for 1921 (typed report of the Superintendent of Yellowstone National Park for the 1920 fiscal year), p. 27.

31. "Forty-six Camps for Tourists to be Built in Park," *Livingston Enterprise*, Sept. 16, 1919.

32. Isador W. Mendelsohn, "Canyon Automobile Camp, Yellowstone National Park," Reprint no. 1019 from *Public Health Reports* (Washington, D.C.: Govt. Printing Office, 1925), pp. 1-9.

33. The number of house trailers brought into the Park reached a prewar high of 1,782 in 1939.

34. Statement of Acting Superintendent Guy D. Edwards in a letter to Mrs. Eleanor Chittenden Cress, November 20, 1930.

35. The Yellowstone Park Camping Company, formed in 1917 through the merger of the Wylie interest (controlled by A.W. Miles) and the Shaw and Powell interests, was an unnatural and uneasy alliance. It was terminated January 8, 1920, by sale to Howard Hays, who continued the operation under the name Yellowstone Park Camps Company. Hays sold to Vernon Goodwin in 1924, and the Vernon Goodwin Company became the Yellowstone Park Lodge & Camps Company when it passed into the hands of H.W. Childs on September 28, 1928.

36. See Shankland, *Steve Mather*, pp. 121-27, for the background of these mergers.

37. Mr. Child ordered the new equipment early in 1917, but had difficulty financing the purchase (116 vehicles with tires and equipment, totaling $427,104.67). An undated memorandum in file "President, 209B" of the Northern Pacific Railroad Company indicates that the money was advanced by the Burlington and Union Pacific roads, secured by a chattel mortage of June 1, 1917.

38. William Morse "Billy" Nichols was Child's son-in-law, a West Point cavalry officer who came to the Park in 1904 but resigned his commission the following year to enter the concession business. He was the head of the Yellowstone Park Company from 1931 to his death, August 6, 1957, at Mammoth Hot Springs.

39. This concern, which was allowed to transport visitors into the Park from Cody, Wyoming, after March 14, 1913, on short-term permits, was the first to motorize (as the Cody-Sylvan Pass Motor Company, a venture entered jointly with F. Jay Haynes in 1916). The partnership was ended by the merger that gave the transportation privilege to the Yellowstone Park Transportation Company.

40. Charles Ashworth Hamilton, who was one of the most successful concessioners the Park ever had—a brusque, warm-hearted businessman—died at his Old Faithful store on May 28, 1957.

41. "Camp Roosevelt to Become a Scientific and Educational Center of Yellowstone Park," *Livingston Enterprise,* Mar. 12, 1921. Edward H. Moorman also comments on this enterprise in his "Yellowstone Park Camps History" (1954), pp. 18-19.

CHAPTER 23

1. *Theodore Roosevelt Cyclopedia,* A.B. Hart and H.R. Ferleger, eds. (New York: Roosevelt Memorial Assoc., 1941), p. 104.

2. Annual Report for 1946 (mimeographed report of the Superintendent of Yellowstone National Park for the 1946 fiscal year), pp. 3-4.

3. See "President, 209B" file, Northern Pacific Railroad Company, St. Paul, Minn. The joint mortgage, dated August 1, 1928, was for $934,000.

4. Ibid.; the Northern Pacific received $19,246.16.

5. M.M. Goodsill, general passenger agent, Northern Pacific Railroad Company, to J.E. Haynes, March 25, 1955, File C-500-4. In this, Mr. Goodsill states: "The last loan financed by the railroads was on a mortgage dated June 1, 1937, which has been repaid, and now the Northern Pacific Railway Company has no financial interest in the Yellowstone Park Company."

6. Annual Report for 1951 (mimeographed report of the Superintendent of Yellowstone National Park for the 1951 fiscal year), p. 8.

7. Report of the Superintendent of Yellowstone National Park, dated July 1, 1953, item 16. (These reports are all filed under no. A2623, Report 10a8.) Cited hereafter as Supt. Report [date].

8. Supt. Report, June 3, 1955, item 11. For a typical reaction see "Should Wyoming Run Park Concessions?" *Salt Lake Tribune,* Feb. 21 and April 6, 1955.

9. "Mission 66 for Yellowstone National Park," mimeographed prospectus of the National Park Service (c. 1956), p. 2.

10. This is spelled out in Contract no. 14-10-0100-603, approved February 3, 1956.

11. Supt. Report, May 28, 1953, item 12. His purchase of the Pryor Stores concession (a 44-year-old concern operated by Mrs. Anna K. Pryor and her sister, Mrs. Elizabeth Trischman) on January 5, 1953, put him in the general store business at Canyon and Mammoth Hot Springs.

12. The decision was rationalized by arguments to the effect that the foundations of the hotel were unsafe. They *had* suffered somewhat from the instability of the site over the forty-seven years the enormous structure was in use, but that chronic difficulty had never been more than maintenance could cope with; the real basis of the decision was financial—a simple choice between a capital investment on which interest had to be paid and one long ago amortized out of existence.

13. The Yellowstone Park Company was purchased by the Goldfield Enterprises on February 4, 1965, and resold several months later to General Hosts.

14. The National Park Service operated a road maintenance camp there after its abandonment by the CCC during World War II.

15. Adolph Murie, *Ecology of the Coyote in the Yellowstone,* Fauna of the National Parks of the United States series (Washington, D.C.: Govt. Printing Office, 1940), 206 pp.

16. Supt. Report, June 15, 1956, item 1.

17. "Management Objectives for Northern Yellowstone Elk," mimeographed release of the National Park Service dated September 19, 1967.

18. "Summary of Yellowstone Bear Protection and Management Policies," mimeographed release of the National Park Service dated September 19, 1967.

19. The number of boats used in the Park increased from 1,242 in 1946 to 4,900 two decades later. Many were owned by persons living near the Park, and for them Lake Yellowstone was the only large body of water within easy reach; thus, they were reluctant to see any part of its waters closed to their craft.

20. Office of the Secretary, "Secretary Udall Maps Long-Range Goals for All Three Types of National Park Areas," mimeographed news release, August 3, 1964.

21. The act of August 25, 1916, establishing the service states:

. . . which purpose is to conserve the scenery and the natural and historic objects and the wildlife therein and to provide for the enjoyment of the same in such manner and by such means as will leave them unimpaired for the enjoyment of future generations.

APPENDIXES AND SOURCES

APPENDIX A: BIOGRAPHICAL

Part I. Members of Important Exploring Parties into the Yellowstone Region

THE FOLSOM PARTY (1869)

David E. Folsom Because his health was not equal to the demands of his academic training, David Folsom became a westerner and a person of influence and substance. He was also in the vanguard of Yellowstone's explorers. Folsom was born at Epping, New Hampshire, in May 1839. He was sent to the Quaker Academy at Vassalboro, Maine, and later to the Moses Brown Quaker School at Providence, Rhode Island. It was there, while he was preparing for a career as a civil engineer, that his health broke down; following his physician's recommendation, he started west. The move temporarily interrupted his friendship with a fellow student named Charles W. Cook.

In 1862, Folsom was headed for the gold mines of Idaho when he heard that the Fisk party was organizing at Fort Abercrombie, on the Red River of the North, for the purpose of pioneering a northern route to the mines. Folsom was accepted as a herder for the train of fifty-two wagons that departed with its escort of soldiers in mid-summer. The ineptness of the man detailed to supply wild meat for the wagon train led Folsom to volunteer his services as hunter for the party. Boyhood hunting excursions in Maine had made him a good woodsman and an excellent shot, so he had no difficulty keeping the 130 expeditioners well supplied.

As the Fisk party was about to cross the Rocky Mountains, word was received that the diggings on Salmon River, which had been their objective, were "played out"; many of its members then turned to a new strike on Grasshopper Creek, where a town called Bannack had already appeared. Folsom spent the winter of 1862-63 there, then moved on to Virginia City and a risky altercation with the outlaw George Ives. Ives' attempt to provoke Folsom into an unfair fight was met in a manner as unexpected as it was untypical of a Quaker background—Folsom floored the man with a pool ball! It was a rash act, from which Folsom escaped with his life only because friends got him out of town until the work of the vigilantes was completed.

Soon discouraged with placer mining, Folsom went to work on the ranch of Henry C. Harrison at Willow Creek, in Madison County, before settling on land in that vicinity. The ordinary vicissitudes of pioneer ranching were compounded by an unending struggle against ferocious grizzly bears. After four years, he turned briefly to employment as a surveyor before he joined his old friend, Charley Cook, in the operation of the ditch company at Confederate Gulch in the winter of 1868-69. This employment led him into the Yellowstone wilderness with Cook and William Peterson, in what was the first step in the definitive exploration of the area now included in Yellowstone National Park.

Following that adventurous trip, Folsom went to work in the office of the surveyor general of Montana Territory at Helena. As a result of this association, he was able to furnish Henry D. Washburn with much information about the Yellowstone region and its wonders (also advancing a suggestion that the area should be reserved for public use); he collaborated with Walter W. deLacy in the 1870 revision of deLacy's *Map of the Territory of Montana, with Portions of the Adjoining Territories,* so that the Yellowstone region was at last delineated with reasonable accuracy. A copy of deLacy's map was carried by the Washburn party. Folsom formed a partnership with deLacy and engaged in land surveying until 1875.

Returning to New Hampshire, Folsom remained there until his marriage to Miss Lucy Jones in 1880. The couple settled in Montana, developing a large sheep ranch on Smith River, near the Cook homestead. Folsom was prominent in public life in Montana. He served as treasurer of Meagher County from 1885 to 1890 and was a state senator in the third and fourth sessions of the Legislative Assembly (actually president pro tem of the Senate during the fourth). He was an appointed member of the commission that supervised the construction of the state capitol at Helena, and, in 1900, he ran for the governorship of Montana but was defeated. David Folsom died on May 18, 1918, in California.

Charles W. Cook The boyhood friend who followed David Folsom into the West was more than a staunch companion on the 1869 exploration of the Yellowstone region; he was the sparkplug of that venture. Charley Cook was born in late February 1839 at Unity, Maine; he attended the Quaker Academy at nearby Vassalboro with his boyhood friend David E. Folsom. Together they went on to the Moses Brown Quaker School at Providence, Rhode Island, where Cook completed his education after David was forced to drop out because of ill health. The spirit of adventure finally swept Charley westward.

Drawn by reports of a rich gold strike near Pikes Peak, Cook made his way to Colorado, only to find there was no fortune awaiting him there. Early in 1864 he joined a band of drovers who were moving 125 head of cattle to Virginia City. The cattle were delivered safely September 22, 1864, just as placer mining in Alder Gulch was at the peak of its frantic activity. There being no more ground available, Cook moved on to Last Chance Gulch (present Helena), and then to Confederate Gulch. There, he found a job managing the Boulder Ditch Company, which supplied water to the placer mines around Diamond City. Soon after taking over in 1865, he employed William Peterson; his old chum, David Folsom, joined him there in the fall of 1868.

Cook first thought of visiting the Yellowstone region in the summer of 1868. An eastern mining man doing business in Diamond City boarded for a time at the headquarters of the ditch company, where he heard some of the rumors of the wonders lying south of Montana's settlements. The guest proposed an exploration of the region, but it was too late to organize a trip that season. However, the notion persisted with Cook. When notice of the intention of a party of citizens from Virginia City, Helena, and Bozeman to explore Yellowstone appeared in the *Helena Weekly Herald* for July 29, 1869, Cook and Folsom sought permission to accompany the expedition; they were greatly disappointed when the project collapsed at the last moment for lack of a military escort. Having already made their preparations for the trip, they decided to go anyhow, and were joined by William Peterson.

The party left Diamond City on September 6, 1869, well armed and outfitted. Interest in the information they brought back induced them to combine their notes in an account suitable for publication. The modest, well written account prepared by Folsom was sent to Cook's mining friend, who had offered to find a publisher; however, attempts to place it with prominent magazines such as *Scribner's* and *Harper's* were rebuffed. It was finally accepted by the Chicago *Western Monthly Magazine,* which used the account in a somewhat abbreviated form, and under Cook's name, in the issue of June 1870.

Cook left the Boulder Ditch Company soon after his return from the Yellowstone adventure, serving briefly as the receiver for a Gallatin Valley flour mill before driving a band of sheep from Oregon to the Smith River valley in 1871. He developed a large ranch called Unity on land he had claimed about ten miles east of Brewer's Springs (now White Sulphur, Montana), and brought his bride (Miss Kennicott of New York) there in 1880. They reared three children.

Charles W. Cook outlived his comrades, and he alone of all the early explorers of the Yellowstone region attended the celebration of Yellowstone Park's Fiftieth Anniversary in 1922. The presence of that tall, spare old man with the craggy face and piercing eyes provided a direct and unforgettable link with the Park's era of definitive exploration.

Cook received the following letter in February 1924:

My Dear Mr. Cook:
   Through the courtesy of Mr. Cornelius Hedges, Jr., and of Congressman Scott Leavitt, I have learned that you are within a few days to celebrate your 85th birthday anniversary. As one of the pioneers of the great inter-mountain west, the first explorer of what is now Yellowstone Park, and one of the men responsible for the founding of the national park system, you have rendered a series of national services of truly notable character. Upon these I wish to extend my felicitations, and my congratulations upon your approaching birthday. I hope you may live to enjoy many more celebrations of the same anniversary.

The tribute was signed by Calvin Coolidge. Cook died on January 30, 1927.

William Peterson The third member of the party that explored the Yellowstone region in the fall of 1869 was less literate than his two companions and has received little notice in the chronicling of that expedition. However, he was an interesting and capable frontiersman. William Peterson was born on December 3, 1834, on one of the Bornholm Islands lying off the Baltic coast of Denmark. Though a farm boy, he finished the schooling required under Danish law before he was fifteen and also developed an adventurous spirit. One day he met a sea captain in the town of Ruma and asked for a place as cabin boy on his ship. A trading voyage to Iceland for tallow, wool, eiderdown, and furs was the beginning of a seafaring life in which Peterson saw much of the world and advanced himself as far as second mate.

After eleven years, Peterson decided to try California. A gold strike in Idaho was the exciting news in California's port at that time, so he continued up the coast to Portland, Oregon, then a small town with muddy streets.

Then he ascended the Columbia by river boat to the Dalles. Peterson had picked up a partner on the boat and they made their way into the mining region, arriving at Elk City in the early summer of 1861. His experience in that area was not untypical of the time and place. He nearly starved to death on one excursion into the wild region at the head of Clearwater River, returning to find that his partner had "struck it rich" on their claim while he was gone and had sold out for several thousand dollars and left the country without dividing with him. Though left destitute, Peterson stuck it out, working for wages, running a packtrain, and serving as watchman for idle mining properties.

When Peterson moved across the Continental Divide into Montana in 1865, he found an occupation with the Boulder Ditch Company at Diamond City, in Confederate Gulch. Thus, at the time of his Yellowstone visit in 1869 he was an old employee of the concern managed by Charley Cook. Each member of the Yellowstone junket had particular skills; Peterson's were a sailor's expertise with fabric and cordage, a packer's mastery of the diamond hitch, and the all-around caginess of a man who had survived for nearly a decade in the rough-and-tumble of the mining frontier. He was also an ideal companion, with just the right mixture of common sense and good humor.

After the expedition, Peterson continued to work for the Boulder Ditch Company to the end of the 1870 season, when he left Diamond City and went to Grasshopper Creek, near Montana's earliest mining town of Bannack. He moved to the Lemhi Valley and went into the cattle business, developing a ranch on a stream that became known as Peterson Creek; he later sold that place and moved to the vicinity of the present town of Salmon. Settling permanently there, William Peterson married Jesse Notewire late in 1888 or early in 1889, and they had two children. Peterson was twice mayor of Salmon and is remembered for building the first electric power plant there. He died November 28, 1919, at Salmon, Idaho.

THE WASHBURN PARTY (1870)

Henry Dana Washburn   Though allowed but thirty-nine years of life, Henry Washburn managed to be both a distinguished soldier and a respected public servant. He was just the right leader for the group of independent, self-reliant spirits who entered the Yellowstone wilderness in 1870.

He was born March 28, 1832, to James and Mary (Cain) Washburn at Windsor, Vermont. That same year his parents moved to Wayne County, Ohio, where he lived until 1850. His public school education was interrupted at the age of thirteen, when he was apprenticed to a tanner, but that trade was not to his liking and he abandoned it to become a school teacher. He was teaching school at Helt's Prairie, near Clinton, Indiana, when he met Miss Serena Nebeker. Washburn took some preparatory work at Oberlin College and got a degree at the New York State and National Law School. He opened a law office in Newport, Indiana, in 1854, and he and Miss Nebeker were married December 28. The young couple lived at Newport and had four children in the years before the Civil War. During that time Washburn supplemented his legal practice by serving as Vermillion county auditor.

At the onset of war in 1861, Washburn raised a company of volunteers at Terre Haute. Before the regiment was mustered into federal service on August 16, 1861, he received the governor's commission as its lieutenant colonel. Washburn's Eighteenth Indiana served in the Missouri campaigns under Generals Fremont and Hunter; campaigned in Arkansas, where Washburn became its colonel on July 15, 1862; and served at the siege of Vicksburg, where exposure to trench life initiated the consumption that later took his life. Washburn was discharged from the army at Savannah, Georgia, July 26, 1865, with the brevet rank of major general.

While still in the army, General Washburn was pressed to run for the seat in the national House of Representatives held by Daniel W. Voorhees. He took leave to campaign in Indiana and was successful despite the election frauds charged to his opponents. Following the war he assumed his seat in the House and was re-elected for a second term. But political life was hard on his war-ravaged health and he refused to run for a third term. He applied to President Grant for the position of surveyor general for Montana Territory in the hope that life in the West would restore his vigor. The other contender for that office was Colonel Philetus W. Norris of Michigan; General Washburn received the appointment April 17, 1869.

Surveyor General Washburn started for Montana in May with his wife, two children, and several relatives. They arrived by steamer at Fort Buford, just within the Montana Territory, one month and two days later, and transferred to the light-draught steamer *Lacon* for the remainder of the voyage to Fort Benton; but the low stage of water in the upper Missouri River prevented the boat from reaching Cow Island; so they turned back after three weeks of fruitless toil over numerous sandbars. On the return trip they were "snagged" and had to defend a sunken boat from Indian attack while laboring on short rations to refloat it. Rescued by their own resources alone, the boat, crew, and passengers were back at Omaha on August 6. The Washburns had accomplished nothing except the loss of their household goods by their voyage of seventy days; so Washburn decided to go on to Helena, Montana, alone while the others returned to their Indiana homes. The surveyor general completed the journey to his post by way of the newly built Union Pacific Railroad to Corinne, Utah, and from thence by bone-jolting stagecoach northward into Montana.

In 1870, General Washburn was gradually involved in events that led to the Yellowstone Expedition for which he proved to be the ideal leader. As Cornelius Hedges later pointed out, he was able to unify and guide a potentially fractious party "with no articles of war to aid in the enforcement of discipline, which was still so essential to the general success and individual safety." His natural ability as a leader, coupled with uniform and impartial consideration for others and his constant willingness to take up a load is undoubtedly what brought the Washburn party through with credit. For General Washburn the strain was too great. He caught cold while searching for Truman C. Everts in miserable weather south of Lake Yellowstone and was forced by ill health to start for his home in Indiana early in January 1871. Despite his illness, he was able to write an account of the Yellowstone adventure. He arrived at the home of his father-in-law in Clinton, Indiana, but lived only a few days longer. He died on January 26, 1871.

Gustavus Cheney Doane As the officer in command of the military escort that accompanied the Washburn party into the Yellowstone wilderness in

1870, Lieutenant Doane unknowingly reached the zenith of a career that was always actuated by a love of adventure. He was born May 29, 1840, at Galesburg, Illinois. His parents moved to Oregon Territory by oxwagon when he was five years old, and in 1849 they were lured south to the gold fields of California. In 1862, young Doane went east with the California Hundred, determined to serve the Union cause. He enlisted in the Second Massachusetts Cavalry on October 30, advanced from private to sergeant by March 23, 1864, and was then commissioned a first lieutenant of cavalry. He was honorably mustered out of service on January 23, 1865. For a time after the war, Doane was a carpetbagger and is said to have been the mayor of Yazoo City, Mississippi. During this period he married, but the union was terminated by divorce in Montana.

Doane returned to military life on July 5, 1868, as a second lieutenant in the Second Regiment, U.S. Cavalry. He was stationed at Fort Ellis, a post established the previous summer for protection of the Gallatin Valley in Montana Territory. When a detail was needed to escort the Washburn party of 1870 into the Yellowstone wilderness, Doane was available at the post that was the logical point of departure. The assignment was routine: "proceed with one sergeant and four privates of Company F, Second Cavalry, to escort the surveyor general of Montana to the falls and lakes of the Yellowstone, and return"; but Lieutenant Doane made a better-than-routine report upon his return. His remarkably thorough description was the first official information on the Yellowstone region and its unusual features. Great interest was created by the report, and as a result, Doane was often referred to as "the man who invented wonderland."

Being a restless, energetic, intelligent man with great powers of endurance, Doane was always busy. He was in demand to escort official parties through the Yellowstone region; he guided the Barlow-Heap and Hayden Survey parties in 1871 and the excursion of Secretary of War William Belknap in 1875. He volunteered to lead scouting parties and developed a force of Crow Indian auxiliaries of considerable value during the Nez Perce campaign of 1877 (the war was a disappointment to Doane because his orders kept him out of the action). Late in 1876, Lieutenant Doane was sent on a winter exploration of the Snake River from its Yellowstone headwaters to the junction with the mighty Columbia with a detail of six men and a homemade boat. He lost the boat—but not his men—in the Grand Canyon of the Snake River, thus ending a venture that could only have matured into tragedy.

On December 16, 1878, Doane married Miss Mary Hunter, daughter of the old pioneer who was the proprietor of Hunter's Hot Springs on the Yellowstone River at present Springdale, Montana. In 1880, he was ordered East to be considered for duty in the arctic as a member of a party that was to implement the Howgate Plan for the study of arctic weather and living conditions. The U.S. Army was to establish and maintain a station at Lady Franklin Bay on Ellesmere Island, less than 500 miles from the North Pole. Doane sailed north in an ancient, leaky tub that had such difficulty reaching the southern tip of Greenland that he relinquished command. He was promoted to the rank of captain on September 22, 1884, and did subsequent service in the Southwest. While doing monotonous duty at dusty outposts, he dreamed of exploration in Africa; he made a serious try for the superintendency of Yellowstone National Park at the time Captain Moses Harris was transferred out. But he was forced to ask for retirement because of damaged nerves in his thigh (perhaps the result of his long service in the saddle) which incapacitated him, and he died of a heart attack on May 5, 1892.

Truman C. Everts Published accounts of Everts' thirty-seven days of wandering lost from the Washburn party south of Yellowstone Lake drew considerable attention to the Washburn party and its discoveries but provided little information about the man who survived those incredible hardships. Truman C. Everts was born at Burlington, Vermont, in 1816. His father was a ship captain and the lad accompanied him as cabin boy during several voyages on the Great Lakes. It is unlikely that Everts received anything more than a public school education. Nothing else is known of Everts' life before the age of forty-eight except that he had been married.

On July 15, 1864, President Abraham Lincoln appointed Everts to be assessor of internal revenue for Montana Territory. Yet he was unable to weather the political intrigues of the Grant administration and lost his patronage position in 1870. Everts lingered in Montana for a time, in the hope of obtaining something else, but by midsummer he had decided to return to the East.

Everts' trip with the Washburn party into the Yellowstone wilderness was in the nature of a vacation between jobs. The details of his harrowing experience appeared as "Thirty-Seven Days of Peril" in *Scribner's Monthly,* (November 1871). Everts was rescued at the last possible moment by Yellowstone Jack Baronett and George A. Pritchett. It would seem that Everts' gratitude to his rescuers would know no limits; yet it did not even extend to the payment of the reward his friends had offered for his rescue, as he maintained he could have made his own way out of the wilderness. Unfortunately, there was more to his ingratitude than that. Several years later Baronett called on Everts in the course of a visit to New York and was so coldly received that he afterward said "he wished he had let the son-of-a-gun roam."

Everts returned to Montana after securing a part interest in the post trader's store at Fort Ellis; but he did not remain there. In 1880, or 1881, he married and settled on a small farm at Hyattsville, Maryland. The couple had a child, Truman C. Everts, Jr., born September 10, 1891. According to this son, Everts was a minor employee of the Post Office Department in later years, and the family went through hard times during the Cleveland administration. Everts died at Hyattsville on February 16, 1901.

Warren Caleb Gillette One of Montana's earliest merchants and entrepreneurs, Warren Gillette was born March 10, 1832, to Dr. Ormel and Julia (Ferris) Gillette at Orleans in Ontario County, New York. He was the eldest of five children. Upon completing public school he entered Oberlin College, Ohio.

Lured by the prospect of gold in 1862, Gillette made his way westward. By the time his party reached Montana City on Little Prickly Pear Creek, it was rumored that gold had been discovered on Grasshopper Creek. Gillette moved there in December 1862 and became a pioneer merchant in Bannack. He brought his goods (an assortment of miner's supplies) directly from Fort Benton by packhorse, gaining valuable experience in freighting and the ways of horse thieves. The store was moved to the new town of Virginia City after gold was discovered in Alder Gulch in 1863, and there

Gillette became associated with James King in a partnership that lasted until 1877.

A project undertaken very early by King and Gillette showed their foresight and ingenuity. All travel between Fort Benton and Helena avoided the impassable Little Prickly Pear Canyon by using a difficult road over Medicine Rock and Lion Mountains, and the partners decided it would be to their advantage to build a toll road through the ten-mile canyon. They had two plows, which cost them $175 each, picks, shovels, and blasting powder; the road was completed in 1866 at a cost of $40,000. Tolls returned that amount within two years and the road remained a profitable enterprise to the expiration of the charter in 1875.

At the time of the Yellowstone expedition, Warren Gillette was considered the best woodsman of the party, and his willingness to remain behind in the Yellowstone wilderness, with two soldiers, to continue the search for the lost Truman Everts was a generous act of a man whose humanity was expressed in his diary: "I hated to leave for home, while there was a possibility of finding poor Everts . . . is he alive? Is he dead? in the mountains wandering, he knows not whither?"

After 1877, Gillette turned to state politics and to sheepraising. He served four times in the Legislative Assembly of Montana Territory, twice on its Legislative Council, and was a member of the convention that framed the constitution for statehood.

Gillette never married; a spinster sister, Eliza, was his housekeeper and companion until her death in 1897. He died at Helena on September 8, 1912.

Samuel Thomas Hauser Samuel Hauser was born January 10, 1833, at Falmouth in Pendleton County, Kentucky, to Samuel and Mary Hauser. A basic education in the public schools of his native state was improved by the careful tutoring of a cousin, who was a Yale graduate. In 1854, Hauser went to Missouri, where he progressed from a railroad surveyor to an assistant engineer, with charge of the work on the Lexington Branch of the Missouri Pacific, prior to the Civil War.

Hauser decided to try his luck at the Idaho gold fields in June 1862. He went from there overland to the Salmon River placers, prospected for a time, and then moved to Grasshopper Creek that fall. A season spent in the town of Bannack convinced Hauser he would have to look elsewhere for his fortune; so he joined James Stuart's Yellowstone Expedition of 1863. The party did not find gold along the lower Yellowstone River, but it did run into hostile Indians, whose night attack on the party came near finishing Hauser. He was struck in the chest by a ball that penetrated a thick notebook he was carrying and came to rest on a rib over his heart. While in the Yellowstone region with the Washburn party, Hauser measured the heights of waterfalls and an eruption of the Beehive Geyser, and sketch-mapped Yellowstone Lake. He also kept a messy but revealing diary of much of the trip.

Hauser, a Democrat, was a delegate to the Democratic National Convention in 1884 and was appointed governor of Montana Territory by President Grover Cleveland in June 1885. He married Miss Helen Farrar, the daughter of a St. Louis physician, in 1871, and they had two children. He died at Helena, Montana, November 10, 1914.

Cornelius Hedges Cornelius Hedges was born October 28, 1831, into the solid New England family of Dennis Hedges. He received his elementary education in the village school and Westfield Academy. As was the custom of the time, he attended classes mainly in winter and spent the growing seasons working on his father's acres. Upon graduating from Yale in 1853, Hedges taught school at the academy of Easton, Connecticut. He entered Harvard Law School, graduated in 1855, and was admitted to the practice of law in the courts of Massachusetts. On July 7, 1856, he married Edna Layette Smith of Southington, Connecticut. Hedges opened a law office in Iowa and assisted in editing a newspaper. He gained a liking for "printer's ink" which lasted a lifetime.

In 1864, Hedges moved his family back to Connecticut and struck out for the gold fields of Montana. He walked all the way from Independence, Iowa, to Virginia City, Montana, hunting along the route of the slow-moving wagon train. He worked several claims with the usual miner's luck before moving on to a new camp where the town of Helena soon came into existence. There, he made the acquaintance of the local sheriff, who turned some legal business his way, allowing him to establish a law office and bring his family to Montana Territory in 1865. By 1870 Hedges was active in Masonic affairs, an elder in the Presbyterian Church, had established a public library, and was an editorial writer for the *Helena Herald*. His diary indicates that the Yellowstone junket in 1870 cost him $280, and that he was uneasy about the expense.

It has been claimed that the national park idea was a direct outgrowth of a suggestion made by Cornelius Hedges beside a campfire at Madison Junction on the evening of September 19, 1870. While there is no doubt that he advanced a proposal for reservation of the area the Washburn party had just passed through, so that it would be held for the public good rather than for private aggrandizement, he was only restating a proposal he had heard Acting Territorial Governor Thomas Francis Meagher make in October 1865. Undoubtedly Hedges' comrades recognized his proposal as a restatement of an idea that had surfaced twice before (David E. Folsom of the 1869 expedition made a similar suggestion to General H.D. Washburn prior to the departure of the 1870 party); thus, Hedges' contribution lay not in a novel suggestion, but in a series of fine articles describing the Yellowstone region that he contributed to the *Helena Herald* on his return. He was a reporter, and it speaks well for Hedges' honesty that he never personally claimed to have originated the park idea, only that "I first suggested the uniting of all our efforts to get it made a National Park, little dreaming that such a thing were possible."

President Grant commissioned Hedges as U.S. attorney for Montana Territory on March 3, 1871, and he became active in the Montana Historical Society in 1873 (serving as recording secretary from 1875 to 1885). He served as superintendent of public instruction for Montana, probate judge of the court at Helena, and Supreme Court reporter.

In 1884, Hedges was a member of the constitutional convention for statehood, and in 1889 he was elected the first Montanan to the state Senate from Lewis and Clark County. His late years were spent almost entirely in the service of the Masonic Order. He died April 29, 1907, at Helena, Montana.

Nathaniel Pitt Langford   See Part III of this Appendix.

Jacob Ward Smith   Jacob Smith was born in 1830 to Jacob and Henrietta Smith in New York City, where his father was a baker. Smith was only two years old when his father died of cholera. His mother married Andrew Lang, a butcher, who taught the boy the trade at a stall in New York's Catherine Street Market. Maturing in the give-and-take environment of the public market Smith was a resilient hustler and an inveterate practical joker, who was merciless with whatever he came to consider a stupidity.

In 1859, Smith moved to Virginia City, Nevada, where he established the City Market. He married Jeanette Furman in San Francisco on October 26, 1861. During the following years, speculation and politics proved more enticing than the butcher business, and Smith rapidly accumulated a modest fortune as a stock broker, speculating in silver. But the decline of the silver mines eventually led to bankruptcy and he moved to Montana Territory in the summer of 1866. He immediately went into the tanning business with John Clough, but the venture ended in failure. The Yellowstone adventure took place in the hiatus that followed.

In 1872, Jake returned to San Francisco at the insistence of his wife, and reestablished himself as a broker. Within a decade he was a millionaire, but lost his considerable fortune just as rapidly. His wife returned to the East with their four children in 1885, and divorced him seven years later. Jake then married Ora C. Caldwell, by whom he had a son before his death January 23, 1897, at San Francisco.

Benjamin F. Stickney   Although his departure from Helena was not such as would inspire confidence, this Montana freighter and miner served the Washburn party of 1870 inconspicuously and well as its chief of commissary.

Benjamin Stickney was born October 23, 1838, in Monroe County, New York, where his parents Abia and Diana Stickney farmed until 1844. In that year the family moved to Ogle County, Illinois, where Stickney's education was obtained by a desultory attendance at a country school.

Between 1859 and 1863, Stickney was employed as a bridge carpenter, a teamster, and a miner. He eventually built up a considerable freighting business which he sold to John A. Largent and Joseph Hill in 1872. Later he engaged in sheep raising. In 1872 Stickney obtained an interest in the Craig ferry, and after 1874 he operated it alone. He also opened a general store in Craig in 1886 and ran it for ten years.

Stickney married Miss Rachel Wareham on November 3, 1873, and they had three children. He died in Florida in February 1912.

Walter Trumbull   Walter Trumbull, who was the oldest son of Senator Lyman Trumbull of Illinois, was born at Springfield in 1846. Upon completion of a public school education there, he entered the U.S. Naval Academy at Newport, Rhode Island; but he resigned his appointment at the conclusion of the Civil War. He then made an extended voyage on the *Vandalia* under Captain Lee, and on his return became a reporter for the *New York Sun*.

Prior to his visit to the Yellowstone Wonderland with the Washburn party of 1870, Walter Trumbull had been employed under Truman C. Everts as assistant assessor of internal revenue for Montana Territory, but was displaced by the Grant administration. Something more than a between-jobs vacation may have prompted young Trumbull to join the Washburn party; there is a hint that he "was familiar with the Yosemite," and his father was a recognized supporter of the Northern Pacific Railroad enterprise. With such a background, the closing sentence of the article he wrote for *The Overland Monthly* of May and June, 1871, takes on greater meaning. "When, however, by means of the Northern Pacific Railroad, the falls of the Yellowstone and the geyser basin are rendered easy of access, probably no portion of America will be more popular as a watering-place or summer resort than that we had the pleasure of viewing, in all the glory and grandeur of its primeval solitude."

There were two other ways Walter Trumbull may have influenced the creation of a Yellowstone National Park. As a special correspondent of the *Helena Herald,* he accompanied William H. Clagett throughout the latter's successful campaign for election as Montana's delegate to Congress, and he thus had excellent opportunities to interest Clagett' in the Yellowstone region. It is even more likely that Senator Lyman Trumbull's support of park legislation was influenced by his son's favorable view.

Walter Trumbull married Miss Slater, a stepdaughter of James H. Roberts of Springfield, and their first son was born in 1879, the year in which Walter went to Zanzibar as assistant consul. It was probably there that his constitution was undermined, leading to the consumption that eventually claimed his life. Trumbull moved to Albuquerque, New Mexico, in the hope of improving his health. The remainder of his life was spent seeking relief from his affliction. He was a patient at the sanitorium at Dansville, New York, and at Battle Creek, Michigan; he died at his father's house in Springfield on October 25, 1891.

William A. Baker The sergeant of Lieutenant Doane's escort was the type of career soldier who held the Old Army together by his competence and loyalty. Born in county Donegal, Ireland, in 1832, Baker was an itinerant peddler prior to his enlistment on November 6, 1854, in Company F, Second Dragoons, Sergeant Baker earned his stripes in rough campaigning during the Civil War, and thus was a well-seasoned noncommissioned officer, experienced with all manner of men, as well as in formal and Indian warfare. He was quiet, efficient, and well liked, and he would have retired from his beloved Company F as a senior NCO at the conclusion of a long and faithful service had he not been shot dead by Private James Murphy on March 31, 1874, in the course of Murphy's attack upon a comrade in the barracks at Fort Ellis.

Charles Moore Charles Moore is distinguished for having made the earliest pictorial representations of Yellowstone features: pencil sketches at Tower Fall and at the Falls of the Yellowstone River. Moore was born in Canada in 1846. He served with the cavalry and with the Battalion of Engineers. He died February 17, 1921.

John Williamson John Williamson, who was born at Frederick, Maryland, in 1843, enlisted at Laramie, Wyoming, on January 19, 1869. The fact that he was picked to accompany Warren C. Gillette and Private Moore on that last, desperate search for the missing Truman Everts hints that he was rugged and resourceful.

George W. McConnell George McConnell was born in Adams County, Indiana, in 1848. On the expedition he was orderly to Lieutenant Doane.

William Leipler William Leipler was born in Baden, Germany, in 1845; he was a skilled pianoforte maker who gave up his vocation to enlist in the Twentieth Regiment of New York Cavalry during the Civil War. Unable to adjust to civilian life at the end of that conflict, he enlisted in Company F, Second Cavalry, on December 7, 1866, to become the most typical of old soldiers. He fought in the Piegan campaign, the Sioux campaign (at Lame Deer, Muddy Creek, and Baker's battle on the Yellowstone River), and in the Nez Perce campaign. When word that Truman Everts had been found reached Fort Ellis, Leipler was one of two soldiers who volunteered to go with the party that brought Everts back to Bozeman.

THE HAYDEN SURVEY (1871)
The United States Geological Survey of the Territories

Ferdinand Vandiveer Hayden While no one man can justly claim the credit for creation of Yellowstone National Park, it is a near certainty that reservation would not have been accomplished without F.V. Hayden. His work supplied the official verification of the Yellowstone "wonders" without which the Congress would not have acted, and no man labored so persistently and effectively to secure them for the people.

Hayden was born at Westfield, in southwestern Massachusetts, on September 7, 1829. His father died when he was ten, and he went to live with an uncle in Ohio. At the age of 16 he was teaching in country schools; at 18 he entered Oberlin College. At Albany Medical School in New York he earned an M.D. degree. For Hayden, medicine proved more of a backdoor to the sciences than a profession. A summer spent collecting tertiary and cretaceous fossils in the White River Bad Lands near Fort Pierre, Dakota Territory, turned Hayden's interest irrevocably toward geology. During the Civil War years, he was a surgeon in the Union Army, from which he was mustered out in 1865 with the rank of brevet lieutenant colonel.

In 1867, Hayden was able to obtain $5,000 of unexpended federal funds for use in conducting a geological survey of the new state of Nebraska. That modest budget launched the Hayden Survey, which was thereafter financed by a combination of appropriated funds and contributions from private sources. When his fledgling organization came under the control of the secretary of the interior in 1869, it received a formal title: The United States Geological Survey of the Territories.

The Washburn expedition of 1870 created a public interest in the Yellowstone region, and Hayden (who had come close to penetrating its mysteries while a geologist with the Raynolds expedition in 1860) capitalized upon that interest by persuading the Congress to grant him $40,000 for a scientific investigation of its features. The work of the Hayden Survey during the summer of 1871 was undoubtedly of crucial importance in obtaining the passage of the act that created Yellowstone National Park on March 1, 1872. Certainly, there would have been no legislation without Hayden's persistent efforts on its behalf during the winter of 1871-72.

The Hayden Survey accomplished important work in Yellowstone Park and the surrounding area in 1872 and 1878 before its merger with the surveys of King and Powell formed the U.S. Geological Survey (1879). It has been claimed that Hayden "worked so rapidly and published so quickly that shoddiness became the hallmark of his reports"; yet, overall, he was essentially correct in his geological interpretation of a staggering amount of the unknown West.

Dr. Hayden continued to work as a geologist with the U.S. Geological Survey until 1886, when failing health caused his retirement. He died the following year.

James Stevenson A subaltern is seldom so well remembered as was the managing director of the Geological Survey of the Territories, the so-called Hayden Survey; but seldom is an organization so beholden to one man for its grand accomplishments. In naming both an island in Yellowstone Lake and a summit of the Absaroka Range for his assistant, Professor Hayden was acknowledging the extent of that debt.

James Stevenson was born December 24, 1840, at Maysville, Kentucky. While employed on the surveys of Lieutenant G.K. Warren and Captain W.F. Raynolds, he came to know Ferdinand V. Hayden and the old trapper guide, Jim Bridger. From the one he gained a scientific curiosity, and from the other a taciturn competence. Intervening winters spent with the Sioux and Blackfoot Indians provided him with a knowledge of their languages and customs which served him well on succeeding expeditions and laid a foundation for his later ethnological studies. The Civil War interrupted his training as a scientific explorer, but it also contributed to his development. Enlisting as a private in the Thirteenth New York Regiment, he rose to the rank of lieutenant during the war years, and was a seasoned leader of men by the end of the war.

In 1866, James Stevenson accompanied Professor Hayden into the badlands of Dakota Territory in search of fossils, and from that time on he was the geologist's assistant in every venture until the Hayden Survey was merged with the surveys of King and Powell to form the U.S. Geological Survey in 1879. His skill in managing the meager finances (supplementing inadequate means by wheedling passes from the railroad and stagecoach companies, borrowing arms, tentage, and wagons from frontier garrisons, and cadging rations from army stores) was genius enough; but he also organized, trained, and often led detachments that moved with dreamlike perfection through a vast expanse of western wilderness, always accomplishing the intended purpose without incident or serious injury.

Upon formation of the Geological Survey in 1879, James Stevenson became its executive officer; but his interest had turned to the study of the American Indian, and he was soon detailed to the Bureau of Ethnology to do research in the Southwest for the Smithsonian Institution. He explored cliff and cave dwellings and lived among the Zuni and Hopi Indians, where his rare tact made it possible for him to gather remarkable collections of pottery, costumes, and ceremonial objects. He was stricken with mountain fever (probably Rocky Mountain spotted fever) in 1885 and never really recovered from it. He died in New York on July 25, 1888.

PERSONNEL OF THE HAYDEN SURVEY

The United States Geological Survey of the Territories

1871

Ferdinand V. Hayden, director
James Stevenson, managing director
Henry Wood Elliot, artist
Cyrus Thomas, agricultural statistician
Antoine Schoenborn, chief topographer
A. J. Smith, assistant topographer
William Henry Jackson, photographer
George B. Dixon, assistant photographer
J. W. Beaman, meteorologist
G.N. Allen, botanist

Robert Adams, Jr., assistant botanist
Albert Charles Peale, mineralogist
Charles S. Turnbull, physician
Edward Campbell Carrington, zoologist
William B. Logan, secretary
F. J. Huse, general assistant
Chester M. Dawes, general assistant
C. De V. Negley, general assistant
J. W. Duncan, general assistant
Thomas Moran, guest

1872

NORTHERN DIVISION

Ferdinand V. Hayden, director
Adolph Burck, chief topographer
Henry Gannett, astronomer
Alexander E. Brown, assistant topographer
E. B. Wakefield, meteorologist
Albert Charles Peale, mineralogist
William Henry Holmes, artist
Walter Brewster Platt, naturalist
A. E. Bingham, general assistant
Joseph Savage, general assistant
T. O'C. Sloane, general assistant
William B. Logan, secretary
Thomas Ticknor, packer
Jack Bean, packer
Steve Hovey, packer
Jim Alexander, packer
Frederick Bottler, hunter

John Raymond, cook
Red Williams, unknown capacity
George Mefford, unknown capacity
Frank Mounts, unknown capacity
John Davis, unknown capacity
Bill Stoner, unknown capacity
Ed Flint, unknown capacity
_____ Springle, unknown capacity
_____ Black, unknown capacity
_____ Greve, unknown capacity
_____ Smith, unknown capacity
_____ Bennett, unknown capacity
_____ Lowe, unknown capacity
J. Crissman, photographer
_____ Eastlake, assistant meteorologist
William Blackmore, guest (English)
William T. Hamilton, guide (Blackmore's)

SOUTHERN DIVISION

James Stevenson, assistant director
Frank Howe Bradley, chief geologist
William Rush Taggart, assistant geologist
Gustavus R. Bechler, chief topographer
Rudolph Hering, assistant topographer
Thomas W. Jaycox, assistant topographer
William Nicholson, meteorologist (Ft. Hall)
John Merle Coulter, botanist
Josiah Curtis, surgeon and microscopist
Clinton Hart Merriam, ornithologist
Edward Campbell Carrington, naturalist
William Henry Jackson, photographer
Charles R. Campbell, assistant photographer
Robert Adams, Jr., general assistant
Philo Judson Beveridge, general assistant

James Scott Negley, general assistant
William Arthur West, general assistant
Sidford Frederick Hamp, general assistant
T. B. Brown, general assistant
Seth Corbett Jones, general assistant
Shepard L. Medara, packer
Alexander Sibley, packer
Granville Turner, hunter
_____ Keyser, cook
_____ Schuman, cook
_____ Goodfellow, unknown capacity
Nathaniel Pitt Langford, guest
Charles Langford Spencer, guest
James Reagles, guest
Richard Leigh, guide

1878

Ferdinand V. Hayden, director
James Stevenson, executive officer
Albert Charles Peale, geologist
William Henry Holmes, geologist and artist
William Henry Jackson, photographer
A. D. Wilson, topographical engineer
Henry Gannett, topographer
F. A. Clarke, topographer
Story B. Ladd, topographer
Joseph E. Mushbach, assistant topographer
Russell West, assistant
F. M. Amelung, assistant
Nelson W. Perry, assistant
Isaac Miller, Jr., assistant
Joe Foster, assistant
John Wilson, assistant

_____ Richardson, assistant
_____ Wells, assistant
_____ Michel, assistant
"Frenchy" _____ , assistant
Steve D. Hovey, chief packer
Tom Cooper, wrangler and packer
George Graves, wrangler and packer
Al Green, wrangler and packer
A. C. Ladd, wrangler and packer
Harry Yount, wrangler and packer
John Raymond, cook
_____ Black, cook
George Boalin, unknown capacity
Clarence Kelsey, guest
E. Eckles, guest (English)

Part II. Persons Prominent in the History of the Yellowstone Region

Walter Washington deLacy Of the many colorful characters who have had a hand in making Yellowstone's history, this talented civil engineer is perhaps the least known. Yet he was a man who accomplished much—as teacher, soldier, surveyor, miner, and cartographer. deLacy might have taken credit for the discovery of Yellowstone had he been less modest.

He was born February 22, 1819, at Petersburg, Virginia, to William and Eliza deLacy of Norfolk. Both parents died while deLacy was a boy, and his upbringing was left to a pair of maiden aunts and a bachelor uncle, who did well by him. At Mount Saint Mary's Catholic College deLacy specialized in mathematics and languages—French, Portugese, and Spanish. An appointment to the U.S. Military Academy at West Point, where he wished to study civil engineering, was denied him through official chicanery. The wrong was righted by a professor who felt a responsibility to the boy's family. He took deLacy to West Point for tutoring by himself and other officers.

In 1839, while deLacy was working as a railroad surveyor, he was called to Washington to take an examination for a commission in the regular army. With the rank of lieutenant, the young man became an assistant instructor in French at the military academy; he soon resigned that position to take a similar one with the U.S. Navy. He was then employed by a group of wealthy men to search for abandoned Spanish silver mines, and he was in the Southwest when war began with Mexico. He took part in that conflict, gaining a captaincy, and, during the following years, he was employed in the West on a number of government projects. During the Indian War of 1856, Governor Isaac I. Stevens of the Territory of Washington appointed deLacy engineer officer responsible for planning and constructing the blockhouses and forts that protected the settlements while the volunteer troops campaigned in Indian country east of the Cascade Mountains.

Having proved himself as a military engineer, deLacy was employed on the construction of the Mullan Road. He set the grade stakes for the crews, and, at the eastern terminus, later laid out the town of Fort Benton at the head of navigation on the Missouri River. deLacy recognized the mineral possibilities of Idaho and Montana, and he followed the succession of stampedes that opened up the northern Rocky Mountains. A prospecting tour in 1863 (with a party he called "the forty thieves") took him across the southwestern corner of present Yellowstone Park. There he saw Shoshone Lake and the Lower Geyser Basin, but failure to adequately publish his discoveries prevented deLacy from getting the credit his explorations merited.

In 1864 the first Territorial Legislature of Montana commissioned deLacy to prepare an official map to be used in establishing the counties, and his map, published in 1865, showed just enough of the Yellowstone region to whet the interest of Montanans (on it was the lake and the Falls of the Yellowstone River, with a "hot spring valley" at the head of the Madison River). The map was periodically improved during the twenty-four years it was in print, and a copy of the 1870 edition (complete with the route of the Folsom-Cook-Peterson party of the previous year and extensively corrected to accord with their observations) was carried by the Washburn party of 1870. (See maps, page 102)

In Montana's Sioux war of 1867, deLacy assumed a familiar role as colonel of engineers for the Territorial Volunteers. In that conflict he displayed his usual quiet bravery by going to the relief of federal troops beleaguered at Fort C.F. Smith on the Bozeman road. Loading a wagon train with Gallatin Valley potatoes and flour for the famishing garrison, he pushed through with a handful of volunteers, despite warnings that the Sioux would gobble him up.

The remaining years of deLacy's life were occupied with surveying and civil engineering. He fixed the initial point and laid out the base line for the public land surveys of Montana, prepared a map for the Northern Pacific Railroad which greatly influenced the choice of a route through the territory, and accomplished a perilous survey of the Salmon River. He was later city engineer for Helena, Montana, and an employee in the surveyor general's office there. He worked to within a few weeks of his death on May 13, 1892.

Collins Jack Baronett "Yellowstone Jack" is best characterized as a soldier of fortune—a man who was sailor, soldier, miner, and guide during his adventurous life. Enough of his life centered on the Yellowstone country to give him the nickname by which he was so well known. Many of the details of Baronett's colorful career come from the biographical sketch that Chittenden included in his 1895 edition of *The Yellowstone*. From it we know he was born in 1829 at Glencoe, Scotland—probably as John H. Baronett—and that he went to sea at an early age. But his nautical career came to an end when he deserted his ship in China in 1850 and made his way from there to the gold fields of California. The lure of gold drew him to other strikes in Australia and Africa, and he made a voyage to the arctic as the second mate on a whaling ship before returning to California in 1855. He served as a courier for General Albert Sidney Johnston in the Mormon War and took part in the Colorado gold rush on the eve of the Civil War. In the war, Baronett's sympathies were with the South, so he joined the First Texas Cavalry. Abandoning the cause in 1863, he took service briefly with the French under Maximilian in Mexico.

Baronett came to Montana Territory in September 1864. He was a member of one of the prospecting parties that crossed the Yellowstone Plateau that fall and he was with the Yellowstone Expedition of 1866. He wintered at Fort C.F. Smith and was one of the men who made their way through the hostile Sioux to the Gallatin Valley to obtain relief for the nearly starved garrison of the northernmost outpost on the Bozeman road. Service as a scout with General Custer's expedition to the Black Hills and another foray into the Yellowstone country in 1869 increased Baronett's familiarity with the region. Thus, when Truman Everts was lost from the 1870 expedition, Baronett was considered the best qualified man to conduct the search. Immediately after the rescue of Everts, Baronett built a toll bridge over the Yellowstone River near its junction with the Lamar River, and he operated it for many years as a vital link in the road to the mining region on Clarks Fork. The care of his bridge was often left in other hands as Baronett guided hunting parties, scouted for the military, and continued his search for elusive mineral riches.

Baronett enjoyed the respect and confidence of his former enemies. He was the preferred guide of General Philip H. Sheridan on several junkets through the Park and was the only member of the original civilian police force to be retained when the army took over management of the area in 1886. He thus became the first scout. Baronett's thirty-five-year association with the Yellowstone region has been justly recognized by coupling his name to a peak that flanks the road to the northeast entrance; otherwise life did not treat him well. His toll bridge, in which he had invested $15,000, was taken from him in 1894, and he spent $6,000 in lawyer's fees to obtain from Congress a niggardly compensation of $5,000. That money was invested in an expedition to Nome, Alaska, during the last great gold rush. But his schooner and his hopes were both crushed in the arctic ice. Thereafter, the old man's health failed rapidly and he was last mentioned as an indigent at Tacoma, Washington, in late January or early February of 1901.

Gilman Sawtell A great peak overlooking Henrys Lake, Idaho, bears the name of the man who was the first settler immediately west of the Yellowstone region and the builder of the first wagon road to its geysers. Gilman Sawtell was born December 10, 1836, to Ebenezer and Sally Sawtell of Groton, Massachusetts. During the Civil War, Gilman served as a sergeant in Company L, Eighth Illinois Cavalry. He married Carrie Livermore near the end of the war, and a son, Eben, was born in Jackson County, Iowa, as the couple migrated westward in 1866.

Gilman Sawtell turned up in the little mining town of Nevada (west of Virginia City, Montana) in 1867 and moved on to Henrys Lake, where he established a ranch and fishery on the northwest side (present Staley's Springs). By the following year he had constructed a rough wagon road to Virginia City, via Raynolds Pass, and had shipped swan cygnets to New York City for the Central Park zoo. In 1871, Rossiter W. Raymond, the federal mineral surveyor for Montana Territory, hired Sawtell to guide his party into the Yellowstone country from Henrys Lake, and in 1872, Sawtell was host to Stevenson's contingent of the Hayden Survey, including the Park's new superintendent, N.P. Langford.

During the summer of 1873, Gilman Sawtell extended his wagon road from Henrys Lake over Targhee Pass to the Madison River and up that stream to the Lower Geyser Basin in Yellowstone National Park. In this, he was assisted by the citizens of Virginia City, who contributed more than $2,000 for the construction of the Virginia City and National Park Free Wagon Road—as it

was called to distinguish it from the toll road that provided a northern apɪ ͜ch
to the new Park. It was estimated that more than 500 persons reached the Park
by the western route during its first season. The ranch at Henrys Lake suffered
during the Nez Perce and Bannock wars of 1877 and 1878 and was abandoned
for a time. When George Marshall began his brief stage service into the Park
in October 1880, he used Sawtell's "home" cabin on Bear Creek (near
Cameron on the Madison River) and the Henrys Lake ranch as stopover points.

Mrs. Sawtell died at Virginia City on December 13, 1884, and the family
property was conveyed to Eben Sawtell in 1890. Thereafter, Gilman Sawtell
lived as an itinerant prospector.

THE ASSISTANT SUPERINTENDENTS
Prior to Passage of the Sundry Civil Bill for 1883

Charles Langford Spencer (1872)

The 16-year-old nephew of Superintendent Langford, whose annual report
for the year 1872 (p. 8), states: "My assistant, Mr. Charles L. Spencer, will
also accept this public tender of my thanks for the able services he rendered
on a trip which was both protracted and toilsome, and afforded him no other
recompense for his assistance than an opportunity to see the wonders of
the park."

David E. Folsom (1873)

An explorer of 1869, appointed by Superintendent Langford as his
assistant in April of 1873, according to a letter written to the secretary of
the interior, from St. Paul, Minnesota, June 19, 1873. (See page 425)

James C. McCartney (1877)

The proprietor of Mammoth Hot Springs Hotel, who was informed by
Superintendent Norris, in a letter written at Washington, D.C., April 19,
1877, "Under authority this day received from the Sec'y of the Interior as
Superintendent of the Yellowstone National Park, you are hereby appointed
assistant Superintendent until my arrival there . . ."

Benjamin P. Bush (1878)

A "member of the scientific association" of Detroit, Michigan, he
accompanied Superintendent Norris to the Park in July 1878, serving as
assistant at $50 per month. Though Mr. Bush had intended to spend the
winter in the geyser basins, he left the Park in mid-October.

Clarence M. Stephens (1879-1882)

The *Bozeman* (Mont.) *Avant Courier* of May 29, 1879, noted the arrival
of Superintendent Norris "and C.M. Stephens, an engineer" at St. Paul,
Minnesota, enroute to the Park, and the superintendent's annual report for
1879 (p. 3), lists him as "assistant," with the date of departure from Detroit
being May 12. Superintendent Conger's annual report for the year 1882
(p. 3), indicates that Stephens was not relieved from his responsibilities in
the Park until May 28, so that his services as assistant exceeded three years.
He was the first employee to pass the winter in the Park (1879-80) and its
first postmaster (appointed March 2, 1880). He also owned the property
where the town of Cinnabar was later built, buying it from the Hendersons
after the Indian Wars and selling to George Huston and Joe Keeney in April,
1883, prior to his return to the East. Stephens Creek is named for him.

George L. Henderson (1882-1885)

A brother of Congressman David B. Henderson, he served as an assistant from about June 1, 1882, to June 4, 1885. He was a widower with a family of four girls and a boy, several of whom were later concessioners in the Park. With his son, Walter, and daughter, Helen, he built the Cottage Hotel at Mammoth Hot Springs (1885), and after the sale of the Cottage Hotel Association in 1889, he served as a lobbyist for the Yellowstone Park Association in Washington, D.C. His literary ability was constantly employed writing for various newspapers.

THE YELLOWSTONE SCOUTS (1886-1918)

E.C. Anderson was employed as an extra scout from April 1 through June 30, 1909.

Henry Anderson was employed as an extra scout from November 1 through December 30, 1910, and from October 2 through November 30, 1911.

Collins Jack Baronett was employed as a regular scout from August 20, 1886, through June 30, 1887, when he resigned (the rigors of patroling on skis had aggravated an old injury to a foot). He was the only man of Superintendent Wear's force of assistant superintendents to be retained by Captain Moses Harris when the military took over administration of the Park (see page 440).

Jesse R. Brown was employed as a regular scout from October 10, 1908, through June 5, 1911, when he was dropped from the roll as "absent without leave." According to Ray Little, he was in trouble over the sale of elk teeth.

Felix Burgess was employed as a regular scout following the disappearance of Ed Wilson in July 1891 (the date of his commission as deputy U.S. marshal for the Park is September 1, 1891). When his service terminated is unknown, but it was after April 19, 1899. Burgess was a tough veteran of the Indian Wars in the Southwest. His capture of the dangerous poacher, Ed Howell, in 1894 brought him a citation from the army and the thanks of the Boone and Crockett Club.

June Buzzell was employed as an extra scout in November 1895; he later engaged in poaching elk in company with Thomas E. Newcomb, another ex-scout (they were tried before U.S. Commissioner Meldrum, found guilty, and fined $50 each on June 27, 1896).

Court B. Dewing was employed as an extra scout in 1917 (period of service unknown); he was listed as a ranger in 1918, serving in that capacity until his death in 1923.

Sellack M. Fitzgerald was employed as an extra scout from September 5 through December 30, 1907. He was earlier one of the assistant superintendents (police) who served under R.E. Carpenter and D.W. Wear in 1885-86.

Samuel D. Graham was employed as an extra scout on August 25, 1902 (length of service is unknown) and re-employed as a regular scout March 4, 1904, continuing in that service until March 9, 1909, when he was promoted to buffalo keeper. He was one of the participants in the classic brawl through which a Yellowstone Park Transportation Company building at Mammoth Hot Springs became known as the Bucket of Blood; he later died insane.

N.C. Hanson was employed as an extra scout from September 1899 through March 22, 1900.

Louis Hartman was employed as an extra scout from October 1, 1890 through March 31, 1901.

Peter Holt was employed as a regular scout in July 1899; his service continued through March 25, 1908 (and perhaps to a later date, since the record is incomplete). Holt gained some notice for his success in capturing buffalo calves from the Park's wild herd. He was later the chief of police for Livingston, Montana, and was killed there in line of duty on August 22, 1929.

Edgar Howell was employed as an extra scout in October and November 1897, in connection with the effort to solve the Solfatara Plateau stagecoach robbery. His services were helpful, but his employment as a federal officer—considering his previous activity as an unscrupulous buffalo poacher and his subsequent conviction for flagrantly ignoring the order of expulsion from the Park—led to severe criticism by Theodore Roosevelt. It was Ed Howell's boast that he brought law and order into Yellowstone Park, and, in a left-handed way, that was correct.

_____ **Jackson** was mentioned by Ray Little as an extra scout; the period of employment is unknown.

Lester Johnson was also mentioned by Ray Little as an extra scout. He was familiarly known as "Cracker" Johnson.

G.M. Leatherman was employed as an extra scout in October 1899.

Raymond C. Little was employed as a regular scout from September 25, 1911, until the end of military administration in the Park. Thereafter, he was a ranger until September 15, 1922, when he resigned from the service. He died May 5, 1961, at Cedar Creek, near Corwin Springs, Montana.

N.J. Malin was employed as an extra scout in November and December 1897.

William F. Manning was employed as an extra scout from September through November 15, 1897. He was probably a resident of the area south of the Park whose service was essentially that of an informer; an entry in the September report from the Snake River outpost states: "Scout Manning doesn't know anything about the Park."

Louis Martin was employed as an extra scout from November 1, 1900, through April 30, 1901.

John E. Mason was employed as an extra scout from April 1 through April 30, 1909.

Donald F. Mattson was employed as an extra scout in 1918 (the period of his service is unknown, but he probably was the last man hired by the army in the capacity of extra scout).

James McBride was employed as an extra scout from September 16, 1900, through February 28, 1901, when he was dropped from the rolls due to illness.

He was re-employed as a regular scout on September 1, 1901, serving to the end of military administration in the Park. He was chief scout from May 1914 on and was a ranger (and also the Park's first chief ranger) until his retirement on December 31, 1938. "Jim" McBride was a friend of John Burroughs and Theodore Roosevelt. He died at Chico Hot Springs, Montana, May 3, 1942.

Silas McMinn was employed as an extra scout from December 9, 1899, through February 13, 1900. He functioned as an informer, for which he received $12 per month. The McMinn Bench, between Mount Everts and the Gardner River, was named for the fact that he mined coal there in the early days of the Park.

R. McTavish was employed as an extra scout on January 1, 1903 (there is no information on the length of his service).

James G. Morrison was employed as a regular scout after taking his discharge from the army in 1895 (he had been a sergeant stationed at the Snake River outpost prior to that). He resigned July 1, 1902, but appears to have served as an extra scout until after April 20, 1904. Morrison settled in Seattle. He died there on October 4, 1951, at the age of 94.

Thomas E. Newcomb was employed as an extra scout in November 1895 and in August 1900, serving as a detective in each instance. He was involved with June Buzzell in poaching park elk in 1896 (for which he was fined $50), and he was heartily disliked by many persons for killing the old Civil War hero, "California Joe," during the Black Hills gold rush.

Ed Romey was employed as an extra scout on the south boundary of the Park during March and April 1902. He was re-employed on October 11, 1902, but there is no indication of his length of service. He was remembered for taking a local poacher by the name of Ed Hunter (the "King of the Forest") with him on several patrols "in order to keep track of him." Romey was an officer on the Yellowstone Forest Reserve after its establishment.

Walter Rubin was employed as an extra scout during November 1911. He returned to Chicago, where he worked as a baker, a guard for Western Electric, and as a city fireman until his death in a street car accident in 1934.

Nathan Rush was employed as an extra scout during November 1897 and re-employed September 1, 1901. (There is no information on the length of his second service.)

Charles J. Smith was better known as "White Mountain Smith" and was employed as an extra scout in 1915 and 1916. He became a ranger in 1917 and was later superintendent of the Grand Teton, Petrified Forest, and the Zion and Bryce Canyon area. His colorful nickname (gained as a stagecoach driver in Yellowstone Park) was reminiscent of his eastern origin. He died May 18, 1962, at Santa Barbara, California.

Frank Stephens was employed as an extra scout in January, February, and March 1902.

Harry Trischman was employed as a regular scout from April 1909 to the end of military administration. He became a ranger September 30, 1916, and served as an assistant chief ranger and chief buffalo keeper before his retirement December 31, 1946. He died March 15, 1950, at Livingston, Montana.

R.A. Waagner, "The Duke of Hell Roaring," was employed as a regular scout from September 16, 1901, through August 1907. He was reputed to be of a noble Austrian family, which accounts for the duke in his nickname; however, the Hell Roaring referred to was not the stream that flows into Yellowstone River within the Park, but a tributary of the West Gallatin River, where he owned land.

George Whittaker was employed as an extra scout in December 1897 and as a regular scout from July 1899 to July 23, 1900, when he resigned to go to the Philippine Islands. He was later a concessioner in the Park, operating stores at Mammoth Hot Springs and the Grand Canyon until April 1, 1932, when he sold to Pryor & Trischman. He died at the Old Soldier's Home at Sawtelle, California, on January 30, 1961.

Charles Wilson, known as "Swede Charley," was employed as an extra scout from November 1 to December 31, 1910.

Edward Wilson was employed as a regular scout on the resignation of C.J. Baronett (probably on July 1, 1887), serving until his suicide in late July 1891. He had been one of the better assistant superintendents (police) employed by D.W. Wear in 1885-86. He made the first winter patrol for protective purposes (1888), thereby proving that winter travel in the back-country was practicable.

James Wilson was employed as a regular scout in place of R.A. Waagner from September 1907 through September 1908.

Nelson Yarnell was employed as an extra scout from January through April 1896.

Part III. Superintendents, Acting Superintendents, and Supervisors of Yellowstone National Park, 1872-1970

Nathaniel Pitt Langford Born August 9, 1832, in Oneida County, New York, Nathaniel Langford was the eleventh of thirteen children in the family of George and Chloe (Sweeting) Langford. His education, obtained in a rural district school, was squeezed into the slack season between fall harvesting and spring plowing. Though his youth included more farming than schooling, he developed into a well-educated young man. Langford moved to St. Paul, Minnesota in 1854, entered the banking business and became widely known in that city.

In June 1862, he joined an expedition bound for the Idaho gold fields under the guidance of James L. Fisk, and in 1863, moved to the new strike at Alder Gulch.

Two months after establishment of the territory of Montana, Langford was commissioned collector of internal revenue on July 15, 1864. He held the position until 1868, when he was removed by President Andrew Johnson, but reinstated by the Senate. Almost before the tumult had died down, Langford resigned his position of collector on the understanding that Johnson would appoint him to the governorship. However, the Senate, having fought to secure one position for him, refused to confirm another.

Following a visit to the Yellowstone region, Langford lectured in the East on the wonders of Yellowstone. When Yellowstone National Park was established, he became its first superintendent, holding that position from May 10, 1872, until April 18, 1877, when he was replaced by Philetus W. Norris. During his superintendency, the Park was neither developed nor protected; indeed, one man, without appropriated funds and already fully employed as U.S. bank examiner for the territories and Pacific Coast states, could hardly be expected to do more than he did: make three brief visits to the area and prepare one report.

Langford married Emma Wheaton, the daughter of a St. Paul physician, November 1, 1876, but his bride died soon after. Eight years later, he married Clara Wheaton, sister of his first wife. After 1885, his life centered in St. Paul, where he engaged in the insurance business and, after 1897, was president of the Ramsey County Board of Control, handling city and county relief matters until October 18, 1909, when he died at the age of 79 from injuries received in a fall.

Philetus Walter Norris The second superintendent of Yellowstone National Park was a fortunate blend of the pioneer and the scientist—just the right man to open a wilderness. He was practical enough to see the immediate need for trails, roads, and buildings, and scholarly enough to record the area's human and natural history; in everything he was enthusiastic and sincere, and his achievements were monumental.

Born at Palmyra, New York, on August 17, 1821, of parents who had New England origins, Norris grew up close to the great falls of the Genesee River, to which he began guiding tourists at the age of ten. That idyllic boyhood was cut short when the family moved to Michigan to take up newly opened lands. The struggle to make a home on the frontier broke his father's health and left the youngster to help his mother support a large family of girls. His formal schooling was neglected and thereafter his education was advanced only by experience and what he could extract from books.

At the age of seventeen, Norris entered the service of the Hudson's Bay Company in Manitoba, and at twenty-one he bought land on the edge of the Black Swamp in northern Ohio. By 1845 he had built a cabin on land laboriously cleared of forest, and it was there he brought his bride, Jane Cotrill of Fayette. Other families located around his homestead, where a post office was established under the name of Pioneer, Ohio, in 1851, with Norris as the first postmaster. The town of the same name came into existence in October 1853 when Norris subdivided and sold part of his land. He built a large frame house, which still stands, on high ground near the site of his early cabin, and lived there until the Civil War. During those years he prospered as an agent for an eastern land company.

Norris volunteered his services for the Union on May 2, 1862, raising a company of the Hoffman Battalion of Ohio Infantry. He was so seriously injured in a West Virginia engagement that it was necessary for him to resign his captaincy January 5, 1863. He served as senator in the Ohio legislature, after which he tried to get a federal position as surveyor general for the newly created territory of Montana. A period of waiting upon his political fortunes was spent with the Sanitary Commission of the Union Army, with which he passed through the bloody Spotsylvania campaign before taking charge of a military prison at Kelley Island. Following the war, Norris undertook the guardianship of the estates of certain fallen Confederate and Union soldiers; by installing drainage and other improvements, Norris turned 10,000 acres of swamp near Detroit, Michigan, into valuable property. Purchasing 1,900 acres around the Prairie Mound, in Hamtramck Township, he laid out a townsite in his name, to which he subsequently moved his family. A flourishing real estate business and a newspaper, the *Norris Suburban,* gave him the means to engage in frequent exploring junkets through the West.

Among the adventures related in a series of articles in his newspaper ("The Great West, a Journal of Rambles over Mountain and Plain") are the story of an ill-fated attempt to penetrate the Yellowstone region early in the summer of 1870 and an account of a successful trip through the new Park in 1875. His observations led him to expose the shortcomings of the first superintendency; as a result, the thankless responsibility was shifted to him. Norris became the second superintendent of Yellowstone National Park on April 18, 1877, serving until February 2, 1882. He was a sincere and energetic administrator who accomplished much for the area. He secured the first appropriation from Congress—$10,000 in 1878—and used the funds to build the Norris Road to the geyser basins and to construct a headquarters building on Capitol Hill. He also explored extensively, and his prolific reporting on the Park's features helped to popularize the area. His scientific curiosity was unusual, leading to significant contributions in ethnology, archeology, and geology.

We have the testimony of G. L. Henderson that the labors of Norris on behalf of the Park materially shortened his life; yet, in many respects, he failed to please. With limited funds for the improvement of the Park, he spread the money thinly in an attempt to give immediate access to most of its interior. As a result, his roads and trails were generally considered inadequate; indeed, some military men thought the work was evidence of malfeasance, or at least incompetence. On the other hand, Norris took an uncompromisingly honest stand in regard to the schemes that later matured into the Star Route Scandal and the Yellowstone Park Improvement Company, thereby alienating essential support. As a result, Norris' enemies were able to have him replaced. He returned to his home to devote his remaining years to the writing of *The Calumet of the Coteau* (1884) and to the investigation of the prehistoric mounds of the Ohio Valley for the Smithsonian Institution. He died at Rocky Hill, Kentucky, on January 14, 1885, and was buried in Elmwood Cemetery at Detroit, Michigan. A handsome memorial marks that grave, but Colonel Norris has others—Norris Geyser Basin, Norris Pass, and Mount Norris—in the great Park he opened. He was a man whose unselfish devotion to the public interest set an example far beyond the standard of his time.

Patrick Henry Conger The personal attributes of the third superintendent of Yellowstone National Park were not equal to the demands of the position. His administration of a little less than two and one-half years is memorable chiefly for its weakness.

Conger was born at Hinesburg, Vermont, on December 22, 1819. At the age of twenty-two he migrated to Galena, Illinois, and then across the Mississippi River into Jackson County, Iowa, where he farmed. He later engaged in business in Dubuque and was there when the Civil War started. Conger's first attempt to enlist was balked by a lung weakness, but he did obtain a position as a deputy U.S. marshal. In that capacity, he worked with the army provost marshal's office in the enlistment of troops for the war. Later, he was accepted for a six-month enlistment with Company A, Forty-fourth Regiment, Iowa Volunteer Infantry.

After the Civil War, Conger settled permanently at Waterloo, Iowa. He supported his large family (three children by his first wife, Sarah Brasher, who died in 1854, and five by his second wife, Julia Bruigher) by holding a succession of patronage positions. He was the agent for the Yankton (Sioux) Indian Reservation for four years, there gaining the military rank of major, and he was connected with various government surveys in the West. From March 1, 1882, until September 9, 1884, he was superintendent of Yellowstone National Park, of which service, historian Hiram Chittenden said:

> Of this Superintendent, it only need be said that his administration was throughout characterized by weakness and inefficiency which brought the Park to the lowest ebb of its fortunes, and drew forth the severe condemnation of visitors and public officials alike. This administration is an important one, however, for it marks the period of change in public sentiment already referred to, and the commencement of reform in the government of the reservation.
>
> (*Yellowstone National Park,* 1895, pp. 131-32)

George L. Henderson, one of the ten assistant superintendents who served under Major Conger, revealed the basis of Conger's troubles: "I recollect that Supt. Conger was bitter against his predecessor Norris and all who spoke of him with respect. His ill will was manifestly shown to all employees who had been under Norris." In that way Conger alienated those who could have helped him and he was left to mire himself in ever-greater difficulties. After his replacement as superintendent of Yellowstone National Park, he returned to his home in Waterloo, Iowa. There, according to his biographer, "he lived in comfortable and honorable retirement" until his death on June 29, 1903, at the age of 84.

Robert Emmett Carpenter The fourth superintendent of Yellowstone National Park was entirely unfit to hold the position. His crass and venal attitude toward management of the Park led to his early removal, but not before great damage was done.

Carpenter was born August 13, 1834, at Harford, Pennsylvania. His education was completed at Wyoming Seminary in his native state, and he entered into business with his brother, C. C. Carpenter, at Fort Dodge, Iowa in 1852. He got the gold fever in 1858 and tried his luck in Colorado, but soon moved on to Texas, where he taught school. Upon the outbreak of the Civil War, Carpenter enlisted in an Iowa regiment with which he served briefly. He was deputy county treasurer and clerk of the board of supervisors for Webster County.

Carpenter was appointed superintendent of Yellowstone National Park on September 1, 1884, through the influence of his brother, Governor Carpenter of Iowa. Chittenden said of him:

In his opinion, the Park was created to be an instrument of profit to those who were shrewd enough to grasp the opportunity. Its protection and improvement were matters of secondary consideration. Instead of remaining at his post during the winter season, he went to Washington, and there, in concert with a member of the Improvement Company, very nearly succeeded in carrying a measure through Congress by which important tracts upon the Reservation were to be thrown open to private occupancy. So confident of success were these conspirators that they even located claims upon the tracts in question, and their names appeared on claim notices posted to designate the localities. Fortunately, the measure failed of passage, but the scandal of Superintendent Carpenter's conduct led to his prompt removal from office.

(Yellowstone National Park, 1895, p. 136)

Following his removal from the superintendency on June 30, 1885, Carpenter appeared openly as a partner of the Hobart Brothers in their construction of a hotel at Old Faithful. This nuisance operation was soon liquidated through purchase by the Northern Pacific Railroad. Carpenter then went to Watertown, South Dakota, where he edited *The Courier News* for six years and was employed as receiver in the U.S. Land Office there. He died at Long Beach, California, on November 6, 1902.

David Walker Wear   The fifth and last civilian superintendent of Yellowstone National Park, prior to the army regime, was an able and uncompromising Missourian; but he came too late upon the scene to undo the mischief of his immediate predecessors.

Wear was born May 31, 1843, at Otterville, Missouri. He was educated for the legal profession and, after reading law in the offices of William Douglas and Judge George W. Miller, was admitted to the bar before he had attained his majority. At the opening of the Civil War, Wear declared for the Union by enlisting as a private soldier. He rose rapidly in the service to the rank of colonel of the Fifty-second Missouri enrolled militia. Following the war, he returned to Missouri where he practiced law at Booneville and St. Louis, and was for a time the assistant attorney for the Missouri Pacific Railroad Company. During this period he also entered a business partnership, and in 1881 he was elected to the Missouri State Senate, serving two terms.

On July 1, 1885, Wear was appointed superintendent of Yellowstone National Park on the recommendation of Senator George Graham Vest, who was eager to correct the abuses that had developed during previous administrations. The *St. Paul Pioneer Press* said about the new superintendent:

Senator Vest has at last got the Yellowstone Park in his grip . . . Mr. Wear is a St. Louis broker . . . honest, driving and capable. He has visited the Park several times; is a semi-misanthrope, hating a great many men and things. *(May 23, 1885)*

That he was just the type of superintendent the Park needed is attested by one of his assistants, D.E. Sawyer, who commented, "For once the park has got a Superintendent. He is the right man . . . doing his duty without fear, favor or affection. A first-class officer as well as a thorough gentlemen."

Wear actually made considerable progress in management of the Park, replacing unsatisfactory assistants, prosecuting poachers and others who habitually disregarded the rules and regulations, and re-establishing a degree of confidence. But dissatisfaction with conditions in the Park was so great that it took only a relatively minor incident to pull him down. The unwarranted abuse of Judge Louis E. Payson, a congressman from Illinois, by a Wyoming justice of the peace at the Lower Geyser Basin, aroused such resentment that Congress refused to appropriate money for the Park in 1886. Without funds for a civilian organization, the secretary of the interior was forced to ask the secretary of war for a detail of troops to manage the area. Accordingly, Wear turned over his responsibilities as superintendent to Captain Moses Harris, Company M, First U.S. Cavalry, on August 20, 1886.

Wear subsequently served in the Bureau of Pensions during President Cleveland's administration, was identified with various movements aimed at improving the city of St. Louis, and re-established a law practice at Booneville; he was a Democrat. His wife was the former Laura Francis Beatty, whom he married in Booneville in 1870; they had one son. Wear died at Booneville on October 20, 1896.

Moses Harris   As the first military officer to serve as acting superintendent of Yellowstone National Park, Moses Harris brought to the assignment the courage, integrity, and common sense that were needed to rescue the Park from a difficult situation.

Harris was born September 6, 1838, in New Hampshire; nothing is known of his life prior to his enlistment in Company G, Fourth U.S. Cavalry, on March 19, 1857. He had reached the rank of sergeant in that unit when he was commissioned a second lieutenant in the First Cavalry on May 18, 1864, and was soon advanced to first lieutenant. For his part in the action at Smithfield, West Virginia, on August 28, 1864, he was subsequently awarded the Congressional Medal of Honor. He was brevetted a captain on November 19, 1864, for meritorious service at the battle of Winchester, Virginia, and held the permanent rank of captain when he took over the superintendency of Yellowstone National Park. Chittenden says,

> The Park was particularly fortunate in its first military superintendent. Captain Harris possessed in a marked degree the qualities required for that position. He was vigorous and uncompromising in suppressing lawlessness, just and impartial in his rulings, untiring in his watchfulness for the public interest. Although his immediate superior, the Secretary of the Interior, originally opposed the use of the military in the Park, he never failed to pay a high tribute to the efficiency with which the new superintendent performed his duties.
>
> *(Yellowstone National Park,* 1964, pp. 117-18)

While Captain Harris did not have the support of adequate laws for the management of the Park, he nevertheless established respect for its rules and regulations by a vigorous use of his power to expel violators, with the result that the editor of *Forest and Stream* was later able to comment: "The Park had been cared for as it never had before." Captain Harris was succeeded by Captain F.A. Boutelle, First U.S. Cavalry, on June 1, 1889. The highest rank Harris reached in his career was major, on July 22, 1892, and he retired from the Eighth U.S. Cavalry on March 7, 1893. He died at Rochester, New York, on June 27, 1927.

Frazier Augustus Boutelle   The second military officer to serve as acting superintendent of Yellowstone National Park was also a product of the Civil

War. Though energetic in his management of the Park, he was the unfortunate victim of political intrigues and thus was soon replaced.

Boutelle was born September 14, 1840, at Troy, New York. Two months after the opening of the Civil War he enlisted as a quartermaster sergeant in Company A, Fifth New York Cavalry. The following year he was commissioned a second lieutenant in that regiment, with which he served until July 19, 1865, when he was mustered out as a captain. Boutelle liked the military life enough to enlist in the regular army as a private on February 12, 1866. He rapidly worked his way up through the ranks and had advanced to the rank of captain by April 24, 1886. He was cited for gallantry in action against Indians at Lost River, Oregon, November 29, 1872, and for conspicuous gallantry and meritorious conduct in the entire Modoc War.

Captain Boutelle's superintendency was undeservedly brief because of his impolitic actions. Chittenden ascribes his downfall to his enforcement of park regulations against a prominent employee of the hotel company, but that is not the whole story. Captain Boutelle was also much too critical of the failure of the secretary of the interior to provide appliances for fighting forest fires in the Park, and there was resentment of his stand in regard to the installation of an elevator in the Grand Canyon of the Yellowstone River. He was replaced by Captain Anderson on February 16, 1891. Captain Boutelle retired August 27, 1895, and died at Seattle, Washington, on February 12, 1924.

George Smith Anderson George Anderson was not only the first West Pointer to serve as acting superintendent of Yellowstone National Park, but also one of the most capable officers ever to manage its affairs. During his administration the Park received the protection of federal law and the activities of poachers were at last curbed.

Anderson was born September 30, 1849, on the family homestead at what is now Bernardsville, New Jersey. His education began in a country school and was fortunately extended two years when he was sent to Mr. William Rankin's Academy at Mendham, where his instructor saw such great possibilities in the boy that he advised Mr. Anderson to apply for a cadetship for his son. George was successfully entered at the United States Military Academy on July 1, 1867, and graduated fifth in his class, gaining an assignment to the Sixth U.S. Cavalry as a second lieutenant on June 12, 1871.

The first four years of Anderson's military career were spent in Kansas and Colorado, where he was concerned with troublesome Indians and miners. In 1874 he received an assignment more in keeping with his interest (which had been in engineering while at West Point) when he was placed on duty with a party surveying a wagon road from Fort Garland, Colorado, to Fort Wingate, New Mexico. It was a difficult assignment that he carried out with such efficiency that he was made the acting engineer officer for the Department of the Missouri in 1875. The following year Anderson served as aide-de-camp to General August V. Kautz, commanding the Department of Arizona, after which he was appointed assistant professor of natural and experimental philosophy at West Point, a post he held for four years. In 1881 he again entered upon a tour of duty in the West, this time seeing service against the Apaches of Arizona. He received his captaincy March 20, 1885, and in 1889 was named to a commission to select small arms for the infantry and cavalry branches, a detail that took him to Europe.

At the time of his appointment to the superintendency of Yellowstone National Park, Anderson was a well-trained and experienced officer who had had the advantage of foreign travel to develop his social graces. Those attributes, joined to his commanding physical appearance, were most helpful to the Park. During his superintendency Anderson was faced with serious problems, such as the attempt to segregate park lands in order to construct a railway to Cooke City, the poaching of buffalo by individuals attempting to take advantage of the fantastically high prices paid for buffalo scalps by taxidermists, and the poor maintenance of the Park's road system. These problems he handled with characteristic energy and zeal, earning the local appellation of Czar of the Yellowstone. He was an outspoken opponent of the railway scheme and helpful to Senator George Graham Vest's effort to obtain laws for the government of the Park. He did strenuous battle with the poachers and took means to perpetuate the buffalo herd; at the same time, he handled problems of road maintenance personally or through overseers responsible to him. His was a vigorous administration that left the Park in very good order at the time of his transfer to other service on June 23, 1897.

Anderson was living at the University Club in New York (he never married) when he suddenly died of a heart attack on March 7, 1915. Following his death, *Forest and Stream* had this to say about him:

> General Anderson was a splendid soldier and a delightful man. He did not know fear, was quick to adapt himself to any situation that arose, and possessed enormous strength and tremendous vitality. Few men had so wide a circle of acquaintance as he; few men were so generally beloved by their associates. With the stature of a giant and the bearing of a soldier, he had the simplicity, directness, and the heart of a little child. *(1918)*

Samuel Baldwin Marks Young   The fourth military officer to serve as acting superintendent of Yellowstone National Park had one of the most unusual and illustrious careers in the U.S. Army. He was also the only man ever to hold the superintendency twice and the only one to hold the titles of acting superintendent and superintendent.

Young was born January 9, 1840, at Pittsburgh, Pennsylvania. Less than two weeks after the outbreak of the Civil War he enlisted as a private in Company K, Twelfth Pennsylvania Infantry, where he rose in rank so rapidly he was made a captain in the Fourth Pennsylvania Cavalry September sixth of that year and was a brevet brigadier general by the war's end. In that struggle he was wounded four times and brevetted three times for gallant and meritorious service in action. Following the war, Young was on frontier duty, participating in many scouts and actions against hostile Indians, and had reached the permanent rank of lieutenant colonel in the Fourth U.S. Cavalry when he was assigned to Yellowstone Park as acting superintendent in 1897. (He came to the Park from Yosemite, where he had been acting superintendent and a terror to local wrongdoers.) A large, blunt, rather positive man, he knew exactly what he was about all the time, and perhaps that is why his administration of Yellowstone passed so smoothly.

General Young retired from military service January 9, 1904, and was appointed superintendent of Yellowstone National Park on June 2, 1907, holding that position until November 28, 1908. He was governor of the U.S. soldier's home in Washington, D.C., from 1909 to 1917, and he died September 1, 1924, at Helena, Montana.

James Brailsford Erwin The fifth military officer to serve as acting superintendent of Yellowstone National Park was a product of the military academy. Though an officer of exceptional ability, he was unable to make any particular contribution to the Park because of his brief tenure.

Erwin was born July 11, 1856, at Savannah, Georgia. He entered the U.S. Military Academy on July 1, 1875, and was assigned to the Fourth Cavalry as a second lieutenant on June 12, 1880. His service with that regiment during the following twenty-three years was marked by graduation from the Cavalry School (with honors) in 1883, campaigns against the Apaches in 1885-86, a brief acting superintendency in Yellowstone Park (November 16, 1897 to March 15, 1899), and hard fighting in the Philippine insurrection. On April 22, 1903, he was transferred to the Ninth Cavalry as a major.

During World War I, he assisted with training of the Sixth Division and commanded the Twelfth Infantry Brigade. He was awarded a Distinguished Service Medal, the French Legion of Honor, French Croix de Guerre, and the rank of brigadier general. General Erwin retired July 11, 1920, and died at Pasadena, California, July 10, 1924.

Wilber Elliott Wilder This officer's brief tour of duty as acting superintendent of Yellowstone National Park was an inconsequential episode in an otherwise remarkably long and active military career.

Wilder was born August 16, 1856, at Atlas, Michigan. He entered the U.S. Military Academy July 1, 1873, and was assigned to the Fourth Cavalry as a second lieutenant on July 15, 1877. He campaigned with that regiment on the western frontier until August 1895, gaining a brevet captaincy February 27, 1890, for his "gallant service in action against Indians" and he later was awarded the Congressional Medal of Honor. During the Spanish American War, Wilder served as colonel of the Fourteenth New York Volunteer Infantry, and his Yellowstone assignment was a mere three months and eight days, preceding duty in the Philippine Islands. Brigadier General Wilder died at Fort Jay, New York, on January 30, 1952, at the age of 96.

Oscar James Brown The seventh military officer to serve as acting superintendent of Yellowstone National Park was also a product of the military academy, and, like his two predecessors, his tenure was too brief to be particularly fruitful.

Brown was born November 25, 1853, at Fairmont, Georgia. He entered the U.S. Military Academy on July 1, 1872, and received an assignment to the Third Cavalry as second lieutenant on June 15, 1877. Appointed to the First Cavalry a few months later, he campaigned against the Bannock Indians in 1878 and the Chiricahua Apache Indians in 1881. His acting superintendency in Yellowstone Park was an interlude of thirteen months between his Spanish American War service as colonel of the Second Georgia Volunteer Infantry and a campaign with the First Cavalry in the Philippines. He died at Fort Sam Houston, Texas, on September 13, 1906.

George William Goode George Goode's tour of duty as acting superintendent of Yellowstone National Park returned him to the scene of earlier service under Captain Moses Harris at the very beginning of the Park's military administration.

Goode was born April 21, 1855, at St. Louis, Missouri. He entered the United States Military Academy on July 1, 1875, and was assigned to the First

Cavalry as a second lieutenant on June 12, 1880. He saw service in the Spanish American War, in which he received a Silver Star citation. His acting superintendency in Yellowstone Park covered a little more than nine months (July 25, 1900, to May 8, 1901). Goode was relieved from active duty November 29, 1918 (his highest rank was that of colonel), and he died at Pasadena, California, on August 20, 1941.

John Pitcher John Pitcher's tour of duty as acting superintendent of Yellowstone National Park (May 9, 1901 to June 1, 1907) corresponds with the golden years of the military administration. Yet that aura probably was due as much to the coincidence of many favorable factors as it was to his efforts.

Pitcher was born September 9, 1854, in Texas. He entered the U.S. Military Academy on July 1, 1872, and was assigned to the Ninth Infantry as a second lieutenant upon graduation. His campaigns included service in the Nez Perce Indian War (1877), the Bannock Indian War (1878), and the Philippine insurrection. He was an accomplished shot with rifle and pistol.

Of Pitcher's handling of park affairs a local editor remarked: "He enjoys the respect and esteem of tourists and others having business in and through the Park in a greater degree than any of his predecessors. While zealously guarding the interests of the Park, he never loses sight of the fact that it is the great national playground and that the people have rights there." However, conditions in and around the Park were very favorable: the railroad had been extended to the park boundary at Gardiner; Chittenden's masterful engineering had completed the road system within the Park and provided an enduring symbol in the basaltic arch erected at the north entrance; the Park stood victorious and peaceful after the long struggle to establish law and order and check the monopolists; the effort to save the American bison in a wild setting appeared successful; and the concessioners were mainly prosperous and happy.

Before the situation changed materially, Colonel Pitcher retired from the regular army. He returned briefly to duty during World War I, and died at Edgewater, Maryland, on October 12, 1926.

Harry Coupland Benson Harry Benson, who served as acting superintendent of Yellowstone National Park for nearly two years (from November 29, 1908, to September 30, 1910), was an anomaly of the military profession—a true intellectual—yet he was a good soldier and administrator.

Benson was born in Ohio, probably in the decade before the Civil War, and he had earned a bachelor of arts degree from Kenyon College prior to entering the U.S. Military Academy on July 1, 1878. He graduated in 1882. He served in the campaign against the Apache Indians in 1885-86, in Cuba during the Spanish American War, and in the Philippine Islands. He was the provost marshal of San Francisco while the city was under martial law following the fire in 1906; he was chief of staff for the Philippine Department from 1912 to 1914 and adjutant for the Western Department from 1917 to 1919. In addition, he found time for further study leading to a degree of master of arts.

A former Yellowstone scout, when asked why Major Benson was called Batty Benson (behind his back, of course) commented: "Well, he would ask a question and answer himself in the same breath." Benson's habit of answering himself was nothing more than a quick, impatient mind that kept him well in advance of his contemporaries. Brigadier General Benson retired April 26, 1919, and he died September 21, 1924.

Lloyd Milton Brett The last military officer to serve as acting superintendent of Yellowstone National Park had a doubly difficult task. He had to prepare the Park for two far-reaching changes: from horsedrawn to motorized transportation and from military to civilian administration.

Brett was born February 22, 1856, in Maine. He graduated from the U.S. Military Academy in 1879. His record as a soldier was outstanding. In a skirmish with Sioux Indians, he earned the Congressional Medal of Honor. He took part in the Apache Indian Campaign in 1885-86. He served in the Spanish American War, the Philippine insurrection, and in World War I, earning distinguished honors.

His six-year service in Yellowstone Park (from October 1, 1910, to October 15, 1916) was very influential in establishing the civilian administration under the new National Park Service. Brigadier General Brett died on September 23, 1927.

Chester Allinson Lindsley The opening years of National Park Service administration in Yellowstone were marked by the enormity of the changeover from military to civilian organization, complicated by the fiscal irresponsibility of Congress and wartime conditions. The Park was fortunate to be in the hands of a civilian employee of many years' experience in the area.

"Chet" Lindsley was born at Franklin, New York, on January 25, 1872. Nothing is known of his life prior to the fall of 1894, when he was employed by Acting Superintendent Anderson as a civilian clerk at the army's headquarters in the Park. He served in that capacity under all the succeeding military superintendents, providing continuity of administrative activities (which would otherwise have suffered from the frequent and complete changing of the detachments stationed in the Park).

When the administration of the Park was handed over to the newly formed civilian service on October 1, 1916, Lindsley was clearly the man for the position of supervisor (a title used until November 1, 1917, when park administrators again were designated superintendents). The two years and nearly nine months during which Lindsley guided the Park, prior to appointment of Horace M. Albright as superintendent on June 28, 1919, is the longest acting superintendency under civilian administration. With Mr. Albright's appointment, Lindsley dropped back to assistant superintendent, a position he held until May 22, 1922. He was then transferred from the National Park Service to the Post Office Department and became postmaster for the Park. Lindsley retired as postmaster on July 1, 1935, with nearly forty-one years of federal service in the Park. He died on November 28, 1938.

Horace Marden Albright Horace M. Albright was born January 6, 1890, at Bishop, California, and was educated in law at the University of California, from which he graduated in 1912. Further study there was interrupted by employment as a confidential clerk to the secretary of the interior in June 1913; his work concerned the establishment of a bureau of national parks. He completed graduate work in 1914 and was admitted to the bar in the District of Columbia and California. As an assistant attorney in the Department of the Interior during 1916-17, Albright was legman for Stephen T.

Mather, assistant to the secretary responsible for the national parks. Albright had a considerable, perhaps even crucial role in the passage of the National Park Service Act of 1916, and, as assistant director (and acting director in 1917-18) of the new organization, he shepherded it through the initial years.

On June 28, 1919, Albright was appointed superintendent of Yellowstone National Park; he held that position until January 12, 1929, when he became the second director of the National Park Service. His years at Yellowstone were filled with challenges; within the Park were problems created by the advent of the automobile; outside were situations threatening the integrity of Yellowstone Park and development of the federal park system. Under Albright's leadership roads were rebuilt to automobile standards, campgrounds were developed, interpretive services were established, and concessioners were encouraged to provide new accommodations, such as service stations, lodge and cabin developments, bathhouses, wood yards, and cafeterias. At the same time, the water and power interests were prevented from encroaching on the Park (which would have damaged park-type conservation beyond any remedy), and the preservation of wilderness superlatives was furthered by Albright's success in establishing Grand Teton National Park. From 1921 to 1926, he acted as field assistant to the director, and from 1926 to 1929 as assistant director (field), dealing with problems of all national parks.

With greater responsibilities as head of the National Park Service, Albright's work on behalf of the national park idea broadened. When he at last withdrew from active direction of the federal park system in 1933, it was well organized and secure under the management of a service with an outstanding sense of mission. Probably his greatest achievement was expanding the park service to include all federal historic sites and structures and the park system of the District of Columbia. Even after he turned to private business as president, general manager, and director of the U.S. Potash Company, Albright retained his interest in the park movement and conservation. His continuing service on behalf of America's wilderness heritage has been well recognized with honorary degrees, awards, and citations, including the American Forestry Association's Distinguished Service Award (1968) and the Audubon Medal of the National Audubon Society (1969). The Horace M. Albright Conservation Lecture Series established at the University of California in 1961, and the Horace M. Albright Training Center established by the National Park Service at Grand Canyon National Park in 1963 will exert continuing influence in coming years.

Joseph Joffe   In the interval between the promotion of Superintendent Horace M. Albright to the position of director of the National Park Service on January 12, 1929, and the appointment of Roger W. Toll as his successor on February 1, 1929, Yellowstone National Park was without a superintendent. Ordinarily, the duties of that position would have been performed by Assistant Superintendent Merrill F. Daum during the changeover, but he was absent on special assignment in the Washington office, and the acting status fell to the assistant to the superintendent, Joseph Joffe. Joffe has been described as "a sort of evener for several superintendents."

He was born in St. Joseph, Missouri, on June 6, 1896. Employment in the Panama Canal Office in Washington, D.C., was followed by a stint in the Navy during World War I, after which he worked for the American Graves Registration Service in Belgium until March 1922. On his return to the United States, Joffe was offered a clerical position in Yellowstone Park by Horace Albright; he thus began a thirty-four-year career as the righthand man of park superintendents until his retirement on March 4, 1960. His smooth handling of correspondence, personnel matters, and public contacts over the years made it possible for the Park's superintendents to undertake far-ranging assignments beneficial to the national park system as a whole. Joffe died at Livingston, Montana, on September 29. 1960.

Roger Wolcott Toll A career ended prematurely by accident is forever haunted by speculation; yet one cannot entirely put aside the feeling that the National Park Service lost a future director in the death of Roger Toll.

Toll was born October 17, 1883, at Denver, Colorado, and was educated at Denver University and Columbia University. Following graduation in 1906, he worked as an engineer until the war. After World War I Toll entered the National Park Service in May 1919 as superintendent of Mount Rainier National Park. Two and one-half years later he was transferred to Rocky Mountain National Park where he was superintendent until his transfer to Yellowstone Park on February 1, 1929, to replace Horace M. Albright.

Superintendent Toll's Yellowstone years are less outstanding than they might have been because of his preoccupation with problems involving the park system as a whole. He maintained an office in Denver, working from there each winter on the inspection of proposed parks and monuments to determine their possible value as units in the national park system. He was serving on a six-man commission to investigate the possibility of establishing international parks and wildlife refuges along the Mexican-American border when he was killed in an automobile accident in New Mexico on February 25, 1936.

John W. Emmert The vacancy in the Yellowstone superintendency created by the tragic death of Roger Toll was filled for three months, on an acting basis, by the Park's assistant superintendent. Jack Emmert was born April 8, 1888, at Hagerstown, Maryland. He studied electrical engineering at George Washington University and was employed at Yosemite National Park from 1912 until his appointment as assistant superintendent of Yellowstone Park in September 1934. Emmert remained at Yellowstone Park as assistant superintendent until April 18, 1943, when he became superintendent of Hot Springs National Park. He was later transferred to Glacier National Park, where he retired in 1958 after forty-six years of dedication to the nation's parks. After a further contribution of his energy and experience to the public good as director of state parks for Idaho, Jack Emmert settled at Coeur d'Alene.

Edmund Burrell Rogers Edmund B. Rogers was born December 28, 1891, at Denver, Colorado, into a pioneer family of that state. He attended public school in his home town, studied for a year at Cornell University, and graduated from Yale in 1915. While a student, he worked for the Topographic Branch of the U.S. Geological Survey; his permanent employment following matriculation was with the Colorado National Bank of Denver. Rogers was a charter member of the Colorado Mountain Club (serving twice as its president), and a love of wilderness places, engendered by that association, finally led him into the National Park Service. He followed Roger Toll as superintendent of Rocky Mountain National Park, and during his seven years in that area the Trail Ridge Road was designed and built; considerable progress was also made in eliminating private landholdings from within the park.

On May 25, 1936, following the death of Roger Toll, Edmund Rogers became superintendent of Yellowstone Park. His management of the first and largest of the national parks lasted twenty years, five months, and six days—a record tenure. His superintendency began on the hopeful side of the Great Depression, struggled through the doldrums of World War II, and had to settle for preserving park values during the postwar resurgence of travel. Those were years dominated by expediency and diplomacy, and the measure of Superintendent Rogers' accomplishment lies in the fact that the Park continued to accommodate a visitation that rose to nearly one and one-half million persons in 1956 (three times the load of 1936), despite appalling obsolescence of physical facilities. In addition to shepherding Yellowstone Park through a period of unusual and protracted trials, Rogers continued to serve the national park system by investigating areas proposed for inclusion and by serving as acting supervisor of recreation and land planning in 1938 and acting superintendent of National Capital Parks in 1939 and 1940.

Edmund Rogers was promoted to the position of special assistant to the director of the national park system following the 1956 travel season, in order to complete a project on which he had worked for many years: compilation of all legislation affecting each area of the national park system. The information eventually filled more than 200 volumes; with completion of that compendium, he retired on July 31, 1960. He died at Denver on January 30, 1972.

Lemuel Alonzo Garrison The task of refurbishing Yellowstone Park in accordance with the ten-year plan known as Mission 66 fell to the man who had headed the committee that activated the plan. His achievements in Yellowstone Park were great, and if they were less than an ultimate solution to the Park's problems, it was because these problems proliferated more rapidly than the means for their control.

"Lon" Garrison was born at Pella, Iowa, on October 1, 1903. His college years included seasonal employment by the forest service in Alaska, where he taught school. There he met and married Inger Wilhelmine Larsen in 1930. Following his graduation from Stanford University in 1932, he went to work for the National Park Service as a seasonal park ranger at Sequoia National Park. His appointment as a permanent park ranger at Yosemite was followed by advancement to district ranger and, in 1939, by transfer to Hopewell Village National Historic Site as the first superintendent of that new area. He served as assistant superintendent for Glacier National Park in 1942 and for the Grand Canyon in 1946; he became superintendent of Big Bend National Park in 1952. Three years later, Garrison was appointed as the first chief of conservation and protection for the National Park Service. While establishing the goals and activities of that branch, he also served as chairman of the steering committee charged with implementing the Mission 66 plan for development of the national park system.

In November 1956, Garrison was appointed to direct Mission 66 in Yellowstone Park as park superintendent. There, where physical facilities for handling rapidly increasing visitation remained at the stage of development reached in pre-depression years, he wrought great change. The new Canyon Village, a project two decades old, was pushed to completion in a year; an entirely new marina development at Bridge Bay on Yellowstone Lake was completed, and work on Grant Village, intended to replace the West Thumb complex, was taken from the planning stage into actual construction. Concurrently, obsolete facilities were removed and their sites restored to a natural appearance. The park road system was given a major overhaul, with particular emphasis on eliminating the many bottle-neck bridges, and transportation to the area was facilitated by construction of a commercial airport adjacent to the Park at West Yellowstone, Montana. Supporting developments—campgrounds, picnicking sites, utilities (including commercial power and telephone service), employee housing, and back-country facilities designed to encourage a broader use of the area—were undertaken throughout the Park.

Less prominent, but equally important, were Garrison's efforts to increase staffing, promote basic research, and solve such biological problems as management of the Yellowstone elk herd, sport fishing, and use of park lakes, particularly Yellowstone Lake. He also strove to gain the understanding and cooperation of interested communities and organizations outside the Park, succeeding so well that he came to be recognized as the spokesman for the conservation movement in the northern Rocky Mountain region. In 1964, when Garrison was transferred to Omaha, Nebraska, to head the midwest region of the National Park Service, he left Yellowstone Park greatly improved and capable of serving many more visitors annually.

During the seven years of Garrison's tenure as Yellowstone's superintendent, park visitation doubled (increasing from one to two million persons annually), while the major concession—the Yellowstone Park Company—became too ailing to hold up its end of the Mission 66 program. Garrison is now director of the Horace M. Albright Training Center at the Grand Canyon.

John S. McLaughlin The closing of Mission 66 and the determination of further objectives in Yellowstone Park fell to a man whose many years with the National Park Service had prepared him for such a role.

John McLaughlin was born at Fremont, Ohio, June 8, 1905. His college years were spent at Colorado State University, where he received a degree in forestry. He entered the National Park Service in 1928 as a park ranger in Yellowstone and became an assistant chief park ranger there in 1930. The following year, McLaughlin transferred to Rocky Mountain National Park as chief park ranger, remaining there until 1936 (except for a year on duty in Washington, D.C., as assistant to the chief forester). In that year he was detailed to the CCC Program in the Western Region, returning to Rocky Mountain National Park as assistant superintendent in 1937. In 1940, he was appointed superintendent of Mesa Verde National Park.

He entered the Army Air Force as a second lieutenant in 1942. Four years later, Major McLaughlin returned to civilian life and the superintendency of Grand Teton National Park. In 1950, he became the assistant regional director, Midwest Region, and in 1955 he accepted the superintendency of Grand Canyon National Park, where he remained until his transfer to Yellowstone Park in 1964.

As a follow-up man, Superintendent McLaughlin had to decide which Mission 66 objectives remained valid in view of the changing conditions within and outside the Park. The available means were then concentrated on the more essential projects. John McLaughlin was transferred to Sequoia-Kings Canyon National Park (where he is now superintendent) in the fall of 1967.

Jack Kenneth Anderson Jack Anderson was born at San Luis Obispo, California, May 24, 1917. He entered nearby San Jose State College with the intention of preparing himself for a career in law. Having entered the U.S. Navy in 1941, Anderson was in Hawaii at the time of the attack on Pearl Harbor. He was returned to the states early in 1943 for flight training. After receiving his wings, he instructed in instrument flying and served as a test pilot in Texas. There he married Virginia Miller.

In 1946, Lieutenant Anderson was influenced by Frank Oberhansley (a former superintendent of Hawaii National Park and a Yellowstone naturalist) to forsake the Navy for a park career. Anderson entered California Poly-Technical College and worked summers as a seasonal ranger at Sequoia-Kings Canyon National Park until 1950, when he received a permanent appointment as a park ranger there. In 1957, he was transferred to Glacier National Park where he served as a management assistant through 1960. Thereafter, he advanced through the superintendencies of George Washington Carver Birthplace National Monument (followed by a special assignment as a task force coordinator in Washington, D.C.) and Grand Teton National Park to the Yellowstone superintendency.

Since Anderson's appointment in 1966, it has become increasingly apparent that continued development of the Park to accommodate the ever-increasing visitation would inevitably destroy many unique features and negate much of the area's charm. Whether or not Yellowstone Park remains relatively unimpaired for the use of future generations depends very largely upon the accuracy with which Superintendent Jack Anderson assesses the problem and the effectiveness with which he meets it.

Part IV. Engineer Officers, Civilian Overseers, and Acting Engineers of Yellowstone National Park, 1883-1918

Daniel Christie Kingman The first officer of the Corps of Engineers assigned the task of constructing and maintaining roads and bridges in Yellowstone Park was handpicked by Major General Philip H. Sheridan to put the work on a professional basis. Kingman established the park road plan that has proven so satisfactory over the years, and set the high standards that have since guided the work of the army engineers.

Daniel Kingman was born March 6, 1852, at Dover, New Hampshire. He graduated from the U.S. Military Academy in 1875. He held the rank of first lieutenant when chosen by General Sheridan to supervise park road development. Upon his arrival in Yellowstone Park on August 13, 1883, Kingman prepared a plan for a double-track wagon road circling the area as the Grand Loop now does. His particular contributions toward the fulfillment of that plan—a figure-eight design that has been the basis of all road development since his time—was construction of the north entrance road by way of the Gardner River, the road from Mammoth Hot Springs to Swan Lake Flat by way of the Golden Gate, with realignment and double-tracking of the road from there to the Upper Geyser Basin, and construction of the Norris Cutoff. The work accomplished under his direction during four seasons in the Park was so superior to any done there previously that the wisdom of entrusting the engineering activities to the army was immediately apparent.

Dan Kingman reached the rank of brigadier general before his retirement from active service March 6, 1916. He died on November 16 of that year at Atlantic City, New Jersey. He is remembered in the name of Kingman Pass, that narrow gap through which he brought the new road from Mammoth Hot Springs out upon Swan Lake Flat.

Clinton Brooks Sears The officer who followed Dan Kingman was fully occupied completing projects initiated by his predecessor, and that, with the brevity of his assignment to the Park (a single working season) allowed him no chance to distinguish himself further. Beyond the fact of his birth at Penn Yan, New York, June 2, 1844, nothing is known of Sears' life prior to his enlistment in Company G, Ninety-fifth Ohio Infantry on July 24, 1862. His Civil War service was interrupted by appointment to the U.S. Military Academy on September 16, 1863; he graduated in 1867. He had reached the rank of captain in the Corps of Engineers by the time of his Yellowstone assignment in 1887. He was retired as a brigadier general and died February 16, 1912, at Boston.

Charles Julius Allen The Park's third engineering officer had the misfortune to take up his responsibility at a time when Congress was remiss in funding the work to which he had been assigned. An unfair, but not unnatural, reaction to his inability was subordination of all his further efforts (and those of two successors) to the irascible Major William A. Jones, who was headquartered at St. Louis. This stultified the work in the Park and wasted a good officer.

Allen was born at Buffalo, New York, on January 31, 1840; he entered the U.S. Military Academy on the eve of the Civil War with the class of 1864. He graduated and had been less than two months in the field when he earned a brevet rank as captain "for highly meritorious service in the sieges of Forts Gaines and Morgan, Alabama." Another brevet brought him the rank of major in 1865. He was commissioned major in the Corps of Engineers during his Yellowstone assignments (the seasons of 1888 and 1889) and retired as a brigadier general. He died June 15, 1915, at Asheville, North Carolina.

William Edward Craighill Another engineer officer—an inexperienced young-ster—also spent a nearly fruitless tour of duty in the Park tied to the apron strings of Major Jones. Craighill was born December 20, 1863, at Baltimore, Maryland. He graduated from the U.S. Military Academy and had been advanced to the rank of first lieutenant in the Corps of Engineers by the time of his assignment to the Park in the fall of 1889 as the representative of Major Jones. It was a brief interlude (a little more than one and one-half years in a career that included service in the Spanish American War. He was retired as a colonel and died November 26, 1916, in Washington, D.C.

A. E. Burns Civilian Overseer Burns supervised construction and mainten-ance of roads in the Park for Major William A. Jones during the seasons of 1893 and 1894. Nothing further is known about him personally, though the unsatisfactory nature of the work performed under his direction (a result he may not have been entirely responsible for) hints that he was only of foreman caliber and not trained to head a field operation of the size of Yellowstone's.

George Smith Anderson Acting Park Superintendent Anderson was directly responsible for construction and maintenance of roads and bridges in the Park from August 29, 1894, when that activity passed out of the control of Major William A. Jones, through June 23, 1897. (A more complete biography is given in Part III of this Appendix.)

Samuel Baldwin Marks Young Acting Park Superintendent Young was directly responsible for construction and maintenance of roads and bridges during his first tour of duty in the Park (June 23, 1897, to May 18, 1898). (A more complete biography is given in Part III of this Appendix.)

James Brailsford Erwin Acting Superintendent Erwin was the last officer to have responsibility for administrative and engineering activities. With his transfer from the Park on March 15, 1899, construction and maintenance of roads and bridges was returned to the Corps of Engineers. (A more complete biography is given in Part III of this Appendix.)

Hiram Martin Chittenden Among the many capable officers of the Corps of Engineers who directed the construction and maintenance of roads and bridges in Yellowstone Park from 1883 to 1918, one man stands out above all others. He prosecuted the work with unusual ability, energy, and imagination, yet also found the time to delve into the area's history; thus, his legacy includes literary as well as engineering contributions.

Hiram Martin Chittenden was born at Yorkshire, in western New York State, on October 25, 1858. His boyhood was spent on a farm where he knew the hard work, rustic pleasures, and village schooling typical of the time and place. He was graduated from the National Military Academy at West Point and as was customary for top-ranking graduates, he was assigned to the Corps of Engineers as a second lieutenant. Two years later Chittenden was promoted to first lieutenant, and in the spring of 1891 was transferred from Missouri River improvement work to Yellowstone National Park, where he was placed in direct charge of construction, repair, and maintenance of roads and bridges. His first tour of duty there covered two summer seasons and was notable for construction of the road between Old Faithful and West Thumb.

Following his return to river improvement work at Columbus, Ohio, Chittenden launched his career as an historian by writing *The Yellowstone National Park* (1895). He was promoted to a captaincy that fall and spent two seasons on a survey of reservoir sites in Wyoming and Colorado. When not occupied with his professional duties, he collected information on the early fur-trade. In 1898 he was detailed to construct the Fort Washakie military road from Wind River Valley to Jackson Lake.

The following year Chittenden was returned to Yellowstone Park for another tour of duty. It was during this second period (1899 to 1906) that his best engineering and literary works appeared. He built a new road from Mammoth Hot Springs to Golden Gate (1899), the concrete viaduct at Golden Gate (1900), Fishing Bridge (1901), the arch at the north entrance (1903), and the road from Canyon to Tower Fall, including the Mount Washburn loop (1905); he also supervised construction of the Sergeant Floyd monument at Sioux City, Iowa, during 1901-02. Chittenden wrote three important histories: *The American Fur Trade of the Far West* (1902), *A History of Early Steamboat Navigation on the Missouri River* (1903), and, with Alfred T. Richardson, *The Life, Letters and Travels of Father Pierre Jean de Smet* (1905). His interest was intense, his research untiring.

When he began work on his fur-trade classic, a friend suggested that retired St. Louis businessman Pierre Chouteau, Jr., might give him access to an invaluable collection of records. The friend arranged a meeting, and the crusty old trader was so taken with the young engineer-historian that he gave him a key to the vault containing the records of the American Fur Company, with permission to come and go as he pleased. Thereafter, Chittenden often spent the hours he should have reserved for sleep in that dusty vault, searching out by lamplight the substance and spirit of the American fur trade.

In 1906 Major Chittenden was placed in charge of all activities of the Corps of Engineers in the Pacific Northwest. From his headquarters at Seattle he directed stream-control and harbor improvement work (including construction of the Lake Washington ship canal) until his retirement for disability in 1910 (with the rank of brigadier general). The remaining seven years of his life were devoted, insofar as his failing health would allow, to work as a private consultant on flood control and in development of the port of Seattle. But he had burned the candle at both ends during his strenuous career and died, after a lingering illness, at the age of 59.

Ernest Dichmann Peek It was inevitable that Chittenden's successor would be obscured by the afterglow of greatness. However, he, too, was an unusual, even talented engineer who would have left his mark upon the Park in any other period than the one that fell to him.

Peek was born November 19, 1878, at Oshkosh, Wisconson. He was graduated from the U.S. Military Academy near the top of his class and never ceased reaching for additional rungs on the ladder to success. He was an eager beaver whose dedication to his military career was absolute. He learned to speak French, German, and Spanish, completed every Garrison School course he could get into, wrangled admission to the Army School of the Line, the Army Staff College, and the Army War College (graduated from all three), and obtained an assignment to observe construction work on the Panama Canal.

There is little doubt the talents of such an officer were wasted in supervising the maintenance of the Yellowstone improvements that Chittenden had put in such excellent condition. There is even evidence that his tour of duty in the Park (March 26, 1906 to October 31, 1908), during which he was advanced to the rank of captain, was less than beneficial for both the man and the area.

But war, for which Peek had trained himself so rigorously, was another matter. He served notably in the Spanish American War and the subsequent Philippine insurrection. During World War I, he organized and maintained the railway system that supported the American First Army in France. He remained in active service until his retirement for disability on October 31, 1942, and died April 22, 1950, at San Francisco.

Wildurr Willing Another engineer officer whose competence probably exceeded his achievements in Yellowstone Park was Wildurr Willing. Willing was born May 1, 1876, at Crystal Springs, Mississippi. He attended the U.S. Military Academy and placed high in the list of graduates. His assignment to engineering work in Yellowstone National Park March 4, 1909, was followed shortly by his advancement to the rank of captain; otherwise, his stint there (it ended November 13, 1910) was not noteworthy. Willing saw service during World War I in the Somme Defensive Sector and with the British Fourth Army. He retired as a colonel and died in New York City on November 19, 1958.

Clarence Hollister Knight The work of preparing the park road system for eventual use by automobile traffic was begun by Clarence Knight, but he was not given the means to make real progress.

Knight was born February 27, 1880, at Akron, Ohio. Upon graduation from the U.S. Military Academy, he was commissioned in the artillery and then transferred to the Corps of Engineers. Prior to his assignment as an engineer officer for Yellowstone Park (June 10, 1911 to June 5, 1914), Captain Knight had served as chief engineer for the army's Philippine Division, and as secretary to the Missouri River Commission. He resigned from military service August 10, 1916, but re-entered for two years as a major in World War I. He died at Clearwater, Florida, on April 3, 1956.

Amos Alfred Fries In contemporary eyes, Amos Fries was a controversial figure. He continued the work of modernizing the park road system, earning both criticism and commendation—the first for his unsuccessful struggle with the slide in the Gardner Canyon, and the second for his improvement of the eastern approach to the Park.

Fries was born March 17, 1873, at Debello, Wisconsin. After graduation from the U.S. Military Academy, he was commissioned in the Corps of Engineers. His tour of duty in Yellowstone Park was from 1914 to 1916. He died in Washington, D.C., on December 30, 1964.

John Wesley Niesz Schulz The last West Pointer to serve as engineer officer for Yellowstone Park did so during war time, when maintenance of the road system was difficult and improvement was impossible.

Schulz was born May 14, 1885, at Wheeling, West Virginia. He was graduated from the U.S. Military Academy and was assigned to the Corps of Engineers. His assignment to the Park in 1917 kept him out of World War I, but he had prominent roles in World War II. He died a brigadier general at Walter Reed Hospital on April 4, 1965.

George E. Verrill Ironically, the officer who handed over the property and responsibilities of the Corps of Engineers in Yellowstone Park to Engineer Arthur W. Burney of the National Park Service—closing out thirty-five years' work on July 1, 1918—was not one of the corps' well-trained professionals but a major held over from the wartime levies. He is known only by the receipts he signed.

Part V. Administrative Personnel of Yellowstone National Park Under the National Park Service (dates of tenure only).

THE ASSISTANT SUPERINTENDENTS

Chester Allinson Lindsley June 28, 1919 to May 21, 1922. (See biographical sketch in Part III of this Appendix)

Leroy Hill May 22, 1922 to August 16, 1927

Peter E. Bilkert May 1, 1924 to September, 1925

Merrill F. Daum　October 16, 1927 to March 31, 1930 (See biographical sketch in Part III of this Appendix)

Guy D. Edwards　April 1, 1930 to August 30, 1934

John W. Emmert　September 13, 1934 to April 18, 1943 (See biographical sketch in Part III of this Appendix.)

Fred T. Johnston　May 17, 1943 to March 28, 1952

Warren F. Hamilton　March 30, 1952 to June 1, 1958

Luis A. Gastellum　June 16, 1958 to December 3, 1964

Julius A. Martinek　November 11, 1962 to May 7, 1967

Richard A. Nelson　February 25, 1962 to May 10, 1964

James M. Carpenter　January 31, 1965 to January 29, 1967

Robert R. Lovegren　February 1967 to May 1969

Vernon E. Hennesay　July 24, 1967, to present

Gary E. Everhardt　May 18, 1969, to present

THE CHIEF RANGERS

James McBride　November 1, 1918 to January 16, 1922 (acting until January 1, 1920)

Samuel T. Woodring　January 16, 1922 to May 15, 1929

George F. Baggley　June 22, 1929 to May 1, 1935

Francis D. LaNoue　July 8, 1935 to May 21, 1943 (acting until March 1, 1938)

Maynard B. Barrows　May 21, 1943 to January 31, 1947 (acting until December 4, 1943)

Francis D. LaNoue　February 1, 1947 to August 21, 1948 (return from military service)

Curtis K. Skinner　September 9, 1948 to April 13, 1952

Otto M. Brown　April 13, 1952 to October 3, 1959

Nelson N. Murdock　March 16, 1960 to June 11, 1961

Oscar T. Dick　June 11, 1961 to February 9, 1963

Wayne R. Howe　February 3, 1963 to June 12, 1966

Harold J. Estey　June 19, 1966, to present

THE PARK NATURALISTS[1] AND CHIEF PARK NATURALISTS[2]

Milton P. Skinner[1] April 1, 1920 to September 21, 1922

Frank E. Thone[1] June 10, 1923 to August 20, 1923 (acting the entire period)

Edmund J. Sawyer[1] March 1, 1924 to January 3, 1926 and February 27, 1926 to March 31, 1928

Dorr G. Yeager[1] April 10, 1928 to April 15, 1931

Alfred H. V. Povah[1] May 2, 1931 to October 31, 1931

Clyde Max Bauer[1, 2] June 16, 1932 to November 15, 1946 (title of Chief Park Naturalist appeared October 1, 1943)

David deL. Condon[2] November 17, 1946 to June 28, 1959

Robert N. McIntyre[2] June 28, 1959 to September 16, 1962

John M. Good[2] February 28, 1963 to April 21, 1968

William W. Dunmire[2] July 14, 1968 , to October 15, 1972

R. Alan Mebane[2] October 29, 1972 to present

THE CHIEF CLERKS[3], SENIOR CLERKS[4], AND ADMINISTRATIVE OFFICERS[5]

Chester A. Lindsley[3] October 16, 1916 to June 28, 1919 (also acting supervisor or superintendent during the period)

Leroy Hill[4] June 28, 1919 to May 22, 1922

Peter E. Bilkert[4] May 22, 1922 to May 1, 1924

Andrew R. Edwin[4] May 1, 1924 to October 6, 1927

Leroy Hill[4] October 6, 1927 to January 1, 1931

Benjamin A. Hundley[3] January 1, 1931 to August 5, 1936

Keith Neilson[3] September 1, 1936 to July 14, 1942

Richard J. Smith[3] July 15, 1942 to September 30, 1943

Parke W. Soule[3] October 8, 1943 to June 4, 1945

Ernest R.I. Anderson[3, 5] June 21, 1945 to November 1, 1965 (title of Administrative Officer appeared February 5, 1953)

Cecil L. Hanner[5] November 7, 1965, to present

THE RESIDENT ENGINEERS[6], PARK ENGINEERS[7], AND CHIEFS OF MAINTENANCE[8]

Arthur W. Burney[6]   July 1, 1918 to May 29, 1926

Merrill F. Daum[6]   May 29, 1926 to October 16, 1927

Cecil A. Lord[6,7]   October 16, 1927 to January 1, 1943 (title of Park Engineer appeared December 7, 1939)

Philip H. Wohlbrandt[7]   January 1, 1943 to April 30, 1956 (acting until February 16, 1943)

Gerald A. Rowe[7]   May 1, 1956 to March 28, 1965

Franklin B. Elliott[8]   August 1, 1965 to May 24, 1969

J. Daniel Nordgren[8]   August 8, 1969, to present

APPENDIX B: LEGISLATIVE

Part I. The Organic Act

(U.S., Statutes at Large, vol. 17, chap. 24, pp. 32-33)

CHAP. XXIV.—An Act to set apart a certain Tract of Land lying near the Head-waters of the Yellowstone River as a public Park.

Be it enacted by the Senate and House of Representatives of the United States of America in Congress assembled, That the tract of land in the Territories of Montana and Wyoming, lying near the head-waters of the Yellowstone river, and described as follows, to wit, commencing at the junction of Gardiner's river with the Yellowstone river, and running east to the meridian passing ten miles to the eastward of the most eastern point of Yellowstone lake; thence south along said meridian to the parallel of latitude passing ten miles south of the most southern point of Yellowstone lake; thence west along said parallel to the meridian passing fifteen miles west of the most western point of Madison lake; thence north along said meridian to the latitude of the junction of the Yellowstone and Gardiner's rivers; thence east to the place of beginning, is hereby reserved and withdrawn from settlement, occupancy, or sale under the laws of the United States, and dedicated and set apart as a public park or pleasureing-ground for the benefit and enjoyment of the people; and all persons who shall locate or settle upon or occupy the same, or any part thereof, except as hereinafter provided, shall be considered trespassers and removed therefrom.

SEC. 2. That said public park shall be under the exclusive control of the Secretary of the Interior, whose duty it shall be, as soon as practicable, to make and publish such rules and regulations as he may deem necessary or proper for the care and management of the same. Such regulations shall provide for the preservation, from injury or spoilation, of all timber, mineral deposits, natural curiosities, or wonders within said park, and their retention in their natural condition. The Secretary may in his discretion, grant leases for building purposes for terms not exceeding ten years, of small parcels of ground, at such places in said park as shall require the erection of buildings for the accommodation of visitors; all of the proceeds of said leases, and all other revenues that may be derived from any source connected with said park, to be expended under his direction in the management of the same, and the construction of roads and bridle-paths therein. He shall provide against the wanton destruction of the fish and game found within said Park, and against their capture or destruction for the purposes of merchandise or profit. He shall also cause all persons trespassing upon the same after the passage of this act to be removed therefrom, and generally shall be authorized to take all such measures as shall be necessary or proper to fully carry out the objects and purposes of this act.

Approved, March 1, 1872.

Signed by:

James G. Blaine, Speaker of the House

Schuyler Colfax, Vice-President of the United States and President of the Senate

Ulysses S. Grant, President of the United States

Part II. Sundry Civil Bill for March 3, 1883

(U.S., Statutes at Large, vol. 22, p. 626)

. . . for every purpose and object necessary for the protection, preservation, and improvement of the Yellowstone National Park, including compensation of superintendent and employees, forty thousand dollars, two thousand dollars of said amount to be paid annually to a superintendent of said park and not exceeding nine hundred dollars annually to each of ten assistants, all of whom shall be appointed by the Secretary of the Interior, and reside continuously in the park and whose duty it shall be to protect the game, timber, and objects of interest therein; the balance of the sum appropriated to be expended in the construction and improvement of suitable roads and bridges within said park, under the supervision and direction of an engineer officer detailed by the Secretary of War for that purpose;

The Secretary of the Interior may lease small portions of ground in the park, not exceeding ten acres in extent for each tract, on which may be erected hotels and the necessary outbuildings, and for a period not exceeding ten years; but such lease shall not include any of the geysers or other objects of curiosity or interest in said park, or exclude the public from the free and convenient approach thereto; or include any ground within one quarter of a mile of any of the geysers, or the Yellowstone Falls, nor shall there be leased more than ten acres to any one person or corporation; nor shall any hotel or other buildings be erected within the park until such lease shall be executed by the Secretary of the Interior, and all contracts, agreements, or exclusive privileges heretofore made or given in regard to said park or any part thereof, are hereby declared to be invalid; nor shall the Secretary of the Interior, in any lease which he may make and execute, grant any exclusive privileges within said park, except upon the ground leased.

The Secretary of War, upon the request of the Secretary of the Interior, is hereby authorized and directed to make the necessary details of troops to prevent trespassers or intruders from entering the park for the purpose of destroying the game or objects of curiosity therein, or for any other purpose prohibited by law, and to remove such persons from the park if found therein . . .

Part III. Wyoming Act

(U.S., Statutes at Large, vol. 26, p. 222)

. . . that nothing in this act contained shall repeal or affect any act of Congress relating to the Yellowstone National Park, or the reservation of the Park as now defined, or as may be hereafter defined or extended, or the power of the United States over it; and nothing contained in this act shall interfere with the right and ownership of the United States in said park and reservation as it now is or may hereafter be defined or extended by law; but exclusive legislation, in all cases whatsoever, shall be exercised by the United States, which shall have exclusive control and jurisdiction over the same; but nothing in this proviso contained shall be construed to prevent the service within said park of civil and criminal process lawfully issued by the authority of said State . . .

From the Act of July 10, 1890.

Part IV. The Lacey Act

(U.S., Statutes at Large, vol. 28, p. 73)

CHAP. 72.—An Act To protect the birds and animals in Yellowstone National Park, and to punish crimes in said park, and for other purposes.

Be it enacted by the Senate and House of Representatives of the United States of America in Congress assembled, That the Yellowstone National Park, as its boundaries now are defined, or as they may be hereafter defined or extended, shall be under the sole and exclusive jurisdiction of the United States; and that all the laws applicable to places under the sole and exclusive jurisdiction of the United States shall have force and effect in said park: *Provided, however,* That nothing in this Act shall be construed to forbid the service in the park of any civil or criminal process of any court having jurisdiction in the States of Idaho, Montana, and Wyoming. All fugitives from justice taking refuge in said park shall be subject to the same laws as refugees from justice found in the State of Wyoming.

SEC. 2. That said park, for all the purposes of this Act, shall constitute a part of the United States judicial district of Wyoming, and the district and circuit courts of the United States in and for said district shall have jurisdiction of all offenses committed within said park.

SEC. 3. That if any offense shall be committed in said Yellowstone National Park, which offense is not prohibited or the punishment is not specially provided for by any law of the United States or by any regulation of the Secretary of the Interior, the offender shall be subject to the same punishment as the laws of the State of Wyoming in force at the time of the commission of the offense may provide for a like offense in the said State; and no subsequent repeal of any such law of the State of Wyoming shall affect any prosecution for said offense committed within said park.

SEC. 4. That all hunting, or the killing or wounding, or capturing at any time of any bird or wild animal, except dangerous animals, when it is necessary to prevent them from destroying human life or inflicting an injury, is prohibited within the limits of said park; nor shall any fish be taken out of the waters of the park by means of seines, nets, traps, or by the use of drugs or any explosive substances or compounds, or in any other way than by hook and line, and then only at such seasons and in such times and manner as may be directed by the Secretary of the Interior. That the Secretary of the Interior shall make and publish such rules and regulations as he may deem necessary and proper for the management and care of the park and for the protection of the property therein, especially for the preservation from injury or spoilation of all timber, mineral deposits, natural curiosities, or wonderful objects within said park; and for the protection of the animals and birds in the park, from capture or destruction, or to prevent their being frightened or driven from the park; and he shall make rules governing the taking of fish from the streams or lakes in the park. Possession within said park of the dead bodies, or any part thereof, of any wild bird or animal shall be prima facie evidence that the person or persons having the same are guilty of violating this Act. Any person or persons, or stage or express company or railway company, receiving for transportation any of the said animals, birds, or fish so killed, taken or caught shall be deemed guilty of a misdemeanor, and shall be fined for every such offense not exceeding three hundred dollars. Any person found guilty of violating any of the provisions of this Act or any rule or regulation that may be promulgated by the Secretary of the Interior with reference to the management and care of the park, or for the protection of the property therein, for the preservation from injury or spoilation of timber, mineral deposits, natural curiosities or wonderful objects within said park, or for the protection of the animals, birds and fish in the said park, shall be deemed guilty of a misdemeanor, and shall be subjected to a fine of not more than one thousand dollars or imprisonment not exceeding two years, or both, and be adjudged to pay all costs of the proceedings.

That all guns, traps, teams, horses, or means of transportation of every nature or description used by any person or persons within said park limits when engaged in killing, trapping, ensnaring, or capturing such wild beasts, birds, or wild animals shall be forfeited to the United States, and may be seized by the officers in said park and held pending the prosecution of any person or persons arrested under charge of violating the provisions of this Act, and upon conviction under this Act of such person or persons using said guns, traps, teams, horses, or other means of transportation such forfeiture shall be adjudicated as a penalty in addition to the other punishment provided in this Act. Such forfeited property shall be disposed of and accounted for by and under the authority of the Secretary of the Interior.

SEC. 5. That the United States circuit court in said district shall appoint a commissioner, who shall reside in the park, who shall have jurisdiction to hear and act upon all complaints made, of any and all violations of the law, or of the rules and regulations made by the Secretary of the Interior for the government of the park, and for the protection of the animals, birds, and fish and objects of interest therein, and, for other purposes authorized by this Act. Such commissioner shall have power, upon sworn information, to issue process in the name of the United States for the arrest of any person charged with the commission of any misdemeanor, or charged with the violation of the rules and regulations, or with the violation of any provision of this Act prescribed for the government of said park, and for the protection of the animals, birds, and fish in the said park, and to try the person so charged, and, if found guilty, to impose the punishment and adjudge the forfeiture prescribed. In all cases of conviction an appeal shall lie from the judgment of said commissioner to the United States district court for the district of Wyoming, said appeal to be governed by the laws of the State of Wyoming providing for appeals in cases of misdemeanor from justices of the peace to the district court of said State; but the United States circuit court in said district may prescribe rules of procedure and practice for said commissioner in the trial of cases and for appeal to said United States district court. Said commissioner shall also have power to issue process as herein before provided for the arrest of any person charged with the commission of any felony within the park, and to summarily hear the evidence introduced, and, if he shall determine that probable cause is shown for holding the person so charged for trial, shall cause such person to be safely conveyed to a secure place for confinement, within the jurisdiction of the United States district court in said State of Wyoming, and shall certify a transcript of the record of his proceedings and the testimony in the case to the said court, which court shall have jurisdiction of the case: *Provided,* That the said commissioner shall grant bail in all cases bailable under the laws of the United States or of said State. All process issued by the commissioner shall be directed to the marshal of the United States for the district of Wyoming; but nothing herein contained shall be construed as preventing the arrest by any officer of the Government or employee of the United States in the park without process of any person taken in the act of violating the law or any regulation of the Secretary of the Interior: *Provided,* That the said commissioner shall only exercise such authority and powers as are conferred by this Act.

SEC. 6. That the marshal of the United States for the district of Wyoming may appoint one or more deputy marshals for said park, who shall reside in said park, and the said United States district and circuit courts shall hold one session of said courts annually at the town of Sheridan in the State of Wyoming, and may also hold other sessions at any other place in said State of Wyoming or in said National Park at such dates as the said courts may order.

SEC. 7. That the said commissioner provided for in this Act shall, in addition to the fees allowed by law to commissioners of the circuit courts of the United States, be paid an annual salary of one thousand dollars, payable quarterly, and the marshal of the United States and his deputies, and the attorney of the United States and his assistants in said district, shall be paid the same compensation and fees as are now provided by law for like services in said district.

SEC.8. That all costs and expenses arising in cases under this Act, and properly chargeable to the United States, shall be certified, approved, and paid as like costs and expenses in the courts of the United States are certified, approved, and paid under the laws of the United States.

SEC. 9. That the Secretary of the Interior shall cause to be erected in the Park a suitable building to be used as a jail, and also having in said building an office for the use of the commissioner, the cost of such building not to exceed five thousand dollars, to be paid out of any moneys in the

Treasury not otherwise appropriated upon the certificate of the Secretary as a voucher there for.

SEC. 10. That this Act shall not be construed to repeal existing laws conferring upon the Secretary of the Interior and the Secretary of War certain powers with reference to the protection, improvement, and control of the said Yellowstone National Park.

Approved, May 7, 1894.

Part V. The Hayes Act

(U.S., Statutes at Large, vol. 28, p. 222)

CHAP. 198.—An Act Concerning leases in the Yellowstone National Park.

Be it enacted by the Senate and House of Representatives of the United States of America in Congress assembled, That the Secretary of the Interior is hereby authorized and empowered to lease to any person, corporation or company, for a period not exceeding ten years, at such annual rental as the Secretary of the Interior may determine, parcels of land in the Yellowstone National Park, of not more than ten acres in extent for each tract and not in excess of twenty acres in all to any one person, corporation, or company on which may be erected hotels and necessary outbuildings: *Provided,* That such lease or leases shall not include any of the geysers or other objects of curiosity or interest in said park, or exclude the public from free and convenient approach thereto or include any ground within one-eighth of a mile of any of the geysers or the Yellowstone Falls, the Grand Canyon, or the Yellowstone River, Mammoth Hot Springs, or any object of curiosity in the park: *And provided further,* That such leases shall not convey, either expressively or by implication, any exclusive privilege within the park except upon the premises held thereunder and for the time therein granted. Every lease hereafter made for any property in said park shall require the lessee to observe and obey each and every provision in any Act of Congress, and every rule, order, or regulation made, or which may hereafter be made and published by the Secretary of the Interior concerning the use, care, management, or government of the park, or any object or property therein, under penalty of forfeiture of such lease, and every such lease shall be subject to the right of revocation and forfeiture, which shall therein be reserved by the Secretary of the Interior: *And provided further,* That persons or corporations now holding leases of ground in the park may, upon the surrender thereof, be granted new leases hereunder, and upon the terms and stipulations contained in their present leases, with such modifications, restrictions, and reservations as the Secretary of the Interior may prescribe.

This Act, however, is not to be construed as mandatory upon the Secretary of the Interior, but the authority herein given is to be exercised in his sound discretion.

That so much of that portion of the Act of March third, eighteen hundred and eighty-three, relating to the Yellowstone Park as conflicts with this Act be, and the same is hereby, repealed.

Approved, August 3, 1894.

APPENDIX C: STATISTICAL

Table I. The Superintendents[1] and Acting Superintendents[2] of Yellowstone National Park, 1872-1972

From a list of "Administrative Officers of Yellowstone National Park," compiled and documented by former superintendent Edmund B. Rogers in October, 1946; additions have been made from official sources.

Nathaniel Pitt Langford[1]	May 10, 1872 to April 18, 1877
Philetus Walter Norris[1]	April 18, 1877 to March 31, 1882
Patrick Henry Conger[1]	April 1, 1882 to September 9, 1884
Robert Emmett Carpenter[1]	September 10, 1884 to June 30, 1885
David Walker Wear[1]	July 1, 1885 to August 20, 1886
Captain Moses Harris[2]	August 20, 1886 to May 31, 1889
Captain Frazier A. Boutelle[2]	June 1, 1889 to February 15, 1891
Captain George S. Anderson[2]	February 15, 1891 to June 23, 1897
Colonel Samuel B. M. Young[2]	June 23, 1897 to November 15, 1897
Captain James B. Erwin[2]	November 15, 1897 to March 15, 1899
Captain Wilber E. Wilder[2]	March 15, 1899 to June 23, 1899
Captain Oscar J. Brown[2]	June 23, 1899 to July 24, 1900
Captain George W. Goode[2]	July 24, 1900 to May 8, 1901
Captain John Pitcher[2]	May 8, 1901 to June 1, 1907
General Samuel B.M. Young[1]	June 1, 1907 to November 28, 1908
Major Harry C. Benson[2]	November 28, 1908 to September 30, 1910
Colonel Lloyd M. Brett[2]	September 30, 1910 to October 15, 1916
Chester Allinson Lindsley[2]	October 16, 1916 to June 28, 1919
Horace Marden Albright[1]	June 28, 1916 to January 11, 1929
Joseph Joffe[2]	January 12, 1929 to February 1, 1929
Roger Wolcott Toll[1]	February 1, 1929 to February 25, 1936
John W. Emmert[2]	February 26, 1936 to May 25, 1936
Edmund B. Rogers[1]	May 25, 1936 to October 31, 1956
Lemuel A. Garrison[1]	November 1, 1956 to February 16, 1964
John S. McLaughlin[1]	March 6, 1964 to October 6, 1967
Jack K. Anderson[1]	October 8, 1967 to Present

Table II.   Visitation to Yellowstone National Park, 1872-1971 (*Compiled from available estimates and official counts*)

Estimates for the years prior to 1890 are based on the following sources:
Letter, Governor Benjamin F. Potts (Montana) to Superintendent Nathaniel P. Langford, November 27, 1873, in National Archives, Washington, D.C.; Annual Report *of Superintendent Philetus W. Norris for the year 1879, p. 22;* Annual Report *of Superintendent Patrick H. Conger for the year 1882, p. 10; Statement of Assistant Superintendent George L. Henderson in* Livingston *(Mont.),* Enterprise *July 16, 1883; p. 1, c. 5.*

Year	Annual	Cumulative
1872	300	300
1873	500	800
1874	500	1,300
1875	500	1,800
1876	500	2,300
1877	1,000	3,300
1878	1,000	4,300
1879	1,030	5,330
1880	1,000	6,330
1881	1,000	7,330
1882	1,000	8,330
1883	5,000	13,330
1884	5,000	18,330
1885	5,000	23,330
1886	5,000	28,330
1887	5,000	33,330
1888	6,000	39,330
1889	6,000	45,330
1890	7,808	53,138
1891	7,154	60,292
1892	7,290	67,582
1893	6,154	73,736
1894	3,105	76,841
1895	5,438	82,279
1896	4,659	86,938
1897	10,825	97,763
1898	6,534	104,297
1899	9,579	113,876
1900	8,928	122,804
1901	10,769	133,573
1902	13,433	147,006
1903	13,165	160,171
1904	13,727	173,898
1905	26,188	200,086
1906	17,102	217,188
1907	16,414	233,602
1908	18,748	252,350
1909	32,545	284,985
1910	19,575	304,470
1911	23,054	327,524

TABLE II _479_

Year	Annual	Cumulative
1912	22,970	350,494
1913	24,929	375,423
1914	20,250	395,673
1915	51,895	447,568
1916	35,849	483,417
1917	35,400	518,817
1918	21,275	540,092
1919	62,261	602,353
1920	79,777	682,130
1921	81,651	763,781
1922	98,225	862,006
1923	138,352	1,000,358
1924	144,158	1,144,516
1925	154,282	1,298,798
1926	187,807	1,486,605
1927	200,825	1,687,430
1928	230,984	1,918,414
1929	260,697	2,179,111
1930	227,901	2,407,012
1931	221,248	2,628,260
1932	157,624	2,785,884
1933	161,938	2,947,822
1934	260,775	3,208,597
1935	317,998	3,526,595
1936	432,570	3,959,165
1937	499,242	4,458,407
1938	466,185	4,924,592
1939	486,936	5,411,528
1940	526,437	5,837,965
1941	581,761	6,519,726
1942	191,830	6,711,556
1943	64,144	6,775,700
1944	85,347	6,861,047
1945	178,296	7,039,343
1946	814,907	7,854,250
1947	932,503	8,786,753
1948	1,013,531	9,800,284
1949	1,133,516	10,933,800
1950	1,109,926	12,043,726
1951	1,166,346	13,210,072
1952	1,330,327	14,540,399
1953	1,326,858	15,867,257
1954	1,328,893	17,196,150
1955	1,368,515	18,564,665
1956	1,457,782	20,022,447
1957	1,595,875	21,618,322
1958	1,442,428	23,060,750
1959	1,408,667	24,469,417
1960	1,443,288	25,912,705
1961	1,524,088	27,436,793
1962	1,923,063	29,359,856
1963	1,870,644	31,230,500
1964	1,929,316	33,159,816

Year	Annual	Cumulative
1965	2,062,476	35,222,292
1966	2,130,313	37,352,605
1967	2,210,023	39,562,628
1968	2,229,657	41,792,285
1969	2,193,894	43,986,179
1970	2,297,290	46,283,469
1971	2,120,487	48,403,956

Table III. Appropriations for Yellowstone National Park, 1878-1951[a]
(Compiled from official sources)

a   *1951 is the last year for which published figures are available.*

The classification of expenditures under the appropriation for Yellowstone National Park into allotments for 1 Administration and Protection, and 2 Construction and Maintenance, became necessary when the army's Corps of Engineers took over the construction and maintenance of park roads and bridges; the superintendent retained control of the A & P funds, while the engineer officer prosecuted his work with the C & M funds.

Redefinition of the classifications, soon after the National Park Service obtained operating control of the Park, broadened the first to include "maintenance" (since such work was performed by regular park crews) and limited the second to "construction" (work then accomplished by contract or force-account).

Bracketed figures include funds from several appropriations

Date	A & P[1]	C & M[2]	Total
June 20, 1878	$	$	$ 10,000.00
March 3, 1879			10,000.00
June 16, 1880			15,000.00
March 3, 1881			15,000.00
March 3, 1881			89.76
August 5, 1882			155.00
August 7, 1882			15,000.00
August 7, 1882			3,180.41
March 3, 1883	16,429.97	23,570.03	40,000.00
July 7, 1884	16,999.98	23,000.02	40,000.00
March 3, 1885	16,790.63	23,209.37	40,000.00
July 15, 1886	934.25	—	934.25
August 4, 1886	—	20,000.00	20,000.00
March 3, 1887	—	20,000.00	20,000.00
October 2, 1888	—	25,000.00	25,000.00
March 2, 1889	—	50,000.00	50,000.00
August 30, 1890	—	75,000.00	75,000.00
September 30, 1890	169.37	—	169.37
March 3, 1891	—	75,000.00	75,000.00
August 5, 1892	—	45,000.00	45,000.00
March 3, 1893	—	30,000.00	30,000.00
May 4, 1894	5,000.00	—	5,000.00
August 18, 1894			30,000.00
March 2, 1895			30,385.75

TABLE III

Date	A & P[1]	C & M[2]	Total
June 8, 1896	[10,565.24]	[89,434.76]	5,000.00
June 11, 1896			35,000.00
June 4, 1897	6,736.74	28,263.26	35,000.00
July 7, 1898	11,356.57	28,643.43	40,000.00
March 3, 1899	5,534.64	34,465.36	40,000.00
June 6, 1900	5,000.00	55,000.00	60,000.00
March 3, 1901	5,000.00	113,000.00	118,000.00
June 28, 1902	5,000.00	250,000.00	255,000.00
March 3, 1903	5,000.00	250,000.00	255,000.00
April 28, 1904	7,500.00	250,000.00	257,500.00
March 3, 1905	7,500.00	133,000.00	140,500.00
June 30, 1906	7,500.00	55,000.00	62,500.00
March 4, 1907	8,000.00	75,000.00	83,000.00
May 27, 1908	10,500.00	65,000.00	75,500.00
March 4, 1909	8,000.00	65,000.00	73,000.00
June 25, 1910	8,500.00	75,000.00	83,500.00
March 4, 1911	8,500.00	70,000.00	78,000.00
July 1,			
August 1, 1912		[11,666.66]	[11,666.66]
August 16,			
August 24, 1912	$ 8,500.00	$ 165,333.34	$173,833.34
June 23, 1913	8,500.00	200,000.00	208,500.00
June 30, 1914			
July 16, 1914	–	[16,666.67]	[16,666.67]
August 1, 1914	8,500.00	238,333.33	246,833.33
March 3, 1915	8,500.00	195,000.00	203,500.00
July 1, 1916	8,500.00	197,200.00	205,700.00
June 12, 1917	10,500.00	167,500.00	178,000.00
July 1, 1918	–	–	334,920.00
July 19, 1919	–	–	255,500.00
November 4, 1919	25,000.00	–	25,000.00
March 6, 1920	43,026.64	3,000.00	46,026.64
June 5, 1920	–	–	278,000.00
	A, P & M	C	
May 24, 1922	281,000.00	80,800.00	361,800.00
1924 FY	–	–	368,000.00
April 2, 1924	27,700.00	–	27,700.00
June 5, 1924	336,800.00	36,000.00	372,800.00
December 5, 1924		30,000.00	30,000.00
January 20, 1925	5,900.00		5,900.00
March 3, 1925	364,503.00	120,297.00	484,800.00
May 10, 1926	373,200.00	134,700.00	507,900.00
January 12, 1927	373,500.00	437,900.00	811,400.00
1928	435,850.00	661,030.70	1,096,880.70
Donation (1928)			23,222.26
1929	453,000.00	343,789.08	796,789.08
Donation (1929)			20,907.81
1930-31			3,362,068.10
Donation (1930)			31,100.00
1931-32			713,745.72

Donation (1931)			8,750.00
1932-33	735,106.00	817,300.00	1,552,406.00
Donation (1932)			1,625.00
FY 1934	224,122.28		224,122.28
1933		194,723.70	194,723.70
1933-35		3,171,848.54	3,171,848.54
FY 1935	366,169.22		366,169.22
June 19, 1934		629,086.00	629,086.00
FY 1936	398,323.94		398,323.94
FY 1937	393,896.34	80,699.00	474,595.34
FY 1938	406,765.00	141,042.00	547,807.00
FY 1939	446,507.38	1,496,050.04	1,942,557.42
FY 1940	886,026.64	86,590.84	972,617.48
FY 1941	580,168.89	84,690.00	664,858.89
Donations			270.00
FY 1942	480,587.54	65,100.00	545,687.54
FY 1943	504,589.00		504,589.00
FY 1944	373,503.00		373,503.00
FY 1945	363,254.00		363,254.00
FY 1946	388,753.85	24,175.00	412,928.85
FY 1947	567,909.35	441,561.00	1,009,470.35
FY 1948	515,523.49	324,433.70	839,957.19
FY 1949	555,495.00	529,048.83	1,084,543.83
FY 1950	791,032.46	1,041,731.86	1,832,764.32
FY 1951	1,147,193.39	195,277.18	1,342,470.57

Table IV. Military Organizations Detailed to Yellowstone Park, 1886-1918

1886	First Cavalry, troop M
1887	First Cavalry, troop M
1888	First Cavalry, troop M (with Lt. Moody and 15 men of the 22nd Infantry at the Upper Geyser Basin after July 22)
1889	First Cavalry, troop M, to First Cavalry, troops A & K
1890	First Cavalry, troops A & K
1891	First Cavalry, troops A & K, to Sixth Cavalry, troops D & I
1892	Sixth Cavalry, troops D & I
1893	Sixth Cavalry, troops D & I
1894	Sixth Cavalry, troops D & I
1895	Sixth Cavalry, troops D & I
1896	Sixth Cavalry, troops D & I
1897	Sixth Cavalry, troops D & I, to Fourth Cavalry troops H & D
1898	Fourth Cavalry, troops H & D
1899	Fourth Cavalry, troops H & D, to First Cavalry, troop M
1900	First Cavalry, troop M, to First Cavalry, troop G
1901	First Cavalry, troop G (with troop F arriving for duty at Nez Perce Creek after August 3)
1902	First Cavalry, troops F & G, to Third Cavalry, troops B & C (with Thirteenth Cavalry, troops A & C, arriving June 3 for temporary duty)
1903	Third Cavalry, troops B, C & D (with troop F arriving June 18, and troop A arriving June 24)
1904	Third Cavalry, troops B, C, D, & F
1905	Third Cavalry, troops B, C, D, & F, to Sixth Cavalry, troop K

TABLE IV

483

1906	Sixth Cavalry, troop K
1907	Sixth Cavalry, troops K & I, to Eighth Cavalry, troops F & G
1908	Eighth Cavalry, troops F & G, to Fifth Cavalry, troops E & F
1909	Fifth Cavalry, troops E & F
1910	Fifth Cavalry, troops E & F, to First Cavalry, troops, E, F, G, & H (with a machine-gun platoon)
1911	First Cavalry, troops E, F, G & H
1912	First Cavalry, troops E, F, G & H
1913	First Cavalry, troops E, F, G & H
1914	First Cavalry, troops E, F, G & H, to "Yellowstone Park Detachment," troops 1 & 2
1915	Yellowstone Park Detachment, troops 1 & 2
1916	Yellowstone Park Detachment, troops 1 & 2
1917	Sixth Cavalry, troop J, to Seventh Cavalry, troops A, B, C & D
1918	Eleventh Cavalry, troops D & G, to the final abandonment of Fort Yellowstone on October 31, 1918

Table V. Estimates of the Number of Buffalo and Elk in Yellowstone National Park, 1877-1915

Page numbers refer to reports of the superintendents and acting superintendents for the indicated years; page numbers for 1877, 1880 and 1891 are those of the versions published with the annual report of the secretary of the interior.

Report	Buffalo	Elk
1877, *p. 843*	"three . . . or four hundred"	"thousands"
1879, *p. 21*		"have increased"
1880, *pp. 608-9*	[3 bands, totaling 600]	"not seriously diminished"
1885, *p. 3*	"neighborhood of two hundred"	"in large numbers"
1886, *pp. 7-8*	"there is an abundance of game"	
1887, *p. 13*	"will not exceed one hundred"	"estimated . . . several thousands"
1888, *pp. 6, 14*	"not less than two hundred"	"many thousands"
1889, *p. 4*	"in undiminished numbers"	
1890, *p. 6*	"a great increase in all"	
1891, *p. 646*	"probably there are 400"	"numbers at 25,000"
1892, *p. 10*	"not less than four hundred"	"estimate of 25,000"
1893, *pp. 13-14*	"four hundred . . . not too high"	"there are 25,000"
1894, *pp. 10-11*	"estimate . . . 200"	"wintered well"
1895, *p. 13*	"two hundred still remain"	"held their own or increased"
1896, *p. 12*	"existence . . . possibly of 50"	"in herds of thousands"
1897, *p. 8*	"estimated at 24"	"increasing"
1898, *p. 11*	"probably 50"	"numerous . . . increasing"
1899, *p. 7*	"fifty or more"	"from 35,000 to 60,000"
1900, *pp. 6-7*	[probably 39]	"are increasing"
1901, *pp. 5-6*	"not . . . more than 25"	"about 25,000"
1902, *pp. 6, 10*	[22 seen]	"considerable increase"
1903, *pp 5-6*	[captive herd of 27]	"loss . . . was very small"
1904, *pp. 5-6*	[captive herd of 39]	[a favorable year]
1905, *pp. 7-9*	[44 captive; 30 wild]	"quite enough"

1906, p. 8	[captive herd of 57]	"loss was very small"
1907, pp. 13-14	[59 captive; 25 wild]	"25,000 . . . a safe estimate"
1908, pp. 9, 11	[captive herd of 74]	"between 25,000 and 30,000"
1909, pp. 10-11	[95 captive; 20 wild]	"between 30,000 and 40,000"
1910, p. 9	[121 captive; 34 wild]	"from 30,000 to 40,000"
1911, p. 10	[147 captive; 35 wild]	"are very numerous"
1912, pp. 10-12	[143 captive; 49 wild]	[census, 27, 801]
1913, pp. 11-12	[captive herd of 162]	[census, 32, 967]
1914, pp. 14-15	[captive herd of 193]	[census, 35, 308]
1915, pp. 18-19	[captive herd of 239]	"estimated total of 37,192"
1916, pp. 30-36	[276 captive; 76 wild]	[census, 29, 544]
1917, pp. 17-19	[330 captive; 67 wild]	[hard winter for elk]
1918, p. 33, 37	[captive herd of 385]	[estimated at 20,000]

Table VI. Number of Visitors Carried by Public Transportation in Yellowstone National Park, 1890-1960

Compiled from the following sources: 1890 - 94, from the estimates of the acting superintendents; 1895 - 1916, from counts published in the Annual Reports *of the Superintendents; and 1917 - 60, from business records of the Yellowstone Park Co.*

| | | | PERCENTAGE BY COMPANIES | | | |
Year	Total	YNPT	Haynes	Wylie	S & P	Indep.
1890	3,904	100.0				
1891	3,577	100.0				
1892	3,645	100.0				
1893	3,076	100.0				
1894	1,734	94.0				
1895	2,744	92.0				6.0
1896	2,862	?				8.0
1897[a]	6,226	74.0				?
1898	3,097	70.9	7.6			26.0
1899	5,315	55.8	7.7	18.3		21.5
1900	4,377	60.7	10.0	18.3		18.2
1901	6,163	56.2	8.2	22.2		11.0
1902	8,419	54.2	16.8	22.2		13.4
1903	8,090	53.7	16.5	21.2		6.8
1904	10,011	60.3	22.4	12.7		8.6
1905[b]	18,922	57.4	14.0	19.4		4.6
1906	12,746	61.0	16.2	13.7		9.2
1907	12,100	52.0	18.7	17.8		9.1
1908	13,803	37.0	26.9	25.0		11.5
1909[c]	27,094	35.9	21.9	28.4		11.1
1910	14,780	34.2	22.4	29.4		13.8
1911	18,954	29.4	29.8	26.4		14.0
1912	18,979	28.4	27.1	31.7		14.4
1913	21,549	27.5	26.7	30.6	11.3	12.8
1914[d]	15,937	24.5	25.8	29.7	15.3	3.9
						4.7

TABLE VI

485

1915	44,742	15.1	45.1	23.6	11.7	4.5
1916e	20,919	100.0				
1917	13,283	100.0				
1918	13,026	100.0				
1919	21,275	100.0				
1920	30,286	100.0				
1921	24,469	100.0				
1922	33,358	100.0				
1923	44,806	100.0				
1924	41,054	100.0				
1925	44,786	100.0				
1926	40,960	100.0				
1927	41,865	100.0				
1928	41,697	100.0				
1929	38,979	100.0				
1930	26,843	100.0				
1931	18,929	100.0				
1932	8,572	100.0				
1933	6,787	100.0				
1934	14,085	100.0				
1935	17,442	100.0				
1936f	19,472	100.0				
1937	20,526	100.0				
1938	18,308	100.0				
1939	17,009	100.0				
1940	17,781	100.0				
1941	18,954	100.0				
1942g	5,687	100.0				
1943	0					
1944	0					
1945	0					
1946	16,076	100.0				
1947	21,910	100.0				
1948	19,493	100.0				
1949	18,760	100.0				
1950	19,951	100.0				
1951	16,514	100.0				
1952	18,015	100.0				
1953	24,239	100.0				
1954	18,868	100.0				
1955	19,398	100.0				
1956	18,977	100.0				
1957	20,638	100.0				
1958	15,425	100.0				
1959	14,603	100.0				
1960	14,594	100.0				

a Visitation increased by the Christian Endeavor tour
b Lewis and Clark Exposition at Portland, Oregon
c Alaska-Yukon Exposition at Seattle, Washington
d Beginning of World War I

e Consolidation of all public transportation in the Park (under the Yellowstone Park Transportation Company)

f Reorganization, merging the Yellowstone Park Transportation Company (1909), Yellowstone Park Hotel Company (1909), Yellowstone Park Boat Company (1911), and Yellowstone Park Lodge and Camps Company (1928) to form the Yellowstone Park Company

g Beginning of World War II

SOURCES

I. BOOKS, PAMPHLETS AND PUBLISHED DOCUMENTS

Abbott, N.C. *Montana in the Making*, Billings, Mont.: Gazette Printing Co., 1931.

Allen, William A. *The Sheep Eaters*, New York: The Shakespeare Press, 1913.

Alter, J. Cecil. *James Bridger, Trapper, Frontiersman, Scout and Guide*, Columbus, Ohio: Long's College Book Co., 1951.

Anderson, A.A. *Experiences and Impressions*, New York: Macmillan Co., 1933.

Anderson, George S. "Report of Superintendent of Yellowstone National Park," in *Annual Report of the Secretary of the Interior*, Washington, D.C.: Govt. Printing Office, 1891.

——————— , *Report of the Superintendent of the Yellowstone National Park to the Secretary of the Interior, 1892*, Washington, D.C.: Govt. Printing Office, 1892.

——————— , *Report of the Superintendent of the Yellowstone National Park to the Secretary of the Interior, 1893*, Washington, D.C.: Govt. Printing Office, 1893.

——————— , *Report of the Acting Superintendent of the Yellowstone National Park to the Secretary of the Interior, 1894*, Washington, D.C.: Govt. Printing Office, 1894.

——————— , *Report of the Acting Superintendent of the Yellowstone National Park to the Secretary of the Interior, 1895*, Washington, D.C.: Govt. Printing Office, 1895.

——————— , *Report of the Acting Superintendent of the Yellowstone National Park to the Secretary of the Interior, 1896*, Washington, D.C.: Govt. Printing Office, 1896.

Barlow, John W., and David P. Heap. *Report of a Reconnoissance of the Basin of the Upper Yellowstone in 1871*. (42d Cong., 2d Sess.; Senate Exec. Doc. 66.) Washington, D.C.: Govt. Printing Office, 1872.

Beal, Merrill D. *The Story of Man in Yellowstone*, Yellowstone Park, Wyoming: Yellowstone Library and Museum Association, 1960.

Benson, Harry C. *Report of the Acting Superintendent of the Yellowstone National Park to the Secretary of the Interior, 1909*, Washington, D.C.: Govt. Printing Office, 1909.

Black, Walter J. *The Best of Ralph Waldo Emerson*, New York: Walter J. Black, 1941.

Bonney, Orrin H. and Lorraine. *Battle Drums and Geysers*, Chicago: The Swallow Press, Inc., 1970.

Boutelle, Frazier A. *Report of the Superintendent of the Yellowstone National Park to the Secretary of the Interior, 1890*, Washington, D.C.: Govt. Printing Office, 1890.

Bowen, A.W. & Co. *Progressive Men of the State of Montana*, Chicago: A.W. Bowen & Co., 1902.

Brackenridge, Henry M. *Views of Louisiana, Together With a Journal of a Voyage Up the Missouri River in 1811,* Pittsburgh: Printed and published by Cramer, Spear and Eichbaum, Franklin head office, 1814.

Brett, Lloyd M. *Report of the Acting Superintendent of the Yellowstone National Park to the Secretary of the Interior, 1911,* Washington, D.C.: Govt. Printing Office, 1911.

——————— , *Report of the Acting Superintendent of the Yellowstone National Park to the Secretary of the Interior, 1912,* Washington, D.C.: Govt. Printing Office, 1912.

——————— , *Report of the Acting Superintendent of the Yellowstone National Park to the Secretary of the Interior, 1913,* Washington, D.C.: Govt. Printing Office, 1913.

——————— , *Report of the Acting Superintendent of the Yellowstone National Park to the Secretary of the Interior, 1914,* Washington, D.C.: Govt. Printing Office, 1914.

——————— , *Report of the Acting Superintendent of the Yellowstone National Park to the Secretary of the Interior, 1915,* Washington, D.C.: Govt. Printing Office, 1915.

Brockman, C. Frank. *Recreational Use of Wild Lands,* New York: McGraw Hill Book Co., 1959.

Brown, Mark H. *The Plainsmen of the Yellowstone,* New York: G.P. Putnam's Sons, 1961.

Brown, Oscar J. *Report of the Acting Superintendent of the Yellowstone National Park to the Secretary of the Interior, 1899,* Washington, D.C.: Govt. Printing Office, 1899.

Carhart, Arthur H. *Water or Your Life,* New York: J.B. Lippincott, 1951.

Carpenter, Frank D. *Adventures in Geyser Land,* ed. H.D. Guie and L.F. McWhorter, Caldwell, Idaho: Caxton Printers, 1935.

Carruth, Gorton, ed. *Encyclopedia of American Facts and Dates* (2nd ed.), New York: Thomas Y. Crowell Co., 1959.

Carter, Clarence E., ed. *The Territories of Louisiana-Missouri, 1803-1806. (The Territorial Papers of the United States,* Vol. XIII), Washington, D.C.: Govt. Printing Office, 1948.

Catlin, George. *Letters and Notes on the Manners, Customs, and Conditions of the North American Indians,* 2 vols., New York: Wiley and Putnam, 1842.

Chittenden, Hiram M. *The Yellowstone National Park,* Cincinnati: Robert Clarke Co., 1895.

——————— , *Improvement of the Yellowstone National Park, Including the Construction, Repair and Maintenance of Roads and Bridges. (Annual Report of the Chief of Engineers for 1899,* Appendix EEE), Washington, D.C.: Govt. Printing Office, 1899.

——————— , *Improvement of the Yellowstone National Park, Including the Construction, Repair and Maintenance of Roads and Bridges, (Annual Report of the Chief of Engineers for 1901,* Appendix FFF). Washington, D.C.: Govt. Printing Office, 1901.

——————— , *The American Fur Trade of the Far West,* 3 vols. New York: Francis P. Harper, 1902.

——————— , *Improvement of Yellowstone National Park, Including the Construction, Repair and Maintenance of Roads and Bridges. (Annual*

Report of the Chief of Engineers for 1902, Appendix FFF.), Washington, D.C.: Govt. Printing Office, 1902.

——————————, *Improvement of Yellowstone National Park, Including the Construction, Repair and Maintenance of Roads and Bridges. (Annual Report of the Chief of Engineers for 1903,* Appendix GGG.) Washington, D.C.: Govt. Printing Office, 1903.

——————————, *The Yellowstone National Park* (4th ed.), Cincinnati: Robert Clarke Co., 1903.

——————————, *Improvement of Yellowstone National Park, Including the Construction, Repair and Maintenance of Roads and Bridges. (Annual Report of the Chief of Engineers for 1905,* Appendix FFF.) Washington, D.C.: Govt. Printing Office, 1905.

Clark, Ella E., ed. *Indian Legends from the Northern Rockies,* Norman, Oklahoma: University of Oklahoma Press, 1966.

Conger, Patrick H. *Annual Report of the Superintendent of the Yellowstone National Park to the Secretary of the Interior, for the Year 1882,* Washington, D.C.: Govt. Printing Office, 1882.

——————————, *Annual Report of the Superintendent of the Yellowstone National Park to the Secretary of the Interior, for the Year 1883,* Washington, D.C.: Govt. Printing Office, 1883.

The Congressional Globe, 42nd Cong., 2d Sess., (1871-72).

Cook, Charles W., David E. Folsom and William Peterson. *The Valley of the Upper Yellowstone; an Exploration of the Headwaters of the Yellowstone River in the Year 1869,* ed. Aubrey L. Haines, Norman, Okla.: University of Oklahoma Press, 1965.

Coues, Elliot, ed. *The Manuscript Journals of Alexander Henry . . . and of David Thompson . . . 1799-1814,* 3 Vols., New York: Francis P. Harper, 1897.

Cramton, Louis C. *Early History of Yellowstone National Park and Its Relationship to National Park Policies,* Washington, D.C.: Govt. Printing Office, 1932.

Dafsman, Raymond F. *The Destruction of California,* New York: Macmillan Company, 1965.

Dines, Glen, *Long Knife,* New York: Macmillan Co., 1916.

Doane, Gustavus C. *Report of Lieutenant Gustavus C. Doane upon the So-called Yellowstone Expedition of 1870,* (41st Cong., 3d Sess; Senate Exec. Doc. 51.) Washington, D.C.: Govt. Printing Office, 1871.

——————————, "Expedition of Lt. G.C. Doane," ed. Merlin K. Potts, *Camp-fire Tales of Jackson Hole,* Moose, Wyo.: Grand Teton Natural History Association, 1960, 20-37.

Dudley, W.H. *The National Park from the Hurricane Deck of A Cayuse, or the Liederkranz Expedition to Geyserland,* Butte, Mont.: Frederick Loeber, 1886.

Dunraven, Windham T.W.-Q. *The Great Divide,* London: Chatto and Windus, 1876.

Emerson, Ralph Waldo. *Essays and English Traits.* (Harvard Classics, ed. Charles W. Eliot, Vol. V) New York: P.F. Collier & Son, 1910.

Erwin, James B. *Report of the Acting Superintendent of the Yellowstone National Park to the Secretary of the Interior, 1898,* Washington, D.C.: Govt. Printing Office, 1898.

Evans, Bergan. *Dictionary of Quotations,* New York: Delacorte Press, 1968.

Ferris, Warren Angus. *Life in the Rocky Mountains, 1830-1835,* ed. P.C. Phillips, Denver: Old West Publishing Company, 1940.

Fisher, S.G. "Journal of S.G. Fisher," *Contributions to the Historical Society of Montana,* Vol. II. Helena, Mont.: State Publishing Co., 1896. 269-82.

Gannett, Henry. *Boundaries of the United States, and of the Several States and Territories* (3rd ed.), Washington, D.C.: Govt. Printing Office, 1904.

Garfield, James A. "James A. Garfield's Diary of a Trip to Montana in 1872," (*Frontier Omnibus,* ed. by John Hakola), Missoula, Mont.: Montana State University Press, 1962. 347-57.

Gerrish, Theodore. *Life in the World's Wonderland,* Biddeford, Maine: no publisher, 1887.

Glover, Richard, ed., *David Thompson's Narrative, 1784-1812,* Toronto: The Champlain Society, 1962.

Goetzmann, William H. *Exploration and Empire,* New York: Alfred A. Knopf, 1966.

Greever, William S. *The Bonanza West,* Norman, Okla.: University of Oklahoma Press, 1963.

Gunnison, John W. *The Mormons, or Latter-Day Saints,* Philadelphia: Lippincott, Grambo & Co., 1852.

Hafen, LeRoy R., ed. *The Mountain Men and the Fur Trade of the Far West.* 10 vols., Glendale, California: The Arthur H. Clark Co., 1965-72.

Haines, Aubrey L. *A History of the Yellowstone National Park Chapel, 1913-1963,* Yellowstone National Park, Wyoming: Superintendent's Church Committee, 1963.

——————— , Charles S. Pope and Erwin N. Thompson, *Norris Soldier Station, Yellowstone National Park: Historic Structures Report,* Washington, D.C.: National Park Service, 1969.

——————— , *Yellowstone National Park: Its Exploration and Establishment,* Washington, D.C.: Govt. Printing Office, 1974.

Hamilton, William T. *My Sixty Years on the Plains,* Columbus, Ohio: Long's College Book Co., 1951.

Hampton, Harold D. *How the U.S. Cavalry Saved Our National Parks,* Bloomington, Ind.: Indiana University Press, 1971.

Harper, Frank B. *Fort Union and Its Neighbors on the Upper Missouri,* [St. Paul, Minn.] : Great Northern Railway Company, n.d.

Harris, Burton. *John Colter, His Years in the Rockies,* New York: Charles Scribner's Sons, 1952.

Harris, Moses. *Report of the Superintendent of the Yellowstone National Park to the Secretary of the Interior, 1887,* Washington, D.C.: Govt. Printing Office, 1887.

——————— , *Report of the Superintendent of the Yellowstone National Park to the Secretary of the Interior, 1888,* Washington, D.C.: Govt. Printing Office, 1888.

——————— , and F.A. Boutelle. *Report of the Superintendent of the Yellowstone National Park to the Secretary of the Interior, 1889,* Washington, D.C.; Govt. Printing Office, 1889.

Harrison, Carter H. *A Summer's Outing,* Chicago: Donohue, Henneberry & Co., 1891.

Hart, A.B. and H.R. Ferleger, eds. *Theodore Roosevelt Cyclopedia,* New York: Roosevelt Memorial Association, 1941.

Hart, Herbert O. *Old Forts of the Northwest,* Seattle, Wash.: Superior Publishing Co., 1963.

Hayden, Ferdinand V. *Preliminary Report of the United States Geological Survey of Montana and Portions of Adjacent Territories, Being a Fifth Annual Report of Progress,* Washington, D.C.: Govt. Printing Office, 1872.

——————————— , *Sixth Annual Report of the United States Geological Survey of the Territories. . . for the Year 1872,* Washington, D.C.: Govt. Printing Office, 1873.

——————————— , *Twelfth Annual Report of the United States Geological and Geographical Survey of the Territories. . . for the Year 1878,* Washington, D.C.: Govt. Printing Office, 1883.

Haynes, Jack E., "Yellowstone's Stage Holdups," (*Brand Book* of the Denver Westerners), Denver, Colo.: The Westerners, 1952, 3 ff.

——————————— , *Yellowstone Stage Holdups,* Bozeman, Mont.: Haynes Studios, Inc., 1959.

——————————— , *Haynes Guide,* Bozeman, Montana: Haynes Studios, 1966.

Heath, Charles A., *A Trial of a Trail, Notes from the Journal of Charles A. Heath,* Chicago: The Franklin Press, 1905.

Heitman, Francis B. *Historical Register and Dictionary of the United States Army,* 2 vols., Washington, D.C.: Govt. Printing Office, 1903.

Henderson, George L. *Yellowstone Park Manual and Guide,* Mammoth Hot Springs, Wyo.: Privately printed, 1885.

Henely, Louise M. *Letters from the Yellowstone,* Grinnell, Iowa: Ray & Frisbie Printers, 1914.

Hodge, Frederick Webb. *Handbook of American Indians, North of Mexico,* 2 parts, Washington, D.C.: Govt. Printing Office, 1910.

Howard, Oliver O. *Nez Perce Joseph,* Boston: Lee and Shepard, 1881.

Inman, Henry. *Buffalo Jones' Forty Years of Adventure.* Topeka, Kans.: Crane & Co., 1899.

[Interior Department]. *Letter from the Secretary of the Interior . . . ,* Jan. 9, 1884. (48th Cong., 1st Sess; Senate Exec. Doc. 47). Washington, D.C.: Govt. Printing Office, 1884.

——————————— , *Letter from the Secretary of the Interior . . . ,* July 3, 1884. (48th Cong., 1st Sess.; Senate Exec. Doc. 207.) Washington, D.C.: Govt. Printing Office, 1884.

——————————— , *Rules and Regulations Governing Forest Reserves Established Under Section 24 of the Act of March 3, 1891,* Washington, D.C.: Govt. Printing Office, 1900.

——————————— , *Laws and Regulations Relating to the Yellowstone National Park,* Washington, D.C.: Govt. Printing Office, 1908.

James, Thomas. *Three Years Among the Mexicans and Indians,* ed. W.B. Douglas, St. Louis: Missouri Historical Society, 1916.

Jones, William A. *Report Upon the Reconnaissance of Northwestern Wyoming, Including Yellowstone National Park, Made in the summer of 1873,* Washington, D.C.: Govt. Printing Office, 1875.

——————————— , *Construction and Improvement of Roads and Bridges in the Yellowstone National Park,* Appendix GGG. *(Annual Report of the Chief of Engineers for 1891.)* Washington, D.C.: Govt. Printing Office, 1891.

——————————— , *Construction and Improvement of Roads and Bridges in*

Yellowstone National Park. Appendix DDD. (*Annual Report of the Chief of Engineers for 1892.*) Washington, D.C.: Govt. Printing Office, 1892.

Jordan, David Starr. *Reconnaissance of the Streams and Lakes of the Yellowstone National Park, Wyoming, in Interests of the United States Fish Commission.* (Bull. of the United States Fish Commission, Vol. IX) Washington, D.C.: Govt. Printing Office, 1890.

————— , *The Days of a Man,* 2 vols. Yonkers-on-Hudson, New York: World Book Co., 1922.

Josephy, Alvin M., Jr. *The Nez Perce Indians and the Opening of the West,* New Haven, Conn.: Yale University Press, 1965.

Kipling, Rudyard. *From Sea to Sea,* Garden City, N.Y.: Doubleday, Page & Co., 1920.

Kley, Michael, *The Grand Old Gal of Yellowstone,* Mammoth Hot Springs, Wyo.: Yellowstone Park Co., n.d.

Knight, Clarence H. *Improvement of Yellowstone National Park, Including the Construction, Repair and Maintenance of Roads and Bridges. (Annual Report of the Chief of Engineers, 1911,* Appendix GGG.) Washington, D.C.: Govt. Printing Office, 1911.

Kurz, Rudolph. *Journal of Rudolph Friederich Kurz,* trans. Myrtis Jarrell and ed. J.N.B. Hewitt. (Bull. 115, Bureau of American Ethnology, Smithsonian Institution.) Washington, D.C.: Govt. Printing Office, 1937.

Langford, Nathaniel P. *Annual Report of the Superintendent of the Yellowstone National Park for the Year 1872.* (42d Cong., 3d Sess.; Senate Exec. Doc. 35.) Washington, D.C.: Govt. Printing Office, 1873.

————— , *Diary of the Washburn Expedition to the Yellowstone and Firehole Rivers in the Year 1870,* St. Paul, Minn.: F.J. Haynes Co., 1905.

Laut, Agnes C. *Conquest of the Great Northwest,* 2 vols., New York: Outing Publishing Co., 1908.

LeRoy, Bruce, ed. *H.M. Chittenden, A Western Epic,* Tacoma, Wash.: Washington State Historical Society, 1961.

Lewis, Meriwether and William Clark. *History of the Expedition Under the Command of Captains Lewis and Clark,* Nicholas Biddle and Paul Allen, ed., 2 vols., Philadelphia: Bradford and Inskeep, 1814.

Ludlow, William. *Report of a Reconnaissance from Carroll, Montana Territory on the Upper Missouri, to the Yellowstone National Park, and Return, Made in the Summer of 1875. (Annual Report of the Chief of Engineers for 1876,* Appendix NN.) Washington, D.C.: Govt. Printing Office, 1876.

Marquis, James. *The Raven,* Indianapolis; The Bobbs-Merrill Co., 1919.

Mather, Stephen T. *Report of the Director of the National Park Service to the Secretary of the Interior, 1918,* Washington, D.C.: Govt. Printing Office, 1918.

Mattes, Merrill J. *Colter's Hell and Jackson's Hole,* Yellowstone Park, Wyo.: Yellowstone Library & Museum Association, 1962.

McCutcheon, John T. *Drawn from Memory,* New York: The Bobbs-Merrill Co., 1950.

Mendelsohn, Isador W. *Canyon Automobile Camp. Yellowstone National Park. (Public Health Reports,* Reprint 1019.) Washington, D.C.: Govt. Printing Office, 1925.

Miles, Nelson A. *Personal Recollections and Observations of General Nelson A. Miles,* Chicago: The Werner Co., 1897.

Miller, Joaquin, ed. *An Illustrated History of the State of Montana,* Chicago: The Lewis Publishing Co., 1894.

[Montana Irrigation Commission]. *Annual Report on Irrigation Possibilities in Montana,* Helena, Mont.: Independent Publishing Co., 1920.

Murie, Adolph. *Ecology of the Coyote in the Yellowstone,* Washington, D.C.: Govt. Printing Office, 1940.

[National Parks Association]. *Essential Facts of the War on our National Parks System,* Washington, D.C.: n.p., 1927.

Norris, Philetus W. *Report Upon the Yellowstone National Park, to the Secretary of the Interior, for the Year 1877,* Washington, D.C.: Govt. Printing Office, 1877.

——————— , *Report Upon the Yellowstone National Park, to the Secretary of the Interior, for the Year 1878,* Washington, D.C.: Govt. Printing Office, 1879.

——————— , *Report Upon the Yellowstone National Park, to the Secretary of the Interior, for the Year 1879,* Washington, D.C.: Govt. Printing Office, 1880.

——————— , "Prehistoric Remains in Montana, Between Fort Ellis and the Yellowstone River," *Annual Report of the Board of Regents of the Smithsonian Institution. . .1878,* Washington, D.C.: Govt. Printing Office, 1880, 327-28.

——————— , *Annual Report of the Superintendent of the Yellowstone National Park, to the Secretary of the Interior, for the Year 1880,* Washington, D.C.: Govt. Printing Office, 1881.

——————— , *Fifth Annual Report of the Superintendent of the Yellowstone National Park,* December 1, 1881, Washington, D.C.: Govt. Printing Office, 1881.

Norton, Harry J. *Wonderland Illustrated; or, Horseback Rides Through the Yellowstone National Park,* Virginia City, Mont.: Harry J. Norton, 1873.

Oberholtzer, Ellis P. *Jay Cooke, Financier of the Civil War,* 2 vols., Philadelphia: George W. Jacobs & Co., 1907.

Osgood, Ernest S., ed. *The Field Notes of Captain William Clark, 1803-1805,* New Haven, Conn.: Yale University Press, 1964.

Peattie, Donald C. *Green Laurels,* New York: The Literary Guild, 1936.

Peek, Ernest D. *Improvement of Yellowstone National Park, Including the Construction, Repair and Maintenance of Roads and Bridges, (Annual Report of the Chief of Engineers, 1908,* Appendix III). Washington, D.C.: Govt. Printing Office, 1908.

Pierrepont, Edwards. *Fifth Avenue to Alaska,* New York: G.P. Putnam Sons, 1884.

Pitcher, John. *Report of the Acting Superintendent of the Yellowstone National Park to the Secretary of the Interior, 1902,* Washington, D.C.: Govt. Printing Office, 1902.

——————— , *Report of the Acting Superintendent of the Yellowstone National Park to the Secretary of the Interior, 1903,* Washington, D.C.: Govt. Printing Office, 1903.

——————— , *Report of the Acting Superintendent of the Yellowstone National Park to the Secretary of the Interior, 1904,* Washington, D.C.: Govt. Printing Office, 1904.

——————— , *Report of the Acting Superintendent of the Yellowstone National Park to the Secretary of the Interior, 1905,* Washington, D.C.: Govt. Printing Office, 1905.

Raftery, John H. *A Miracle in Hotel Building,* Mammoth Hot Springs, Wyo.: Yellowstone Park Co., [1912].

Raymond, Rossiter W. *Mineral Resources of the States and Territories,* Washington, D.C.: Govt. Printing Office, 1869.

Raynolds, William F. *The Report of Brevet Brigadier General W.F. Raynolds on the Exploration of the Yellowstone and the Country Drained by that River.* (40th Cong., 1st Sess.; Senate Exec. Doc. 77.) Washington, D.C.: Govt. Printing Office, 1868.

Richardson, James D. *A Compilation of the Messages and Papers of the Presidents, 1789-1902,* 10 vols., Washington, D.C.: Govt. Printing Office, 1903.

Roosevelt, Theodore. *Outdoor Pastimes of an American Hunter,* New York: Charles Scribner's Sons, 1923.

——————— , *Theodore Roosevelt, An Autobiography,* New York: Charles Scribner's Sons, 1923.

Ross, Alexander. *The Fur Hunters of the Far West: A Narrative of Adventure in the Oregon and Rocky Mountains,* 2 vols., London: Smith, Elder and Co., 1855.

Russell, Obsorne. *Journal of a Trapper, or, Nine Years in the Rocky Mountains, 1834-1843,* ed. L.A. York, Boise, Idaho: Sims-York Co., 1921.

——————— , *Osborne Russell's Journal of a Trapper,* ed. Aubrey L. Haines, Portland, Oregon: Oregon Historical Society, 1955. [and Lincoln, Neb.: University of Nebraska Press, 1965.]

Ruxton, George F. *Life in the Far West,* ed. LeRoy Hafen, Norman, Okla.: University of Oklahoma Press, 1959.

Schmide, Carl E. *A Western Trip,* Detroit, Mich.: Herold Press, 1910.

Shankland, Robert. *Steve Mather of the National Parks,* New York: Alfred A. Knopf, 1951.

Sheridan, Phillip H. and W.T. Sherman. *Reports of Inspections Made in the Summer of 1877,* Washington, D.C.: Govt. Printing Office, 1878.

——————— , *Report of Lieut. General P.H. Sheridan of His Expedition Through the Big Horn Mountains, Yellowstone National Park,* etc., Washington, D.C.: Govt. Printing Office, 1882.

——————— , *et al. Report of an Exploration of Parts of Wyoming, Idaho, and Montana in August and September, 1882,* Washington, D.C.: Govt. Printing Office, 1882.

Simon, James R. *Yellowstone Fishes,* Yellowstone National Park, Wyo.: Yellowstone Library and Museum Association, 1962.

Smalley, E.V., compiler. *Northern Pacific Railroad; Book of Reference,* New York: G.P. Putnam's Sons, 1883.

Smith, Fred G. *Impressions,* Minneapolis, Minn.: Augsburg Publishing House, 1925.

Smith, Wallace. *On the Trail in Yellowstone,* New York: G.P. Putnam's Sons, 1924.

The Standard Historical Society. *The Standard History of the World,* 10 vols., Cincinnati: Standard Historical Society, 1931.

Stanley, Edwin J. *Rambles in Wonderland; or, Up the Yellowstone and Among the Geysers and Other Curiosities of the National Park,* New York: D. Appleton and Co., 1878.

——————— , *Rambles in Wonderland,* 5th ed., Nashville, Tenn.:

Publishing House of the Methodist Episcopal Church, South, 1898.

Steege, Louis C. and Warren W. Welch. *Stone Projectile Points,* Colorado Springs, Colo.: Northwestern Plains Publishing Co., 1961.

Steele, David M. *Going Abroad Overland,* New York: G.P. Putnam's Sons, 1917.

Stone, Mrs. E.A. *Uinta County, Wyoming: Its place in History,* Laramie, Wyo.: The Laramie Printing Co., 1924.

Stout, Tom. *Montana, Its Story and Biography,* 3 vols., Chicago: The American Historical Society, 1921.

Strahorn, Carrie A. *15,000 Miles by Stage,* (2nd ed.) New York: G.P. Putnam's Sons, 1915.

Strong, William E. *A Trip to the Yellowstone National Park in July, August, and September, 1875.* Washington, D.C.: privately printed, 1876.

Stuart, Granville, *Montana As It Is,* New York: C.S. Westcott & Co., Printers, 1865.

Stuart, Robert. *The Discovery of the Oregon Trail,* ed. Phillip Ashton Rollins, New York: Scribner's Sons, 1935.

Synge, Georgina M. *A Ride Through Wonderland,* London: Sampson, Low, Marston & Co., 1892.

Thoreau, Henry David, "Walking" (1862), (*Harvard Classics,* ed. Charles W. Eliot, Vol. XXVIII.) New York: P.F. Collier & Son, 1910. 407-38.

Tilden, Freeman. *Following the Frontier,* New York: Alfred A. Knopf, 1964.

Timmons, William. *Twilight on the Range,* Austin, Texas: University of Texas Press, 1962.

Topping, Eugene S. *The Chronicles of the Yellowstone; An Accurate, and Comprehensive History,* St. Paul, Minn.: Pioneer Press, 1883.

Trefethen, James B., *Crusade for Wildlife,* Harrisburg, Penn.: Stackpole Co., 1961.

[Truman, Harry S.] *Published Papers of the Presidents, Harry S. Truman, 1950,* Washington, D.C.: Govt. Printing Office, 1965.

Turrill, Gardner S. *A Tale of the Yellowstone; or, In a Wagon Through Western Wyoming and Wonderland,* Jefferson, Iowa: G.S. Turrill Publishing Co., 1901.

[United States Army]. *Rules, Regulations and Instructions, for the Information and Guidance of Officers and Enlisted Men of the United States Army, and of the Scouts Doing duty in the Yellowstone National Park,* Washington, D.C.: Govt. Printing Office, 1907.

[United States Congress]. *Hearings Before the Committee on Public Lands, House of Representatives—Irrigation Easements, Yellowstone National Park* (66th Cong., 2nd Sess.; H.R. 12466). Washington, D.C.: Govt. Printing Office, 1920.

——————— , *Hearings Before the Committee on Irrigation, United States Senate—Dam Across the Yellowstone River,* (66th Cong., 3rd Sess.; Senate 4529) Washington, D.C.: Govt. Printing Office, 1921.

[United States Engineers]. *Instructions to Foremen of Working Parties . . . ,* Yellowstone National Park, Wyo.: Corps of Engineers, U.S. Army, 1906.

[United States Life Saving Service]. *Report of the United States Life Saving Service, for Fiscal Year 1889,* Washington, D.C.: Govt. Printing Office, 1889.

[United States Weather Bureau]. *Annual Meteorological Summary With Comparative Data, 1927—Yellowstone Park, Wyoming,* comp. Edgar H. Fletcher, Salt Lake City, Utah: Weather Bureau Office, 1928.

Van de Water, Frederic F. *The Family Flivver to Frisco,* New York: D. Appleton and Co., 1927.

Van Tassell, Charles, *Truthful Lies* (2nd ed.), Bozeman, Mont.: Chas. Van Tassell, 1913.

Victor, Francis Fuller. *River of the West,* Hartford, Conn.: R.W. Bliss & Co., 1870.

Wallace, R.C. *A Few Memories of a Long Life.* No place: Privately printed, 1900.

[War Department]. *Report on Survey for Wagon Road in Yellowstone National Park* (60th Cong., 1st Sess; H.R. Doc. 502). Washington, D.C.: Govt. Printing Office, 1908.

——————— , *New Roads in Yellowstone National Park,* (62d Cong., 2d Sess.; Senate Doc. 871). Washington, D.C.: Govt. Printing Office, 1912.

Ware, Eugene F. *The Indian War of 1864,* New York: St. Martin's Press, 1960.

Wear, David W. and Moses Harris. *Report of the Superintendent of the Yellowstone National Park to the Secretary of the Interior, 1886,* Washington, D.C.: Govt. Printing Office, 1886.

Wheat, Carl I. *Mapping the Trans-Mississippi West,* (From the Civil War to the Geological Survey, Vol. V), San Francisco: The Institute of Historical Cartography, 1963.

Wylie, William W. *Yellowstone National Park; or, The Great American Wonderland,* Kansas City, Mo.: Ramsey, Millett & Hudson, 1882.

[Wyoming Territory]. *Laws Appertaining to the Yellowstone National Park,* Cheyenne, Wyo.: The Leader Printing Company, 1884.

Yard, Robert S. *Our Federal Lands,* New York: Charles Scribner's Sons, 1928

[Yellowstone Boundary Commission]. *Final Report of the Yellowstone National Park Boundary Commission,* Washington, D.C.: Govt. Printing Office, 1931.

Young, Samuel B.M. *Report of the Acting Superintendent of the Yellowstone National Park to the Secretary of the Interior, 1897,* Washington, D.C.: Govt. Printing Office, 1897.

——————— , *Annual Report of the Superintendent of the Yellowstone National Park to the Secretary of the Interior, 1907,* Washington, D.C.: Govt. Printing Office, 1907.

——————— , *Report of Superintendent of the Yellowstone National Park to the Secretary of the Interior, 1908,* Washington, D.C.: Govt. Printing Office, 1908.

II. MAGAZINE ARTICLES

[American Forests], "The Dawn of Conservation," *American Forests* 41 (September 1935), 446-49.

Baker, Ray S., "A Place of Marvels," *Century Magazine* 66 (August 1903), 490.

Brayer, Herbert O., "Exploring the Yellowstone with Hayden, 1872," *Annals of Wyoming* 14 (October 1942), 253-98.

Bruette, William A., "Another Raid on the Yellowstone," *Forest and Stream* (September 28, 1929).

Burt, Struthers, "The Battle of Jackson's Hole," *The Nation* 122 (March 3, 1926), 225-27.

Clough, Wilson O. "Wyoming's Earliest Place Names?" *Annals of Wyoming* 37 (October 1965), 211-220.

Connery, Thomas M., "The Winter Tragedy of the Yellowstone," *The World Wide Magazine* (June 1919), 143-47.

Cooper, Suzanne T., "Summertime Revisited," *American Heritage* 14 (June 1963), 35-49.

deLaguna, Frederica, review of the symposium on "Early Man in the Western American Arctic" (1962), *American Anthropologist* 66(4), 950.

Drake, O.S.T., "A Lady's Trip to the Yellowstone Park," *Every Girl's Annual* (1887), 346-49.

[Engineering News], "Reinforced Concrete Arch Bridge Over the Yellowstone River, Yellowstone National Park," *Engineering News* 51 (January 14, 1904), 25.

Evermann, Barton W., "Two Ocean Pass," *Popular Science Monthly* 47 (June 1895), 183.

Everts, Truman C., "Thirty-seven Days of Peril," *Scribner's Monthly* 3 (November 1871), 1-17.

Ferris, Warren Angus, "Rocky Mountain Geysers," *Western Literary Messenger* 2 (July 13, 1842), 12-13.

——————————, "Life in the Rocky Mountains," *Western Literary Messenger* 3 (January 6, 1844), 196.

Finck, Henry T., "A Week in Yellowstone Park," *The Nation* 45 (September 11, 1887), 167.

——————————, "Yellowstone Park in 1897," *The Nation* 65 (October 7, 1897), 276-77.

——————————, "Yellowstone Park as a Summer Resort," *The Nation* 71 (September 27, 1900), 248-50.

Fisher, James, "The Idea of Wilderness," *The Listener* (London) 67 (April 1962), 721-23.

Folsom, David E., "Valley of the Upper Yellowstone," *Western Monthly* 4 (July 1870), 60-67.

Forbes, Stephen A., "Mysterious Music in Yellowstone Park," *The Literary Digest* 90 (September 18, 1926), 26.

Forest and Stream 19 (January 4, 1883), 441.

Forest and Stream 19 (January 11, 1883), 462.

Forest and Stream (March 13, 1884).

Forest and Stream 26 (June 24, 1886), 425.

Forest and Stream 28 (February 17, 1887), 61.

Franklin, W.S., "The Yellowstone," *Science,* N.S. 37 (March 21, 1913), 446-47.

Gibbon, John, "The Wonders of the Yellowstone," *Journal of the American Geographical Society of New York* 5 (1874), 112-37.

Gray, John S., "Last Rites for Lonesome Charley Reynolds," *Montana* 13 (Summer 1963), 42-50.

Gregg, William C., "The Cascade Corner of Yellowstone Park," *The Outlook* 129 (November 23, 1921), 469-76.

Haines, Aubrey L., "The Bridge That Jack Built," *Yellowstone Nature Notes* 21 (January-February 1947), 1-4.

——————— ,"McGuirk's Medicinal Springs," *Yellowstone Nature Notes* 21 (March-April 1947), 22-23.

——————— , "The Bannock Indian Trails of Yellowstone National Park," *Archaeology in Montana* 4 (March 1962), 1-8.

——————— , "Lost in the Wilderness," *Montana Magazine* 22 (Summer 1972), 31-41.

Haynes, C. Vance, Jr., "Fluted Projectile Points: Their Age and Dispersion," *Science* 145 (September 25, 1964), 1408-13.

Haynes, Jack E., "The First Winter Trip Through Yellowstone National Park," *Annals of Wyoming* 14 (April 1942), 89-97.

——————— , "That Man, Yankee Jim," *The Rotospoke* 4 (December 28, 1954), 2-3.

Hedges, Cornelius, "An Account of a Trip to Fort Benton in October, 1865, with Acting Governor Thomas F. Meagher to Treat with the Blackfeet Indians," *Rocky Mountain Magazine* 1 (November 1900), 155-58.

Henderson, A. Bart, "The Yellowstone Diaries of A. Bart Henderson," ed. by A.L. Haines, *The Yellowstone Interpreter* 2 (January-February, March-April, May-June 1964), 8-14, 20-26, 33-40.

Henderson, C. Hanford, "Through the Yellowstone on Foot," *Outing* (May 1899), 161-67.

Hofer, Thomas E., "Yellowstone Park Notes," *Forest and Stream* (December 19,1897).

Hough, Emerson, "Greater Yellowstone," *The Saturday Evening Post* 190 (December 1, 1917): 61, 64.

Hultkrantz, Ake, "The Shoshones in the Rocky Mountains," *Annals of Wyoming* 33 (April 1961):19-41.

Huth, Hans, "Yosemite: The Story of an Idea," *Sierra Club Bulletin* 33 (March 1948): 47-78.

Jaager, T.A., "Death Gulch a Natural Bear Trap," *Appleton's Popular Science Monthly* 54 (February 1899): 475.

Jashemski, Wilhelmina, "Pompeii," *Natural History* 73 (December 1964): 30-41.

Kintrea, Frank, "When the Coachman Was a Millionaire," *American Heritage* 18 (October 1967): 21-25, 75-79.

Kuppens, Francis X., "On the Origin of the Yellowstone National Park," *The Jesuit Bulletin* 41 (October 1962): 6-7, 14.

Langford, Nathaniel P., "The Wonders of the Yellowstone," *Scribner's Monthly,* (May, June 1871): 1-17, 113-28.

——————— "The Ascent of Mount Hayden," *Scribner's Monthly* 6 (June 1873): 129-57.

Lillard, Richard G., "The Siege and Conquest of a National Park," *The American West* 5 (January 1968): 28-32, 67-72.

[Literary Digest], "Speak Up Quickly for the Yellowstone," *The Literary Digest* 65 (June 5, 1920): 90-93.

——————— , "The Fight for the Yellowstone Waters," *The Literary Digest* 67 (October 23, 1920): 90-91.

——————— , "Neighbors for a Night in Yellowstone Park," *The Literary Digest* 82 (August 30, 1924): 44-46.

Malouf, Carling, "Historic Tribes and Archaeology," *Archaeology in Montana* 8 (January-March, 1967): 1-16.

Martindale, Phillip, "An Additional Note on the Wickiups," *Yellowstone Nature Notes* 4 (May 31, 1927): 4.

Mattes, Merrill J., "Behind the Legend of Colter's Hell: The Early Exploration of the Yellowstone National Park," *Mississippi Valley Historical Review* 36 (September 1949): 251-82.

Matthews, Albert, "The Word Park in the United States," Publications of the Colonial Society of Massachusetts 8 (April 1904): 378-81.

McIntosh, A.C., "Who Owns Yellowstone Park?" *The American Mercury* 37 (April 1936): 493-96.

Mitchell, S. Weir, "Through the Yellowstone Park to Fort Custer," *Lippincott's Magazine* 26 (July 1880): 21-41.

Monihan, R.S., "Ocean to Ocean—by Automobile," *American Heritage* 13 (April 1962): 54-65.

Moriarity, James R., "Transitional Pre-Desert Phase in San Diego County, California," *Science* 155 (February 3, 1967): 553-55.

Munson, Lyman E., "Pioneer Life in Montana," *Contributions to the Historical Society of Montana* 5 (1904): 214-16.

Murphy, Robert, "Triumph of the Trumpeters," *National Wildlife* 5 (June-July 1967): 42-47.

Nash, Roderick, "The American Wilderness in Historical Perspective," *Forest History* 6 (Winter 1963): 2-13.

The Nation 14 (March 7, 1872): 153.

The Nation 25 (October 18, 1877): 233-34.

[Outdoor America], "The Jackson Hole Plan," *Outdoor America,* (November-December 1944).

[Outlook Magazine], "The Looters of Yellowstone Park, Hands Off," *The Outlook* 144 (October 20, 1926): 229-30.

——————————, "Yellowstone Park and the Nation," *The Outlook* 145 (January 19, 1927): 77-80.

Partoll, Albert J. "The Flathead Indian Name in Montana Nomenclature," *Montana Magazine* 1 (January 1951): 37-47.

[Pond, Peter] "Adventures in American Northwest," *Journal of American History* 1 (1907): 362-63.

[Potts, Daniel T.], "Early Yellowstone and Western Experiences," *Yellowstone Nature Notes* 21 (September-October 1947): 49-56.

Reinhardt, Richard, "The Case of the Hard Nosed Conservationists," *American West* 4 (February 1967): 52-54, 85-90.

Remington, Frederic, "Policing the Yellowstone," *Harper's Weekly* 39 (January 12, 1895): 35-38.

Roosevelt, Theodore, "Three Capital Books of the Wilderness," *The Outlook* 102 (November 30, 1912): 712-15.

Ross, George T., "Yellowstone Park Extension," *Outdoor America* (December 1927): 8.

Sawyer, Edmund J., "Death of Ranger Charles Phillips," *Yellowstone Nature Notes* 4 (April 30, 1927): 1-2.

Scribner's Monthly 4 (May 1872): 120-21.

Sedgewick, Henry D., Jr., "On Horseback Through the Yellowstone," *The World's Work* 6 (June 1903): 3575.

Smith, Hugh M., "Mysterious Acoustic Phenomena in Yellowstone Natio— ¹ Park," *Science* N.S. 63 (June 11, 1926): 586-7.

Sutton, Horace, "The Bear Facts," *The Saturday Review* 38 (July 9, 1955): 29.

Swain, Donald C., "The Founding of the National Park Service," *The American West* 6 (September 1969): 6-9.

Swanson, Earl H., Jr., "Cultural Relations Between Two Plains," *Archaeology In Montana* 7 (April-June 1966): 1-2.

"T.E.S." [Thomas E. Sherman], "Across the Continent. II–The National Park," *Woodstock Letters* (1882): 25-42.

Thayer, Wade W., "Camp and Cycle in Yellowstone Park," *Outing* (April 1898): 17-24.

Thomas, Lately, "The Operator and the Emperors," *American Heritage* 15 (April 1964): 4-8, 83-88.

Thomas, Thomas H. "Yellowstone Park Illustrated," (2 parts) *The Graphic* (August 11 and 18, 1888): 157-64, 189-93, 196.

Thoreau, Henry David, "Chesuncook," *Atlantic Monthly* 2 (June, July, August, 1858): 1-12, 224-33, 305-17.

Trumbull, Walter, "The Washburn Yellowstone Expedition, No. 1," *Overland Monthly* 6 (May 1871): 431-37.

———————, "The Washburn Yellowstone Expedition, No. 2," *Overland Monthly* 6 (June 1871): 489-96.

Weikert, Andrew J., "Journal of the Tour Through the Yellowstone National Park, in August and September 1877," *Contributions to the Historical Society of Montana* 3 (1900): 153-74.

Wheeler, Olin D., "Walter Washington deLacy," *Contributions to the Historical Society of Montana* 2 (1896): 241-51.

———————, "Yellowstone's Semi-Centennial," *Western Magazine* 18 (February 1921): 28-33.

White, John L., "D. J. 'Kid' O'Malley . . .," *Montana* 17 (July 1967): 60-73.

Whitmell, Charles T., "The American Wonderland, the Yellowstone National Park," *Report and Transactions of the Cardiff Naturalists Society* 17 (1885): 77-106.

Wister, Owen, "Old Yellowstone Days," *Harper's Monthly* 172 (March 1936): 471-80.

III. NEWSPAPER ARTICLES

Anonymous articles are listed chronologically under the name of the newspaper in which they appeared. Newspapers are alphabetized by title.

Avant Courier (Bozeman, Mont.)

[Mammoth Hot Springs], Sept. 13, 1871.

[Toll road construction], Oct. 26, 1871.

"Mammoth Hot Springs," Nov. 2, 1871.

"Hon N.P. Langford . . . ," Nov. 9, 1871.

"The Cataracts and Geysers of the Upper Yellowstone–Why they Should be Given in Perpetuity to Montana," Dec. 7, 1871.

"A Natural Wonder," Jan. 25, 1872.

[New route to geysers], Aug. 22, 1872.

[Hayden survey party], Oct. 17 and Nov. 28, 1872.

"To Wonderland," Dec. 20, 1872.

[Toll road to the Park], July 11, 1873.

"Important Exploration," Aug. 15, 1873.

"Deer Lodge Party," ". . . return from the Geysers," ". . . en route to the Springs" and "Return of the Tourists," Sept. 12, 1873.

"Killing Bear by Wholesale" and "Vandalism", Sept. 26, 1873.

"Virginia City . . . Free Wagon Road, Oct. 3, 1873.

"National Park," Dec. 12, 1873.

"For the Mammoth Hot Springs," July 10, 1874.

"Important Cut-off," Aug. 7, 1874.

"Sudden Death," Sept. 18, 1874.

[Specimen collecting], Aug. 20, 1875.

"Navigation on the Yellowstone," Dec. 31, 1875.

"A Cactus Canticle," Feb. 18, 1876.

[Add—Steamer Yellowstone], Mar. 17, 1876.

"Wonderland, Scenes of Bloodshed," Sept. 6 and 13, 1877.

"Stewart's Story . . . ," Sept. 27, 1877.

"Andy Weikert has arrived . . .," Oct. 25, 1877.

"From Wonderland," Nov. 1, 1877.

"The Cunning Fox Caught at Last," Mar. 20, 1879.

"Eastern Montana Boom," Feb. 26, 1880.

". . . mail route," Aug. 5, 1880.

"A Fraud on Tourists to the Park," Aug. 12, 1880.

"A Newsy and Interesting Letter . . .," Aug. 19, 1880.

"Another 'Faber-Pusher' After Col. Norris," Sept. 9, 1880.

"The Yellowstone Park—Its Management," Sept. 30, 1880.

"The Yellowstone National Park" and "Management of the Yellowstone . . .," Dec. 23, 1880.

"Peterfunk Windy Norris' Report," Mar. 3, 1881.

"The Yellowstone Park," Aug. 25, 1881.

"They Went Bicycle Riding," Oct. 27, 1881.

"Sheridan on the Yellowstone Region," Dec. 22, 1881.

"Railroad . . . to the Yellowstone Park," Jan. 26, 1882.

"O. [C.] T. Hobart . . . ," Feb. 2, 1882.

"Another Norris Hoodoo" and "Railroad Racket," Feb. 9, 1882.

"Subsiding of the Wind," Feb. 16, 1882.

"Newsy Letter from Upper Yellowstone," Apr. 6, 1882.

"Save the National Park from Ruin," May 4, 1882.

"G.L. Henderson . . . ," June 1, 1882.

"Major Conger . . . ," June 8, 1882.

"A couple of Dakota men . . . ," Sept. 7, 1882.

"Wonderland Tourists . . . ," Sept. 28, 1882.

"The National Park Enterprise," Oct. 5, 1882.

"Jas. McCartney . . . ," Oct. 19, 1882.

"Yellowstone Park," Dec. 15, 1882.

"The Company of Capitalists . . . ," Dec. 21, 1882.

"Letter from Yellowstone Park," Dec. 28, 1882.

"Harry Horr's Hot Spring Claim" and "Game Features of the Yellowstone . . . ," Jan. 11, 1883.

"Slaughtering Game . . . ," Jan. 25, 1883.

"Park Items," Feb. 15, 1883.

"Game in the Park" and "The Yellowstone Contract," Feb. 22, 1883.
"The Yellowstone Lease," Mar. 22, 1883.
"Park Pencilings," Apr. 12 and 19, 1883.
"House Building in the Park," May 17, 1883.
"That perennial sage brush blossom . . .," May 24, 1883.
"Park Appropriations and Appointments," June 7, 1883.
"A good story . . .," Sept. 13, 1883.

Billings Gazette (Mont.)
"Lovell Man Recalls Early-day Work on Yellowstone Park Roads," 1956 (clipping).

Box Elder Valley Press (Mont.)
"Yellowstone Expedition of 1819 a Miserable Failure," June 2, 1922.

Bozeman Daily Chronicle (Mont.)
"Hearing Opens on Teton Park," Aug. 9, 1938.

Budget Review (Douglas, Wyo.)
"Senator Tom Cooper Has Plan to Extend Park," Aug. 25, 1927.

Butte Daily Miner (Mont.)
"The Interior Department today . . .," Mar. 15, 1891.

Chicago Weekly News (Ill.)
"In Yellowstone Park," Aug. 23, 1883.

Christian Science Monitor (Boston, Mass.)
"The Yellowstone Trail," June 12, 1917.

Daily Morning Chronicle (Washington, D.C.)
"Yellowstone River," Jan. 20, 1871.

Denver Post (Colo.)
"Denver Man Arrested . . .," May 22, 1915.
"Caught! The Lone Highwayman," Jan. 5, 1916.

Free Press (Detroit, Mich.)
"Ickes Defends National Park," June 18, 1933.

Frontier Index (Fort Sanders, D.T.)
"The Greatest Bear Story Yet," Mar. 6, 1868.

Frontier Index (Laramie, D.T.)
"California," May 5, 1886.
"Brevities Communicated from the Sanctum of the American Libertarian," June 16, 1868.

Frontier Index (Julesburg, Neb.)
"Remarkable Discovery," July 26, 1867.

Frontier Index (Green River, D.T.)
"The Great Shoshone Falls of Snake River," Aug. 21, 1868.

Great Falls Tribune (Mont.)
"Yellowstone Boundary Commission Named," Apr. 9, 1929.

Helena Daily Herald (Mont.)
"Departure of the Expedition," Aug. 18, 1870.
"Yellowstone Party Heard From," Sept. 23, 1870.
"The Yellowstone Expedition," Sept. 27 and 28, 1870 (both reprinted in issue of Sept. 30).
"Arrival of Warren C. Gillette," Oct. 3, 1870.
"The Lost Man—$600 Reward," Oct. 6, 1870.
"The Yellowstone Expedition," Oct. 26, 1870.
"Correspondence," Nov. 11, 1870.
"The Yellowstone Banquet," Nov. 14, 1870.
"A Grand Lecture," Nov. 17, 1870.
"Around Montana," July 10, 1871.
"The Yellowstone Scientific Expedition," July 11, 1871.
"A National Park," Jan. 16 and 31, 1872.
"Our National Park," Feb. 28 and Mar. 1, 1872.

Helena Weekly Herald (Mont.)
"The Headwaters of the Yellowstone," Dec. 12, 1867.
"Good Story—We clip from an eastern paper. . . ," Dec. 26, 1867.

Idaho Republican (Blackfoot)
"The Ford," Nov. 18, 1919.

Jackson Hole Courier (Jackson, Wyo.)
"Many Outsiders Interested in Park Extension," Apr. 24, 1918.
"Renewal of Effort to Incorporate Tetons in Y.N. Park—Albright Forecast," Dec. 12, 1922.
"Pertinent Facts—Lundy Memorial," Feb. 28, 1929.
"Park Extension to Follow 'The Jackson Hole Plan,' "May 31, 1934.
"Why Give it Away?" Jan. 27, 1938.
"Park Extension Compromise?" Sept. 1, 1938.

Livingston Enterprise (Mont.)
"Yellowstone Park Guides," June 6, 1883.
"Local Layout," June 29, 1883.
"Montana News," July 26, 1883.
"The Editor's Excursion," Aug. 1 and 6, 1883.
"Rufus Hatch's Party," Aug. 11, 1883.
"Another 'Heap Big Chief,' "Aug. 13, 1883.
". . . notices are posted," Aug. 17, 1883.
[Arthur-Crosby dialogue], "Frank Leslie Depicts Arthur. . . ," "Arrival of the Hatch Party," "Details of the Killing at Gardiner" and "Completion of the Northern Pacific," Aug. 23, 1883.
"Weber's Capture," Aug. 24, 1883.
"Local Layout," Aug. 25, 1883.
"Going to Kidnap the President," Aug. 27, 1883.
"Villard's Guests," and "Under the head, 'Stealing our Park . . .'" Aug. 29, 1883.
"By Telegraph", Aug. 31, 1883.
"Local Layout," Sept. 1, 1883.
[Editorial], and "The National Park Branch," Sept. 3, 1883.

"The Hatch Party," Sept. 4, 1883.

"The Decoration," Sept. 6, 1883.

"Local Layout," Sept. 19, 1883.

"Slang Words and Phrases," Sept. 22, 1883.

"About Hotel Waiters," Oct. 3, 1883.

"Ridicule Cannot Kill," Oct. 15, 1883.

"The Yellowstone Name," Oct. 23, 1883.

"Uncle Rufus' Recent Pilgrimage," Nov. 22, 1883.

[Real estate transactions], Dec. 1, 1883.

"Yellowstone Park to Have a New Superintendent," Dec. 20, 1883.

". . . Villard's junket," Dec. 29, 1883.

"Railroad to Cooke City," Jan. 5 and 18, 1884.

"President Arthur's Health," Jan. 8, 1884.

"National Park Matters," Jan. 12, 1884.

"Query—is the road . . . ," Jan. 22, 1884.

"Park Paragraphs," Jan. 26, 1884.

"In Memoriam," Jan. 29, 1884.

"Report on the National Park," Feb. 4, 1884.

"Up-River Mishaps," Feb. 23, 1884.

"The man who was killed . . . ," Feb. 26, 1884.

"The Park Improvement Company's Affairs," Mar. 11, 1884.

"Receiver Appointed," Mar. 21, 1884.

"The Redman's Welcome to Villard," Mar. 28, 1884.

"Cinnabar and Clark's Fork . . . ," May 3, 1884.

"Mr. Bassett . . . ," May 4, 1884.

"What Hulme Says," May 8, 1884.

"An Interview with Hatch," May 12, 1884.

"The Clark's Fork Railroad," May 31, 1884.

"A Possible Solution," June 12, 1884.

"The Forest Reserve," June 14, 1884.

"Settled at Last," July 5, 1884.

"Major Conger Asked to Resign," July 19, 1884.

"The Park Superintendency," July 21, 1884.

". . . Mr. Carpenter who has been appointed," July 26, 1884.

"Park Notes," Nov. 15, 1884.

"Trouble in the Park," Dec. 13, 1884.

"The Park Arrests," Dec. 20, 1884.

"That Horse," Feb. 21, 1885.

"News from the Mountains," Mar. 14, 1885.

"Superintendent Carpenter's Resignation Asked for," "The Charges Against
    Carpenter" and "The Other side of the Story," Apr. 18, 1885.

"Gossip and Comment," May 23, 1885.

"Doings in Wonderland," June 13, 1885.

"The Yellowstone Park," June 20, 1885.

"Congressman O'Neal Talks . . . ," July 11, 1885.

"Enthusiastically Descriptive," July 18, 1885.

"Gossip and Comment," Aug. 1, 1885.

"Local Layout," Aug. 8, 1885.

"Gossip and Comment" and "Rounding up Offenders," Aug. 15, 1885.

"Bear Hunting in the National Park," Aug. 18, 1885.

"An Unextinguished Camp Fire," Aug. 20, 1885.
"The Park Pioneer Pinafore" and "Babcock & Miles . . .," Aug. 22, 1885.
"Alluding to his Yellowstone Park excursion . . .," Sept. 5, 1885.
"Noticed in the Park," Sept. 19, 1885.
"Arrested in the Park," Nov. 7, 1885.
"Alpine the Hunter," Nov. 14, 1885.
"Yellowstone Park," July 7, 1888.
"The Immortal 15" and "Last Saturday, a shooting . . .," Sept. 22, 1888.
[Poem], Feb. 18, 1893.
"Capt. Baronette," Apr. 20, 1901.
"Pathfinder Crew Arrives," May 25, 1911.
"Park to Park Highway," June 29, 1911.
"New Lake in Wonderland," Aug. 1, 1911.
"Will Hold Meet in Yellowstone," Aug. 8, 1911.
"Would Admit Autos to the Y.N. Park," Aug. 9, 1911.
"Blythe Tells Funny Stories," Sept. 13, 1911.
"Many Churches Unite in Dedication . . .," June 26, 1913.
"Yellowstone Park May be Enlarged," Oct. 23, 1917.
"Three Times More Flivvers," Mar. 17, 1918.
"Forty-six Camps for Tourists," Sept. 16, 1919.
"Plan Entrances for Cooke Road," Apr. 14, 1920.
"Appealing to the East," Apr. 30, 1920.
"Cooperation Builds Trail . . .," May 9, 1920.
"Caterpillar Plow Clears Park Roads," June 2, 1920.
"Lest We Forget . . .," June 8, 1920.
"Camp Roosevelt to Become a Scientific and Educational Center . . .," Mar. 12, 1921.
"A Great Figure of the Yellowstone . . .," June 30, 1923.
"Park County Authorities to Go Before the Legislature With a Plea for Annexation of Land," Jan. 16, 1929.
[Presidential Proclamation], Nov. 3, 1932.

Los Angeles Times (Calif.)
"Californian Appointed Park Director," July 6, 1919.

Miles City Star (Mont.)
"First Objective, Hold Water in Montana," July 28, 1937.

Montana Post (Virginia City)
"The Very Latest," May 11, 1867.
"Who Will Say Now We Are Not in Danger?", May 18, 1867.
"Gone With Provisions," May 25, 1867.
"From Bozeman," June 1, 1867.
"The Upper Yellowstone," Aug. 24, 1867.

Montana Standard (Butte)
"Cars Safer Than Horses," Sept. 14, 1966.

Newark Call (N.J.)
"Natural Beauty of Yellowstone," Mar. 31, 1918.

New North-West (Deer Lodge, Mont.)
"Geyser Land," Dec. 28, 1871.
"The Park Again," Mar. 9, 1872.

"The Splendors of the West," Mar. 16, 1872.
"N.P. Langford . . . ," June 15, 1872.
"Life With the Nez Perce—The Capture and Adventures of [Shively] . . . ,
    Sept. 14, 1877.
"Yellowstone Park Improvements," Feb. 22, 1889.

New York Herald
"Science and Art. Wonders of Montana . . . ," Jan. 22, 1871.

New York Times
"Travels in Montana," Jan. 22, 1871.
"John D., Jr., Upheld in Teton Park Acts," May 7, 1934.

New York Daily Tribune
"The Wonders of Montana," Jan. 23, 1871.

Niles Register (Philadelphia, Penn.)
    "From the West," Oct. 6, 1827.

Northside News (Jerome, Idaho)
"Idaho Could Use Water from the Park," June 30, 1933.

Philadelphia Gazette and Daily Advertiser (Penn.)
"Communicated for the . . . ," Sept. 27, 1827.

Pioneer Press (St. Paul, Minn.)
[List of Appointments] , June 2, 1883.

Post Enterprise (Sheridan, Wyo.)
"Teton Measure Before Senate," Dec. 8, 1928.

Post Register (Idaho Falls, Idaho)
"Plans Made to Tap Lake," Nov. 16, 1934.

Record Herald (Helena, Mont.)
"Vast Development of Yellowstone and Missouri River Watersheds Pro-
    posed to Public Works Body," Sept. 4, 1935.

Record-Herald (Salmon, Idaho)
"Teton National Park New Proposal for Congress," Aug. 22, 1928.

Republican (Rawlins, Wyo.)
"Wyoming's Wonderful Asset," Sept. 8, 1827.

Rigby Sentinel (Idaho)
"Wyoming Opposes Plan to Divert Water to Idaho," Feb. 13, 1937.

River Press (Fort Benton, Mont.)
"Steamboats Coming to Fort Benton had Varied and Interesting Stories,"
    Aug. 21, 1946.

Rocky Mountain Daily Gazette (Helena, Mont.)
"The Mineral Springs of . . . ," July 24, 1871.

Rocky Mountain Weekly Gazette (Helena, Mont.)
"Yellowstone Expedition," Oct. 3, 1870.

Salt Lake Tribune (Utah)
"Should Wyoming Run Park Concessions?", Feb. 21 and Apr. 6, 1955.

Spokane Statesman-Review (Wash.)
"Park Rangers Succeed Cavalry," June 6, 1919.

Sundance Gazette (Wyo.)
"Uncle Sam's Big Menagerie," Nov. 25, 1898.

Tribune (Pocatello, Idaho)
"Kosanke Plan," June 21, 1933.

Tribune-Leader (Cheyenne, Wyo.)
"Yellowstone Waters Cut from Parley," June 18, 1936.

Virginia Tri-Weekly Post (Mont.)
"Niagara Eclipsed," Feb. 4, 1868.

Washington Post (D. C.)
"Ex-Congressman Guy R. Pelton . . .," July 28, 1890.
"Yellowstone Hotels," Aug. 10, 1890.
"The Yellowstone Park Scandal," Aug. 27, 1890.

Wonderland (Gardiner, Mont.)
"Dudes are Amused" and "Eight hundred men . . .," Aug. 21, 1902.
"Fort Yellowstone," Jan. 29, 1903.
"The Corner Stone was Laid," April 30, 1903.
"Uncle John Yancey," May 5, 1903.

World (N.Y.)
"Roosevelt's Life in the Wilderness," Apr. 24, 1903.

Wyoming State Tribune (Cheyenne)
"Congressman Mondell Writes Jackson Hole Rancher Favoring Park Extension" and "Maxwell Struthers Burt, Author, Traveller, Rancher, Answers Mondell Letter," Nov. 5, 1919.

By-line articles are listed alphabetically under name of author.

"Botanicus" [Robert Adams, Jr.], "The Geological Survey," *The Inquirer* (Philadelpha, Pa.) Sept. 19, 1872.

Burdet, Bob, "In the National Park," *Livingston Enterprise* (Mont.) July 28, 1888.

Davis, John C., "Yellowstone Park," *Courier-Journal* (Louisville, Ky.) Apr. 13, 1884.

Haines, Aubrey L., "Stagecoach Days in the Yellowstone," *Cody Enterprise* (Wyo.) June 14, 1962.

Hedges, Cornelius, "Mount Everts," *Helena Daily Herald* (Mont.) Oct. 8, 1870.

—————————, "The Great Falls of the Yellowstone," *Helena Daily Herald,* Oct. 15, 1870.

—————————, "Hell Broth Springs," *Helena Daily Herald,* Oct. 19, 1870.

————————— , "Pictures of the Yellowstone Country—Sulphur Mountain and Mud Volcano," *Helena Weekly Herald,* Oct. 27, 1870.

—————————, "Yellowstone Lake," *Helena Daily Herald,* Nov. 9, 1870.

Henderson, George L., "The Park Pioneer . . .," *Livingston Enterprise* (Mont.) Aug. 22, 1885.

—————————"Haynes' Winter Expedition," *Helena Independent* (Mont.) Feb. 6, 1887.

————————— , "Naming a Geyser," *Daily Herald* (Norristown, Pa.) Jan. 19, 1889.

————————— , "Thoughts of Old," *Livingston Post* (Mont.) Jan. 11, 1900.

Hough, Emerson, "Winter in the Rockies," *Chicago Tribune* (Ill.) Dec. 23, 1894.

"M.E." [Eastlake], "From the Far West," *Western Home Journal* (Lawrence, Kan.) July 1872.

Miller, Robert E., "Mushbach, Veteran Explorer, Tells of Early Days in Park," *Montana Record-Herald* (Helena) Nov. 30, 1929.

Panton, S.P., "Early Days in Yellowstone Recalled by N.P. Surveyor," *Wolf Point News* (Mont.) Nov. 23, 1939.

Savage, Joseph, "From the Yellowstone Expedition," *Western Home Journal* (Lawrence, Kan.) Aug. 1, 1872.

————————— , "The Wonders of the Yellowstone," *Western Home Journal,* Sept. 19, 1872.

Sheppard, W.B., "History of A Bill," *Evening Post* (N.Y.) Sept. 25, 1919.

Sunderlee, Charles R., "A Thrilling Event on the Yellowstone," *Helena Daily Herald* (Mont.) May 18, 1870.

Trumbull, Walter, "Yellowstone Papers—No. One," *Rocky Mountain Daily Gazette* (Helena, Mont.) Oct. 18, 1870.

————————— , "Yellowstone Papers—No. Two," *Rocky Mountain Daily Gazette,* Oct. 19, 1870.

————————— , "Yellowstone Papers," *Rocky Mountain Weekly Gazette,* Oct. 24 and 31, 1870.

Van Dyke, Henry, "Rivers, Ranches and Reservations," *New York Times Book Review and Magazine,* Oct. 2, 1921.

Walsh, William H., "Bath's Soldier Boy," *Bath Independent* (Maine) Dec. 1895.

Weaver, David B., "The Upper Yellowstone," *Montana Post* (Virginia City) Aug. 31, 1867.

IV. UNPUBLISHED MATERIALS

Albright, Horace M., "Annual Report of the Superintendent of Yellowstone National Park to the Director of the National Park Service, October 29, 1919," Bound file, Yellowstone National Park Reference Library.

————————— , "Annual Report of the Supt. of Yellowstone National Park to the Director of the National Park Service, 1921." Bound file, Yellowstone National Park Library.

————————— , Letter to C.W. Farnham, July 28, 1924. Copy in files of Yellowstone National Park.

————————— , "Monthly Report of the Supt. of Y.N.P. for the month of August 1925." Bound file, Yellowstone National Park Reference Library.

————————— , "Annual Report of the Supt. of Y.N.P. to the Director of the National Park Service, 1925." Bound File, Yellowstone National Park Reference Library.

————————— , Letter to I.H. Larom, January 24, 1929. Copy in files of Yellowstone National Park.

————————— , Letter to W.C. Gregg, February 1, 1929. Copy in files of Yellowstone National Park.

————————— , Letter to Edmund Seymour, September 28, 1929. Copy in files of Yellowstone National Park.

———————— , Letter to the author, July 1, 1963.

Allinder, W.L., Letter to Joseph Joffe, May 3, 1946. Original in files of Yellowstone National Park.

[Anonymous], Letter to G.C. Anderson, January 26, 1891. Yellowstone National Park Archives.

Arthur, George W., "An Archaeological Survey of the Upper Yellowstone River Drainage, Montana," Agricultural Economics Research Report No. 26, Montana Agricultural Experiment Station, Bozeman, October 1966.

Askevold, E., Summary of the Development of the Yellowstone Park Hotel Company and Yellowstone Park Transportation Company, January 30, 1917, in file "President, 209B," Northern Pacific Railroad Company, St. Paul, Minn.

Atchison, William Emory, "An Epic of the Middle West," ed. by Charles H. Ramsdell and mimeographed by J.E. Haynes, St. Paul, Minn., February 1, 1933.

Bassett, W.H., Letter to Moses Harris, July 23, 1888. Letter Box 4, Doc. no. 654, Yellowstone National Park Archives.

Batterman, C.S., Letter to G.S. Anderson, August 2, 1893. Letter Box 4, Doc. no. 681, Yellowstone National Park Archives.

Belknap, William W., Letter to Commanding Officers of Posts on the route of the Geological Explorations by Professor Hayden, March 25, 1871. Records of the Geological and Geographical Survey of the Territories ("Hayden Survey"), Record Group 57, Letters Received from Govt. Agencies. (M 623, roll 14, frame 319), National Archives, Washington, D.C.

Bigford, R., Letter to S.B.M. Young, June 17, 1908. Letter Box 33, Yellowstone National Park Archives.

Billings, Frederick, Letter to J. M. Ashley, March 27, 1871. Northern Pacific Railroad Papers (Land Department), Minnesota Historical Society, St. Paul.

Blackmore, William, "Diary—1872—Fourth Visit to the United States," photocopy of a transcript of parts 5, 6 & 7, Yellowstone National Park Library.

Bonnell, Fred, Interview with the author at Mammoth Hot Springs, Wyo., September 1, 1963.

Borton, Raymond E. "Irrigation on the Crow Reservation . . ." Mimeographed Thesis. Montana State College, Bozeman, 1964.

Boutelle, Frazier A., Letter to the Secretary of Interior, July 31, 1889. Letter Book 214, Yellowstone National Park Archives.

———————— , Letter to the Secretary of Interior, August 29, 1890. Letter Book 214, Yellowstone National Park Archives.

———————— , Letter to the Secretary of Interior, September 11, 1890. Letter Book 215, Yellowstone National Park Archives.

Brackett, Julia S., Interview at Livingston, Mont., November 9, 1950. Transcript in Yellowstone National Park Reference Library.

Brett, Lloyd M., Letter to Secretary of the Yellowstone Park Hotel Co., December 1, 1912. Letter Box 68, Yellowstone National Park Archives.

———————— , Letter to the *Western Motor Car Company,* August 10, 1914. Letter Box 43, Yellowstone National Park Archives.

Brooks, Blayne, Interview by the author at Mammoth Hot Springs, July 7, 1964.

Burley, D.E., Letter to L.M. Brett, June 25, 1915. Letter Box 43, Yellowstone National Park Archives.

Carpenter, Robert E., Notice to G.J. Jackson, Jack Rutherford and R.E. Cutler, October 30, 1884. Letter Box 9, Doc. no. 1411, Yellowstone National Park Archives.

Chambers, William, Jr., Report to P.H. Conger, November 14, 1883. Letter Box 9, Doc. no. 1346, Yellowstone National Park Archives.

Chittenden, Hiram M. "The 'National Park Range' of Mountains; What is its Rightful Name?" Typed MS., Yellowstone National Park Reference Library.

————————, "Echoes on Frontier Days—Holdups." Manuscript, n.d. Yellowstone National Park Reference Library.

————————, Letter to Capt. George Anderson, March 28, 1895. Letter Box 10, Doc. no. 2243, Yellowstone National Park Archives.

————————, Letter to Editor of *Forest and Stream,* February 14, 1899. Typed copy in Miscellanies VI: 106-22, Yellowstone National Park Library.

————————, Letter to E.A. Hitchcock, April 23, 1903. Yellowstone National Park Archives.

————————, Letter to John Pitcher, April 5, 1904. Original in Yellowstone National Park Archives.

————————, "The Yellowstone," n.d. Typescript in Yellowstone National Park Reference Library.

Clark, William. "A Map of Part of the Continent of North America . . . Compiled from the information of the best informed travellers through that quarter of the Globe . . .," 1806-11. MS no. 303-IV, Coe Collection, Beinecke Library, Yale University.

Coleman, Lee L., Interview by the author, at Mammoth Hot Springs, Wyo., March 20, 1961.

Conger, Patrick H., Office memorandum [1883]. Letter Box 9, Doc. no. 1555, Yellowstone National Park Archives.

Cook, Charles W. "Remarks of C.W. Cook, Last Survivor of the Original Explorers of the Yellowstone Park Region, on the Occasion of His Second Visit to the Park in 53 years, During the Celebration of the Park's Golden Anniversary," Official transcript, July 14, 1922, Yellowstone National Park Reference Library.

Coyne, Thomas E., Letter to G.C. Crowe, February 2, 1933. Original in file of Yellowstone National Park.

Curran, Patrick J., "Yellowstone Park Association, 1886-1896," MS dated August 23, 1968. Minnesota Historical Society, St. Paul.

Daum, Merrill F., Letter to J.E. Haynes, April 4, 1929. Copy in the files of Yellowstone National Park.

Dean, James H., Report to P.H. Conger, July 14, 1884. Letter Box 9, Doc. no. 1359, Yellowstone National Park Archives.

————————, Report to P.H. Conger, August 14, 1884. Letter Box 9, Doc. no. 1356, Yellowstone National Park Archives.

————————, Report to P.H. Conger, August 26, 1884. Letter Box 9, Doc. no. 1355, Yellowstone National Park Archives.

————————, Report to P.H. Conger, September 3, 1884. Letter Box 9, Doc. no. 1354, Yellowstone National Park Archives.

deLacy, Walter W., Letter to Major Martin Maginnis, May 9, 1874. Copy, Montana Historical Society, Helena.

DeSmet, Pierre-Jean. [Untitled map]. Jesuit Archives, Missouri Province. IX: De Smetiana. C-B: Atlas, No. 5, St. Louis University.

—————————— , "Chart of the Head of Yellow Stone." Drawn by James Bridger, 1851. Jesuit Archives, Missouri Province. IX: DeSmetiana, C-B: Atlas, No. 10, St. Louis University.

Doane, Gustavus C., Letter to Henry D. Washburn, August 12, 1870. Original MS, Hauser Papers, Montana Historical Society, Helena.

—————————— , "Expedition of Lt. G.C. Doane, 1876-77." A typescript from the original diary is in Yellowstone National Park Reference Library.

Dupuis, James, "Diary, Nov. 1, 1918 to Sept. 3, 1922." Original held by Mrs. Eva Ann Meyers, Bozeman, Mont.

Ebert, Hugh, "Memorandum to the Chief Ranger, Yellowstone National Park," April 12, 1944. Yellowstone National Park Reference Library.

Edwards, Guy D., Letter to Mrs. E.C. Cress, November 20, 1930. Original in the files of Yellowstone National Park.

Fish, Edmund I., Report to P.H. Conger, April 29, 1884. Letter Box 9, Doc. no. 1421, Yellowstone National Park Archives.

—————————— , Report to P.H. Conger, May 12, 1884. Letter Box 9, Doc. no. 1420, Yellowstone National Park Archives.

—————————— , Report to P.H. Conger, May 18, 1884. Letter Box 9, Doc. no. 1417, Yellowstone National Park Archives.

—————————— , Report to P.H. Conger, June 4, 1884. Letter Box 9, Doc. no. 1418, Yellowstone National Park Archives.

—————————— , Report to P.H. Conger, November 11, 1884. Letter Box 9, Doc. no. 1431, Yellowstone National Park Archives.

[Fort Yellowstone]. "Record of Property Purchased, Expended." Ledger 62, Yellowstone National Park Archives.

—————————— , "Record Book of Interments at the Post Cemetery, at Fort Yellowstone, Wyo., " Ledger 155, Yellowstone National Park Archives.

—————————— , "Maintenance Record-book of the Post Quartermaster, 1886-1912." Ledger 167, Yellowstone National Park Archives.

—————————— , Circulars of Instruction, 1901-1908. Letter Book 239, Yellowstone National Park Archives.

Fromm, R.J., "An Open History of Fish and Fish Planting in Yellowstone National Park," n.d. Typescript in the Yellowstone National Park Reference Library.

Frost, Ned. Jr., Conversation with the author, June 27, 1968.

Garrison, Lemuel A., Memorandum to the Chief of Interpretation, October 25, 1961. Original in the files of Yellowstone National Park.

General Services Administration. [Personnel records]. Federal Records Center, St. Louis, Missouri.

Gibbs, Jas. S. and John D. Ripley. Letter to S.B.M. Young, June 12, 1907. Letter Box 33, Yellowstone National Park Archives.

Gibson, Francis M. [Pocket diary, August 7-27, 1882]. MS in Yellowstone National Park Reference Library.

Gillette, Warren C. "Diary of Warren Caleb Gillette (1870)," Original MS, Montana Historical Society, Helena.

Godfrey, Lorenzo D., Report to P.H. Conger, August 15, 1884. Letter Box 9, Doc. no. 1437, Yellowstone National Park Archives.

Goodsill, M.M., Letter to J.E. Haynes, March 25, 1955. File C-500-4, Northern Pacific Railroad Company, St. Paul, Minn.

Haas, R.P. Letter to Superintendent of Yellowstone National Park. August 12, 1929.

Haines, Aubrey L., "Preliminary Report on the Rigler Bluffs Prehistoric Indian Site, 24 PA 401," November 26, 1962, typed MS in Yellowstone National Park Reference Library.

Haines, Aubrey L. "A Preliminary Report on High-altitude Indian Occupation Sites Near the North Boundary of Yellowstone National Park," December, 1963, typed MS in Yellowstone National Park Reference Library.

——————, "A Supplemental Report on High-Altitude Indian Occupation Sites Near the North Boundary of Yellowstone National Park," January 6, 1965, typed MS in Yellowstone National Park Reference Library.

Hampton, Harold D., "Conservation and Cavalry: A Study of the Role of the United States Army in the Development of a National Park System, 1886-1917." Ph.D. dissertation, University of Colorado, 1965.

Harris, Moses. Letter to the Secretary of Interior, October 4, 1886. Letter Book 213, Yellowstone National Park Archives.

——————, Letter to the Secretary of Interior, March 23, 1889. Letter Book 214, Yellowstone National Park Archives.

——————, Letter to H.L. Muldrow, April 11, 1889. Letter Book 214, Yellowstone National Park Archives.

Hauser, Samuel T. "Diary of Samuel T. Hauser, Aug. 17 to Sept. 4, 1870," MS no. 249, Coe Collection, Bienecke Library, Yale University.

Haynes, Jack E., Anecdotes related to the author, 1961.

Healy, John. Papers, Montana Historical Society, Helena.

Hedges, Cornelius. Eulogy on Henry D. Washburn, presented at the Methodist-Episcopal Church, Helena, Mont., January 29, 1871. Hedges Papers, Montana State Historical Society, Helena.

Henderson, A. Bart. "Journal of the Yellowstone Expedition of 1866 Under Captain Jeff Standifer . . . Also the Diaries Kept by Henderson During his Prospecting Journeys in the Snake, Wind River and Yellowstone Country During the years 1866-72." MS no. 452, Coe Collection, Bienecke Library, Yale University.

Henderson, George L., Letter to P.H. Conger, June 11, 1884. Letter Box 9, Doc. no. 1454, Yellowstone National Park Archives.

——————, Report to P.H. Conger, June 28, 1884. Letter Box 9, Doc. no. 1453, Yellowstone National Park Archives.

——————, Report to P.H. Conger, August 10, 1884. Letter Box 9, Doc. no. 1448, Yellowstone National Park Archives.

——————, "Cottage Hotel Register," MS journal kept at Mammoth Hot Springs, 1882-1886. Ledger 141, Yellowstone National Park Archives.

Henneberger, John, "To Protect and Preserve: A History of the National Park Ranger," MS examined in October 1965 through kindness of the author.

Hinkley, H.C., Statement, October 23, 1887. Letter Box 78, Yellowstone National Park Archives.

Hitchcock, E.A., Letter to John Pitcher, April 6, 1902. Letter Box 21, Yellowstone National Park Archives.

Hofer, Thomas E., Letter to C.A. Lindsley, July 25, 1923. MS in Yellowstone National Park Reference Library.

———————— , Letter to LeRoy Hill, February 5, 1927. MS in Yellowstone National Park Reference Library.

———————— , Letter to H.M. Albright, March 27, 1926. MS in Yellowstone National Park Reference Library.

Holmes, William H., "W.H. Holmes, Artist to the Survey of the Territories," (notes abstracted by him from his 1872 diary) June 25, 1928. Copy in Yellowstone National Park Reference Library.

Horr, H.R., J.C. McCartney and J. Shaffer. Letter to Columbus Delano, March 28, 1872. Records of the Office of the Sec'y of Interior Relating to Yellowstone Natl. Park, 1872-1886 (File Microcopy no. 62, roll 1), National Archives, Washington.

Horr, H.R., Letter to Secretary of Interior, May 25, 1874, Records of the Office of the Sec'y of Interior Relating to Yellowstone Natl. Park, 1872-1886 (File microcopy no. 62, roll 1), National Archives, Washington.

———————— , Letter to D.W. Wear, July 6, 1885. Letter Box 5, Doc. no. 1049, Yellowstone National Park Archives.

[Interior Department]. Letter to Supt. P.H. Conger, June 2, 1882. Letter Box 1, Doc. no. 12, Yellowstone National Park Archives.

———————, Letter to P.H. Conger, January 18, 1884. Letter Box 1, Doc. no. 78, Yellowstone National Park Archives.

———————— , Letter to P.H. Conger, April 18, 1884. Letter Box 1, Doc. no. 30, Yellowstone National Park Archives.

———————— , Letter to P.H. Conger, August 16, 1884. Letter Box 1, Doc. no. 158, Yellowstone National Park Archives.

———————, Letter to P.H. Conger, September 22, 1884. Letter Box 1, Doc. no. 132, Yellowstone National Park Archives.

———————— , Letter to Tate and Scott, November 15, 1884. Letter Box 1, Doc. no. 118, Yellowstone National Park Archives.

———————— , Letter to R.E. Carpenter, November 15, 1884. Letter Box 1, Doc. no. 117, Yellowstone National Park Archives.

———————, Letter to D.W. Wear, May 25, 1886. Letter Box 1, Doc. no. 184, Yellowstone National Park Archives.

———————— , Letter to Moses Harris, April 17, 1889. Letter Box 2, Doc. no. 333, Yellowstone National Park Archives.

———————, Letter to F.A. Boutelle, September 24, 1890. Letter Box 2, Doc. no. 236, Yellowstone National Park Archives.

———————— , Letter to D.B. May, October 15, 1890. Letter Box 2, Doc. no. 405, Yellowstone National Park Archives.

———————— , Letter to D.G. Stivers, July 20, 1891. Letter Box 2, Doc. no. 332, Yellowstone National Park Archives.

———————— , Commission of C.J. Jones, dated July 8, 1902. Original in the Yellowstone National Park Reference Library.

———————— , Letter to C.J. Jones, July 8, 1902. Letter Book 235:92, Yellowstone National Park Archives.

———————— , Letter to John Pitcher, July 6, 1905. Letter Book 237:58-59, Yellowstone National Park Archives.

———————— , Letter to C.J. Jones, September 12, 1905. Letter Book 237: 142-43, Yellowstone National Park Archives.

———————— , "Secretary Udall Maps Long-Range Goals for All three types of National Park Areas," August 3, 1964. Mimeographed news release.

Jackson, William T., "The Early Exploration and Founding of Yellowstone National Park," Ph.D. dissertation, University of Texas, 1940.

James, William. Letter to Moses Harris, August 27, 1887. Letter Box 78, Yellowstone National Park Archives.

Jenkins, Henry Del. Interview with the author at Jackson, Wyo., July 3, 1961. Audio tape in Yellowstone National Park Reference Library.

——————— , "The Lucky Cowboy," MS copied in part by permission, July 3, 1961.

Joffe, Joseph, "Personnel Lists, 1918 to June 1928, incl." Joffe file, Yellowstone National Park Archives.

Jones, Charles J., Letter to John Pitcher, July 5, 1903. Letter Box 20, Yellowstone National Park Archives.

——————— , Letter to John Pitcher, August 7, 1904. Letter Book 237: 60-64, Yellowstone National Park Archives.

——————— , Letter to Secretary of Interior. September 5, 1905. Letter Book 237:125, Yellowstone National Park Archives.

Jones, Jefferson. Information supplied Jack E. Haynes in 1952, concerning the 1887 stagecoach holdup.

——————— , Information supplied Jack E. Haynes, December 1953, from a file on "Territorial Post Offices and Their Dates of Establishment."

Jones, William A., Letter to G.S. Anderson, September 17, 1891. Letter Box 5, Doc. no. 1070, Yellowstone National Park Archives.

Joyner, Newell F., [Notes Collected by Newell Joyner Concerning Various Explorers, Etc.], August 16, 1930. Typescript in Yellowstone National Park Reference Library.

Kellner, John, Letter to G.S. Anderson, March 29, 1891. Letter Box 9, Doc. no. 1540, Yellowstone National Park Archives.

King, Mrs. Albert A., Letters to the author, July 20 and September 7, 1966.

Kirk, L.R., Letter to T. Paul Wilcox, August 23, 1937. U.S. Commissioner's Papers, Yellowstone National Park Archives.

Kirkbride, J.B., Letter to Moses Harris, November 15, 1887. Letter Box 78, Yellowstone National Park Archives.

Kittams, Walter, "Problems of Surplus Elk in Yellowstone National Park," a mimeographed report of the park biologist, 1948.

Kopac, Emil, Letter to D. deL. Condon, August 15, 1949. Original in files of Yellowstone National Park.

Langford, Nathaniel P., Letters to Will Doolittle, April 22, and November 14, 1865. Original MS in "Langford Papers, 1707-1942," Minnesota Historical Society, St. Paul.

——————— , Letter to Samuel T. Hauser, May 8, 1865. Original MS, Montana Historical Society, Helena.

——————— , Personal Diary for the Years 1870 and 1871. Original MS in "Langford Papers, 1707-1942," Minnesota Historical Society, St. Paul.

——————— , "Notes of Lectures Given by N.P. Langford During the Winter of 1870-71" [title added at a later date]. Original MS, Yellowstone National Park Reference Library.

——————— , Letter to Columbus Delano, July 27, 1872. Records of the

Office of the Sec'y of Interior Relating to Yellowstone Natl. Park, 1872-1886 (File microcopy no. 62, roll 1), National Archives, Washington.

————————, Letter to Secretary of Interior, September 7, 1874, Records of the Office of the Sec'y of Interior Relating to Yellowstone Natl. Park, 1872-1886 (File microcopy no. 62, roll 1), National Archives, Washington.

————————, Letter to Cornelius Hedges, February 26, 1905. Hedges Papers, Montana Historical Society, Helena.

LeHardy, Paul. "Autobiography of Paul LeHardy" (a typescript of pages 95-104 furnished from the original by his son, May 16, 1961). Copy in Yellowstone National Park Reference Library.

Liek, Harry, William Wiggins, Herman Biastoch, John Bauman, Rudy Grimm, Bill Wright, and Bob Robinson. Reminiscences at the retirement of Harry Liek, n.d. Audio tape in Yellowstone National Park Reference Library.

Lindsley, Chester A., Letter to W.M. Nichols, May 6, 1914. Letter Box 23, Yellowstone National Park Archives.

————————, "Monthly Report for October, 1916." Letter Box 89, Yellowstone National Park Archives.

————————, "Annual Report of the Acting Superintendent of Yellowstone National Park to the Superintendent of National Parks, 1916." Bound file, Yellowstone National Park Reference Library.

————————, "The Chronology of Yellowstone National Park, 1806 to 1939," a typescript in Yellowstone National Park Reference Library.

Little, Raymond G., Interview with the author at Gallatin Gateway, Mont., April 12, 1961.

Mallon, Henry, et al., Interview by the author at Mammoth Hot Springs, Wyo., July 5, 1961. Audio tape in the Yellowstone National Park Reference Library.

Malouf, Carling, "Preliminary Report, Yellowstone National Park Archeological Survey, Summer 1958," mimeographed by Montana State University, Missoula, January 5, 1959.

Marble, Charles, "Fifty Years in and Around Yellowstone Park, and Miscellaneous Notes" (1932). Typescript in Yellowstone National Park Reference Library.

Marshall, George W., Biographical statement in Bancroft Library, c. 1885 (Photostat furnished Yellowstone National Park Reference Library October 12, 1938).

Marshall, Robert B., Letter to L. M. Brett, October 13, 1916. Yellowstone National Park Archives.

McCartney, James C., Affidavit, May 15, 1891. Letter Box 6, Doc. no. 1137, Yellowstone National Park Archives.

McGuirk, Matthew. Affidavit, May 18, 1891. Letter Box 6, Doc. no. 1149, Yellowstone National Park Archives.

Meldrum, John W., Interviewed by J.E. Haynes, at Mammoth Hot Springs, Wyo., October 14, 1925. Author's notes.

————————, Abstract of the preliminary hearing in the case of the *United States* vs. *Guz Smitzer, alias Little Gus, and George Reeb, alias Morphine Charley*, n.d., Yellowstone National Park Reference Library.

Merry, Edward T., Letters to the author, June 8 and August 1, 1966.

Moore, Frank, Statement, October 27, 1887. Letter Box 78, Yellowstone National Park Archives.

Moorman, Edward H., "Yellowstone Park Camps History," Mimeographed reminiscence (1899-1948), dated April 2, 1954. Copy in Yellowstone National Park Reference Library.

Murri, Ernest, Interview by John Douglas and Garth Nelson at Ashton, Idaho, May 5, 1968. Audio tape in the Yellowstone National Park Reference Library.

Musser, M.K., Letter to the Superintendent, October 1, 1935. Original in the files of Yellowstone National Park.

[National Park Service], "Map Showing Proposed Enlargement of Yellowstone National Park and Development of Southern Entrance" (1918). Copy in Yellowstone National Park Reference Library.

——————————, "Mission 66 for Yellowstone National Park," c. 1956. Copy in files of Yellowstone National Park.

——————————, "Summary of Yellowstone Bear Protection and Management Policies," September 19, 1967. Copy in files of Yellowstone National Park.

——————————, "Management Objectives for Northern Yellowstone Elk," September 10, 1967. Copy in files of Yellowstone National Park.

Nettleton, A.B., Letters to F.V. Hayden, June 7, June 16, October 27, 1871. Records of the Geological Survey of the Territories ("Hayden Survey"), Record Group 57. Letters Received (M 623, roll 2, frames 120-2, 127-8, 155), National Archives, Washington, D.C.

Norbeck, Peter. Letter to H. M. Albright, April 23, 1931. Original in files of Yellowstone National Park.

Norman, G.L., Letter to the Superintendent, June 9, 1967. Original in files of Yellowstone National Park.

Norris, Philetus W., Letter to J.C. McCartney, April 19, 1877, Record Group 79, National Archives.

——————————, Letter to Assistant Secretary Bell, October 13, 1880. Letters Received, Dept. of Interior, Appointments Division, National Archives.

——————————, "Meanderings of a Mountaineer, or, The Journals and Musings (or Storys) of a Rambler over Prairie (or Mountain) and Plain." MS prepared from newspaper clippings (1870-75), and annotated about 1885. P.W. Norris Collection (HM 506), Henry E. Huntington Library, San Marino, Calif.

Northern Pacific Railroad Company. Notes made from records of the Mechanical Division. St. Paul, Minn., February 15, 1967.

——————————, Notes made from file "President, 209A," Headquarters Office, St. Paul, Minn., February 15, 1967.

——————————, Notes made from file "President, 209A-1," Headquarters Office, St. Paul, Minn., February 15, 1967.

——————————, Notes from file "President, 209B," Headquarters Office, St. Paul, Minn., February 15, 1967.

——————————, Notes from file "President, 210-A," Headquarters Office, St. Paul, Minn., February 15, 1967.

Noyes, Albert L., [Diary, July 4 to October 2, 1902], MS in Yellowstone National Park Reference Library.

Ogston, Edward E., Interview by the author, June 20, 1966. Audio tape in Yellowstone National Park Reference Library.

Orton, A.W., "Some Scattered Thoughts on the Early Life of N.P. Langford." Typed MS, copy in Yellowstone National Park Reference Library.

Owens, William O., "The First Bicycle Tour of the Yellowstone National Park." Typescript dated February 12, 1934, in Yellowstone National Park Reference Library.

Peale, Albert C., "A.C. Peale, U.S.G.S. 2", July 21 to October 24, 1872, MS notebook, Yellowstone National Park Reference Library.

Phillips, W. Hallett, Letter to the Secretary of Interior. Letters Received, Department of the Interior, P. and M. Division, 1885-6, National Archives, Washington.

Pitcher, John, Letter to the Department of Dakota (Army), November 28, 1906. Letter Book VIII (Interior): 25-28, Yellowstone National Park Archives.

——————, Letter to John F. Yancey, May 31, 1902. Letter Book XI:396, Yellowstone National Park Archives.

Potter, Mrs. Lena, Interview by the author, at Gardiner, Mont., April 20, 1962.

Potts, Benjamin F., Letter to N.P. Langford, November 27, 1873. Records of the Office of the Sec'y of Interior Relating to Yellowstone Natl. Park, 1872-1886 (File microcopy no. 62, roll 1), National Archives, Washington.

Potts, Daniel T., Letter to Robert Potts, July 8, 1827. Original MS Yellowstone National Park Reference Library.

Reeves, Mary., Letter to her mother, August 2, 1889. MS in Yellowstone National Park Reference Library.

Rogers, Edmund B., "Annual Report, 1937; Yellowstone National Park." Bound file, Yellowstone National Park Reference Library.

——————, "Annual Report, 1946; Yellowstone National Park." Bound file, Yellowstone National Park Reference Library.

——————, "Annual Report, 1947; Yellowstone National Park." Bound file, Yellowstone National Park Reference Library.

——————, "Annual Report, 1951; Yellowstone National Park." Bound file, Yellowstone National Park Reference Library.

——————, "Report of the Superintendent of Yellowstone National Park, May 28, 1953." File A-2623, Report 10a8, Yellowstone National Park Archives.

——————, "Report of the Superintendent of Yellowstone National Park, July 1, 1953." File A-2623, Report 10a8, Yellowstone National Park Archives.

——————, "Report of the Superintendent of Yellowstone National Park, June 3, 1955." File A-2623, Report 10a8, Yellowstone National Park Archives.

——————, "Report of the Superintendent of Yellowstone National Park, June 15, 1956." File A-2623, Report 10a8, Yellowstone National Park Archives.

Roosevelt, Theodore, Letter to G.S. Anderson, January 21, 1895. Letter Box 6, Doc. no. 1282, Yellowstone National Park Archives.

——————, Letter to S.B.M. Young, January 22, 1908. MS in Yellowstone National Park Reference Library.

Sanders, Everett, Letter to H.M. Albright, February 26, 1929. Original in files of Yellowstone National Park.

Sawtell, Gilman, Letter to George G. Boutwell, January 5, 1874. Records of the Sec'y of Interior Relating to Yellowstone Natl. Park, 1872-1886 (File microcopy no. 62, roll 1), National Archives, Washington.

Scales, Bill, Letter to the Chief Ranger of Yellowstone National Park, May 20, 1963. Original in Yellowstone National Park Reference Library.

Scott, W.F., Letter to S.B.M. Young, August 24, 1907. Letter Box 33, Yellowstone National Park Archives.

["Scott"], Note to Joe Joffe, February 28, 1929. Original in files of Yellowstone National Park.

Server, Fred E., "Diary of a Trip Through Yellowstone Park, Down the Snake River to Fort Hall and Back to Fort Ellis, 1876-77." Copy of typescript furnished by Montana State University Library, Bozeman.

Sexton, Jno. W., Telegram to N.P.R.R. Land Office, November 11, 1871. Northern Pacific Railroad Papers (Land Department), Minnesota Historical Society, St. Paul.

Shield, Rexford M., Interview by the author at Mammoth Hot Springs, August 29, 1962. Audio Tape in Yellowstone National Park Reference Library.

Skinner. Milton P., Letter to C.P. Russell, January 25, 1932. Original in files of Yellowstone National Park.

Smith, Charles J., [Reminiscence recorded at Zion National Park, Utah, April, 1952]. Copy in Yellowstone National Park Reference Library.

Smith, L.A., Letter to author. July 19, 1967.

Stephens, Clarence M., Letter to Secretary of Interior, May 18, 1882. Letter Box 1, Doc. no. 13. Yellowstone National Park Archives. .

Stevenson, James., Letter to Prof. J.D. Butler, February 28, 1886. Records of the Geological and Geographical Survey of the Territories ("Hayden Survey"), Record Group 57, National Archives, Washington, D.C.

Stivers, D. Gay, Letter to Moses Harris, March 28, 1889. Letter Box 3, Doc. no. 514, Yellowstone National Park Archives.

[Superintendent of YNP], "Journal," 1901-03. Ledger 143, Yellowstone National Park Archives.

——————————, "Journal," 1903-21. Ledger 142, Yellowstone National Park Archives.

Taylor, Chloe, Letter to her daughter, May 3, 1871. Original MS in possession of James Taylor Dunn, former Librarian, Minnesota Historical Society, St. Paul.

Taylor, Dee C., "Preliminary Archaeological Investigations in Yellowstone National Park," a report submitted in fulfillment of Contract No. 14-10-232-320 between the National Park Service and Montana State University, Missoula, 1964.

Terry, William H., Report to P.H. Conger, November 26, 1883. Letter Box 9, Doc. no. 1571, Yellowstone National Park Archives.

——————————, Report to P.H. Conger, December 6, 1883. Letter Box 9, Doc. no. 1343, Yellowstone National Park Archives.

——————————, Report to P.H. Conger, December 11, 1883. Letter Box 9, Doc. no. 1517, Yellowstone National Park Archives.

——————————, Report to P.H. Conger, December 15, 1883. Letter Box 9, Doc. no. 1569, Yellowstone National Park Archives.

Thomas, George., "My Recollections of the Yellowstone Park," an account of events in the spring and summer of 1883. MS [1938], Yellowstone National Park Reference Library.

Toll, Roger W., "Annual Report for Yellowstone National Park, 1933." Bound file, Yellowstone National Park Reference Library.

—————————, Memorandum, n.d., Yellowstone National Park Archives.

Turpin, Francis Lynn, "A Trip Through Yellowstone Park, 1895." MS in Montana State University Library, Bozeman.

[United States Army Command], Records of Army Posts. Record Group 98, National Archives, Washington.

[United States Commissioner], Records of Judge John W. Meldrum, 1894-1935. Yellowstone National Park Archives.

Vandercook, R.O., "A Bicycle 'Odyssey,' " [1892]. MS in the Yellowstone National Park Reference Library.

Waters, Ella C., Letters to G.L. Cline, W.C. Rivers and E.J. Lamartine, September 10, 1888. Letter Box 3, Doc. nos. 626-7, Yellowstone National Park Archives.

Weimer, Josiah W., Report to P.H. Conger, December 27, 1883. Letter Box 9, Doc. no. 1424, Yellowstone National Park Archives.

—————————, Report to P.H. Conger, July 20, 1884. Letter Box 9, Doc. no. 1590, Yellowstone National Park Archives.

—————————, Report to P.H. Conger, July 27, 1884. Letter Box 9, Doc. no. 1588, Yellowstone National Park Archives.

—————————, Report to P.H. Conger, Aug. 10, 1884. Letter Box 9, Doc. no. 1586, Yellowstone National Park Archives.

—————————, Report to D.W. Wear, July 18, 1885. Letter Box 9, Doc. no. 1584, Yellowstone National Park Archives.

—————————, Report to D.W. Wear, August 29, 1885. Letter Box 9, Doc. no. 1581, Yellowstone National Park Archives.

—————————, Report to D.W. Wear, Nov. 7, 1885. Letter Box 9, Doc. no. 1580, Yellowstone National Park Archives.

Welch, Max R., Special Report to Commanding Officer, Fort Yellowstone, August 16, 1897. Report Box 130, Yellowstone National Park Archives.

Wheat, Joe Ben, Letter to Otho Mack, Gardiner, Mont., June 24, 1962.

Wheeler, Olin D., Letter to H.M. Chittenden, September 4, 1913. Copy in Yellowstone National Park Reference Library.

Whittaker, George, "Scout's Diary. . . December 19, 1897, to May 29, 1898." MS no. 31, Yellowstone National Park Archives.

Williams, Jack R., et al., "National Park Service Insignia and How the Uniform Grew," March 1966. Mimeographed at Aztec Ruins National Monument, New Mexico.

Wineman, Mode, "Through Yellowstone National Park into Jackson Hole Country," 1908. MS diary in Yellowstone National Park Reference Library.

Wormington, Marie H., Letter to Otho Mack, Gardiner, Mont., January 1963.

Wylie, William W., [Yellowstone National Park History]. MS donated to Montana State University Library January 7, 1967.

Yeager, Dorr G., "Some Old Timers of the Yellowstone" (1929). Typescript in Yellowstone National Park Reference Library.

[Yellowstone National Park], "Record of Auto Permits—All Gates, 1915," Ledger 158, Yellowstone National Park Archives.

—————————, "A History of the Educational Department in National Parks," [1930]. Typescript in museum files, Yellowstone National Park.

Yellowstone National Park Reference Library. Pamphlet File.

——————— , Scrapbook no. 1.

——————— , Scrapbook no. 2.

Yellowstone Park Association. Notes made from records held by Hugh D. Galusha, Helena, Mont.

Yellowstone Park Transportation Company. Notes made from records held by Hugh D. Galusha, Helena, Montana.

Young, Samuel B.M., Letter to the Adjutant General of the Army, July 14, 1897. Letter Book 218:286-87, Yellowstone National Park Archives.

——————— , Letter to A.B. Cox, August 7, 1907. Letter Box 33, Yellowstone National Park Archives.

——————— , Letters to E.C. Waters, August 7, 1907. Letter Book 229: 286, 287, Yellowstone National Park Archives.

——————— , Letter to "Agent of the Yellowstone Lake Boat Company," June 15, 1908. Letter Box 33, Yellowstone National Park Archives.

INDEX

Absaroka Range, 200, 314, 315, 320, 331

Abundance, Lake, 88

Academy of Sciences, 58

Acker, W.B., 289

Ackers, Pvt. _____ , 196, 197

"aerial sounds," 92

airplane: first landing, 275; as a prime carrier, 372-73

airport: West Yellowstone, 373

Albright, Horace M., 285, 287, 289; as superintendent, 296, 303, 304, 308, 310, 323, 324, 329, 330, 352, 356, 359; as director, 331, 333, 334; biography, 458-59

"Albright forecast," 324-25

Aldridge, Mont., 147, 178, 205

"Alexis" (nom de plume): article by, 21

Allard herd (buffalo), 72

Allen, Col. B.F., 280

Allen, Maj. Charles J., 216, 253; biography, 464

Allinder, W.I., 153, 154

Alton, Dr. _____ , 16

Alum Creek, 68, 69, 129

American Automobile Association, 246, 265

American Bridge Company, 228

American Civic Association, 256, 284, 285

American Forest Congress, 94

American Forestry Association, 94

American Museum Association, 310

American Society for the Advancement of Science, 346

Amethyst Mountain, 25

Anderson, A.A., 99

Anderson, E.C., 445

Anderson, Capt. George S.: as acting superintendent, 19, 60, 62, 63, 65, 67-71 _passim,_ 81, 91, 95, 104-5, 127, 162, 170, 174, 175, 182, 191, 195, 217, 219-22 _passim,_ 238, 243, 281, 338; biography, 454-55, 464-65

Anderson, Henry, 290, 445

Anderson, Jack K.: biography, 463

antelope, 81, 82, 230, 332; killing of, 54, 55; protection of, 83; numbers of, 84

Antelope Creek, 381

Apex Mine, 197

Apollinaris Spring, 108, 109, 146, 147, 260

Appian Way (Roman), 213

approach roads: described, 350-51, 354-55

appropriation: lack of, 3, 227, 281, 285, 286, 287, 290; for engineering, 213, 216, 217, 220, 224, 228-29, 247; for NPS, 285; listed (1878-1951), 480-82

area of park: changes listed, 417n33

Armstrong, _____ (U.S.R.R. commissioner), 34

Arnica Creek, 126

"Arthur's seat," 106

Artist Point, 274, 374

Ashton, Idaho, 314, 333

assistant superintendents: (police), 3, 4, 27, 182, 184, 185; (NPS), listed, 467-68

Aster Creek, 194

Astringent Creek, 62, 63, 194

Atlantic Creek, Wyo., 92

automobile campgrounds, 304, 359, 361, 375, 376, 378; at Canyon, 359; at Fishing Bridge, 359, 361, 362, 365; at Lake, 359; at Mammoth, 359, 361, 362, 365, 369; at Old Faithful, 359, 361, 365; at West Thumb, 365

automobiles, 246, 247, 248, 256, 259, 261-74 _passim,_ 293; excluded from park, 246, 264, 410n14; first to enter, 263-64; admission sought, 265; admission of, 267, 269, 273, 286, 287, 348, 354, 411n21, 419n3; regulation of, 269; first entry (official), 269, 271; checking of, 281, 286, 291, 296, 299-300, 351

automobile tourists, 347-55 _passim_

avalanches (snowslides), 6, 179, 181, 197, 213

Bach, Edward N., 46, 49, 229

ABOUT THE AUTHOR

Aubrey L. Haines was born in Portland, Oregon. After graduating from the University of Washington with a degree in forestry, he was employed as a park ranger in Yellowstone National Park. Following four years of service with the United States Army Corps of Engineers during World War II, he returned to Yellowstone and, in 1946, was appointed assistant park engineer. In 1959 he was promoted to the newly-created position of park historian, remaining in that post until he retired in 1969.

Mr. Haines is the author of *Osborne Russell's Journal of a Trapper*, Oregon Historical Society (reprinted by the University of Nebraska Press) and *Yellowstone National Park, Its Exploration and Establishment*, National Park Service. He has edited *The Valley of the Upper Yellowstone*, University of Oklahoma Press, and *The Discovery of Yellowstone Park*, University of Nebraska Press.

Since his retirement, Mr. Haines has served as a consultant on historical research for the National Park Service and the Bureau of Outdoor Recreation. He lives with his wife in Bozeman, Montana.